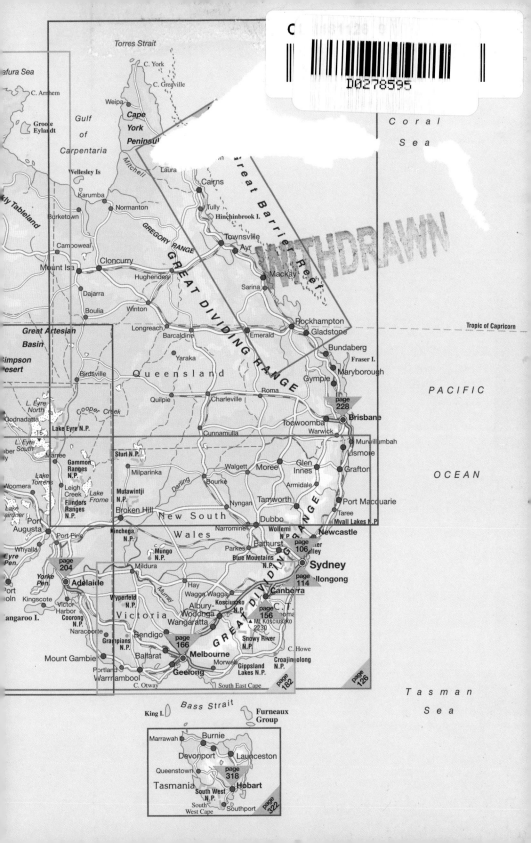

INSIGHT GUIDES
AUSTRALIA

NEXT 92 km

DISCOVERY
CHANNEL

APA PUBLICATIONS **L**

Part of the Langenscheidt Publishing Group

INSIGHT GUIDE
AUSTRALIA

ABOUT THIS BOOK

Editorial

Project Editor
Joanna Potts
Managing Editor
Alyse Dar
Series Editor
Dorothy Stannard

Distribution

UK & Ireland
GeoCenter International Ltd
Meridian House, Churchill Way West
Basingstoke, Hampshire RG21 6YR
Fax: (44) 1256 817988

United States
Langenscheidt Publishers, Inc.
36–36 33rd Street, 4th Floor
Long Island City, New York 11106
Fax: (1) 718 784 0640

Australia
Universal Publishers
1 Waterloo Road
Macquarie Park, NSW 2113
Fax: (61) 2 9888 9074

New Zealand
Hema Maps New Zealand Ltd (HNZ)
Unit 2, 10 Cryers Road
East Tamaki, Auckland 2013
Fax: (64) 9 273 6479

Worldwide
**Apa Publications GmbH & Co.
Verlag KG (Singapore branch)**
38 Joo Koon Road, Singapore 628990
Tel: (65) 6865 1600. Fax: (65) 6861 6438

Printing

Insight Print Services (Pte) Ltd
38 Joo Koon Road, Singapore 628990
Tel: (65) 6865 1600. Fax: (65) 6861 6438

©2009 Apa Publications GmbH & Co.
Verlag KG (Singapore branch)
All Rights Reserved
First Edition 1992
Fifth Edition 2007; revised 2008

CONTACTING THE EDITORS

We would appreciate it if readers
would alert us to errors or out-
dated information by writing to:
**Insight Guides, P.O. Box 7910,
London SE1 1WE, England.
Fax: (44) 20 7403 0290.
insight@apaguide.co.uk**

www.insightguides.com

The first Insight Guide pioneered
the use of creative full-colour photography in travel guides in 1970.
Since then, we have expanded our
range to cater for our readers' need
not only for reliable information about
their chosen destination but also for
a real understanding of the culture
and workings of that destination.
Now, when the internet can supply
inexhaustible (but not always reliable)
facts, our books marry text and pic-
tures to provide those much more
elusive qualities: knowledge and dis-
cernment. To achieve this, they rely
heavily on the authority of locally
based writers and photographers.

How to use this book

Insight Guide: Australia is structured to convey an understanding
of the country and its culture and
to guide readers through its sights
and activities.

◆ The **Best of Australia** at the front
of the guide helps you to prioritise
what you want to do.

◆ The **Features** section, indicated
by a yellow bar at the top of each
page, covers the country's history,
culture and people in a series of
informative essays.

◆ The main **Places** section, indicated by a blue bar, is a complete
guide to all the sights and areas
worth visiting. Places of special interest are coordinated by number with
the maps. Restaurant listings are
included at the end of each chapter.

◆ The **Travel Tips** listings section,
with an orange bar, provides a
handy point of reference for information on travel, hotels, shops,
restaurants and more.

The contributors

When a country has changed in as many ways as Australia over the past few years, it's not enough simply to update a travel guide – you need to rewrite and rephotograph large portions of it. That's what we've done for this major new edition, bringing together a team of experts from all corners of Australia who have pooled their invaluable inside knowledge.

Melbourne-based **Jerry Dennis** put together the new chapters for Victoria, Queensland, Tasmania and the Great Barrier Reef. Dennis has written and photographed for many Insight Guides and edited three recent titles on New South Wales, Queensland and Tasmania.

Ute Junker, a freelance writer and editor, worked on the history and culture chapters, Modern Australian Cuisine, New South Wales and Canberra.

Sydney-based journalist **Kerry McCarthy** applied her knowledge of her adopted city's best beaches and shopping districts, and also worked on the Urban Aussies chapter.

Tania Sincock, writer and self-confessed "greenie", updated Flora and Fauna, Sports, South Australia (where she grew up) and contributed to the Travel Tips section.

Dorothy Stannard, executive editor at Insight Guides and editor of Insight's guide to Perth, worked on the Western Australia chapter.

The Northern Territory chapter was updated by **Ron Banks**, a Darwin-based writer and former journalist at the *Western Australian* newspaper.

Their contributions build on the work of the following Australia-based writers for previous editions: **John Borthwick** (the original chapters on Australia's remarkable history); **Paul Phelan** (Queensland, the Great Barrier Reef; **Amanda Burdon** (Sydney and New South Wales chapters, and the photo feature on Sydney's museums); **Victoria Kyriakopoulos** (Melbourne and Victoria); **Amanda Gryst** (South Australia); **Dennis Schulz** (Northern Territory, Aboriginal Art and Australia's Wildlife); **Victoria Laurie** (Western Australia); and **Rick Eaves** (Tasmania).

Other past contributors include **Joe Rollo**, **Robert Mayne**, **Vic Waters**, **Paul Phelan**, **Robert James Wallace**, **Christine Long** and **Harriet Salisbury**, **A.D. Aird**, **Charles Perkins**, **Craig McGregor**, **Mungo McCallum** and **Lesley Thelander**.

Picture research was by **Hilary Genin**. The book was indexed by **Isobel McLean** and proof-read by **Sylvia Suddes**.

Map Legend

— - -	International Boundary
– – – –	State Boundary
–·–	National Park/Reserve
– – – –	Ferry Route
✈	Airport
🚌	Bus Station
P	Parking
ℹ	Tourist Information
✉	Post Office
† ⚲ ♂	Church/Ruins
⚲ ⚑	Mosque
✡	Synagogue
⚲ ♂	Castle/Ruins
∴	Archaeological Site
∩	Cave
★	Place of Interest

The main places of interest in the Places section are coordinated by number with a full-colour map (e.g. ❶) and a symbol at the top of every right-hand page tells you where to find the map.

INSIGHT GUIDE
AUSTRALIA

CONTENTS

A map of Australia is on the inside front cover and a map of Sydney City Centre faces the inside back cover.

Lifesavers
at Bondi
Beach,
Sydney

Travel Tips

THE BEST OF AUSTRALIA

Awe-inspiring scenery including perfect beaches, dramatic deserts and classic city-scapes; fantastic galleries, festivals and gourmet delights... here, at a glance, are our top recommendations for a visit

MAJOR HIGHLIGHTS

- **Sydney Harbour, NSW** With its balance of scenic beauty and human ingenuity, there is no better advertisement for the country. *Page 107*
- **Sunrise and sunset at Uluru, NT** Enjoy feelings of insignificance as the sun bathes the immense rock in glorious shades of red. *Page 273*
- **Snorkelling at the Great Barrier Reef, Qld** Take a fish's eye view of the world's largest natural reef. *Page 256*
- **Cruising the Yellow Water Billabong, Kakadu, NT** The finest natural wildlife viewing anywhere in Australia. *Page 277*

- **Driving the Great Ocean Road, Vic** Take in some of Australia's most spectacular coastal scenery. *Page 183*
- **Wildflowers of WA** Western Australia's vibrant wild flower displays are most spectacular during the spring (August through to November). *Page 312*

BEST GALLERIES

- **Aboriginal rock art galleries at Kakadu, NT** The astounding rock art galleries, particularly at Nourlangie and Ubirr rocks, display some of the earliest paintings by man. *Page 272*
- **National Gallery of Australia, Canberra** Repository of many of the finest artworks in the country, including excellent Asian and Aboriginal collections. *Page 157*
- **National Gallery of Victoria, Melbourne** The gallery has been split over two sites, one houses national and one houses international works. *Pages 168 & 172*

- **South Australian Museum, Adelaide** Extensive Aboriginal and Pacific exhibits and a broad survey of regional natural history. *Page 207*

ABOVE: glorious Uluru. **LEFT:** spoilt for choice at the Great Barrier Reef. **BELOW:** ancient rock art at Kakadu National Park.

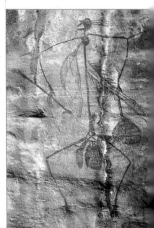

BEST ISLANDS

● **Tiwi Islands, NT** Accessible only by boat or plane through organised tours, the islands are rich in Aboriginal culture. *Page 282*

● **Kangaroo Island, SA** Seals, penguins, echidnas, kangaroos, emus and koalas all live here. *Page 219*

● **Lord Howe Island, NSW** This heavily forested isle has numerous walking trails, as well as diving and snorkelling facilities. *Page 136*

● **Maria Island, Tas** A 19th-century penal colony, Maria Island is vehicle-free, so pack walking boots or hire a mountain bike at the ferry point. *Page 322*

● **Fraser Island, Qld** Endless beaches on this giant sand bar. *Page 238*

● **Magnetic Island, Qld** Just over the water from Townsville but a world away. *Page 241*

NATIONAL PARKS

● **Kakadu, NT** Scenic splendour, ancient Aboriginal culture and paintings and an incredible array of flora and fauna. *Page 277*

● **Cradle Mountain, Tas** One of Australia's must-see destinations is well set up for visitors. *Page 332*

● **Flinders Ranges, SA** Rugged Outback, including spectacular Wilpena Pound – a raised valley surrounded by quartzite hills. *Page 213*

● **Great Barrier Reef Marine Park, Qld** The largest natural feature on Earth. The 20 or so resort islands inside the Great Barrier Reef Marine Park offer many attractions. *Page 256*

● **Ningaloo Reef, WA** Western Australia's largest coral reef, Ningaloo is an unspoilt delight for divers. *Page 302*

● **Kings Canyon, NT** The 350 million-year-old canyon is best seen during the magnificent four-hour Canyon Rim Walk. *Page 272*

● **Blue Mountains, NSW** A string of hill towns give access to one of the state's natural wonders. *Page 119*

BEST WALKS

● **Overland Track, Tas** A rite of passage for many, the walk is a 6-day (or more) journey from Dove Lake in Cradle Valley to the southern end of Lake St Clair. *Page 333*

● **Mount Warning, NSW** Climb at dawn and catch the first rays of light to hit the Australian mainland. *Page 135*

● **Coogee Beach to Bondi Beach, NSW** Spectacular coastal walk in Sydney taking in the many beaches that help give the city its character. *Page 118*

● **Wilson's Promontory, Vic** "The Prom", as it is affectionately known, features more than 80 km (50 miles) of walking tracks to long sandy beaches, forested mountain slopes, and heaths and marshes. *Page 196*

TOP: Blue Mountains, NSW.
ABOVE: beautiful Magnetic Island, Queensland.
LEFT: kitted out for a scenic walk.

BEST BEACHES

- **Whitehaven, Whitsunday Island, Qld** As beaches go, Whitehaven is pretty unbeatable. *Page 259*
- **Shark Bay, WA** A World Heritage Site, Shark Bay has marine wildlife galore. Hand feed dolphins at the bay's Monkey Mia. *Page 301*
- **Noosa, Qld** As well as being an excellent surfing beach, Noosa benefits from a national park on one side, and shopping strip on the other. *Page 236*
- **Wineglass Bay, Freycinet NP, Tas** This is a breathtaking sweep of white sands and azure sea. The best views are from Wineglass Bay lookout. *Page 323*
- **Maslin's Beach, SA** The backdrop of sandstone cliffs makes this family-orientated beach one of the most beautiful in the state. *Page 211*
- **Bells Beach, Vic** famed worldwide for its Easter surf contest. *Page 183*
- **Cable Beach, WA** A ride on a camel train along the beach at sunset is a great experience. *Page 305*

BEST COLONIAL TOWNS

- **Richmond, Tas** One of the very best preserved Georgian towns in all of Australia. *Page 321*
- **Broome, WA** The timber dwellings of Chinatown serve as a reminder of Broome's pearling days. *Page 304*
- **Ballarat, Vic** An old gold-mining town. The Eureka Centre recreates the day in 1854 when gold was discovered. *Page 187*
- **The Rocks, Sydney** Site of the first European settlement, today The Rocks is

an open-air museum. *Page 108*
- **Hahndorf, SA** Pretty German town established in 1839 in the Adelaide Hills. *Page 209*
- **Charters Towers, Qld** Attractive former gold-mining town with splendid colonial buildings. *Page 241*

BEST FESTIVALS

- **Adelaide Fringe, SA** Rapidly expanding in size and popularity, the Adelaide Fringe festival attracts exhibitions and acts from around the world. *Page 206*
- **Floriade, Canberra** Spectacular floral displays at Australia's biggest Spring festival. *Page 373*
- **Henley on Todd Regatta, Alice Springs** Waterless regatta held on the dry bed of the Todd River. Has to be seen to be believed. *Page 271*
- **Melbourne International Comedy Festival, Vic** The third biggest comedy festival in the world takes over Melbourne for one month each year. *Page 372*
- **Wooden Boat Festival, Tas** This biennial event draws wooden-boat builders and lovers from across the globe. *Page 372*
- **Gay and Lesbian Mardi Gras, Sydney** Hugely popular and flamboyant street parade. *Page 116*

ABOVE: Wineglass Bay. **LEFT:** ye olde sign. **BELOW:** the Brokeback Mormons join Mardi Gras.

BEST MARKETS

● **Sydney Fish Market, NSW** The ultimate seafood experience; Sydney's Fish Market has fish auctions, market stalls, restaurants and even a cookery school. *Page 114*

● **Adelaide's Central Market, SA** A giant covered area packed with more than 200 shops and stalls, the main attraction is the wealth of local produce that SA is famed for. *Page 208*

● **Sunday Bondi Markets, Sydney** The Markets have helped establish more than a few of the most successful Sydney designers. *Page 117*

● **Queen Victoria Market, Melbourne** A buzzing place where locals after fresh produce or deli specialities, mix with tourists seeking souvenir clocks in the shape of Australia. *Page 174*

● **Mindil Beach Market, Darwin** The Asian food stalls at this sunset market, held every Thursday, are marvellous. *Page 280*

BEST WINE REGIONS

● **Margaret River, WA** This picturesque region is famous for superb estate-grown and bottled wines. This is crafted wine and a far cry from the mass-production of Australia's eastern states. *Page 294*

● **Barossa Valley, SA** The 60 local wineries in this region include some of the most famous names in the business. *Page 211*

● **Hunter Valley, NSW** There are more than 120 wineries in the Hunter Valley and wine tourism – tastings, tours and accommodation – is big business. *Page 130*

● **The Yarra Valley, Vic** 55 wineries dot the gently rolling countryside. Tours can be arranged or you can dip in to the odd cellar door as you pass through. *Page 190*

● **Clare Valley, SA** Jesuit priests began making sacramental wines here in 1848. Today there are more than 20 wineries and 40 cellar doors. Many are boutique wineries whose labels are taking their place on some of the world's finest wine lists. *Page 212*

LEFT: Sydney Fish Market.
RIGHT: enjoying a tipple.
BELOW: BYO is a great way to save money.

MONEY-SAVING TIPS

Entertainment: Concessions are often offered to senior people (over-60s) and students, allowing big savings on all kinds of shows and events as well as cinema and theatre tickets and other admission fees. If you qualify, carry any relevant identifying card with you, though many places will take you at your word. Also note that small cinema chains will often be cheaper than the larger chains.

Cheap eating: There is so much good quality fresh produce in Australia and it is worthwhile putting together a picnic if you plan to be out all day (weather-permitting) rather than pay for lunch out. The best and cheapest place to buy this is at markets rather than supermarkets, which tend to be a lot more expensive. Some of the most affordable and best quality restaurant food can be found in and around Chinatown in larger cities.

BYO: There are restaurants and cafés across Australia which do not have licences to sell alcohol but are happy for you to bring your own (advertised as BYO), for which they add a small corkage charge to the bill. This not only allows wine buffs to drink exactly what they want with their meal but also seriously reduces the cost of dining out, especially if you choose a clean-skin (minimum labelling) wine, which are great value. Even some establishments that do have licences will allow BYO wine, but the corkage tends to be set abit higher and you need to look at the marginal benefits.

DOWN-UNDER

It's the world's largest island, or the earth's
oldest continent. Either way, Australia
is a place like no other

*Australia is like an open door with the blue beyond. You just walk out of the
world and into Australia.* —D. H. Lawrence (1922)

Australia is the perfect place to suffer jet-lag. Waking up to the bush
dawn, as the kookaburras begin their maniacal laughs and the golden
light pierces the gumtrees, is one of the great outdoor experiences.
Even in Sydney, a 6am stroll by the harbour as the first ferries roll past the
Opera House will convince you that this may be the most gorgeous city on
earth. This dawn beauty is just as well, since, even in the age of the jetliner,
Australia's distance from almost everywhere else is the central fact of its
existence – the source of its greatest strengths and weaknesses.

It always has been so, ever since a great chunk of earth broke
off from Gondwanaland and Australia's landscapes and animals began to evolve into exotica. For 50,000 years the Australian Aborigines wandered these far shores, unmolested by the
rest of the planet. In the 1780s the British knew exactly what to
do with such profound isolation: take the dregs of their society,
the criminals and the politically unsound, and expel them to
the uttermost ends of the earth. The strangeness of the landscape, the heat, the rain (or endless droughts), the strangeness
of it all… who would voluntarily choose to live in such a place?

All that has changed, of course. Today, Australians tend to be
thankful for their distance from Europe and the United States, and embrace
their (relative) proximity to Asia. The quirks of their homeland – the egg-
laying mammals, the ghostly trees, the savage deserts, the spiders, even the
menagerie of deadly snakes – have become a source of endless fascination.

Thinking of their history, which was once considered dull and uneventful,
Australians now agree with Mark Twain that it is a rip-roaring affair, so
colourful that it might well have been invented. And culturally, Australians
now look to their own resources – hardly indifferent to the rest of the world,
but confident in their contributions. Living in this supposedly upside-down
land – the Antipodes, "the exact opposite or contrary" – can hardly fail to
provide a unique view of the world. ❏

PRECEDING PAGES: a Pacific surfer catches the wave; Sydney Harbour,
seen from McMahons Point. **LEFT:** Weano Gorge in the Karijini National Park,
Western Australia. **ABOVE:** a cold beer promotes the "no worries" attitude.

AUSTRALIA'S ANCIENT LANDSCAPE

Australia has been a continent for around 50 million years.
But the history of the land can be traced back much
further, to a time when the world was young

Australia's topography, so forbidding to the first European settlers who arrived over 200 years ago and now so compelling to more recent arrivals, takes us back to the earliest history of our planet. Certain rocks have been dated back 3,500 million years, while large chunks of the landscape suggest earthly movements dating back more than 1,000 million years.

Whereas much of Europe and the Americas have the landscapes of youth – snow-covered peaks, rushing waterfalls, geysers, active volcanoes, giant gorges and mountain lakes – Australia's blunted, stunted, arid lands speak of an age which must be treated with respect. It is a land in which even the animals and plants, developed in isolation, are strikingly different.

Forces of nature

The last great geological shifts in Australia took place some 230 million years ago, before the Permian period. It was then that the forces of nature convulsed the earth's crust and created alpine ranges whose peaks extended above the snow line. Since then, modest convulsions on the eastern and western fringes have created low ranges (now known as tablelands), and volcanoes have occasionally erupted – but, generally speaking Australia was already a sleeping giant when the rest of the world's landforms came into being. Barring unforeseen geological circumstances, it will also be the first continent to achieve equilibrium, a flattening of the land to the point where rivers cease to run, there is no further erosion, and landscape becomes moonscape.

Australia began to take shape 50 million years

ago when it broke away from the great southern continent later known as Gondwanaland. This landmass at one time incorporated Africa, South America and India. Australia broke free and drifted north, reshaping itself into a continent. The centre was rising from a shallow sea to unite what had been a series of islands. One of these islands, the Great Western Plateau, had been the only constant during much of this change, sometimes partly submerged but always the stable heart of the continent.

Today that plateau spreads over almost half the continent, a dry and dramatic expanse of pristine beauty. It takes in the Kimberley and Hamersley ranges, the Great Sandy Desert, Gibson Desert and the Great Victoria Desert,

LEFT: a dry lake at sunrise.
RIGHT: Murchison Gorge, Kalbarri National Park.

and, although its topography has changed greatly, it houses the artefacts of ancient times.

A rock found near Marble Bar yielded the remains of organisms which lived 3,500 million years ago – the oldest form of life yet discovered. A dinosaur footprint is frozen in rock near Broome, and in the Kimberley, once a coral reef in a shallow sea, landlocked ocean fish have adapted to fresh water.

The Lowlands

The central eastern lowlands, stretching south from the Gulf of Carpentaria, form a sedimentary basin that has often been encroached upon

by the sea. Although this is a catchment area of 1.5 million sq. km (600,000 sq. miles) for rivers running inland off the eastern range, much of the water is lost through evaporation or into the vast chain of salt lakes and clay pans. The largest of the salt lakes, Lake Eyre, is also the lowest part of the continent at 15 metres (50 ft) below sea level.

Much of the lowlands are so exceptionally harsh and inhospitable that it is difficult to imagine that beneath the surface lies the Great Artesian Basin, from which bores are tapped to provide water for livestock. The most ancient part of the basin area is the Flinders Ranges of South Australia, in which there are rocks and remains dating back 1,000 million years.

The Highlands

Because of its immense age, Australia can no longer boast a true alpine range. The Great Dividing Range that runs parallel with the east coast for more than 2,000 km (1,250 miles) is as diverse as any found on earth, tropical at one end and subalpine at the other.

Mount Kosciuszko, at 2,230 metres (7,315 ft), is the highest point, but equally majestic are the rainforests of the north and the moors of Tasmania. The Glass House Mountains in southern Queensland were formed by volcanoes about 20 million years ago, while the granite belt bridging the Queensland–New South Wales border and the Warrumbungle Mountains was born in similar circumstances a short time later.

In fact, Australia's last active volcano, in Victoria, died only 6,000 years ago – a few ticks ago, really, on the geological clock. In Tasmania the effects of volcanic activity and two ice ages have created a distinctive wilderness.

The Coast

The coastline of Australia is as spectacular and as varied as the centre. It ranges from the limestone cliffs at the edge of the Nullarbor Plain to the jagged rock formations of Tasmania and western Victoria, from the mangrove swamps of the north to the spectacular beauty of the Great Barrier Reef – a lagoon which runs almost 2,000 km (1,250 miles) down the Queensland coast and contains more than 2,000 coral reefs. ❏

FLORA AND FAUNA

Australia's vegetation is dominated by the eucalyptus, the humble gum tree, in its more than 500 forms. It's hard to escape the smell, feel and sight of this tree, often stunted, knotted and offering little shade.

The marsupials have developed in isolation in extraordinary ways, and into 120 different species – from the red kangaroo and the gliders that fly between trees, to tiny desert mice. The platypus and echidna are the world's only egg-laying mammals; the Queensland lungfish can breathe both above and under water. Like the lungfish, which may be the fish that first stepped onto land and ultimately became humankind, Australia has clear links to a time when the world was young.

LEFT: storm at Katherine Gorge, Northern Territory.
RIGHT: Aborigines occupied caves like this for tens of thousands of years.

ONE-OF-A-KIND WILDLIFE

Australia has been an island long enough for evolution
to take a unique path. The result is a range of plants
and animals that are found nowhere else on earth

ustralia's splendid isolation has had a profound effect on the evolution of animals and plants in the southern continent. The sheer age of the landmass and its division by sea from other continents allowed Nature to have her way, independent of what was happening elsewhere. Consequently, Australian wildlife took on a unique character that prospered until the arrival of the white man and the onset of the technological age.

There are no better examples of this than the Australian mammals. Mammals are warm-blooded and furred, and almost all give birth to their young alive and suckle them. There are three groups: marsupials, monotremes and placentals. In Australia, marsupials are by far the most prominent. Their young are born not fully developed, and so are kept securely in a pouch until they are strong enough to move around independently. Kangaroos, possums and wallabies are examples of Australian marsupials.

Duck-billed platypus

Monotremes are probably the most unique type of mammals. Rather than giving birth to live young, they lay eggs. However, they do suckle their young and display many other mammalian traits. The amphibious duck-billed platypus is a monotreme, as is the echidna (also known as the spiny anteater).

The placental group comprises all the familiar large mammals that exist on earth. While they proliferate on most continents, very few examples can be found among the native Australian fauna. The native dog, the dingo, is a member of the placental group but was only introduced into Australia by Aboriginal immigrants sometime within the past 20,000 years.

Most marsupials are herbivorous, but there are some that include insects, small reptiles or smaller mammals in their diets. The larger members of the carnivorous group are the native "cats" and "wolves".

In fact, these animals have no relation to the cat or dog families but their names do suggest some sort of confusion on the part of the early white settlers. Examples include the Tasmanian devil and the Tasmanian tiger (thylacine). The latter is a wolf-like carnivorous creature thought to be extinct – except by a few die-hards who occasionally report uncertain sightings in wilderness areas.

The herbivores abound and represent the cuddly postcard image of Australian wildlife. The shy koala is an example, as are the many varieties of possum, including the ringtail and the sugar glider. But undoubtedly the best known are the macropods, or hopping marsupials, such as the kangaroo, wallaby, wallaroo and kangaroo rat. The familiar kangaroo profile is probably the greatest Australian symbol of them all.

Before the arrival of the white man the kangaroo population was controlled by the climate and environment. In times of drought, female kangaroos intuitively did not come into season, thereby putting restraints on the expansion of the herd. This helped preserve food supplies. In times of plenty the kangaroo population increased. However, this fine balance

laid-back marsupial is now completely protected.

The wombat is related to the koala, but instead of making its home up a tree and dining on gum leaves, it uses its powerful digging paws to make burrows under stumps, logs or in creek banks. It lives on roots, leaves and bark.

Snakes and lizards

Reptiles figure prominently in Aboriginal legend and diet, particularly the venomous snakes such as the taipan, tiger snake, death adder and brown snake. Non-venomous varieties such as the carpet snake and green tree snake abound.

was altered when artificial irrigation of the grasslands created more food. While the kangaroos grew in number and competed with sheep and cattle for the available food, farmers sought ways to keep the 'roos off their properties.

The retiring koala, despite its often misused title, is not a bear but is yet another exotic example of Australia's herbivorous marsupials. Its habit of sleeping openly in the forks of gum (eucalyptus) trees made it an easy target for hunters seeking its fur. So great was the slaughter that urgent steps were taken to save the koala in the 1920s. This

LEFT: male red kangaroos compete in a sporting manner to mate with females.
ABOVE: coastal banksia on Fraser Island beach.

SAVING AUSTRALIA

A recognisable conservation movement emerged in Australia in the late 1970s, around the time of the nation-wide campaign to protect Tasmania's Franklin River from being dammed. The movement gathered impetus during the 1980s and has managed to ensure many wild places are now safe for future generations to enjoy. Notable victories include the protection of such international icons as Fraser Island, Kakadu, the Daintree Rainforest, Tasmania's Southwest National Park and the Great Barrier Reef.

In recent times, governments have tended to sacrifice the environment for the interest of big business and the struggles continue around such issues as uranium mining and the logging of Australia's old-growth forests.

Lizards, ranging from the tiniest of skinks to goannas more than 2 metres (6 ft) long, proliferate in Australia. The most exotic is the frill-necked lizard, which has a frock of skin around its neck erected into a broad collar when confronted with danger. It should not be confused with the bearded dragon, named for its mane of prickly spines. Many city dwellers welcome the presence of the blue-tongued lizard in their gardens. It hunts snails and insects and, while it is not as faithful as a dog, it is cheaper to keep.

Australia has more than its share of frogs and toads, many similar in appearance to those of Europe and North America, and many peculiarly Australian. Sadly, the most infamous amphibian is the Queensland cane toad. This giant was introduced to eradicate a cane parasite but has become such an unwelcome intruder in its own right that environmentalists are searching for ways to eradicate the species. It's yet another example of the destabilising effect that introduced species have had on the local environment.

The Great Barrier Reef

In the far north of Queensland, the Great Barrier Reef is a natural wonderland blessed with numerous fish, shell and polyp species peculiar to Australian waters *(for more on the Reef's*

VARIETIES OF PLANT LIFE

From the tropical growth of northern Queensland's steamy jungles to the delicate blossoms of New South Wales's cool southern tablelands, there is seemingly no end to the variety of plant life promoted by the country's vast climatic and geographical differences.

There are some types of plant that thrive almost anywhere in Australia, regardless of climate, soil type or mankind's presence. The most abundant is the acacia, or wattle. And visitors might note the presence of grass-trees in almost all areas. These are sometimes called "black boys" because of the spear-like vegetation that juts from the centre, often to a height of 5 metres (16 ft).

Like many of the continent's animals, Australian flora has been affected by the introduction of foreign trees, grasses, shrubs, and plants. Some of these types have flourished unchecked, completely altering the ecological balance of entire regions. However, many city- and country-dwellers are becoming aware of the importance of native plant life.

In the cities, the replanting of native trees has encouraged bird and insect life to return to these areas with the resultant re-germination process for which the birds and the bees are so celebrated. More than 200 years after the pineering botanist Joseph Banks went into raptures about this botanical wonderland, teachers are leading Australian children out into the wild to experience and appreciate the beauty and uniqueness of their local wildlife.

ecosystem, see pages 256–63). But one doesn't have to go snorkelling in the Reef to sample the coastal wildlife. A scramble over any coastal rock platform will reveal shellfish, starfish, anemones, crabs and even the occasional octopus.

Australia's early explorers were almost as intrigued by the strange bird life as they were by kangaroos and koalas. On the east coast in particular, flocks of raucous parrots plunder the fruit trees. They include brilliantly plumed rosellas and lorikeets. The eccentric bowerbird builds a structure or bower on which he performs to win the attention of a female. He adorns his court with brightly coloured trinkets (preferably

development consumed coastal habitats, but protective measures have saved many from the threat of extinction.

Visitors to Australia expecting to see kangaroos bounding through the streets of the cities and koalas scuttling up the nearest telephone pole will be disappointed. Like most wildlife, Aussie animals are generally shy of man. Of course, you can go to any of the city zoos such as Sydney's Taronga Park or the Melbourne Zoo and see most forms of local wildlife from platypus to black snake. If you don't have the time to spend weeks in the bush studying creatures in their natural environment, a suitable

blue) such as stones, glass or objects collected from gardens or houses.

Eagles, hawks, crows and cuckoos of native origin can all be observed. The opening up of the southern continent helped Europeans to map the migratory habits of numerous northern-hemisphere species which were known to "fly south for the winter".

The size of the continent and the variety of habitats allow for many species of waterfowl. Some were hunted by the early settlers, and

compromise is a visit to any of the larger nature reserves that exist on the fringes of the cities. Here, in natural surroundings and often under the guidance of a park ranger, you can observe examples of Australia's wondrous animals. As many native mammals are nocturnal, it is worth considering a night tour if it is on offer.

Ubiquitous flora

As for the flora: well, it's almost everywhere. From a stroll through the leafy outer suburbs of Sydney or Melbourne, to a bushwalk in the jarrah forests of Western Australia or a camping trip in the Tasmanian wilderness, you can easily expose your senses to the great Aussie bush. You will find many of the species are those that

LEFT: koalas resting in the branches of a eucalyptus tree, Lone Pine Sanctuary, Brisbane.
ABOVE: blue-tongued lizards are a common sight.
RIGHT: the rainbow lorikeet, pretty and precocious.

qualify as rare exotica in Europe or America.

The range of Australian eucalyptus is immense, ranging from low, stunted, scrub-like bush to the great towering varieties of the highland forests. The mountain ash eucalyptus found in the forests of Victoria and Tasmania is the tallest flowering plant on earth, growing to 70–90 metres (230–300 ft) or more. There are ghost gums, so named because under the light of the moon they appear silvery-white, and rock-hard ironbarks, capable of blunting the toughest timber saws. The name "eucalyptus" includes a very wide range of trees in all climates and terrains.

It is from the gold and green of the acacia, or wattle, that Australia draws its national colours. So hardy is the wattle that it is usually one of the first varieties to rejuvenate after a season of bushfires. In season, wattles bathe the bush in gold with their blossoms.

Trees under threat

Unlike the softwood varieties of Europe and North America, most Australian trees have very hard timber. This made clearing the land an extremely arduous task for the early settlers. When the pioneers encountered softer timber such as cedar, they proceeded to fell it.

In Tasmania, the mighty Huon pine was found to be one of the best building timbers in the world. It is especially prized by boat-builders. The jarrah forests of south Western Australia are currently under threat from mining and from culling. Jarrah and the tough karri are also superb building timbers, and foresters are exploring ways to guarantee their proliferation by combating a disease called "die-back".

A concerted drive to replant some of the tree life laid waste in the name of agricultural development is currently in process and trees are making a comeback.

The deserts might appear to be vast infertile wastes in the dry season, but it only takes a good downpour to turn them into paradises of wild flowers. The seeds can lie dormant in the soil for years, waiting for moisture to bring them to life. One region noted for its variety of wildflowers is the southern corner of Western Australia. The area has become so famous that commercial growing of some of the more exotic types has become a minor local industry. ❑

ABOVE: The largest carnivorous marsupial in the world, "devils" measure about 90 cm (35 inches) from head to tail. This nocturnal predator-scavenger has a loud, screeching call and, for its size, the most powerful bite of any living mammal. 400 years ago it was widespread throughout Australia, but now is found only in Tasmania. Its population has been ravaged since 1996 by Devil facial tumour disease.

BELOW: The snake-necked turtle (also known as the long-necked turtle) does not draw its neck straight back into its shell but tucks it in sideways. It is carnivorous and uses its long neck to strike like a snake.

AUSTRALIA'S NATURAL-BORN KILLERS

Australia is a land where lethal killers abound…or crawl or slither or float or dive. Scorpions hide beneath rocks across the continent, great white sharks devour the occasional abalone diver off South Australia, saltwater crocodiles stalk fishermen (as do box jellyfish) in the Northern Territory, the poisonous blue-ringed octopus waits on the reefs, and the venomous funnel-web spider lurks in the gardens of suburban Sydney.

And as if that weren't enough, Australia possesses more species of venomous snakes than any other country on earth. It is home to 40 snake species – 12 of them, like the stunning copperhead *(pictured above)*, can inflict a fatal wound. The inland taipan, or fierce snake, takes the prize as the world's deadliest snake: it is 50 times more venomous than the cobra. This rich reptilian diversity is not limited to the mainland: 32 known varieties of poisonous sea snakes reside offshore.

However, dangerous liaisons between humans and these creatures are rare, with most sightings of killer animals confined to city zoos. In the wild, most animals prefer escape to confrontation with potentially lethal human beings.

ABOVE: The lethal Sydney funnel-web spider, despite its name, is found throughout the eastern coastal region.

BELOW: A blind, burrowing desert-dweller, the marsupial mole swims through the sand, leaving no burrow. The young are nurtured in the pouch, which has evolved to open backwards so that it doesn't fill with sand.

ABOVE: The duck-billed platypus is an agile swimmer, propelling itself with webbed forefeet. The male has a venomous claw on its hind legs and is the only mammal capable of poisoning. It is found from Queensland to Tasmania.

LEFT: To attract its mate, the bowerbird spends hours building a bower with walls of sticks and decorating the floor with colourful ornaments including shells, berries, flowers, or even glass or plastic. The female will then inspect each bower and will mate with the male who has impressed her the most.

DREAMTIME AND DISCOVERY

Living in harmony with the land, Australia's Aborigines developed a culture rich and complex in its customs, religions and lifestyles, which was abruptly interrupted by the arrival of the British in 1788

Long before the ancient civilisations in the Middle East, Europe and the Americas flourished, more than 50,000 years before European, Asian or Middle Eastern navigators recorded visits to the shores of "The Great South Land", Australian Aborigines occupied this continent – its arid deserts and tropical rainforests, and especially its major river systems and coastal plains and mountains. Estimates by anthropologists put the population of Aborigines, prior to 1770, at more than 300,000.

Their ancient traditions thrived in a kinship and close spiritual bond with every living thing and even with inanimate objects such as rocks, rivers and other geographical features.

The dawn of creation

Dreamtime is the basis of all traditional Aboriginal thought and practice. It is the Aborigines' cultural, historical and ancestral heritage. In their mythology it is an age that existed long ago and yet remains ever-present as a continuing, timeless experience, linking past, present and future. Dreamtime was the dawn of all creation when the land, the rivers, the rain, the wind and all living things were generated.

Tribal elders were responsible for maintaining the clan's group identity through its totemistic religion. Groups of people formed special bonds with a totem, usually an animal or a plant which acted as a protector and a symbol of group identity. Through special ceremonies and other social and religious practices, the elders transmitted their knowledge.

PRECEDING PAGES: rock paintings at Nourlangie Rock.
LEFT: an early impression of an Aboriginal camp.
RIGHT: an Aboriginal man plays the didgeridoo.

HUNTERS AND GATHERERS

Aborigines lived in clans of 10 to 50 or more people. Their life in the harsh landscape of Australia was based on hunting by the men and fishing and gathering by the women. A good hunter knew intimately the habits of the creatures he stalked, was an expert tracker and understood the seasons and the winds.

Each tribe recognised the local landmarks and their links with the rich mythology of the Dreamtime (or Dreaming). Various geological aspects were sacred sites with their own personality and significance. The Aborigine considered himself, nature and the land inseparably bound and interdependent. In this state of unity, he (and she) achieved a balance with the environment.

The Aborigines celebrated the adventures of their Dreamtime spirit heroes through their paintings, songs and sacred dances. The rock paintings were of special significance, bearing the strongest psychological and ritual values. As no Aboriginal language was written, these paintings, along with the oration of legends by tribal leaders, were responsible for passing the Dreamtime stories from one generation to the next.

The Aboriginal ceremony of celebrating with song and dance was called *corroboree*. The male dancers were expert in mimicking the movements of animals; with these skills they reconstructed legends, heroic deeds or famous hunts. Bodies were elaborately painted, and songs were chanted to the accompaniment of music sticks and boomerangs clapped together.

Basic dance themes dealt with hunting and food gathering, or sex and fertility. Sometimes they took a humorous vein but more often they dealt seriously with the procreation of life. Some tribes used a long, hollow piece of wood which, when blown, emitted a weird droning sound. This was the didgeridoo, whose sound was said to resemble the calling of the spirits.

Aborigines believed that a person's spirit did not die upon physical death, and that ceremonies were essential to ensure that the spirit left

EARLY EXPLORERS

The Greeks, the Hindus and Marco Polo had all speculated upon the location and nature of the "Great South Land". The Arabs, the Chinese and the Malays had probably come and gone, as had the Portuguese. The Dutch came, looked and left, disappointed at not finding "uncommonly large profit".

At the end of the 17th century, the English explorer and privateer William Dampier was appalled by the bleak landscape of the northwestern coast, inhabited by "the miserablest people on earth".

The fertile east coast was missed by just a few kilometres by both the French explorer Louis Antoine de Bougainville and the Spaniard Luis Vaez de Torres.

the body and became re-embodied elsewhere – in a rock, a tree, an animal, or perhaps another human form. Thus each person was the centre of an intricate web of relationships which gave order to the entire world.

Aboriginal culture had prepared the people for everything they might expect to face in life – except the coming of the white man.

The impact of Captain Cook

When James Cook, a 41-year-old Royal Navy lieutenant, dropped anchor in 1770 in that east coast bay, so teeming with exotic new life forms

ABOVE: *Fishing*, portrayed by John Heaviside Clark.
RIGHT: Captain Cook, as depicted by Nathanial Dance.

that he decided to call it Botany Bay, he verified by flag and map an idea that Europe had craved.

Cook had been sent by the Admiralty to Tahiti, at the request of the Royal Society, to observe a transit of the planet Venus. Among the company of 94 on his second-hand coal ship *Endeavour* were Daniel Carl Solander and Joseph Banks, two of the great botanists of the age.

After Tahiti, Cook sailed southwest to New Zealand and spent six months charting both islands. He was then free to return to England by either the Cape or the Horn. Instead, he and his officers decided upon a route that would lead towards the unknown, the fabled South Land.

On 28 April 1770, *Endeavour* anchored in Botany Bay for one week. No naturalists before or since Solander and Banks have ever collected in such a short time so many new specimens of plant, bird and animal life. Meanwhile, the sailors ate their fill of seafoods, causing Cook at first to name the place Stingray Harbour Bay. He later changed it to Botany Bay because of Solander and Banks's discoveries.

A claim for the king

Sailing north, Cook sighted and named (but did not enter) Port Jackson, Sydney's great harbour-to-be. On 22 August, at Possession Island off the tip of Cape York, he hoisted the British colours and claimed the whole of the eastern side of the continent under "the name of New South Wales" for George III.

Upon reaching London in 1771, Cook reported to the Admiralty that he had found the east coast of New Holland, but not the Great South Land – if indeed such a place existed. During his voyage of 1772 to 1775, he destroyed the historical myth of the Great South Land by using the westerlies to circumnavigate the Antarctic. In 1779, he died at the hands of Polynesians in the Hawaiian islands, which he also discovered.

The First Fleet

In May 1787, 11 small ships of "the First Fleet" under Captain (later Governor) Arthur Phillip sailed from Portsmouth. Eight months later, the 1,000 passengers arrived at Botany Bay. Three-quarters of them were convicts, since Britain had been forced to find a new dumping ground for rebels, poachers, prostitutes and murderers

CAPTAIN JAMES COOK

James Cook was stern and hot-tempered; physically, he was tall, dark and handsome. He was also, in the parlance of his time, a "tarpaulin", an officer who had prospered without the boost of an aristocratic birth.

Born in 1728, the son of a Yorkshire farm labourer, at 18 he had been apprenticed onto North Sea colliers. Enlisting in the Royal Navy in 1755, he distinguished himself as a navigator and a master, particularly on the St Lawrence River in Quebec, Canada, during the Seven Years' War with France.

A courageous and proud man, Cook was driven more by a sense of duty and personal excellence than by greed or God. All supplies of fresh food which his crew obtained he "caused to be equally divided among the whole company generally by weight, so the meanest person in the Ship had an equal share with myself [Cook] or anyone on board." As for the soul-snatching men of the cloth, he would never permit a parson to sail on any of his ships. Reflecting during his homeward journey upon the state of the Australian Aborigine, he took a remarkably enlightened view, writing the classic description of the noble savage: "In reality they are far more happier than we European; being wholly unacquainted with not only the superfluous but the necessary Conveniences so much sought after in Europe… the Earth and sea of their own accord furnishes them with all things necessary for life."

after it lost Maryland and Georgia in the American War of Independence. The auguries for Australia's future were not those of the Promised Land.

A quick survey showed two things: Cook's description of the waterless place had been far too generous; and two ships of Comte de la Perouse were also there, possibly shopping for a new continent on behalf of France's Louis XVI. Phillip hurriedly sailed 20 km (12 miles) up the coast to Port Jackson and (after a few toasts and a fusillade) raised the flag for George III on 26 January 1788.

After 30 months of isolation and famine, locked in by the natural prison of this alien bush, the settlement was down to half rations. When a ship finally appeared, to their despair, it was carrying not supplies but 222 elderly and ill female convicts. Fortunately, the supply ships of the Second Fleet were close behind.

The birth of Sydney

The tents at Sydney Cove were replaced by brick and timber huts. Phillip tried to lay out a town along orderly lines, but conformity was not in the nature of its inhabitants. Short cuts soon became streets and, despite later attempts at order, the convenient jigsaw that resulted can

still be observed today as the ground plan of Sydney's high-rise pile-up.

Sydney Town expanded west towards the fertile farming lands of Parramatta, but was still hemmed in by the impenetrable escarpment of the Blue Mountains. Explorers fanned out by land and sea to open new pastures and farms, and to find even more isolated and savage prisons, such as Norfolk Island. This had originally figured in British strategy as a potential source of flax, hemp and masts for its Pacific naval and trade fleets. The plan failed, and the island's true "success" was as a hell-hole of sadism.

New South Wales was still costing London dearly (£1 million in the first 12 years), but it was turning a profit for its local landowners

A TOUGH BEGINNING

Officers, marines, transportees, sheep, goats and cattle were disgorged in 1788 into a cove that is now overlooked by the Sydney Opera House.

The surgeon-general to the fleet rhapsodised that Port Jackson was "the finest and most extensive harbour in the Universe." It is said that even the convicts raised a cheer of joy. It is also noted that two Aborigines shouted "Warra! Warra!" (Go Away!); no one heeded.

Thus the colony stumbled to life. These first New South Welshmen found that their seed-wheat, which had been damaged at sea, failed to germinate in the sandy soil. Their cattle grew wild, and the sheep fell foul of convicts, Aborigines and dingoes.

and the officers of the NSW Corps, otherwise known as "the Rum Corps". The Corps resisted the extortionate demands of trading-vessel masters, and developed its own monopolies. The colony had become such a vat of drunkenness, and the demand for Bengal rum, which the Corps controlled, was so great that rum almost became the currency of the colony.

Captain Bligh fails again

Governor William Bligh (of *Bounty* fame) was despatched to clean up the Rum Corps' act, and to encourage free settlers to come to Sydney. However, the Corps, at the bidding of a farmer

death at the end of a noose would often have been more merciful. In attempting to escape, some became the interior's first explorers. Pathetically, they fled into the bush, some believing that China lay beyond the Blue Mountains or that a colony of free whites dwelt inland. The only sure way of escape from the pathological violence on Norfolk Island was to commit murder in the hope of being hanged.

Transportation to Australia's penal settlements had ceased by 1868. By then 160,000 convicts had arrived; only 25,000 were women, a distortion which left its stamp in the harsh, male-dominated "frontier" society for decades.

and officer, John Macarthur, pulled the second of the famous mutinies in Bligh's career, and in 1808 deposed him.

New South Wales and its satellite penal settlements at Moreton Bay (now Brisbane), Norfolk Island and Van Diemen's Land (Tasmania) entered the 19th century with a reputation as "hell on earth" – a reputation which the British hoped would function as a deterrent.

Irish rebels, Tolpuddle Martyrs and petty thieves caught for stealing buckles or loaves of bread were thrown together in Australia, when

LEFT: Sydney Cove soon after settlement.
ABOVE: a new barracks built to house Australia's many convicts.

LACHLAN MACQUARIE

The initial brutality shown to convicts was tempered by the high-mindedness and reforms of Governor Lachlan Macquarie (1810–21), by the hopes of some emancipists (freed convicts) that morality and dignity could prevail, and by a growing prosperity through trade. Macquarie, a paternalistic autocrat, stifled the Rum Corps' monopoly on the import of spirit, established the colony's own currency (1813) and first bank (1817), and encouraged the first crossing of the Blue Mountains (1813). His programme of public works and town planning (265 projects in 11 years) owes much to Francis Greenway, an emancipist transported to Sydney as a forger, who became the colony's leading architect.

Domestic exploration

A continent of 7.7 million sq. km (3 million sq. miles), much of it searing desert or dense scrub, could not be explored easily. Before the crossing of the Blue Mountains in 1813, most significant exploration took place by sea. Two British sailors, Bass and Flinders, guessed correctly at the separation of Tasmania from the mainland. The French ships of Baudin in 1802, and later of Dumont d'Urville in 1826, scared the colonial authorities into establishing settlements in Tasmania and Western Australia respectively. Once the Great Dividing Range had been penetrated in 1813, the drive for new lands, minerals and the

glory of being "first there" – wherever "there" happened to be – lured men on.

Early explorers believed that the westward-flowing rivers of the NSW interior led towards a vast inland sea. In 1830 Charles Sturt and his party set out on the Murrumbidgee River, following its current into the Lachlan and Murray rivers, finally reaching Lake Alexandrina near the South Australia coast. After travelling more than 1,000 km (600 miles) they were within sight of the sea, but were unable to reach it. Instead they had to row against the current towards their starting point.

Their 47 days' rowing, on meagre rations and against flood tides, left Sturt temporarily blind, but is one of the most heroic journeys in Aus-

Edward John Eyre made an extraordinary journey in 1840, on foot, east to west along the coast of the Great Australian Bight. He began with an assistant, John Baxter, and three Aborigines. Some 4½ months and 2,000 km (1,250 miles) later, after an appalling journey mostly through desert, he and one Aborigine, called Wylie, walked into Albany on King George Sound. Baxter had been murdered by the other two, who then ran away.

There are many such explorers' tales of courage and folly, some still carved as messages on tree trunks, or buried beside dried-up billabongs. Others are just blood on the sand of the inland deserts.

In 1842, a 29-year-old Prussian draft dodger, Ludwig Leichhardt, landed in Sydney. He did not have good qualifications for an aspiring explorer: he could neither shoot nor see very well, and he also had a poor sense of direction. He did, however, know how to spot potential benefactors.

By 1844, he had found sufficient backers for an ambitious northwesterly thrust across Queensland and into the Northern Territory. His ambition was to open up the land from Brisbane to Port Essington (Darwin), a distance of 4,800 km (3,000 miles). With 10 companions, Aboriginal guides and a bullock team, he ran into innumerable difficulties, lost his provisions, and saw three of his men speared (one fatally) by natives.

Fourteen months after their departure, and long after being given up for dead, Leichhardt and his party staggered into Port Essington. Returning by sea to Sydney these "men from the grave" were fêted as national heroes; the Prussian government even pardoned Leichhardt for his military desertion.

In April 1848, he set out again, this time on a proposed transcontinental trek from Roma in southern Queensland to the Indian Ocean. His party of seven men and 77 beasts was never seen again, and their fate was to become one of the great mysteries of the Australian bush. The first search parties could only report that the missing men had probably been speared by Aborigines in western Queensland. But the search continued for years, spurred on by finds of skeletons, relics and pack horses. Stories of a wild white man living among Queensland Aborigines in the 1860s suggested that one member, Adolf Classen, survived for some years.

Between 1852 and 1938, nine major searches were conducted for survivors or evidence of what happened to Leichhardt's party. But the desert has never relinquished the tale of Leichhardt's fate. The city of Sydney has, however, named one of its suburbs after him.

tralian exploration. The myth of an inland sea had been dispelled.

By 1836, the vast river systems of the south-eastern continent had been charted. Tasmania had been explored, and the genocide of its natives had begun. A decade later most of New South Wales, half of Queensland, and the southern and northern coasts had been explored.

Heroes and villains

This era is rich in tales of intrepid adventurers, some driven by the urge to explore unknown territory but most motivated by dreams of finding riches. One such tale of misadventures is

with him, and from Innamincka on Cooper's Creek, he forged ahead in 60°C (140°F) heat. They reached the Gulf of Carpentaria in February 1861 and immediately began retracing their footsteps. Grey died on the way.

The three emaciated survivors finally reached their earlier camp at Innamincka where they had left another companion, Brahe. But Brahe, who had waited four months for them, had departed only seven hours earlier. After rejecting the potential assistance of local Aborigines, Burke and Wills died soon after in the implacable Stony Desert. Only King, cared for by Aborigines, survived to tell the story. ❑

now deeply ingrained in Australian folklore.

In August 1860, Robert O'Hara Burke and W.J. Wills left Melbourne with a well-equipped team and a camel train (imported from Afghanistan). Their intention was to be the first party to cross the continent from coast to coast.

Burke was brash, inexperienced, supremely confident and a glory-seeker. Too impatient to wait for the supply camels to keep up, he took Wills and other team members, Grey and King

LEFT: Matthew Flinders and George Bass charting the Bass Strait.
ABOVE: John Wills, John King and Charles Grey set out on their ill-fated exploration of the interior, 1860.
RIGHT: Aborigines in Sydney in the early 1800s.

THE NEW SETTLERS

The transportation of convicts was phased out between 1840 and 1868. By 1860, the continent had been divided into five separate colonies, with each exhibiting at times more loyalty to Mother London than to its neighbouring siblings.

A major force within the colonies was the "squatocracy", the rich officers, emancipated convicts and free settlers who had followed the explorers into the fertile hinterlands. They had simply laid claim to or "squatted" upon enormous tracts of land, often 8,000 hectares (20,000 acres) and more. Like the merino sheep they introduced to their stations, the squatters both lived off and were "the fat of the land".

FROM GOLD RUSH TO WORLD WAR

After gold was discovered in the 1850s, a sudden influx
of immigrants set out to make their fortune and a similar
boom in outlaws set to relieve them of it. Then, in
1901, the six quarrelling colonies became a nation

In 1851 Edward Hargraves, an Australian forty-niner (a fortune seeker of the 1849 California gold rush) returned home. He was certain, given the geological similarities he had observed, that gold must also exist in New South Wales. (Unbeknown to him, gold had been found 10 years earlier by a Rev. W.B. Clarke, but news of the discovery had been suppressed. Upon seeing the gold, the Governor, Sir George Gipps, had said: "Put it away, Mr Clarke, or we shall all have our throats cut!")

The announcement on 15 May 1851 of "Gold Discovered!" near Bathurst, 170 km (106 miles) west of Sydney, sent shock waves through the Australian colonies. The rush of prospectors to Bathurst was so great that the population of Victoria immediately nosedived. Melbourne employers offered a £200 reward for the discovery of gold near *their* city.

By July the prize had been claimed, and before the end of the year incredibly rich fields were in production in Victoria at Ballarat, Bendigo and Castlemaine. For the businessmen of Melbourne, the finds were a mixed blessing. While the prices of flour, blankets, bread, shovels and mining gear doubled and tripled, there was often no one to sell them. Melbourne and Geelong were almost emptied of men.

The Roaring Days

The scene in the goldfields was one of frantic activity, where teams of four or six men worked a claim, digging, shovelling, washing and cradling from dawn to dusk. When the miners hit town, they careened around the streets on horseback or in cabs. At one Melbourne theatre, reported an eyewitness, the actors "were obliged to appear before the footlights to bear a pelting

shower of nuggets – a substitute for bouquets – many over half an ounce, and several of which fell short of the mark into the orchestra."

Gold rushes flared like bushfire around the continent during the next two decades, and then sporadically for the rest of the century. The last great find was the Kalgoorlie-Coolgardie field in Western Australia in 1892–93. It was not only the shop assistants of Sydney and the sailors of Port Phillip who caught gold fever. In 1852 alone, 95,000 hopefuls from around the world flooded into New South Wales and Victoria.

ABOVE: *The Prospector* dreams of riches in an 1889 painting by Julian Ashton.
RIGHT: troopers storm the Eureka Stockade in 1854.

The Eureka Stockade

At Ballarat, near Melbourne, the early gold dig-gers smarted under the imposition, whether they struck gold or not, of a £1 a month licence fee. Raids by thuggish police who enforced the licence fee *and* collected half the fine from defaulters added to their rancour.

In October 1854 a miner was kicked to death by a local publican, who (despite strong evi-dence against him) was cleared of the crime. Mass meetings attended by up to 5,000 miners railed against these injustices. The men demanded the granting of universal franchise and the abolition of licence fees. They formed the Ballarat Reform League and on 29 Novem-ber made a bonfire of their mining licences.

The lieutenant-governor of Victoria, Sir Charles Hotham, sent in the "traps" (police-men) and troopers. Five hundred diggers built a stockade and swore to "fight to defend our rights and liberties." In the early hours of 3 December 1854, a force of 300 infantry, cavalry men and mounted police savagely attacked the sleeping stockade, whose defenders had dwin-dled to 150. Within 15 minutes it was all over. Six soldiers and 24 miners were dead.

Eventually an amnesty was proclaimed for the rebels, and the licence fee was abolished.

BUSHRANGERS AND REBELS

The gold rush created a new boom in bushranging – highway robbery. Many an "old lag" (ex-convict), as well as poor settlers, saw that gold need not necessarily be dug from the ground. The proceeds from "bailing up" a stagecoach or gold wagon could be good, and the work was a lot cleaner than digging. One Victorian gang in 1853 relieved the gold escort of 70,000 grams (over 2,400 oz) of gold and £700 in cash; three gang members were also sent to the gallows.

In the 1860s the most famous of the "Wild Colonial Boys" were the bushrangers Ben Hall, Frank Gardiner and John Gilbert. Well-armed and superbly mounted – often on stolen racehorses – they pulled off audacious raids. In November 1864, Hall's gang of three, working the Sydney–Melbourne road, rounded up 60 travellers at once. Then came the prize for which they were waiting – the armed mail coach. While one bushranger covered the 60 captives, Hall and Gilbert shot the police guard and robbed the coach. Several of the captives came out of the bush, not to aid the police but to watch the shoot-out.

From their first appearance, bushrangers were often sheltered by the rural poor, many of whom were Irish immigrants or the descendants of political transportees. Their strong republican sentiments led them to regard some of the outlaws as rebels against the same enemy – the British, Protestant landlords and authorities.

While the incident is replete with tragedy and some farce, the Eureka Stockade and its flag continue to evoke the ideals of revolt against colonialism and bourgeois authority. As Mark Twain commented, Eureka was "the finest thing in Australian history… another instance of a victory won by a lost battle."

The Federation is born

In September 1900, Queen Victoria regally proclaimed that, on 1 January 1901, not only a new century but also a new nation would be born.

A federal government for the six Australian colonies was generally welcomed, what with the Russians and the increasingly strong Japanese prowling the Pacific. With Australia not wishing to step too far out of line, its Constitution was tame. The Queen remained head of state, retaining the power over all foreign affairs. British parliamentary legislation could overrule any laws passed by the Commonwealth, and legal appeals ultimately were settled in London. Few Australians objected to this arrangement, for each of the six colonies felt more at ease in its dealings with the motherland than with the other colonies.

For her part, Mother Britain did not let the new nation escape the interests of imperialism.

THE KELLY GANG

Ned Kelly was born in 1854 and grew up among impoverished Irish farmers near Benalla, northern Victoria. He first ran foul of the law in 1877 when he shot a constable in the wrist. Teaming up with his brother Dan and two friends, Joe Byrne and Steve Hart, he fled to the bush and turned outlaw. The following year, in a shoot-out at Stringybark Creek, Ned killed three of a party of four police who were hunting him. From then on, the Kellys became part of Australian folklore.

Ned saw himself as a Robin Hood, a defender of the free against the oppressive British overlords. Instead of robbing coaches, his gang bailed-up whole towns, cutting the telegraph and robbing the bank before escaping.

The gang hid out in the Wombat Ranges, but in June 1880, on hearing that a train-load of police was on the way to arrest them, they captured the town of Glenrowan, Victoria, and held the townsfolk prisoner in the hotel.

A furious shoot-out erupted between the Kellys and the cops. Wounded, Ned donned his suit of home-made armour and attempted to escape. Instead, he stumbled into the police who at first thought they were seeing a ghostly apparition. Ned was shot down but not killed. The police torched the hotel and the other three members of the Kelly Gang died within it, rather than surrender.

Four months later in Melbourne, Kelly was sentenced to death. He was hanged on 11 November 1880.

She expected, and got, continuing support in her military involvements, and ample returns on her substantial investments in Australia.

The quest for a capital

The new nation needed a capital. Sydney and Melbourne each wished it to be in its own state, and neither of the longstanding rivals would permit it in the other's. After considerable back-biting, a separate Australian Capital Territory was established at a point between the two cities, 320 km (200 miles) from Sydney on the beautiful Monaro Tablelands. Some suggested naming the capital Shakespeare – hardly an ap-

teers had been despatched to Europe via Egypt. Many were to die at Gallipoli *(see page 40)*.

The Australian "Diggers" (soldiers) were deployed in France, on the Western Front, from April 1916. In the grisly attacks, through mustard gas and frozen winters, their losses were appalling – 23,000 dead in nine weeks in the First Battle of the Somme, 38,000 at Ypres, 10,000 at Bullecourt. The new nation was being cut down.

Many Australians were now questioning the sense of supporting Britain in what they saw as a "sordid trade war". But a deciding factor was the presence at Australia's helm of a feisty and dogged little man who was loved and loathed

propriate choice considering the anti-intellectual cultural cringers who formed a vocal part of the Australian population. In 1913 the Aboriginal word "Canberra" was chosen instead.

The Great War

When Britain declared war on Germany on 4 August 1914 Australia, as a member of the British Empire, was automatically at war, too. The response by both Labor and Liberal parties was immediate. By the end of October the First Australian Infantry Force of 20,000 volun-

LEFT: *Bailed Up*, painted by Tom Roberts at the end of the 19th century.
ABOVE: Allied forces at Gallipoli in 1915.

THE CHINESE INFLUX

The vast majority of Diggers were British, but of the other nationalities the Chinese were the most numerous. In the five years from 1854, more than 40,000 flocked to the Victorian fields. The Chinese lived in their own communities, were usually diligent labourers, and produced only one Chinese bushranger, San Poo.

By 1887, Asian immigration had been stifled. Australia inaugurated "the White Australia Policy" with federation and nationhood in 1901. The Immigration Act allowed an impossibly tough dictation test in any European language to be given to all non-European arrivals. It was not until 1966 that there was any genuine reversal of this race-based exclusion.

with equal passion: William Morris ("Billy") Hughes, or "the Little Digger".

In 1916 Hughes had pledged a supply of 16,500 Australian troops a month. Such a number could be raised only through conscription – previously, recruitment had been voluntary. The proposal was defeated narrowly in a referendum, and Hughes was expelled from his own Labor Party. He set about forming a national coalition government and held a second referendum in December 1917. Again he was defeated, but again he bounced back, winning a seat at the Versailles Peace Conference.

Of the 330,000 Australian troops who had

fought in the war, 226,000 (68.5 percent) were casualties, a greater percentage by far than had been suffered by any other Allied nation.

The Great Depression

Between 1929 and 1933 every government in Australia, both state and federal, was thrown out of office by an electorate deciding to "give the other mob a go – they couldn't be worse." But nor could they do any better, for the Great Depression had arrived. Thirty percent of the country's breadwinners were on "Susso" (sustenance benefits). Wearing war surplus greatcoats, hundreds were tramping the Outback roads as "swagmen" looking for rural work.

Australia's economy was based heavily upon the export of wheat and wool, and upon continued borrowings from Britain. When world prices for primary products slumped by 50 percent, and when Britain withdrew £30 million from the Australian economy, the result was traumatic, especially for the poor.

Sir Otto Niemeyer of the Bank of England was despatched to scold Australians for living at an unsustainably high standard, to advise wage cuts and retrenchments, and to make sure that the interest was still paid on his loans.

World War II

When Britain again went to war against Germany in September 1939, Australia once more automatically entered the conflict. A Second Australian Infantry Force was raised and despatched to the Middle East.

In 1939 Australia's prime minister, the leader of the United Australia Party, was Robert

THE DEATH TOLL OF GALLIPOLI

While Australia's troops trained in Egypt, Winston Churchill (then First Lord of the Admiralty in London) conceived a plan that was intended to relieve Turkish pressure on Russia's troops by forcing an entrance to the Black Sea. He wished to take the Dardanelles, and ordered the waiting Australian, New Zealand, French, British, Indian and Gurkha divisions to attack from the sea.

The Turks, warned of these intentions, were entrenched in fortified positions along the ridges of the Gallipoli Peninsula. Their commanders, Mustafa Kemal and the German Liman von Sanders, were able safely to direct their fire upon the exposed beaches below.

From 25 April 1915, when they landed, until 20

December, when they withdrew, the British and Allied forces were pinned to the near-vertical cliffs and narrow coves. There was horrendous carnage and epic heroism.

During the eight months of fighting at Gallipoli, 78,000 were wounded and 33,500 killed on the side of Britain and its allies. Of the dead, 8,587 were "Anzacs" (belonging to the Australian and New Zealand Army Corps). Australians often overlook the fact that almost as many French died there, and twice as many Britons, Indians and Nepalis; also that 250,000 Turks fell.

Nevertheless, out of this baptism by mud, shrapnel and gallantry arose Australia's first coherent sense of nationhood and identity.

Gordon Menzies, a clever, witty barrister and a deeply conservative Anglophile. He had earned the nickname of "Pig-Iron Bob" by selling pig iron to the re-arming Japanese, of whom Australia had become increasingly nervous. Japan was now threatening Southeast Asia and had marked Australia for invasion.

While Australian air, land and sea forces fought in Britain, the Mediterranean, North Africa, Greece and the Middle East, Japan began to move south, first into French Indochina. Australian forces were sent to Malaya, the Dutch East Indies, Darwin and Rabaul (New Guinea) to try to stem the Japanese tide.

Britain could be of no real assistance against an imminent Japanese invasion.

Japanese planes bombed Darwin on 19 February and Broome on 3 March. Arms and food caches were established in the north of the continent. Australia faced the very real threat of invasion by Japanese troops.

The Australian war cabinet then outraged Churchill by diverting the 7th Australian Division from the defence of British Burma to the New Guinea and Pacific theatres. If it is true that the Australian nation was born at Gallipoli, it is no less true that with the fall of Singapore it finally came of age.

In Canberra, "Pig-Iron Bob" was reviled for his Chamberlain-like pre-war appeasement of the Axis powers. By October 1941 a Labor Government under John Curtin was in power.

A nation comes of age

The Japanese attack on Pearl Harbor confirmed Australia's great fear: to be isolated and white in an Asia at war. When Singapore fell on 15 February 1942, 15,000 of the 130,000 captured troops were Australian. The country was faced with the fact that a distant and beleaguered

The tide turns

The tide began to turn against Japan in May 1942 when a combined American and Australian fleet checked a Japanese force at the Battle of the Coral Sea. The US victory at Midway in June assured Allied control of the Pacific, but on New Guinea, Japanese foot soldiers were closing in on Australia's main base at Port Moresby. After months of guerrilla combat and hand-to-hand jungle fighting, the Australian troops finally pushed them back.

Of the 1 million Australian servicemen and women who had enlisted, almost 10,000 died in Europe and more than 17,000 in the Pacific. Of those taken prisoner by the Japanese, 8,000 did not survive the Japanese camps. ❑

LEFT: a World War I poster encourages South Australians to enlist.

RIGHT: Sydney Harbour Bridge was completed in 1932.

THE MODERN ERA

Over the past 60 years, Australia has witnessed a trebling
of the population, industrial booms and economic
slumps, rigid conservatism and progressive liberalism

Australian history since World War II has been an up-and-down saga – a rise to undreamed-of affluence in the 1950s and '60s when the wool prices boomed, followed by unexpected cracks in the great suburban dream. Today the image of the country as a conservative, Anglo-Saxon society somehow finding itself lost in Asia has been completely recast. But the road towards a cosmopolitan, liberal, middle-class Australia has been tortuous. For a small country – population-wise – of which it was said "nothing ever happens", there has been a succession of booms, recessions, political crises, wars, culture shocks and social changes.

The 1940s were the most difficult years in Australia's history, the long war against Japan emphasising the country's vulnerability. The war also shook up Australian society internally; many women served in the armed forces, or worked in factories or office jobs that had previously been reserved for men, and were reluctant to go back to the old inequality between the sexes. Ex-servicemen didn't want to go back to the old order either.

Radical changes

In 1946, Australians voted an activist Labor government, led by Ben Chifley, back into power with plans for an expanded social welfare programme. In quick succession, Chifley set up a government-owned airline, took initiatives in housing and education (the Australian National University was opened in Canberra), and ordered massive work projects such as the Snowy Mountains Scheme, which provided hydroelectric power for southeast Australia.

The most radical and revitalising change, however, occurred in immigration. The spectre of a Japanese invasion in World War II had convinced Australians that the country's population must increase. Labor's immigration minister, Arthur Calwell, embarked upon one of the most spectacular migration programmes of the 20th century. Half of the assisted migrants were to be British, but the other half could come from anywhere – as long as they were white. More than 2 million migrants arrived between 1945 and 1965, helping Australia's population to leap from 7 to 11 million.

The nation still clung to its White Australia policy, and Calwell himself was a racist. (He made the infamous wisecrack, when asked whether he would permit Asian immigration, "Two Wongs don't make a white.") The policy was modified slowly in later years until it was formally abolished in 1973. So rapid has been the overturning of these anachronistic attitudes that at the present time one-third of all immigrants are Asian. The effect of this change in policy was to be far-reaching *(see panel below)*.

Into the modern world

Still, mainstream Australian culture changed slowly. In the 1950s, Australia remained a rigid society, one which had grown up in comparative isolation and was complacent and illiberal. It was still dominated by men, despite the postwar challenge from women: male rituals like

Church, dominated morals; divorce was legal, but it was condemned and hard to obtain; abortion remained illegal, the province of backstreet doctors. The nation was burdened with a suffocating puritanism which Australians labelled "wowserism". Censorship was strict (James Joyce's *Ulysses* and D.H. Lawrence's *Lady Chatterley's Lover* were banned, and had to be smuggled into the country). The language was stamped with prejudices, many directed at migrants and refugees ("reffos").

Politically, the decade is referred to as the "Boring Fifties". A revived conservative party – known as the Liberal Party, and led by the

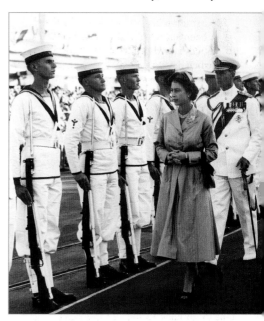

sport, drinking and brawling predominated; homosexuals were persecuted as "poofters" and anyone with a beard or long hair was dubbed a "weirdo". Male values such as mateship were extolled while "the missus" was expected to stay at home and look after the kids. It seemed, visually and ethically, a very working-class society, a land of boots and felt hats, of men in dank pubs calling each other "mate" or "sport".

The churches, especially the Roman Catholic

LEFT: migrants sail into Sydney harbour in 1949.
ABOVE: prime minister Ben Chifley with his 1948 Holden, Australia's first mass-produced car.
RIGHT: Queen Elizabeth II inspects Royal Australian naval personnel in Perth in 1962.

A FLOOD OF IMMIGRANTS

In 1945 Australia had been a conformist, predominantly Anglo-Saxon country in which 98 percent of inhabitants had a British background. Suddenly it was confronted with massive contingents of Italians, Greeks, Germans, Dutch and Yugoslavs who could hardly speak English and who set up their own communities, shops and newspapers. It all happened with surprisingly little friction, although with great hardship on the part of the so-called "New Australians". They were the workforce behind much of the intense development of the 1950s and 1960s, providing manual labour in steelworks, mines, factories and on the roads, as well as on major national projects such as the Snowy Mountains Scheme.

rabid Anglophile Robert Menzies, who proclaimed himself "British to his boot-straps" – was able to tap into the growing Cold War hysteria and attack the Labor Party for being riddled with Communists.

When rising unemployment threatened to turn the Liberals out of office, Menzies decided to plump for safe, middle-of-the-road policies that would disturb neither extreme of the electorate. The Labor Party split in 1955 on ideological lines and effectively kept itself out of power for another 17 years.

"Development" became the national slogan; there were posters everywhere stressing peace,

prosperity and progress, and even the arrival of rock 'n' roll from the United States didn't seem to disturb the social equanimity. There were a few rebel groups, such as the bodgies (male) and widgies (female), who did such radical things as ride motorcycles and listen to Elvis, but it was hardly more than a milk-bar menace. Another nonconformist group was the Sydney "push", a group of freethinkers and libertarians who gathered at pubs and coffee shops and scorned the suburban coma ward which surrounded them. They wrote poetry and bawdy songs and, though mainly a male group, produced two remarkable women –

THE FLIGHT OF THE FREE SPIRITS

Every year from the late 1950s, thousands of young Australians left on their equivalent of the "Grand Tour" of London and other cities in Europe, seeking the excitement and the sort of mind-broadening experience which, despite the immigration programme, was unavailable at home.

They could hardly be blamed. The newsreels of the time, seen now, are embarrassingly nationalistic, racist and sexist. The pubs closed at 6pm sharp each weekday, producing the infamous "six o'clock swill", when men crammed into pubs and guzzled as much as they could between the end of work and closing time (women wouldn't have been allowed in even if they'd wanted to). Off-course betting was illegal, so SP (starting price) bookmakers flourished

alongside sly-grog joints, where liquor could be bought after hours. On the positive side, during the 1950s Australia enjoyed the most even income distribution of any Western industrialised nation.

Well into the 1960s, the district of Earls Court in London became an Aussie ghetto; Rolf Harris, the entertainer, started his climb to fame by singing Tie Me Kangaroo Down, Sport at the Down Under Club; unique talents like Barry Humphries, Clive James and Robert Hughes all fled Australia. The nation's best artists and writers – Patrick White, Germaine Greer and Sidney Nolan among them – turned themselves into expatriates. At the time it seemed that little was happening back in Oz.

Germaine Greer, author of *The Female Eunuch*, and the late Lillian Roxon, author of the first *Rock Encyclopedia*.

The affluent 1960s

Meanwhile, Australia had begun turning itself from a nation of primary industry (sheep, wheat and cattle) to one of manufacturing. Between 1940 and 1960 the number of factories doubled; fridges, washing machines, vacuum cleaners and cars became available to the great mass of the population for the first time.

By the mid-1960s, Australians were enjoying, after the North Americans, the highest stan-

In the meantime, the shape of Australian society was being entirely changed. In the early 1960s the number of white-collar workers exceeded, for the first time, the number of blue-collar workers and then streaked far ahead. This booming group typically lived in comfortable suburban homes, owned cars and TVs, had bank accounts, and voted Liberal (Australian for "Conservative").

Australia, regarded for so long as a working man's paradise, had almost unnoticed transformed itself into one of the most middle-class nations in the world.

But, amid the prosperity, many were deject-

dard of living in the world. They were also living in the most urbanised nation on earth, with three-quarters of the population in cities – more than half of that on the eastern seaboard.

Links with the Old Country were weakened when Britain joined the European Economic Community, leaving Australia out in the cold; trade with the US and Japan grew to fill the gap. The 1951 ANZUS security treaty had brought Australia and New Zealand securely within the USA's sphere.

LEFT: Barry Humphries as Edna Everage before she bestrode the international stage as a Dame.
ABOVE: feminist Germaine Greer offers some biting criticism of contemporary dolls.

ed over the fate of Australia and the consequences of its new-found wealth. Donald Horne wrote a book called, with heavy irony, *The Lucky Country* – a land that had squandered its opportunities and abandoned its best egalitarian traditions to wallow in complacency. The Australian social ideal of communality was changing and with it, apparently, the Australian character.

A time of change

Cracks began to appear in the bland facade of Australian contentment. In 1962 Australia had become involved in the Vietnam War and in the next 10 years sent 49,000 conscripts, chosen by lottery, off to the jungles of Southeast Asia – where 499 were killed and 2,069 wounded. As in the United States, the anti-war movement breathed life into all forms of liberalisation, pushing Australia into an era of crisis and questioning *(see box below)*.

When the Labor Party, led by Gough Whitlam, finally won office in 1972 under the slogan "It's Time", it seemed to many that a clean break with the past had occurred and a promising new, progressive era was about to begin.

Labor moved quickly to abolish military conscription, to end Australia's involvement in Vietnam, to recognise China and to begin the long process of reconstructing the social

welfare system. Everything appeared to be happening at once, with plans underway for a universal health-care system, increased support for the arts (resulting in a spate of Australian films), and the formal end of White Australia.

But Whitlam didn't reckon on the economic and social impacts of big government spending. He managed to win another election in 1974 but was confronted with a sudden and unexpected world recession provoked by an oil price hike. Australians suddenly faced growing inflation and unemployment and the the government was beset by a series of damaging scandals, including an attempt to borrow four billion petrodollars through a questionable intermediary.

Political crisis

Labor had been hobbled in its programme by a Conservative majority vote in the Senate. In 1975 the Liberal-National Country Party opposition, led by Malcolm Fraser, used this power to deny the government its money supply. Whitlam refused to resign, and the nation was thrust into the gravest political and constitutional crisis of its history. This was resolved in a controversial manner: the governor-general, Sir John Kerr, as the Queen's representative in Australia, dismissed Whitlam and called another election. It was an act that many considered illegal – in spirit, if not in the letter of the Constitution.

Fraser won the subsequent election, consolidated his power and swore he would take politics off the front page.

The Spirit of the 1960s

Student power, the women's movement, black power and sexual liberation groups began challenging the conservative consensus. The rigid censorship of books and films was slowly dismantled, allowing Australians the opportunity to pore over previously forbidden classics of literature such as *Lolita* and *Portnoy's Complaint*.

Aborigines had been allowed to vote in federal elections in 1967, but a "freedom bus" drove through Queensland and New South Wales in protest against the deep-rooted, systematic discrimination against black people. At the same time, it was found that 10 percent of Australians were living in chronic poverty; they included Aborigines, single parents, the sick and handicapped and the jobless.

At the same time, migrants had begun transforming the staid British social customs of their host country. At an obvious level arrived the introduction of delicatessens, continental European food, open-air cafés, new varieties of music and a hectic sort of cosmopolitanism hardly imaginable before World War II. More profoundly, the migrants also opened Australians up to new ideas and new ways of looking at the world that have gradually altered the national character.

Spurred on by the new spirit, a revived Labor Party was arguing for new policies on a grand scale and was being led by its most inspiring politician for years, the towering, bushy-browed, charismatic Gough Whitlam.

Change is the constant

In 1983 a new Labor era began when Australians voted in a government led by Bob Hawke, an ex-union leader, ex-Rhodes scholar and ex-world champion beer drinker (2½ pints in 11 seconds). Hawke later wrote that this feat did most for his political career in a country "with a strong beer culture". The Labor Party had become more right-wing, economically liberal and in closer touch with the increasingly powerful white-collar unions and business.

For the next 13 years, it ruled with little challenge (with Paul Keating taking over the prime ministership in 1991). Consensus became the "banana republic" if fundamental changes to the economy weren't made. Labor presided over a push towards free-market policies, yet was able to maintain some degree of social justice by keeping Australia's welfare system intact.

Diplomatically and economically, Australia linked itself much more closely to Asia, while on the home front Asian immigration was stepped up, shifting the emphasis away from European immigration. Women were admitted to more positions of power, and Aboriginal "land rights" (control over their native homelands) was put on the national agenda. The celebration of the Bicentennial of British set-

catchword, with the government brokering historic accords between business and unions, promising unprecedented industrial peace, and finally introducing a national health care system for all, Medicare.

This new-look Labor government had to deal with an ever-sliding Australian economy, starting off with a series of devaluations of the Aussie dollar (the "Pacific peso", as it wryly became known). Keating warned that the country would turn into a Latin American-style

LEFT: Gough Whitlam listens to the Governor-General's edict dismissing his government in 1975.
ABOVE: World Expo '88, held in Brisbane, had the theme "Leisure in the Age of Technology".

tlement in 1988 was a landmark of Australian self-confidence, but also a cause for some national soul-searching. In 1992, a High Court ruling, known as the Mabo case, finally abolished the historical fiction of *terra nullius* – the colonial doctrine that said Australia was uninhabited when the British first arrived – and opened the way to Aboriginal land claims *(see Aborigines Today, pages 68–9)*.

The 1980s and 1990s saw a flowering of the Australian arts, with local film makers and writers increasingly taking on an international profile. Australians also began talking seriously about becoming a republic at last – an initiative driven by the news that Sydney would host the Olympic Games in 2000.

Despite the steady achievements of these years, Australian voters had wearied of Labor and in 1996 voted in a Liberal-National Coalition government, led by the determinedly conservative John Howard, with a large majority. In economic matters, Howard has been pushing for a freer market and smaller government, while also capturing swinging voters with economic support. Conservatism also held out in the 1999 status referendum, as Australia entered the new millennium voting against becoming a republic and (by the narrowest of majorities) opting to keep the Queen as head of state.

Australia's economic outlook has improved steadily with the "globalisation" initiatives of successive recent governments, a booming resources industry and the often controversial privatisation of the transport, energy and communications monoliths. In recent years the Australian dollar has regained considerable ground against the US "greenback". The country celebrated its new-found confidence in the euphoria of Sydney's staging of the 2000 Olympics. Dubbed the "best Games ever" by the IOC president, the games were an unequivocal success, both as a mark of Australia's sporting prowess and as the ulti-

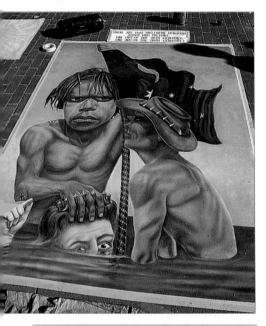

GOVERNMENT AND POLITICS

Australians are triple-governed – by local councils, state and federal parliaments. Any time they're asked, they vote politicians as the least trustworthy profession. There's a growing belief that a small nation of 20 million can't produce enough talent to run three levels of government.

Judging by the acres of newsprint and airspace devoted to the topic, the nation is obsessed with politics, though no more than a few thousand people are paid-up members of political parties. Everyone votes in the national (federal) elections because they have to: federal law made it compulsory in 1924, and unless you have a good excuse, you will receive a small fine for not voting.

mate high-profile evidence of Australia as an attractive travel destination.

Climate change controversy

The government's refusal to sign the Kyoto Agreement on climate change despite overwhelming evidence of global warming, has aroused international condemnation. Many voters see the connection between Howard's reluctance to act on environmental issues and their experiences of water shortages and bush fires, and are unhappy with his response.

ABOVE LEFT: the Queen is a victim of pavement art.
ABOVE: a banner keeps alive the racial issue.
RIGHT: prime minister John Howard and wife Janette.

Australia's treatment of refugees has also been criticised. The 2001 Tampa incident – when the captain of a Norwegian freighter, who rescued a group of Afghan refugees from their sinking boat off the Australian coast, was refused permission to deliver the refugees to Australia – made international headlines, not least because it was a direct contravention of Australia's obligations under international law. Australia has developed an "outsourcing" policy, intercepting refugees on their way to Australia and redirecting them to small South Pacific nations. But many of these island nations are already dependent on Australian aid, and are ill-equipped to deal with boatloads of refugees.

At the start of the century the government's policy of "Mandatory Detention" – the forced detainment of immigrants without a valid visa at hugely expensive, prison-like detention centres – was brought to the attention of the world's media through high-profile hunger strikes by some of the detainees. While the international press has since moved elsewhere, the centres continue to be deeply controversial and to many Australians to be at odds with the country's recent history of receiving and welcoming immigrants. ❑

JOHN HOWARD'S CONTROVERSIAL REIGN

John Howard, a Sydney-born lawyer, became Australia's second longest-serving prime minister after Robert Menzies. A buoyant economy and a disorganised Labor party helped keep him in office, despite an increasing disillusionment among the electorate about many of his policies. In 2007, the Labour Party, led by centre-left Kevin Rudd, won the election thus bringing Howard's 11-year reign to an end.

In the latter years, Howard championed a foreign policy more closely aligned with that of the United Kingdom and the United States. Perhaps the government's most divisive decision was the continued presence of Australian troops in Iraq and the perceived connection of this presence to a recent spate of terrorist attacks across the Western world. The 2002 Bali bombings, in which 202 people, including 88 young Australians, died, was an enormous shock to a country previously considered insulated from the possibility of attack.

The combination of these factors coupled with an already present degree of prejudice raised tensions with Australia's considerable Muslim community. These tensions bubbled over in the 2005 riots in the Cronulla area of Sydney, and remained a point of friction.

In the rough trade of Australian politics, Howard was able to push through legislation in a number of controversial areas – such as gun control, sales tax reform, compulsory trade unionism, tight immigration controls, and aboriginal land ownership.

Decisive Dates

50 million years ago: Australia breaks free from the landmass that includes Antarctica, and drifts north.
50,000BC: The first Australians arrive, overland from New Guinea (some authorities place it earlier).
40,000BC: Tools from this period, found by Nepean River, are the oldest evidence of human occupation.
12,000BC: Tasmania and New Guinea are separated from the mainland as seas rise after the last ice age.
8000BC: Returning boomerangs are perfected and used for hunting for the first time in South Australia.
2000BC: The dingo arrives in Australia.

AD150: Geographer Ptolemy decides there must be an unknown southern land *(terra australis incognita)*.

EARLY VISITORS

9th century: Seafarers from China possibly reach Australia's north coast.
11th century: Macassar fishermen regularly visit Australia in search of the sea cucumber, a valuable delicacy.
1290s: Marco Polo's journal refers to a land south of Java, rich in gold and shells.
1516: Portuguese establish colony on Timor, 500 km (310 miles) to the north; possibly visit north coast.
1606: Dutchman Willem Jansz, sailing east from Java, lands on the western side of Cape York Peninsula – the first verifiable European landing.

1642: Abel Tasman names the west coast of Tasmania Van Diemen's Land. *Terra Australis Incognita* becomes *Hollandia Nova* (New Holland) on maps.
1688: English buccaneer William Dampier lands on the northwest coast.

COLONISATION AND EXPLORATION

1770: Captain Cook lands at Botany Bay, then sails north, charting 4,000 km (2,500 miles) of coast. He names it New South Wales and claims it for Britain.
1773: First picture of a kangaroo seen in Britain.
1788: First Fleet arrives in Sydney Cove, with a cargo of convicts. First white child is born in Australia.
1790: Second Fleet arrives.
1793: First free immigrants arrive in Australia.
1797: Merino sheep brought from Cape of Good Hope.
1803: Publication of *Sydney Gazette and New South Wales Advertiser*, Australia's first newspapers.
1801–3: Matthew Flinders circumnavigates Australia, proving it is a single island.
1811: Rev. Samuel Marsden exports the first commercial cargo of wool to England.
1813: Australia's own currency is established. First crossing of the Blue Mountains.
1817: The name Australia is adopted (instead of New Holland). First bank is established in Sydney.
1829: First settlers land at Fremantle, and found Perth two days later. Western Australia becomes a colony.
1830: All Aborigines in Tasmania are rounded up and herded into reserves.
1831: Publication of *Quintus Servinton,* the first Australian novel, by Henry Savery, a former convict.
1836: Colony of South Australia established; Adelaide founded the following year.
1837: A year-old village on the Yarra River is named Melbourne (still part of New South Wales).
1838: Myall Creek Massacre: 28 Aborigines are butchered by white farmers.

GOLD RUSHES AND GROWTH

1842: New South Wales becomes a self-governing colony. Copper discovered in South Australia.
1850: Southern part of NSW becomes a separate colony called Victoria.
1851: Gold discovered, first in east-central NSW, then throughout Victoria.
1854: Battle at the Eureka Stockade between state troopers and miners protesting against licence fees.
1855: Van Diemen's Land becomes Tasmania.
1859: Northern part of New South Wales becomes a separate colony, Queensland. European rabbits intro-

duced near Geelong; by 1868 they have eaten most of western Victoria's vegetation.

1860: First south–north crossing (Melbourne to Gulf of Carpentaria) by the Burke and Wills Expedition.

1861: First Melbourne Cup horse race, watched by 4,000 people.

1863: South Australia takes over the administration of Northern Territory (formerly part of NSW).

1868: Transportation of convicts ends.

1880: Bushranger Ned Kelly is captured and hanged.

1882: Australian cricketers beat England for first time.

1883: Silver discovered at Broken Hill, NSW. Queensland takes possession of Papua (New Guinea).

1891: Delegates from the six colonies meet in Sydney to draft a Constitution for Australia.

1893: Gold rush in Kalgoorlie, Western Australia.

1895: Banjo Paterson writes *Waltzing Matilda*.

1896: Athlete Edwin Flack represents Australia at the first modern Olympic Games.

A NEW NATION

1901: The six colonies become a federation, the Commonwealth of Australia (population 3,370,000). The first Commonwealth Parliament sits in Melbourne.

1911: The federal government takes over the administration of Northern Territory.

1914–18: 330,000 Australians serve in World War I; 60,000 are killed, 165,000 wounded.

1915: Australian troops take a major part in the Gallipoli siege; more than 8,000 are killed.

1923: Chemist Cyril Callister creates Vegemite, Australia's national food.

1927: Parliament House opens in Canberra and the federal parliament moves there from Melbourne.

1928: Royal Flying Doctor Service founded by Rev. John Flynn in Cloncurry, Queensland.

1930: The Great Depression; 25 percent of the Australian workforce is unemployed.

1932: Sydney Harbour Bridge opens.

1939: Australia declares war on Germany. Australian Air Force is active in Britain, navy operates in Mediterranean, Australian troops fight in North Africa.

1941: Australia declares war on Japan.

1942: 15,000 Australians captured when Singapore falls to Japan. Japanese bomb Darwin.

1950: Immigration peaks at 150,000 new arrivals.

1954: Elizabeth II is the first reigning monarch to visit.

1956: Olympic Games held in Melbourne.

1959: Danish architect Jørn Utzon wins the competition to design Sydney Opera House. Population of Australia reaches 10 million.

1965: Conscription re-introduced.

1967: Aborigines granted Australian citizenship and the right to vote.

1973: Sydney Opera House is finally completed. Australian Patrick White wins Nobel Prize for Literature.

1974: Darwin flattened by Cyclone Tracy.

1975: Papua New Guinea is granted independence.

1985: Uluru (Ayers Rock), Kata Tjuta (The Olgas) and surrounding desert are returned to Aborigines.

1986: Australian film *Crocodile Dundee*, starring Paul Hogan, grosses $116 million in USA.

1988: In Australia's Bicentennial year, Queen

Elizabeth II opens new Parliament House in Canberra.

1995: Australians protest strongly over French nuclear testing in the South Pacific.

1999: Australians vote against becoming a republic.

2000: Olympic Games are held in Sydney.

2001: Centenary of the Federation.

2002: The Bali bombing kills 88 Australians.

2003: Australia's Liberal government supports US military action in Iraq.

2004: Government announces new cruise missile programme is to be the region's potentially most lethal.

2005: Racially motivated youth violence hits Sydney.

2006: Melbourne hosts the Commonwealth Games.

2007: Kevin Rudd leads the Australian Labour Party to victory in the November elections.

2008: Rudd apologises to the Stolen Generations. ❏

LEFT: the First Fleet in Sydney Cove in 1788.
RIGHT: Aboriginal athlete Cathy Freeman prepares to light the flame for the 2000 Olympic Games.

THE URBAN AUSSIE

Most of the population live in cities and suburbs, and most of them on the coast. But that doesn't stop Australians dreaming of the wide-open Outback

According to myth, the "true Aussie" is a sun-bronzed stockman or jillaroo, riding the Outback range with a trusty sheep-dog – which is like imagining all Americans to be tobacco-chewing cowboys, and French-men going about in berets and striped shirts. Truth to tell, Australia is the most urbanised country on earth, with 80 percent of the popu-lation living in cities (66 percent in the state capitals). More precisely, it's the most subur-banised country on earth. The Great Australian Dream, still enjoyed by a huge portion of the population, is to live on your own plot of land, with a brick house, red-tile roof, hoist wash-ing line and a barbie in the backyard.

Clinging to the coast

Most Australians now work in office jobs, and wouldn't recognise a trough of sheep dip if they fell in it. And although many still see the Out-back as somehow embodying the most distinc-tive part of the country, relatively few have visited it, let alone considered living there. Even Patrick White, who set famous novels such as *Voss* in the furthest red-sand-and-spinifex deserts, never actually saw them (he got his images from his friend Sidney Nolan's paintings). White settled in Sydney's eastern suburbs, 2,834 km (1,761 miles) from Uluru.

The fact is that Australians have clung to the coast rather naturally, shrugging off the priggish, cramped and tight-lipped spirit of the first British settlers and openly embracing the more sensual and hedonistic spirit of their Mediterranean envi-

PRECEDING PAGES: on the beach at Bondi.
LEFT: ready for action at Surfers Paradise, Queensland.
RIGHT: a charity bed race in Melbourne.

ronment. At least in the 21st century, the coast – and specifically the beach – has a far more pow-erful claim on Australian souls than the Outback. "How shall I put this delicately?" asks Sydney writer Robert Drewe. "Most Australians of the past three generations have had their first sex-ual experience on the coast. So is it surprising that for the rest of their lives the sexual and lit-toral experiences are entwined in their memo-ries; that most Australians thereafter see the beach in a pleasurable light?" It is to the sea that Australians return at each crucial stage of their lives: as lovers, on honeymoon, as parents. It is to the sea that they were taken as children, and to the sea that they return in old age, to the endless retirement villages of the Queensland shores.

And how could it really be otherwise, in a country with such a climate and geography? It would take a serious effort of will not to lap up the perfect skies, the sea breeze, the glorious mounds of prawns and oysters, the bodies laid out on the sands and saturated in SPF 30+. Under the Antipodean sun, more austere national traits succumb to the easy-going, tolerant, obsessively casual Australian manner. It's no surprise to see a first-generation immigrant from Glasgow turn into a surfie overnight, or the daughters of black-shrouded Muslim women lolling bikini-clad in the outdoor beer garden of a pub, or the sons of Puritanical Ger-

POSTCARD FROM AUSTRALIA

Bruce Chatwin wrote to Paul Theroux: "You must come here. The men are awful, like bits of cardboard, but the women are splendid."

end of the road, and residents may keep an eye out for funnel-web spiders, possums in the roof and snakes in the garden.

Despite the occasional natural menaces, relaxation is part of the territory in Australia. It takes something truly grim to rouse most people to anger – and there's always a swim, or a beer, or a crisp Chardonnay to calm them down.

mans dilute the work ethic so they can spend a few days each week windsurfing.

Leisure has become crucial to the Australian way of life – while working 9–5 provides the means, it is at the weekends when Aussies truly come into their own. And few other places give people such opportunities to use their leisure well. Nature is close in Australia as nowhere else: in Sydney with its 70 metropolitan beaches, in Melbourne with one-third of its area devoted to parkland, in Darwin where 4-metre (13-ft) crocodiles are regularly fished from the harbour. Some visitors still arrive expecting kangaroos to hop across the tarmac. This may not be so, but even in the red-brick back blocks of suburbia a national park might begin at the

From railway workers to restaurant waiters, the most common response to questions these days is a breezy "No worries", "Too easy" or "Not a problem" – the latest incarnation of the 1950s slogan "She'll be right, mate". Politics is a matter to shake your head at ("The bastards are all the same" is the common refrain at election time). Economics, however, has become a matter of fascination, and cab drivers and supermarket clerks can talk with authority on economic rationalism and exchange rates.

From convicts to democrats

Every country is shaped by its past, and few have had a stranger start than Australia's, as the dumping ground for Britain's petty thieves. As

Robert Hughes remarked in *The Fatal Shore*, it's one of the great ironies of history that a land founded by felons should evolve into one of the world's most law-abiding societies. Few cities of equal size around the world are as safe, tidy and downright civil as Australia's.

Social commentators have tried to draw conclusions from the country's awkward origins: that the convict legacy instilled a disdain for authority, leading to its powerful union movement, or that it led to a blunt conformism, accepting serious curtailments of civil liberties for most of the 20th century. Hughes comes up with the formula "skeptical conformists": Aus-

Diverting as such theories are, the truth is that few modern Australians can really trace their lineages to convict times; most are the descendants of free English, Scottish and Irish settlers after the 1850s, or the wave of immigrants from the rest of the world a century later. Although the convict "stain" was once a matter of horror – an ignoble memory that any respectable society would excise, particularly from school books – the opposite is true in Australia today. Anyone who can dig up a convict ancestor now wears the fact as a badge of honour. In Sydney's Hyde Barracks Museum, schoolchildren eagerly type their

tralians like to think of themselves as rowdy rebels, talking big at the pub or behind authority's back, but obey with little question when it comes to the crunch, tugging the forelock while seething with contempt.

Other, more jaded social commentators might say that Australia's beginnings as a penal colony have made it a corrupt place from day one. Many Australian officials, from police officers to immigration rubber-stampers, have a surprising arrogance; there is none more self-satisfied, it sometimes seems, than the petty Aussie clerk who is able to say "No".

LEFT: urban kangaroos in Perth, made of bronze.
ABOVE: dining alfresco on Melbourne's Brighton Beach.

RISING TENSIONS

In recent years events like the Bali bombs and the war in Iraq have caused racial and religious tensions to shift. Where previously Aboriginal groups were the scapegoats for the ills of urban Australia, now the sizeable Lebanese communities are being targeted as troublemakers, despite living peacefully in Australian cities for decades. Tensions came to a head in December 2005 and beach riots broke out in Sydney's eastern suburbs. The majority of the country was openly sickened by the riots, but for a place that professes an idyllic paradise of sun and opportunity for all, it's a worrying development.

names into a computer bank to see if they too bear the felon's mark.

Colonial machismo

The traditional image of Australians as sturdy bush workers may have little to do with modern life, but it has been potent nonetheless. It's the local version of the great frontier myth that crops up in the United States, parts of South America and South Africa. By the 1890s, writers, poets and painters were suggesting that a distinctive "national spirit" had been forged in the great empty wilderness, and that this "New Man" was typified by a Kiplingesque

of the most sexist societies in the developed world. The worst manifestation of the crass male spirit was known as the "Ocker Aussie" – the beer-swilling, pot-bellied, narrow-minded, "poofter"-bashing, provincial redneck, who watched footie at the pub while the sheila stayed at home minding the kids. Barry Humphries satirised the type with Bazza MacKenzie, the simple-minded tourist who was always ready for a schooner and a chunder. Paul Hogan started his TV career in stubby shorts and an Aussie Rules sleeveless shirt as an Ocker with a sense of humour, before elevating the image with more wit and irony in the *Crocodile Dundee* films.

mishmash of colonial values: naturally democratic, excelling at sports, blunt in his language, sardonic, self-reliant, independent, not over-educated or burdened by musty traditions. Above all, an Aussie trusted his mates, who were bound to one another by an almost mystical bond. This image transmuted over the years from the miners of the gold rushes to the Outback drover and the ANZAC "Diggers" of Gallipoli.

The one obvious drawback of this as a national myth was that it did not include women. The contribution of women on the frontier, or in the arts, or in the factories during wars, tended to be brushed aside, so that by the 1950s Australia had earned a reputation as one

THE RISE OF GAY CULTURE

Visitors hoping to find the "last refuge of unselfconscious masculinity" – as Ocker Aussies termed it – may be disappointed. In recent times, gay culture has exploded in the country – especially in Sydney, which now has a higher concentration of gays than San Francisco. At the first Gay Mardi Gras parade in 1978, police blockades were set up and 53 marchers were taken into custody. Today, the annual parade is the highest-attended event in the country, usually luring 300,000 to watch floats of fabuously attired transvestites and lesbian nuns on Harley-Davidsons ("Dikes on Bikes"). In fact, Australia has turned into one of the most permissive and tolerant of societies.

Like the long-ingrained racism, sexism abated with the general loosening-up of society in the 1970s. These days, many Australians poke fun at the Ocker image. Others, such as those who perceive themselves as the "Urban Elite" with fashionable inner Sydney or Melbourne addresses, simply cringe. Aussie women have always been strong characters – perhaps even more blunt, independent and self-reliant than the men so loudly proclaimed themselves to be, out of sheer necessity – so in recent years they have easily taken the lead in many fields. Still, as in other Western nations, women remain sadly under-represented in politics and top management positions.

of up front (as a social equal supposedly would). Public officials, even prime ministers, are often known by their first names. The other side of the egalitarian coin is known as the "tall-poppy syndrome": a national resentment of high achievers and an inescapable urge to bring them down.

But is Australia a classless society? Patently not. There may be none of the rigid divisions of the British or the gross inequalities of the American system, but there are serious divisions of wealth and opportunity – and many believe that the gaps are increasing.

According to pessimists, the great settler's

Australian dreams

Perhaps the myth dearest to the Australian heart is that this is the most naturally democratic of societies – the frontier past, and distance from the Old World, have naturally levelled Aussies to equals.

Certainly the outward signs are there. Waiters may still call you "mate" (and service can be a problem: diners must sometimes work hard, if they wish to be served, to convince waiters that they feel in no way superior). Taxi drivers can still get cranky if you sit in the back seat instead

LEFT: schoolgirls on the way home by ferry.
ABOVE: older girls riding out at Sydney's Gay and Lesbian Mardi Gras.

dream of Australia as the "millennial Eden" is being eroded. In a haphazard way, Australians have committed themselves to avoiding the errors of Europe and the US, and guaranteeing an unusual measure of social justice. But Australians are becoming increasingly materialistic, and less generous in their vision of society as a place where the weaker are protected. Australia's great narrative historian, Manning Clark, had a bleak vision of his compatriots before he died in the 1990s: "Mammon had infected the ancient continent of Australia," he intoned, in the manner of an Old Testament prophet. "The dreams of humanity had ended in an age of ruins."

Just don't try telling that to an Aussie on a sunny day. She'll already be at the beach. ❑

LIFE IN THE BUSH

The old stereotypes of rural Australia are disappearing fast, but there's still a distinct attitude of mind among those who live "out there"

Ten-year droughts, Biblical-style floods, bushfires whistling through the scrub – the same natural processes that allowed the Aborigines to eke out an existence from the land have made life unpredictable for most farmers. Yet despite constant threats of bankruptcy, few give up. They stick to the land, aided by their own brand of black humour and the solace of Saturday night at the pub.

Rural Australia – sometimes referred to as West of the Divide, The Bush, Back o'Bourke, Beyond the Black Stump or The Mulga – is in some respects an Antipodean myth. Most Australians rise each morning to spend another city day at the factory or office, a far cry from the days when men tramped "the Wallaby Track" (the old sheep station shearing circuit), with belongings in a "swag" on the shoulder and a faithful blue-heeler cattle dog padding alongside.

Visitors from overseas wanting to "go bush" will find many specialised tourism operators catering for just that urge. Everything's available, from luxury air, bus and rail tours to motorised four-wheel drive backpacker parties with ghetto-blasters and plenty of chilled beer.

The Outback has resorts ranging from remote fishing camps to the accommodation conglomerates at Uluru (Ayers Rock) offering everything from camp sites to five-star luxury.

Schizophrenic attitudes

The Australian romanticising of the bush on the one hand and distaste for it on the other can be traced back to the turn of the 20th-century author and poet Henry Lawson, one of the country's literary folk heroes; and to another, Andrew Barton (Banjo) Paterson.

After a wretched childhood on the western

New South Wales goldfields, Lawson kept returning to the bush to reinforce his dislike of it. He hated the unrelenting grey-green of the eucalyptus, the monotony and hopelessness (his word) of the countryside. Lawson railed against the heat on the track to Hungerford, the "bloody flies", the thieving publicans, the greedy bosses, the arrogant squatters and the brutal police. He did, however, love the "bush battlers", the staunch early unionists and the great Outback tradition of mateship – male-bonding in the wild.

In his poems, such as *Past Carin'*, Lawson put the fear into city people about living "out there". But the bush people felt that Lawson was speaking truly for them. Paterson had a more humorous approach, but also praised the "back country" and its people. Their attitudes continue to permeate the nation's thinking.

Some urban Australians seem to believe that the Outback and its 170,000 farmers and graziers are stuck in an 1890s time warp. In fact, Aussie farmers are highly mechanised agribusiness people, mustering cattle by helicopter and trail bike, flying their own planes, and adept at using the internet to run their businesses.

Another blind spot concerns the colour of cowboys. The best have always been black (although until the 1960s they were often paid half of what white stockmen received). As jackaroos, boundary riders, shearers and trackers, Aborigines have

olate emu in a chicken-wire cage. It can be found in any small country town where the architecture is at least semi-colonial, which supplies a broad rural area, and where you can still believe that the inhabitants come out of the pages of Henry Lawson or Banjo Paterson.

Bush mischief

Many of the old clichés about laconic, resourceful, friendly country people still have a good deal of truth. And there's a helpfulness in the bush that is not always immediately apparent to the visitor, thanks to a little bush mischief on the side. Any enquiry for directions, for

contributed skill and labour to Australia's rural prosperity, particularly in the Northern Territory and Western Australia. With the recent granting of land rights, Aborigines have taken over cattle stations and found a degree of independence.

The country mentality

Despite all the changes, it is still another world outside the Australian cities. And these days one doesn't have to pack a swag to find it. It is not a matter of tracking to the "dead heart"of the Outback, where the only establishment within 500 km is a lone pub with warm beer and a des-

instance, can be met with a slow "buggered-if-I-know" reply, followed almost immediately with an entertaining series of precise directions. Australians would never deliberately misdirect visitors, for, in the Outback, misdirection may result in death, by either starvation or thirst.

Given the harshness of Outback life, little wonder that the bushie is pretty taciturn, or that, when he "spins a yarn" in a flat nasal monotone, it usually has little to do with success. In most stories, the anti-hero doesn't quite make it. "And then, stone the crows, after he'd got the mob of sheep across the river and saved the boss's daughter from the flood, the dopey bugger fell off his horse and broke his neck. Goes to show, don't it?"

Out Bush, some things will never change. ❏

LEFT: camping out in South Australia's Outback.
ABOVE: the best cowboys, reputedly, are Aborigines.

A MULTICULTURAL SOCIETY

In the past 50 years the population has doubled and diversified. Immigrants have not always found it easy, but today's rich ethnic mix is seen as one of Australia's assets

When a survey in 1939 showed that the Australian population was comprised of 98 percent Anglo-Celtic stock, local newspapers proudly proclaimed that Australia was the most "British" country on earth. In this monochromatic society, the only unusual accents were those of the "new chums" from corners of Ireland or the Scottish highlands; foods were rarely more exotic than Yorkshire pudding; Christmas was a time for huge Dickensian meals of roast beef or pork, no matter how brutally tropical the weather.

All that changed after 1945, when Australia embarked on one of the most ambitious – and successful – immigration programmes of the modern era. The migrants were drawn first from the Mediterranean and Baltic countries of Europe, then in the 1970s from around the world. Since the programme began, more than 6 million settlers from almost 200 countries have made Australia their home.

Immense diversity

Almost one-quarter of the population was born overseas; 15 percent speak a language other than English at home. In recent years, more than 40 percent of settler arrivals have come from Asia, with British and Irish immigrants making up only 18 percent. The humanitarian programme is gradually adding even more diversity to the population. In the 1990s, most of these arrivals came from the Balkans; lately African arrivals have topped the list.

Just as the United States and Argentina were

transformed by immigration in the 1890s, so the post-war influx has radically changed the structure and habits of Australian society. Take a seat on the Manly ferry and you're just as likely to be sitting next to the daughter of a builder from Athens as you are to a journalist from Naples, a car salesman from Thailand or a doctor from Lebanon. And the guiding principle of Australia's immigration policy, and of society in general, has generally become "multiculturalism" – tolerance and respect for all cultures and races.

But, although the multicultural society is a *fait accompli*, just how to balance the demands of such a heterogeneous population can be a delicate task. Ethnic loyalties are encouraged, but the first loyalty must be to the Australian

LEFT: Polish-Australians perform at a Sydney festival.
RIGHT: two bus drivers – one Vietnamese and one Sikh, but both Australian citizens.

legal and parliamentary system; multiple languages are promoted, but English is the official tongue; and any coercive cultural practices, such as arranged marriages, are illegal.

The closing door

Even as late as the 1970s, Australia welcomed almost anyone who applied as an immigrant, with the government even financially assisting the passage. These days, more emphasis is laid on skills: of the 134–144,000 target set for one recent year, 87,000 places were reserved for skilled migrants, with 46,000 places in the family category and 13,000 humanitarian places.

If the statistics are cold, the issue isn't. Immigration is still a major point of debate. Should there be more immigrants or fewer? More refugees? More from Asia? Scarcely a week goes by without a politician or an academic adding controversially to the discussion.

The process for a potential immigrant can be laborious. Applicants are tested for their suitability to settle successfully, assimilate into the community and find work. Points are allocated for such categories as age, employability, English-language skill and so on.

Employability usually gets the highest weighting because of the greater contribution

A TALE OF TWO ASIANS

Every immigrant to Australia faces the challenge of building a new life and, often, learning a new language. John Lam arrived in 1979 from Vietnam to join an aunt and uncle. For his first two months he stayed in a migrant hostel, receiving A$36 a week in benefits, plus food and some clothing. After that, he moved in with his aunt and uncle, starting work in a kitchen, and then eventually became a barman. He now speaks good English, owns a house with his two brothers and two sisters, and has become an Australian citizen.

Other Asian immigrants find the cultural transition more difficult. "The first two weeks, I was sick, totally homesick," recalls William Ho, originally from Hong Kong.

"The country was new and I had no friends here. I had to start all over again."

A highly placed restaurant manager in Hong Kong, Ho arrived in 1981, having become interested in Australia through a friend, a chef. The friend knew that the owner of one of Australia's best Chinese restaurants was looking for a manager. Ho contacted the owner by mail and employer sponsorship was arranged. The entire process took about five months.

Despite a shaky start, he adapted and began to find bright spots in his changed life. Even so, Ho is not over his homesickness. He still thinks Hong Kong is the best place in the world to eat…

skilled migrants make to the economy. The programme is aimed at attracting "young, skilled and talented people" and does not discriminate on the basis of ethnic origin, sex or religion.

The New Australians

When Australia became a nation in 1901, racial purity was top of the agenda; the notorious White Australia policy, instituted by the Immigration Restriction Bill, was one of the first measures to be passed by the new parliament. It would govern migration for decades, and would not be formally overturned until 1973.

Thus the first wave of non-British immi-

blades and black-clad widows, would be the death of the pure, Arcadian, boiled potatoes-and-mutton Aussie way. How right the prophets were! Yet try denying Anglos their right to cappuccino, Gucci labels, lasagne or Greek restaurants, and they'll feel threatened indeed. The newcomers were also industrious to the point of exhaustion. By the 1960s, many entrepreneurs at the corner restaurant, milk bar or take-away food store were from Southern Europe. This energy received mixed reactions: admiration from many, but also resentment from some traditionally relaxed Anglo-Australian "natives".

Typical of this wave of European immi-

grants, brought over in the 1950s and 1960s, was drawn from Europe – mostly from Greece and Italy. Some 275,000 of these "New Australians" arrived in those years – although now, of course, they are Old Australians. Some 5 percent of the population is now of Italian descent, while Melbourne is often touted as the second-largest Greek city in the world.

This was not without its problems; many Anglo-Australians feared that the "dagos", "wogs" and "Ities", with their garlic, switch-

grants is Teresa Cupri, who emigrated from Italy with her family as a teenager in 1970. It took her family two years to receive permission to migrate from Naples. When it was finally granted, there weren't enough places for all 10 members. The family had to be divided; the elder children, including Teresa, went with their father, and the others followed with their mother about six months later.

The entire family paid only A$50 for the government-assisted passage, and were initially put up in a barrack-like hostel in Sydney. Teresa went to work in a factory three days after their arrival; she remembers some unpleasant name-calling at the time, the down-side of the immigrant experience. Poor conditions and low pay led her to seek

LEFT: a family celebrating the Iranian New Year in Sydney's Observatory Park.
ABOVE: Tiwi islanders outside an Aboriginal design store in Nguiu, Northern Territory.

another job, which she found in a nursing home. She stayed there for five years, learned English, and has been working steadily ever since.

With her husband Johnny – another Italian-Australian – Teresa now owns a popular pasta restaurant. The adult members of her family own their own homes; several of her siblings also have their own businesses. For them, hard work has produced the promised comforts, despite their impoverished beginnings. Although many Italian immigrants circulate amongst fellow countrymen, Teresa and Johnny do not have the time, and links with the community have grown weak. They have become integrated into Australian society: their children will not even speak Italian as a second language.

The polyglot nation

Even during the 19th century, there had been some exceptions to Australia's monocultural facade. There was a large Chinese population that had come to Australia during the gold rushes of the 1850s (and had survived the bitter resentment of Anglo miners, which occasionally erupted into violent attacks).

Several wine-growing valleys of South Australia, settled by Silesians in the 1840s, are still Teutonic in architecture, art and community fes-

OLD ATTITUDES

In the 19th century, racism was as deep-rooted in Australia as in the Western world – and the "Asian hordes" to the north of the empty country were looked on with particular dread by the first settlers. Imperialists were terrified that the Chinese would sweep down to occupy their near-empty continent; unionists feared that bosses would bring in cheap labour from Asia or the Pacific, destroying their workers' standard of living and creating a plantation economy. At the turn of the 20th century even the otherwise progressive Australian Labor Party stood on a xenophobic platform. In marked contrast to its family and skills programme, the humanitarian programme accepts very limited numbers – Australia still fears the invading hordes.

tivals. Remote Broome at the top of Western Australia was full of Japanese pearlers. But these remained exceptions to the rule until the boom in different cultures that Australia received in the 1970s, once it truly opened its doors to the rest of the world, particularly to Asia. By the 1990s, one-third of all immigration was from Asian countries, and the proportion is expected to increase. The new arrivals do not always find it easy to adapt, but their cultural influence is increasingly obvious in all regions.

Other ways of settling

There are also thousands of Australian men who have married women from foreign countries and brought them here. Often known as "mail-order brides" (because of the way introduction agencies used to advertise their Thai, Filipina, Fijian and Malaysian clients in Australian newspapers, to be brought over on the basis of a photo), these women join a long tradition of "imported spouses". Many ethnic groups, from Italians to Arabs to Indians, whose men or women may prefer to marry within their own community, have long arranged their own version of "mail-order" partners from "the old country".

For those for whom all legal avenues have failed, there is illegal immigration – often by arriving as a tourist and then staying on

and television broadcasting network – Special Broadcasting Service (SBS) – began in the 1980s to transmit in a Babel of languages (with everything subtitled in English). Throughout the main cities, SBS Television's evening news is regarded as the most wide-ranging and balanced coverage on offer. Many viewers stay tuned to catch variety shows from Brazil, films from Israel, comedies from China. Today, SBS has become perhaps the most public manifestation of Australia's cultural diversity.

Overall, the Australian experience of immigration has been one of the most successful in history: the massive influx has been absorbed

beyond the legal period. It is estimated that there are 50,000 illegal immigrants in Australia, many of whom remain undetected for years. They are often resented as "queue-jumpers" by other immigrants, who may wait years for their own family reunion approvals. When apprehended, they face the choice of rapid departure or mandatory deportation. The single biggest group is British tourists overstaying their visas.

As a result of these immigration waves, 2 million Australians speak a language other than English when they are at home. An ethnic radio

into society with remarkably little friction. Indeed, it has been widely accepted as the key to the country's vitality.

Ethnic energy

As Professor Jerzy Zubzycki – a Polish-born professor at the Australian National University – recently said, immigration "has become the most dynamic and constructive and self-renewing feature of Australian society. We need to share our country with others, but also unashamedly want the talent, energy and industry of diverse groups of immigrants, to help us develop a potential which is plainly abundant. The tolerance of our ethnic diversity is the principal means available to us to reach this goal." ❑

LEFT: cooking yum cha in Sydney's Chinatown.
ABOVE: Turkish breadmaking, Perth's Subiaco Market.

ABORIGINES TODAY

Captain Arthur Phillip reported that the first words the
Australian Aborigines said to his men in 1788 were
"Warra! Warra!" (Go away!) Given the subsequent cultural
attrition, their first reaction was remarkably prescient

For Aboriginal groups, "land rights" have always been the top priority. The land is a crucial part of their being, and the responsibility for protecting significant sites is central to their spiritual life. Yet they have been pushed from their traditional homes, and seen sacred sites mined, built on, flooded or destroyed.

There have been attempts at partial restitution. The Northern Territory Land Rights Act, passed in 1975, allowed Aborigines to make claims to vast swathes of the Outback on the basis of traditional ownership. The act also gave them significant control over mining and other activities on their land. Royalties from mining were distributed to Aboriginal groups, and land rights acts have been passed in various states.

Growing resentment

Political awareness grew steadily from the 1930s, culminating in the Freedom Rides of the mid-1960s, when young activists rode in buses through Outback Queensland and New South Wales bringing their message to remote communities. An "Aboriginal Embassy" was set up in front of Canberra's Parliament House; demonstrations resulted in violent clashes with police, pushing the Aboriginal plight on to the front pages and into white middle-class homes.

By the early 1970s, this new-found political consciousness forced the government, led by Gough Whitlam, to come up with a new policy: "self-determination". This allowed Aborigines to make decisions affecting their own future, retain their cultural identity and values, and achieve greater economic and social equality.

The Department of Aboriginal Affairs was established in 1972, followed by the Aboriginal Development Commission (ADC) in 1980. The

underlying concept was to bring increasing economic independence to Aboriginal people by fostering the development of business enterprises.

It didn't happen overnight. In 1988, while the rest of Australia celebrated 200 years of white settlement at the Bicentennial, Aboriginal activists staged peaceful protest marches. White Australians were forced to admit that, for the Aborigines, the colonial "invasion" had been an unmitigated disaster. The bicentennial helped push Aboriginal issues into the forefront of the national political agenda.

LEFT: traditional, highly structured *corroboree* dance ceremonies still take place.
RIGHT: a family at Katherine, Northern Territory.

Rights and wrongs

The most symbolic change occurred in 1992, when the High Court of Australia overturned the legal fiction of *terra nullius*. Ignoring the fact that Australia had been occupied for 60,000 years, this Latin declaration of "no man's land" had been the basis of Australia's settlement. The judges agreed that "native title" had always existed for land that had been continuously occupied by Aborigines, and in 1993 the government set up a Native Title Tribunal to regulate claims.

But the tribunal has achieved little: because 19th-century missionaries had moved Aboriginal peoples around, often splitting up clans by force, few Aboriginal groups could prove continuous occupation of their lands.

Inevitably, the growth of an "Aboriginal industry", comprising politicians, city-based do-gooders and opportunistic Aboriginal leaders, had been nurtured by communal guilt. But welfare dependency was seen by many as a dead end. More promising was the creation of successful Aboriginal businesses, from shopping centres and cattle stations to craft shops.

But the problems facing the large proportion of Aborigines who live in remote communities – slums, illiteracy, low wages, child abuse, alcohol and drugs – resist simple solutions. Life

HOW ABORIGINES LOSE OUT

After more than 200 years of European settlement, Aboriginal Australians are the country's most disadvantaged group. Statistics show the sad results of the colonial experience: the average life expectancy for Aborigines is 15 years shorter than that for other Australians; they have three times the infant mortality rate and a far higher incidence of both communicable diseases, such as hepatitis B, and "lifestyle" diseases such as heart failure; an unemployment rate six times the national average; half the average income level; and a large proportion living in sub-standard housing or temporary shelters. Aborigines are also 16 times more likely to be imprisoned than other Australians.

expectancy for the average Aboriginal male is 20 years less than for Australian males in general.

Success stories

Many Aborigines, however, have successfully entered Australian society on their own terms. Neville Bonner became a senator of the Commonwealth Parliament and pastor Sir Doug Nichols was appointed Governor of South Australia. Evonne Goolagong-Cawley became a Wimbledon tennis champion, athlete Cathy Freeman won a gold medal in the 2000 Olympics, and Oodgeroo Noonuccal (formerly Kath Walker) was a prominent artist and author. Writers such as Herb Wharton and Evelyn Crawford are immensely popular. ❑

WHERE THE PAST MEETS THE PRESENT

From Dreamtime to polymer paints...the artworks being created by modern Aborigines carry within them thousands of years of myth and tradition

It's contemporary yet traditional. It's today but it's timeless. Attaching a single label to modern Aboriginal art can be as difficult as establishing the meanings behind the symbols. But it does provide us with a unique cultural vision of Australia, as deep and enduring as any on earth. The international explosion in Australian Aboriginal art began in the early 1970s as a spark in Northern Territory, first in various groups in Arnhem Land and in the desert community of Papunya, west of Alice Springs. In Arnhem Land, missionaries encouraged tribal people to paint their designs, derived from traditional rock art and body decoration, on bark panels stripped from trees. Meanwhile in central Australia, teacher Geoffrey Bardon introduced polymer paints to desert-dwellers, producing an entirely new genre of art: the strongly symbolic dot style was born. Today the National Gallery in Canberra, the state galleries and private galleries in all the major cities feature desert and Top End art.

More recently, other northern Aboriginal communities have also earned distinguished reputations for their artisans: Tiwi islanders for their carving and distinctive painting (the picture above shows a Tiwi decorating a shell); representations of WA's Kimberley region, as characterised by artists Rover Thomas and Paddy Carlton; blazing acrylics from Eubana Nampitjin of Balgo Hills. Works by the recently deceased Emily Kngwarreye put the central Australian community of Utopia on the map; her niece Kathleen Petyarre continues that tradition with her intricately detailed paintings, prints and batiks, which can be viewed at numerous galleries throughout Australia.

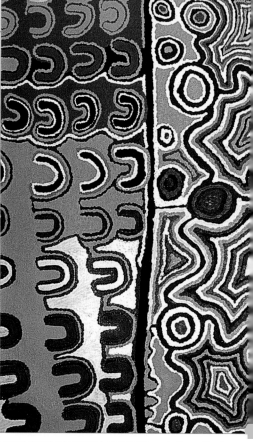

ABOVE: Aboriginal art continues to adapt and take on new themes. Though dots remain prolific in paintings from Balgo Hills, a colourful design element has recently emerged, as characterised by this triptych by the Tjakamarra brothers.

LEFT: Pukamani burial poles are still carved today as an enduring gesture of respect for the dead. The number of poles produced reflects the individual's standing in the community. A plethora of poles, all bearing striking graphic designs, are erected at the funeral of an important elder.

ABOVE: Art is omnipresent on Bathurst and Melville Islands. Modern icons decorate public buildings, from the local primary school to the fabrics showroom of Tiwi Designs. The artists take a pragmatic approach to prospective sites for their work – corrugated iron, the classic Australian building material, remains a favourite texture to display Tiwi graphic design.

A PICTURE BOOK OF HISTORY

Aboriginal rock art is recognised as the world's oldest and longest continuous living tradition. The ancient art is found all across Australia in the form of paintings or engravings on rock. Archaeologists continue to argue over their age, but some of the earliest paintings, in red ochre in northern sandstone shelters, could be 50,000 years old. In 1996 in the Kimberley region of Western Australia, an engraving site was dated at over 110,000 years old, sending archaeologists back to the drawing board and rewriting the history of modern human movement. Arnhem Land and neighbouring Kakadu National Park in the Northern Territory provide the finest Aboriginal rock art experiences. At Ubirr shelter in Kakadu, many of the paintings were made well before the last ice age, 8,000 years ago. A layer of animal depictions (some of species now extinct) lie beneath red dynamic figures racing across the shelter. Over them are splashed X-ray paintings of barramundi fish, their internal organs accurately detailed. Over them are sailing vessels, documenting the European arrivals in Australia. Each layer reads like a page in the history of the continent.

RIGHT: Muntja Nungurrayi, from WA's Balgo desert community, was recognised in Europe as a modern-day master until her death in 1997. Though virtually unknown as an artist at home, her paintings drew their inspiration from the role of ritual in her lifestyle and the secret nature of tribal "women's business".

RIGHT: On the Northern Territory's Tiwi Islands, carving and painting wooden sculptures is a natural extension of the production of Pukamani burial poles (see far left).

BELOW: A modern painting in the dot style, on display in Fremantle, WA, employs traditional elements such as the tortoise and lizards, and also alludes to the ancient hand silhouettes found in Aboriginal rock art. The Carnarvon Range in Queensland has some excellent examples of ancient silhouette art.

LEFT: St Theresa's church on Bathurst Island, Northern Territory, is a perfect example of the fusion of Roman Catholicism with Tiwi beliefs and culture. The cross is still a prominent feature at the altar, but instead of a more staid European-style design, St Theresa's cross is highly decorated in colourful Tiwi designs and motifs.

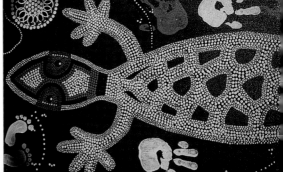

THE ARTS

In music, drama, literature, film and the visual arts,
Australia has absorbed influences from around
the world – and has at last found its own voice

The first century of Australian European culture was, unsurprisingly, entirely derivative. The white convicts and their white jailers took little notice of the black Aboriginal culture that had been in existence in Australia for at least 50,000 years before their arrival. Georgian English art was transplanted to Australian soil at the same time as European crops.

The first great turning point in Australian cultural history was the 1890s, which saw a tremendous upsurge in Australian nationalism. This was reflected in the arts, especially in literature. This was the period when *The Bulletin* magazine's school of balladists and short-story writers got under way, helped by balladists such as Banjo Paterson, who wrote *The Man From Snowy River*, and Henry Lawson, Australia's finest short-story writer. Many of them celebrated the bush, and its male traditions such as mateship, Aussie nationalism and the underdog, at the expense of the ruling Anglophile "bunyip aristocracy". Joseph Furphy wrote his novel *Such Is Life* (said to be the last words of Ned Kelly, the bushranger and folk hero, before he was hanged) at this time.

Australian literature is born

At a more popular level, Steele Rudd began writing his *On Our Selection* series, about life on poverty-stricken bush properties. A little later, C.J. Dennis started celebrating city larrikins in his poems about Ginger Mick and The Sentimental Bloke.

This creative leap was the start of a distinctive Australian literature, which continued strongly

LEFT: Sydney Symphony Orchestra at the Opera House.
RIGHT: the award-winning author Peter Carey.

in the 20th century through the novels of Henry Handel Richardson, Miles Franklin, Christina Stead and Eve Langley, the short stories of Barbara Baynton, Gavin Casey and Peter Cowan, and the poetry of Christopher Brennan, Kenneth Slessor, R.D. Fitzgerald, Douglas Stewart and Judith Wright, to the writers of the present day.

A similar nationalistic burst could be seen in the other arts in the 1890s. Louis Esson began writing plays in self-consciously Australian idiom. A recognisable Australian school of landscape painting emerged and crystallised later in the work of Sir Arthur Streeton, Tom Roberts and the "Heidelberg School" (named after the Melbourne suburb, not the German town). Dame Nellie Melba, the first of a line of Australian opera divas, made an international name singing French arias in Italian in British concert halls and gave her name to an ice-cream dessert, the "Peach Melba". Low, May and Hop began drawing for *The Bulletin*. Australians made *Soldiers of the Cross*, which is said to be the world's first feature movie, and the film industry flourished.

By the time of federation in 1901, Australian architecture had developed an indigenous style based upon the bush homestead, with high-pitched galvanised roofs and shady verandahs. By 1910, however, most urban Australians were living in the rows of terraced houses, decorated with cast-iron balconies, or in the suburban red-brick or fibrocement bungalows that were to become the dominant local architectural style.

In the late 1920s and early 1930s, an important change took place. At the very time that Australia was beginning to break free politically and culturally of British domination, it came under the influence of the United States. In doing this, Australia was taking part in the internationalisation of an immensely influential American culture, the influence of which is still felt today.

An Australian cultural resistance

Despite this, a vernacular Australian culture continued to develop and strengthen itself. In a

ARTISTS IN EXILE

For much of the 20th century, Australia was regarded as a cultural wasteland – by the rest of the world and, oddly, by many Australians themselves. In the 1940s, '50s and '60s, local artists often went overseas – almost always to London – to make a name for themselves. Exiles included opera singer Joan Sutherland, novelist Patrick White, painters Sidney Nolan and Albert Tucker, ballet dancer Robert Helpmann, sculptor Clement Meadmore, and many others.

Australian audiences at that time, the expatriates lamented, showed a general lack of sophistication and appreciation for the "high" arts in comparison with their European contemporaries.

The artistic scene changed dramatically in the 1970s, with a flowering of all forms of creativity that lured many of the expatriates home. In the early 21st century, most Australian artists prefer to remain in their own country. This is partly because their audiences have grown tremendously, to the point where it is now possible to make a living in Australia, at least with government arts subsidies, from the Australia Council. Partly it is because mass communications such as the internet have made it possible for them to stay in Sydney or Melbourne, or even away from the big cities, and still, quite often, reach an international market. Now pretty much every town will have at least one gallery or outlet for local artists and Australians find themselves in demand.

sense, it had merely added the American to the British, European and Asian ingredients already stirred into the local mix. There was considerable resistance to some of the American input: the traditional arts kept very close to their British and European sources. American culture, though glamorous, was regarded as inferior.

Sometimes cultural resistance took strange forms. For example, many of Australia's 19th-century bush songs and ballads had either died out or faded into the background; American country and western music (or hillbilly music, as it was then called) became popular in country towns. Aussie hillbilly singers began imitating

The next big bang

The late 1960s and 1970s were the next great period of Australian cultural growth, and the reasons are complex. The perils of World War II gave a boost to Australian nationalism; the 1960s and early 1970s were a time of economic growth and growing self-confidence. Meanwhile, the nation's isolation seemed to have come to an end; a massive immigration programme brought millions of migrants from Britain and Europe.

There was a sense of the old, stale moulds, which had contained Australian life for so long, being broken open. The traditional connection with British high culture was weakening, and

the Americans. They adopted names like Tex Morton, Buddy Williams and Slim Dusty and began writing their own songs about outlaws, pubs, bushrangers, tall tales, and country myths.

Before long, Australia had developed its own hybrid style of country music, along with its own country music stars, records and radio stations. Slim Dusty's *The Pub with No Beer* became a smash hit in the late 1950s and has been a perennial bestseller ever since.

LEFT: *The Ship That Never Was*, Tasmania's longest running play, tells how convict shipwrights escaped in 1834 by hijacking a ship they had just built.
ABOVE: the Bangarra Dance Theatre combine Aboriginal and Western traditions.

the American input seemed to have been partly absorbed. In retrospect, all the right ingredients seemed to be there for a cultural take-off.

The poets, as usual, led the way. At first they were dominated by academics such as A.D. Hope and James McAuley. These were followed by a loose collection of poets, such as David Malouf, Tom Shapcott, Bruce Dawe, Les Murray, Gwen Harwood, John Tranter and Robert Adamson, who adopted a freer, more vernacular approach to their verse and concentrated more on specifically Australian themes.

In the novel, progress was steadier, perhaps because it was dominated for so long by the late Patrick White. The 1974 Nobel Laureate influenced younger novelists, especially through his poetic prose style. A new generation of writers, including David Ireland, Thomas Kenneally, Glenda Adam and David Malouf, have taken their own idiosyncratic approaches, as have Tim Winton, David Foster, Kate Grenville and Fotini Epanomitis and a string of Aboriginal writers. Some, including Peter Carey, have enjoyed considerable international acclaim.

Centre stage

With a burst of dramatic talent and new government incentives, the film industry became Australia's biggest cultural export. The business generated $1.5 billion in 2000 and indications are that the film industry can expect a bright future.

The most celebrated movies range from the brutal post-apocalpytic *Mad Max* series starring Mel Gibson to period pieces (Gillian Armstrong's 1979 version of the Miles Franklin classic, *My Brilliant Career*; Peter Weir's atmospheric *Picnic at Hanging Rock* in 1975); from Jane Campion's suburban *Sweetie* (1989) to George Miller's 1996 talking pig, *Babe*. Baz Luhrmann's dazzling dance comedy *Strictly Ballroom*, the drag-queen frenzy of *Priscilla, Queen of the Desert* and the kitschy vision of *Muriel's Wedding* rounded off the eclectic 1990s.

Australian actors such as Nicole Kidman, Cate

ANTIPODEAN RHYTHMS

Classical music in Australia has always been a matter of performance rather than composition. The nation has several well-established symphony orchestras, chamber groups and opera companies, including The Australian Opera. Despite the limited opportunities, contemporary - composers such as Richard Meale, Peter Sculthorpe, Nigel Butterley, George Dreyfus, Anne Boyd and Moya Henderson frequently have their work performed here and in other countries. Ballet has shared in the recent growth in the "high" arts, helped by the work of such dancer-choreographers as Graeme Murphy and Kai Tai Chan.

In recent years, Australia has become as well known for its rock bands as its films; the local pub music scene, especially in Melbourne and Sydney, is extraordinarily healthy. Performers such as Nick Cave, Powderfinger, The Cruel Sea, Jet and Wolfmother started off on the pub circuit and now enjoy international success. Other groups that made it big overseas include The Easybeats, the Seekers, the BeeGees, Skyhooks, Mental as Anything, AC/DC, INXS and Men at Work. Midnight Oil became a self-consciously Australian group, politically committed to an independent, nuclear-free country. The Aboriginal band Yothu Yindi, with didgeridoos and tribal dancers, is unmistakably Northern Territory. One of Australia's best-known exports (in Europe, at least) is Kylie Minogue, a former teenage soap star and now pop icon.

Blanchett, Toni Collette, Geoffrey Rush, Eric Bana, Guy Pearce, Heath Ledger and Hugh Jackman have become big names in Hollywood, following in the footsteps of Judy Davis and Mel Gibson, and Russell Crowe, though born in New Zealand, has spent most of his life in Australia.

There are also actors and directors who prefer to create work that reflects the realities of modern Australia. In the early noughties, for instance, a spate of indigenous-themed films was released, including *Rabbit-Proof Fence* (Philip Noyce's 2002 tale of three aboriginal girls trekking across the outback to escape from menial jobs), *The Tracker*, *Yolngu Boy*, *Beneath*

War II, a group of figurative painters emerged which for a long time was identified as "the Australian School". Its practitioners included Sidney Nolan, whose series on Ned Kelly, the outlaw bushranger, became national icons; Albert Tucker, whose cover illustration helped make Donald Horne's *The Lucky Country* a bestseller; Arthur Boyd, Lloyd Rees and Clifton Pugh.

In the early 1970s Sydney became the centre for an abstract expressionist movement which drew upon earlier painters such as Ian Fairweather and Godfrey Miller, and was soon experimenting with hard edge, colour field and lyrical expressionist modes. Eric Smith,

Clouds and *Australian Rules*. In 2006, Rolf de Heer, the director of *The Tracker*, won international praise for *Ten Canoes*, the first Australian film to feature an entirely indigenous cast and to be spoken entirely in indigenous languages.

Images on canvas

Painting and sculpture enjoyed such popularity in the mid-1970s that it was commonplace to talk of an "art boom", with buyers and business investors paying very high prices for local works.

Melbourne was the early focus; after World

LEFT: Aboriginal band Yothu Yindi blends traditional instruments with rock music.
ABOVE: *Rabbit-Proof Fence*, a socially aware movie.

William Rose, John Coburn and Stanislaus Rapotec were followed by a new breed of younger painters such as Brett Whiteley, David Aspden, Michael Johnson and Tim Storrier.

In Melbourne, Fred Williams established himself as the most important landscape painter of the post-war years – possibly in the history of Australian painting – with his haunting, semi-abstract depictions of the Outback.

Probably the best-known contemporary Australian artist is Tracey Moffatt, born in Brisbane in 1960. Her painterly films and photographic works have won international critical acclaim and been widely exhibited. She has always been strong on ideas, and some of her recent work has examined fame and celebrity. ❏

BIG THINGS

It's big, it's sometimes clever, and it's the ultimate way for a town to put itself on the map when it really doesn't have much else going for it

The first Big Thing in Australia was in New South Wales. It was at Coffs Harbour on the north coast that the Big Banana was erected in 1964 as a way of attracting custom to a plantation on the Pacific Highway. It was ludicrous, it was tacky and it immediately struck a chord with passers-by. It became a destination in itself, and once that happened every desperate or mediocre enterprise that had no other distinguishing feature considered adopting the idea.

New South Wales was fertile ground for Big Things and many a small company or local council has jumped on the bandwagon. At the last count there were close to 40 of the things around the state. Other states quickly following suit. Some "Big Things" are quite distinguished feats of engineering and construction, some are more simple but still alluring, and some are quite frankly, rubbish. Originality doesn't count for much either; in NSW there are two sheep, two chickens and three bottles, while in Queensland the Big Things take on more of a B-movie quality with two crabs and three crocodiles. It's one of those phenomena that seems amusing enough the first time you encounter one, but it's just possible that the march of the Big Things is getting out of hand. Still, keep your eyes open and look out for that serendipitous moment when the Big Potato looms over the horizon, or take a more planned approach and invest in the book *Big Things* by David Clark.

ABOVE: The Big Peanut is in Queensland on the Kennedy Highway between Tolga and Mareeba outside a produce shop otherwise entirely bereft of character. The peanut makes you stop for a photo. Then you buy vegetables. See, function fulfiled.

BELOW: it all began in NSW with the Big Banana on the Pacific Highway just outside the resort of Coffs Harbour, and it must still be one of the most visited of all the Big Things with claims that millions have passed through it in the 40+ years since it was built. There's a café and a shop selling absolutely everything that could possibly carry the banana insignia. You can see the real, smaller, things on a monorail trip around the plantation.

ABOVE: Ballina's Big Prawn in NSW displays an attention to detail that sets it apart from some of its more slapdash rivals. The ultimate in local publicity, this Big Thing sits astride a restaurant, which serves – you've guessed it – seafood.

RIGHT: The Big Golden Guitar in Tamworth, NSW, pays its way by reminding visitors of the Country Music Festival for the 11 months of the year when the place isn't swamped by musicians in cowboy hats. As if Big Things weren't creepy enough, this one also has its own wax museum – the Gallery of Stars – which displays wax models of figures from country music.

BIG THINGS AS ART FORMS

While it could be argued that they go against the ethos of the Big Thing as the epitome of tackiness, there are a couple of examples of Big Things which have been put together by serious artists. Pro Hart was probably the most famous of the Broken Hill artists and it was he who constructed the Big Ant in 1982. It is now on a high plinth that resembles a winding tower over a mine shaft, situated in Lions Park opposite the Visitor Information Centre in Broken Hill. The other artist is Brett Whitely, who was responsible for *Almost Once*, the pretentious name for what ought to be dubbed the Big Matchsticks. There are two of them, one pristine, the other the charcoal remains of a spent match; both are several metres high. You can find them in Sydney on the Domain Sculpture Walk behind the Art Gallery of New South Wales.

ABOVE: The famous Big Merino on the outskirts of Goulburn has hit a spot of bother. It used to be on the Hume Highway and attracted a lot of passing trade to its shop and museum complex. However, a bypass has been built around the town and business is slow. The solution is to move it a few hundred metres down the road so that it's visible from the highway again. Pleasant as it is to contemplate a Big Sheepdog being brought in to shoo it on its way, the reality is more prosaic: it will be taken apart, trucked down the road and then bolted back together again. Visitors can go inside the structure, climb some steps and look out of the eyes.

ABOVE: Queensland's Big Cane Toad is on Sarina's main street, but isn't quite big enough to cause the pile-ups of distracted drivers that would really put the town on the map. However, its rusty steel bulk is sturdy and nigh-on indestructible, which is also a fine metaphor for the real-life cane toad – introduced in 1935 to deal with a plague of beetles but which has spread relentlessly, eating everything in its path.

ABOVE: Wauchope is a small town a few kilometres inland from Port Macquarie on the Oxley Highway. It is no doubt a pleasant place but wasn't going to feature in this book. But it's got the Big Bull and now it does. See, works a treat.

RIGHT: Tully's Golden Gumboot in Queensland would have been big enough to handle the town's record rainfall of 7.93 metres (26 ft) in 1950. Aptly enough, the Golden Gumboot is also the name of a competition between Tully and the neighbouring towns of Innisfail and Babinda for the title of the wettest town in Australia. Since 1970 the winning town has been awarded with a gumboot (normal-sized). Tully built the giant gumboot in 2003 to publicise this little known bout of inter-town rivalry. As the picture indicates, there are stairs inside the boot that allow visitors to climb to the rim. They'd just better hope it's owner doesn't come looking for it.

MODERN AUSTRALIAN CUISINE

It took a long time to happen, but food in Australia
is now distinguished for its quality, imagination
and a truly multinational diversity

Not so long ago, the term "Australian
cuisine" conjured grisly images of meat
pies, Vegemite sandwiches and sausage
rolls. Then, almost out of the blue, Australia
transformed itself into a paradise for foodies
(antipodean gourmands). Few places in the
world have restaurants that can compare with
the variety, quality and sheer inventiveness of
Australian ones. From formal dining rooms to
tiny beach-side cafés, creations such as "seared
kangaroo fillet with wilted beetroot greens and
roasted onion" pop up on menus; even the most
basic corner diners, which once served up ham-
burgers and chips, dish up focaccias with fresh
King Island cheeses and exotic fruits.

In fact Australia's culinary establishment
may be the most adventurous in the world.
Each capital city has seen a swarm of "Mod
Oz" restaurants with inventive chefs at the
helm and an audience of willing epicures.

This renaissance is due to two factors: the
wealth of superlative Australian produce –
including native foods – and the plethora of international cuisines brought to Australia by its
immigrants, in particular, those from Asia. The
mix of traditional flavours from around the world
has provided an astonishing flurry of innovation.

Slow start

But the Australian palate, like the nation, is relatively young, and the current sophistication follows a bleak culinary history. The early settlers
struggled to maintain their stolid British or Irish
diets, subsisting on salted meats – either roasted,
stewed or baked into pies. Various early recipes
indicate that native animals were eaten but, apart
from kangaroo (whose tails make a fine soup),
were rarely appreciated. The unfamiliar harsh-

ness of the Australian bush bred tough bellies
used to tinned beef and damper (the most basic
bread of flour, water and a pinch of salt).

During the Gold Rush days of the 1850s,
Chinese immigrants recognised the potential
for cultivation and grew a great variety of herbs
and vegetables (on some occasions, their industry saved white mining camps from starvation).
Even the tiniest country town still has its Chinese restaurant, which for decades saved the
citizens from complete culinary deprivation.

Even in the 1960s, the only things approaching an Australian cuisine were a couple of sweet
confections – pavlova (meringue pie shell filled
with fruit and cream) and lamingtons (sponge
cubes covered with chocolate and coconut). Of

course, there was always Vegemite – the black, salty yeast spread that most Aussies were weaned on, though abhorred by most others – but this hardly made up a culinary identity. Thanks to the climate, the "barbie" (barbecue) did become an Australian institution, but British roast dinners were turned out every Sunday; and on Christmas Day, in steaming hot summers, the hot roast turkey graced every table.

From famine to feast

Today, the acknowledged basis of Australian cuisine is the quality of its ingredients. Aussies were slow to recognise the wealth of seafood in their

ular produce: King Island cream, Sydney rock oysters, Bowen mangoes, Coffin Bay scallops, Tasmanian salmon, Illabo milk-fed lamb. Each state has its acknowledged specialities, which travellers should take advantage of. Tropical Queensland produces a wealth of exotic fruits (try Bowen mangoes and papaya in season), succulent reef fish, mudcrabs and Moreton Bay Bugs (shellfish, not insects). The Northern Territory can add the white-fleshed barramundi and Mangrove Jack to the list of tropical fish, while in Darwin, buffalo and crocodile are regularly served as steaks and burgers. New South Wales has Hunter Valley wines, Balmain Bugs

waters, but now a range of fresh fish is on every menu. Small farms devote themselves to gourmet beef and poultry, while the quality of everyday vegetables tends to be better than anything grown on organic farms in Europe or the United States. And far from pining for imports of French cheese, Greek olives or Italian wine, for example, Australians are now producing their own – and often finding them to be of superior standard.

Like Italy and France, Australia can be divided into regions that are known for partic-

Three characteristics of eating in Australia: the fabulously fresh seafood (**LEFT**), opportunities to eat outdoors (**ABOVE**), and excellent Asian food (**RIGHT**).

and perfect Sydney rock oysters (the acknowledged top of the oyster line). Victoria produces some of the tenderest meats, such as Gippsland beef and Meredith lamb, Mallee squab and corn-fed chicken. Tasmania is one of the least-polluted corners of the globe, and has gained national attention for its salmon, trout, cheeses, oysters and raspberries. South Australia is home to the Barossa Valley wine industry, Coffin Bay scallops, olive oils, tuna and cultivated native foods. Finally, Western Australia has received rave reviews for its superb new wines from the southwest and for goat's cheeses.

The massive migration from Mediterranean countries after World War II made the first real dent on Australia's palate. Italians in particular helped revolutionise cooking, introducing wary Aussies to the wonders of pasta, garlic and olive oil. Today, each capital city has its concentration of Italian restaurants – Melbourne's Lygon Street and Sydney's Leichhardt being the most famous – serving authentic, well-priced food. Meanwhile, classic French methods became the undisputed basis of fine cooking.

This was only the beginning. The extension of immigration in the 1970s added myriad new cuisines. The great "melting pot" – or perhaps more appropriately "salad bowl" – of Australian society meant that restaurants were sud-

ramundi. And although pies 'n' peas are now thankfully low on the food chain, you can still get a version at the occasional retro-chic diner.

Towards a modern cuisine

With the sudden wealth of new ingredients from all quarters – including "bush tucker" *(see facing page)* – enterprising chefs in the 1990s proceeded to defy the rules by mixing flavours from completely different ethnic traditions. Modern Australian cuisine was born, also referred to as "Pacific Rim" and "fusion".

Potent Asian flavours such as lemongrass, coriander, chilli and cardamom can be added to

denly opened by Lebanese, Turkish, Balkan, Hungarian and Spanish chefs. But the biggest impact by far has been made by the Asians.

Regional Chinese, Thai, Vietnamese, Japanese and Indian restaurants are now Australia's biggest success stories, with Korean, Sri Lankan, Singaporean and Indonesian cuisines waiting in the wings. Every capital city offers pristine teppanyaki Japanese dining rooms, and take-away lakhsa stalls. Singapore-style "food courts" have sprung up everywhere; even local supermarkets now stock Thai and Indian ingredients.

Not that Australia has tossed off its British heritage altogether – just spruced it up a bit. Your fish 'n' chips might still come in folded newspaper, but inside is the freshest grilled bar-

many essentially European dishes. By the same token, a Modern Asian cuisine has emerged as Asian chefs substitute traditional ingredients for unusual local ones: Cantonese stir-fried kangaroo meat, perhaps, or barramundi in a Thai green curry. And with the added options from the Mediterranean, young Australian chefs are currently afire with their own powers of invention, turning out dishes like angel-hair pasta with Balmain Bugs, prawns and lime mascarpone, and ocean-trout tartare on potato rösti with wasabi. Some chefs have acquired celebrity status, and restaurants' fortunes rise and fall depending on which name is currently in the kitchen. ❑

ABOVE: practising the art of picknicking.

Bush Tucker

n one of Sydney's finest restaurants, you may come across a dish called "Anabaroo, Mango and Burrawong Soup". It's a blend of three foods from the Northern Territory: water buffalo, roasted in an elastic net to keep the high water-content meat intact; the tropical mango; and bur-rawong, a native nut that was first mentioned in the journals of the 19th-century Outback explorer Ludwig Leichhardt.

Next on the menu might be reef fish served in a tart sauce of green billyoat plum – an Aussie fruit found by researchers to have 5,000 times the vitamin C content of an orange per gram. Or quan-dong-rowbumba – a duck cooked in a sauce made from the South Australian peach quandong, orange extract and brandy. And you may start off with emu pâté, smoked possum or witchetty grubs...

It's all part of the new Australian fascination with "bush tucker" – or, in its more gourmet incar-nation, "native cuisine". Restaurants are now mer-rily discovering ingredients from the great storehouse of the Outback and mixing them with European and Asian traditions.

Of course, Aborigines have been using the same ingredients for 50,000 years. Europeans first tasted many Aboriginal recipes in the earliest colo-nial days, when the members of the First Fleet in Sydney were on the brink of starvation, waiting for food from Britain. Some settlers turned to Aborig-ines for help, and learned ways of surviving in the bush. But once the supply lines were established to the Mother Country again, most settlers turned back to their porridge and stodge.

Only the bushmen on the frontiers of settlement kept up the cooking traditions using native Austral-ian materials – at least up to World War II, when supermarkets and frozen foods made it to the Out-back. Even in the 1930s, a cookbook written by an Englishwoman included recipes using everything from possum and rosella to kangaroo meat.

Until the early 1990s, the only native plant food harvested commercially was the macadamia nut (which even most Australians thought was Hawai-ian). The native spinach, or samphire, had been taken back to Europe by Sir Joseph Banks on Cap-tain Cook's voyage in 1770 and was common in French cooking – but could not be found in the mar-kets of its homeland.

RIGHT: this fast-food chef uses local ingredients.

Today it is known that, of Australia's 20,000 plant species, some 20 percent are edible. A vast untapped reserve of native flora now turns up on menus: riberries, bunya nuts, wild rosellas, Kakadu plums, lilipili, bush tomatoes. New herbs include native pepperleaf, aniseed myrtle and wattle seed – a flavouring agent for ice cream and cakes.

Although some three million kangaroos are shot each year in the Outback, the sale of kangaroo meat was only recently legalised in Australia (despite the fact that for years it was exported to Europe and the United States). It has become ex-tremely popular, partly because of its low fat con-tent: the flesh can be as low as 1 percent fat,

compared with 25 percent in marbled red meat.

Along with crocodile, possum and emu, the list of new ingredients includes baby eels, freshwater yabbies and witchetty grubs. The latter are often pan-fried and served on a bed of alfalfa sprouts, in a curved Aboriginal plate *(coolamon)*. The correct way to eat the grub is by hand, holding the head between the fingers. It tastes like a cross between prawns, peanuts, pork crackling and chicken skin.

Few other dishes are quite so exotic as witchetty grubs. In fact, most dishes are based on familiar culinary ground – seducing nervous palates with more Western, time-honoured favourites. Which is why your emu pâté will probably come with a com-pote of mango, and lamb, barramundi and prawns still feature prominently on the food line-up. ❑

MORE THAN 200 YEARS OF WINEMAKING

It's only comparatively recently that they have attracted international attention, but Australians have been making wine for more than 200 years

Australia's wine industry dates back to the First Fleet, which arrived in Sydney Cove in January 1788 bearing grape vines from the Cape of Good Hope and convicts from Britain. The vineyards spread from Sydney and today grapes are grown and wine is made in all six states and two territories. Most of the European varieties are grown by some 7,000 grape growers in 158,549 hectares (352,331 acres) of vineyards.

Riesling, Chardonnay and Semillon are the most favoured white varieties; reds include Cabernet Sauvignon, Shiraz and Pinot Noir. Climatic conditions provide excellent ripening, with an abundance of flavour and high alcohol levels – often too high for those who feel 15 percent is excessive for table wines.

Winemakers use stainless steel and temperature control to retain flavour and purity and maintain consistency. Imported oak, mainly American and European, is used for dry reds and some dry whites for maturation. The Australian harvest is from January to May.

Australian wine exports reached a staggering $2.4 billion in 2003, led by surging demand from the USA. There are now more than 1,600 wineries in Australia, many of them small family operations. But around 80 percent of all wine production comes from the Big Four conglomerates – Southcorp Wines, which owns Penfolds, Lindeman, Seppelt, Leo Buring and Rouge Homme brands; BRL-Hardy, a public company controlling Chateau Reynella, Leasingham, Berri, Renmano and Hardy's; Orlando Wyndham, owned by France's Pernod Ricard; and Mildara Blass (owned by Fosters Brewing) with Mildara, Wolf Blass and Rothbury Estate. The Big Four wines dominate the export market.

LEFT: Demand for Australian wines has been growing so fast that many winemakers have had trouble coping. The Big Four have achieved huge marketing success abroad. This has created a situation where wine drinkers with limited knowledge of wines will now choose an Australian bottle of wine simply because they recognise the brand and not because of the quality of grape. On the other hand, the new breeds of Australian wine now represent a serious challange to traditional European markets. Shiraz (known as Syrah when it's grown in France's Rhone Valley) is the most popular red wine grape, and is the variety used in Penfolds famous Grange.

ABOVE: Clare Valley winemaker Neil Pike takes a sample of red wine. Australian winemakers put a lot of time into individual barrel selection and blending to ensure the quality of the wine is up to their chosen standard.

LEFT: The ancient art of coopering is alive in the Barossa Valley. Penfolds' chief cooper, Bob Butler, uses fire to shape staves of American oak to create a strong and air-tight barrel. Despite modern advances in wine-making, the industry still incorporates traditional methods.

ABOVE: Mountadam's vineyards are at High Eden, several hundred metres above the Barossa Valley, SA. The purple flowers are Salvation Jane – a rather picturesque weed.

FLYING WINEMAKERS

Australia's vintage takes place at the opposite end of the year to the European and North American harvests – which allows talented Australian winemakers to visit the northern hemisphere's winemaking areas to share their new-found expertise. High temperatures during the Australian summer, when the grapes are ripening, are both a blessing and a problem. The sunshine means higher sugar levels, which in turn translate into high alcohol content and plenty of ripe flavours in the finished wines. But hot weather during the December–February period can also stress and damage ripening grapes. Because of this, the effects of global warming represent a serious threat to the Australian wine industry. Many big vineyards are harvested by machines at night, so that the fruit can be taken to the crusher while cool.

Aussie winemakers have had to develop special skills in high-technology wineries – such as Lindeman's big Karadoc winery in Victoria *(above)* – to keep ferments under control and retain the high fruit levels of their wines. The success of these new techniques has meant that many of them are now being exported, mainly to France, Italy and Spain, by Australians (nicknamed "flying winemakers") during the European vintage.

RIGHT: The Hunter Valley's wineries, 160 km (100 miles) from Sydney, are popular with tourists. Indeed tourism in the Lower Hunter Valley is as important to the local economy as anything produced by the viticulturalists.

RIGHT: Barrels of sherry age at Morris Wines, Rutherglen, Victoria. Established in 1859 and now in it's fifth generation of winemakers, Morris is one of the best producers of fortified wines, including amazing muscats. Although the Australian industry was founded on fortified wines, they have waned in popularity.

ABOVE: Barrel cellars at Yeringberg winery in the Yarra Valley, east of Melbourne. The winery was established in 1862, when the area was enjoying a wine boom. Tragedy struck a few decades later when the vine louse phylloxera, imported from Europe, nearly destroyed the Victorian wine industry. Some of the vineyards were replanted in 1969 and today Victorian wine is flourishing again. Yeringberg wines are generally produced in relatively small quantities and a good vintage from the vineyard can be highly desirable.

WHERE SPORT IS SUPREME

If you want to join in the local conversation – especially with Australian males – you need to know how the local team is getting on

In Australia, sport is more than an outlet for excess energy. The 19th-century macho physical culture has transmuted into competition on the game field. In the 20th century, sport was the language in which Australians first shouted: "Hey world, here we are!"

A working knowledge of any major sport still offers the easiest entry to the often male-dominated Aussie pub. In fact, wherever males gather – in pubs, clubs or the workplace – sport tends to be the major topic of conversation. They bet on it and brag about it, they eulogise or verbally crucify its performers, analyse its conduct and speculate about its future. One thing they never do is tire of it.

The golden 1950s

This sports fixation might seem a giant charade if it weren't for an Australian sporting tradition based on real achievements. The 1950s was a period of Australian dominance in world swimming and tennis, plus its arrival as a force to reckon with in track and field, cycling, boxing, sculling and golf. The climax to this golden era came in 1956: Australia dusted the United States 5–0 in the Davis Cup tennis final, while at the Melbourne Olympic Games, Aussie athletes won 35 medals – 13 gold, eight silver and 14 bronze – an astonishing number for the small population.

The cricket mania

It is only in summer, when cricket grabs the public's imagination, that Australians are more or less united in their sporting focus. Spectator interest settles squarely on the national team in its Test Match encounters with the West Indies, India, Pakistan, New Zealand, South Africa and,

most crucially, the traditional rival, England.

A Test Match normally takes five days to complete and even then it frequently finishes in a draw. Yet the game is followed with religious zeal. Radios blare the ball-by-ball commentary at the beach; pub discussions focus on the latest catch in the slips; and cricket receives extra TV coverage, day in, day out.

In the more than 100 years since Australia played its first Test series against England, nobody has been better at the game than a slightly built fellow by the name of Donald Bradman. "The Don", as he was known, was the greatest batsman ever, racking up century after century in matches with apparently effortless ease. During the 1930s and 1940s, Bradman was to cricket what Pelé later was to football or Babe Ruth had been to baseball.

A Test series is played over three, four, five or sometimes six matches, with the battlegrounds moving between Sydney, Melbourne, Adelaide, Brisbane and Perth. Ground capacities range from 30,000 to 100,000; lovers of the game say there are few greater sporting moments than to experience the opening "over" of an England v Australia Test before a capacity crowd. A Test Match is never as boring as it sounds: the combination of sun, partisan passion and beer can make cricket crowds boisterous, humorous and sometimes downright dangerous.

and barbecues, enjoying the game at an entirely different and less frenetic pace, some of them no doubt fuelling and foiling their Bradman fantasies with a can or four of the amber fluid (beer).

Aussie Rules footie

On the surface it seems incongruous that a country so fond of cricket, with all its esoteric customs and traditions, could have given birth to a game as apparently anarchic as Australian Rules football. The sport may be virtually unknown beyond Australia's shores, but in the southern states it is a passion, particularly in Melbourne: the city may have only 3.5 million

If a five-day Test sounds too much to take in, consider watching a "limited-over" or one-day game. As the name implies, these are whambam affairs that come and go in a heated rush and often wring participants and spectators dry with their tension and drama. These games often continue into the evening, under floodlights.

While international test cricket is the top of the pyramid, the game is also played at multiple levels, from the Sheffield Shield (interstate matches) down through district ranks to the junior and social levels. On any summer Sunday you'll find the social plodders, with their attendant picnics

LEFT: a dedicated fan of the Sydney Roosters.
ABOVE: Tasmania makes a pitch for more big games.

inhabitants, yet "Aussie Rules" ranks among the most popular football leagues of any codes anywhere in the world.

It is estimated that, each winter Saturday in Melbourne, one person in 16 attends an Australian Football League (AFL) game and thousands more follow the saturation TV coverage. September's AFL grand final is one of the great sporting experiences, rivalling an English FA Cup Final or an American Super Bowl for colour, passion and atmosphere.

While Victoria is the traditional showcase of Australian Rules football, teams from interstate (notably Sydney, Brisbane, Adelaide and Perth) have dominated the finals in recent times. The other states also get a chance to flex their might during the State-of-Origin games. These are inter-state representative games in which each state picks its best players, including those who have departed for the glory and lucrative semi-professional pay packets offered by interstate AFL clubs.

The art of non-compromise

In Sydney and points north, footie of a different kind is the winter preoccupation. Rugby League started as a professional alternative to Rugby Union. It's played in a half-dozen provinces of a half-dozen countries, and to that degree qualifies as an international sport.

appeal rests in its strong gladiatorial image and macho confrontations as pairs of teams slam into one another head-to-head – although fans believe that a dazzling backline movement resulting in a try (touch-down) is one of the real joys in sporting life. The Aussie national side, known as the Kangaroos, regularly hops through tours of France and Great Britain unbeaten.

God's own game

According to its devotees, Rugby Union is "the game they play in heaven" – which is remarkable considering its relative popularity in New South Wales and Queensland, where angels are in

League attendances are nothing like as large as those of the AFL, but the Sydney clubs – such as St George, the Western Suburbs, Manly and Parramatta – keep their players fabulously well-paid through the revenue of their slot machines and licensed clubs. In Brisbane and Sydney, the game found its roots in the working-class inner suburbs and, despite media overkill, hasn't significantly broadened its social base.

Rugby League is a physical rather than cerebral game. Modern strategy is based on an uncompromising style of defence that prompted one American football coach to observe: "Our guys could never stand up to that sort of constant punishment." You don't have to play this game to feel how much it hurts. The game's

AUSSIE RULES OK?

The game now known as Australian Rules football originated from a crude brand of Gaelic football played by miners on the Victorian goldfields in the 1850s. In 1858 H.C.A. Harrison and T.W. Wills formed Melbourne Football Club, after drawing up a set of rules borrowed liberally from other football codes. Initially, part of the rationale was to keep cricketers fit during winter.

In 1866 the game's first official rules were established, although they were altered over and over again in subsequent years. The spectacular series of kicks and catches at the heart of the game have led its detractors to dub the game "aerial ping-pong". A maximum of 18 players per team can be on the field at any one time.

short supply. The game's popular interest is at state rather than club level. Two or three times a year, the New South Wales and Queensland teams engage in a brutal battle that makes the Eureka Stockade seem like a tea party. If you enjoy football, it's worth taking the opportunity to see the Wallabies (the national side) in action.

At club level, Rugby Union projects a social spirit often lacking in the professional codes. Compared with League, the game has a "silver-tail" (upper-crust) image based partly on its strength in the universities and private schools. The "flying Ella brothers" of the 1970s were a contradiction to the class rule, three gifted Ab-

Johnny Famechon, Lionel Rose, Jimmy Carruthers, Jeff Fenech and Jeff Harding punched portholes in the fabric of world boxing. The spartan long-distance runners include Herb Elliot, Robert de Castella, Steve Monaghetti, Cathy Feeman and world triathlon champion Michellie Jones.

But it has been those sports which pit the individual against the elements which have brought out the best in Australians. With such a vast coastline and fine summers, it's not surprising that swimming has been a top sport: kids are tossed into the pool almost as soon as they can walk. In the 1950s, Dawn Fraser

original athletes from Sydney's inner southern suburbs who all wound up wearing the gold shirts of the Australian team.

Great individualists

The 1950s and '60s brought forward a rash of tennis talents, including Rod Laver, John Newcombe, Evonne Goolagong-Cawley and Pat Cash, and more recent hopes include Adelaide's Lleyton Hewitt. World-famous golfers have included Bruce Devlin, Graham Marsh, Peter Thomson, Jan Stephenson and Greg Norman.

LEFT: Lleyton Hewitt, a former World No 1.
ABOVE: Australian Rules star Adam Goodes, of the Sydney Swans, in action at a grand final.

became Australia's darling as much for her cheeky anti-establishment attitude as her victories. In the 1970s, Shane Gould followed in her wake, with a slew of Olympic medals. Australia's latest swimming hero is Ian Thorpe, who won three gold and two silver medals in the 2000 Olympics, and in 2003 became the first swimmer ever to win three consecutive world titles in one event, the 400 metres freestyle. At the 2004 Olympics "Thorpie" added another four medals to his Olympic tally: two gold, one silver and one bronze. Now retired, Thorpe has been credited with inspiring a whole new generation of swimmers.

Aussies have ruled international surfing almost since its inception as a competitive sport, with Mark Richards' four world titles marking him as one of the world's greatest-ever competition surfers. Names like Nat Young and Tom Carroll have permanent niches in a national "surfing hall of fame". Hang gliding and sailboarding are two relatively new sports in which Aussies have also excelled.

Australian motor racing has produced Formula One world champions in Jack Brabham (three-times winner) and Alan Jones, plus motorcycle champs Wayne Gardner, Daryl Beattie and Michael Doohan. Yet the real local heroes of the track are the touring car drivers. The class attracts heavy sponsorship and wide television coverage for its championship series, the highlight of which is the Bathurst 1000 held in October, an endurance event that attracts an international field of drivers. The Formula 1 Grand Prix is held on Melbourne's Albert Park circuit in early March.

The history of soccer in Australia bears little comparison to other forms of football. The game first kicked off more than a century ago among British migrants, then more or less stagnated until post-World War II, with the arrival of migrants from Southern Europe. Now most clubs in the National Soccer League are dominated by players from the Italian, Greek, Croatian, Slavic, Maltese, Dutch and Macedonian communities. The national team, the Socceroos, continue to edge their way up the international ladder, their success in the 2006 World Cup revived the sport's popularity at home.

A nation of punters

It is often said that Aussies would gamble on just about anything – including which of two flies crawling up a wall would reach the top first. But there's only one race in the year that captures the imagination of all and puts millions of dollars through the bags of bookmakers and the agencies of the Totalizator Agency Board (TAB). That race is the Melbourne Cup.

At 3.30pm Melbourne time on the first Tuesday in November, the whole of Australia stops for the running of this classic horse race. The (3,200-metre) two-mile event has become an international thoroughbred classic since it was first held at Melbourne's Flemington course in 1861. It's a public holiday in Victoria, and even the process of government is suspended so that the nation's decision-makers can watch the live telecast. ❑

LEFT: The American Champ Car series has been taking over the streets of Surfers Paradise since 1991. The race is held every October and lures thousands of petrol heads.

BELOW: One of the biggest events in the yachting calendar is the Sydney-Hobart Race which sees the Sydney Harbour foreshore packed every Boxing Day as spectators see off the contestants. The stormy Bass Strait usually leads to a high attrition rate.

AUSSIE RULES

For years Australian Rules Football was the preserve of Victoria, until it was decided that if the sport was to survive, it would need to build up its fan base. As part of this process the Fitzroy Lions from north Melbourne merged with Brisbane Bears in 1996 and the Brisbane Lions were born. Similar moves saw teams established in the other mainland states, but for some time the dominant clubs still came from Victoria. This began to change when the West Coast Eagles from Perth won championships in 1992 and 1994, but the real shift in attitudes came with the astonishing success of the Brisbane Lions, when the team won three consecutive Grand Finals from 2001 to 2003 under coach Leigh Matthews. With success came loyalty from local fans, and nowadays the team can attract 30,000 to the Gabba in Brisbane. The season runs from March to September, and there's always a willing local to explain the arcane rules to an overseas visitor.

ABOVE: The State of Origin series between Queensland and New South Wales is the highlight of the Rugby League calendar. The matches are played as a best of three every June and inspire passionate support from inhabitants of both states.

RIGHT: Cricket has always been popular in Australia and with the ongoing success of the national side – apart from the odd blip against England – it shows no sign of losing its appeal. The big event is the New Year's Test Match at the SCG (Sydney Cricket Ground) against whichever side is touring that year. Every four years it will be an Ashes game when passions are really roused. The state team has been consistently successful over the years and currently includes fast-bowling pin-up Brett Lee *(pictured)* in its line-up.

RIGHT: Newly retired Ian Thorpe may still be the poster boy of Australian swimming, but it's Queenslander Grant Hackett who's quietly breaking records and securing championships at a rate which suggests he may one day eclipse his great rival and Olympic teammate. As winner of the 1,500 metres freestyle at both the 2000 and 2004 Olympics, Hackett has established himself as one of the greats of distance swimming. He was made team captain of Australia as well.

RIGHT: Harness racing, or the "Trots", doesn't arouse particular interest in itself; however, it's not really about the sport. The Trots, unlike other horse racing, can run at night and that means more betting time.

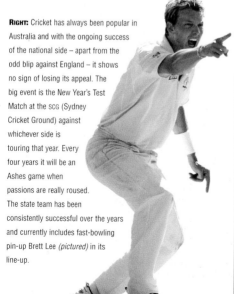

SURF CULTURE

Introduced to Australia in 1912 by Duke Kahanamoku of Honolulu, surfing has become a way of life for many of Australia's coastal dwellers

On a good day at Noosa Heads, Manly or countless other Australian beaches, thousands of surfers of all ages and on all kinds of equipment clog the line-ups. Surfing today is as mainstream as tennis, golf, cricket or football and kids on the coast grow up riding every kind of surf craft imaginable. If you come across a Saturday morning "nippers" (junior surf life-saving session), with kids who look as if they're barely out of nappies charging in and out of the waves, you would swear they're breeding a new, genetically modified amphibious race here. Webbed hands and feet and gills are surely only a few generations away.

The old surf clubs with their prime beach-front positions are still the social hubs of the Australian coast, where you can enjoy a cheap meal, a cold beer, or succumb to the dreaded "pokies" (fruit machines), all with unmatched ocean views. The old, framed black-and-white photos of past surf champions peer down curiously, echoing earlier, simpler times. The world-wide boom of the surf industry means that professional surfers have the opportunity to set themselves up financially for life. Young surfers barely out of their teens drive luxury 4WD vehicles and buy million-dollar mansions.

For the quintessential Australian surf experience, have a surf lesson, sit under a pandanus tree with a pie and a chocolate milk, go for another surf, then retreat to the surf club for a steak and a beer as the sun sets over the ocean. Just see if you don't feel strangely good about the world again. Then go to bed, wake up and do it all again.

ABOVE: There are surf schools at all major surf beaches. With a reasonable level of fitness and balance you'll be on their feet in a lesson or two.
BELOW: Kids on the Australian coast grow up learning how to play on the ocean and their confidence in the water is almost frightening. Most surf beaches will have junior surf clubs and will provide starter lessons designed for children.

BELOW Peter Townend, the original Coolangatta kid, was pro surfing's first world champion. Intense local rivalry in the 1970s between Queensland's Coolangatta surfers pushed riders to heights that would propel them to fame.

BRIEF HISTORY OF SURFING

Australian surfing as we know it began at Sydney's Freshwater Beach, when visiting Hawaiian champion Duke Kahanamoku *(right)* put on his historic display in 1914. However, there is some evidence of a surf culture among indigenous Australians. The foundation meeting of the Greenmount Surf Club in 1908 paid tribute to a local Aboriginal man, called Churaki, for the many daring rescues he carried out in the surf prior to the club's formation.

Surf life-saving clubs were formed in the early 1900s to protect public safety, and quickly grew as social hubs for the emerging beach culture. Surfboards were built for ocean rescues and manned by teams of earnest paddlers, but proved poorly designed for rough ocean conditions.

Surf clubs remained unchallenged as the seat of beach culture until the 1950s, when a group of Americans visited Australia to coincide with the 1956 Melbourne Olympics. Their surf-riding displays on revolutionary, short, light Malibu boards reverberated around the country. Freshly inspired surfers rejected the conservatism of the surf clubs for the freewheeling lifestyle of the wave-chasing surfie. In the late 1960s and early 1970s, surfing's image reached an all-time low, associated as it was with laziness, drug use and anti-social behaviour. Beneath the hippy trappings, however, surfer rivalry was pushing the sport to greater heights. In the late 1970s, Australia's success in the first ever international competitions made the dream of pro-surfing a distinct possibility. Today, lucrative careers with million-dollar salaries and worldwide superstardom beckons the most successful surfers.

ABOVE: Hawaiian champion Duke Kahanamoku and Elizabeth Latham, his tandem board rider, pose alongside an early surfboard. Duke Kahanamoku is credited with bringing surfing to Australia.

RIGHT: Australia's first official surf life-saving club was founded at Bondi Beach, Sydney, in 1906. Today the organisation Surf Life Saving Australia has over 100,000 members and has over 300 clubs dotting the continent's coastline. The surf life-savers perform an essential role on the beaches of Australia and now employ all manner of devices – including jet skis and motorboats – to patrol the waters. When they're not on duty, surf life-saving clubs also organise competitions that test the strength and skills of their members. These competitions are very popular and often draw big crowds.

ABOVE: A surfer "riding a tube", so called because it requires the surfer to position themselves on the wave just as it tips over, forming a barrel in which to surf.

RIGHT: Mick Fanning, one of today's Coolangatta kids takes on a wave.

BELOW: The Quiksilver Pro 2006 hits Queensland's Gold Coast. International riders follow the competitions round the world and with prize monies of up to US$280,000 available at the Quiksilver Pro alone, professional surfing has become a lucrative sports career.

PLACES

The world's largest island, or its smallest continent – whichever way you look at it, Australia's vastness is inescapable. In area it matches Europe or the continental USA. And, just as a traveller might not plan to journey from London to Moscow or from New York to Los Angeles in a week or two, travel in Oz takes a little time – and some judicious selection. The following chapters will help you make those choices.

With only 20 million inhabitants, almost all living in eight major cities, Australia is also one of the world's emptiest corners. Nowhere else is it so easy to escape the crowds as in Australia: there are more than 600 national parks, 16 World Heritage areas, vast swathes of countryside where you could pitch a tent for six months and never see another soul. Indeed, in much of the Outback the sheer loneliness can be the greatest danger.

The way to see Australia, therefore, is by choosing your destinations thoughtfully, flying across the greatest distances and dipping into the wilderness with care. Almost every international traveller arrives in Sydney – Australia's biggest city and, despite the protestations of rivals Melbourne (the old financial centre) and Canberra (the official seat of government), fast becoming its de facto capital. Number two on any list of "greatest hits" is the Great Barrier Reef – the world's largest living organism, sprawling along the Queensland coast. Next comes Uluru, or Ayers Rock – the world's largest monolith, looming mysteriously in the

A detailed guide to the entire country, with main sites cross-referenced by number to the maps

middle of the Outback plains. Finally, there's Darwin in the wild, monsoonal "Top End", jumping-off point for Kakadu, with its rich Aboriginal culture, tropical wetlands and giant saltwater crocodiles.

These high-profile attractions are just some of the reasons why international visitors flock to Australia. This book divides the country into its official states and territories – the arbitrary lines set up by British colonial administrators in the 19th century remain the divisions today. In New South Wales, consider a trip beyond Sydney to the Blue Mountains or the northern beaches. Victoria has the cultural sights of Melbourne as well as mountains and a spectacular coastline to explore. In South Australia, visit the wine country of the Barossa. Queensland may have the Reef, but it also has the world's oldest rainforests and the wilderness of Cape York.

The red-earth Outback is most famous in the Northern Territory, but Western Australia has the breathtaking Kimberley and 3,000 km (1,800 miles) of virtually uninhabited coastline. Or you can pop "overseas" to the island of Tasmania, the most pristine corner of Australia, with the finest bushwalking and the most spectacular ruins of the convict era.   ❏

PRECEDING PAGES: the Pinnacles, Nambung National Park, Western Australia; the Three Sisters in the Blue Mountains; enjoying a warm evening opposite The Rocks in Sydney.
ABOVE: P&O's *Oriana* is welcomed into Sydney Harbour.

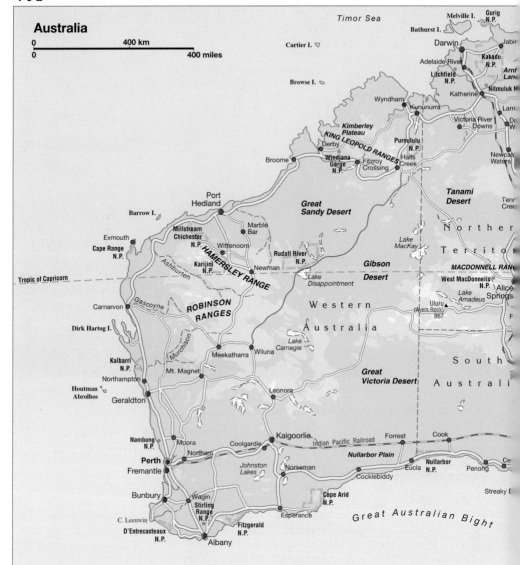

Australia

0   400 km

0   400 miles

Timor Sea

Cartier I.

Browse I.

Melville I.

Gurig N.P.

Bathurst I.

Darwin   Jabir

Kakadu N.P.

Adelaide River

Litchfield N.P.

Arnh Lan

Wyndham   Kununurra

Katherine   Nitmuluk N

Larri

Kimberley Plateau

Victoria River Downs

Da W

KING LEOPOLD RANGES

Derby

Purnululu N.P.

Windjana Gorge N.P.

Fitzroy Crossing

Halls Creek

Newca Waters

Broome

Great Sandy Desert

Tanami Desert

Tenn Cree

Port Hedland

Barrow I.

Marble Bar

N o r t h e r

Exmouth

Millstream Chichester N.P.

Wittenoom

T e r r i t o

Cape Range N.P.

HAMERSLEY RANGE

Rudall River N.P.

Lake MacKay

Ashburton

Karijini N.P.

Newman

Gibson Desert

Lake Disappointment

MACDONNELL RAN

West MacDonnells N.P.

Alice

Tropic of Capricorn

Carnarvon

Gascoyne

ROBINSON RANGES

W e s t e r n

Uluru (Ayers Rock) 867

Lake Amadeus

Alice Springs

Dirk Hartog I.

Murchison

A u s t r a l i a

F

Meekatharra   Wiluna

Lake Carnegie

S o u t h

Kalbarri N.P.

Mt. Magnet

Great Victoria Desert

A u s t r a l i

Northampton

Leonora

Houtman Abrolhos

Geraldton

Nambung N.P.

Moora

Coolgardie

Kalgoorlie   Forrest   Cook

Northam

Indian Pacific Railroad

Perth

Johnston Lakes

Norseman

Nullarbor Plain

Nullarbor N.P.

Eucla

Ce

Fremantle

Penong

Bunbury

Wagin

Cocklebiddy

Stirling Range N.P.

Streaky E

C. Leeuwin

Cape Arid N.P.

D'Entrecasteaux N.P.

Fitzgerald N.P.

Esperance

Great Australian Bight

Albany

I N D I A N   O C E A N

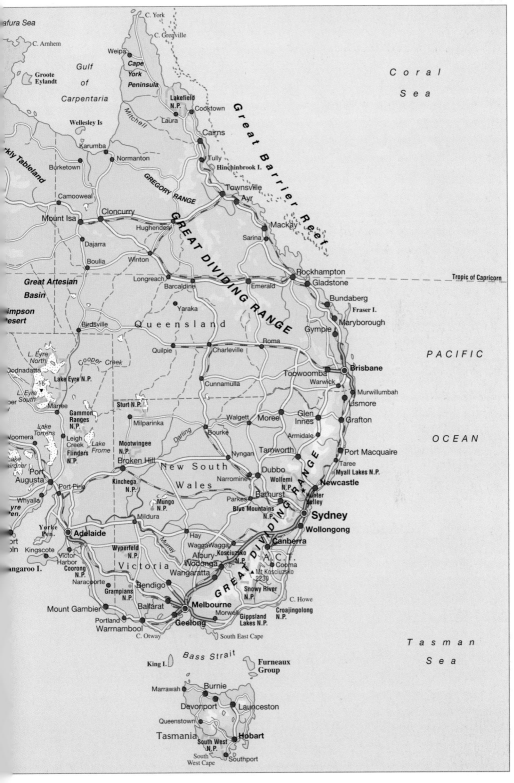

SYDNEY

The glittering harbour with its coat-hanger bridge, the pearly sails of the Opera House, the bronzed lifesavers at Bondi Beach... most of the symbols that define Australia are located here

Map
on page
106

Sydney is where Australian hedonism finds its most spectacular backdrop, a city where leisure has been elevated to an art form. Yet Australia's largest metropolis, with over 4 million people, can still baffle expectations. The natural beauty of the harbour and beaches often stands in stark relief to the man-made landscape: the narrow, traffic-clogged streets, the lacklustre architecture of its inner city, the endless orange-roofed expanse of its suburbia. If this is your first stop in Australia and the flight path of your aircraft takes you in a loop west of the city, with the Opera House and the Harbour Bridge cast in miniature against the harbour, chances are you'll be smitten.

A magnet for talent

To its critics – who mostly live in its traditional rival, Melbourne – Sydney is all glitz, obsessed with superficial show, appearances above substance. But none of this seems to matter to most Sydneysiders, and even less to visitors. The city continually lures the wealthiest, smartest and most artistically talented from the rest of Australia, and increasingly, the world, while real-estate values go through the roof. Everybody wants to live in "the capital of the Pacific Rim."

Yet few of the world's great cities have had such an unpromising start. On 26 January 1788, a fleet of 11 ships under the command of Captain Arthur Phillip landed a seasick gaggle of male convicts and their jailers – an unsavoury group of naval recruits well schooled in rum, sodomy and the lash – while the local Aborigines let out furious howls and threw stones to drive them away. The officers pitched their tents east of the freshwater Tank Stream at Sydney Cove, the prisoners and their guards to the west (creating a social division that lasts to this day, with the wealthier suburbs of the east versus the have-nots of the west). Two weeks later, the women convicts disembarked with the many children that had been born on the voy-

LEFT: Sydney's spectacular New Year's Eve fireworks.
BELOW: the Aquarium

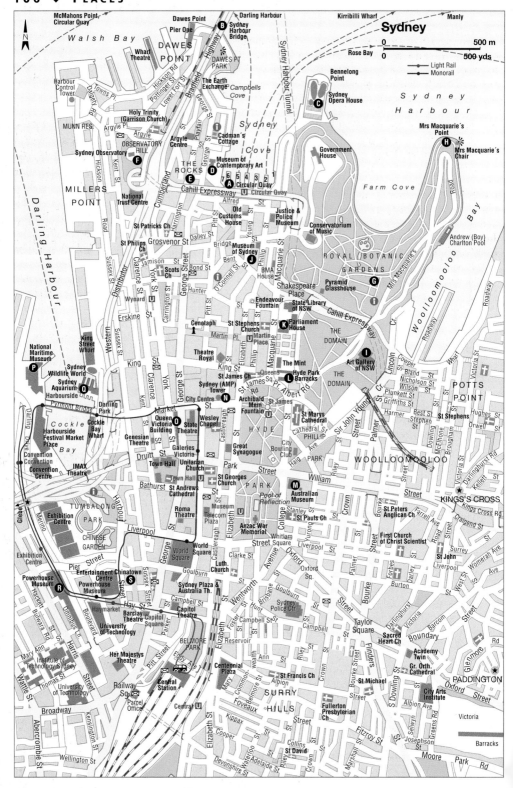

Sydney

age. An extra rum ration was handed out, a violent storm began, and the 736 felons of the young colony – along with not a few of their randy guards – embarked on a drunken orgy.

Today the site of this Hogarthian display is one of the most visited spots in Sydney: **Circular Quay Ⓐ**. This is the gateway to **Sydney Harbour** and the place where everyone should begin a visit. Ferries, Jetcats, water taxis and tour boats of every stripe plough in and out of its docks, taking passengers up and down the grand waterway of Port Jackson, described by Phillip as "the finest harbour in the world, where a thousand ship of the line may ride with the most perfect security." To get a feel for Sydney, hop on a ferry, take a seat outside and, for the first trip, don't get off at all; all ferries eventually return home to the quay. There's a great view of Sydney's two familiar icons.

The Harbour Bridge

First to be constructed was the **Harbour Bridge Ⓑ**. The widest single-span bridge in the world, it was erected during the depths of the 1930s Depression as a symbol of hope in the future. It became dubbed the Coathanger, the Toast Rack and the Iron Lung (the latter for the number of people given work on its construction, which kept Sydney breathing). These days, despite dire predictions that rust is rotting it away from the inside, the bridge is still the major link between Sydney's northern and southern suburbs (there's also an underground tunnel).

The southeastern pylon on the Harbour Bridge is home to the **Pylon Lookout** museum (daily 10am–5pm; tel: 02-9240 1100; www.pylonlookout.com .au; entrance fee), which leads up to a viewing platform with superb views of the harbour and city. Small-group guided climbs to the bridge's summit, each lasting 3½ hours, can be booked through BridgeClimb (daily; tel: 02-8274 7777). Unless you're seriously scared of heights, spend the cash and do the climb. You'll forget all about the

deeply unattractive jumpsuits that are compulsory for safety once you see the priceless view from the top.

The Opera House

The second symbol, began construction in 1959, and today is probably the most photographed site in Sydney. The **Opera House Ⓒ** (guided one-hour tours daily, every half-hour 9am–5pm; two-hour backstage tour including breakfast, daily at 7am; tel: 02-92507111; www.sydneyoperahouse.com; entrance fee) is without a doubt one of the world's most spectacular buildings (or, as art critic Robert Hughes would have it, "the biggest environmental site-specific sculpture south of the Equator"). It was designed by Jørn Utzon, a Dane, after an international competition – although nobody at the time quite knew how it would be built. It was the first large-scale project to make extensive use of computer technology but, even so, the construction was fraught with difficulties. Costs escalated. Utzon became caught up in the petty-minded moneygrubbing of Australian politics, and resigned in

Map on page 106

Luna Park sits on the water under the northern end of the Harbour Bridge. Built in 1935, it is modelled on the amusement park at New York's Coney Island.

BELOW: the Opera House.

Ken Done (pronounced as in "bone") is a popular local artist and designer who has a gallery in The Rocks exhibiting his paintings. A shop sells clothes, ceramics and other items featuring his work.

BELOW: Circular Quay and the city from the terrace of the Opera House.

disgust in 1966. A state lottery raised the necessary cash, and by the time the completed building was opened by the Queen in 1973, it had cost $102 million – 15 times its initial budget. But few have ever complained about the price since. The Opera House became an immediate icon for Australia's new-found cultural independence.

Also overlooking the harbour, the Gothic Revival style is exemplified by **Government House** (by guided tour only, on the hour and half hour; Fri–Sun 10.30am–3pm; tel: 02-9931 5222; www.hht.net.au; free), formerly home to state governors and now open to the public. The ground-floor state rooms have some beautiful 19th- and 20th-century furniture and decoration.

Apart from the docking ferries, Circular Quay is a lively scene, packed with buskers, pedlars and office workers relaxing on their lunch breaks during the day, and busy with after-work drinkers and dining tourists at night. Just around the waterline lies the squat, yellow **Museum of Contemporary Art ⓓ** (MCA; daily 10am–5pm; tel: 02-9245 2400; www.mca.com.au; free), whose

outdoor café is the ultimate lunch address on a sunny day. This is the country's only museum devoted entirely to contemporary art in all its myriad forms. Those who might be inflamed by the idea of a video showing football star David Beckham asleep in a Madrid hotel room as a work of art might be tempted to keep their distance. But even if Sam Taylor Wood isn't your thing, the museum still won't disappoint: there's always a mix of styles and new exhibitions to keep you interested.

The Rocks

Behind it begins Sydney's most historic district, known as **The Rocks ⓔ** after the sandstone bluffs from which the first convicts cut golden bricks for public buildings (take a look up the **Argyle Cut**, slicing straight through the cliffs – the pick marks are still easily identifiable). Almost immediately the area became the colony's main port, and warehouses grew up along the waterfront, backed by merchants' shops, offices, hotels, banks, bars and brothels that went along with the seafaring trade of the 19th century. But respectability always eluded The Rocks and by the 1960s the area had long outlived its original mercantile function.

Today The Rocks is virtually an open-air museum, where you can absorb Australia's early history with a leisurely stroll – although the entire area is now unashamedly devoted to tourism. Avoid the markets on a Saturday unless you want to be stuck there for hours dodging the crowds. If you really want to visit, make it an evening excursion – you're spoilt for choice for overpriced but top-notch restaurants.

Sydney's oldest building

Next to the MCA is the tiny stone **Cadman's Cottage** (Mon–Fri 9.30am–4.30pm, Sat & Sun 10am–4.30pm; free), built in 1816 and believed to be Sydney's oldest building, now housing a museum and an information centre. Only a small number of buildings remain from the first half of the 19th

century. Many more date from the Victorian era, when cargoes of wool, wheat and gold provided a rich source of income that allowed architectural flourishes of the period to blossom. The contrast beween these ornate buildings and the simple, embellished stonework of the Georgian era is striking.

The Argyle Cut passes the **Argyle Centre**, a convict-era storehouse that is now a boutique shopping centre; the **Garrison Church**; and eventually leads up a steep path to **Observatory Hill** ❻. Although a fort was built on the hilltop in 1803 for officers in case of a convict uprising, the oldest building still standing is the Signal Station, which was erected in 1848. In 1855 the hill became the site for the Sydney Observatory (daily 10am–5pm; tel: 02-9221 3485; www.sydneyobservatory.com.au; free), which began as a time-keeping device. Since 1982 the Observatory has been a museum of astronomy, with an imaginative **3-D Space Theatre** (daily 10am–5pm, tour bookings essential; tel: 02-9221 3485; entrance fee).

Today Observatory Hill is a picnic spot with fine harbour views, making it a favourite viewing point for tourists and locals to watch the fireworks on New Year's Eve. Further towards Millers Point lies a network of narrow streets that have traditionally been home to wharf workers. The **Hero of Waterloo** and **Fortune of War** compete for the honour of being Sydney's oldest pub, with the **Palisade** one of the most atmospheric.

The Botanic Gardens

Following the waterline in the opposite direction from the quay leads you past the Opera House to the **Royal Botanic Gardens** ❼ (daily sunrise–sunset; tel: 02-9231 8111; www.rbgsyd.nsw.gov.au; free) – a vast, voluptuous collection of Antipodean flora, including some truly majestic Moreton Bay figs. Hidden amongst the sculpted lakes and exotic fronds is an excellent café-restaurant. If you decide to picnic on the lawns, be warned – the strutting, long-beaked ibis are notorious lunch burglars.

From **Mrs Macquarie's Point** ❽ one gazes out at the tiny island of **Fort Denison**. This is also the site of the

Map on page 106

Bunting flutters on the old warehouses at The Rocks to celebrate Australia Day on 26 January.

BELOW: the Royal Botanic Gardens.

An installation at the Museum of Sydney symbolises links between Aboriginal and European cultures.

BELOW: the controversial monorail.

summer Open Air Cinema (one month every year; www.stgeorgeopenair.com.au), where you can sip champagne and watch a recent movie from a screen that seems to rise out of the harbour. You'd be hard-pressed to find a more beautiful backdrop to a cinema, but get in quick because tickets sell out fast.

Paths continue through the gardens to the **Art Gallery of New South Wales** ❶ (Thur–Tues 10am–5pm, Wed 10am–9pm; tel: 02-9225 1744; www.artgallery.nsw.gov.au; free). This imposing edifice is crowned with the celestial names of Leonardo da Vinci, Michelangelo, Botticelli and the like, although not one of these artists is represented in the collection. What the gallery does mainly contain is the country's finest grouping of Australian art and the garden setting makes it perfect for an afternoon of browsing.

Sydney's **Central Business District** – the "CBD" as many refer to it – is an oddly anonymous hodgepodge of glass skyscrapers and architectural styles from the past two centuries, all squeezed onto a street plan drawn up in Georgian times. It is best seen by stroll-ing up Young Street from the quay, past the 1846 classical revival **Customs House** (Mon–Fri 8am–midnight, Sat 10am–midnight, Sun 11am–5pm; tel: 02-9242 8595; www.cityofsydney.nsw.gov.au/customshouse; free) – now a cultural forum with an on-site lending library and roof-top restaurant – evoking Syd-ney's early days as a great imperial port.

Museum of Sydney

You then pass the **Museum of Sydney** ❶ (daily 9.30am–5pm; tel: 02-9251 5988; www.hht.net.au; entrance fee), which has entertaining sight-and-sound exhibits from the city's earliest days to today *(see pages 124–5).* Built on the site of the original Government House, remnants of the foundations (unearthed by accident in 1983) can now be seen inside the museum.

Cut over to Macquarie Street for a view of official Sydney: in quick suc-cession come the **State Library** (Mon–Thur 9am–8pm, Fri until 5pm; Sat, Sun 10am–5pm; tel: 02-9273 1414; www.sl.nsw.gov.au; free) – which, although not the prettiest building in town, con-tains some of the most important archives of Australiana; **Parliament House** ❶ (Mon–Fri 9am–5pm; tel: 02-9230 2111; www.parliament.nsw.gov.au; free) – the seat of the New South Wales state government; **Sydney Mint;** and **Hyde Park Barracks** ❶.

The barracks now houses one of Syd-ney's most popular museums (daily 9.30am–5pm; tel: 2-8239 2311) entrance fee). Designed in 1817 by con-vict architect Francis Greenway and completed in 1819, the building was first used to house hundreds of prison-ers. Exhibits relating to the convict sys-tem include a re-creation of the prisoners' cramped canvas-hammock sleeping quarters.

At the end of Macquarie Street lies **Hyde Park**, with the powerful art deco **Anzac War Memorial**. To the east of the park on College Street stands the **Australian Museum** ❶ (daily 9.30am–5pm; tel: 02-9320 6000; www.austmus.gov.au; entrance fee), the oldest (1827)

Map on page 106

and one of the largest in the country. It is the foremost showcase of Australian natural history, and also includes an extensive Aboriginal section. Only a fraction of its collections are ever displayed, but the museum mounts ever-changing exhibitions designed to captivate visitors, and children in particular.

Sydney Tower

Cut back across Hyde Park towards Pitt and George streets, the two main arteries of the CBD and where you'll find some very respectable shopping. The controversial needle of **Sydney Tower ⓝ** is regarded as a phallic eyesore by many, but it has great views from the summit, plus the inevitable revolving restaurant – great for an after-hours cocktail.

Covering an entire city block is the **Queen Victoria Building ⓞ** (daily 9am–6pm; Thur until 9pm; Sun 11am–5pm; tel: 02-9264 9209; www .qvb.com.au; free). Built during the 1890s Depression as Sydney's main market, the arcade was lovingly restored in the 1980s as the city's leading collection of chic stores. The stained-glass windows, Byzantine arches and plaster ornamentaion have made the QVB, according to Pierre Cardin, "the most beautiful shopping centre in the world." Along with some chain stores and designer stores, you'll be able to feast on a few Australiana shops and the odd specialist boutique.

Darling Harbour

Slithering its way past the QVB is the controversial monorail – which, despite protests that it turns Sydney into a Disneyland, and promises by politicians that it will be torn down, shows no sign of slowing. This is the easiest way to get to **Darling Harbour**, largest of the city's modern developments. In the 1800s, this was the "back door" to Sydney, where most trading ships docked. It is now a touristy collection of shops and restaurants, with a **Maritime Museum ⓟ** (daily 9.30am–5pm, Jan until 6pm; www.anmm.gov.au; free; *see pages 124–5*), **Aquarium ⓠ**

(daily 9am–10pm; tel: 02-8251 7800; www.sydneyaquarium.com.au; entrance fee), **Exhibition Centre** and **Chinese Garden** thrown in for good measure.

The Aquarium is the best place to see Australia's extraordinary aquatic life without getting wet – or eaten. As well as crocodiles and tanks full of multi-coloured tropical fish, the Aquarium has transparent tunnels that take you underwater for a spectacular, fish-eye journey through various habitats teeming with sea creatures – the Great Barrier Reef, a seal sanctuary and the Open Oceanarium – where sharks, sea turtles and stingrays glide alongside.

After decades of trying to curb illegal gambling, the state government allowed a giant casino to be built, not far from the Maritime Museum in Pyrmont. **Star City Casino** (open 24 hours; tel: 02-9777 9000; www.starcity.com.au) brings a touch of Las Vegas to Sydney's waterfront. Whether or not that's a good thing depends on your personal taste.

Transfer to the Light Rail at the casino and get off two stops later at the **Fish Market** in Pyrmont (tel: 02-9004 1100; www.sydneyfishmarket.com.au). The

Sydney Tower

BELOW:
the Queen Victoria Building, home to chic stores.

Harbour-hopping

Sydney's green-and-yellow harbour ferries are perhaps the world's most pleasant form of commuter transport, and should be taken whenever possible. A surprising amount of the city can be seen by hopping from wharf to wharf.

A five-minute ride directly opposite Circular Quay (the main ferry terminal) leads to the North Shore suburb of **Kirribilli**, where the prime minister and governor-general have official residences (and both are known to pop in to the legendary Kirribilli fish-and-chip shop for a meal beneath the bridge pylons).

On the other side of the bridge, **McMahons Point** is held to have the best view in Sydney (the Opera House is framed beneath the bridge); running up to north Sydney, **Blues Point Road** is a string of cafés much favoured by yuppies, ostentatiously barking into their mobile phones.

Only slightly longer is the ride to **Cremorne Point**, a dramatic promontory with a leafy harbourside walk to Mosman (considered by aficionados to be one of the best hikes in Sydney), where a ferry can be caught back to the quay.

Also accessible by ferry is **Taronga Park Zoo** (daily 9am–5pm; tel: 02-9969 2777; www.zoo.nsw.gov.au; entrance fee). Surrounded by virgin bush, this must be one of the most beautiful zoo sites on earth, with another heart-stopping panorama of the city (taronga is an Aboriginal word for "view across the water"). There are more than 5,000 animals in the collection, including the full panoply of local critters (this is your best chance for seeing a platypus, for example, and many a snake that you would rather not encounter in the wild). In summer, classical, jazz and swing concerts are held in the zoo's gardens.

Around half of Sydney's beaches are actually within the harbour (nets are set up to keep the sharks at bay). One of the best, near the entrance to Middle Harbour, is **Balmoral**, which also has the famous Bathers's Pavilion restaurant on its shores. **Nielsen Park** at Vaucluse is a favored picnic spot, while **Lady Jane** allows nude bathing. **Camp Cove**, on the southern side near the harbour entrance permits topless bathing and is popular with families.

The most famous ferry ride of all is to **Manly**; it crosses through the open sea between the Heads, and on a rough day waves can dwarf the boats. The name was given by Captain Phillip in 1788 when he was struck by the "manly" bearing of the Aborigines he met there. In the 1930s, the isthmus became Australia's favourite holiday resort "seven miles from Sydney and a thousand miles from care." The family atmosphere has lingered, with a bustling pedestrian mall and reasonably priced eateries. There is an 11-km (8-mile) harbourside walk to the Spit from here (catch a bus back). On West Esplanade are **Manly Art Gallery and Museum** (Tues–Sun 10am–5pm; tel: 02-9976 1420; www.manlyweb.com.au; entrance fee), with a good selection of Australian paintings, and **Oceanworld** (daily 10am–5.30pm; tel: 02-8251 7877; www.oceanworld.com.au; entrance fee) where visitors can watch huge sharks and giant stingrays being fed.

From Circular Quay a high-speed catamaran, the RiverCat, now speeds down the river to **Parramatta** ("where the eels lie down" in the original tongue) – technically a city in its own right, although Sydneysiders persist in regarding it as a suburb. Parramatta still has several colonial buildings scattered through it, including Old Government House; an Explorer bus meets the RiverCat at the docks and transports passengers to the attractions.

Acting as a tourist attraction and famous Sydney icon, the ferries themselves aren't just a pretty face. More than 38,000 Sydneysiders use the harbour transport to get into the city every day for work and they provide the quickest route to some seriously popular suburbs. ❑

LEFT: a harbour ferry approaches Circular Quay.

ultimate seafood experience, Sydney's Fish Market mixes fish auctions, market stalls, restaurants and seafood cooking school to make up the largest market of it's kind in the southern hemisphere. Weekly behind-the-scenes tours run on Mondays and Thursdays (entrance fee).

From here you can either take a stroll back to the monorail, or take the Light Rail back to Paddy's Markets, which leads to the **Powerhouse Museum ®** (daily 10am–5pm; tel: 02-9217 0111; www.powerhouse.com; entrance fee), a huge space devoted to science and technology, with lots of interactive displays *(see pages 124–5)*. From there, it is a short stroll back into Sydney's **Chinatown ⑤**, with its wall-to-wall Asian food.

Away from the centre

In many ways, it is the assortment of "inner-city suburbs" (as they are oddly called) that show Sydney at its most genuine. In the late 19th century, row after row of terraced houses were thrown up as cheap accommodation for workers – usually with small gardens, tight porches and elaborate iron-lace decorations. In the early 20th century several families at a time would squeeze into these places, and as soon as they could, most moved out to the more spacious outer suburbs in search of the Aussie dream. But from the 1970s gentrification began apace.

In the inner west lies **Glebe ❶**, whose main thoroughfare, Glebe Point Road, is lined with boutiques and cafés – many catering to students from the nearby **University of Sydney**, a leafy haven which was built in a self-conscious Oxbridge style. Harbourside **Balmain** was once the raunchiest of working-class suburbs, with industrial dockworks and 41 pubs, one for every 366 residents. There are now 24 pubs, but the leafy ambience is decidedly more upmarket. It can be reached by regular ferry from Circular Quay, and is an ideal spot for a Sunday stroll (the 19th-century waterfront residences are particularly impressive – they featured in Peter Carey's novel *Oscar and Lucinda*).

Kings Cross

The inner east is more of a mixed bag. In Victorian times, **Kings Cross ❷** was an elegant, tree-lined suburb; in the 1920s and 1930s "The Cross" was Sydney's bohemian mecca, but the Vietnam War and the drug boom turned it into the city's sleazy red-light strip, albeit now on the decline. The recent addition of a horde of backpackers' hostels has hardly lifted the atmosphere.

A jaunt up **Darlinghurst Road** late on a Friday and Saturday night past the smack-addled prostitutes, drunken yobbos, cheap strip joints (with mottos like "point yer erection in our direction") and fast-food parlours is without doubt Sydney's least attractive tradition. Despite the grotty backdrop, The Cross also houses some of the city's most popular nightspots and best restaurants, not to mention a smattering of exclusive members-only (unless you're a gorgeous blonde, model, or musician) bars, such as the infamous Hugo's on Bayswater Road. Don't be too wary of the area. It is worth exploring, although safer in a group, and some

Maps
City 106
Area 114

TIP

The Sydney Visitors' Centre at Darling Harbour (tel: 02-9286 0111) is located behind the IMAX Theatre, under the expressway. It is open 9.30am–5.30pm for general advice and information about tickets for a variety of city attractions.

BELOW:
the less salubrious side of Kings Cross.

BELOW:
hanging out on Campbell Parade.

of the nightspots are pulsating pits of all-night dancing and cocktails.

Not a place to be at night, **William Street** is replacing the Paddington Street end of Oxford Street as the designer boutique capital of Sydney, with stylishly designed shop fronts popping up every month. Either side of Darlinghurst and William the streets are filled with pretty, well-maintained homes, and **Victoria Street** houses more great eateries, fashionable bars and chic fashion stops.

Running out into the eastern suburbs as far as Bondi Junction and it's sprawling shopping centre, **Oxford Street** has become another crucial promenade. It begins in the suburb of Darlinghurst, where hip bars and cool attitudes coexist with the best haircuts and the smallest dogs in town.

It is also where Sydney's gay community reigns supreme, most majestically where Oxford Street meets Taylor Square. Gay-friendly clubs, bars and shops snuggle happily together here, and every February the area hosts the **Sydney Gay and Lesbian Mardi Gras** parade. Thousands of Sydneysiders line the street, peek over balconies and try

and nab a spot on a roof terrace while the flamboyant floats, processions, dancers and acts strut their funky stuff. A million more watch the event on TV from the comfort of their living rooms. Considering that homosexuality was illegal in NSW until 1982, prejudices seem to have been swept aside and locals of all backgrounds come out to applaud the efforts of the carefully constructed party.

Paddington

As Oxford Street enters **Paddington** ❸, the change in atmosphere is quite palpable. For many years now "Paddo" has been the address to have for young Sydneysiders. The colonial-style housing is chic (although not cheap!) and the boutiques, bars and restaurants that line Oxford are a weekend opportunity for the well-heeled and even better-dressed to show off their uber-trendy taste. It is not unusual to see the Paddo elite rummaging around the **Paddington Bazaar,** Sydney's oldest market, held in the grounds of the Uniting Church on a Saturday (10am–4pm), dressed in head-to-toe labels, straight

from the covers of *Vogue*. However, the fairly recent addition of Bondi Junction's huge shopping mall has hit Paddo hard. The Sydney faves of Sass & Bide, Scanlon and Theodore and Lisa Ho survive, but more and more owners of small businesses are paying their last month's rent and closing up shop as they struggle to compete with the convenience of Bondi Junction or the ludicrously high rent rates. But if you love to people-watch almost as much as you love shopping for shoes you will appreciate the community feel of Oxford Street – and it beats being stuck in an air-conditioned mall when there is Sydney weather to soak up.

As you reach the summit of Oxford, before it heads along the dual carriageway to Bondi, you hit **Centennial Park**. A favourite spot all year round for those wanting some greenery, whether you want to run, rollerblade, picnic, cycle, horse-ride or just relax in a café with a coffee in the company of some very yummy eastern suburbs mummies, you can do it here. Great all-year round, in midsummer Centennial is also home to the Moonlight Cin-

ema (www.moonlight.com.au), a delightful opportunity to watch new blockbusters and old classics, while lounging on a comfy bean bag in the park. Take a picnic (there are some great delis on Oxford) and a bottle of wine and relax in the great outdoors. An unmissable treat for a summer night.

Sydney's beaches

From Paddington, it is a short bus or taxi ride to any of the eastern beaches – of which the most famous is certainly **Bondi** ❹ (pronounced *Bond-eye*). It was from this great arc of sand in the late 1880s that the first Sydney "cranks" braved the ocean – breaking an old law that forbade swimming during daylight hours as indecent. The breakthrough came in 1902, when Manly newspaper proprietor William Gocher defied the ban and invited arrest. A similar challenge to the ban came the following year from a Waverley clergyman and a respectable bank clerk, and crowds of Sydneysiders soon followed suit. In 1906, the world's first lifesaving club was set up, and 20 years later, crowds of up to 100,000 people were reported at

Life-saver mural on Bondi Pavilion.

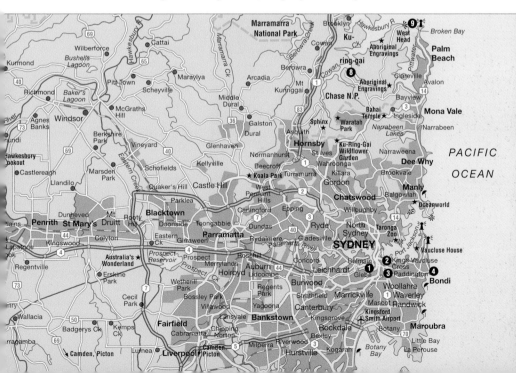

Sydney's suburbs have plenty of good surf beaches.

BELOW: the golden arc of Bondi Beach.

Bondi on summer days. With its wide golden sands, ragged sandstone headlands and reliably fine rollers, Bondi had become another potent Sydney icon. This iconic status was added to during the 2000 Olympics when Bondi beach played host to the beach volleyball competition.

The place is at its best, not surprisingly, in summer. Activity kicks off at dawn, with the joggers on the promenade, bodybuilders by the shore and surfies catching a few waves before work. Sun-worshippers arrive early, closely followed by busloads of Japanese tourists. The Bondi Pavilion opens up, selling ice creams and souvenirs; picnickers arrive with their fish and chips; and the activity continues until well after dark, when lovers take over the sands.

Bondi is also a suburb. **Campbell Parade**, the main beachfront thoroughfare, is a motley string of 1930s-era storefronts that seems to resist all improvement ("one of the great disappointments of Sydney," according to the writer Jan Morris). In the mid-1990s, talk of a "Bondi Renaissance" began as

the suburb leapt to new heights of fashionability, and strings of "New Australian" restaurants opened on the North Bondi end. But still, the parade hangs on to its raffish, sand-gritted personality – and most Sydneysiders really would have it no other way.

The Bondi markets

The **Sunday Bondi Markets**, held each week 10am–5pm in the grounds of the Bondi Beach Public School, have helped establish many successful Sydney designers, and young hopefuls set up stalls each week in hope of being discovered. As if to emphasise the link, the streets behind the busy tourist trap of the parade are now lined with the fashionistas' boutiques, and are a great place to bag an expensive one-off.

But despite its historic and iconic status, the face of Bondi is changing. Slightly further away from the city than is comfortable – especially in summer when the 40-minute bus ride can take twice that time thanks to the throngs of tourists – Bondi is being eclipsed by some of the other eastern suburbs beaches, which are just as beautiful (although all much smaller than Bondi), but don't attract the crowds. The easiest way to see them all in a day is to walk it. **Coogee** is your best option to start from in summer because it is quicker to get to from the city on a bus.

After a recent face-lift Coogee, once known as a poor cousin to trendy Bondi, is coming into its own with great restaurants and bars popping up all the time. The beach itself is flanked by the historic Wylie's Baths and although the waves are not for surfers, there's many a boogie boarder to be found at the weekend. Deep Blue is probably the most high-class Coogee eatery, but A Fish Called Coogee can't be beaten for quality.

Following the coast along, you'll see the small beach of **Gordon's Bay**, after which you will hit **Clovelly**. Including a saltwater swimming pool and one of the best kiosks on the strip (try their $5 milkshakes), Clovelly is

popular with families because generally it doesn't get the big waves and it is a favourite spot for snorkelling. The Clovelly Hotel pub is also well known for its fantastic lunch and dinner menu – best served on one of their two decks – and you can rest assured that if there is a big sports game on, it will get some airplay on one of their massive screens.

Continue on through the stunning Waverly Cemetery until you come to **Bronte**. As well as being home to Aussie director Baz Luhrmann (and actor Heath Ledger in the past), Bronte attracts parties of people throughout summer thanks to a crowd of free gas barbecues and some killer surf.

Next up is **Tamarama** beach, before you turn the corner to find yourself at Bondi. The walk is best in summer when there is little wind and before the sun hits its peak but, just in case, there are plenty of cafés and kiosks along the way to sustain you. If you are here in November, do not miss Sculpture by the Sea, a free exhibition of contemporary sculpture, which starts at Bondi and runs all the way to Bronte.

Watsons Bay

North of Bondi, New South Head Road runs to **Watsons Bay**, whose pub has the finest outdoor beer garden in Sydney, with views across the bobbing yachts to the city skyline. Next door is Doyle's, Sydney's oldest and best-known fish restaurant. It is a stiff hike up to **South Head** at the mouth of Port Jackson, but worth it. The sheer cliffs of The Gap are a favoured suicide spot. On a brighter note, the beaches along this stretch of the coast are always crowded, but lovely, and most have shark nets throughout summer.

The route back to the city goes through one of the most exclusive suburbs, **Vaucluse**. It centres around a magnificent mansion, **Vaucluse House** (Fri, Sat and Sun 9.30am–4pm; entrance fee), built in 1827 for the statesman, poet and explorer William Charles Wentworth. The tea rooms are charming, as are the garden picnic grounds. Swanky **Double Bay** is synonymous with Old Money, although there is also a large central European contingent that has made the grade.

Map on page 114

The original owner of Vaucluse House, William Charles Wentworth, was born in 1790. The son of a convict, he took part in the first successful inland exploration across the Blue Mountains and co-founded the colony's first independent newspaper, The Australian, *in 1824.*

BELOW:
an aerial view shows Sydney's suburban sprawl.

Royal National Park

Only 32 km (20 miles) from Sydney, the **Royal National Park** (daily 7.30am–8.30pm; tel: 02-9542 0648; entrance fee) was established in 1879 and is the world's second-oldest national park – after Yellowstone in the USA.

The Royal packs incredible natural diversity into a relatively small area. Offering riverside picnics, great surf beaches, clifftop heathland walks, rainforest cycle tracks, and much more, the park also has more than 60 camping sites.

A daily entrance fee is charged, although if you're going to be spending a lot of time visiting the national parks, an annual pass is more economical.

There is a strict code of care when it comes to conserving the natural beauty of the parks so read up on the rules and live by them while you're there.

The Blue Mountains

Just 65 km (40 miles) west of Sydney lie the **Blue Mountains**, the range that divides the populous, beach-fringed coastal plain from Australia's notoriously flat, harsh interior. It was an effective barrier to the colony's first explorers, whose efforts to conquer this section of the Great Dividing Range were thwarted by the rugged sandstone cliffs. The footsteps of the trio who in 1813 successfully found the narrow passes are now followed westwards by the main route out of Sydney, the **Great Western Highway**. Today those three pioneers – Blaxland, Wentworth and Lawson – are remembered in the names of towns along the highway as it winds up into the mountains. It was not until the 1920s that this "rude peculiar country" took off as a holiday destination for fashionable Sydneysiders. Small European-style guest houses sprang up, catering to honeymooners and families escaping the summer heat. In 1932, a group of bushwalkers came across a farmer about to cut down a gorgeous blue gum forest in the Grose Valley. They begged him to stop, and in the end offered to buy the

land. It was the beginning of a movement that has since protected almost 1 million hectares (2½ million acres) of Australia's most magnificent wilderness.

Despite the almost impenetrable barrier the Blue Mountains presented to early travellers, they are in fact a sandstone plateau reaching a height of only about 1,100 metres (3,600 ft). Erosion has let the stone fall away to form sheer cliff faces punctuated by picturesque waterfalls. The **Blue Mountains National Park** (tel: 02-4787 8877; vehicle fees apply), totalling 247,000 hectares (950 sq. miles), is well served by bushwalking tracks and picnic and camping spots. Small towns are riddled with fine restaurants, old-style cafés and antique stores catering to weekenders.

Leura

As you drive up from Sydney, first stop should be **Leura ❺**, a classic Blue Mountains hamlet; it's a tidy, picturesque railway town that makes an ideal lunch break. The region's main town, **Katoomba ❻**, is perched on the edge of the Jamison Valley, and shows off its natural wonders to the best advantage at

TIP

If you visit the Blue Mountains at the end of September, take time to stop in Leura during the town's Garden Festival, when many of the beautiful private gardens open to the public (tel: 02-4757 2539).

BELOW: check off the Three Sisters – a must-do for every visitor to the Blue Mountains.

Echo Point, which overlooks one of the state's most photogenic rock formations, the **Three Sisters**. Always busy with tourists, Echo Point has a well-equipped tourist information centre. A great place to take a breather before or after a hike, it might also be wise to take a picnic, especially if you are feeding a hungry family. That or budget for a big bill.

High on the list of breathtaking experiences is the **Scenic Railway** that shafts down into a tree-clad gorge and is claimed to be the world's steepest railway. There are many footpaths for one-day walks in the area – an excellent choice is hiking down the "Golden Stairs" to the rock formations known as the **Ruined Castle**.

Katoomba has a giant cinema with a screen as tall as a six-storey building; its feature on the Blue Mountains is quite stunning.

Some 10 minutes' drive further west along the highway looms the **Hydro Majestic Hotel**, an art deco former casino that catered to high society in the 1920s now being restored. **Blackheath ❼** has some of the best guesthouses and restaurants. Follow the signs to **Govetts Leap**, a spectacular lookout over the Grose Valley.

The village of **Mount Victoria** is located at the height of the Blue Mountains. Like so many of the surrounding areas, the preservation of the historic buildings makes this spot a pleasure to wander through, or bed down for the night in one of the beautiful cottages – priceless views guaranteed.

Jenolan Caves

As the road drops from the mountains down the steep Victoria Pass, it narrows to cross a convict-built bridge that was part of the first road through to the rich wool, wheat, cattle and sheep country. A little way on, and 46 km (29 miles) south of the highway, are the magnificent Jenolan Caves, a mighty series of underground limestone halls encrusted with stalactites and stalagmites. In the 1920s, this was the premier honeymoon spot for young Australians, who regarded the arduous journey and difficult conditions as a badge of honour.

On the highway, 12 km (7½ miles) past the Jenolan Caves turn-off, there are signposts to a monument to the inge-

Map on page 114

Leura's Everglades gardens (37 Everglades Ave, tel: 02-4784 1938, daily 10am– 5pm) integrate local and European trees and plants.

LEFT: the Skyway cable car crosses Jamison Valley. **BELOW:** Leura Post Office now houses a restaurant.

Map on page 114

St Matthew's Church in Windsor was designed by the ex-convict architect Francis Green in the early 19th-century.

BELOW:
fishing in the Hawkesbury River.

nuity used in solving one of the 19th century's greatest engineering problems at **Lithgow**. It is the railway line which originally conquered the steep descent out of the Blue Mountains, known as the **Zig-Zag Railway** – so named for its unique method of overcoming the almost sheer mountain side. The zig-zag line was finished in 1869, but was abandoned in 1910 for a more modern descent. Dedicated train buffs have eventually restored the line to give day excursions travelling back into railway history (for details tel: 02-6355 2955).

There are also some picturesque colonial towns on the edge of the Blue Mountains. Peppered with historic buildings the atmosphere of these hidden settlements is truly unique. Acting like a kind of time capsule of Australian colonial history, the **Hawkesbury** area was established in 1794 when settlers arrived to farm their 30 acres (12 hectares). Many of the descendants from these original settlers still work and live in the district, giving it a truly rustic Aussie atmosphere.

There are countless bushwalking and camping opportunities in the town of Windsor, as well as the new Hawkesbury Regional Gallery (The Deerubbin Centre; Mon, Wed–Fri 10am–4pm, Sat & Sun 10am–3pm; tel: 02-4560 4444; free), and **Richmond** also offers camping, canoeing and swimming.

Historic towns

Between Sydney and the Blue Mountains lie several historic towns. In 1805 John Macarthur was granted nearly 2,000 hectares (5,000 acres) to raise sheep in **Camden**, the beginning of the nation's wool industry. The Camden-Campbelltown-Picton region is still known as Macarthur Country, and **Camden Park House** (1835) is owned by descendants of John Macarthur; it is open to groups by appointment – tel: 02-4655 8466 – with an open day in the third week of September. Camden (pop. 8,000) is the centre of a dairy region focused on the Nepean River Valley.

Sixteen km (10 miles) southwest of Camden, tiny **Picton** also has numerous remnants of 19th-century settlement. Upper Menangle Street is listed by the National Trust as "representing a typical country town street" of 100 years ago. It is a fine base from which to explore the scenic surrounding region.

North of Sydney

An hour's drive north of Sydney lie some of New South Wales' most beautiful national parklands, at **Ku-ring-gai Chase National Park ❽** (tel: 02-9472 8949; vehicle fee payable). Hundreds of Aboriginal carvings dot the cliffs here, which often give sweeping views of the countryside and Cowan Creek: the easiest to reach are on the **Basin Trail** off West Head Road. At the mouth of the Hawkesbury River is **Broken Bay ❾**, a favourite recreational area, where boaters and picnickers flock at weekends.

Palm Beach, home of the Aussie TV soap *Home and Away*, is one of Greater Sydney's smarter neighbourhoods, and its beach is rated highly by surfers. If you're short of time, you can visit this area by seaplane; these leave from Rose Bay in the city, landing in Pittwater. ❏

RESTAURANTS & BARS

Restaurants

Across the Harbour Bridge

Aqua Dining
Corner Paul & Northcliff streets, Milsons Point
Tel: 02-9964 9998
www.aquadining.com.au
Open: L & D daily. $$$
With a blinder of a position above the Olympic swimming pool by the Harbour Bridge, Aqua could probably get away with serving any old rubbish. But this is ambitious modern cooking with a high success rate. Pricey wine though.

Milsons
17 Willoughby Street, Kirribilli
Tel: 02-9955 7075
www.milsonsrestaurant.com.au
Open: L Mon–Fri, D Mon–Sat. $$$
Up by the northern end of the bridge sits this reliable purveyor of modern Australian cooking.

Chinatown & Haymarket

Dragon Star Seafood
Level 3, Market City, 9–13 Hay Street, Haymarket

PRICE CATEGORIES

Prices for a three-course dinner with a half-bottle of house wine:
$ = under A$50
$$ = A$50–$80
$$$ = A$80–120
$$$$ = over A$120
L = lunch, D = dinner, BYO = bring your own alcohol

Tel: 02-9211 8988
L & D daily. $
Sydney's biggest Chinese restaurant and dim sum venue. Go for brunch on Sunday and watch the waiters communicate by walkie-talkie as they serve some 800 patrons. BYO.

Golden Century
393–399 Sussex Street, Haymarket
Tel: 02-9212 3901
www.goldencentury.com.au
L & D daily. $
Chinese-style seafood at its best, and with all the hustle and bustle of a Hong Kong dim sum restaurant.

Circular Quay to Bennelong Point

Aria
1 Macquarie Street, East Circular Quay
Tel: 02-9252 2555
www.ariarestaurant.com
Open: L Mon–Fri, D daily. $$$$
Contemporary cooking with a healthy French influence scores a lot of points in this smart restaurant right on Circular Quay and with outstanding views.

Guillaume at Bennelong
Sydney Opera House, Bennelong Point
Tel: 02-9241 1999
www.guillaumeatbennelong.com.au
Open: L Thur–Fri, D Mon–Sat. $$$
This award-winning restaurant offers modern French cuisine from

Guillaume Brahimi. For food and setting it can't be beaten. Must book.

Downtown Sydney

Bilson's
Radisson Plaza Hotel, 27 O'Connell Street
Tel: 02-8214 0496
www.bilsons.com.au
Open: L Mon–Fri, D Mon–Sat. $$$$
The extravagant classic French-based cuisine from Tony Bilson is absolutely scrumptious.

Botanic Gardens Restaurant
Royal Botanic Gardens, Mrs Macquarie's Road
Tel: 02-9241 2419
Open: L daily. $$
Another lovely setting, this time in the Botanic Gardens. Serves accomplished fusion cooking, but patience may be needed.

The Summit
Level 47, Australia Square, 264 George Street
Tel: 02-9247 9777
www.summitrestaurant.com.au
Open: L Sun–Fri, D daily. $$$
Revolving restaurant with amazing views, decorated in space-age style. You wouldn't even notice if the food was poor, but it isn't.

Hyde Park to Surry Hills

Beppi's
Yurong Street (corner Stanley Street), East Sydney
Tel: 02-9360 4558
www.beppis.com.au
Open: L Mon–Fri, D Mon–Sat. $$

This traditional restaurant, popular with the media, is the finest in Sydney's Little Italy. Opened in 1956 by Beppi Polese and family-run to this day.

Diethnes
336 Pitt Street, Hyde Park
Tel: 02-9267 8956
www.diethnes.com.au
Open: L & D Mon–Sat. $
One of Sydney's oldest Greek restaurants. Old favourites like moussaka and lamb casserole, complemented by Greek coffee and baklava. Busy but friendly.

Longrain
85 Commonwealth Street, Surry Hills
Tel: 02-9280 2888
www.longrain.com
Open: L Mon–Fri, D Mon–Sat. $$$
Spacious 100-year-old warehouse with chic ambience and some terrific food: a fusion of Thai and Chinese.

Marque
355 Crown Street, Surry Hills
Tel: 02-9332 2225
www.marquerestaurant.com.au
Open: D Mon–Sat. $$$
Elegant French cuisine from master chef Mark Best. For sophisticated food with imagination, there's nowhere better.

Millers Point, Darling Harbour & Wynyard

Machiavelli
123 Clarence Street
Tel: 02-9299 3748
www.machiavelli.com.au
Open: L & D Mon–Fri. $$$

Big, loud Italian restaurant. The massive antipasto dishes are the city's best.

The Malaya
39 Lime Street, King Street Wharf, Darling Harbour
Tel: 02-9279 1170
www.themalaya.com.au
Open: L Mon–Sat, D daily.
$$$
Authentic Malaysian cuisine – reputedly the best laksa in town. Dine by the water, or inside in an open-plan setting.

Tetsuya's
529 Kent Street
Tel: 02-9267 2900
www.tetsuyas.com
Open: L Sat, D Tues–Sat.
$$$$
Held in awe by locals, Tetsuya Wakuda combines French and Japanese cooking techniques with the freshest of Australian ingredients to produce Sydney's most exciting food. Book way ahead.

The Wharf
Pier 4, Hickson Road, Walsh Bay
Tel: 02-9250 1761
www.wharfrestaurant.com.au
Open: L & D Mon–Sat. $$
Interestingly eclectic food in a casual industrial space propped out over the water.

Zaaffran
Level 2, Harbourside Shopping Centre, Darling Harbour
Tel: 02-9211 8900
www.zaaffran.com.au
Open: L & D daily. $$
Australia's only 5-star Indian restaurant. Traditional, home-style Indian cooking, presented with a contemporary flair.

Pyrmont

Flying Fish
Jones Bay Wharf, 19–21 Pirrama Road, Pyrmont
Tel: 02-9518 6677
www.flyingfish.com.au
Open: L Tues–Fri & Sun, D Tues–Sat. $$$
Old wharf building, offset by theatrical lighting. Fish prepared with flair.

The Rocks

Bel Mondo
Gloucester Walk (up Argyle Stairs from Argyle Street),
Tel: 02-9241 3700
www.belmondo.com.au
Open: D Mon–Sat. $$$
Once you've found it, watch the chef preside over the preparation of Italian-style food in an open kitchen on a raised dais.

est.
Establishment Hotel, 252 George Street
Tel: 02-9240 3010
www.merivale.com/establishment/est
Open: L Mon–Fri, D Mon–Sat. $$$$
Enjoy Peter Doyle's brilliantly accomplished modern cuisine in classy surroundings, with an adjoining sushi restaurant, cigar bar and an elegantly retro downstairs bar. Top marks.

Quay
Overseas Passenger Terminal, The Rocks
Tel: 02-9251 5600
www.quay.com.au
Open: L Tues–Fri, D daily.
$$$$
Inspired cuisine with an unmistakable French influence.

Sailors Thai
106 George Street,

Tel: 02-9251 2466
Open: L Mon–Fri, D Mon–Sat. $$$
Beautifully crafted Thai street food. There's a cheaper option in the downstairs canteen.

Yoshii
115 Harrington Street,
Tel: 02-9247 2566
www.yoshii.com.au
Open: L Tues–Fri, D Mon–Sat. $$$$
Simplicity and experimentation are the two key ingredients at this award-winning Japanese restaurant.

Inner suburbs (Kings Cross, Darlinghurst)

Balkan Seafood
217 Oxford Street Darlinghurst
Tel: 02-9331 7670
Open: D Tues–Sun. $$
Some of the best and cheapest seafood in town, cooked the Croatian way. BYO.

Bayswater Brasserie
32 Bayswater Road, Kings Cross
Tel: 02-9357 2177
Open: L Fri, D Mon–Sun. $
A long-established eatery, serving good quality modern Australian cuisine.

Café Sel et Poivre
263 Victoria St, Darlinghurst
Tel: 02-9361 6530
Open: B, L & D daily. $
Good-value French cuisine, served with gusto. Opens daily at 7am for breakfast.

Oh! Calcutta!
251 Victoria Street, Darlinghurst
Tel: 02-9360 3650
Open: L Fri, D daily. $$
Bistro-style restaurant

at the heart of the tourist district, serving subtle modern Indian food with an Australian twist. BYO.

Glebe

Boathouse on Blackwattle Bay
End of Ferry Road, Glebe
Tel: 02-9518 9011
Open: L & D, Tues–Sun. $$$
Some of Sydney's best seafood in a converted boathouse on the edge of the harbour.

Eastern suburbs

Claude's
10 Oxford Street, Woollahra,
Tel: 2-9331 2325
Open: D Tues–Sat $$$$
An upmarket but low-key restaurant with discreet celebrity-friendly atmosphere, serving possibly the best French food in Sydney with wonderful desserts. BYO

Pier
594 New South Head Road, Rose Bay
Tel: 02-9327 6561
Open: L & D daily. $$$
Consistently voted Sydney's best seafood restaurant, this beautifully sleek outfit hovers over the harbour waters.

Northside

Chequers
Mandarin Centre, 65 Albert Avenue, Chatswood
Tel: 02-9904 8388
Open: L & D daily. $$
A popular Chinese *yum cha* and seafood eatery with a core of devoted local regulars. BYO.

Jonah's

69 Bynya Road, Palm Beach
Tel: 02-9974 5599
Open: B Sat–Sun, L & D
daily. **$$$**
Popular, long-established restaurant in a
romantic setting with
outdoor dining and
water views. Modern
Australian and seafood
cuisine. Not cheap, but
good value.

Minato

47 East Esplanade, Manly
Tel: 02-9977 0580
Open: D daily. **$**
A very economical
Japanese dining experience in beachy surroundings. BYO.

Southside

Sean's Panorama

270 Campbell Parade,
Bondi Beach
Tel: 02-9365 4924
Open: B, L Sat–Sun,
D Mon–Sat. **$$**
An eccentric little
place at the north end
of Bondi Beach. The
modern Australian
menu is very good and
the weekend breakfasts are legendary.
BYO.

Western suburbs

Pho Minh

42 Arthur Street, Cabramatta
Tel: 02-9726 5195
Open: L & D daily. **$**
One of the many Vietnamese noodle eateries in Cabramatta,
basic but spacious,
with very economical
prices. Also has a
seafood menu, and
simple, no-fuss service.

RIGHT: lunch beside the seaside.

Indulgence

96 Philip Street, Parramatta
Tel: 02-9689 2288
Open: L & D daily. **$$$**
Modern Australian
cuisine and steakhouse in historic,
colonial Parramatta.
Has live music, outdoor dining and bar.

Cafés, Bars & Pubs

Downtown Sydney

Hyde Park Barracks Café

Queen Square,
Macquarie Street
Tel: 02-9222 1815
Open: L daily. **$$**
Over the road from
Hyde Park, this large
café has a historic,
colonial feel. Modern
Australian cuisine.
Fully licensed.

Haymarket/Hyde Park

Civic Hotel

388 Pitt Street (corner
Goulburn Street)
Tel: 02-8080 7000
www.civichotel.com.au
Open: L & D Tues–Sat,
bar till late. **$$**
The Civic's 1940s
pub with an attractive,
retro style, hosts live
music, club sessions
and jazz.

Three Wise Monkeys

555 George Street (corner
Liverpool Street)
Tel: 02-9283 5855
www.3wisemonkeys.com.au
Open: daily. **$**
A pub in the thick of
things. Attracts young
locals as well as fashion-conscious international backpackers.

The Rocks

Hero of Waterloo

81 Lower Fort Street
Tel: 02-9252 4553
Open: daily. **$**
A truly historic Rocks
pub and a local landmark. If you want to
experience a true-blue
Australian hotel, this
much-loved watering
hole is a prime choice.

Suburbs

Bar Coluzzi

322 Victoria Street,
Darlinghurst
Open: daily until late. **$**
A local landmark.

Piccolo Bar

6 Roslyn Street, Kings Cross
Open: daily till late. **$**
A tiny place in the thick
of Kings Cross street
activity, and something
of an institution.

Royal Hotel

Five Ways, Paddington
www.royalhotel.com.au

Tel: 2-9698 8557
Open: L & D daily. **$$**
Situated in the pleasant, villagey Five Ways.
Ornate Victorian architecture and affordable
pub food.

Hotel Bondi

178 Campbell Parade,
Bondi Beach
Tel: 2-9130 3271
Open: L & D daily until late. **$**
This is the real Bondi –
loud, friendly, sun and
sea-soaked, despite
its yuppification.

SYDNEY'S MUSEUMS

From the depths of archaeology and shipwrecks to the heights of modern aviation and architecture, the city's museums offer a range of experiences both traditional and contemporary

Although it's built on the site of Australia's oldest building – the first Government House – the experience offered by the Museum of Sydney (opened 1995) is thoroughly modern in its exploration of Sydney life. You can still look down into the remains of Governor Arthur Phillip's 1788 house, but state-of-the-art technology is a key feature. Hologram-like ghosts speak to you of colonial times, and a 33-screen video display and soundtrack delivers towering vistas of Sydney's natural environment. The culture of the region's indigenous people, the Eora, is widely recognised, and the museum also tells stories of trade, art, architecture and everyday life – but without relying on boring interpretive panels. Instead, each exhibit is accompanied by excerpts from private journals and literary works, to encourage you to make your own connections with Sydney's rich character.

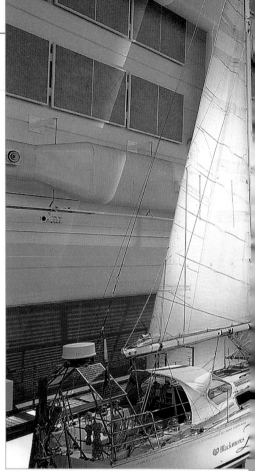

For a more traditional museum experience, navigate around the National Maritime Museum at Darling Harbour. Designed by Sydney architect Phillip Cox to resemble billowing sails, the museum charts the relationship Australians have had with the sea over 50,000 years. It contains a permanent Aboriginal gallery (Merana Eora Nora) and also covers early European exploration, trade, Australia's naval history, immigration, sport and leisure. You can see the America's Cup-winning yacht *Australia II*, a naval destroyer and the world's fastest boat, among many others.

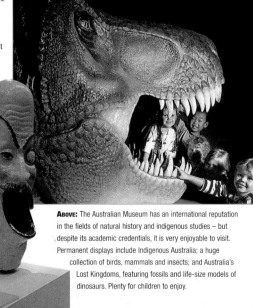

RIGHT: *The Crazy Crooners* are part of a Museum of Sydney exhibit on city sights. They are from an early sideshow in Luna Park, the northside amusement park that opened in the 1930s, closed in the 1960s and reopened for business in 2004. The museum offers a unique insight into the city's history. Exhibitions, films and displays tell stories of Aboriginal culture, colonial life, environment, trade, the law, and everyday dramas.

ABOVE: The Australian Museum has an international reputation in the fields of natural history and indigenous studies – but despite its academic credentials, it is very enjoyable to visit. Permanent displays include Indigenous Australia; a huge collection of birds, mammals and insects; and Australia's Lost Kingdoms, featuring fossils and life-size models of dinosaurs. Plenty for children to enjoy.

ABOVE: Australia's history, society and daily life has been shaped by the sea. The National Maritime Museum covers everything from Aboriginal seafarers to early European explorers, from submarines to surfboards. There are boats outside in Darling Harbour, including the destroyer Vampire and the submarine Onslow, and a wealth of nautical artefacts inside.

BELOW : *The Edge of the Trees* sculpture outside the Museum of Sydney, by Janet Laurence and Fiona Foley (Sydney's first public artwork to be a collaboration between a European and an Aboriginal Australian), represents human memory and experience, drawing on Eora culture and Sydney's many cultural influences. The story of Sydney's indigenous people is woven through the fabric of the museum.

POWER TO THE PEOPLE

Australia's largest and most popular museum, the Powerhouse, contains more than 30,000 objects in 25 galleries on the themes of science, technology, decorative arts and social history. Since opening in 1988 on the site of the old Ultimo power station, it has become home to one of the country's largest transport collections: visitors can travel in time from the Industrial Revolution to the frontiers of space, through exhibits that include 12 operating steam engines and a life-size model of NASA's space habitation module.

Some of the museum's rare decorative art work includes Thomas Hope's Egyptian suite (*circa* 1800), a stunning Wedgwood collection and a model of the Strasbourg clock. There are also impressive re-creations of a bush hut and the interior of a country pub.

For a more hands-on experience, children and adults alike are encouraged to sample more than 100 interactive demonstrations on topics as diverse as the chemistry of smell, lace-making and computer animation.

LEFT: Although it looks like a piece of contemporary art, the Trade Wall in the Museum of Sydney maps the varied items available in the 1830s and today, from Malayan raisins and New Zealand manganese to Turkish figs and West Indian rum. Sydney has been a busy international trading port for over 200 years and the wall highlights the effect the influx of foreign items has had on Australian tastes and culture.

RIGHT: The 180-year-old giant wooden figurehead from the battleship HMS *Nelson* passed from the Royal Navy to the Victorian Colonial Navy to the Royal Australian Navy, and was restored in 1988 for display in the National Maritime Museum. The figurehead is modelled on Vice Admiral Lord Horatio Nelson, most famous for his part in the Napoleonic Wars, and especially in the Battle of Trafalgar, where he was also killed.

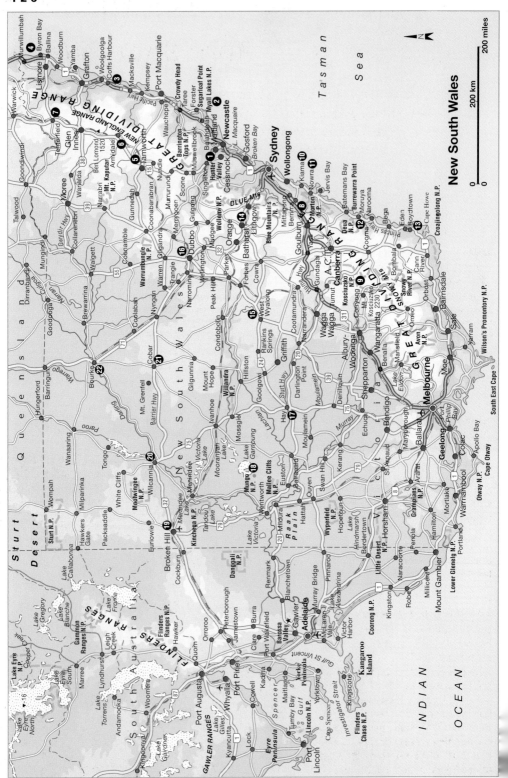

New South Wales

NEW SOUTH WALES

New South Wales's greatest asset is its diversity. From Sydney you can head north for tropical banana plantations, south for snow-capped mountains or west for the vast expanses of the Outback

To many visitors, the names "Sydney" and "New South Wales" are synonymous. However, there's a lot more to Australia's most populous state than its capital city. While Sydneysiders may have the harbour as their playground, elsewhere in the state you can unwind by hiking in the local rainforest, going diving on a coral reef, or just counting the cattle as they come in for the muster. Similarly, while Sydney may be enjoying a balmy day, there may be snow on the southern Alps, spiralling dust storms sweeping across the sunbaked towns in the western Outback, while monsoons flood the lush farming country of the northeast.

We have divided the state (usually written as "NSW") into six separate regions. These are: the Pacific Highway to the north coast (with a detour to the Hunter Valley), New England, the Southern Highlands, the Snowy Mountains, the south coast, and the western slopes and plains.

The Pacific Highway

For generations, the Pacific Highway has been Sydney's track of dreams, its escape route to the sun. Generations of Sydneysiders have made the regular pilgrimage up the coast, fleeing the winter chill, the big-city hustle, or just the tedium of the everyday. Not so long ago, the road passed through country that was still largely undeveloped: after the outskirts of Sydney thinned out into nothingness, you were in a place where the bush and the breezes did most of the talking.

These days, the Pacific Highway has been transformed into a traffic-laden artery that cuts through expanding coastal towns and seafront subdivisions. However, motorists may still enjoy a flickering parade of gum trees in the late afternoon light, along with occasional glimpses of the Pacific Ocean's white-lace hems (despite its name, the Pacific Highway is generally several kilometres from the coast).

With the pedal to the metal, you can

Map: opposite page

BELOW: a truck kicks up dust on a dirt road in the Outback.

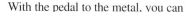

Fishing at Brisbane Water, Gosford.

BELOW: the beach, plus swimming pool, at Newcastle.

make the drive to Queensland in 12 hours, but it's much better to give yourself the time to explore the unpredictable patchwork of boutique wineries and old-fashioned milk bars, country pubs and fish and chips shops, fabled surf spots and vast tropical plantations. Three days is the bare minimum needed to experience at least some of the coast, but if you want to do some serious exploring, five days is recommended.

The trip north starts at Sydney Harbour Bridge. Northbound traffic soon throttles down into the four lanes of the Pacific Highway; at peak hours, this artery is clotted every few minutes at stop lights and suburban intersections, although at other times it flows freely. After negotiating past the Volvos and Saabs of the well-heeled upper North Shore, you finally hit the beginning of the Newcastle Freeway at **Wahroonga**.

Where the highway crosses the **Hawkesbury River** at **Brooklyn**, a vista of ridges, valleys and arms of open water spreads east and west. This is a popular weekend playground for many Sydneysiders, who rent cabin cruisers and drift among the bays and inlets.

Many companies offer cruises; a highlight is the River Boat Mail Run, the local post service departing from Brooklyn, which also carries passengers.

Upstream lies **Wiseman's Ferry**, where former convict Solomon Wiseman opened the first ferry across the river in 1827. A free car ferry takes you to the rugged bush-clad sandstone cliffs of **Dharug National Park** (tel: 02-4320 4200). Walkers, cyclists and horse riders can travel a stretch of the Great North Road, literally carved out of the rock by convicts in the 1830s.

The commercial hub of this central coast region (a mixed bag of retirees, new industries and Sydney commuters) is a detour away at the not-terribly-alluring **Gosford**. But beyond the urban sprawl are the orchards and forests of the **Mangrove Mountain** area, plus a string of beautiful beaches to escape to. Nearby is the **Australian Reptile Park** (daily 9am–5pm; tel: 02 4320 1022; www.reptilepark.com.au; free).

At **Doyalson**, the Pacific Highway heads along a ridge between the ocean and **Lake Macquarie**. Frequently overlooked by tourists, the lake (particularly its western shore) is a fascinating relic of a past age, when working folk could afford water frontages. The mining village of **Wangi Wangi**, for many years the retreat of the artist Sir William Dobell, is a classic example of lake-shore charm.

Newcastle

The second-largest city in New South Wales, **Newcastle**, was long lumbered with a reputation as an unsophisticated industrial hub. But when steel production stopped in 2000, the town worked hard to reinvent itself as a cultural centre. Helped by a lively waterfront development, beautifully preserved heritage buildings and a large student population to liven things up, it is developing as a destination in its own right. It also makes a great base to explore the region, with easy access to the boating and bushlands of Lake Macquarie to the south and expansive, wild Myall Lakes

Map on page 126

to the north, not to mention its own impressive surf beaches. As a bonus, there are the prosperous wineries of the lower **Hunter Valley ❶**, one of Australia's premier wine-growing districts.

Many of its hillsides were originally settled in the pursuit of coal. Coal mining is still a thriving local industry, along with aluminium smelters, giant open-cut mines and power stations, providing a surprising flipside to the area's famed wine industry *(see page 130)*. Turning off from Newcastle, you reach **Maitland**, a city rich in historic buildings. From Maitland, the road leads through one winery after another, with most of them centred around **Pokolbin**.

As the highway heads deeper into the valley, the pace of life slows down. **Singleton** is a mixture of modern and old civic buildings and private homes. It is a delightful place.

The town of **Scone** (rhymes with *own*) is pretty but unremarkable save for its "horsiness". This is the home of thoroughbred stud farms, horse shows and the sport of polo. Much of New England is "squatter" territory, where the sons and daughters of the landed gentry (or aspiring "wannabes") continue the traditions of Mother England – political conservatism, good riding skills and bad dress sense. Scone hosts major polo tournaments, at which champagne flows freely between the chukkas.

While the Hunter Valley is very pleasant to visit, its scenery is not that spectacular; in high summer, its low hills can become unbearably hot. Many Australian wine buffs now prefer to head an hour's drive further east to visit the lesser-known vineyards around **Mudgee**. The picturesque village of **Gulgong** makes an ideal base; it was the childhood home of the poet Henry Lawson, and has a centre devoted to him, and a pioneer museum.

Port Stephens

Back on the Pacific Highway, north of Newcastle the road crosses the Hunter River at Hexham and skirts the western shore of **Port Stephens**. Two and a half times the size of Sydney Harbour and blessed with both calm swimming coves and ocean beaches perfect for surfing, Port Stephens is home to a number of popular resorts such as the

Hunter Valley's wide choice of wineries.

BELOW: Segenhoe Stud Farm, Scone.

The Hunter Valley wine industry

Although the state of South Australia produces more than half of Australia's fine domestic wine, New South Wales's Hunter Valley is the next most important wine region in terms of both size and quality. In the past, the area specialised in particularly dry red and white wine, but with the expansion of the vineyards to the upper Hunter, Rieslings and fine full-bodied reds are also produced here. There are now more than 120 wineries in the lower Hunter at Pokolbin and seven in the upper Hunter near Denman.

The Australian wine industry actually had its beginnings 160 km (100 miles) to the south. By 1827 the Macarthur family was making wine in considerable quantities at Camden, west of Sydney, but real commercial production of Australian wine did not begin until the later 1830s – in the Hunter Valley.

Over the past few decades, local winemakers have embraced new technology with enthusiasm, enabling them to combat the heat at vintage time and to produce wines of a remarkable consistency – an essential requirement of supermarket buyers in Europe and the USA. They may not always be subtle but, because the grapes ripen in hot, sunny, rain-free conditions, where the wines acquire more fruit, more flavour, more alcohol and less acidity, they do have a wildly exuberant flavour.

Semillon does especially well in the Hunter Valley. With about five years' ageing, it offers wonderful oak-infused flavours, plus a rich, honeyed lime-like fruit. Shiraz also produces strong, spicy reds here and, being a less fashionable grape than Cabernet Sauvignon, can offer good value for money.

A tour of the region should begin at the Vintage Hunter Wine and Visitors Centre at **Pokolbin** (Mon–Sat 9am–5pm, Sun 9am–4pm; tel: 02-4990 0900; www.winecountry.com.au). This impressive facility includes a visitor information centre, the Hunter Valley Wine Society, the Wine Country Café and a Wine Interpretive Centre. This is a great place to pick up information and maps, and for anyone with limited time, the Wine Society showroom allows you to taste a few wines from one of the region's vineyards.

The wineries are spread over quite a large area around Pokolbin, and 80 km (50 miles) further up the valley near **Muswellbrook**. Most offer tasting facilities; more than 40 of them also have restaurants, including such acclaimed dining rooms as Robert's at Peppertree, and Esca Bimbadgen. The wineries differ considerably in size, from the internationally famous names such as Lindemans and Tyrrell's to small boutique wineries which offer distinctive, limited-edition wines. Many of the latter are available only by a personal visit, during which you might buy your bottle from the person who tended the vines, picked the grapes, supervised the fermentation and stuck on the labels.

A pleasant way to discover the valley is to tour the wineries of the lower Hunter, spend the night at one of the 180-plus lodgings in the area, and drive on for a second bout of liver and brain damage at Muswellbrook the next day. The Hunter Valley offers a broad range of accommodation, from five-star golf resorts to chic country cottages. Alternatively, you can do your exploring by bicycle (rentable at Pokolbin).

The table wines of the region are uniformly good, and an ideal lubricant for your picnic lunches in the rolling hills. The prices may be higher than those in discount bottle shops in Sydney, but the surroundings are infinitely more relaxing. ❏

LEFT: grape growing on an industrial scale.

sophisticated **Nelson Bay**, and quieter settlements such as **Tea Gardens** and **Hawks Nest**. The bay's most famous attraction is its large population of bottlenose dolphins. Between May and November it also offers whale-watching opportunities. The aquatic reserves at **Fly Point** and **Halifax Point** are popular with divers, and the surrounding bush offers ample walking trails.

Myall Lakes

About 40 km (25 miles) north of Port Stephens you reach Bulahdelah, the gateway to the beautiful **Myall Lakes** ❷. Preserving the blue pearls of Myall Lakes was an early victory for conservationists. Here paperbarks, palms and other wetland vegetation crowd the shores, while the waterways are filled with bird life said to be the most exotic in the state. Surrounding the chain of lakes is national parkland where nature lovers may camp in the wild. The beach at the tiny community of **Seal Rocks** is one of the most scenically exquisite along the whole NSW coast.

Seal Rocks is the first of a string of beaches at the northern end of the lakes

leading to the holiday resort of **Forster**, the southernmost of the North Coast beach towns. Travelling north also entails crossing river after river, for the NSW coast is crenellated with the mouths of waterways which carry runoff from the Great Dividing Range. The further north you go, the rivers become more and more romantic, their shores wilder, their bars and tides more spectacular.

Taree, about a two-hour drive from Newcastle, is a thriving market town in the dairy-rich **Manning Valley**. The beautiful Manning River runs through the middle of town and, if you follow it west to **Elands**, after an hour's drive you find yourself at **Ellenborough Falls**, one of the highest single-drop falls in Australia.

The Manning and other valleys of the mid-North Coast are timber centres providing native woods and pine from vast forests which stretch westwards onto the New England Plateau. Here the highway winds through miles of forest, and it is worth a detour along the well-made coast road from Kew to **Port Macquarie**. These are some of the prettiest beaches in the state, with

Map on page 126

To lessen the impact of walkers, national parks in New South Wales provide boardwalks over fragile terrain.

BELOW: relaxing in the bow net on a dolphin-watching expedition.

rocky outcrops and golden sands. On the western side of the road there is yet another chain of ocean lakes, ideal for fishing and boating.

However, North Coast tourism has taken its toll on the landscape at Port Macquarie (a former penal settlement, founded in 1821, and still full of historic sandstone buildings). Garish motels, retirement villages and time-share resorts dot the headlands, and red-brick suburbia has taken over the flatlands to the west. But, for all its superannuated qualities, there is still much to like about "Port" – good restaurants, top-quality accommodation and easy access to uncrowded beaches. At **Wauchope**, a few miles up the Hastings River, there is a replica of an old sawmilling village, **Timbertown**.

The highway again snakes inland and through the forests. It is worth making the 24-km (15-mile) detour to take in the resort of **Crescent Head** – a pretty, peaceful town with fine surf and good golf. For a real escape, head south from Crescent on the old dirt coast road for 10 km (6 miles) to a grassy headland and beach known as

Racecourse. There's no sign, but a ranger appears from nowhere after a day or two to collect a modest camping fee. Given the joys of an empty beach, uncrowded waves and occasional dolphin sightings, the fee is a gift.

Nearby is the town of **South West Rocks**, perched on a picturesque headland, and the famous **Trial Bay Gaol**, dating back to 1886, which held convicts and, later, German war internees.

Beyond Trial Bay a distinctly tropical feel begins to permeate the air and, from **Macksville** north, banana plantations are a common sight. Houses are built on stilts, Queensland-style, in order to catch the cooling breeze and keep things dry. Everywhere the dominant colour is a lush green, and the roadside signs tell you this is paradise. It isn't, but it's a step in the right direction. While you're filling the tank in Macksville, pop around to The Star pub, which sits right on the banks of the Nambucca River, as pretty and profane an ale house as you'll find anywhere.

On the coast, just south of Macksville, is the small town of **Scotts Head** with a long, clean beach and a caravan park.

Coffs Harbour

The timber port of **Coffs Harbour ❸** is reputed to have Australia's best climate, and has developed into a major centre of North Coast tourism. Unfortunately, most motorists know Coffs only as the city of the Big Banana, another manifestation of Australia's bizarre tourist gigantism (*see pages 78–9*). Upmarket resorts in the area include **Australis Pelican Beach Resort**, **Quality Resort Nautilus**, **Novotel Pacific Bay** and **Opal Cove**, while those with a taste for adventure can join whitewater professionals for a day of rafting action on the nearby **Nymboida River**.

Coffs is more or less the midway point between Sydney and Brisbane – around seven and six hours' driving distance, respectively. Travellers often plan to stay here overnight only, but end up staying a whole week. The town is alive with restaurants and

BELOW:
the beach at
South West Rocks.

pubs, bars and discos, particularly in the strip from the jetty to Park Beach. Parasailing, four-wheel-drive tours into the surrounding forests, the beach, golf and galleries fill the days.

Inland, the Bellingen Valley offers scenic pleasures quite different from the coast. Some parts of this valley, particularly the pebbled river banks, look more like the northern hemisphere than east-coast Australia.

Bellingen

The beautiful village of **Bellingen** (which features dramatically in the climax of Peter Carey's novel *Oscar and Lucinda*) is, along with Nimbin to the north *(see page 134)*, the heart of alternative culture in NSW, although concessions have been made to capitalism since the real-estate boom hit and idyllic communal farms became worth millions. Bellingen retains a relaxed atmosphere and a strong alternative bent. Browse the local arts and crafts at the Old Butter Factory or the beautifully restored Hammond and Wheatley Emporium department store. If you're in the area in August or October

you can take in the local jazz or global music festivals.

From Bellingen, take the Dorrigo Road to the small town of **Dorrigo**, a great base for exploring the **Dorrigo National Park** (tel: 02-6657 2309). The park is a fragment of the massive rainforest that covered the area until the 1920s, when loggers cleared the area in their search for Australian cedar, a timber so valuable it was known as "red gold". From the Dorrigo Rainforest Centre (daily 9am–5pm), you can take a number of walks including the Skywalk, a wooden walkway stretched high over the forest canopy that is also open for nocturnal excursions.

The Pacific Highway swings inland yet again through the forests, this time emerging at **Grafton**, a lovely old town shaded with jacaranda trees (a wonderful sight in late October and early November) and situated on a bend of the Clarence River, 65 km (40 miles) from its mouth. Grafton has some delightful 19th-century architecture enhanced by its wide, tree-lined streets. This is flood country, and the houses close to the river are tropical bungalows

Map on page 126

Jacaranda trees in bloom, Grafton.

BELOW: the 1909 Hammond & Wheatley Emporium in Bellingen.

*Acute local aware-
ness of the harmful
effects of the sun
means that most
children wear body-
suits on the beach.*

BELOW: a surf
shop at Byron Bay.

on stilts. Like several towns away from the coast, Grafton has been bypassed in the tourist boom, and prices for food and lodging are still reasonable.

North of Grafton, the highway follows the line of the Clarence River across flatlands to the coast, with rambling old houses peering out from behind fields of sugar cane. The village of **Maclean**, built on several hills a few miles upriver from Yamba, is quaint, quiet, and a great spot from which to view the workings of the Clarence with its fishermen and cane haulers. Fifteen minutes down a straight bitumen road is the resort of **Yamba**, once a sleepy hollow and now filled with shoddily built "weekenders" and more garish motels. But the pub on the headland and the beaches spread below are first-rate. Down the coast a few kilometres from Yamba is the village and famous surf point of **Angourie**, with its rocky coastline and "Blue Pools".

After a stretch of alternating river and cane scenery, the Pacific Highway clips the coast again at **Ballina**, the southernmost beach town in a string reaching to the Queensland border, col-

lectively known as the Summerland Coast. Ballina, the scene of a minor gold rush in the 19th century, has now found more consistent treasure as a bustling tourist centre and fishing port.

The Pacific Highway heads due north through magnificent rolling hills, but the alternative coastal route takes in some equally breathtaking coastal scenery, including the village of **Lennox Head**, ranked as one of the top 10 surfing spots in the world (the big waves come from May to July).

Byron Bay

The area's big tourist magnet is **Byron Bay ❹**, the easternmost town in Australia and a popular tourist destination.

In the 1960s, Byron was still a quiet rural community with an alternative bent. Today, its magnificent setting, with almost 30 km (19 miles) of sandy beaches fringed by a fertile hinterland, has made it a mecca for the rich and the famous. Some, like *Crocodile Dundee* star Paul Hogan, own property here; others ensconce themselves in the area's impressive array of luxury retreats.

The town is just as popular with the less well-off, who spend their time bodysurfing or relaxing in the sun, a laid-back lifestyle that has made the town a magnet for unemployed youth. In a classic case of biting the hand that feeds, the local council has been battling to limit the number of visitors, but thus far without success.

Come to town on a crowded festival weekend and you may even sympathise with the council. Byron has a packed roster of festivals, devoted variously to blues, writers, films, jazz, and many more besides, during which times the town can get uncomfortably full.

The town's growth has not marred its natural beauty. While the beaches are a major attraction, the hinterland features a number of national parks and nature reserves, including **Tyagarah** and **Broken Head** nature reserves, **Arakwal National Park** (tel: 02-6685 8665) and **Cape Byron Headland**. Then of course there's the underwater world. Byron's

most famous dive spot, the **Julian Rocks Aquatic Reserve**, is considered second only to the Great Barrier Reef on the east coast. This is where temperate waters and tropical waters meet, giving divers the opportunity to view an astonishing array of marine wildlife. A few gruesome incidents where divers have been taken by sharks have done little to lessen its popularity.

The best-known attraction in Byron's hinterland is **Nimbin**, Australia's original alternative community, the town where the 1973 Aquarius Festival launched Australia's hippy culture. While much of the town is still caught in a 1970s time warp, with luridly painted houses and shops and the scent of patchouli in the air, its drug community has moved on from marijuana to hard-core heroin. The overt drug peddling makes many visitors uncomfortable, and they tend not to linger.

A better option is to spend some time exploring the local area. The winding roads between Nimbin and Lismore, through undulating landscape covered in lush rainforest, offer some of the most scenic drives in the state.

These pockets of rainforest, left untouched by the early settlers, were the focus of Australia's first anti-logging protest in the late 1970s.

Mount Warning

The rich soil is a legacy of the giant, shield-shaped volcano that once covered the entire area. The remnant of its central vent is a 1,157-metre-peak (3,780-ft) called **Mount Warning** in English, **Wollumbin** ("cloud catcher") in the local Bandjalung language. Its peak is the first spot in Australia to catch the rays of the rising sun, and offers dazzling views over the district. Also worth exploring are the **Border Ranges and National Park** (tel: 02-6632 0000; vehicle entry fee) and the **Nightcap National Park** (tel: 02-6627 0200), including the 100-metre (328-ft) high Minyon Falls.

The border town of **Tweed Heads** has only recently emerged from the shadow of its flashier sister across the Queensland border, Coolangatta, but the tourist boom now proceeds apace. The end of one journey is the beginning of the next. As you cross the Tweed River,

Map on page 126

Patriotic statues at Tweed Heads.

BELOW:
the lighthouse at Cape Byron, the easternmost point of Australia.

Two Gems in the Pacific

Two of Australia's tiniest tourist areas are also among the most attractive. Although Norfolk and Lord Howe are South Pacific islands, these are not atolls of palm trees and corals. Rather, they are lush green specks on the vastness of the ocean, rather like a bonsaied version of Tasmania.

The sea life around the islands is quite phenomenal. In the surrounding waters, warm and cool currents collide, spawning a wealth of marine creatures including giant clams, sea turtles, clownfish, lionfish, tuna, butterfly fish and a wrasse known as the doubleheader, a species that is unique to the island's waters. Not surprising then that diving is a major draw to the islands.

A rich and fascinating cultural heritage, relaxed lifestyle and rolling green pastures characterise **Norfolk Island**, 1,700 km (1,050 miles) northeast of Sydney. No one lived here until a British penal settlement was established in 1788.

The most bizarre event in Norfolk's history occurred after the British Government decided, in 1852, that the settlement was too expensive to maintain and evacuated all the inhabitants. At about the same time, on remote Pitcairn Island the descendants of the Bounty mutineers and the Polynesian women they took with them from Tahiti in 1789

(after dumping Captain William Bligh) were finding it difficult to grow enough food for their increasing population. So they were relocated to Norfolk Island in 1856, although a few later returned to Pitcairn.

Today there are fewer than 1,800 people on the 3,500-hectare (8,750-acre) island, but many of them share the same set of Bounty surnames. Indeed, so many Christians, Quintals, Youngs, McCoys, Adamses, Buffetts, Nobbses and Evanses crowd the telephone book that it's the only one in the world to publish subscribers' nicknames.

Norfolk is a self-governing territory within Australia. The tourist clutter of **Kingston** is the island's only town. Surprisingly, tax-free shopping here is very cheap, especially for fashionable wool and cashmere sweaters.

Down by the waterfront, the buildings of the early settlements are still in good condition – some are still used as government offices. The evening sound and light show along these buildings, which are remnants from a savage time, is well worth your while.

Norfolk Island doesn't promise a wild time. However, you feel close to history here, and there is enough to do to warrant several days' stay on the island. Diving is a popular activity, and Fletcher Christian's descendant Karlene Christian, at the Bounty Dive Shop, takes daily diving groups.

Accommodation on the island ranges from basic and cheap to quite up-market. There are regular flights from Sydney and Brisbane, and Norfolk can be a very pleasant interlude on the way between Australia and New Zealand.

Lord Howe Island

Much smaller than Norfolk Island, crescent-shaped **Lord Howe Island** is only 11 km (7 miles) long and 2 km (1¼ miles) wide, with a population of about 300. Visitors usually travel on bicycles.

This heavily forested and partially mountainous isle often has a cap of cloud on top of the highest peak, Mount Gower (875 metres/2,870 ft), at the southern end. There are numerous walking trails, many birds and some unique vegetation. There are good reasons to take a tour with a local guide, since it takes a resident expert to decipher the island's rich botany and bird life. As on Norfolk, there are also facilities for diving, snorkelling and, of course, holidaying.

Lord Howe, which is part of New South Wales, is only 600 km (430 miles) off the NSW coast, about level with Port Macquarie. ❏

LEFT: feeding the fish, Lord Howe Island.

he North Coast of NSW falls behind, and what opens ahead is a very different beast: the Queensland Gold Coast.

New England

At **Murrurundi** the New England Highway climbs up, leaving the Hunter Valley to enter the Great Dividing Range, the vast upheaval which separates the coastal plains from the tablelands along the entire length of New South Wales. The town itself is set in a valley of the Liverpool Ranges, and seems constantly shrouded in mist.

The road winds further into the ranges and onto the New England Plateau, eventually reaching the city of **Tamworth ❺**. This pretty centre, surrounded by hills, is the largest in the northwest with a thriving local economy based on sheep and cattle. Tamworth's role as a commercial centre for outlying farms and ranches prompted a local radio announcer to establish a promotion on the cowboy theme. In the early 1970s he organised a country music festival and started calling Tamworth "the country music capital of Australia". At first, most residents

were appalled at the thought of being stereotyped as hillbillies, but the annual festival is now the town's major tourist drawcard. If you're in the area, it is worth a detour to Tamworth just to dine at Monty's (Marius Street, tel: 02-6766 7000), one of Australia's best regional restaurants.

Not far from Tamworth, along a road that follows the bends of the Peel River, is the old gold-mining town of **Nundle**. Abandoned diggings and the ghost-town atmosphere make it well worth a detour. North of Tamworth the New England Highway passes through spectacular country, with rugged peaks and long plains dotted with quaint old mining towns. **Uralla**, once a thriving gold centre, houses the grave of the legendary bushranger Captain Thunderbolt, shot during a battle with police at nearby Kentucky Creek in 1870.

As its name suggests, the **New England Tableland** bears striking similarities, in both topography and climate, to "the old country", England. Its altitude gives it frosty mornings nine months of the year, occasional snow and a year-round freshness.

Map on page 126

TIP

Follow Scenic Drive 19 for about 11 km (7 miles) east out of Uralla, until you reach the privately owned village of Gostwyck. Beautiful little Gostwyck Chapel, set on the banks of a willow-edged stream, is covered with trailing vines that blaze red around April.

BELOW: Tamworth Town Hall.

Nowhere is this more evident than in the city of **Armidale** , a university town greened by parks and gardens, with two cathedrals and tree-lined streets. As well as the University of New England, Armidale has one other college and three boarding schools, establishing it as the major NSW seat of learning outside Sydney. The student population has given Armidale an air of youthfulness in contrast to its stately Victorian architecture.

The highway out of Armidale leads along a ridge to the watershed of the Great Dividing Range, 1,320 metres (4,330 ft) above sea level, at **Guyra**, then on to the junction with the Gwydir Highway at **Glen Innes**, famous for its fine gemstones. Almost a third of the world's sapphires are mined in this area and, although most of the good spots are on commercial lease, you can search for sapphires, garnets, jasper, agate and numerous other stones at many places. The town itself features magnificent ornate buildings and is fringed by five lovely parks. The mist-shrouded **New England National Park** (tel: 02-6657 2309), east of Armidale, is beautiful.

Tenterfield  is the next major town along the route, once chiefly famous as "the birthplace of Federation" (because Sir Henry Parkes first called for the Australian colonies to unite in a speech made in the School of Arts here in 1889), but now more famous as the birthplace of Peter Allen's grandfather. The late, expatriate Aussie singer topped the charts in the early 1980s with a soppy eulogy to his grandfather called *Tenterfield Saddler*. For all that, it is a rather ordinary country town in which there is not a great deal except memories.

The Southern Highlands

The Hume Highway is the main road running south from Sydney to Melbourne, along the inland route. **Mount Gibraltar**, a denuded volcanic plug known locally as "The Gib", rises above Mittagong and the surrounding terrain, marking the gateway to the Southern Highlands. Few people take the time to stop in Mittagong; they're heading either for the limestone Wombeyan Caves nearby, or the collection of picturesque country towns that have made the Southern Highlands a favourite weekend getaway for Sydneysiders.

The first one you'll come to is **Bowral**, 5 km (3 miles) from **Mittagong**, which combines wide small-town streets with elegant big-city-style boutiques. A fashionable resort for well-to-do Sydneysiders in the 1880s, it is still favoured by a similar crowd today, which explains why the town has one of the most sophisticated dining scenes outside Sydney. Other attractions include the **Tulip Festival** in September–October and the **Bradman Museum** (daily 10am–5pm; tel: 02-4862 1247; www.bradman.org.au; entrance fee) on Jude Street, which details the career of Australia's most revered sportsman, cricketer Don Bradman, who died in 2001. The nearby **Mount Gibraltar Reserve** offers the chance to spot wombat and brush-tailed possum.

The gem of the Southern Highlands is **Berrima** , a small village pre-

served just as it was in the first half of the 19th century. It is off the Hume Highway, about 8 km (5 miles) west of Bowral, and most of it is protected by historic trusts. The township was established in 1831, and today many of its impressive old sandstone buildings have been converted to antique and craft galleries; most of those with historical artefacts are open from 10am to 5pm daily. These include the Surveyor General Inn (1834), said to be the oldest continuously licensed pub in Australia; the Court House (1839), now the information centre and museum (daily 10am–4pm; tel: 02-4877 1505; www.berrimacourthouse.org.au; free); the Gaol (1839), now a prison rehabilitation training centre; the Church of Holy Trinity (1849); and St Francis Xavier's Roman Catholic Church (1851).

Goulburn

The big country town of **Goulburn** is located 200 km (120 miles) southwest of Sydney, about midway between the Southern Highlands and the national capital of Canberra. For most of its life Goulburn has been a staging post for travellers along the Hume Highway. In 1992 that period ended when the extended freeway skirted the town, and Goulburn today is a much more relaxed place since the semi-trailers stopped rumbling through. Livestock, wool, wheat and potatoes provide the economic foundation for the town, whose peaceful Georgian homes and two classical cathedrals belie its 19th-century history as a centre of police action against the bushrangers who plagued the surrounding roads for decades. **Towrang Stockade**, 10 km (6 miles) to the north, is sparse ruins today; outlaws like Ben Hall and Frank Gardiner gave this once-formidable penal settlement a wide berth.

Iron hitching posts still stand outside some of the graceful commercial buildings on the main street of **Yass**. Hamilton Hume, the explorer after whom the Hume Highway is named, spent the last 40 years of his life here; his **Cooma Cottage** can be inspected (Mon, Thur–Sun 10am–4pm; tel: 02-6226 1470; entrance fee) and his tombstone can be visited in the local cemetery.

Gundagai, where the Hume crosses the Murrumbidgee River, has one of

Map on page 126

Bowral holds an annual Tulip Festival.

BELOW: "the Don's" statue at the Bradman Museum.

Sir Donald Bradman

Australia's finest cricketer and batsman, Donald George Bradman, affectionately known as "the Don", was born in Bowral in the Southern Highlands in 1908. He attracted attention at an early age, batting golf balls against a local water tank with only a thin strip of wood. He made his Test cricket debut in 1928, at the relatively early age of 20. Two years later, he scored a record 334 not out in a Test against England and, in a match against Queensland, the highest first-class innings ever achieved (452 not out) – a record he would continue to hold until 1959.

His international career spanned 20 years, during which he played in 52 Tests and captained Australia for over a decade. His unequalled reputation stems from his unique batting average of 99.94 runs per innings – he made more than 35,000 runs throughout his career.

Sadly, in his final Test, he famously needed only a further four runs to reach an average of 100, but was dismissed for a "duck" (zero runs) on the second ball. Bradman retired from the game in 1948 and continued to work as a stockbroker as well as serving as a selector for the Australian cricket team. He died in 2001 in Adelaide at the age of 92.

TIP

On an average day, you'll have to wait your turn for a photo opportunity by the cairn that marks the busy summit of Mount Kosciuszko. But there's a grassy knoll a little further down where you can sit on the granite rocks and enjoy the view.

BELOW:
skiing in the
Snowy Mountains.

those quintessentially Australian names that songwriters find irresistible – it features in a number of tunes, from the classic *Road to Gundagai* to *When a Boy from Alabama meets a Girl from Gundagai*. The town has a colourful history – it was moved from its original site after Australia's worst flood disaster in 1852, when 89 people died – and was the favoured hunting ground for the bushranger Captain Moonlight, who was tried at the courthouse in 1879. The town's most famous attraction is the statue of the dog on the tuckerbox, a statue that has retained Aussie icon status long after the poem that inspired it has been forgotten.

The Snowy Mountains

Some might argue that the Snowy Mountains don't really live up to their name. They're not particularly snowy, at least by international standards – the ski resorts at **Perisher Blue**, **Thredbo** and **Charlotte Pass** often rely on snow-making machines for back-up during the short ski season. Nor are the peaks particularly impressive. Although it dominates the skyline, Australia's highest mountain, **Mount Kosciuszko** (pronounced *koz-ee-oss-ko*) is a not-quite-soaring 2,230 metres (7,315 ft) high. However, **Kosciuszko National Park** (tel: 02-6450 5600; vehicle entry fee), the largest protected area in the state, is well worth a visit, with a number of beautiful walks, some of which can be accessed by the Thredbo ski lifts.

Whether you're coming down the Monaro Highway from Canberra or along the Snowy Mountains Highway from the coast, the town of **Cooma**, at the intersection of the two highways, makes a good base and has a number of nice heritage buildings.

Some prefer to base themselves at **Jindabyne**, 60 km (37 miles) west of Cooma on the shores of the lake of the same name. The original town of Jindabyne is buried under the lake – a picturesque history that made it the perfect setting for Ray Lawrence's acclaimed film, *Jindabyne*. Intrepid divers explore lake-bed remnants, including abandoned trucks and the few homesteads that weren't relocated before flooding.

The creation of Lake Jindabyne was part of the Snow River Hydroelectric

Park Life

With more than 600 national parks or nature reserves in the state under the aegis of the NSW National Parks and Wildlife Service, you won't find it difficult to find a patch of accessible nature. At 44 of them you will have to pay a daily entry fee for your vehicle. Everywhere else you're free to come and go as you please. Where there is a fee it's sometimes a matter of purchasing a "pay and display" ticket, so make sure you have plenty of coins on you. It is worthwhile calling the park office (telephone numbers provided in text) ahead of your visit to check whether there are current fire restrictions that could mean all or part of the park is shut. For full information on any or all of the parks, visit: www.nationalparks.nsw.gov.au.

Project, a 25-year, $820-million scheme to provide energy for Sydney, Melbourne, and the rest of southeastern Australia while diverting water to irrigate vast stretches of the Riverina district west of the mountains. Regarded as one of the great achievements of civil engineering, 100,000 people worked on the scheme, mainly immigrants from 30 different countries.

The timber town of **Tumut** on the Snowy Mountains Highway is known for its autumn colours and its May Festival of the Falling Leaves.

South of Tumut, the highway enters the national park and skirts the eastern shore of **Blowering Reservoir**, venue of numerous water-ski and speed-boat records including the fastest (510 kph/317 mph) and longest (1,673 km/ 1,040 miles) runs.

Further on, the **Yarrangobilly Caves** (tel: 02-6454 9597) have become one of the Snowy Mountains' leading attractions. About 260 caves have been discovered in a 2.5 by 12 km (1½ by 7½ mile) limestone belt around the 300-metre (1,000-ft) deep Yarrangobilly River valley. Few caverns anywhere can rival the variety and beauty of their calcite formations. Six caves are open to the public for inspection, five of them by guided tour only.

The road climbs rapidly into **Kiandra**, 90 km (56 miles) from Tumut. Now a desolate road junction, it has two 19th-century claims to fame: it was the site of Australia's highest goldfield (1,414 metres/4,639 ft), and the location of its first ski club. In fact, the 15,000 miners who lived in tents and shanties on these slopes around 1860 were holding competitive ski races before anyone in Europe. They strapped fence palings – "butter pads" – to their boots to move around the surrounding countryside in the winter months. The Kiandra Snow-Shoe Club, established in 1882, numbered among its members the poet Banjo Paterson.

Travellers proceeding towards Melbourne should turn west at the Kiandra junction. The road climbs to

Cabramurra, the highest town (about 1,500 metres/4,900 ft) in Australia. From this point, it's downhill 63 km (39 miles) to the park's western gateway of **Khancoban**. From January to April, this road is a delightful trail through fields of wildflowers, forest stands of mountain ash and snow gum, a number of lovely blue lakes, and frequent herds of kangaroos.

The South Coast

NSW's South Coast remains less developed than its northern counterpart, the occasional boutique winery and eco-resort notwithstanding, but amid its authentic mix of fishing ports and vacation towns, steel mills and cheese factories, primal forest and coal works, there's plenty to justify the journey. Those travelling **Highway One** (the Princes Highway) are only a short detour away from a windswept peninsular national park and an island whose best-known denizens are little penguins. Because the highway south stays close to the coast, it is more scenic than the better-known Pacific Highway north from Sydney.

Map on page 126

A monument in Jindabyne to Sir Paul Edmund Strzelecki (1797–1873), the Polish explorer.

BELOW: Thredbo village before the snow arrives.

TIP

One of the finest vistas in Australia is to be had from Cambewarra Lookout in Morton National Park, just past the village of Kangaroo Valley, where a sweeping landscape of escarpment rainforest interspersed with tracts of dairy farmland greets the eye.

BELOW:
Kiama's Blowhole.

Departing the metropolis, the Princes Highway spectacularly skirts the rim of the **Illawarra Plateau** until descending suddenly to **Wollongong**, a major industrial city in an impressive natural setting. Some may argue that the smokestacks of the nation's largest steel works provide an unsightly backdrop to the otherwise pristine scene of surf and sandstone cliffs, but the heavy industry is the bread and butter for 10 percent of Wollongong district's population of 255,000.

That population is spread along 48 km (30 miles) of coastline from Stanwell Park in the north to Shellharbour in the south, but is mostly concentrated in the southern Wollongong and **Port Kembla** townships, which have a steel works, a copper smelter and an artificial harbour.

Back in 1797, explorer George Bass anchored in tiny **Kiama Bay** and remarked on a "tremendous noise" emanating from a rocky headland. Today, the **Blowhole** is the most popular attraction of the fishing and market town of **Kiama** . When seas are sufficiently high to force water geyser-like through a rock fissure, the spout can reach an amazing 60 metres (200 ft) in height. Beware – visitors have been swept to their death off these rocks.

Kangaroo Valley

Southwards, a short distance of 20 km (12 miles) west of **Berry** ("The Town of Trees"), is **Kangaroo Valley**, a lovely historic township set in an isolated vale among heavily forested slopes. Established in 1829, today it is a favourite haunt of picnickers, bushwalkers and spring wildflower lovers. The **Pioneer Settlement Museum** (tel: 02-4465 1306; free) at Hampden Bridge contains a reconstructed 1880s dairy farm, a settler's hut and pioneering farm equipment. Kangaroo Valley is the gateway to the magnificent **Morton National Park** (tel: 02-4887 7270; vehicle entry fee), which encompasses a large part of the Shoalhaven escarpment.

Nowra ⑪ is the hub of the Shoalhaven district, 162 km (101 miles) south of Sydney. A regional farming centre and an increasingly popular focus of tourism, this riverbank city is 13 km (8 miles) from the mouth of the Shoalhaven River. Regional attractions

Hyams Beach

The best-known of all the beaches is Hyams, on the southern shores of the bay, which has the whitest sand in the world according to the *Guinness Book of Records*. This is also Jervis Bay's style capital. The bay's sparkling waters, its underwater topography of arches, caves and rock stacks, and a marine population that includes groupers, wrasses, sharks, cuttlefish and sea dragons, also make this one of the state's finest dive sites.

Most of the dive sites are located on the seaward faces of the northern and southern headlands that guard the approaches to the bay. Shore diving is possible from Hyams Beach and Green Patch, but the best sites require a boat.

Dive operators in Huskisson can supply all the gear, as well as providing regular boat trips.

include *HMAS Albatross*, Australia's last naval air training station; **Greenwell Point**, where fresh oysters can be purchased from local growers at the co-operative; and the **Nowra Raceways**, three separate modern tracks for horse racing, trotting and greyhounds. The horse-racing track is known as Archer Raceway after the home-bred winner of the first two Melbourne Cups (1861 and 1862). Archer's stall is maintained as a veritable shrine at Terara House, a private property east of the town.

Jervis Bay

Surrounded on all sides but the southeast by 50 km (30 miles) of headland and beaches, **Jervis Bay** (pronounced Jarvis) is one of the South Coast's most idyllic holiday spots. Once a port that rivalled Sydney Harbour (Port Jackson) as the colony's most important harbour, these days it's home to the Royal Australian Naval College, HMAS *Creswell*. Technically, this is part of Australian Capital Territory – co-opted under an act that stipulated the capital must have access to the sea – but that matters not a jot to tourists who are drawn here by the

bay's blindingly white, tranquil beaches, the rugged cliff-side landscapes, and the heaths, wetlands and forests that fringe the bay. Picnic in the **Booderee Botanic Gardens** (daily 8am–5pm; free), Green Patch or Illuka beaches, or sign up for a bush tucker tour with the Wreck Bay Aboriginal Community. The clear waters and varied marine life, including soft corals, sponge gardens and giant cuttlefish, make it a popular destination for scuba divers.

Ulladulla is a rapidly growing beach resort and fishing port which supplies much of Sydney's fresh fish daily. The importance of its fleet can be credited to Italian immigrants of the 1930s who created the town's artificial harbour.

Batemans Bay, another 85 km (53 miles) south, is a tourist, crayfishing and oystering centre at the mouth of the Clyde River. The wildlife refuge on the Tollgate Islands, just offshore, is frequented by penguins, while kangaroos frolic on Pebbly Beach at dawn and dusk. At **Old Mogo Town**, east of the Princes Highway near Mogo, 12 km (7½ miles) south of Batemans Bay, an old mine, a steam

Map on page 126

The crenellated bridge leading to Kangaroo Valley

BELOW: the bay at Ulladulla.

The skeleton of killer whale Old Tom, who used to help whalers in their hunt, is now on display in Eden.

BELOW: one of the beaches at Narooma.

engine and a century-old stamper battery (ore crusher) attract modern-day fortune-seekers. Kids will love **Mogo Zoo** (daily 9am–5pm; tel: 02-4474 4930; www.mogozoo.com.au; entrance fee), a privately owned zoo specialising in endangered animals including snow leopards, jaguars, red pandas, and Bengal and Sumatran tigers.

Moruya ⓬, like Nowra to the north, is established several kilometres inland on the tidal waters of a river mouth. Its first home, Francis Flanagan's Shannon View (1828), is still occupied, and the Uniting Church (or Wesleyan as it was known in the past) was built in 1864 of local granite. The 130-year-old granite quarry on the north side of the Moruya River once supported a town of its own. Among its notable "clients" has been Sydney Harbour Bridge.

As the Princes Highway winds through the hills into **Bodalla**, 38 km (23 miles) south of Moruya, it's hard to miss the little town's **Big Cheese**. Some 4½ metres (15 ft) high and equally wide, it was sculpted from metal in early 1984 to bolster the community's image as a cheesemaking centre. The region's two largest cheese manufacturers produce almost 10,000 tonnes of fancy and cheddar cheese annually.

The waters off the Eurobodalla area, around the small coastal resort towns of **Narooma** and **Bermagui** – especially those around **Montague Island**, 8 km (5 miles) off Narooma – yield record tuna, shark and kingfish catches. **Central Tilba**, 29 km (18 miles) southwest of Narooma, is a beautifully preserved hamlet. Each of the village's two dozen wooden buildings, classified and protected by the National Trust, is as it was in the late 19th century. The ABC Cheese Factory is open (daily 9am–5pm; free) for cheese tasting, and ancient equipment is on display. Central Tilba was established in the 1870s when gold was discovered on Mount Dromedary. There are fine coastal views from the 825-metre (2,700-ft) mountain top, reached by a walking track.

Bega

The lush dairy country continues around **Bega**, the far South Coast's biggest town, and famous for its eponymous cheese. There's probably a by-law that forbids visitors to leave without sampling the local product: play it safe and take in a factory tour and cheese tasting at the Bega Cheese Heritage Centre (daily 9am–5pm; tel: 02-6491 7777; www.begacheese.com.au; free) or watch milking demonstrations on the revolving platform at the Brogo Valley Rotolactor Dairy, 23 km (15 miles) north of Bega (Mon–Wed 2–5pm, daily during school holidays; free).

Merimbula and its sister town of **Pambula**, on the so-called "Sapphire Coast", offer fine surfing, boating, fishing, and oystering. **Eden**, the last sizeable town before you cross the Victoria state border, is located on **Twofold Bay**, once a thriving whaling port and now host to whale-watching tours. The **Eden Killer Whale Museum** (Mon–Sat 9.15am–3.45pm, Sun 11.15am–3.45pm; tel: 02-6496 2094; www.killerwhalemuseum.com.au; entrance fee) on Imlay Street recalls those 19th-century days. Twofold

Bay – the world's third-deepest natural harbour – is home to a fine fishing fleet, a fish-processing factory and the controversial Japanese-sponsored Harris-Daishow woodchip mill on the south shore of the bay.

During its whaling era, Eden had stiff competition as a port from **Boydtown** ⑬, established in 1842 by the banker-adventurer Ben Boyd on the south side of Twofold Bay. Boyd dreamed aloud that his settlement would one day become the capital of Australia. He established a steamship service to Sydney and erected many buildings, but in 1850 his empire collapsed. Boyd went bankrupt, fled Australia to the Solomon Islands, and was never heard of again.

All that remains of the grand scheme today are the **Seahorse Inn** – a magnificent building with stone walls a metre (3 ft) thick, Gothic arches and hand-carved doors and windows – and **Boyd's Tower**, a 31-metre (102-ft) sandstone lighthouse built in 1846 but never lit. The 8,950-hectare (22,110-acre) **Ben Boyd National Park** (tel: 02-6495 5001; vehicle entry fee) encompasses the coastal headlands north and south of Twofold Bay. Its highlights include stunning red sandstone cliffs, rich animal and bird life, and lovely wildflowers.

Map on page 126

Western slopes and plains

The route due west from Sydney, along the Great Western Highway, passes through the Blue Mountains *(see pages 118–20)* and enters the vast grazing land that begins where the mountains end. **Bathurst** ⑭, Australia's oldest inland city, was a major pastoral centre even before the heady gold rush of the 1850s. It is once again a major centre of rural production, although its elegant 19th-century buildings and its lively student population, courtesy of the local campus of Charles Sturt University (split between Bathurst and Wagga Wagga), give it a more sophisticated ambience than one might expect.

There's a packaged Gold Rush experience at **Bathurst Goldfields** on the city's scenic **Mount Panorama**, where old-time diggings have been set up, and gold-panning demonstrations are given. A bit more authentic is do-it-yourself panning at **Hill End** or

The discovery of a large nugget by a Mr Austin at Ophir in 1851 triggered Australia's first gold rush. More mayhem ensued when another discovery was made in Victoria six months later.

BELOW: Bathurst Courthouse is the home of the Bathurst Historical Museum.

Sofala, ghost towns north of Bathurst. Take a drive around the town and inner suburbs to see the civic buildings and grand mansions built from the profits of Australia's first gold rush.

In Bathurst, the scenic drive around Mount Panorama becomes a world-class motor-racing circuit for the 1,000-km (600-mile) touring car race and V8 race in October. Just over 50 km (30 miles) from Bathurst is the intensively photographed village of **Carcoar**, where more than 20 restored colonial buildings nestle in a picturesque little valley.

The highway runs through mainly sheep and wheat country to **Cowra**, a prosperous agricultural centre on the Lachlan River. Cowra has strong links with Japan. During World War II, Japanese prisoners of war were interned in a camp there, and in 1944 it was the scene of a suicidal mass break-out attempt in which nearly 231 prisoners were killed. The care local people gave to the graves of the dead prisoners impressed the Japanese, who later repaid them with the gift of a classically laid-out garden – the **Japanese Garden and Cultural Centre** (daily 8.30am–5pm; tel: 02-6341 2233; entrance fee), a colourful Oriental showpiece in the gold-brown central west of New South Wales.

Wagga Wagga

South of Cowra lies **Wagga Wagga**, shortened to Wagga (rhyming with *logger*) by just about everyone. Although it may seem like a sleepy country town, Australia's most populous inland city has a number of attractions, including the impressive Botanic Gardens, which have a walk-through aviary with over 300 bird species; the **Wagga Wagga Art Gallery** (open Tues–Sat 10am–5pm, Sun noon–4pm; tel: 02-6926 9660; www.waggaartgallery .org; free) that houses the National Art Glass Collection; Charles Sturt University, which runs a prestigious wine course from its on-campus winery; and even a sandy river beach, on the banks of the Murrumbidgee close to the town's main street.

From Cowra, the highway becomes a basic two-lane blacktop, running fairly straight for 1,000 km (600 miles) or so, until the approaches to Adelaide. Here you enter the true "sunburnt country", the "land of sweeping plains" of Dorothea Mackellar's famous poem. If you've yet to see any kangaroos, you'll probably spot them here – although they're likely to be caught in the glare of your headlights. Those cute warning signs have a serious purpose: 'roos are a dangerous hazard on these roads, particularly at night.

The harshness of the elements is burnt into the wild-west appearance of **West Wyalong ⑮**, 161 km (100 miles) west of Cowra. Motorists should spurn the bypass and drive down the main street of the former gold-mining town. The quaint town of **Orange** is, predictably, a fruit-growing centre – but, not so predictably, the crops are apples and cherries rather than citrus fruits (it was named after the Duke of Orange). The extinct volcano **Mount Canobolas**, 14 km (9 miles) southwest of Orange, is a 1,500-hectare (600-acre) flora and fauna reserve with walking trails, picnic areas,

TIP

Spring blossoms transform Cowra's Japanese Garden in early October, when it becomes the focus of *Sakura Matsuri*, the town's annual cherry blossom festival. The festival also features traditional Japanese foods, arts and crafts, kite flying, tea ceremonies, martial arts and *shakuhachi* flute recitals.

BELOW:
the Japanese Garden at Cowra.

waterfalls and a 360-degree view of the countryside from the summit.

The town of **Parkes**, 93 km (58 miles) west of Orange, is known for its Observatory, housing a 64-metre (210-ft) radio telescope which played a role in the 1969 moon landing, an episode of Australian history that inspired the 2000 movie comedy *The Dish*.

The **Ophir Goldfields**, 27 km (17 miles) northeast of Orange, were where Australia's first payable gold was discovered in 1851 and are now an official fossicking area. Banjo Paterson's birthplace is marked by a memorial 3 km (2 miles) off the highway on the Ophir Road.

Dubbo

The Mitchell Highway runs through undulating terrain around **Wellington**. The **Wellington Caves**, 8 km (5 miles) southwest of the town, have huge stalagmite formations in their limestone caverns. The last truly productive agricultural area is around the thriving city of **Dubbo** ⓰, in the middle of the wheat belt, with large sheep and cattle properties and irrigated farms.

Dubbo's main attraction for tourists is the **Western Plains Zoo** (daily 9am–5pm; tel: 02-6881 1400; www .westernplainszoo.com.au; entrance fee), which is an excellent wildlife park associated with Sydney's Taronga Park Zoo. Animals are placed in settings as near as possible to their native conditions, and penned by moats rather than cages or fences. Australia has an inordinate number of jails as tourist attractions, and Dubbo is no exception: the **Old Dubbo Gaol** (open daily 9am–5pm; tel: 02-6801 4460; www.olddubbogaol.com.au; entrance fee), which was closed in 1966 after almost 80 years, has been restored, complete with gallows, and is open for self-guided inspection tours.

Narromine, 39 km (24 miles) on from Dubbo and on the edge of the western plains, is a major citrus-growing area, and the local Citrus Packers Co-operative will let visitors have a look around. The terrain here provides thermal air lifts, making the area ideal for gliding. In the **Macquarie Valley Irrigation Area**, the town of **Trangie** is the centre of a large cotton-growing industry, and visits can be arranged to

Map on page 126

Western Plains Zoo was set up as a sister facility to Sydney's Taronga Zoo and is a key breeding centre.

BELOW: colonial-style architecture at Wagga Wagga railway station.

the nearby Auscott Cotton Farm. Harvesting and ginning take place from late April to June, the best time to visit.

The scenery starts to turn dry brown at **Nyngan** on the Bogan River, where the Barrier Highway begins. Here motorists should start keeping an eagle eye on the fuel gauge. There's only one fuel supply (at Hermidale) over the 128 km (80 miles) to Cobar; only one stop (at Topar) between Wilcannia and Broken Hill; and few service stations from there to Yunta in South Australia.

Hay

It's a desolate drive on to **Hay** ⓱. Banjo Paterson's bitter poem *Hay, Hell and Booligal* was inspired by the almost treeless horizons and the sun-parched tedium, broken only by the sight of an occasional emu, goanna or flock of budgerigars. The town, about halfway from Sydney to Adelaide, is a well-watered oasis on the banks of the Murrumbidgee River. For many years it was an important river crossing on the stock route to Victoria; it also served as a major link in the legendary Cobb and Co. passenger coach network

and is now the centre of an extensive horticultural and wool-producing area. An old Cobb and Co. coach, used until 1901, is on display at the coach-house, corner of Lachlan and Moppett streets, and Hay's Gaol Museum has a great array of pioneering memorabilia.

Balranald is another spot of green on the Murrumbidgee. Head north to visit the **Willandra Lakes World Heritage Site**, a 370,000-hectare (950,000-acre) system of Pleistocene lakes that contains the longest continuous record on Aboriginal habitation in Australia, stretching back 40,000 years. The dry lakes contain ancient hearths and middens, and the world's oldest evidence of cremation – a first sign of civilisation – dating back 26,000 years. The most accessible part of Willandra is **Mungo National Park** ⓲ (tel: 03-5021 8900; vehicle entry fee), about 150 km (93 miles) north of Balranald. Its star attraction is the **Walls of China**, a geological phenomenon of 30-metre (100-ft) high walls of white sand running for 30 km (19 miles).

A good base for visiting the park is the sleepy town of **Wentworth**, once

TIP

Serious birdwatchers can expect to find close to a hundred species at Willandra Creek, as well as grey and red kangaroos, the largest of Australia's marsupials.

BELOW: the Walls of China in Mungo National Park.

Map on page 126

one of the interior's most important towns. Its position at the confluence of the Murray and Darling rivers meant it controlled the river trade between NSW, Victoria and South Australia, until it was superseded by the coming of the railways. It is a pleasant enough base, although most of the so-called attractions, such as Old Wentworth Gaol and Pioneer World, can easily be skipped.

Broken Hill

Head north from Wentworth for 265 km (165 miles) and you'll reach New South Wales' most remote outpost: **Broken Hill ⑲**. In this far corner, locals set their watches to South Australian time, half an hour behind. Although it belongs to NSW geographically and administratively, most of Broken Hill's trade and communication is conducted through Adelaide, which lies much nearer than faraway Sydney.

The city looms large in Australia's industrial history, with legendary unions eventually dominating the city with the Barrier Industrial Council. Its mineral wealth played the largest part in changing the nation from a strictly pastoral outpost to a more industrial base.

Delprat's Mine (tours Mon–Fri 10.30am, Sat 2pm; tel: 08-8088 1604; entrance fee), BHP's original dig, an almost black hill that dominates the city, gives the non-claustrophobic a chance to don a hard hat, lamp and boots for a guided tour. The route heads 120 metres (390 ft) underground in pits that were started in the early, dangerous days of hand drilling. With former miners as guides, visitors will get a feel of the industry's terrible hardships. You can see reproductions of mine workings at **White's Mining Museum** (daily 9am–5pm; tel: 08-8087 2878; entrance fee), off the Silverton Road.

But not everything in Broken Hill is related to the great black hill. This Outback town has become an unlikely font of the arts, and is now home to several locally famous painters including Pro Hart, Jack Absalom and Hugh Schulz. Among the 27 galleries in the city, **Pro Hart's** (Mon–Sat 9am–5pm, Sun 1.30–5pm; tel: 08-8087 2441; www.prohart.com.au; free) is the most exotic. Besides a wide range of paintings by Hart himself, it also

Cooling-off time in Bell's Milk Bar, Broken Hill.

BELOW: Broken Hill's redundant Junction Mine.

How The Hill began

It all began in 1883 when a boundary rider and amateur geologist, Charles Rasp, stumbled across a lump of silver ore on a rocky outcrop he described as a "broken hill". From the claim that he and his syndicate pegged grew the nation's largest company, the Broken Hill Proprietary Co. Ltd.

Although it diversified widely and had completely moved out of Broken Hill by 1939, BHP is still spoken of with distaste in the city for its abrasive attitude to the workforce – the stuff of legend.

"The Hill" turned out to be the world's largest silver, lead and zinc lode and, while other mining towns have tended to peter out over the years, this one is still going strong. It has yielded more than 147 million tonnes of ore from its 8-km (5-mile) long lode.

houses much of his private collection which includes works by Monet, Rembrandt, Dalí, Picasso, Dobell, Drysdale and Tom Roberts.

Broken Hill has also become a centre for one of Australia's unique institutions – the **Flying Doctor Service**, which carries medical attention across the vast distances of the Outback by aircraft.

At night, head for the licensed clubs to play the "pokies" (poker machines). A good deal of the city's social life revolves around the Musicians, Sturt, Legion and Social Democratic clubs, which welcome visitors and have good dining and bar facilities.

In red, rocky country it may be, but Broken Hill still has its beach resort at **Lake Menindee**, 110 km (68 miles) away. This is the city's part-natural and part-artificial water-supply system. The lake and a system of other lakes and channels cater for yachting, power boating and swimming; it combines with the adjacent **Kinchega National Park** (tel: 08-8080 3200; vehicle entry fee), home to many water birds.

The restored ghost town of **Silverton**, a mining centre 23 km (14 miles) from

Broken Hill, is not just an attraction for tourists; it's becoming a regular star in Outback movie epics. With repainted shop and hotel signs, it has appeared in *A Town Like Alice*, *Mad Max II* and *Razorback*. The predictable result is that an Outback Hollywood is evolving. Also in the Silverton area is the 100-year-old **Daydream Mine** (tours daily 10am–3.30pm; tel: 08-8088 5682; entrance fee), where inspections include walking down into the old workings.

For the braver traveller with a bit more time, it's possible to drive right off the beaten track from Wilcannia to Broken Hill, with a detour through the opal fields. It's a rewarding diversion, but not one to be taken lightly because of its lack of sealed roads, fuel and water.

Mutawintji National Park

From Broken Hill, it's about 265 km (165 miles) to **Mutawintji National Park** (tel: 08-8080 3200), a surprising patch of greenness in the barren Bynguano Ranges. Strange and colourful rock formations surround ancient Aboriginal campsites, tools, engravings and paintings, which are explained in films shown at the visitor centre. Visitors must check in with the resident ranger on arrival. There are camping facilities, but no power, and ranger-guided tours are available during the cooler months.

White Cliffs, 297 km (185 miles) from Broken Hill, is a lunar landscape of craters created by opal diggings, and where fossickers with permits can have a scrounge around. Many residents live underground to escape the scorching winds and extreme temperatures, and some of them don't mind showing off the interiors of their white-walled subterranean settlements, which can be surprisingly luxurious. The best accommodation at White Cliffs is, of course, an underground motel or subterranean bed-and-breakfast.

The historic buildings and wharf remnants at **Wilcannia** ⑳, 98 km (61 miles) south of White Cliffs, are reminders of the days when its position on the Darling River made it a major inland

BELOW: sunset over a lake in Kinchega National Park.

port and earned it the title of "Queen City of the West". The lift-span bridge on the approach to the town is an interesting relic of those days: machinery lifted the roadway straight up to allow paddle steamers to pass beneath.

Take the highway from Wilcannia to Cobar, and about 40 km (25 miles) before town, you'll find the turn-off to the **Mount Grenfell Aboriginal cave paintings** (tel: 02-6836 2692). Drive 30 km (19 miles) along a good dirt road to the cave, a shallow overhanging rock shelter, for rare examples of the techniques of pigments applied by finger, in human, bird and animal outlines, and hand stencils.

Cobar

Cobar ㉑ typifies the resilience of the area's people as well as its hardy flora and fauna. From being a rip-roaring town of 10,000 people and 14 hotels not long after copper mining began there in the 1870s, its fortunes have fluctuated: 100 years later its population was less than 4,000 and only one mine was operating; today the figures are 7,000 people and four mines. The Eleura lead, zinc and silver mine (which was opened in 1983) boosted the town's population and economy. The **Great Cobar Heritage Centre** (Mon–Fri 8.30am–5pm, Sat & Sun 9am–5pm; tel: 02-6836 2448; entrance fee), in an old two-storey mining company office, gives a fascinating insight into the area and its people.

Cobar's Great Western Hotel is the epitome of country hotels with its massive first-floor verandah. Classification by the National Trust means that the exterior retains its original timberwork and iron lace but, on the inside, accommodation has been transformed into modern motel-style units. Regulars lining the counter of the public bar are always ready for a yarn with strangers.

North of Cobar, the Mitchell Highway meets the Darling River at the small and pleasant township of **Bourke** ㉒. Once an important port, Bourke has become immortalised in the colloquial expression, "out the back o'Bourke", signifying a place so remote that it is exceeded only by going "beyond the black stump". Take in the emptiness that surrounds Bourke, and you'll get a sense of what the Outback really means. ❑

Map on page 126

Camels can cope well in the Outback's harsh conditions.

BELOW: where Mad Max drops in for a tinny.

RESTAURANTS & BARS

South East NSW

Albury

The Commercial Club
618 Dean Street
Tel: 02-6057 2000
www.commclubalbury.
com.au
Open: L & D daily. $
This massive social
club has a choice of
eating. A-la-carte Dining
Room is the silver-
service venue or there
are the progressively
cheaper Sevens
Restaurant and Reflec-
tions Café.

Batemans Bay

On the Pier
Old Punt Road
Tel: 02-4472 6405
www.onthepier.com.au
Open: L daily, D Mon–Sat. $$
Simple but stylish
cooking in a building
that sits right over the
water.

Berry

Berry Wood-fired
Sourdough Bakery
23 Prince Alfred Street
Tel: 02-4464 1617
www.sourdough.com.au
Open: B & L Wed–Sun. $
Produce from the

PRICE CATEGORIES

Three-course dinner with a
half-bottle of house wine:
$ = under A$50
$$ = A$50–$75
$$$ = over A$75
B = Breakfast, L = lunch, D
= dinner, BYO = bring your
own alcohol

bakery is sensational
and there's a fine deck
to enjoy it on. BYO.

Eden

Wheelhouse
253 Imlay Street
Tel: 02-6496 3392
Open: L & D daily (closed
Mon May–Aug). $$
Down at the wharf
where the fleet comes
in, the Wheelhouse is
well set to grab the best
of the local fish. It does
so and then, with mini-
mal fuss, creates
mouth-watering platters.

Jervis Bay

Fresh at the Bay
64 Owen Street, Huskisson
Tel: 02-4441 5245
Open: L daily. $
Good pastries and
coffee along with the
usual rolls and wraps.

The Gunyah
Paperbark Camp, 571
Woollamia Road, Huskisson
Phone: 02-4441 7299
www.paperbarkcamp.
com.au
Open: D daily. $$
Dinner plus B&B is a
sensible choice at this
eco-resort. Dinner in
the elevated dining
room is a successful
mix of contemporary
cooking with indigenous
bush flavours. BYO.

Kiama

55 on Collins
Shop 1, 55 Collins Street
Tel: 02-4232 2811
Open: B & L daily,
D Mon–Tues, Thur–Sat. $$

Effortlessly retaining
the mantle of best
restaurant in Kiama, 55
employs good local pro-
duce in innovative and
satisfying combina-
tions. Allow room for
one of the fabulous
desserts. BYO.

Narooma

Lynch's Restaurant
135 Wagonga Street
Tel: 02-4476 3022
Open: L & D daily. $$
Slightly old-fashioned
feel to this small
restaurant but the food
is always interesting,
sometimes inspired.

Thredbo

Credo
Riverside Cabins
Tel: 02-6457 6844
www.credo.com.au
Opening times dependent
on snow and weather
conditions. $$
This attractive chalet of
timber and glass offers
large helpings from a
small but interesting
menu. Beautiful outlook
and sound cooking.

Wollongong

Diggies Beach Café
1 Cliff Road, North Beach,
North Wollongong
Tel: 02-4226 2688
Open: L daily, D daily in
summer. $
Find a spot in this
lovely old listed build-
ing, grab a coffee and a
well-crafted snack, and
just hang out and watch
the beach life.

Central NSW
and Coast

Bathurst

The Crowded House
1 Ribbon Gang Lane
Tel: 02-6334 2300
Open: B & L Mon–Sat, D
Tues–Sat. $
www.crowdedhousecafc.
com.au
In a converted church
school with a lovely
enclosed courtyard, the
Crowded House claims
its "modern Australian
food is French based
with a Mediterranean
influence". Both food
and ambience excel.

Cowra

Neila
5 Kendal Street
Tel: 02-6341 2188
www.alldaydining.com
Open: D Thur–Sat. $$$
A short menu of unclut-
tered dishes is devoted
to local produce. The
results are exquisite.

Nelson Bay

The Point
Sunset Boulevard,
Soldiers Point
Tel: 02-4984 7111
www.thepointrestaurant.
com.au
Open: L & D daily. $$$
There aren't many
places on the East Coast
where you can watch the
sun setting over the
water. This is one, and it
can be done over some
rather excellent cooking,
with an emphasis on
seafood. BYO.

Newcastle

Café Supply
Corner Watt & King streets
Tel: 02-4929 2222
Open: B & L daily,
D Tues–Sat. **$$**
A dowdy old bank has
been transformed into
an exciting contempo-
rary meeting and eating
place. From the vanilla
risotto at breakfast,
there's invention on the
menu. BYO.

Orange

Selkirks
179 Anson Street
Tel: 02-6361 1179
www.selkirksrestaurant.com.au
Open: D Tues–Sat **$$$**
Firmly grounded in well-
matched local food and
wine, Selkirks serves
up inventive and sophis-
ticated meals in this old
Federation home.

Terrigal

Dekk
3–5 Kurrawyba Avenue
Tel: 02-4385 3100
www.dekk.com.au
Open: L & D daily. **$$$**
Trendy atmosphere and
modern dining with real
attention to detail.

New England and North Coast

Armidale

Lindsay House
128 Faulkner Street
Tel: 02-6771 4554
www.lindsayhouse.com.au
Open: D Wed–Sat. **$$**
Using local ingredients,
chef Sandy Phillips pre-
pares what's regarded
as the town's best food.

RIGHT: a seafood treat.

Bangalow

Utopia
13 Byron Street
Tel: 02-6687 2088
Open: B & L Tues–Sun,
D Fri–Sat. **$$**
A welcoming space
where ingredients are
kept simple but there's
always a twist. BYO.

Byron Bay

dish
corner of Jonson and Marvel
streets
Tel: 02-6685 7320
www.dishbyronbay.com.au
Open: D daily. **$$$**
Stylish but casual
restaurant and raw bar
with a good wine selec-
tion. Booking essential
in peak season.

Nimbin

Rainbow Cafe
64A Cullen Street
Tel: 02-6689 1997
Open: B & L daily. **$**
Co-operative-run and
packed with vegetarian
offerings, although not
exclusively.

Tamworth

Cafe 2340
15b White Street
Tel: 02-6766 9466
Open: B & L daily. **$**
Fresh ingredients in
satisfying combinations.

Monty's
Quality Hotel Powerhouse,
Marius Street
Tel: 02-6766 7000
Open: D Tues–Sun **$$**
Before relocating to Tam-
worth, chef Ben Davies
worked in Europe, win-
ning a Michelin star
three times.

Western Outback

Bourke

Port o' Bourke Hotel
33 Mitchell Street
Tel: 02-6872 2544
Open: L & D Mon–Sat. **$**
Good pub food in this
friendly old hotel.

Broken Hill

**Barrier Social &
Democratic Club**
218 Argent Street
Tel: 08-8088 4477
Open: B, L & D daily. **$**
The "Demo" is one of
several social clubs
around town and the
competition means that
you can get sizeable
bistro meals very
cheaply. The Sturt Club
at 321 Blende Street
(08-8087 4541) is also
worth a look.

Griffith

Michelin
72 Banna Avenue
Tel: 02-6964 9006
Open: B Sun, L Tues–Sun,
D Tues–Sat, D. **$$**
Sophisticated and sleek
– both the space and
the menu. Michelin
would not look out of
place in Sydney and
could hold its own in
elevated company.

Hay

Jolly Jumbuck Bistro
Riverina Hotel,
148 Lachlan Street
Tel: 02-6993 4718
Open: L & D daily. **$$**
Smart dining room of
bare brick and polished
wood. Classic bistro fare
explains its popularity.

Tibooburra

Tibooburra Hotel
Briscoe Street
Tel: 08-8091 3310
www.outbacknsw.com.au/
tibooburra.htm
Open: L & D daily. **$**
A friendly welcome and
huge meals to satisfy
the most demanding of
itinerant stockmen.

White Cliffs

**White Cliffs
Underground Motel**
Smith's Hill
Tel: 08-8091 6677
www.undergroundmotel.
com.au
Open: D daily. **$**
Reasonable three-
course dinners; the
bistro has a more
informal menu.

CANBERRA

The capital of Australia is a place conceived by accident, built by bureaucrats and located on a compromise. Considering all that, it's a remarkably pleasant place to visit

Map on page 156

uring one of his visits to Australia's national capital, the Duke of Edinburgh declared that **Canberra** (pop. 322,000) was "a city without a soul" – a royal snub the citizens of Canberra have not forgotten. In January 2003, raging bush fires spread into the city, destroying 530 homes and 30 farms, and killing four residents. The community spirit in the aftermath demonstrated that even if Canberra were "a city without a soul", its residents still had hearts. But it is not a soul that Canberra lacks – it is more a sense of purpose. Like many administrative capitals, it is an artificial city, constructed not around any existing settlement, but simply out of thin Monaro air.

Intense rivalry

The reason it was built at all can be traced to colonial jealousy: in 1901, at the time of the federation of the six Australian colonies, there was intense rivalry (which still exists) between Sydney and Melbourne over which was the chief city of Australia. After some wrangling, the founding fathers solved the problem by the compromise of inventing a new capital at an equally inconvenient distance from both. Thus a small and hitherto undistinguished valley in the southern tablelands of New South Wales was selected as the site.

Visitors often complain that they can never find the centre – even when they are actually standing in it. Canberra, the political, diplomatic and administrative capital of the Commonwealth, is simply not built as a commercial city, and so far it has stubbornly refused to look or act like one. In fact, what it looks most like, apart from a spread of pleasantly wooded suburbs, is a kind of semi-dignified Disneyland, complete with a **Captain Cook Memorial Water Jet** Ⓐ which flings water 140 metres (460 ft) into the air. Visitors are either impressed or bemused by the city's uncluttered, circular road system that tends to lead the unwary around in circles. Of equal

LEFT: the Carillon on the shore of Lake Burley Griffin.
BELOW: the Cook Memorial shows the routes taken by his various expeditions.

Free guided tours of Parliament House take about 45 minutes and include both Houses, the Great Hall and the roof.

wonder is the absence of external TV antennas and the lack of front fences – both decreed aesthetically incompatible with Canberra's image.

Similarly, new homes are supplied with young native trees in order to promote the city's reputation as a leafy suburbia. In contrast to the absence of planning in other Australian cities, the zeal with which the bureaucracy has monitored and moulded this city's character does impress. As a result, Canberra is a city of showcase architecture. The capital's main attractions are clustered in a relatively small area, in close proximity to **Lake Burley Griffin**, and a walk around the lake will provide great views of the city and parliaments.

Parliament House B, which cost more than $1 billion and is adorned with many art and craft works, was completed in 1988, in time for the bicentennial celebrations. It is built into the side of Capital Hill on the lakeside, its roof grassed in order to blend in, and extensive areas can be visited (daily 9am– 5pm). When parliament is sitting, anyone can watch

Australian parliamentary democracy in action from the Public Galleries. The livelier of the two chambers is the House of Representatives, and the best time to be there is Question Time. This is generally held at 2pm, for which you'll need to book by calling the Sergeant-at-Arms' office on 02-6277 4889 by 12.30pm on the day required.

Old Parliament House

Its predecessor, **Old Parliament House C** on King George Terrace, now houses the **National Portrait Gallery** (daily 9am–5pm, tel: 02-6270 8236; www.portrait.gov.au; entrance fee) as well as visiting exhibitions and music performances. Past exhibitions have been dedicated to pop star Kylie Minogue, Australian sporting heroes, some of the greats of Australian portraiture and even *Fuzzy Prime Ministers of Australia* – the complete line-up of prime ministers, captured for posterity in hooked-wool rugs.

On either side of the glass-like pond at the front of the building is the **Aboriginal Tent Embassy**, first set up here in the 1970s to focus attention on the Aboriginal land-rights campaign and a per-

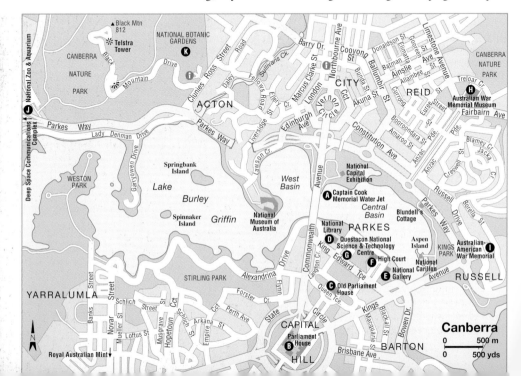

manent fixture since 1992. Depending on your point of view, it's either an icon or an eyesore; but it does serve to remind visitors of how many Aboriginal people feel that they do not share equally in the fruits of modern Australia.

National institutions

Also on the lake front are the **National Library**  (Mon–Thur 9am–9pm; Fri–Sat 9am–5pm, Sun 1.30am–5pm, free guided tour at 12.30pm Thur only; tel: 02-6262 1111), which has 4½ million books and whose displays include a model of Captain Cook's *Endeavour*; the **National Gallery** (daily 9am–5pm; tel: 02-6240 6411; www.nga.gov.au; free), which has a fine collection of Aboriginal art and a Sculpture Garden; the **High Court** (daily 9.45am–4.30pm), grandiose enough to echo a Moghul palace; and the **Questacon National Science and Technology Centre** (daily 9am–5pm; tel: 02-6270 2800; www.questacon.edu.au; entrance fee), which has many enjoyable hands-on displays.

On the Acton Peninsula is one of Canberra's newest attractions. The **National Museum** (daily 9am–5pm;

tel: 02-6208 5000; www.nma.gov.au; free) opened in 2001 and houses an eclectic collection of artefacts. Highlights include the world's largest collection of Aboriginal bark paintings, convict clothing and leg irons, and a raft used by Vietnamese refugees who landed in Australia in the 1970s. Perhaps the oddest exhibit is the oversized heart of the racehorse Phar Lap, whose record-breaking achievements captured the country's imagination during the Great Depression until his premature death, apparently due to arsenic poisoning.

Children have their own gallery, **KSpace FutureWorld**, at the National Museum. Here they can use touch-screen computers to design cities and vehicles, then watch their designs come to life on a 3D theatre screen. On Aspen Island, the **Carillon** tower, a 53-bell gift from Britain, plays muzak-like selections to the residents at weekends.

North of the lake, the **Australian War Memorial Museum** (daily 10am–5pm; tel: 02-6243 4211; www.awm.gov.au; free) looks oppressive but has a collection of relics, weapons, documents and photographs said to be one

Map: opposite page

The National Gallery's Sculpture Garden is freely accessible from the path around Lake Burley Griffin.

BELOW: the National Museum of Australia.

Capital insights

On the opposite shore from the National Library at Regatta Point, just by the bridge, is the **National Capital Exhibition** (daily 9am–5pm; tel: 02-6257 1068; www.nationalcapital.gov.au; free) – essential if you want to make sense of the layout of Canberra. The exhibition offers fine views of the city and contains some curious sidelights to the shaping of the capital. According to the original plan, the surrounding hills were to be planted with flowering shrubs in different colours: Mount Ainslie in yellow, with plantings of wattle and broom, Black Mountain in pink and white with flowering fruit trees, and Red Hill – in red, of course. The plan was never implemented with any enthusiasm, although Red Hill does live up to its name, with its springtime flush of scarlet bottlebrush and *callistemon lanceolatus*.

Map on page 156

TIP

Every year during January and February the National Botanic Gardens hosts a summer concert series, on weekends starting at 6pm. Call the Gardens' visitor centre, tel: 02-6250 9540, for more information.

BELOW: a memorial to air crew in the grounds of the war memorial.

of the best of its kind in the world. The **Australian-American War Memorial** ❶ on Kings Avenue is known to local people as "Bugs Bunny" because the winged eagle that adorns its summit bears a resemblance to the rabbit.

West of the lake, the **National Zoo and Aquarium** ❹ on Lady Denham Drive (daily 10am–5pm; tel: 02-6287 8400; www.zooquarium.com.au; entrance fee) is worth a visit and includes a wildlife sanctuary.

In the midst of all the high-minded architectural efforts, Canberra retains considerable charm. It remains one of the few cities (as opposed to towns) in Australia where it's still possible, occasionally, to see kangaroos in the streets. For those who miss out on this spectacle, the nearby **Tidbinbilla Nature Reserve** offers a range of Australian flora and fauna.

National Botanic Gardens

Nature lovers should also visit the **National Botanic Gardens** ❻ (daily, 8.30am–5pm; 02-6250 9540; free) at Black Mountain Reserve, which contain a huge range of Australian plants over 40 hectares (100 acres), the best of its kind in the country. The surrounding bush is one of the city's great attractions.

The city has acquired an impressive range of restaurants of many national cuisines, and several international-class hotels (such as the fabulous Art Deco Hyatt). Nightlife is improving, too: there are 300 cafés, restaurants and bars (including some 24-hour bars), a variety of cinemas and theatres, a casino, and some good music, ranging from classical to rock. For half the year you can watch the Australian Parliament in session – which, when the "pollies" go at each other hammer and tongs, is the best free show in town.

Around Canberra

Canberra is a good jumping-off place for outdoor entertainment. There are easy day trips to old mining and farming towns such as **Captains Flat** and **Bungendore**.

A few hours' drive to the south, along the Alpine Way, are the **Snowy Mountains**, Australia's best ski area in winter and the setting for spectacular bushwalking in summer. About the same distance east is the **south coast** of New South Wales, with some of the prettiest and least-spoilt beaches.

The **Deep Space Communications Complex** at **Tidbinbilla** (daily 9am–5pm; www.cdscc.nasa.gov; free), is active in the command, tracking and recording of a number of NASA space exploration projects, and is open to visitors. There are also a number of optical and radio telescopes in the surrounding countryside. Many of them, including those at the renowned Mount Stromlo Observatory, were destroyed in the 2003 bushfires; however, rebuilding is underway.

Although the city is Australia's capital, it can seem surprisingly casual, with low-key security. The best times to visit are spring, when it's green and covered with blossom and wattle, and autumn, when the weather is balmy and the yellowing leaves of the deciduous trees are strikingly beautiful. ❑

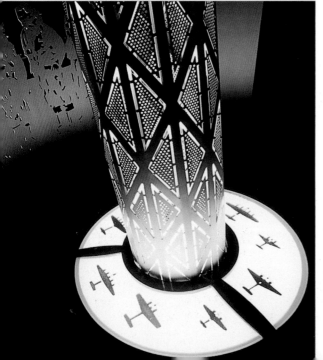

RESTAURANTS & BARS

Restaurants

City (Civic)

Aubergine
18 Barker Street
Tel: 02-6260 8666
www.auberginerestaurant
.com.au
Open: L Mon–Fri, D daily.
$$$
Courgette's sister restaurant, French and italian influences and choice of menus.

Courgette
54 Marcus Clarke Street
Tel: 02-6247 4042
www.courgette.com.au
Open: L Mon–Fri,
D Mon–Sat. **$$$**
Classy eatery where simple but stylish decor and the gentlest murmur of voices suggests reverence for the food about to appear. Quite appropriate for some of the city's most imaginative modern cooking.

Mezzalira
Melbourne Building,
20 West Row
Tel: 02-6230 0025
www.mezzalira.com.au
Open: L Mon–Fri ,
D Mon–Sat. **$$**
The Trimboli family has some exquisite regional cooking. BYO.

Milk and Honey
Center Cinema Building, 29
Garema Place
Tel: 02-6247 7722
www.milkandhoney.net.au
Open: B & L daily,
D Mon–Sat. **$$**
There's café eating or a more formal restaurant menu in the two split-level dining areas of this bright modern enterprise with its ironic references to 1970s styling. Good food too.

Tasuke
Sydney Building, 122 Alinga
Street
Tel: 02-6257 9711
Open: L & D Mon–Sat. **$**
This tiny place looks like a sandwich bar but inside some of Canberra's finest and freshest Japanese food is lapped up by the cognoscenti. BYO.

Barton

Ottoman Cuisine
9 Broughton Street (corner
Blackall Street)
Tel: 02-6273 6111
Open: L Tues–Fri,
D Tues–Sat. **$$**
With such a huge menu of superbly executed Turkish delights, it may be prudent to put yourself in the hands of the chef and settle for one of the "banquets". This is where Canberra's chefs eat on nights off.

Dickson

Fekerte's
74/ 2 Cape Street, Dickson
Tel: 02-6262 5799
Open: L Tues–Fri,
D Tues–Sun. **$**
Effortlessly cornering the market in Ethiopian cuisine, Fekerte Tesfaye cooks up a range of wholesome meaty offerings as well as a comprehensive selection of excellent vegetarian options. BYO.

Parkes

The Ginger Room
Old Parliament House (enter
by Queen Victoria Terrace)
Tel: 02-6270 8262
www.gingercatering.com.au
Open: D Tues–Sat. **$$**
Impressive, elegant Pacific-rim eating in the refurbished former private dining room of Old Parliament House.

Kingston & Griffith

Artespresso
31 Giles Street, Kingston
Tel: 02-6295 8055
www.artespresso.com.au
Open: B Sat & Sun,
L Tues–Fri, D Tues–Sat. **$$**
It's café meets bistro meets restaurant – but the modern Australian food is reliably good whatever you're after. BYO.

Manuka

Abell's Kopi Tiam
7 Furneaux Street
Tel: 02-6293 4199
Open: L & D Tues–Sat. **$**
A lot of Malaysian and other regional classics produced with aplomb in this busy but friendly restaurant. BYO.

Cafés, Pubs & Bars

City (Civic)

Blue Olive Café
56 Alinga Street
Tel: 02-6230 4600
Open B, L & T Mon–Sat. **$**
In the lovely old Melbourne Building, loads of great snacks with an emphasis on home-baked bread and cakes. BYO.

Café Essen
Shop 5, 6 Garema
Arcade
Tel: 02-6248 9300
Open: B, L & D daily. **$**
Primarly a coffee house, this old favourite does great breakfasts. BYO.

The Phoenix
23 East Row
Tel: 02-6247 1606
Open: L & D daily. **$**
Not very large, but the Phoenix is a popular pub with a friendly and relaxed atmosphere. There's occasionally live music and usually some local art on the walls.

Kingston

Silo Bakery
36 Giles Street
Tel: 02-6260 6060
www.silobakery.com.au
Open: B & L Mon–Sat. **$**
A popular and lively café is part of this excellent bakery. Some Mediterranean leanings.

TWO PARLIAMENTS

Canberra was specially designed and built as a seat of government. To add a bit of excitement to their administrative dream, its founders created not one parliament but two

When consideration is given to the number of working politicians per head of population, Australia is one of the most over-governed countries in the world. It should come as no surprise, then, that in the Australian Capital Territory and its city of Canberra there are two complete national parliament buildings, not to mention the ACT legislative assembly. Admittedly Old Parliament House has been pensioned off from active government, but its bulky presence in the centre of the city reinforces the feeling that this is a place where legislators rule the roost, where each facet of the city is dedicated to the smooth running of the machinery of power.

Opened in 1927, Old Parliament House was the home of the Federal government for 60 years until 1988. Since then the imposing building has become a museum of its previous incarnation and also holds visiting exhibitions. Tours are available of both buildings and it's always worth securing a spot in the public gallery if either house of the new Parliament House is in session, particularly if there's a chance to witness Prime Minister's question time. The same applies in Sydney, only for the State Parliament where, again, there are two houses. If Prime Minister's question time fails to entertain, Canberra's Parliament House also holds a national collection of over 5,000 specially commissioned works of art and heritage objects, ranging from paintings to sculptures and tapestries by Australian artists.

BELOW: The annual Canberra Balloon Fiesta each March sees the sky above the capital filled with colourful craft. A ready supply of hot air is believed to be incidental to the location.

ABOVE: long-serving Prime Minister John Howard at the dais in the House of Representatives in Federal Parliament.
BELOW: the distinctly home-grown national crest.

BELOW: In an echo of the Westminster system the Senate or upper house is fitted out in red, the lower house in green.

A PLACE OF PROTEST

On the afternoon of 26 January 1972 – Australia Day – a tent was set up on the lawn in front of Old Parliament House as part of an Aboriginal protest against government tardiness in dealing with issues of land rights and compensation for indigenous people. Thus was born the Aboriginal Tent Embassy, which existed on and off for many years, and has been permanent since 1992. The original protestors felt like "aliens in our own land, so like the other aliens we need an embassy". The site, despite claims that it is an eyesore, has now taken on such symbolic significance as the focus for Aboriginal struggle that its future seems reasonably assured. It would, in fact, take a foolhardy politician to order its removal, especially after its listing on the National Estate by the Australian Heritage Commission in 1995.

ABOVE: The mosaic in front of Parliament House is derived from a painting by acclaimed Aboriginal artist Michael Nelson Tjakamarra of the Northern Territory's Papunya community. *Possum Wallaby Dreaming* is made up of over 90,000 pieces. The artist also has a huge painting in the foyer of Sydney Opera House.

BELOW: A panel in the exhibition area of Parliament House celebrates the role of women in parliament since the election of the first MP, Enid Lyons from Tasmania, in August 1943. The first woman senator, Dorothy Tangney of Western Australia, took up her seat at the same time. In the 21st century one in four of the members of the lower house are women, while in the senate the proportion is around 30 percent. Australia is yet to have a woman prime minister.

Women in the Federal Parliament

RIGHT: In Walter Burleigh Griffin's carefully planned city a line can be drawn from the centre of Parliament House through Old Parliament House, the Australian War Memorial and on to the peak of Mount Ainslie, as can be seen from this view from the main entrance to Parliament House. Visitors can also take in the scene from the grassed-over roof of the building (although heightened security concerns have largely put an end to unsupervised wandering on the roof), but the favourite spot is the Queen's Terrace Café on the first floor. The design for the new parliament was chosen by an international competition that attracted over 300 entries. The winning design was the work of New York-based Italian architect, Romaldo Giurgola, whose concept was a circular building that "would nest into the hill".

MELBOURNE

The capital of Victoria is Australia's most "European" city, a 21st-century metropolis with an abundance of 19th-century charm and a passion for culture and sport

Map
on page
166

That Melbourne continues to feature at or near the top of the *Economist*'s most liveable city table never surprises its residents even if denizens of the harbour city across the border affect disbelief. **Melbourne ❶** doesn't compete on brash big-ticket items like a harbour or opera house, but quietly gets on with being the sporting, cultural and eating capital of Australia. It's also a shopping magnet for many Australians and some travel from Sydney, lured by boutiques known for their one-off designs. For visitors, that's one hell of a combination and justifies an extended stay.

Newcomers will not find the most picturesque city. The Yarra River isn't the sparkling focal point that rivers are in some cities. Novelist Anthony Trollope considered the Yarra (or Yarra Yarra as it was) during a visit in 1871: "It seems to have but little to do with the city. But it is popular with rowers, and it waters the Botanical Gardens".

River development

That may be changing, however. There has been extensive development on the river over the past few years, with the Southgate development, Federation Square and a massive programme at Docklands. During the 2006 Commonwealth Games, the river was the centrepiece of the opening ceremony and subsequently attracted thousands each night for a sound and light show.

Trollope also complained that "there are no hills to produce scenery, or scenic effect. Though you go up and down the streets, the country around is flat – and for the most part uninteresting. I know no great town in the neighbourhood of which there is less to see in the way of landscape beauty." Well, say locals, if he'd looked up from St Kilda beach, he'd have seen the Dandenong Mountains. But Melbourne is more about hidden charms. There are copious parks and gardens that encourage you to linger, and leafy suburbs proliferate.

PRECEDING PAGES: the city from the Yarra River. **LEFT:** South Bank café sculpture. **BELOW:** Moomba Waterfest parade, held in March.

Indeed, suburbs are intrinsic to an understanding of the city. One of the city's most famous exports, Dame Edna Everage, may skewer them mercilessly but this city is the sum of its neighbourhoods. And when Edna was born out of Barry Humphries' appalled fascination with the monocultural suburbia he grew up in with its "politics of niceness", nobody could have anticipated that by 2006 the city he scorned would have so thoroughly embraced his creation as to approve the naming of a city laneway Dame Edna Place.

Power shifts

But Melbourne now is not the city it was in the 1950s of Edna's debut. At that time the majority of Australia's biggest companies were based in the Victorian capital and most overseas enterprises followed suit. Here was the seat of the Establishment where background and connections determined your entry to the corridors of power. There is still some residue of those times; stockbrokers, lawyers, bankers and company directors are more often than not the product of the city's elite

grammar schools and colleges. Pitch up at the wrong barbecue and you'll still find men, and it's usually men, bragging about their private school and casually dropping the names of their more successful classmates.

But the balance has shifted. Sydney now has the majority of major company headquarters and, with the exception of the mining companies and banks, the trend is in that direction. So Melbourne has had to reinvent itself.

Much of the impetus for this has come from changes in the population. Migration has always influenced the growth of the city and the Anglo-Celtic dominance that lasted up to World War II has steadily diminished with consecutive waves of migrants from Italy, Greece, the Balkans, Lebanon, Turkey, China, Vietnam and Eastern Europe. The genteel, refined European tastes of the past are still there, but they have been spiced by a more vibrant and outgoing approach to life.

The Melbourne that Ava Gardner described in the 1960s, while shooting an adaptation of Nevil Shute's *On The Beach*, as the perfect place to make a

Rowers on the Yarra River. Melbourne has a strong sporting history and hosted the 1956 Olympics and 2006 Commonwealth Games.

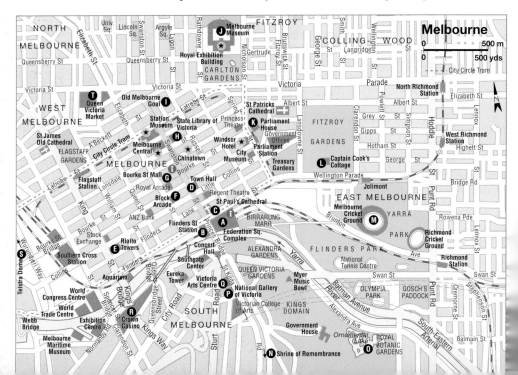

film about the end of the world, is now a city of cool bars, radical architecture and sophisticated inhabitants.

Free men from the start

Unlike Sydney, Melbourne was not founded as a penal colony. Instead, the city's early settlers were free men intent on building a new and prosperous life for themselves. In June 1835, John Batman, a land speculator from Tasmania, sailed his schooner into Port Phillip Bay, rowed up a broad river and declared: "This will be the place for a village." With a payment of goods including blankets, mirrors and axes, he persuaded the local Aborigines to "sell" him 600,000 acres (240,000 hectares) of prime land and drew up a document to legalise the purchase. This was later discounted as a farce by the British government, which accused Batman of trespassing on Crown Land.

A year later, the settlement beside the Yarra was named in honour of Lord Melbourne, Britain's prime minister. The first land sales took place soon after, and small properties at the centre of the settlement sold for £150. Two years on the same properties were changing hands for £10,000.

If it was these auspicious beginnings that laid the foundation for Melbourne, it was the discovery of gold at nearby Ballarat in 1851 that propelled the sudden growth in population and prosperity which determined its true character. This was also when it's role as Australia's financial centre was established. The finds drew thousands of fortune-seekers from Europe, the USA and China and gold fever swept the country. But in time the alluvial gold ran out, and thousands of diggers left the goldfields to make Melbourne their home. The population more than quadrupled in 10 years, and the gold revenue financed new development in a rapidly expanding city determined to grow in a grand style.

When Mark Twain visited on a lecture tour in 1895, he was entranced by what he saw: "It is a stately city architecturally as well as in magnitude. It has an elaborate system of cable-car service; it has museums, and colleges, and schools, and public gardens, and electricity, and gas, and libraries, and

Map: opposite page

The Windsor Hotel on Spring Street is a Victorian Heritage Hotel and dates from 1883

BELOW: two familar visual aspects of Melbourne – its graffiti and its wrought ironwork.

theatres, and mining centres and wool centres, and centres of the arts and sciences, and boards of trade, and ships, and railroads, and a harbor, and social clubs, and journalistic clubs and racing clubs, and a squatter club sumptuously housed and appointed, and as many churches and banks as can make a living. In a word, it is equipped with everything that goes to make the modern great city."

Ironically, by this time depression was setting in. However, Federation in 1901 saw the city take on the mantle of political capital until the move to Canberra in 1927. The Depression of the 1930s was followed by a spell of industrial growth and development, given extra impetus by post-war migration. By the time that it hosted the 1956 Olympics, Melbourne was more than ready to take its place on the world stage. Substantial investment in the local equivalent of Francois Mitterrand's *grands projets* – particularly under Liberal Premier Jeff Kennett in the 1990s – transformed the city for the new millennium and even shifted its geographical axis.

![TIP]

Melbourne is peppered with interesting little shops and boutiques. To get a real feel for the city you might consider taking a shopping tour around the less obvious streets and areas. Hidden Secrets Tours operates a number of "fashion walks" (tel: 03-9329 9665; www.hiddensecretstours.com).

BELOW:
Flinders Street Station seen from St Paul's Cathedral.

Federation Square

The completion of **Federation Square** (tel: 03-9655 1900; www.fedsquare .com) in 2004 gave Melbourne its first popularly embraced public space. The ornately Victorian **Flinders Street Station** had been the city's signature building for years and "under the clocks" was the traditional rendezvous point for a night out, a practice immortalised in a song of that name by seminal local band Weddings Parties Anything. But station steps are not necessarily the best place to loiter. Federation Square, on the other hand, has plenty of space, places to sit, cafés and bars, and is right opposite the station.

Its design has its detractors, some of them vehement, but no-one can deny its impact on the city. Built above unsightly railway yards, it serves to unite the Central Business District (CBD) with the Yarra. At its heart is a gently scalloped piazza paved with variegated sandstone, which inclines towards a small stage and a giant video screen. Concerts and public events attract large crowds and there are occasions, such as the Socceroos successful run in the 2006 soccer World Cup, when so many want to party that numbers have to be limited.

The buildings behind, designed as "shards" sticking out of the ground, look as if they have been crazy-paved in a combination of glass, stone and zinc. The riches within include a branch of the National Gallery of Victoria – **The Ian Potter Centre** (Tues–Sun 10am–5pm; tel: 03-8620 2222; www.ngv.vic.gov.au; free), which is one of those buildings that is totally unpredictable once you get inside. Walls are coming at you from all angles and there's no clue as to what may be around the next corner. Somehow it all works; the daylight comes in where it should and the art – all Australian – is displayed sympathetically. The **Australian Centre for the Moving Image** has screenings, exhibitions, even video games; the programming is sometimes populist and always eclectic (Mon–Fri

Map on page 166

10am–5pm, Sat–Sun 10am–6pm; cinema times as advertised; tel: 03-8663 2200; www.acmi.net.au). There is also the **Edge** performance space and a variety of bars, cafés and restaurants.

Behind Fed Square (as it quickly became known) is **Birrarung Marr**, an area of parkland on the river bank designed to acknowledge the original Aboriginal occupants of the land. Rock carvings and sculptural representations of shields and spears reflect the various tribes. Further on, the striking **Federation Bells** installation is worth seeing and hearing, and the opening of a new bridge through to the Melbourne Cricket Ground should ensure that many more people will get to enjoy them.

Taking the tram

Melbourne's CBD is on an easily navigable grid and easily walkable. There is also the **Circular Tram**, a free service that operates in a loop round the edge of the CBD. The tram system is one of Melbourne's great resources and, if you pick your route judiciously, a great way to discover the city.

St Paul's Cathedral ᴄ, opposite Federation Square, was built between 1880 and 1891 to a design by William Butterfield, who never bothered to travel over from England to see it. The stained glass and tiled floors are amongst the highlights.

On the other corner of Flinders and Swanston streets, **Young and Jackson's** pub is a Melbourne institution, renowned for the 19th-century nude portrait *Chloe* on the first floor which was considered rather racy in its day. Make your own assessment.

Continue down Swanston Street to **Melbourne Town Hall ᴅ**. Typical of the grand public buildings erected on the back of the gold boom, it comes into its own during the International Comedy Festival every April when various performance spaces are carved out of its halls and meeting rooms and it takes on a real club atmosphere.

Collins Street crosses Swanston Street at this point and, were you to go uphill past the magnificent **Regent Theatre** – pop into the foyer if it's open – you would come to what's known as the "Paris end", where a bunch of exclusive boutiques and

Melbourne's traditional green and gold trams are the best way to get around the city.

BELOW: a medley of facades at Federation Square.

BELOW: strolling past the colourful Melbourne Museum.

designer stores hang around in a group, hoping to mug wealthy tourists. To avoid that, go in the opposite direction.

Should you want an overview of the city, continue down for several blocks to the **Rialto Towers** Ⓔ where a fast lift will take you to the observation deck on the 55th floor (Sun–Thur 10am–10pm, Fri–Sat 10am–11pm; tel: 03-9629 8222; www.melbourne360rialto.com.au; entrance fee). Not only can you see for miles around, but you also get a chance to bemoan the fact that the new **Eureka Tower** across the river is much taller but doesn't have an observation deck at all.

Shopping arcades

Have a look at the remarkable gothic revival facade of the ANZ **Bank Building** at the junction with Queen Street on the way back and make for the **Block Arcade** Ⓕ between Elizabeth and Swanston Streets. In this Victorian marvel, thrill to the mosaic floors, etched glass roof, and the original shop fittings. The **Hopetoun Tearooms** has been purveying refreshment to refined shoppers for generations. Wind through to Little Collins Street and

cross the road to **Royal Arcade**. You'll run the gamut of the slightly cartoonish statues of Gog and Magog, just behind you as you enter.

The far end opens into **Bourke Street Mall** Ⓖ, the epicentre of old-style city shopping with the flagship department stores of the Myer and David Jones chains. At the Elizabeth Street end, the old GPO building has been successfully converted into a high-end shopping complex. The Myer store runs back across two blocks and has a bridge over to the recently reconfigured **Melbourne Central** retail hub which completely encloses the 1890 Shot Tower.

The Swanston Street entrance to Melbourne Central faces the imposing **State Library of Victoria** Ⓗ (Mon–Thur 10am–9pm, Fri–Sun 10am–6pm, public holidays 10am–6pm; tel: 03-9669 9888; www.slv.vic.gov.au; free), which has had a fortune spent on it in renovations. The **Reading Room** copies the one in the British Museum.

The **QV Centre**, next to the library, is another mega shopping development, which includes AFL **World**

(daily 10am–6pm; tel: 03-8660 5555; www.aflworld.com.au; entrance fee), devoted to Aussie Rules Football.

Follow Latrobe Street beside the library and left on Russell Street you will find **Old Melbourne Gaol ①** (daily 9.30am–5pm; tel: 03-9663 7228; www.nattrust.com.au; entrance fee). This is where Ned Kelly met his end and his death mask is on display along with some of his armour. The building is grimly atmospheric as it is, but extreme thrill seekers can join a monthly overnight ghost hunt if they dare.

Return along Russell Street until you reach Little Bourke Street, Melbourne's **Chinatown**, a buzzing and colourful lane with some rather good eateries. Turn left on Spring Street and continue to the end where the **Carlton Gardens** across the road lead up to Australia's first World Heritage-listed structure, the **Royal Exhibition Building**. Access is normally only available for special events but, if you get a chance, nip in and have a look.

Melbourne Museum

On the far side, that striking modern pavilion is the **Melbourne Museum ①** (daily 10am–5pm; tel: 03-8341 7777; www.melbourne.museum.vic.gov.au; entrance fee). The largest museum in the country, there is masses to see and all presented so alluringly that you can spend hours here without realising it.

The children's section is pitched just right but other areas appeal to all ages, especially the Australia Gallery which hops with surprising ease from a wacky tin model of the MCG to the stuffed remains of legendary racehorse, Phar Lap. There's an IMAX cinema too.

Victorian piles

Return to Spring Street and the state's seat of government at **Parliament House ⑭** (tours 10, 11am, noon, 1, 2, 3pm, 3.45pm; tel: 03-9651 8911; www.parliament.vic.gov.au; free), another grandiose Victorian pile which still awaits the dome originally designed for it. Probably in vain. Tours are available

unless the houses are in session, in which case try for the public gallery.

The **Princess Theatre** opposite is typical of its era, even down to the ghost story; ask at the box office. Continue along Spring Street to, yes, another monolithic public building. This is the Old Treasury, containing the **City Museum** (Mon–Fri 9am–5pm, Sat–Sun 10am–4pm; tel: 03-9651 2233; www.citymuseummelbourne.org; entrance fee). The permanent exhibits are linked to the history of the building and its role as repository of gold, and there are broader-themed temporary displays. **Treasury Gardens**, alongside, crawls with possums after dark.

Walk through to **Fitzroy Gardens** where, under towering old trees, you will find **Captain Cook's Cottage ⑫** (daily 9am–5pm; tel: 03-9419 4677; www.melbourne.vic.gov.au; entrance fee). Not hard to discover Australia if you were brought up there, you might think. But no, the whole thing was disassembled in Yorkshire, shipped round the world and rebuilt in Melbourne, making it the only 18th-century building in town. Elsewhere in the gardens

Map on page 166

The Old Melbourne Gaol also runs night tours four nights a week.

BELOW: the World Heritage-listed Royal Exhibition Building.

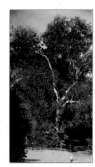

The most famous plant in the Botanic Gardens is the "Separation Tree", an old river Eucalyptus around which a public party took place in 1851 to celebrate independence of Victoria from New South Wales.

RIGHT: a racegoer observes the action at the Victoria Derby Day.

look out for the model **Tudor Village**, sent as a gift from the people of Lambeth in London, grateful for Australian food parcels during World War II; and the **Fairies' Tree**, a tree trunk carved with cute little figures. A twee trunk.

Across Wellington Parade the Melbourne Cricket Ground, better known as the MCG , beckons. Try to get in to see some kind of sporting action, but if not, there are tours (Gate 3; daily 10am–3pm if no event; tel: 03-9657 867; www.mcg.org.au). The stadium can seat 100,000.

Return to Federation Square, turn left over the river, and go down St Kilda Road. Directly ahead of you, the grey stone building is the **Shrine of Remembrance** (daily 10am–5pm; tel: 03-9661 8100; www.shrine.org.au; free). Built over six years from 1928 to commemorate the dead of World War I, it is aligned so that once a year at 11am on the 11 November – Remembrance Day a beam of light shines on to the Stone of Remembrance and illuminates the word "love". A visitor centre was cleverly constructed in the shadow of the main building.

Just across the way is the Observatory Gate, one of the entry points to the **Royal Botanic Gardens** (daily Nov–Mar 7am–8.30pm, Apr, Sept, Oct 7.30am–6pm, May–Aug 7.30am–5.30pm; tel: 03-9252 2300; www.rbg.vic.gov.au; free). Enthusiasts will enjoy the specialist areas, like the cactus garden or the cycad collection, but many simply wander through the beautifully tended grounds and drink in the tranquillity of the lakeside. An excellent children's garden opened in 2006.

Arts precinct

Return to St Kilda Road and cross over to the bluestone bulk of the **National Gallery of Victoria** (Wed–Mon 10am–5pm; tel: 03-8620 2222; www.ngv.vic.gov.au; free). This is, in fact, NGV **International**, which houses the NGV's collection of work from overseas as opposed to the Ian Potter Centre at Federation Square which specialises in Australian works. Stick your fingers in the water wall at the entrance, as generations have before you, and take your pick of the permanent exhibits or the visiting shows (for which a charge

Sports Society

If Australians are sports mad, then Melbourne must be the asylum. It's not just the obsession with the sports themselves, but the determination to make every contest an event.

The first Tuesday of November is a public holiday because that's when the Melbourne Cup is run. But that is just day in the Spring Racing Carnival and each year the crowds at Flemington Racecourse are increasing so that in 2006, the record-breaking 129,000 crowd was not at Cup Day at all, but at the previous Saturday's Derby Day.

The Boxing Day cricket invariably sells out at the MCG but, again in 2006, for an exciting Ashes series where Australia was pitched against England, all the first four days of the test match sold out in advance. That's 400,000 people.

The story's the same for January's Open tennis championship. And the Australian Rules Grand Final at the MCG in September is probably the biggest event of them all. Aussie Rules, or the "footie," dominates Melbourne for seven months of the year. Every office has its tipping competition and everyone has to "barrack" for a team, irrespective of age or gender. Ironically, in this very Victorian sport (10 of the 16 teams are from the state), at the time of writing the trophy had not been won by a home side for seven years.

Map
on page
166

is usually levied). Leonard Hall's stained-glass ceiling of the **Great Hall** accounts for all the people lying on their backs within, and beyond is the doorway to the **Sculpture Garden**.

Next door, distinguished by the huge mesh spire above it, is the **Arts Centre Q**. This cultural power house has three theatres presenting **Melbourne Threatre Company** productions and visiting opera, dance and drama companies. **Hamer Hall** is the city's formal concert venue.

At the river turn left along the South Bank and stroll through the **Southgate** development where shopping and eating opportunities abound. The promenade provides good views over the city.

You may want to consider crossing one of the footbridges over the river to visit the absorbing **Immigration Museum** (daily 10am–5pm; tel: 03-9927 2700; www.immigration.museum.vic.gov.au; entrance fee), or to **Melbourne Aquarium** (daily 9.30am–6pm; tel: 03-9620 0999 www.melbourneaquarium.com.au; entrance fee).

Crown Casino R (daily, 24 hours; tel: 03-9292 8888; www.crowncasino.com.au; free) on your left seems to go on forever and given the turnover on the tables and through the one-arm bandits, or "pokies" as they're known, the management probably hopes it will. Shops, restaurants, show venues and a cinema can be found inside.

Docklands

The architecturally stimulating **Melbourne Exhibition Centre**, or "Jeff's Shed" as the locals call it, since it was one of Premier Jeff Kennett's projects, comes next. On the river bank beyond is the distinctive outline of historic ship, the *Polly Woodside*, currently being renovated by the National Trust.

Stay on the path by the water round to **Docklands**, the latest area of Melbourne to be given an overhaul. You cross the river on the serpentine **Webb Bridge**, so called because of the steel spider's web effect of its canopy, and then follow the path through a sculpture garden that eventually leads to **Victoria Harbour** with the **Telstra Dome S** sports stadium on your right and glistening new developments of offices, apartments and restaurants on

*Melbourne
Exhibition Centre
aka Jeff's Shed.*

BELOW: the Royal Botanic Gardens.

your left. The area is still finding its feet but it's worth wandering down for a look if only because it's so unlike anything else in Melbourne.

It's time to hop on the Circle Tram clockwise to the junction of Latrobe and Queen streets. Walk north up Queen Street until reaching the extensive sheds of **Queen Victoria Market** ❶ (Tues, Thur 6am–2pm, Fri 6am–5pm, Sat 6am–3pm, Sun 9am–4pm; tel: 03-9320 5822; www.qvm.com.au). It is a buzzing place where locals after fresh produce or deli specialities mix with tourists seeking souvenir clocks in the shape of Australia. At weekends it has a holiday atmosphere.

Little Italy

A short distance to the north, **Lygon Street** in Carlton, just 10 minutes by tram from the city centre, is sometimes known as **Little Italy**. It was this area that the waves of post-war Italian migrants adopted as their own and at certain times of the year, such as when the blessed Ferrari team is in town for the Grand Prix, streets are closed and the partying doesn't let up. Today

A colourful store on Brunswick Street.

BELOW: Queen Victoria Market.

Lygon Street is touristy, but a lively community of professional people and academics from adjacent Melbourne University keeps the place grounded. Coffee bars, bistros, trattorias, noisy pubs and pool rooms, as well as edgy fashion boutiques, contribute to a vibrant atmosphere.

Brunswick Street, a few blocks to the east, is hipper. In the evenings Melburnians drift here from around the city with bottles of wine tucked under their arms, looking for the latest BYO restaurant. There are cuisines from around the world, as well as Modern Australian. Wine bars, pubs with local bands and comedy nights, hip designer clothes stores, tiny retro fashion shops, gay and lesbian bookshops, artists' cafés of the type popular in the 1950s and '60s, full of earnest characters confused by daylight, all happily co-exist. Intersecting Brunswick Street, Johnston Street is Melbourne's Spanish quarter, lined with tapas bars that pulsate at night with salsa and flamenco.

Melbourne Zoo in Parkville, west of Lygon Street, has been a favourite since it opened in 1862 (Elliott Avenue; daily 9am–5pm; tel: 03-9285 9300; www.zoo.org.au; entrance fee). It has a comprehensive collection of indigenous animals, displayed in sympathetic surroundings, as well as species from further afield. Its new elephant enclosure manages to recreate an Asian setting and the foodcourt is themed to match.

St Kilda

St Kilda has always meant fun. Often sleazy, frequently illicit, but fun nonetheless. This bayside suburb is Melbourne's urban beach. There may not be surf to speak of, and few would brave a dip in the water, but the sand is clean and the beachfront on weekends is rather like Los Angeles' Venice Beach: rollerbladers and cyclists speed past, models preen themselves in the sun, bodybuilders work out on the grass. Fight for an outside table at a beachfront restaurant, or walk along

Map
on page
166

the jetty for a distant view of the city skyline (there's a café at the end).

Roller coaster

Acland Street is famous for its cafés and cake shops. It displays the palate-delighting influences of Vienna and Warsaw, Budapest, Prague and Tel Aviv reflecting the strong Jewish presence, but many other nationalities are crowding in. At the end of the street, **Luna Park**'s gap-toothed grin invites you to try the clattering roller coaster (summer Fri 7am–11pm, Sat 11am–11pm, Sun 11am–6pm, winter Sat–Sun 11am–6pm; tel: 03-9525 5033; www.lunapark .com.au; pay for rides).

The **Upper Esplanade** hosts a Sunday arts and crafts market, while in **Fitzroy Street** the restaurants take over the footpaths, Mediterranean-style, with their tables and umbrellas.

On the other side of the bay, over the Westgate Bridge (or take a ferry from St Kilda or Southgate), is **Williams-town**, with the atmosphere of a bayside town, plenty of cafés, restaurants and great views back to the city. On the outskirts lies one of Mel-bourne's best museums: **Science-works** (2 Booker Street, Spotswood; daily 10am–4.30pm; tel: 03-9392 4800; www.scienceworks.museum.vic.gov.au; entrance fee), set in the grounds of an old pumping station. Its hands-on displays include House Secrets, which reveals what's really going on under the surface of a domestic environment.

Top market

North of St Kilda, **Prahran** has one of Melbourne's best markets (163 Commercial Road; Tues, Thur, Sat dawn–5pm, Fri dawn–6pm, Sun 10am–3pm; tel: 03-8290 8220; www.prahranmarket.com.au) and, in **Chapel Street**, a shopping strip that runs from op-shop (charity shop) sleaze to designer chic, with prices rising as you move north into South Yarra and affluent Toorak.

Como House (corner Williams Road and Lechlade Avenue, South Yarra; daily 10am–5pm; tel: 03-9827 2500; www.nattrust.com.au; entrance fee) is a graceful colonial mansion built in 1847, set in grounds that demand that you go equipped with a picnic. ❑

The grinning way in to Luna Park, site of an amusement park since 1906.

BELOW:
Colourful acts at the "Espy" in St Kilda.

Music City

As well as having a throbbing local scene, Melbourne is a must-visit destination for international performers of all genres. It's partly down to the local audiences who love their music, know what they like, and are also pretty relaxed about trying something new. And it's a lot to do with the venues.

Every inner-city suburb seems to have two or three pubs or clubs where something will be happening most nights of the week. Old favourite the Esplanade Hotel – or "Espy" – in St Kilda will book hundreds of acts a year across its various bars. The Corner in Richmond, the Prince of Wales in St Kilda, the HiFi Bar in the city, and the Northcote Social Club in High Street, Northcote, present big-name overseas acts in intimate settings.

RESTAURANTS & BARS

Restaurants

Central Melbourne

ezard
187 Flinders Lane
Tel: 03-9639 6811
www.ezard.com.au
Open: L Mon–Fri, D
Mon–Sat. $$$$
Five awards in 2006 alone
is evidence of Teage
Ezard's success with
contemporary cooking.

Flower Drum
17 Market Lane
Tel: 03-9662 3655
Open: L Mon–Sat, D daily.
$$$
Coming off years of being
regarded as the absolute
pinnacle of Melbourne din-
ing, this Cantonese eatery
still has its adherents.

Grossi Florentino
80 Bourke Street
Tel: 03-9662 1811
www.grossiflorentino.com
Open: L Mon–Fri, D
Mon–Sat. $$$$
If it's rich, florid surround-
ings and brilliant execution
of Italian classics you're
after, then this is the place.

**Pellegrini's Espresso
Bar**
66 Bourke Street
Tel: 03-9662 1885
Open: B, L & D Mon–Sat. $
An Italian cafe that appears
to channel the 1950s and
has been around long
enough to do it with com-
plete conviction.

Taxi
Transport Hotel, Federation
Square
Tel: 03-9654 8808
www.transporthotel.com.au
Open: L & D daily. $$$

Occasion dining *par excellence* in this eyrie above
Fed Square. Input from Australia (Michael Lambie) and
Japan (Ikuei Arakane) combines to brilliant effect and,
in so doing, appears to
attract every celebrity in
town. At least, the discern-
ing ones.

Vue de Monde
Normanby Chambers,
430 Little Collins Street
Tel: 03-9691 3888
www.vuedemonde.com.au
Open: L Tues–Fri, D
Tues–Sat. $$$$
With accolades and awards
suggesting that this must
be Oz's best restaurant,
tables can be booked
months ahead. The reward
for those who get to sample
the obligatory degustation
menu is sublime, adventurous modern cooking.

Docklands &
South Bank

Kobe Jones
427 Docklands Drive,
Docklands
Tel: 03-9329 9173
www.kobejones.com.au
Open: L Mon–Fri, D daily.
$$$
Interesting Japanese food
with influences ranging
from Australia to California.
Alternatively enjoy one of
their innovative cocktails
while enjoying the restau-
rant's fantastic views over
the water.

Livebait
55b Newquay Promenade,
Docklands
Tel: 03-9642 1500
www.livebait.com.au

Open: L & D daily. $$
Accomplished fish restau-
rant that makes the most
of its waterside setting on
the quay at Docklands.

Red Emperor
Southgate, South Bank
Tel: 03-9699 4170
www.redemperor.com.au
Open: L & D daily. $$
Southgate's ambitious and
successful Chinese.
Panoramic views of the city
and the Yarra.

Rockpool Bar & Grill
Crown Complex, South Bank
Tel: 03-8648 1900
www.rockpool.com
Open: L & D daily. $$$$
Melbourne's first exposure
to the Neil Perry phenome-
non is a subtle variation on
his Sydney flagship. A
meatier menu and flasher
environment are the points
of difference.

South Melbourne &
Port Melbourne

**Colonial Tramcar
Restaurant**
Departs corner Normanby
Road & Clarendon Street,
South Melbourne
Tel: 03-9696 4000
www.tramrestaurant.com.au
Open: L & D daily. $$$
The fun is in rattling around
Melbourne for three hours
in a historic tram while
plates are ushered back-
wards and forwards to your
table. Fine dining can wait.

The Graham
97 Graham Street, Port
Melbourne
Tel: 03-9676 2566
www.thegraham.com.au
Open: L & D daily. $$

Small menu executed to
perfection in this converted
pub which, in friendliness
and service, is difficult to
surpass.

North Melbourne

The Court House
86–90 Errol Street, North
Melbourne
Tel: 03-9329 5394
www.thecourthouse.net.au
Open: L & D Mon–Sat. $$
A relaxed pub conversion
that has quietly moved to
the front ranks with its
French-infused cuisine.

Fitzroy & Carlton

Interlude
211 Brunswick Street,
Fitzroy
Tel: 03-9415 7300
www.interlude.com.au
Open: L Tues–Fri, D
Mon–Sat. $$$
It's a culinary adventure to
embark on one of Robin
Wickens' lengthy tasting
menus where bald descrip-
tions, such as "pea and
ham", craftily undersells a
brilliant re-imagining of com-
mon ingredients.

Matteo's
533 Brunswick Street,
Fitzroy North
Tel: 03-9481 1177
www.matteos.com.au
Open: L Sun–Fri, D daily. $$
A stylish neighbourhood
restaurant that sets the
bar high with its adventurous menu.

Three, One, Two
312 Drummond Street,
Carlton
Tel: 03-9347 3312
www.312.com.au

Open: L Fri–Sun, D Tues–Sat. **$$$**

Melbourne culinary legend Andrew McConnell's new home instantly made its mark with its ambitious and intelligent juxtapositioning of prime ingredients.

Shakahari
201–3 Faraday Street, Carlton
Tel: 03-9347 3848
Open: B, L & D daily. **$**
Legendary vegetarian establishment that serves its niche impressively and is imaginative enough to appease the unconverted.

South Yarra

Botanical
169 Domain Road, South Yarra
Tel: 03-9820 7888
www.thebotanical.com.au
Open: B, L & D daily. **$$$**
Adventurous menu accomplished perfectly makes Botanical one of the reliables if you want to impress someone in a cool and relaxed environment.

St Kilda

Café di Stasio
31 Fitzroy Street, St Kilda
Tel: 03-9525 3999
Open: L & D daily. **$$**
This busy Italian has been thrilling St Kilda for years and shows no signs of losing its touch.

Circa the Prince
2 Acland Street, St Kilda
Tel: 03-9536 1122
www.circa.com.au
Open: B & D daily, L Sun–Fri **$$$$**
A dramatic dining room and some of the most accomplished cooking in the city

RIGHT: for excellent value, head to Chinatown.

usually delight the most demanding of patrons.

Donovans
40 Jacka Boulevard, St Kilda
Tel: 03-9534 8221
www.donovanshouse.com.au
Open: L & D daily. **$$$**
A cross between a boathouse and a common room, Donovans consistently comes up with splendid modern Australian cooking to match the peerless beachside setting.

Mr Wolf
9–15 Inkerman Street, St Kilda
Tel: 03-9534 0255
www.mrwolf.com.au
Open: L Tues–Fri, Sun, D Tues–Sun. **$**
Pizzas with a difference, and varied, child-friendly menu.

Soulmama
St Kilda Seabaths, 10–18 Jacka Boulevard, St Kilda
Tel: 03-9525 3338
www.soulmama.com.au
Open: L & D daily. **$**
Choose your dishes, fill your bowls and then pay according to weight. Relaxed vegetarian canteen by the sea.

Stokehouse
30 Jacka Boulevard, St Kilda
Tel: 03-9525 5555
www.stokehouse.com.au
Open: L & D daily. **$$$**
Another St Kilda staple, Stokehouse will always attract people to its beachside location, but there's some seriously good Mediterranean cooking going on behind the scenes.

Bars

Central Melbourne

The Gin Palace
190 Little Collins Street

Tel: 03-9654 0533
Open: L & D daily. **$**
Plush decadence is the look behind the anonymous door in the city centre.

Manchester Lane
36 Manchester Lane
Tel: 03-9663 0630
www.manchesterlane.com.au
Open: L Mon–Fri, D Mon–Sat, bar Mon–Sat till late. **$$$**
Great food and elegantly hip bar area. Live music every evening with dinner.

Melbourne Supper Club
161 Spring Street
Tel: 03-9654 6300
Open: D daily. **$**
Clubby, with deep sofas and discreet alcoves. A wonderful refined place to end a night on the town.

Fitzroy & Carlton

The Night Cat
141 Johnston Street, Fitzroy
Tel: 03-9417 0090
www.thenightcat.com.au

Open: Thur–Sun 9pm til late. Live band venue featuring music for dancing to: funky soul, Cuban and salsa. Sofas for those who would rather watch.

St Kilda

Dogs Bar
54 Acland Street, St Kilda
Tel: 03-9525 3599
www.dogsbar.com.au
Open: B, L & D daily. **$**
The ground floor of a lovely old dwelling oozes atmosphere and warmth. A local favourite in St Kilda.

PRICE CATEGORIES
Three-course dinner with a half-bottle of house wine: **$** = under A$50 **$$** = A$50–$80 **$$$** = A$80–120 **$$$$** = over A$120 B = breakfast, L = lunch, D = dinner, BYO = bring your own alcohol.

MELBOURNE'S ARCHITECTURE

Australia's second city has many fine buildings, with elegant 19th-century survivors and striking new towers

Melbourne grew on the back of the great wealth created by the 1850s gold rush. By 1880, when the population stood at 250,000, the city was illuminated by more than 1,000 gaslights. The following 10 years saw a building boom on a scale unprecedented in Australia. This period, known as "Marvellous Melbourne", was heralded by the International Exhibition of 1880, for which the splendid Melbourne Exhibition Building was created. By the turn of the century Melbourne was regarded as one of the major cities of the world, rich in theatres, churches, arcades, rows of terraced houses and magnificent gardens.

Collins Street, Melbourne's best-known thoroughfare, still contains a number of grand buildings from the Victorian era. The street's development began around 1849, when doctors and dentists began building residences and consulting rooms. At the eastern end, near Parliament House and the Treasury, the impressive stone buildings and trees on the footpaths led this area to be called the Paris End. The dignified 19th-century buildings still standing on Collins Street include banks, offices, theatres, churches and the Melbourne Club.

The face of the city began to change in 1959 with the construction of Melbourne's first skyscraper. The skyline is now dominated by modern glass and concrete towers, although many grand Victorian buildings remain at their feet. The 1990s saw a return to city living, with the renovation and conversion of warehouses and historic buildings for residential use. More recently, the river has seen significant development and in 2006 was the focus of the opening ceremony for the Commonwealth Games.

ABOVE: The building of Parliament House began in 1856 but was not finished until 1930, and a dome in the original design was never completed. The grand interior is one of the finest in Australia.

BELOW: An angelic feature of the Princess Theatre, completed in 1886. The theatre retains its classical facade, although the interior was remodelled in 1922.

LEFT: The ornate facades of the Rialto and Winfield buildings on Collins Street are dwarfed by the Rialto Towers, once Australia's tallest buidling but now itself dwarfed by Eureka Towers – which has to content itself with the title of Australia's tallest residential building (both have been beaten by Queensland's Q1 building). The area around Collins Street has numerous impressive examples of Victorian gothic revival architecture and many buildings are listed on Australia's Victorian Heritage Register.

THE ADVANCE OF THE MODERN

With many of Australia's leading architectural firms based in Melbourne, it's not surprising that the city is rich in modern architecture. The latticework laser-lit spire of the Victorian Arts Centre *(far left)* is not just a beacon for the impressive arts precinct it adorns, but a symbol of modern Melbourne.

The rejuvenation of the south bank of the Yarra – including the Southgate Center, the Crown casino and entertainment complex with its elegant ovoid tower, and the Melbourne Exhibition Centre – has completed what is generally recognised as one of the most exciting waterfront developments in Australia.

Melbourne has many modern office towers worthy of note, among them Rialto Towers (with an observation deck and impressive views of the city); 101 Collins Street, with arguably the city's most impressive foyer; the former BHP House at the corner of William and Bourke streets, which uses expressed steel on its exterior; the AMP building on the opposite corner; the twin towers of Collins Place; the Melbourne Central shopping precinct, which houses the historic Coop's shot tower and factory inside a glass cone *(above)*; and Melbourne's first skyscraper, ICI House in Nicholson, built in 1959 and one of the first curtain-wall buildings in Australia.

Left: The Windsor Hotel, opened in 1887 and still popular, is a landmark of Victorian architecture. It has a memorable facade, staircase and attractive domed restaurant. The hotel also has an impressive roll-call of famous guests and, because of its positioning opposite Parliament House, has entertained more than its fair share of past and present political leaders. In 1898 the hotel was at the centre of Australian politics when it played host to the signing of the state and nation's Constitution.

Below: The City Baths, splendidly restored in 1990, were built in 1903–4 and originally contained separate men's and women's swimming pools, slipper baths, spray baths, Jewish Mivka baths and Turkish baths. The Baths now house the CBD's largest swimming pool as well as a gym and workout studio.

Above: The Melbourne Exhibition Centre opened in 1995. Its main hall measures 84 x 360 metres (275 x 1,180 ft); outside, a stunning 60-metre (200-ft) cantilevered steel blade proclaims its presence. The Exhibition Centre is linked by a covered footbridge to the Convention Centre on the opposite side of the river.

Right: Flinders Street Station has been the hub of Victoria's railway system since it was completed in 1911. There has been a train station at the site since 1894, but the current design was chosen in a competition in 1902. Flinders Street has recently undergone much-needed renovation and is looking better than ever. The clock tower is a favourite meeting place for Melburnians, although the popularity of nearby Federation Square is threatening to steal its title.

VICTORIA

All the destinations in Victoria are within a day's drive of Melbourne – alpine mountains, desert plains, pristine beaches, historic wineries, gold-mining villages and quaint spa towns

Around 5 million people live in Victoria, the smallest of the mainland states, which makes it heavily populated by Australian standards. Three and a half million are in Melbourne though, so parts of Victoria can still feel pretty empty. Squashed down in the bottom right corner of the country, its northern border defined over hundreds of kilometres by the Murray River, Victoria is at its emptiest in the north west where the Mallee, a semi-arid land of open plains, is given over to sheep, grain and national parks; and in the east, where the end of the Great Dividing Range curls round to peter out a few kilometres short of Melbourne. This high country of timber and cattle farming gets busier in winter as snow opens up the ski fields.

Victoria stuttered into life with the first permanent European settlement at Portland in 1834. Two years later pastoralists started crossing the Murray from the east and, with Melbourne growing, population increase was rapid. Aboriginal numbers, though, fell rapidly as introduced diseases and firearms took their toll.

In 1851 Victoria seceded from New South Wales. Within weeks gold was discovered and the new state's population and prosperity boomed. Indeed, the countryside is still littered with colonial mansions, and the towns with stately public buildings and hotels.

For a small state, Victoria packs in a lot of attractions. The Great Ocean Road, the Goldfields and Wilson's Promontory are amongst the best known but there are also coastal resorts, wineries, the inland ports of the Murray and some wonderful mountain scenery. With good roads and comfortable distances to cover, Victoria is an easy state to explore.

West of Melbourne

From Melbourne the Princes Freeway speeds through the plains along the western shore of **Port Phillip Bay**. For a glimpse of opulence, take the exit to

Map on page 182

LEFT: a dramatic way to view the Grampian Ranges.
BELOW: the Queenscliff Hotel.

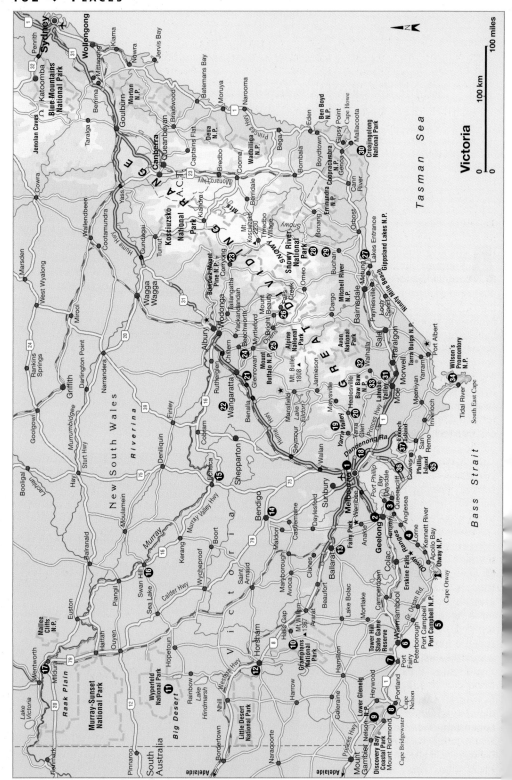

Victoria

Werribee Park (daily Nov–Apr 10am–5pm; May–Oct Mon–Fri 10am–4pm, Sat–Sun 10am–5pm; www.parkweb.vic.gov.au; entrance fee). In a 60–room Italianate mansion built in 1877 by the pastoralist Chirnside family, visitors can see a vivid example of flamboyant wealth. The extensive grounds are set off by a sculpture walk and, in addition each autumn, the entrants to the Helen Lampriere Sculpture Prize are on display, often creating quirky juxtapositions with their surroundings. There are more sedate pleasures to be found in the adjoining **Victoria State Rose Garden**.

Nearby, the **Werribee Open Range Zoo** (daily 9am–5pm; tel: 03-9731 9601; www.zoo.org.au; entrance fee) recreates African savanna with safari buses carrying you amongst the animals.

Geelong and the coast

As you drive on, the volcanic **You Yangs** dominate the skyline. Get closer to them by detouring to **Anakie**, home of **Fairy Park** (daily 10am–4pm; tel: 03-5284 1262; www.fairypark.com; entrance fee), "Australia's first and oldest theme park", where dioramas from fairy tales unfold by the winding path to the top of a granite crag. Very low-tech by today's standards but young kids love it and there's an excellent playgound, including the irresistible "do not touch this button".

Return to the highway and Victoria's second city. In its early days **Geelong** ❷ rivalled Melbourne as an outlet for Western District wool and later became an important manufacturing centre. After years of somnolence the city has shaken itself up – particularly by the waterfront, where quirky sculptures and a renovated pier are the focus.

A drive along the waterfront shows Geelong past and present – the old mansions, wool stores and piers, and the new industries, wharves and container terminal. Along the Barwon River are fine homes such as **Barwon Grange** (Fernleigh St; Wed, Sun 11am–4pm; tel: 03-5221 3906;

www.nattrust.com.au; entrance fee) refurnished in the style of 1855, when it was built by a merchant shipowner.

For a whiff of nostalgia, take the Bellarine Highway out of Geelong and travel to **Queenscliff** ❸. This was "Queen of the Watering Places" in the 1880s when paddlesteamers brought the fashionable to the handsome turreted hotels. There is still a haughty grandeur to the place. The Queenscliff fort, with red-brick walls and cannon, was built in the 19th century to defend Melbourne against a Russian invasion.

The road on to **Anglesea** meanders through seaside settlements, sleepy in winter and pulsing with life in summer. **Torquay** is the surf centre of Victoria, and **Bells Beach** is famed worldwide for its Easter surf contest.

Beyond Anglesea, whose main claim to fame is the mob of kangaroos that live on the golf course, is the start of the **Great Ocean Road**, 200 km (125 miles) of the state's most spectacular coastal scenery.

A favourite weekend spot from Melbourne is **Lorne** ❹, set on a picturesque bay with a bush backdrop and

Map: opposite page

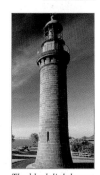

The black lighthouse at Queenscliff guards the treacherous entrance to Port Phillip Bay. It was prefabricated in Scotland and shipped to Australia in 1863.

BELOW: bushwalking in Great Otway National Park.

Some of the Twelve Apostles.

BELOW:
Hopetoun Falls in the Great Otway National Park.

several restaurants and shops, marred only by an over-large resort hotel. The annual Pier-to-Pub Swim in January attracts entrants from across the nation.

In the **Great Otway National Park**, tracks wind through eucalyptus forest and fern gullies to waterfalls and lookouts. Walks vary from a gentle stroll along the St George's River to rock-hopping along to the Cora Lyn Cascades. A three-hour hike up to the **Erskine Falls** can be strenuous. The less energetic can reach a lookout by car.

Along the coast at **Kennett River**, a 6-km (3½-mile) drive leads to the **Grey River Scenic Reserve**. It's a short walk (1.5-km/1 mile round trip), one of the best in Victoria, up a fern gully amid towering blue gums.

For a panoramic view of the **Otway Ranges**, turn inland at **Skenes Creek** and drive up into the hills. After 15 km (9 miles), turn left into the fern and mountain-ash forest along Turton's Track. When the country opens out again you are on a ridge. On the left, wooded spurs reach down to the sea; on the right are the volcanic lakes and plains of the Western District.

From **Apollo Bay**, with its mixed artsy and fishing vibe, the Great Ocean Road leaves the coast to wind through the forest behind Cape Otway. Find the **Otway Fly** (daily 9am–5pm; tel: 03-5235 9200; www.otwayfly.com; entrance fee), and enjoy a walk through the forest canopy on 600 metres (660 yards) of steel walkway, 25 metres (82 feet) above the ground. At **Cape Otway** a tour of the **Lighthouse** (daily 9am–5pm; tel: 03-5237 9240; www.lightstation.com; entrance fee), which has watched over the hazardous entrance to the Bass Strait since 1848, is worthwhile. The setting is sublime.

The Twelvish Apostles

Beyond Princetown lies the spectacular coastline of **Port Campbell National Park ⑤**, where breakers have battered the soft limestone cliffs, creating grottoes and gorges, arches and sea sculptures rising from the surf. The road gives only occasional glimpses of the drama below, which includes the stark rock stacks of **The Twelve Apostles** – or possibly eleven after the collapse of one in 2005 – and the spray billowing

through the fallen arch of **London Bridge**. Stop at all the vantage points, follow the various trails at **Loch Ard Gorge**, and make the most of the new visitor centre.

Beyond Peterborough and the dramatic **Bay of Islands** lies **Warrnambool ⑥**, once a busy port and now a holiday centre. People flock here in winter to see the Southern Right Whales off Logans Beach. Around the lighthouse is the **Flagstaff Hill Maritime Village**, a recreated 19th-century port with its chandlers, shipwrights and sailmakers (daily 9am–5pm; tel: 03-5559 4600; www.flagstaffhill.com; entrance fee). The spectacular *Shipwrecked* sound and laser show runs nightly at dusk. **Warrnambool Art Gallery** (Mon–Fri 10am–5pm, Sat–Sun noon–5pm; tel: 03-5559 4889; www.warrnambool.vic.gov. au; free) has a large collection of Australiana.

Beyond Warrnambool is **Tower Hill State Game Reserve**, a volcanic crater containing smaller cones where ducks nest, emus share your picnic and there's a good chance of seeing koalas. At dusk the 'roos come out as well.

Port Fairy

Along the coast is the fishing-village charm of **Port Fairy ⑦**, where brightly painted boats tie up at the jetty with their catches of crayfish and crab. Port Fairy was named by Captain James Wishart who brought his tiny cutter, the *Fairy*, into the Moyne River to find shelter during a sealing expedition in 1810. Sealers and, later, whalers built stone cottages which still nestle under the tall Norfolk Island pines shading the streets. You can drink at the **Caledonian Inn**, which opened in 1844 and has been in business ever since.

Griffiths Island, at the mouth of the river, was a whaling station, but is now a rookery for thousands of mutton birds that return in September from the north Pacific. The young hatch in January, and every evening till they leave in April you can watch the adult birds swoop in from the sea to feed their chicks, if you can see them – it can get very dark by the time they arrive and you simply hear a low whirring as they cruise past your head.

Portland ⑧ – big wharves on a broad bay and solid 19th-century blue-

Map on page 182

The jetty at Port Fairy.

BELOW:
Loch Ard Gorge.

stone buildings – was a whaling station when Edward Henty arrived in 1834 and ploughed the first furrow in Victorian soil. Take the cliff walks at **Cape Nelson** and view the moonscape bluff of **Cape Bridgewater**, where wind and water have fashioned a petrified forest from scrub.

The coast road to South Australia skirts **Mount Richmond**, a sand-covered volcano ablaze with wildflowers in spring. It borders **Discovery Bay Coastal Park**, with its vast rolling sand dunes and stretches of unspoilt beach, and runs along the southern margin of **Lower Glenelg National Park ❾**, known for its gorge and delicate cave formations. You can drive or take a boat tour from **Nelson** up the gorge to the caves. The park is rich with 700 species of native plants, but most of it can be explored only by river or on rough, sandy tracks.

The Grampians

Pass through the wool town of **Hamilton** – see the **Big Wool Bales** – towards **Halls Gap**, where the ranges of the **Grampians National Park ❿**

rise abruptly to dominate the surrounding plains. These craggy mountains are a series of rocky ranges thrown up by the folding of a sandstone mass into an uncommon cuesta formation – spectacular escarpments on the east side and gentle slopes to the west. Erosion has shaped bizarre rock sculptures, and waterfalls cascade over the sheer face.

Many scenic points are accessible by car, but there is wilderness aplenty for the more adventurous and walking tracks to suit all grades of hiker. You can drive past **Lake Bellfield**, where koalas feed in the manna gums, to the highest peak in the ranges, **Mount William** (1,167 metres/3,829 ft). A 1.5-km (1-mile) walk takes you to the summit. Return to Halls Gap via the Silverband Road to take in some of the highlights of the **Wonderland Range**.

On Mount Victory Road, short detours lead to **Reid Lookout**, high over the Victoria Valley, and home to kangaroos and emus. A 15-minute walk along the cliff top brings you to **The Balconies**, outcrops of sandstone that hang like giant jaws over the precipice.

TIP

With the desert on one side and the sea on the other, Victoria is notorious for its changeable and unpredictable weather. Be prepared for cold winds, rain and searing heat all in the same day.

BELOW: winter in the Grampians.

As the road winds through the forest, stop at the viewpoint for the **McKenzie Falls** or take the walking track to the falls along the river, before going on to **Zumstein**. Walter Zumstein, a beekeeper and bush-lover who was a pioneer in this valley in the early 20th century, befriended the kangaroos, and each afternoon their descendants still leave the forest to be fed.

The Wimmera

The Western Highway travels through the heart of **The Wimmera**, the granary of Victoria. This sweep of golden wheat fields in an area the size of Wales stretches west to the South Australia border and north to the sand dunes and dry lakebeds of **Wyperfeld National Park** ⓫. It is dotted with small townships, soaring silos, and populated by more sheep than people.

Horsham ⓬ is a small town, with the excellent **Horsham Regional Art Gallery** (Tues–Fri 10am–5pm, Sat–Sun 1–4.30pm; tel: 03-5382 5575; www.horsham.net.au/gallery; donation) and the **Botanic Gardens** starring.

Return east along the Western Highway towards **Ararat**. The town's first settler named a nearby peak Mount Ararat "for like the Ark, we rested there." Two French settlers, who saw that the soil and climate between Ararat and Stawell resembled that of France, planted the first vines in 1863, and wines, both red and sparkling white, have been produced at **Great Western** ever since. The road continues past forested hills to **Beaufort**, notable for its iron-lacework band rotunda topped with a clock tower.

The Eureka Stockade

Ballarat ⓭ is within an hour's drive of Melbourne, a far cry from the jolting day-long journey along potholed tracks that faced the miners bound for the gold-diggings in the 1850s.

On the southern side of the city, a signpost points to the **Eureka Centre** (daily 9am–4.30pm; tel: 03-5333 1854; www.eurekaballarat.com; entrance fee). At the site, a diorama brings to life the day in December 1854 when the name Eureka was etched into Australian history (*see page 37*).

The bar at Craig's Royal Hotel, Ballarat.

BELOW: yesteryear recalled at Ballarat.

Aboriginal Art

More than 40 Aboriginal art sites have been found in caves and rock shelters in the Grampians. Some of the more accessible are in the **Victoria Range**, where you can see hand stencils in red ochre in the **Cave of Hands**, and a variety of paintings including animals, human figures and a kangaroo hunt in the **Glenisla Shelter**. Many of the geographical features of the region are woven into the Dreamtime legends, including the splitting of one of the Grampian ranges by Tchingal, a giant emu, to create **Roses Gap**. You can learn more about the area's traditional inhabitants at the **Brambuk Aboriginal Cultural Centre**, a striking building 2 km (1¼ miles) south of Halls Gap (daily 9am–5pm; free; tel: 03-5361 4000; www. brambuk.com.au; free).

TIP

Buy a Gold Pass at Sovereign Hill for admission to all the sights, including the Gold Museum and an underground mine tour. There's also a *son et lumière* show twice nightly, recreating the Eureka Stockade battle.

BELOW: panning for gold at Sovereign Hill, Ballarat.

The rumbustious life of those times is recreated in the mocked-up gold-mining town of **Sovereign Hill** (daily 10am–5pm; tel: 03-5337 1100; www.sovereignhill.com.au; entrance fee).

In the main street, resembling Ballarat in the 1850s with its old-fashioned wooden shops, apothecary and confectioners, you can watch blacksmiths, tinsmiths and potters at work; sample a digger's lunch at the New York Bakery; or have a drink at the United States Hotel next to the Victoria Theatre where Lola Montez danced her famous and risqué "spider dance". Take a ride on a Cobb & Co. coach and pan for gold in the creek. After a look around the Red Hill gully diggings, slake your thirst at the "lemonade" tent – the sly-grog shop where diggers celebrated their luck or drowned their sorrows. Then walk along the underground tunnel of the Quartz Mine, typical of the company mines where, in later years, the real money was made. It is a ridiculously enjoyable day out and can be topped off with the *Blood on the Southern Cross* sound and light show that recreates the drama of the Eureka Stockade.

Ballarat was born in the boom time, and its wide streets, verandahs and iron lace, towers and colonnades give it grace and distinction. **Ballarat Fine Art Gallery** (40 Lydiard St; daily 9am–5pm; tel: 03-5320 5858; www.balgal.com; entrance fee) is renow-ned for its Australian paintings, and the **Botanic Gardens** beside **Lake Wendouree** sport Italian statues and a blaze of begonias.

Gold towns

Other "golden" towns lurk to the north of Ballarat, where thousands of men dug their 12 ft by 12ft (13.4 sq metres) claims with ant-like ardour. **Clunes**, the scene of the first gold strike on 1 July 1851, has an ornate town hall, and elegant banks and bluestone churches. **Daylesford**, a picturesque town on Wombat Hill, is known (along with its neighbour Hepburn Springs) as the spa centre of Australia. Nowadays, it's also known as a thriving weekend retreat for Melburnians, including a strong gay and lesbian contingent.

In **Castlemaine** the Greek temple-style market building and other fine edifices date from an era of promise never quite fulfilled. A short ride on one of the steam trains of the **Victorian Goldfields Railway** (Sun, some Wed; tel: 03-5475 2966; www.vgr.com.au) will take you to **Maldon**, the National Trust's first "notable town in Australia". Its gold-rush era streetscapes are terrific, as much for their tranquillity as their remarkable state of preservation.

In **Bendigo** , some of the richest quartz reefs in the world created a Victorian extravaganza. The scarlet **Joss House** is an interesting reminder of the thousands of Chinese who came to the "Big Gold Mountain", bringing with them temples, tea-houses and festivals. The colourful Chinese dragon, Sun Loong, is 100 metres (328 ft) long and the star of the Bendigo Easter Fair. Elsewhere there are extravagant hotels, another

good art gallery (42 View St; daily 10am–5pm; tel: 03-5434 6088; www.bendigoartgallery.com.au; donation) and the **Central Deborah Goldmine** (corner High and Violet streets; daily 9.30am–5pm; tel: 03-5443 8322; www.central-deborah.com; entrance fee) where you can take an underground tour.

The Murray

Echuca 🟕, 88 km (55 miles) north of Bendigo, was an important port on the **Murray River** and its magnificent old timber wharf is now a major draw for visitors. You need a ticket to get in (daily 9am–5pm; tel: 03-5482 4248; www.portofechuca.org.au; free) but it allows access to displays in two historic pubs and can be boosted to include a cruise on one of the historic paddle steamers. A cruise is *de rigueur* and allows you to relive the days when these mighty vessels, laden with cargo and passengers, made the river a busy thoroughfare, before the railways made them obsolete. Think about renting a houseboat and making the river, lined with tall red gums, your home for a few days. Back on land, **Sharps Magic Movie House and Penny Arcade** (daily 9am–5pm; tel: 03-5482 2361; www.sharpsmoviehouse.com.au; entrance fee) in the historic precinct behind the wharf lets you relive the simple pleasures of pre-electronic entertainment.

The Murray Valley Highway loosely tracks the river as it heads north west and rejoins it at **Swan Hill 🟖** where the principal pull is the **Pioneer Settlement** (daily 9.30am–4pm, daily in school hols; tel: 03-5036 2410; www.pioneersettlement.com.au; entrance fee), a collection of original historic buildings transplanted to this site to create a typical township of the 19th century. Time rushes by as you stroll in and out of shops and houses. You can cruise on a paddle steamer and, at dusk, take in a sound and light show.

It is another 196 km (122 miles) to the city of **Mildura 🟗**. While many Australian centres claim the biggest of something, Mildura aims for the longest bar in the world – 91 metres (298 ft) long, at the **Workingman's Club**; the largest fruit-juice factory; and the largest deckchair ever built (in front of a main-street motel).

Map on page 182

In the last quarter of the 19th century, up to 30 steamboats were carrying gold-mining and other supplies along the Murray River. Then rail freight took over.

BELOW: the Murray River.

Mildura is an exceptionally pleasant and friendly city, with its great climate and water pastimes of fishing, swimming and boating. The town, and the irrigation system that drew settlers to the area, were established by two American brothers, George and William Chaffey. William's imposing homestead, **Rio Vista**, can be seen at **Mildura Arts Centre** (199 Cureton Ave; daily 10am–5pm; tel: 03-5018 8330; www.miduraarts.net.au). His other legacy is that, in US style, Mildura has streets with numbers rather than names.

The Murray River, of course, is the dominant attraction, and you can take to it and its series of locks with two-hour trips on the steam-driven *Melbourne*, day cruises on the *Rothbury*, lunch and dining cruises on the 1877 vintage *Avoca*, and five-day excursions on the *Coonawarra*. There is also a wide range of houseboats for hire.

From here the Calder Highway runs back to Melbourne.

The Dandenongs

About 50 km (31 miles) east of Melbourne lie the **Dandenong Ranges** ⓲.

Here, the mountain bluffs are riddled with fern gullies and art galleries, while small towns like **Belgrave** and **Olinda** make lovely destinations for day trips, offering antique shops and cafés serving cream teas.

Attractions include the **William Ricketts Sanctuary**, where romantically idealised Aboriginal spirit figures have been carved from wood by an elderly white sculptor and placed in a forest setting, and **Puffing Billy**, a narrow-gauge steam train that plies a 24-km (15-mile) track from Belgrave to Gembrook (Mon–Fri 9am–5pm; tel: 03-9754 6800; www.puffingbilly.com.au).

The **National Rhododendron Gardens** at Olinda (daily 10am–5pm; tel: 03-8627 4699; www.parkweb.vic.gov.au; entrance fee) are at their spectacular best in October and November but worth a visit all year.

Directly north of the Dandenongs, the **Yarra Valley** ⓳ now claims 55 wineries in its gently rolling countryside. Organised wine-tasting tours can be arranged or you can dip in to the odd cellar door as you pass through. One to look out for is **Yering Station**

The Murray River supported many native fish such as the Murray cod and the silver perch. But the introduction of other varieties, particularly carp, destroyed aquatic plants and became a threat to the native fish, many of which have become threatened species.

BELOW: Puffing Billy runs from Belgrave to Gembrook.

(38 Melba Highway; Mon–Fri 10am–5pm, Sat–Sun 10am–6pm; tel: 03-9730 0100; www.yering.com) was Victoria's first vineyard but is now a sparkling modern enterprise with a dramatic architect-designed centre and stunning views. Having the sumptuous **Chateau Yering** hotel with its excellent restaurants next door only adds to its appeal.

Yarra Glen is a relaxed centre to the area and a stop at the historic **Grand Hotel** is recommended. Take the road towards Healesville and pause at the **TarraWarra Museum of Art** (Tues–Sun 11am–5pm; tel: 03-5957 3100; www.twma.com.au; entrance fee), which has changing exhibitions in its sleek, airy, award-winning space.

Only 61 km (38 miles) from Melbourne is **Healesville** ⓴, best known for the **Healesville Sanctuary** (daily 9am–5pm; tel: 03-5957 2800; www.zoo.org.au; entrance fee). This world-renowned open-air zoo was established in 1934 to study and breed native fauna and has played a key role in helping to replenish Australia's endangered wildlife.

Travel north on the Maroondah Highway and, after 24 km (15 miles) turn off to **Marysville**. This is the base for Melbourne's closest ski field, the cross-country resort of **Lake Mountain**. A winding road through **Yarra Ranges National Park** leads to the pretty village of **Warburton**.

For downhill skiing, return to the Maroondah Highway and work round to the northeast towards **Mansfield**, an important grazing and timber centre and the gateway to **Mount Buller** (1,808 metres/5,932 ft), Victoria's largest ski resort. It lies just 3 km (2 miles) from **Lake Eildon**, a 130-sq. km (50-sq. mile) body of water formed from the damming of five rivers to irrigate thousands of square miles of farmland. Today the lake is a paradise for waterskiers and fishermen angling for trout, perch and Murray cod.

Kelly Country

Take the Midland Highway north and join the Hume Highway eastward. This is the heart of "Kelly Country", the stamping grounds of the legendary Ned Kelly. Today, travellers on the

Map on page 182

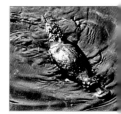

For a rare chance to see the duck-billed platypus in a fairly natural environment, visit the Healesville Sanctuary, the first place to breed this notoriously shy creature in captivity.

BELOW: the Ned Kelly statue at Glenrowan.

The Kelly Trial

Glenrowan Inn, 16 km (10 miles) south west of Wangaratta, was the site of Ned Kelly's last stand. Kelly's comrades were killed in a shoot-out with police as the inn burned to the ground, and Ned himself was brought to trial in Melbourne, subsequently to be hanged in the gaol there in November 1880.

Glenrowan has rather gone to town on its role in all this. **Kellyland** features computerised mannequins judderingly re-enacting the last stand at regular intervals throughout the day. Outside a gigantic, technicolour Ned Kelly, in full armour and clutching his gun, looms over a block of tacky shops pushing Kelly kitsch. Many heinous crimes have been linked to Australia's most infamous bushranger, and there's no sign of it ending any time soon.

Rutherglen exported wine to England and France in the 19th century, but few vineyards survived an invasion of the phylloxera mite at the turn of the 20th century. Some vintners stubbornly persisted, finding the soil and climate ideal for sherries and dessert wines – they discovered they could ripen their grapes late in the season to a high sugar level.

BELOW:
watch the birdy.

Hume Highway through **Glenrowan** ㉑ can't miss his presence *(see panel, previous page)*.

Benalla, which calls itself the "Rose City" after the thousands of bushes that bloom from October to April. These add colour to the unusual **Benalla Art Gallery** (Bridge St; daily 10am–5pm; tel: 03-5762 3027; www.benallaartgallery.com; free) overlooking the Broken River.

Wangaratta ㉒ is a skilfully planned agricultural centre with a population of 17,500 on the Ovens River. Today it is noted for its wool mills, two interesting 19th-century churches, and the Wangaratta Jazz Festival which draws crowds every spring.

All towns here have one thing in common – a history linked to gold. In 1853, when gold was discovered in the valley of the Ovens River, dozens of prosperous mining settlements sprang into life almost overnight. By 1870, most of them had folded as the precious mineral became harder to find, but some of the towns survive as vital reminders of a thrilling history in a valley better known today for its wines.

Chiltern was originally established in the 1850s as Black Dog Creek. With its wide streets flanked by shops with Old West-style facades, the town has proved a popular filmset. Today its main claim to fame is **Lake View Homestead** (Sun noon–4pm; tel: 03-5726 1611; www.nattrust.com.au; entrance fee), the childhood home of novelist Ethel Richardson, who, as Henry Handel Richardson, wrote some of Australia's classic works, including *The Fortunes of Richard Mahony*.

Some 16 km (10 miles) northwest of Chiltern is **Rutherglen**, centre of Australia's oldest vine-growing district and still the foremost producer of fortified wines.

On the border

Wodonga is the Victorian half of Australia's fastest-growing inland metropolis. Its big brother, **Albury**, across the Murray River in New South Wales, gives the twin cities a combined population of about 85,000. Hub of the Riverina district, which produces prodigious quantities of grain, fruit and livestock, Albury

marks the site where the explorers Hume and Hovell discovered the Murray in 1824 after trekking south from Sydney.

The Murray Valley Highway passes through **Tallangatta**, at the eastern tip of **Lake Hume**. It is a new town, built in 1956 to replace the former community flooded by the damming of the Murray River and the creation of the lake. Traces of the old township – lines of trees, streets, even some buildings – eerily reappear at times of low water. The lake, four times the size of Sydney Harbour, is now a playground for swimmers, waterskiers, fishermen and birdwatchers.

Corryong ㉓, the last town before the border with New South Wales, features the **Man From Snowy River Folk Museum** (103 Hanson St; daily 10am–noon, 2–4pm; tel: 02-6076 1114; entrance fee); its varied collection includes what has been enticingly described as "the most recognised snow-ski collection in Australia".

To the south is the village of **Nariel Creek**, where folk-music festivals are held on an old Aboriginal corroboree ground on New Year holidays and Victorian Labour Day weekend. Northwest of Corryong (access from Cudgewa) is **Burrowa Pine Mountain National Park** with rugged walks and views of the Snowy Mountains.

Beechworth

Return west, where the entire township of **Yackandandah** has been classified by the National Trust. Miners who came from California and the Klondike in the 1860s helped to give the place a lingering air of the American West. Today it is the centre of Victoria's largest strawberry industry.

Nestled in the midst of rolling hill country is northeast Victoria's best-preserved gold town, **Beechworth** ㉔. No fewer than 32 of its buildings have been classified by the National Trust, including the towered **Post Office** (1867) with its Victorian stone construction,

Tanswell's Commercial Hotel (1873) with its handsome facade and wrought-iron verandah, and the **Robert O'Hara Burke Memorial Museum** (1856; daily 9am–5pm; tel: 03-5728 8067; entrance fee), part of the historic precinct on Loch Street. This museum exhibits myriad relics and memorabilia of the gold-rush era – when 3 million ounces of gold were garnered in just 14 years – along with other pioneer objects, and there is even a life-sized recreation of a section of Beechworth's former main street. During its heyday the town had 61 hotels and a theatre which hosted international acts.

Mount Buffalo

South from Beechworth is a region of considerable natural beauty, the beginning of Victoria's high country. **Myrtleford** is the thriving centre of a walnut, tobacco and hop-growing region. **Mount Buffalo National Park** ㉕, a vast plateau at 1,370 metres (4,495 ft), becomes a huge snowfield in winter, a carpet of wildflowers in spring, and a popular spot for bushwalking in the summer and autumn.

Map on page 182

"The Man from Snowy River" started life in 1890 as a poem by bush poet Banjo Paterson. It became a silent film in 1920 and a popular modern version in 1982 spawned a sequel in 1988, a TV series in the 1990s and a stage musical. The poem was celebrated in the opening sequence of Sydney's Olympic Games.

BELOW:
Mount Buffalo National Park.

Winter fun in Falls Creek.

Bright, a town of 5,000 famed for its autumn colours, is a short distance away. Oaks, maples and other hardwoods promote a serenity which belies its violent gold-rush days, including the notorious 1857 Buckland riots when white prospectors brutally ousted Chinese miners from their claims.

Mount Beauty is the gateway to the largest of the alpine resorts at smart **Falls Creek** ㉖ in **Alpine National Park**, where the après ski is as important as what happens on the slopes. Working south along the Great Alpine Road, **Mount Hotham** has downhill and cross-country runs, while **Dinner Plain** is an arresting 1980s resort.

Continue for 160 km (100 miles) of attractive high country motoring until the road joins the Princes Highway.

Bairnsdale

A couple of kilometres west is **Bairnsdale**, the commercial centre of **East Gippsland**, 285 km (177 miles) east of Melbourne. A sheep, dairy and timber centre, it is best known for its fine **Botanic Gardens** and the "Sistine Chapel" murals in **St Mary's Catholic Church**. Nearby **Paynesville**, a boating resort, features the bizarre yet interesting **Church of St Peter**: a sailors' house of worship, it has a spire like a lighthouse, a pulpit shaped like the bow of a boat, and a sanctuary lighting fixture that was once a ship's riding lamp.

The Princes Highway westwards runs all the way to Sydney but the only time it touches the coast in Victoria is at **Lakes Entrance** ㉗. This resort is situated at the narrow man-made inlet to the **Gippsland Lakes**, a long string of interconnected lagoons stretching west along the inner shore of the Bass Strait for some 80 km (50 miles). They are separated from the sea only by a narrow band of dunes and hummocks called **Ninety Mile Beach**.

The normal population of Lakes Entrance increases by a factor of six in summer as holidaymakers pack the motels and caravan parks. Up-market accommodation is on offer at quiet **Metung**, a few kilometres to the west.

Fishing, boating and swimming are the main draws, while cruise boats offer regular sightseeing tours of the lakes. Sometimes called the "Victo-

Map
on page
182

rian Riviera", the area has consistent temperatures of about 20°C (68°F) in winter. The **Gippsland Lakes Coastal Park**, a reserve of dunes and heath along the lakes' seaward edge, and the **Lakes National Park**, a bird-filled woodland on a sandy peninsula between Lake Reeve and Lake Victoria, help protect natural features.

Snowy River National Park

Logging trucks seem to congregate at **Orbost**, a prosperous town of about 3,000 people near the banks of the lower Snowy River.

Snowy River National Park ❷⓼, in the mountains above, is popular with whitewater canoeists, who relish the challenge of riding the water through the deep gorges that contribute to the spectacular scenery of this often overlooked area. The Princes Highway then winds through its most remote stretch, 208 km (129 miles) of mountains and rainforest, to reach the state border.

At Nowa Nowa, 22 km (13 miles) from Lakes Entrance, a winding road will take you to **Buchan** ❷⓽. It hosts a rodeo over Easter, and a lumberjacks' contest in May, but its main attraction is its limestone caves, unquestionably the finest in Victoria. There are 350 here, but only three are open to the public, including the **Fairy Cave**, whose numerous honeycombed chambers are embedded with ancient marsupial bones (tours daily; tel: 03-5155 9264; www.parkweb.vic.gov.au; entrance fee).

The southeast

At the hamlet of Genoa near the NSW border, a sealed side road turns south towards **Mallacoota**. This tiny resort town, much beloved by fishermen and nature lovers, is at the end of a 24-km (15-mile) journey off the Princes Highway at Victoria's south-easternmost tip. It is surrounded by **Croajingolong National Park** ❸⓪, 86,000 hectares (212,500 acres) of rocky cliffs and open beaches, rain-forest, open woodland and health,

stretching some 100 km (60 miles) from the NSW border to Sydenham Inlet. Numerous nocturnal mammals (including possums and gliders) and many snakes – some venomous – make their homes in the park; hundreds of bird species include lyrebirds, oystercatchers, sea eagles and kingfishers. The pub at the charming village at **Gipsy Point** overlooks the inlet between Mallacoota and Genoa.

It's time for the long trek back towards Melbourne. The string of small cities along the Princes Highway from **Sale** comprises the **Latrobe Valley** ❸⓵, whose coal produces about 90 percent of the electricity for Melbourne and Victoria. The valley sits upon the world's largest deposit of brown coal and open-cut mines and the steaming towers of power stations are everywhere.

Moe, the valley's largest and most modern city, is the site of **Old Gippstown** (daily 9am–5pm; tel: 03-5127 3082; www.gippslandheritagepark.com.au; entrance fee), an 1850s theme park, where industrial and agricultural structures and machinery have been transplanted to a garden setting. To see the

In some of the limestone caves near Buchan (not those open to visitors) explorers have found tools and rock engravings dating back 17,000 years.

BELOW: Buchan's limestone caves.

"The Prom" – as Wilson's Promontory is generally known.

BELOW:
Phillip Island.

real thing, and with a more dramatic backdrop, make your way to the tiny mountain community of **Walhalla** ㉜, where what was once Victoria's richest gold mine sits in a beautiful valley, now almost deserted.

Long Tunnel Extended Gold Mine is open for tours (daily; entrance fee) and there's plenty more to keep you in this lovely spot.

Mount Baw Baw ㉝, the nearest downhill ski resort to Melbourne, is a short distance to the northwest on the map, but to actually get there is a long and complicated drive down towards Moe and up again.

The Prom

The final swathe of goodies are to be found along the coast. **Wilson's Promontory** ㉞, a huge granite peninsula that represents mainland Australia's furthest thrust towards Antarctica, is the most popular national park in Victoria. "The Prom", as it is affectionately called by regular visitors, features more than 80 km (50 miles) of walking tracks to long sandy beaches, forested mountain slopes, and

heath and marshes packed with bird, animal and plant life. An estimated 100,000 people visit the park each year and access is managed carefully, but even the hot spots of **Tidal River**, **Squeaky Beach** and **Picnic Bay** rarely feel crowded. Just don't expect to find a camping spot in peak season without booking months ahead (tel: 03-5680 9555; www.parkweb.vic.gov.au).

The historic township of **Port Albert** to the east is worth a look for the **Port Albert Hotel** (1842) and the old timber jetty – at which eager 19th-century Chinese gold miners once disembarked. The **Gippsland Regional Maritime Museum** (daily Sept–May, Jun–Aug Sat–Sun 10.30am–4pm; tel: 03-5183 2520; entrance fee) is housed in the old Bank of Victoria.

Penguin Island

For many travellers, the most interesting stop in this final stretch to Melbourne is **Phillip Island** ㉟. It is connected to the mainland fishing community of **San Remo** by a bridge under which a flock of pelicans gathers daily for a feed. In an area about 104

sq. km (40 sq. miles), there is a bewildering array of tourist attractions.

Phillip Island was the site of Australia's first motor-racing circuit (1928), and it still attracts crowds today when it hosts the Australian 500cc Motorcycle Grand Prix in October and the V8 touring car championship shortly afterwards. Among other attractions are koala and bird sanctuaries, scenic offshore rock formations, historic homesteads, pottery shops, and sports – from surfing, diving, sailing and fishing to golf, tennis, bowling and croquet. The relaxed north-coast summer resort town of **Cowes** is the tourist centre.

However, unquestionably the biggest regular attraction for Phillip Island visitors is the **Penguin Parade** *(see panel below)*. About 1.5 km (1 mile) off the western tip of the island are the **Seal Rocks**, the breeding ground for Australia's largest colony of fur seals. Early December – the peak of the breeding season – is the best time to watch the 5–6,000 seals through coin-operated telescopes in the kiosk on the clifftop at Point Grant.

The Mornington Peninsula

The most popular weekend destination for Melburnians is the **Mornington Peninsula** ㊱, which stretches down the eastern side of Port Phillip Bay. The Nepean Highway follows the bayside coast through a whole series of small resorts, all with beaches, some with bathing huts (although not as photogenic as the ones at **Sandringham**, closer to the city, that make it on to all the postcards). **Sorrento**, towards the tip of the peninsula, is the most attractive settlement and proudly offers a bayside beach as well as the more rigorous waters of the ocean. A ferry makes the short trip across the mouth of the bay to Queenscliff.

Further up on the eastern side of the peninsula sits **French Island** ㊲. It used to be a prison farm and retains some of the old buildings. Most of the land is given over to the national park, with farming taking up the remainder, and it's one of the most peaceful places in the state, with hardly any cars. Visitors travel around by bike. Ferries to the island leave from Stony Point, or Cowes on Phillip Island. ❑

Map on page 182

On the Bass Highway, near the turn-off for Phillip Island, there's a museum dedicated to Megascolides Australis, the largest worm in the world, which grows to 3.5 metres (11 ft) long and 2.5 cm (1 inch) thick. You can't miss the Wildlife Wonderland – it's shaped like a worm. It also includes Wombat World and other wildlife.

BELOW: a little penguin on Phillip Island.

Penguins on Parade

Every day at **Summerland Beach** on Phillip Island, hundreds of little penguins – we're not to call them fairy penguins any more – waddle from the waters of the Bass Strait to their protected burrows in the sand. Wings outstretched, they strut in small groups up a concrete ramp past throngs of curious human onlookers. This has developed into a serious, packaged tourist spectacle: there can be days when humans outnumber the penguins. In response to this there are now elite ticketing options, involving a "penguin sky box" or a small-group "more personalised intimate wildlife experience", which sees richer tourists led to a quiet beach by their own ranger. (Daily dusk; bookings 10am–5pm; tel: 03-5951 2800; www.penguins.org.au.)

RESTAURANTS & BARS

Restaurants

Werribee

Joseph's
Mansion Hotel, Werribee Park
Tel: 03-9731 4130
www.mansionhotel.com.au
Open: B, L & D daily. $$$
Imaginative and sound modern European cooking that adds significantly to the pleasure of the mansion's grand environs.

PRICE CATEGORIES

Three-course dinner with a half-bottle of house wine:
$ = under A$50
$$ = A$50–A$80
$$$ = A$80–A$120
$$$$ = over A$120
B = breakfast, L = lunch, D = dinner

Geelong

Fishermen's Pier
Yarra Street
Tel: 03-5222 4100
www.fishermenspier.com.au
Open: L & D daily. $$
Geelong's buzzing waterfront is augmented by this temple to seafood. A couple of meat dishes are thrown in for refuseniks.

2 Faces
8 Malop Street
Tel: 03-5229 4546
Open: D Tues–Sat. $$$
Seafood features here, too, in dishes such as bouillabaisse, but the preparation tends more towards the complex and offbeat. It's a small intimate place.

Queenscliff

Athelstane House
4 Hobson Street
Tel: 03-5258 1024
www.athelstane.com.au
Open: B, L & D daily. $$
Behind the scenes some serious work goes into food this good. Out front the atmosphere is relaxed and informal – a counterbalance to Queenscliff's formal Victorian dining rooms.

Vue Grand Hotel
46 Hesse Street
Tel: 03-5258 1544
www.vuegrand.com.au
Open: B, L & D daily. $$$
It would be hard to find a more imposing setting than this. The cooking ventures to match it with bold colours and flavours.

Lorne

Ba Ba Lu
6a Mountjoy Parade
Tel: 03-5289 1808
Open: B, L & D daily. $
A lively Spanish bar and restaurant where the tapas will fill a corner and the mains will fill a backpacker.

Port Fairy

Portofino on Bank
26 Bank Street
Tel: 03-5568 2251
Open: D Mon–Sat. $$$
Exquisite North-African influenced fine dining with a twist.

Dunkeld

Royal Mail Hotel
Corner Glenelg Highway & Parker Street
www.royalmail.com.au
Tel: 03-5577 2241
Open: B, L & D daily. $$$
Generally regarded as the best restaurant in the Grampians, a brief acquaintance with Cameron Goad's sharp handling of contemporary Mod Oz cooking should be enough to explain why. An acclaimed wine list completes the picture.

Ballarat

Lake View Hotel
22 Wendouree Parade
Tel: 03-5331 4592
Open: B, L & D daily. $
With views like this they could serve any old rubbish to hungry punters, so be grateful that such splendid café fare is on offer. More sophisitication in the evening.

Daylesford

Lake House
King Street
Tel: 03-5348 3329
www.lakehouse.com.au
Open: B, L & D daily. $$$
There's theatre in the presentation and drama on the plate at this award-winning gourmand's delight. The insistence on the absolute best local produce goes a long way to explaining the quality.

Bendigo

The Bridge
49 Bridge Street
Tel: 03-5443 7811
www.thebridgebendigo.com.au
Open: L & D daily. $$
The beautiful modern din-

LEFT: the range of local wines can be bewildering.

ing room matches the food in this beautifully renovated landmark pub.

Echuca

Oscar W's

101 Murray Esplanade, Echuca Wharf
Tel: 03-5482 5133
www.oscarws.com.au
Open: L & D daily. $$$
At the top of the wharf with magnificent views of the paddle steamers chugging along the Murray below, Oscar W's scores on the food front too. Deceptively simple dishes feature idiosyncracies that denote a chef right at the top of his game.

Mildura

Stefano's

Mildura Grand Hotel, Seventh Street
Tel: 03-5023 0511
www.milduragrandhotel.com.au
Open: D Mon–Sat. $$$
A dining room of such renown that Melburnians make special trips out to enjoy it. You can see why. Each day's menu evolves according to the produce available so everything is fresh.

Yarra Valley

Eleonore's at Chateau Yering

42 Melba Highway, Yering
Tel: 03-9237 3333
www.chateauyering.com.au
Open: L Sat–Sun, D daily. $$$
This formal dining room makes eating an occasion and the food deserves the reverence that that implies. The next-door café is a recommended alternative.

Healesville

Healesville Hotel

256 Maroondah Highway
Tel: 03-5962 4002
Open: L & D daily. $$$
Marvellously atmospheric dining room in this old hotel with great pub grub. Good wines, too.

Marysville

Marysville Patisserie

7 Falls Road
Tel: 03-5963 3368
Open: B & L Wed–Sun. $
This village-centre bakery is a great place to recharge after a morning's skiing.

Beechworth

Beechworth Bakery

27 Camp Street
Tel: 03-5728 1132
www.beechworthbakery.com
Open: B & L daily. $
People queue for this local landmark. Its success has spawned a chain of six outles across the state.

Bright

Simone's

98 Gavan Street
Tel: 03-5755 2266
www.simonesrestaurant.com.au
Open: D Tues–Sat. $$$
Italian expertise applied to seasonal local produce to stunning effect.

Bairnsdale

The River Grill

2 Wood Street
Tel: 03-5153 1421
Open: B & L daily, D Thur–Sat. $$
Lots of the best regional produce, including much from Bass Strait, served in a chic, contemporary setting.

Lakes Entrance

Nautilus

Western Boat Harbour
Tel: 03-5155 1400
Open: D Tues–Sat. $$$
Famed floating fish restaurant that piques interest with spice and ingenuity.

Phillip Island

Chicory

115 Thompson Avenue, Cowes
Tel: 03-5952 2655
www.chicory.com.au
Open: L & D Thur–Tues. $$
Classy urban cuisine in a friendly environment.

Mornington Peninsula

Salix

Willow Creek Vineyard, 166 Balnarring Road, Merricks North
Tel: 03-5989 7640
www.willow-creek.com.au
Open: L daily, D Fri–Sat. $$
Excellent food to complement the local wines in this local favourite.

Smokehouse Sorrento

182 Ocean Beach Road
Tel: 03-5984 1246
Open: D Wed–Sun. $$
A pizza restaurant with enough twists to keep it packed for most of the summer and at weekends.

Bars

Benalla

North Eastern Hotel

1–3 Nunn Street
Tel: 03-5762 3252
www.northeasternhotel.com
Open: L Wed–Sun, D daily. $
Good-quality pub food in this attractive old hotel.

Metung

Metung Hotel

1 Kurnai Avenue
Tel: 03-5156 2206
www.metunghotel.com.au
Open: L & D daily. $$
On the water, this pub is well liked by both locals and visitors.

RIGHT: traditional fish and chips.

South Australia

This state, with its multinational culture, is
renowned for food, wine and festivals. It is also
blessed with a Mediterranean coastal climate,
great beaches and awesome stretches of Outback

Try a word-association test on most
Australians: say "South Australia". The first response is likely
to be "wine". The second could be
"Adelaide Festival", and the third
might be "Flinders Ranges" or "Nullarbor Plain". The mix suggests the
unlikely variety of this remote corner:
the state covers the gamut of Australian
landscapes and culture, from the pastures of the coast, with its easy-going
capital city, to the endless vineyards of
the Barossa Valley and the barren
beauty of the Coorong. No other Australian state has such a high proportion
of classic Outback desert to arable land,
and this vast hinterland has seen some
strange sights.

Ancient landscapes

If you love the outdoors, then getting
out in the timeless landscapes of the
Outback is really something special.
You could find yourself enjoying a
desert sunset as you bathe in the warm
springs at Dalhousie in the far north,
sleeping undergound in subterranean
Coober Pedy or dealing with feelings
of insignificance when you're the only
person for miles. The vast landscapes
of South Australia's Outback are
steeped in Aboriginal history and culture and are pretty much untouched by
the modern world. This is where you
can experience the quintessential Australia that you may have seen in popular films such as *Rabbit Proof Fence* or
Priscilla Queen of the Desert.

A big country town

Both visitors and locals often refer to
Adelaide ❶ as a big country town.
Maybe it's the clean air, the friendly
locals who smile at you on the street,
the views of the green Adelaide Hills
from the central business district
(CBD), or maybe it's the space; the
roads are wide, there's plenty of parks
and the suburbs don't suffer from
dense high-rise living. Combine this
with a cheaper cost of living than the
major cities on Australia's east coast
and you've got one very livable city.

Maps:
Area 210
City 204

Preceding Pages:
vines and horses in
South Australia.
Left: forest road on
Kangaroo Island.
Below:
Adelaide's Queen
Victoria Fountain.

TIP

The City Loop Bus
(route 99C) is a conve-
nient way to see the
sights of Adelaide's
CBD, and it's free. It
operates daily at regu-
lar intervals and takes
in many of they city's
attractions including
the Central Market and
North Terrace. Visit the
Adelaide Metro Info-
Centre (corner of King
William and Currie
streets) for timetables.

Situated roughly one-third of the way from Sydney to Perth, this city of 1.2 million people is ideally placed to ignore the rest of the world – which, for most of its history, it did quite happily. Among Australians, Adelaide used to epitomise conservatism with a small "c". In the 1970s the city went through a cultural revival under the premiership of Don Dunstan and for a while Adelaide led Australia on social and cultural reforms. While a legacy of world-class festivals and food and wine still remains, other parts of the Adelaide scene have not quite kept up.

Adelaide should be savoured slowly. It is possible to rock around the clock in Adelaide, if you know where to go, but it can be done better elsewhere (except at festival time, when no other Australian city can compare – *see page 206*). For most of the year, to get the most out of Adelaide you should shift down a gear or two, move at a leisurely pace and meet it on its own terms.

One's first impression of Adelaide is its sheer prettiness. This isn't an accident of nature. The city was laid out in a choice location according to the grand design of a British Army engineer, Colonel William Light, who founded the city in 1836. He came with a bevy of free settlers who had the express idea of founding a Utopia in the Antipodes. Sadly, Light – who was suffering from tuberculosis – was given a breakneck two-month deadline to choose a location and survey it. He managed the feat, choosing an inland site that was controversial at first, but his health collapsed; he had to retire, and died soon after.

The "City of Light" still follows his original design. From the air the original city resembles a lopsided figure eight, with residential North Adelaide on one side of the Torrens River and the central business district on the other.

North Adelaide has some of Australia's grandest homes. It was intended as an exclusive enclave for the transplanted English gentry, who shipped out grand pianos and chandeliers to put in their colonial salons. Despite the prevailing local opinion that many were the "idiot sons" for whom there was no room in the old country, the gentry more or less thrived, in spite of itself, on the mineral and ag-

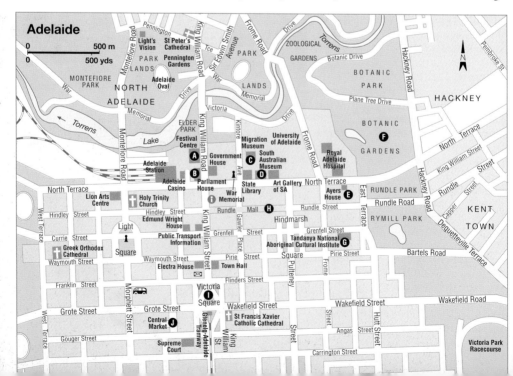

Map: opposite page

ricultural wealth of South Australia. On this side of the Torrens is historic **Adelaide Oval**, the most beautiful cricket ground in the country, and well worth a visit during the summer cricket season. At the northern end of the Oval stands the neo-Gothic **St Peter's Cathedral**.

South of the river, the central business district was designed for walking; it measures one imperial square mile and is surrounded by extensive parklands, studded with majestic gum trees, which act as a scenic buffer between the city centre and the suburbs. This leafy "moat" means it is quite impossible to enter or leave the city without passing through restful greenery. The two halves are connected by King William Street, at 42 metres (138 ft) wide, the broadest main street of any Australian capital city – one reason for the lack of traffic jams.

The main intersection in Adelaide is where North Terrace crosses King William Street. Most major attractions are within a few minutes' walk of this intersection.

The **Adelaide Festival Centre Ⓐ** (tel: 08-8216 8600; www.afct.org.au) is the oldest multipurpose performing arts centre in Australia. Its four performance spaces host a variety of events and one-off shows including the nation's premier arts festival. The centre overlooks **Elder Park** by the River Torrens – once a rather unimpressive trickle, but dammed to form an artificial lake. Visitors can choose to take a two-person pedal boat out on the river or cruise to the zoo onboard the cruise boat *Popeye*, an Adelaide tradition that dates back to 1935; a 40-km (25-mile) cycle and walking track also runs along the river.

Back on North Terrace is the monumental **Parliament House Ⓑ**, completed in 1939, which is open to visitors (guided tours 10am and 2pm weekdays, when parliament is not sitting; free). Across the road is **Government House** (closed to visitors), the official residence of the governor of South Australia.

The eastern wing of **North Terrace** is the cultural heart of Adelaide with museums and galleries situated within easy walking distance from one another. Just behind the **State Library**, which houses a tribute to Australian cricket legend Sir Donald

St Peter's Cathedral.

BELOW: the convention centre on the Torrens River.

Festival Frenzy

Sydney, Melbourne and Perth all have their arts festivals, but none compares in size, prestige or sheer excitement to Adelaide's. The Adelaide Festival of Arts is held in March on even-numbered years and trades on the city's natural advantages. Few places in the world have such an extraordinary range of performance spaces, from the gleaming white Festival Centre to the outdoor amphitheatres and intimate lofts. The weather is nigh-perfect, with dry, hot days and clear, star-studded nights – and you can walk to every venue within about 15 minutes.

The festival actually operates on several levels. The "official" festival lures the high-profile international acts, and kicks off with free weekend concerts in Rundle Park, followed by firework displays. Tickets to the official shows are very reasonable compared with the prices charged in Sydney and Melbourne, and there is usually a string of free events.

At the same time, the Adelaide Fringe is for lesser-known performers and artists. It is second in size only to Edinburgh's annual shindig: literally thousands of acts arrive from all over Australia, Europe and North America. Its popularity has seen it become an annual event. The chaotic, organic nature of the Fringe is what gives Adelaide its buzz. The focus tends to be around the bars and restaurants of Rundle Street East, where the festivities continue until dawn at the Fringe Club, but buskers and performers spread throughout the city.

With nearly 500 events in the programme, every spare corner of indoor space is devoted to some art exhibition, and every stretch outdoors to a site-specific installation. By any standards, it's a remarkable happening.

At the same time as the Festival of Arts, Adelaide hosts Writers' Week, an event that lures the literary heavies from around the globe. It is entirely free, with readings by famous authors and book launches held in the Pioneer Women's Memorial Gardens on King William Street, across from the Festival Centre.

Although nothing quite matches the festival for action, things are not too quiet in South Australia for the rest of the time. Also every March, Adelaide hosts an enormous World Music Festival, known as Womadelaide, in Botanical Park. Tasting Australia is a huge biannual food and wine festival held in Adelaide every odd year in October .

The Adelaide Festival of Ideas is a more recent addition to the abundance of celebrations, and takes place every odd year during the winter. It attracts some of the world's leading writers and thinkers such as ex-prime ministers, journalists, political commentators and university professors. A typical festival could touch on such varied topics as the Middle East, globalisation, cloning, theology or extraterrestrials.

The Barossa Valley hosts its own music festival every October. Most of its recitals are classical in nature and held in Lutheran churches – although the accompanying indulgent meals and fine wines might well have appalled the region's dour founding fathers.

Then, in early April in odd-numbered years, the Barossa Vintage Festival is a thanks-giving celebration for the region's grape harvest. The seven-day event, based in Tanunda, includes lavish tastings, grape picking and treading contests and a vintage fair.

Between May and October most wine-producing areas hold food, wine and music festivals, the most notable being the Clare Valley Gourmet Weekend in May; McLaren Vale holds several, including the Sea and Vines festival in June. ❏

LEFT: outdoor concert during Adelaide Festival.

Bradman, the **Migration Museum**  (Mon–Fri 10am–5pm, Sat & Sun 1–5pm; tel: 08-8207 7580; www.history.sa.gov.au; entrance fee) is an excellent place to explore South Australia's cultural diversity.

The **University of Adelaide** could have been transplanted from Oxford, ivy-covered walls, dreaming spires and all. The **South Australian Museum**  (daily 10am–5pm; tel: 08-8207 7500; www.samuseum.sa.gov.au; free) houses the world's largest collection of Aboriginal artefacts, as well as an extensive Pacific exhibit and a broad survey of regional natural history (the building can be identified by the huge whale skeletons displayed behind glass walls). Next door, the **Art Gallery of South Australia** (daily 10am–5pm; tel: 08-8207 7000; www.artgallery.sa.gov.au; free) has a renowned collection of 35,000 works. It displays a comprehensive collection of Australian art including landscapes by Sir Hans Heysen and Aboriginal Western Desert dot paintings.

North Terrace was once lined with houses like **Ayers House** . The home of Sir Henry Ayers, who con-

trived to be premier of South Australia seven times – an Australian record – and after whom Ayers Rock (Uluru) was named, is now a restaurant and living museum protected by the National Trust (Tues–Fri 10am–4pm, Sat, Sun 1–4pm; tel: 08-8223 1234; entrance fee). The elegant bluestone mansion contains 40 rooms dating from 1846 to the 1870s, and the hand-painted ceilings and ornate chandeliers of the dining room and ballroom are particularly remarkable.

To the north of Ayers House lie the **Botanic Gardens**  (daily; guided walks daily 10.30am; tel 08-8222 9311; entrance charge for Bicentennial Conservatory only), 16 hectares (40 acres) of lawns, trees, shrubs and lakes, with an impressive rose garden and some exceptional botanical buildings as well, from the old Palm House brought from Germany in 1875 to the extraordinary Bicentennial Conservatory of 1988.

South of Ayers House, in Grenfell Street, is **Tandanya Aboriginal Cultural Institute**  (daily 10am–5pm; www.tandanya.com.au; entrance fee), the city's venue for theatre, dance, talks,

Map on page 210

An invitation to dine in the South Australian Outback.

BELOW: the 1875 Botanic Gardens Palm House.

demonstrations and constantly changing exhibitions of arts and crafts, representing all aspects of contemporary Aboriginal culture. The Institute has a shop selling native arts and crafts, and a café where visitors can try "bush tucker".

The lively, busker-filled **Rundle Mall** was the country's first traffic-free shopping mall, an idea of former state premier Don Dunstan, who in the 1960s turned Adelaide from a musty provincial centre into "the Athens of the South". He also originated the Festival Centre and introduced some of the most progressive state laws in Australia – laws to recognise Aboriginal land rights, decriminalise homosexuality and guarantee equal opportunity. Dunstan shocked staid old Adelaide, and much of Australia besides (on one occasion, he caused a media frenzy when he wore what were described as "pink hot-pants" to parliament).

In the centre of the city's square mile, King William Street opens out into **Victoria Square** , which is where you can catch the tram to the beachside suburb of Glenelg. Just to the west is Adelaide's **Central Market** (Tues 7am–5.30pm, Thur 9am–5.30pm, Fri 7am–9pm, Sat 7am–3pm) – easily one of the most colourful in Australia. A giant covered area packed with more than 200 shops and stalls, it sells cheap fruit, vegetables, cheeses, meats, spices and a variety of esoteric imported foods. But the main attraction is the wealth of local produce that South Australia is famed for, from Maggie Beer's pâtés and Adelaide Hills cheeses, to gourmet delights from the Barossa Valley and fresh local fish such as the delicately sweet King George whiting. There's plenty of tastings to be had as well. It's no wonder this is one of Adelaide's most popular attractions for both locals and visitors. There are also stalls selling books, crafts, jewellery and clothing, alongside cafés and cheap eateries.

The market encompasses Adelaide's **Chinatown**, which spills out into Gouger Street, one of the city's main restaurant strips. The others include O'Connell Street (North Adelaide), Rundle Street (East End) and Hindley Street (West End). Between them, they

The fountain outside Adelaide Arcade used to sit at the intersection of Rundle Mall and Gawler Place. When state Premier Don Dunstan opened the mall in 1976 the fountain flowed with champagne, much to the delight of 10,000 onlookers.

BELOW: an enticing stand in Adelaide's covered market.

provide a fine choice of Chinese, Indian, Turkish, Italian, Malaysian, Japanese, Greek, African, Vietnamese, Russian, Lebanese, Thai and Australian eateries. Adelaide reputedly has more restaurants per capita than any other Australian city and it would be a shame not to visit as many as possible during your trip.

Hills and beaches

Cosmopolitan though it can be, Adelaide never loses that country-town feeling. You can drive across the city in half an hour, and you can be in beautiful countryside in a fraction of the time it takes to leave other major cities in Australia. Take any one of a dozen roads up into the **Adelaide Hills** and you can happily get lost in leafy, winding laneways. The hills are littered with small commuter suburbs such as **Blackwood**, **Aldgate** and **Crafers**, some of them strikingly pretty. There are pubs with hilltop views and restaurants like Windy Point where you can dine overlooking the expanse of the city's twinkling lights.

Adelaide Hills offer something for most tastes; there are bushwalks, mar-

kets, wineries, award-winning restaurants, wildlife parks and Birdwood's **National Motor Museum** (daily 10am–5pm; tel: 08-8568 4000; entrance fee), which is the largest of its kind in Australia. You an easily spend a day lapping up the pretty German town of **Hahndorf** and its surrounds, a favourite weekend excursion for Adelaideans.

Another Adelaide ritual is to take the Glenelg tram from the city centre to the beach. The ride takes about 20 minutes and, while **Glenelg** has seen better times and now suffers from overdevelopment, the beach is wide, white and wonderful.

Adjacent to the final tram stop near the Glenelg Town Hall at Moseley Square, you'll find **The Rodney Fox Shark Experience** (daily 10am–5pm; tel: 08-8363 1788; www.rodneyfox.com.au; entrance fee). The museum showcases the fearsome great white shark which are locals in this part of the world. If Glenelg is too crowded for your liking, Adelaide is blessed with a coastline border fringed by spacious, clean beaches that stretch for miles. **Henley Beach** is a popular, more low-key option, and

Maps:
City 204
Area 210

Among the 400 vehicles in the National Motor Museum is an 1899 Shearer, built in Mannum, South Australia, and still running. Also on display is a Talbot which completed an epic 51-day journey from Darwin to Adelaide in 1908.

BELOW: Glenelg's uncrowded beach.

Nocturnal Walks

Warrawong Sanctuary (Tues–Sun from 10am; tel: 08-8370 9197; www.warrawong.com; entrance fee), situated just 25 minutes outside of Adelaide in the Adelaide Hills, is a thriving home for more than 100 of Australia's native species.

As most native mammals are active mainly at night, the Warrawong Sanctuary's guided nocturnal tour is an excellent way to get to know the local wildlife. The bilby, which has replaced the bunny as the local symbol for Easter, is one of the endangered marsupials that you will see on the tour. Winter nocturnal tours run from 5–6.30pm. Summer nocturnal tours run from 7.30–9pm. There are also a number of self-guided walks all year round between 10am–4pm.

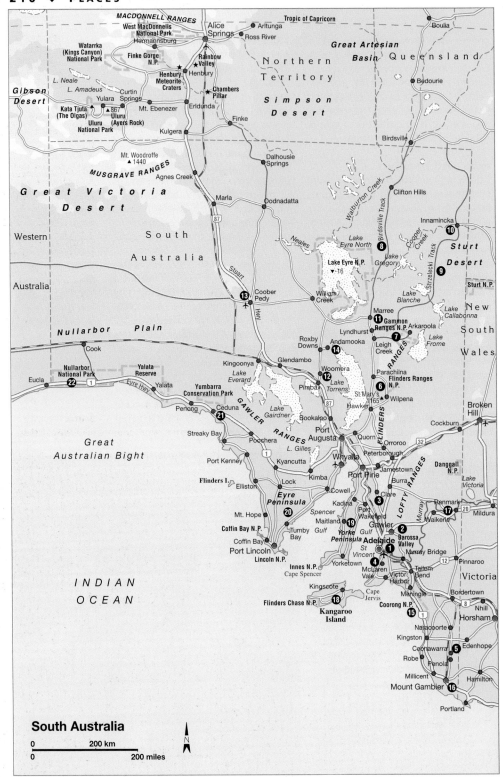

MACDONNELL RANGES

West MacDonnells National Park

Alice Springs

Arltunga

Tropic of Capricorn

Boulia

Watarrka (Kings Canyon) National Park

Finke Gorge N.P.

Hermannsburg

Ross River

Great Artesian Basin

Queensland

Rainbow Valley

Northern

Henbury Meteorite Craters

Henbury

Territory

Simpson Desert

Bedourie

L. Neale

L. Amadeus

Curtin Springs

Chambers Pillar

Gibson Desert

Yulara

Mt. Ebenezer

Kata Tjuta (The Olgas)

867

Erldunda

Uluru (Ayers Rock)

Uluru (Ayers Rock) National Park

Finke

Birdsville

Kulgera

Mt. Woodroffe ▲ 1440

Dalhousie Springs

MUSGRAVE RANGES

Agnes Creek

Clifton Hills

Innamincka ⑩

Great Victoria Desert

Marla

Oodnadatta

Walburton Creek

Birdsville Track

Sturt Desert

South Australia

Stuart Hwy

Neales

Lake Eyre North

⑧

Lake Gregory

Cooper Creek

⑨

Sturt N.P.

Western

Australia

Lake Eyre N.P. ▼ -16

Strzelecki Track

New South Wales

Nullarbor Plain

Cook

Coober Pedy ⑬

William Creek

Lake Blanche

Lake Callabonna

Marree

⑪ Gammon Ranges N.P.

Arkaroola

Nullarbor National Park

Yalata Reserve

Lyndhurst

Leigh Creek

RANGES

Lake Frome

Eucla

⑳

Eyre Hwy

Yalata

Roxby Downs

Andamooka

⑭

Sturt N.P.

Yumbarra Conservation Park

Ceduna

Kingoonya

Glendambo

Woomera

⑫

Pimba

Parachilna

Flinders Ranges N.P.

Great Australian Bight

Penong

Lake Everard

Lake Torrens

St Mary's 1165 ⑥

Wilpena

Streaky Bay

Poochera

Lake Gairdner

Bookaloo

Hawker

FLINDERS

Port Kenney

L. Gilles

Port Augusta

Quorn

Orroroo

Cockburn

Broken Hill

Flinders I.

Elliston

Lock

Kyancutta

Kimba

Cowell

Whyalla

Peterborough

32

Danggali N.P.

Eyre Peninsula

⑳

Mt. Hope

Spencer

Kadina

Port Pirie

Jamestown

Burra

LOFTY

Lake Victoria

Coffin Bay N.P.

Tumby Bay

Gulf

Maitland

⑲

Port Wakefield

Clare

③

RANGES

Renmark

⑰

Waikerie

Mildura

Coffin Bay

Port Lincoln

Lincoln N.P.

Yorke Peninsula

Gawler

Barossa Valley ②

Murray

20

Pinnaroo

Innes N.P.

Cape Spencer

Yorketown

St Vincent

Adelaide ①

Murray Bridge

Tailem Bend

12

Victoria

INDIAN OCEAN

Kingscote

Cape Jervis

McLaren Vale ④

Victor Harbor

Meningie

Bordertown

Nhill

Flinders Chase N.P. ⑱

Kangaroo Island

Coorong N.P.

⑮

Naracoorte

Horsham

Kingston

Coonawarra

⑤

Edenhope

Robe

Penola

Millicent

Hamilton

Mount Gambier ⑯

Portland

South Australia

0   200 km

0   200 miles

N

Map on page 210

after a dip or a walk you can dine on some fish and chips at the grassy, beach-side square.

If you like to feel the sun on your skin, drive down Main South Road (A13) for 20 km (12 miles) until you see the turn-off on the right to **Maslin's Beach**. It's an official nudist beach and its backdrop of sandstone cliffs makes it one of the most beautiful seaside settings in the state. Maslin's is friendly and family-oriented, but be warned: the gulf waters are fed by the Southern Ocean and the water can be brisk.

Valleys of vines

Adelaide sits amid the country's greatest wine regions, of which the **Barossa Valley ❷** is easily the most famous. It was named in 1837 by Colonel William Light, Adelaide's far-sighted planner, because it reminded him of the countryside in Spain where he had fought against Napoleon's army in the Battle of Barossa. The valley was settled in the 1840s by Germans seeking freedom to worship in the Lutheran Church. They brought the first vine cuttings with them and more than 150 years later, wine drinkers worldwide thank them for their forethought.

It takes just over an hour to drive to the Barossa Valley, which lies 60 km (35 miles) northeast of Adelaide. Along the way you will pass the actual Jacob's Creek, where the famous winery gets its name from, and then row after row of vines belonging to one of the 60 local wineries which include some of the most famous names in the business – **Peter Lehman**, **Yalumba**, **Grant Burge**, **Penfolds** and **Wolf Blass**.

Nearly all the wineries have tasting and salerooms, and many have barbecue and picnic areas as well as restaurants and cafés. Like a well-stocked cellar built up over many years, the wineries are spread the length of the Barossa Valley Way which links most of the main towns in the region.

An alternative to the direct route from Adelaide to the Barossa via Gawler, is to choose the scenic drive via the Adelaide Hills which takes you through Cudlee Creek, onto Williamstown and then **Lyndoch**, which is the first major town in the valley. The enjoyable drive

Vineyard sign in Barossa Valley.

BELOW:
the Barossa Valley.

Jacob's Creek, one of the world's most popular wine brands, is produced by Orlando Wines whose grapes were first planted by immigrants from Bavaria in 1847. In 1989 Orlando was bought by France's Pernod Ricard.

BELOW: winemaker Hans de Haan.

takes you past some of the city's reservoirs. Just beyond Williamstown, stop at the **Whispering Wall**, which is not only an engineering feat but an acoustic phenomenon. The wall is curved in such a way that whisperings at one end can be clearly heard at the other which is 140 metres (460 ft) away.

From Lyndoch in its forest setting, the Barossa Way continues on to **Tanunda**, the most distinctly German town in the region, which is renowned for its fine butchers and bakeries. Following the road to Nuriootpa, you can take a detour to the left down Samuel Road to visit **Maggie Beer's Farm Shop** (daily 10.30am–5pm; tel: 08-8562 4477; www.maggiebeer.com.au). Maggie is one of Australia's leading celebrity cooks and a Barossa icon – at her farm shop you can catch a daily cooking demonstration at 2pm or pick up some picnic supplies.

Back on the road it's not far to **Nuriootpa**, the commercial centre of the Barossa Valley. Keep following the road to Angaston, where the popular Barossa Farmer's Market takes place each Saturday morning.

Many Barossa wineries not only produce excellent vintages but also have magnificent grounds and buildings, like the palm groves at **Seppeltsfield**, picturesque **Chateau Yaldara**, and the two-storey historic blue-marble buildings at **Yalumba**.

Bethany Winery has panoramic views of the valley while **Rockford Wines** is one of the last bastions of traditional basket-press wine making.

Clare

Although the Barossa is the best-known wine-producing area in Australia, it is only one of five major wine regions within easy driving distance of Adelaide. **Clare ❸** is the centre of the wine area of the Clare Valley/Watervale region about 130 km (80 miles) north of Adelaide. Jesuit priests fleeing persecution in Silesia settled in the Clare Valley in 1848 and began making sacramental wines at Sevenhill Cellars. Today there are more than 20 wineries and 40 cellar doors in a 25-km (15-mile) strip. The region is famed for its Rieslings but you will also find some fine Shiraz and Cabernet Sauvignon.

Many are boutique wineries whose labels are taking their place on some of the world's finest wine lists.

Some of the more renowned names in the business include Neil Paulett, Jeffrey Grosset, David O'Leary, Neil Pike and Mount Horrocks.

More than 60 cellar doors are dotted throughout **McLaren Vale** ❹, 42 km (26 miles) south of Adelaide. Cartographers battle to fit all the vineyards on the map; they read like a wine lover's roll of honour: Geoff Merrill, Hardy's Tintara and Wirra Wirra . This region is renowned for its reds, although there is plenty on offer to please lovers of white wine, including some fine Sauvignon Blanc and Viognier.

In the southeast of the state, on the way between Adelaide and Melbourne, the vineyards of the **Coonawarra** ❺ area are justly famed for their reds. Vineyards at **Keppoch** and **Padthaway** are becoming equally well-known. **Padthaway Estate Homestead**, now an exclusive hotel, is an imposing stone mansion in an oasis of green English-style gardens. The property was taken up as a sheep run in 1847, and the homestead was built in 1882. Today a number of vineyards spread over the acres where sheep once grazed.

The orchards of the **Riverland**, on the Murray River, produce nearly half of the state's wine grapes. The specialities of the region are brandies and fortified dessert wines. **Berri Estates** is the largest winery in the southern hemisphere while smaller wineries include Bonneyview Wines at Barmera.

The most famous is **Banrock Station** near Kingston-on-Murray, which is well worth a visit. Their eco-friendly philosophy is reflected in the design of the visitor centre, which has information on how the winery helps to fund environmental programmes. The winery overlooks restored wetlands, which you can explore at leisure.

North from Adelaide

If you're not too keen on driving the vast distances of the Outback on your own, then you could choose to watch the scenery glide past you from the comfort of the **Ghan** (see pages 269– 70), one of the world's great rail journeys. It links Adelaide to the Red Centre, before con-

Map on page 210

TIP

Bundaleer Forest Weekend, held in March, is a music festival where artists perform outdoors in the forest. Hearing the Adelaide Symphony Orchestra while sitting on hay bales at sunset is a memorable experience. The forest is 10km (6 miles) south of Jamestown and about 2½ hours' drive from Adelaide. www.bundaleerweekend.com.au

BELOW:
Chateau Yaldara.

tinuing onto the tropical Top End. The Ghan gets its name from the Afghan camel traders who pioneered travel from Adelaide to the Red Centre.

The **Flinders Ranges** extend from near Port Pirie, where Mount Remarkable (975 metres/3,150 ft) is the first major peak, to past Mount Painter in the desert and salt lakes to the north. At the top of the **Spencer Gulf**, the road turns away from the ocean and heads into the arid heart of the continent. Here lies **Port Augusta** which, with Port Pirie and Whyalla, forms the basis of South Australia's industrial heart, known as the Iron Triangle. From Port Augusta, the road runs northeast through **Quorn**, then on to **Hawker**, the nearest township to the northern Flinders Ranges. You can travel between Port Augusta and Quorn on the steam locomotive of the historic **Pichi Richi Railway** which operates on the oldest section of the Ghan track.

By a fortunate coincidence, the most spectacular feature of the Flinders Ranges is also the most accessible. **Wilpena Pound** at the southern end of the **Flinders Ranges National Park**

❻ is a raised valley surrounded by quartzite hills. St Mary's Peak is the highest point in the ranges at 1,165 metres (3,758 ft).

The only way into the pound is on foot: there are a number of hikes that begin at the Wilpena visitor centre. By comparison with the thin, rocky soil and arid landscape outside, the pound floor is richly vegetated. In fact, Wilpena Pound attracts considerably more rainfall than neighbouring regions. Although the exterior walls of the pound are steep, the inside slopes are relatively gentle. The six-hour return hike up St Mary's Peak rewards you with breathtaking views. Although Wilpena Pound looks like a crater, it is the result of folding rocks, not the impact of a celestial object.

If Wilpena is your only destination in the Flinders, it is worth your while taking the time to detour north past the natural rock feature known as the Great Wall of China, then through **Parachilna Pass** to join the main Leigh Creek Road before heading south. Coming out of the pass, you emerge onto plains that typify central

In Aboriginal "Dreaming" (mythology) the encircling walls of Wilpena Pound were created by two snakes who came to rest here. St Mary's Peak is seen as the head of one of them.

BELOW: leisurely pursuits at Port Augusta.

Australia; from here, as you look back, the open lip of Wilpena Pound clearly shows its strikingly symmetrical form.

The northern end of the Flinders Ranges more closely resembles the other mountains of central Australia. The base for exploring the **Gammon Ranges National Park 7** is **Arkaroola**, a small settlement geared to the needs of tourists. Gorges and valleys filled with wildflowers and endless variations on the recurrent themes of rock, eucalyptus and folded hills prevail.

The sky at night

The rugged wilderness and abundant wildlife of the northern Flinders are easily explored by foot or four-wheel-drive. There are some good vantage points where you can see the Flinders Ranges stretching south for miles. But some of the best views are at night. Cloudless skies and no light pollution create the ideal conditions to explore the night sky and there are three observatories at Arkaroola as well as astronomy tours to get you on your way.

The roads north into the Outback – the **Birdsville Track 8** or the **Strz-**

elecki Track **9** – are rough adventures, aiming towards the distant Queensland border. Not everyone likes the desert, but those who do will find the continual but almost imperceptible changes in scenery endlessly fascinating.

Along the Strzelecki Track, the last stop in South Australia is **Innamincka 10**, a settlement with a population of fewer than 200 people where the only two buildings of note are the general store and the pub. Locals will be able to direct you to the Dig Tree *(see page 251)*, a few kilometres to the east on the border with Queensland, which marks the spot where a supply of food was left for starving members of the ill-fated transcontinental expedition, led by Bourke and Wills. Camping by Coopers Creek after a few beers at the pub is now the embodiment of the Outback.

The Birdsville Track lies deep in the Australian psyche. It was developed as a route for driving cattle from western Queensland to Marree, SA, where they could be loaded onto railcars heading south. **Marree 11** itself was a trading depot for the Afghan camel drivers

Map
on page
210

TIP

You should not attempt the Strzelecki, Oodnadatta or the Birdsville tracks without extensive Outback driving experience, a four-wheel-drive vehicle and a lot of preparation. The Strzelecki Track has no petrol, water or supply station for 500 km (300 miles) between Lyndhurst and Innamincka.

BELOW:
down the lonely
Strzelecki Track.

BELOW:
an opal miner's dugout home at Coober Pedy.

who opened much of central Australia. Following the Oodnadatta Track northwest from Marree follows part of the original route that these Afghan traders took. The track skirts around the southern end of **Lake Eyre**, which is Australia's largest lake when there is water in it – it has filled to capacity only three times in the past 150 years.

At 15 metres (50 ft) below sea level, Lake Eyre is the lowest part of the continent, a bowl that collects the monsoon rains of northern Australia.

The lake can be accessed at William Creek, whose pub bursts with character. Dalhousie Springs is an Outback oasis and is worth a 180-km (112-mile) detour (one-way) off the track north of Oodnadatta.

Driving this far north into the Outback of South Australia you will eventually cross the **Dingo Fence** which was completed in 1885 to keep dingoes to the north and out of the fertile sheep country of south-east Australia. It is the world's longest fence stretching 5,320 km (3,300 miles) from the Great Australian Bight in South Australia to southeast Queensland. It's questionable whether it has been successful – dingoes can still be found in the southern states – while it is thought feral animal populations in the south are booming due to lack of competition from native predators

On the sealed Stuart Highway, which stretches 1,370 km (850 miles) from Port Augusta to Alice Springs, the tiny settlement of **Pimba** marks the turn-off to **Woomera** ⑫, the rocket and research base that was opened to the public in 1982 with displays detailing the early days of rocketry. (Woomera is the Aboriginal term for spear launcher). The Woomera Prohibited Area is adjacent to the town and spans 127,000 sq. km (49,000 sq. miles) – about the size of England. British nuclear tests took place at Maralinga, at the western reaches of the area, during the 1950s.

Coober Pedy

Coober Pedy ⑬, halfway to Northern Territory on the Stuart Highway, is the best-known town in Outback South Australia. This is the world's largest opal field (for white opals), where the

relentlessly hot climate (sometimes soaring to 50°C/122°F or more) has forced the inhabitants to live underground in dugouts.

At first glance, the town looks like a hard-hit battlefield. The almost treeless terrain consists of hundreds of mounds of upturned earth and abandoned mines where fossickers have rummaged through the landscape in search of precious gems. If you should arrive during one of the regular dust storms that sweep across the area, you could be excused for believing the apocalypse was nigh. But beneath the surface there are homes, shops, restaurants and even churches. There is an underground hotel, too, suitable only for non-claustrophobics.

Visitors should note the beautiful natural patterns in the bare clay walls (and the lack of windows, compensated for by good air conditioning).

Unfortunately, the rapid increase in traffic aiming for the centre has changed Coober Pedy into a near-caricature of its early self. For a more genuine experience of an Outback opal town, venture off the beaten track to **Andamooka** ⓮, due north from Woomera, where fewer than 500 people dwell, but be aware that any rainfall can quickly leave you stranded. The striking ochre coloured hills of the **Breakaways** lie 33 km (20 miles) north of Coober Pedy. This arid landscape was an inland sea 70 million years ago.

Coorong and beyond

To the southeast of Adelaide, around the mouth of the Murray River, lies an indefinable maze of sandbanks and estuaries. This is the **Coorong National Park** ⓯, a haven for many waterfowl. The main features are the sand dunes of the **Younghusband Peninsula** that separate the shallow waters of the Coorong from the Southern Ocean, and the **Coorong** itself (*karangh* or "narrow neck" to the Aborigines), a long, thin neck of water stretching 120 km (75 miles) from Lake Alexandrina and Lake Albert at the mouth of the Murray River

to the saltpans and marshy ponds at the southern end.

If you lack a four-wheel-drive vehicle, it's a half-hour walk across the dunes to the ocean beach, an endless area of golden sand left mostly to the seagulls, oystercatchers, pelicans and occasional fishermen. A great number and variety of waterfowl feed on the water plants in the lagoons and drink at the freshwater soaks. For thousands of years Ngarrindjeri Aboriginal people lived here, netting fish in the lagoons, collecting cockles on the beach and fashioning reeds into rafts and baskets. You may come across their ancient shell middens in the sand dunes – you should not interfere with them in any way.

To explore the Coorong fully, you need time, preferably a boat and, in the heat of summer near the drying salt flats, a strong nose. The spirit of the Coorong was well captured in the 1976 film *Storm Boy*.

South of the Coorong is a series of seaside holiday resorts, with this part of the coast renowned for its shellfish. At **Kingston** you can buy delicious fresh lobster at the jetty. In **Robe**, once

Ore slags grow tall at Coober Pedy.

BELOW:
a paddle-steamer on the Murray River.

TIP

There are several
paddlewheel vessels
(the *Proud Mary*,
Murray Princess and
Murray River Queen)
running five- and six-
day cruises along the
river. Houseboats can
be hired at Renmark,
Loxton, Berri and
Waikerie. More details:
www.murrayriver
.com.au

BELOW: the tram
to Granite Island.

an important port and retaining much
of its early character, the Caledonian
Inn, licensed in 1858, still caters to
weary travellers.

A stone near the harbour commem-
orates the thousands of Chinese who
disembarked here in the 1850s and
tramped hundreds of kilometres
through the bush to the Victorian gold
diggings, to avoid the £10 arrival tax
imposed at Victorian ports. Robe tends
to be full in school holidays and over-
flows at Christmas and on New Year's
Eve, but is a lovely, peaceful spot for
the rest of the year.

Mount Gambier nestles on the
side of a 5,000-year-old extinct volcano. Within its rim lie three craters,
four lakes, and the mystery of why the
largest, **Blue Lake**, turns from winter
grey to brilliant azure from November
through to March. Outside the city are
the Tantanoola limestone caves.

Further north, the **Naracoorte Caves**
(fee for cave tours; tel: 08-8762 2340)
contain not only beautiful limestone
formations but also a fossil cave where
the traces of many extinct animals are
being unearthed. They include giant

kangaroos, a wombat the size of a hip-
popotamus and a marsupial lion.

The Riverland

Renmark , northeast of Adelaide
near the Victorian border, was the
birthplace of the Murray River irrigation area in 1887. The drive along the
Sturt Highway roughly follows the
river through extensive orchards and
vineyards supported by the Murray's
waters. Half of South Australia's
grapes and 90 percent of the state's
stone fruit and citrus are grown in the
Riverland. River transport is prominent
here, too, with the paddleboat days
remembered in the old steamer moored
as a floating museum.

Barmera and nearby Lake Bonney are
the recreational heart of the Riverland.
Lake Bonney attracts a wide variety of
watercraft: mainly windsurfers and sailing boats. In 1964, the pace increased
considerably when Sir Donald Campbell used the lake for an attempt on the
world water-speed record.

The air currents from the plains
around **Waikerie** have made it one of
the world's leading soaring centres. In
summer, when sun-heated air rises in
powerful thermals, gliders can be seen
throughout the region. For flights, check
with the Waikerie International Soaring
Centre (tel: 08-8541 2644; www
.waikeriaglidingclub.com.au). Waikerie's Aboriginal name means "many wings",
after the giant moth "wei kari". It could
easily refer to the abundant bird life in
the nearby **Hart Lagoon**.

Peninsulas and islands

The deeply indented coastline of
South Australia has made a set of natural divisions, each with its own
appeal. The **Fleurieu Peninsula**,
south of Adelaide beyond McLaren
Vale, is a popular holiday area for
South Australians. **Victor Harbor** is
the main resort – its hotels, motels and
guest houses are often full during
school holidays. Among Victor's
attractions are the little penguin
colony on **Granite Island** (connected

to the mainland by a causeway with a horse-drawn tram), an adventure park and winter whale watching.

Cape Jervis, at the end of the peninsula, is the stepping-off point for Kangaroo Island ⓲. Until the end of the last ice age, 9,000 years ago, the island (Australia's third largest, after Tasmania and Melville) wasn't separated from the mainland. Even now, the finger of the Dudley Peninsula on the island appears to be reaching towards Cape Jervis. The island's main towns are Kingscote, American River and Penneshaw. Fishing, exploring the scenery and observing wildlife are the main activities for visitors. Seals, sea lions, penguins, echidnas, kangaroos, emus and koalas all live here in abundance. Nightly processions of little penguins can be seen on the beaches around Kingscote and Penneshaw, and you can walk among one of Australia's largest colonies of sea lions at Seal Bay. At the large Flinders Chase National Park, the only enclosures are to keep the persistent wildlife away from picnickers.

From the gentle sandy beaches of the Dudley Peninsula to the pounding surf on the headland of Cape du Couedic, Kangaroo Island has a wide range of terrains. The lighthouse at the cape was built in 1906 as an essential navigation aid for coastal shipping. Near it lie two unusual features: Remarkable Rocks, a collection of granite boulders worn by the sea into fantastical shapes, some resembling animals and birds, others akin to Henry Moore sculptures; and Admirals Arch, a 20-metre (64-ft) maw rimmed with fang-like blackened stalactites, frame a maelstrom of surging waves. These are primeval sites at odds with the placid nature of other parts of the island.

Yorke Peninsula

A loop of picturesque towns, Yorke Peninsula ⓳ takes in the east-coast port of Ardrossan with its attractive water access and, down the coast, Edithburgh with its splendid clifftop views and its famous old pub, the Troubridge Hotel. The town's cemetery includes the graves of the 34 victims of the 1909 wreck of the *Clan Ranald*. The scenic route south to Yorketown is a

Map on page 210

Playful seals on Kangaroo Island.

BELOW: the Remarkable Rocks, granite formations in Flinders Chase National Park.

One transport firm made the Guinness Book of Records *in 1999 by hauling 45 trailers, weighing more than 600 tons, for 8 km (5 miles) using one truck. In real life, few road trains haul more than six trailers in the Outback, and these will be transferred to individual trucks before they reach an urban destination.*

BELOW:
salt deposits
around Lake Eyre.

magical drive offering great coastal views of offshore reefs popular with local scuba divers. Yorketown is a small farming town surrounded by a series of salt lakes.

Towards the southwestern extremity of the peninsula is the great horseshoe-shaped sweep of **Pondalowie Bay**. Located in a national park, the bay is a fishing, diving and surfing paradise made even more appealing by its remoteness. A full seven hours' drive from Adelaide, it is a great place to camp and enjoy the beauty of the Southern Ocean coastline.

The ports of the Yorke Peninsula's west coast indicate its importance as a grain-growing area. It was from places such as **Port Victoria** that great wind-jammers left to race back to Britain and Europe with their cargoes of grain. Farming and fishing still play important parts in the peninsula's modest economy, but mineral wealth contributed a colourful chapter to the area's history. The discovery of copper at **Kadina** and **Moonta** led to the mass migration of Cornish miners and their families from southwest England.

Along with the port town of **Wallaroo**, the two hamlets grew as solid Cornish communities with strong Methodist influences, catering to 30,000 people. The boom period has long passed but the contribution of the Cornish Cousin Jacks and Cousin Jills, as they were known, remains an indelible part of the peninsula's heritage.

The long road west

Of all the great Australian highway routes, the 2,000-km-plus (1,240-mile-plus) stretch from Adelaide to Perth is the one most frequently flaunted, with "We crossed the Nullarbor" stickers displayed on car and van windows. However, the road itself is no longer the challenge – rather it's the cost of fuel to propel a vehicle across several thousand kilometres of nothingness.

On the drive west towards Perth, the **Eyre Peninsula** ⑳ and the attractive township of Port Lincoln exert strong pressure to detour. Explorer John Eyre ploughed through the area in 1841 and, although burnt almost to a frazzle by the harshness of the hinterland, he was impressed by the spectacular coastline. The peninsula has its own historical charm in places like **Coffin Bay**, famous for its delicious oysters, and **Anxious Bay**. **Port Lincoln** itself has a large tuna-fishing fleet, cruises, and great white shark diving tours. Some of the shark scenes from *Jaws* were filmed here.

At **Point Labatt**, on the Flinders Highway, is the only seal colony on mainland Australia. If you would like to get a little closer, dolphin and sea lion swimming tours depart from Baird Bay in the warmer months.

Ceduna ㉑ is the centre of a large pastoral industry, but surfers from both east and west coasts know it as a favoured stopping-off place in their pursuit of waves. It's blessed with golden beaches; Cactus is the break surfers speak of with the greatest reverence. But be warned, great white sharks prowl this coastline and shark

Map on page 210

attacks have occurred. The navigator Matthew Flinders named nearby **Denial Bay** when he realised it was not the access to the elusive "Inland Sea" that was rumoured to exist.

Inland from Ceduna is the 106,000-hectare (262,000-acre) tract of **Yumbarra Conservation Park**. Its sandy ridges and granite outcrops appear inhospitable but the local wildlife, particularly emus and kangaroos, find it ideal. In winter the top of the bight is also a favourite spot for whale-watching. Head of Bight whale-watching centre (tel: 08-8625 6201; www.headofbight.com.au), 25 km (15 miles) east of Nullarbor, offers a great opportunity to get out of the car and stretch your legs. Southern right whales are regularly seen from the spectacular cliffs here during the winter.

Ceduna is South Australia's most westerly town. From here to Norseman in Western Australia it is 1,232 km (765 miles), and any other point shown on a map along the way is nothing more than a water storage base or a fuel station. That's what makes crossing the Nullarbor Plain such an intimidating prospect.

There are no trees on the plain (*nullarbor* is Latin for "no tree"), as the limestone is unable to hold rainwater.

Crossing the desert

The **Eyre Highway** hugs the coastline on its long route to Western Australia, passing through the **Nullarbor National Park** ㉒ during the last stretch of South Australia. For the earlier pioneers, the coastal route was much harsher than the alternative of the interior. While vast stretches of the coastline are devoid of fresh water, limestone sinkholes in the plain might have provided ready supplies.

The desert is also traversed by the Trans-Australian railway, one of the world's great rail journeys, with one straight section that stretches 479 km (298 miles), making it the world's longest. It is part of the Indian Pacific passenger rail service that links Sydney to Perth *(see page 345)*

A lasting impression of the coastline of the **Great Australian Bight** is the sheer cliff formations that make the coastal strip near the Western Australian border so spectacular. ❏

TIP

Overtaking a road train requires strong nerves and you shouldn't even try on dirt roads. Courteous truckers will blink their right-turn indicator to indicate that the road ahead is clear.

BELOW: a road train stirs up the dust on the Eyre Highway.

RESTAURANTS & BARS

Restaurants

Central City

Auge
22 Grote Street
Tel: 08-8410 9332
www.auge.com.au
Open: L Tues–Fri, D
Tues–Sat.$$$
Award-winning modern
Italian cuisine in a
smart setting.
Espresso and juices
available all day from
the impressive bar –
perfect for a brief shop-
ping respite.

Botanic Gardens
Restaurant and Kiosk
Botanic Gardens
North Terrace
Tel: 08-8223 3526
www.botanicgardenrestaurant
.com.au
Open: L daily.$$

On a fine day there's
no better choice for
lunch than the patio of
this superb restaurant.
Black swans bob on
the lake by your table,
while scents from the
gardens add to the
dreamlike setting. Wan-
dering in the rose gar-
den after lunch
provides an ideal end
to the meal.

Blake's
The Hyatt Regency
Tel: 08-8238 2381
Open: D Mon & Wed–Sat.
$$$
Has one of the coun-
try's most famous
wine lists.

The Grange
Hilton Adelaide
233 Victoria Square
Tel: 08-8217 2000

www.adelaide.hilton.com
Open: D Wed–Sat. $$$
Chef Cheong Liew has
gained an international
reputation as a pio-
neer of east-west
fusion and he contin-
ues to win accolades
for his innovative and
imaginative menus.

Red Ochre Restaurant
War Memorial Drive, North
Adelaide
Tel: 08-8211 8555
www.redochre.com.au
Open: L Mon–Fri,
D Mon–Sat. $$
Specialising in bush
tucker/native Aus-
tralian produce. The
place to sample wal-
laby shanks or emu
pâté. Waterfront loca-
tion on Torrens Lake
and city views.

Rigoni's
27 Leigh Street
Tel: 08-8231 5160
Open: B, L & D Mon–Fri. $
An Italian brasserie
which is a real scene
for journos, politicians
and hangers-on. Break-
fast, lunch and dinner,
7am till late.

Universal Wine Bar
285 Rundle Street
Tel: 08-8232 5000
Open: L, D Mon–Sat. $$
Slick and stylish with an
impressive wine list and
ever-changing menu.

The Oxford Hotel
101 O'Connell Street
Tel: 08-8267 2652
Open: L daily, D Mon–Sat. $
A great bistro offering
excellent service and
outside dining.

Rundle Street East

The Austral Hotel
205 Rundle St
Tel: 08-8223 4660
www.theaustral.com
Open: L, D daily. $
Modern Australian pub
cuisine.

Lemon Grass Bistro
289 Rundle St
Tel: 08-8223 6627
Open: L Mon–Fri, D daily. $
An up-market Thai con-
cern where kangaroo
and crocodile fillet sit
alongside more tradi-
tional menu options.

Cibo Espresso
218 Rundle Street
Tel 08-8232 9199
www.ciboespresso.com.au
For rich Italian coffee
and pastries look out
for the red awning and
umbrellas.

Amalfi Pizzeria
Ristorante
29 Frome Street
Tel: 08-8223 1948
Open: L Mon–Fri
D Mon–Sat. $
Amalfi's turns out
authentic Italian spe-
cials to its loyal supper
crowd. Here you'll find
a real cross-section of
Adelaide nightlife, and
the good-natured staff
add to the appeal.

Gouger Street

Ying Chow
114 Gouger Street
Tel: 08-8211 7998
Open: L Fri, D daily. BYO. $
One of the best-value
restaurants in town and
a favourite of many
young Adelaidians, this

busy, casual place serves first-rate regional Chinese dishes at low prices.

Paul's Restaurant
79 Gouger Street
Tel: 08-8231 9778
Open: L Mon–Fri, D daily, BYO. **$**
Simply prepared fish and chips.

Stanley's Fish Café
76 Gouger Street
Tel: 08-8410 0909.
Open: L & D daily. **$$$**
King George whiting, garfish and tommy ruffs are some of the tastiest catches to look out for on the menu.

The Tap Inn
Kent Town Hotel, 76 Rundle Street, Kent Town
Tel: 08-8362 2116
www.tapinn.com.au
Open: L, D daily. **$$**
A multimillion dollar refurbishment has transformed this old local favourite into an outlandish venue complete with indoor golf-driving range. The golf theme continues into the Sand Bunker Beer Garden, where the schnitzels are so big they hang off the plate.

Hutt Street

Chianti Classico
160 Hutt Street
Tel: 08-8232 7955
www.chianticlassico.com.au
Open: D daily. **$$**
A popular, family-orientated restaurant offering pasta and other classic Italian dishes.

Good Life. Modern Organic Pizza
170 Hutt Street
Tel: 08-8223 2618
www.goodlifepizza.com
Open: L Tues–Fri, D Mon–Sat. **$**
Pizzas made using locally-sourced free-range and organic ingrediants. Toppings are tasty and imaginative – free-range chicken with potatoes, garlic and rosemary, or smoked salmon with preserved lemons and caper mayonnaise, to pick two.

Worth Leaving Town

The Magill Estate Restaurant
78 Penfold Road, Magill
Tel: 08-8301 5551
www.penfolds.com.au
Open: L Fri, D Tues–Sat. **$$$**
About 8 km (5 miles) from the city, the restaurant at Penfolds Magill Estate is highly recommended. Fine dining with views of vineyards and the city. Splurge on a glass of Penfolds Grange Hermitage.

Star of Greece
The Esplanade, Port Willunga
Tel: 08-8557 7420
Open: L Wed–Sun, D Sat (Summer only). **$$**
The spectacular setting, perched on the cliffs of Adelaide's southern beaches, is enhanced by a funky, ad hoc atmosphere and a menu that uses some of the best local ingredients. The food

is not Greek – it is named after a ship that ran aground off the coast. Limited openings outside summer period.

Adelaide Hills

Bridgewater Mill
Mount Barker Road, Bridgewater
Tel: 08-8339 9200
www.bridgewatermill.com.au
Open: L Thur–Mon. **$$$**
Dine alfresco in the historic setting of this Adelaide Hills winery which is a regular best Australian restaurant finalist in *Gourmet Traveller* magazine. The mill also houses the cellar door and tastings for Petaluma wines.

Windy Point Restaurant
Windy Point Lookout, Belair Road, Belair
Tel: 08-8278 8255

Open: D Mon–Sat. **$$$**
Located just above the look-out area at Windy Point, the restaurant has fantastic panoramic views over the city. Seasonal food and a wine list sourced mainly from SA.

Zorro's Charcoal Grill
60 Main Street, Hahndorf
Tel: 08-8388 1309
Open: L Thur–Mon. **$$$**
Hearty Serbian cooking with the emphasis on grilled meat. On Sundays, the roast is cooked on a huge spit.

PRICE CATEGORIES
Three-course dinner with a half-bottle of house wine:
$ = under A$50
$$ = A$50–A$75
$$$ = over A$75
B = breakfast, L = lunch, D = dinner, BYO = bring your own alcohol

LEFT: kangaroo, cooked Thai-style.
RIGHT: a snack at Jacob's Creek visitor centre.

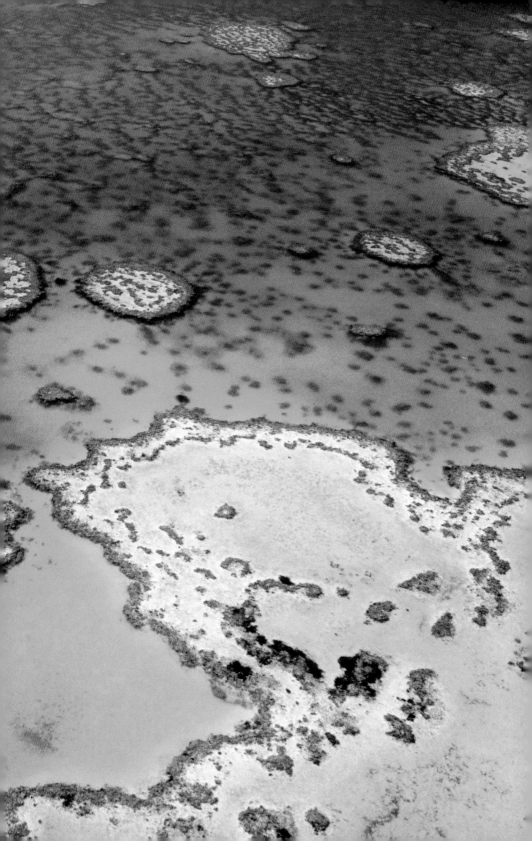

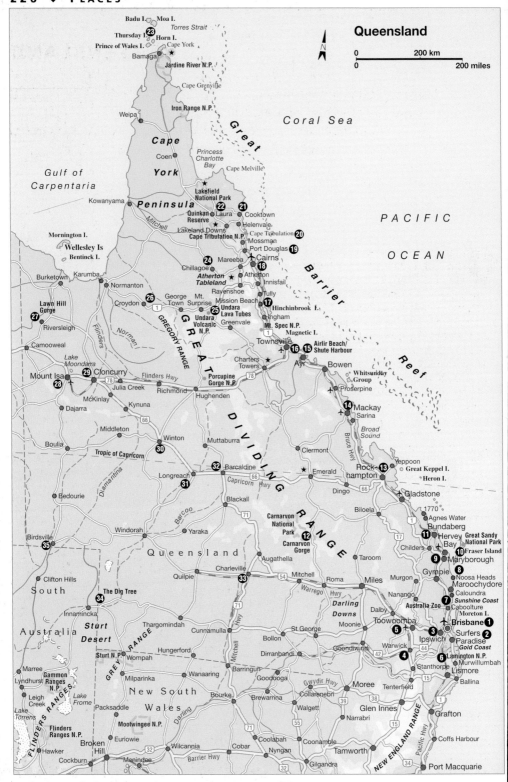

Queensland

0 — 200 km

0 — 200 miles

Torres Strait
Badu I. — Moa I.
Thursday I. — Horn I. 23
Prince of Wales I.
Bamaga
Cape York
Jardine River N.P.

Coral Sea

Cape Grenville

Weipa

Cape

Coen

York

Princess Charlotte Bay
Cape Melville

Gulf of Carpentaria

Kowanyama

Lakefield National Park

Peninsula

Quinkan Reserve 22 21 Cooktown
Laura
Helenvale
Lakeland Downs
Cape Tribulation N.P. Cape Tribulation 20
Mossman
Port Douglas 19

PACIFIC

Mornington I.
Wellesley Is
Bentinck I.

Chillagoe 24 Mareeba Cairns 18
Atherton Tableland Atherton
Innisfail

OCEAN

Burketown
Karumba

Ravenshoe
Mission Beach
Tully 17 Hinchinbrook I.
Ingham
Mt. Spec N.P.
Magnetic I.

Normanton
George Town Mt. Surprise
25 Undara Lava Tubes
Undara Volcanic N.P.
Greenvale

Barrier

Croydon 26

Lawn Hill Gorge
27
Riversleigh

Townsville
16 15 Airlie Beach/Shute Harbour

Reef

Camooweal

Charters Towers
Ayr
Bowen
Whitsunday Group

Lake Moondarra
Mount Isa 28 29 Cloncurry
Julia Creek
Flinders Hwy
McKinlay Kynuna
Richmond Hughenden
Porcupine Gorge N.P.

Proserpine

Dajarra

Mackay 14
Sarina

Broad Sound

Middleton
Winton

Boulia

Muttaburra

Clermont

Tropic of Capricorn 30

Barcaldine 32
Capricorn Hwy
Emerald

Rock-hampton 13
Yeppoon
Great Keppel I.
Heron I.

Longreach 31
Dingo

Bedourie

Blackall

Gladstone

Birdsville 35

Windorah
Yaraka

Carnarvon National Park
Carnarvon Gorge 12
Taroom

Biloela

1770
Agnes Water
Bundaberg 11 Hervey Bay
Great Sandy National Park
Childers Fraser Island
9 10 Maryborough
Gympie 8
Noosa Heads
Maroochydore

Queensland

Augathella

Clifton Hills

South

Australia

The Dig Tree
34
Innamincka

Charleville 33
Quilpie
Mitchell
Roma Miles
Murgon
Nanango
Darling Downs
Dalby
Toowoomba 5
Warrego Hwy

Caloundra
Australia Zoo 7 **Sunshine Coast**
Caboolture
Moreton I.
Brisbane 1
Ipswich 3 Surfers Paradise 2
Gold Coast
Lamington N.P. 6 Murwillumbah
Lismore

Marree
Lyndhurst
Leigh Creek
Gammon Ranges N.P.
Lake Torrens
Lake Frome
FLINDERS RANGES
Flinders Ranges N.P.
Hawker
Cockburn

Sturt Desert
Sturt N.P.
Milparinka
Packsaddle
Wompah
Hungerford
Wanaaring

Thargomindah
Cunnamulla
Bollon
Barringun
Goodooga

St George
Moonie
Dirranbandi
Goondiwindi

Warwick 44 4
Stanthorpe

Ballina

Broken Hill
Euriowie
Wilcannia
Menindee

Mootwingee N.P.

Bourke
Brewarrina
Walgett
Collarenebri

Moree
Narrabri

Glen Innes
Tenterfield

Grafton

New South Wales

Cobar
Nyngan
Coolabah
Coonamble
Gilgandra

Tamworth
NEW ENGLAND RANGE

Coffs Harbour

Port Macquarie

QUEENSLAND

This is Australia's holiday state, the most visited destination after Sydney. Its major attractions include magnificent beaches, the Great Barrier Reef and unique rainforest areas

Queensland represents a sizeable chunk of Australia. At over 2,000 km (1,240 miles) from top to bottom and 1,450 km at its widest point, its 1.73 million sq. km (667,000 sq. mile) area could happily contain an assortment of European countries or a few hefty American states. It is unsurprising then that within its confines can be found such a range of terrain: unsullied tropical rainforest, broad expanses of dusty cattle-grazing country – indistinguishable from desert at times, the ragged peaks of the Great Dividing Range, rolling hills and, to cap it all, some great beaches. Plus, tethered along the eastern shoreline, just beyond a scattering of achingly beautiful desert islands, is one of the world's natural wonders, the Great Barrier Reef.

Sun seekers

Queensland's proud claim to be the Sunshine State has been readily accepted not just by overseas visitors but also by other Australians who have been flocking to the state for their holidays for years. When winter arrives many dwellers in the cooler southern states hanker for a spot on one of the endless golden beaches on Queensland's vast coastline. And once they've tasted paradise it's a short step to opt for the "sea change" – the exchange of the perceived drab urban existence for the Technicolor joys of perpetual summer. Some move at once, others wait for retirement. Either way, a pattern of migration has long been established. However, it has accelerated to the point where more than 200 people a day are now resettling in the sun.

Border crossing

Incomers can be found all along the coast but the clearest concrete (in every sense of the word) evidence is to be found in the developments to the north and south of Brisbane, on the Sunshine and Gold coasts. Queenslanders call the new arrivals "Mexicans" (people from south of the border). This

Map on opposite page

PRECEDING PAGES:
Hardy Reef.
BELOW:
soldiers preparing
for an Anzac Day
ceremony in
Anzac Square.

The riverside skyscrapers of Brisbane's central business district.

laconic approach is in part a response to those migrants who claim they can be identified by the relative ease with which they can spell their own names.

Brisbane

It's not just the coastal resorts that are burgeoning. The state capital, **Brisbane ❶** (or "Brissie" as it's known to the locals), is Australia's third-largest city and has been transformed over the past few years. Close to half of the state's 4 million people are to be found within its ambit, scattered over a series of low hills with the Brisbane River at its heart. Until recently there was much in the claim that it was "the world's biggest country town", but visitors today will find an urbane and cosmopolitan city, where café culture is sweeping the once musty streets, and reinvigorating the suburbs.

Like Sydney and Hobart, this easygoing city emerged from nightmarish beginnings. A convict settlement was established at nearby Moreton Bay in September 1824, when the first party of prisoners – the "hardest cases", convicted of further crimes since arriving in Australia – arrived from Sydney. Many of the convicts died, victims of the tyrannies of the guards, hunger, tropical disease and an indifference towards prolonging their own lives.

The first convict establishment was at Redcliffe, but due to a shortage of water the penal settlement moved up the river to the site of today's city centre. It was named after Sir Thomas Brisbane (then Governor of New South Wales). The present government and shopping precincts overlie the original convict settlement.

Today's central business district (CBD), in an area cupped by the river, is a mixture of stately colonial buildings and eye-catching modern architecture, with lungs provided by the City Botanic Gardens at one end and Roma Street Parkland at the other.

The visitor information centre (corner Albert and Queen streets; Mon–Thur 9am–5.30pm, Fri 9am–7pm, Sat 9am–5pm, Sun 9.30am–4.30pm; tel: 07-3006 6290) can help with the usual sackloads of brochures and then it's a matter of pounding the streets.

A quick overview of the city's history

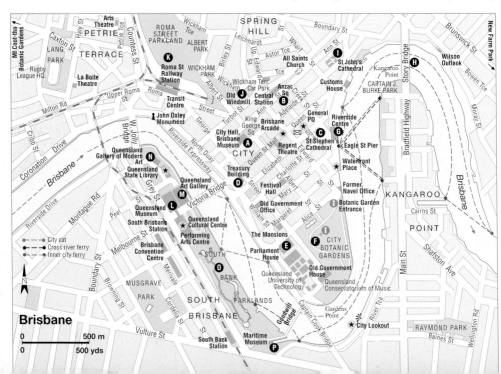

can be gleaned inside one of the more prominent landmarks. The **Brisbane Museum** (daily 10am–5pm; tel: 07-3403 8888 for City Hall; free) is housed in the appropriately overbearing pile that is **Brisbane City Hall** Ⓐ on King George Square. While you're there it's worth taking the elevator up to the viewing platform in the clocktower to have a look at the city. The square itself is home to a motley collection of sculptures and the earthed-in fountains and pools provide reminders of the long-term drought that is afflicting the country.

The historic centre

Anzac Square Ⓑ in Ann Street is a place for reflection. A perpetual flame commemorating the city's war dead is aligned directly between the clock towers of the Central Railway Station and the **General Post Office**. The latter, with its Corinthian colonnades, can be accessed through tranquil Post Office Square. Follow the narrow lane flanking the building to Elizabeth Street and **St Stephen's Cathedral** Ⓒ. Within this precinct you will find the gracefully weathered Pugin's Chapel, also known as old St Stephen's Church, completed in 1850 to a design by celebrated Victorian (the era, not the state) Gothic architect Augustus Welby Pugin. Beside it reposes the more substantial cathedral that replaced it as Brisbane's seat of Catholicism in 1874.

Returning to the GPO and heading west, the shopping hub of **Queen Street Mall** stretches towards the river. The foyer of the Regent Theatre is an unmissable paean to kitsch medievalism, which has survived virtually unchanged since 1929. Another slice of history remains in the refined Edwardian-style **Brisbane Arcade**, built in 1924 and now the city's oldest surviving shopping arcade.

Architectural historians acclaim the **Treasury Building** Ⓓ as the finest example of Italian renaissance style in the country. Walk south along George Street to **The Mansions**, a group of 1890 terraced houses with handsome red-brick facades and pale sandstone arcading, now occupied by classy shops and restaurants.

Further down George Street is Queensland's **Parliament House** Ⓔ

Maps:
Area 226
City 228

Inside City Hall is a museum "for and about the people of Brisbane". Free concerts are given here.

BELOW:
St Stephen's
Cathedral.

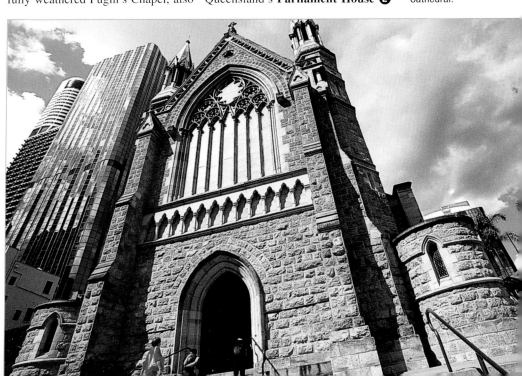

TIP

Eagle Street Pier is the departure point for paddlewheeler cruises on board the *Kooka-burra River Queens I* and *II*. Lunch cruises depart daily at noon; dinner cruises Mon–Sat 7pm, Sun 6.30pm (tel: 07-3221 1300; www.kooka burrariverqueens.com).

BELOW:
the Story Bridge at night from the Riverside Centre.

(Mon–Fri 9am–5pm, Sat–Sun 10am–2pm; www.parliament.qld.gov.au; free), begun in 1865. To the frustration of the architect, Charles Tiffin, who had won a nationwide contest with his design on French renaissance lines, it took 24 years of sporadic building to see the work completed. There are conducted tours when Parliament is not sitting. When it is in session (usually May–Oct) a gallery pass enables you to sit in on debates which, given the abrasive nature of the state's politics, can be riveting. Another Tiffin design, **Old Government House**, is now part of Queensland University of Technology and can be found down the road.

Dropping away to the left is the inviting green expanse of the **City Botanic Gardens F**. Originally a vegetable garden for the penal settlement, its 20 hectares (50 acres) of formal lawns and flora now provides respite from the city's bustle for hoards of office workers, students and tourists. Highlights include an avenue of weeping willows planted over 150 years ago, and a boardwalk through mangroves growing on the river bank.

The river

Leaving the gardens at the north-eastern corner, pass the Former Naval Offices, follow the riverside pathway and take in the views. Eagle Street Pier is the starting point for various sight-seeing cruises and then comes the acclaimed modernist pile that is Harry Seidler's **Riverside Centre G**. It houses, among other things, some fine eateries. A short distance further on lies the Customs House – now a function centre – opened in 1889 and crowned by a distinctive copper dome.

Looming ahead is Brisbane's most distinctive structure, the **Story Bridge H** joining Kangaroo Point with the CBD. Tram tracks were removed in 1959 but otherwise it stands unchanged since its opening on 6 July, 1940. At the time, it symbolised progress in an era of political and economic uncertainty and even now, it radiates pride and permanence. Test its sturdiness and your fortitude by booking a bridge climb (tel: 07-3514 6900; www.storybridgeadventures.com.au).

Walking across the bridge is rewarded with fine views back across

the city, but the easier way to **Kangaroo Point** is to hop on to one of the buzzing water ferries, the River Cat. Once across, there are plenty of adventure activities on offer at the old **Brisbane Naval Stores**, or you can just enjoy a pleasant stroll through the parkland where sculptures of varying degrees of accomplishment are lurking. Climb up the cliff steps for more, spectacular views and a glimpse of the historic **St Mary's Anglican Church**.

CBD completists, however, will defer such delights and follow the road north behind the Riverside Centre, turn left up Wharf Street and investigate **St John's Cathedral ❶** in Ann Street. Watch as stonemasons toil on Australia's last uncompleted Gothic-style cathedral. Work started in 1901, new bays were completed in 1968 and, although the facade is well-advanced, there are years of work ahead.

Just down Ann Street, **All Saints Church** (1862), is the oldest Anglican church in Brisbane. Cross into Wickham Terrace, nod in a knowing manner at Wickham Terrace Car Park, which won architect James Birrell awards for his innovative use of concrete, and amble along to the **Old Windmill ❷**. Built in 1829 and one of only two convict buildings surviving from the first wave of construction, it is small and unprepossessing. A design flaw meant it never worked as a windmill, so to grind corn for the settlement convicts were put to work turning a treadmill. It soon earned the soubriquet, the "tower of torture".

Continue along Wickham Terrace for 300 metres (330 yards) or so and take a path into **Roma Street Parkland ❸**. Here the Roma Street railway shunting yards have been converted into a splendidly diverse area of waterfalls, lakes, misty crannies of tropical vegetation, and cultivated floral displays that attract their own ecosystem of insects and birds.

The nearby old residential area of **Spring Hill** is an attractive maze of early houses, some of them old "Queenslanders" – distinctive shady wooden homes built on stilts to maximise the circulation of cooling air. Worth seeking out are the Spring Hill Baths in Torrington Street, the first public baths in the state and sufficiently atmospheric to feature heavily in the film *Swimming Upstream*.

South Bank

Across the river to the west of the CBD is one of Brisbane's most vibrant areas, the rapidly evolving South Bank with its impressive complex, the **Queensland Cultural Centre** and the sprawling pleasure gardens of South Bank Parklands. Cross over from the CBD by the Victoria Bridge and on the right can be found four key attractions. The **Queensland Museum**'s ❹ (daily 9.30am–5pm; tel: 07-3840 7555; www.southbank.qm.qld.gov.au; free) several million items include everything from *Muttaburrasaurus*, the most complete dinosaur skeleton found in Australia, to the tiny aeroplane Bert Hinkler flew from England to Australia in 1928. The museum also contains the **Dandiiri**

Map on page 228

Sculpture in front of Queensland Art Gallery.

BELOW: the artificial Streets Beach in South Bank Parklands.

Queensland Maritime Museum has a fine collection of vessels to investigate, including a Torres Strait pearling lugger and the Royal Australian Navy frigate, Diamantina. *The 1925 steam tug,* Forceful, *makes regular trips down the Brisbane River to Moreton Bay (tel: 07-3844 5361).*

RIGHT: a DJ in Fortitude Valley.

Maiwar Centre devoted to Aboriginal and Torres Strait Islander cultures.

At the **Queensland Art Gallery** (Mon–Fri 10am–5pm, Sat–Sun 9am–5pm; tel: 07-3840 7303; www.qag.qld.gov.au; free), core exhibitions are supplemented by touring art shows. A second, sister gallery, the **Queensland Gallery of Modern Art** (opening hours and details as before), or GoMA as it is known, opened in late 2006 and exhibits modern and contemporary works in a sparkling purpose-built structure.

The **State Library** holds important historic archives. To the left after crossing the bridge is a fine **Performing Arts Centre** and behind it the Convention and Exhibition Centre.

Sands in the city

The site of the 1988 World Expo, **South Bank Parklands**, has put many of the former Expo pavilions to innovative use. Attractions in the 16 hectares (40 acres) of riverside parkland include a diverse array of restaurants that take maximum advantage of the city's weather. Brisbane, once a culinary desert, now enjoys a reputation for chefs who take advantage of the state's natural resources: giant mud crabs, macadamia nuts, coral trout, oysters, mangoes and other delicacies.

South Bank even has a large swimming lagoon at Streets Beach, complete with imported sand.

Stick with the promenade by the river and at the end of the striking Goodwill Bridge, which takes pedestrian traffic across to the CBD, you will find the **Queensland Maritime Museum** (daily 9.30am–4.30pm; tel: 07-3844 5361; entrance fee) with its collection of all things nautical, including a handful of vessels moored by the bank.

Urban Brisbane, gives way quickly to nature. Just 8 km (5 miles) west of the centre, the **Mount Coot-tha Botanic Gardens** consist of over 57 hectares (141 acres) of ponds and parkland, where thousands of plant species thrive. Further west, rainforest-cloaked mountains shelter the city and offer a generous choice of picnic spots, bush walks and wilderness areas; all within half an hour's drive of the city centre.

Fortitude Valley

Many of Brisbane's suburbs clamour for your attention, none more brazenly than Fortitude Valley to the north of the CBD. Once Brisbane's premier commercial and retail hub – with some grand old buildings to match – it has been reborn as a cosmopolitan precinct of cool bars, funky eateries, pounding clubs, sweaty music venues and residential apartments. Street action radiates around the sidewalk cafés in **Brunswick Street Mall** though new bars have begun surfacing in some of the surrounding blocks. Either way, the precinct pumps at weekends when the bohemian and fashionable let their well-coiffeured hair down.

Family (MacLachlan St) claims a 33,000-watt sound system and runs at weekends; the Press Club on Brunswick Street sees itself as cooler; on Ann Street The Zoo is the live band venue; and the Wickham Hotel is the gay HQ, although many other venues cater to the market.

Chinatown Mall in Duncan Street provides a range of Asian gastronomical possibilities including Thai, Malaysian, Korean and Japanese...but not so much Chinese. Excellent Chinese restaurants do operate within Chinatown but, in general, Chinese restaurateurs and shopkeepers have gravitated to Sunnybank, a well-to-do fringe suburb with a large expatriate Chinese community.

To the east, downstream along the Brisbane River, you can reach the various beaches of **Moreton Bay** and the islands (some unpopulated) that make this a vast fishing and sailing paradise. Moreton Island features Mount Tempest, at 285 metres (935 ft), the world's highest stabilised coastal dune.

The Gold Coast

South of Brisbane, the 32-km (20-mile) stretch of coast from South Beach, just above Surfers Paradise, down to Coolangatta – bushland just two generations ago – is the fastest-growing tourist and residential area in Australia. The beaches, particularly **Burleigh Heads** set in a national park, are strikingly gorgeous, and from a heady apartment or hotel room on the umpteenth floor of a high-rise at **Surfers Paradise** ❷ the sight of sands stretching away to the north and south can be breathtaking. Down below, though, it's somewhat different. On the beach you can feel crowded in by towers thrown up with little evident architectural merit; height is the only yardstick and the current leader is the

Q1 building, completed in 2005. Its claim to capture "the aura of modernity evident in world-famous buildings by architects such as Renzo Piano and Frank Lloyd Wright" seems to be the height of folly. Which, incidentally, is 323 metres (1,060 ft).

Comparisons between Surfers Paradise and Ipanema, Miami and Cannes also seem wide of the mark. There's little sense of the style or class that such parallels might suggest. Stores are functional at best, tacky souvenir shops abound and patches of waste ground are purloined for haphazard collections of glorified fairground attractions, such as the Flycoaster or the Vomatron Sling Shot, both to be found on the corner of Gold Coast Highway and Cypress Avenue.

Night time is when the place really comes into its own, possibly because you can't see it so well. Party-goers take over the streets, casinos and restaurants; the clubs start buzzing and hedonism is given full reign. Unsurprisingly, the beaches can be pretty quiet in the morning and that's when families are out in force.

Maps:
City 228
Area 226

TIP

Descendants of the Kombumerri people, who once inhabited the area around Burleigh Heads, run various guided tours that explain the significance of rock formations and middens (Paradise Dreaming; tel: 07-5578 3044).

BELOW:
catching a wave at Burleigh Heads.

Away from Surfers, the super-rich are indulged at **South Beach** in the six-star (sic) resort, Palazzo Versace. Further south numbers of international visitors diminish and domestic tourists and hard-core surfies dominate.

Theme parks

The Gold Coast scores strongly with its family-oriented theme parks. Performing dolphins and a dynamic waterski show are the main pulls at **Sea World** (Seaworld Drive, The Spit; daily 10am–5.30pm; tel: 07-5588 2205; www.seaworld.com.au; entrance fee); **Dreamworld**, a large amusement park

The ultimate blonde at Movie World.

with a reassuringly Australian atmosphere, combines laid-back fun with adrenaline-pumping rides as well as a section devoted to the Wiggles (daily 10am–5pm; tel: 07-5588 1111; www.dreamworld.com.au; entrance fee); **Wet 'n' Wild** is a huge aquatic park with a mind-boggling variety of moist rides and adventures (daily May–Aug 10am–4pm, Sept–Apr 10am–5pm, 27 Dec–25 Jan until 9pm; tel: 07-5573 2255; www.wetnwild.com.au; entrance fee). But surpassing them all as a

BELOW: Wet 'n' Wild's Super 8 Aqua Racer.

tourism drawcard is **Warner Brothers' Movie World**, where startling rides such as Superman Adventure and the Wild West Falls Adventure are augmented by stunt shows and special-effects displays (daily 10am–5.30pm; tel: 07-5573 8485; www.movieworld.com.au; entrance fee).

Finally, the **Australian Outback Spectacular** packages up "a genuine Aussie Outback experience" which is, of course, nothing of the kind (Tues–Sat 7.30pm; tel: 07-5573 8289; entrance fee). None of these parks is cheap, but you can easily spend a day in each of them so arrive early and get value for money.

For an antidote to excess, the **Currumbin Wildlife Sanctuary** (28 Tomewin St, Currumbin; tel: 07-5534 1266; www.currumbin-sanctuary.org.au; entrance fee) offers every variety of indigenous fauna and the chance to act as a perch for flocks of lorikeets at feeding time.

The Darling Downs

Inland from Brisbane, the countryside is almost entirely ignored by tourists. Here, the tablelands give way to the Darling Downs, a vast area of beautiful, rolling plains and rich soil. **Ipswich ❸**, now an easy commute from Brisbane, is an old railway town whose history is well displayed at the Workshops Rail Museum (North Street; daily 9.30am–5pm; tel: 07-3432 5100; entrance fee), but there are plenty of other interesting features on its heritage trail.

The pleasant city of **Warwick ❹** serves as a livestock industry hub. The second-oldest town in Queensland retains a good deal of historical character, much of it linked to prosperity deriving from the discovery of gold nearby. There are some beautiful buildings but its most famous feature is the month-long Rose and Rodeo Festival, which attracts the country's best cowboys every October.

Hilly **Toowoomba ❺** is not just Queensland's largest inland conurba-

tion but also a garden city of some note. Situated on the rim of the Great Dividing Range, with the Darling Downs laid out before it, Toowoomba is colourful all year but sensational when spring flowers bloom.

Lamington National Park ❻, in the McPherson Ranges directly behind the Gold Coast, is vast and offers some fabulous bushwalking through dramatic rainforest. Occupying part of the rim of an ancient volcano, Lamington has a wide range of ferns and hundreds of species of orchid.

The Sunshine Coast

North of Brisbane there are more of the contrasts between the sublime and the kitsch that characterise the Gold Coast, but with the Sunshine Coast the balance is very different. The beaches are just glorious, but the resorts are less brash. Examples of kitsch, many inherent in tourist constructs, tend less towards theme parks and more to the peculiar Australian creation of "Big Things" *(see pages 78–9)*.

Follow the Bruce Highway out of Brisbane and as the suburbs are left behind look out for the unique geological formations of the **Glass House Mountains** looming up on your left, which dominate the landscape for several kilometres. Walks up them or drives between them are to be recommended. And it's the Glass House Mountains Road you'll want anyway for the **Australia Zoo** ❼ (daily 9am–4.30pm; tel: 07-5436 2000; www.australiazoo.com; entrance fee), near Beerwah. Entirely synonymous with "crocodile hunter" Steve Irwin, the organisation is now having to adjust to life after his death in 2006. The intention appears to be to continue virtually unchanged as both a tribute to Irwin and as a focus for the environmental work that he so assiduously promoted.

Back on the highway a cartoon Aussie boozer, the **Ettamogah Pub**, reacquaints us with the trashy, while **Aussie World** (daily 9am–5pm; tel: 07-5494 5444; www.aussieworld.com.au; entrance fee), next door, is really a glorified fairground. Stay inland and take the Nambour Tourist Drive. Six km (4 miles) south of Nambour, marvel at an enormous fibreglass pineapple. Buy

Map on page 226

Map on page 226

TIP

If you like a thrill you can explore the Sunshine Coast on a Harley Davidson, in a souped-up trike or in a vintage Tiger Moth. **Freedom Wheels** (tel: 07-5448 4200; mob: 0403 680 507; www.freedom wheels.com.au) offers excursions lasting from an hour to a full day, as well as extended tours combining the thrill of both Harley Davidson and Tiger Moth.

BELOW:
the Ettamogah Pub tilts in all directions.

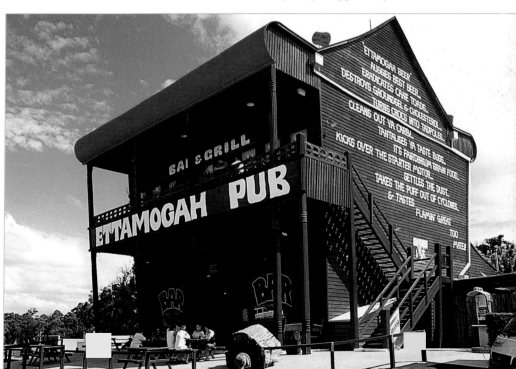

TIP

Noosa Visitor
Information Centre
(Hasting Street, Noosa
Heads; tel: 07-5447
4988) provides infor-
mation about accom-
modation as well as
events like the Noosa
Long Weekend in
June, the Celebration
of Food and Wine in
May and Noosa Jazz
Festival in September.

BELOW:
Noosa from the air.

local fruit, tour a pineapple farm, and learn about the pineapple industry in a theatrette inside the structure. This is but one of dozens of "Big Things" that litter, predominantly, eastern Australia. and, in its attention to detail, it's one of the less tacky. Really.

Coastal towns

All this can distract visitors from what is one of the most gorgeous stretches of Queensland's coastline. The action begins at **Caloundra**, where Bribie Island lies just across the Pumicestone Channel, but, more importantly, where the serious surf beaches begin. Caloun-dra is now a blossoming family resort. Further up, Mooloolaba is also seeing a spate of high-rise development. Beaches all along this stretch are gems. Try seeking out the unspoiled Mar-coola Beach at Coolum, a relaxed and up-market settlement.

Many visitors stick with the Sun-shine Highway all the way to **Noosa Heads** ❽. Noosa has been called the Cannes of Australia, a heady blend of beauty, sophistication and wealth. Nestling beside the usually tranquil

waters of Laguna Bay, Noosa for many people comes close to distilling the essence of the Australian Dream.

Today it is a collection of townships strung along the coast. The perfectly cylindrical waves that wrap around the points of Noosa's National Park rank among the world's finest, and surfers were the first to populate the area. Names of local beaches – Ti-tree Bay, Granite Beach, Fairy Pool, Devil's Kitchen – captured the enchantment of Noosa.

Publicity soon lured a different clique – the wealthy early retirees of Sydney, Melbourne and Adelaide. From the moment they saw Noosa Heads, these refugees from colder climes began buy-ing up large tracts of the best land. Today, the village of Noosa is lined with glitzy restaurants and boutiques, although it can't seem to shake off the raffish charm of old. Only a few metres from Hastings Street, Noosa's main business thoroughfare, swimmers still float lazily in a sea so clear you can see whiting and flathead scud across the bottom. Sheltering Noosa from the pre-vailing southeasterly winds is the head-

land, gateway to the 334-hectare (825-acre) Noosa National Park, an area of woodland and marshes on the south bank of the Noosa River.

Highway 1, the main coastal route from Brisbane to Cairns, stretches for 1,703 km (1,058 miles) and, although it is being continually improved, don't think of it as a "highway" in the American or European sense; much of it is just a good-quality undivided two-lane road. Distances between coastal centres can be vast and, by comparison with more populated areas in the south of Australia, rural Queensland remains something of a rough diamond. Still, small diversions from the route north will reveal magnificent uncrowded beaches, pristine rainforests, tropical islands (anything from uninhabited to home for overpriced resorts), authentic country pubs, splendid fishing and diving, mouth-watering local tucker and, obviously, more Big Things.

Travelling north

Highway 1 runs through **Gympie**, a one-time gold-mining town which hosts a week-long Gold Rush Festival every October, then to atmospheric **Maryborough** ➒ which has a railway museum and some fine old Victorian buildings. From nearby Hervey Bay, a barge will carry you and your vehicle over to **Fraser Island** ➓ *(see overleaf)*.

Childers, on the highway to the north, is a National Trust-listed town surrounded by rolling hills covered in sugar cane. The town encapsulates the region's early architecture. A turn-off to Woodgate Beach and Woodgate National Park, about 40 km (25 miles) down the side road, pays dividends.

The next major town north is **Bundaberg** ⓫ on the coast, 45 km (28 miles) from Highway 1. For millions of Australians "Bundy" is synonymous with rum and here, in the heart of sugar country, is the distillery that put the town on the map. An inexpensive tour provides an insight into the production process, a visit to a museum and a taste of the product (Whittred Street; Mon–Fri 10am–3pm, Sat–Sun 10am–2pm; tel: 07-4131 2999; www.bundabergrum.com.au; entrance fee). There is much else to see

Map on page 226

The Bundaberg Rum Distillery (Whittred Street, tel: 07-4131 2999) runs free tours on the hour Mon–Fri 9am–5pm, Sat 9am–3pm.

BELOW: a grand old Victorian "Queenslander" in Maryborough.

Fraser Island

Fraser is the world's largest sand island, and its ecology is unlike that of any other – a fact that put it on the UN's World Heritage list in 1992. Instead of barren desert, the entire interior is covered with a rich patchwork of forests whose muscular vegetation manages to survive on the nutrients in only the top 15 cm (6 inches) of soil.

The island's landscape changes every few hundred metres, from classic Aussie scrub and reed-filled swamps surrounded by 60-metre (200-ft) satinay trees, to expanses of lush rainforest, with plants so dense that they almost block out the sunlight. Amid the forests are some 40 freshwater lakes, including both "perched" (above sea level) and "window" lakes (at or below sea level). Some of them have water the colour of tea, while others are perfect blue with blinding white sands – **Lake Mackenzie**, for example, looks like a scene from the Caribbean.

This magnificent island has been reshaping itself again and again over thousands of years. Enormous sand dunes creep like silent yellow glaciers, consuming entire forests then leaving them behind, petrified and ghostly. But plant life always revives in their wake; there are more independent dune systems on Fraser, showing sand and vegetation in different stages of interaction, than anywhere else on earth.

The island won a permanent place in the white Australian psyche in the 1830s, when some shipwrecked British sailors were probably killed here by local Aborigines; the lone survivor, Eliza Fraser, spent many months living with local people before being "rescued" by an escaped convict. British settlers then used the island as a sort of natural prison camp for Aborigines. When fine wood was discovered soon after, the British herded the Aborigines off, killing many, it is said, by driving them into the sea.

For the past 30 years, Fraser Island has been at the centre of one of Australia's most vicious conservation disputes. In the 1970s came the battle to stop mining (the sands are rich in rutile and zircon); in the 1980s there was a long, and finally successful, campaign to ban logging on the island.

There are still arguments about how to manage the booming number of annual visitors – from 10,000 in the early 1970s to 350,000 today. There can be few other World Heritage sites so readily available to the public, and the island's four ranger stations are kept busy trying to manage the place in such a way that visitor pressures don't do more damage than logging did.

Fishermen head for **Waddy Point**, while nature-lovers seek out the soft sands of the deserted beaches (swimwear optional). The **Great Sandy National Park**, covering 840 sq. km (325 sq. miles), is a jigsaw of lakes, dunes, forest and beach, unlike anything else in the world. You can rent a canoe at Boreen Point or Elanda Point.

For a small fee, anyone can bring a four-wheel drive vehicle over from the mainland, bounce along the island's trails, rip up and down **Seventy-Five Mile Beach** on the east coast and camp in designated areas. (Note that a four-wheel drive is essential; tyre pressure should be reduced for beach travel, which should be attempted only at low tide. Oh, and count on getting "bogged" at least once during your visit.) There are plenty of organised tours for those daunted by off-road driving.

Non-tented sleeping options include Kingfisher Bay Resort, which is shrewdly conceived to repose so lightly amid scrub and natural lagoons as to be barely noticeable from the beach or from passing yachts. Even with 1,000 guests, it maintains an uncrowded sense of serenity and has become the accommodation of choice for affluent greenies. ❑

LEFT: driving on the beach on Fraser Island.

around town, including a selection of museums and a turtle hatchery. From Bundaberg, cruises and flights operate to **Lady Elliot Island**, 85 km (53 miles) away, on the southern end of the Great Barrier Reef (see page 257).

The twin coastal resorts of **Agnes Water** and **Town of 1770** have become popular fishing and boating centres as well as being the departure point for visits to Eurimbula and Deepwater national parks with their pristine coastal landscapes.

Pass up the next detour, to the surprisingly attractive industrial centre of **Gladstone**, unless you happen to be interested in the world's largest aluminium plant ($355 million to construct) or you are one of the fortunate heading out by ferry or helicopter to Heron Island (see page 257).

Carnarvon Gorge

The Dawson Highway, heading west from Gladstone, is the route to one of Queensland's most outstanding national parks at **Carnarvon Gorge** ⑫. This 30-km (16-mile) sandstone gorge has a profusion of palm trees,

cycads, ferns and mosses as well as fine examples of Aboriginal rock paintings. One contributor to Insight's Queensland guide tells of taking a trip to the far west of the state but only getting as far as Carnarvon Gorge because it was too beautiful to leave.

Rockhampon

Back on Highway 1, and north of the Tropic of Capricorn (marked by a roadside spire), **Rockhampton** ⑬ is the commercial heart of central Queensland. A colourful former mayor of "Rocky", Rex Pilbeam, had a baggynecked Brahman bull cast in concrete and erected at the northern entrance to the city (the Brahman is the breed favoured by cattlemen to the north), and a similar sculpture of a Hereford (the breed favoured by farmers in the south) at the southern end. When the beasts were made, Pilbeam – anticipating "playfulness" by local lads – had several spare sets of testicles placed in storage. Hooligans struck the Brahman almost immediately. They were dumbfounded when workmen bolted on a replacement appendage the same day.

Map on page 226

Rockhampton has stunningly wellpreserved old hotels and warehouses down by the river. You can pick up heritage trail leaflets from any visitor centre in town.

BELOW: Carnarvon Gorge has well maintained walking trails.

The Gem Fields

Fortune hunters should head 270 km (170 miles) inland from Rockhampton to **Emerald**, a centre for the farming of cotton, citrus fruits, grapes and fodder crops. It is also a gateway to the famous central Queensland gem fields, where scores of latter-day pioneers fossick for precious stones. There's nothing fancy about the gem fields; in tents, caravans and tumbledown tin shacks the miners have traded traditional comforts for the freedom and excitement of their own frontier, their rewards being sapphire, topaz, amethyst and jasper. These are the largest sapphire-producing fields in the world, and some fossickers have struck it rich in their first week. Most haven't. Various fossicking parks give visitors a chance to try their hand.

Townsville has some impressive Art Deco buildings.

BELOW: indolent island-hopping.
RIGHT: the water park on Townsville's Strand.

Rockhampton has a population of about 60,000, with modern pubs and office blocks interspersed among older buildings – and what buildings. The National Estate lists Quay Street in its entirety on its heritage register, and superb colonial homes are found in Agnes Street. Look out too for the excellent collection of Australian art at **Rockhampton Art Gallery** (62 Victoria Parade; Tues–Fri 10am–4pm, Sat–Sun 11am–4pm; tel: 07-4927 7129; free), and the outstanding Botanic Gardens. Pick up a heritage guide from the visitor information centre in the old Customs House on Quay Street.

The starting point for **Mackay 14**, 333 km (207 miles) to the north, is the large tourist information centre set in a replica of the Richmond Sugar Mill, the first in the area. Fanned by tropical breezes and surrounded by a rustling sea of sugar cane, Mackay is a pleasant city of wide streets and elegant old hotels. A stroll through the centre reveals an assortment of Victorian buildings interspersed with several displaying the sleek lines of 1930s art deco. North of the centre there are some fine beaches and the shiny new Marina Village.

Airlie Beach 15 and neighbouring **Shute Harbour**, 135 km (84 miles) to the north, act as the gateway to the Whitsunday Islands *(see page 258)*. There are fine eateries and accommodation from backpackers hostels to four-star resorts. This is the place to find a berth on one of the many island-hopping yachts.

Townsville

Eyebrows used to be raised at the idea of visiting **Townsville 16**, but these days the state's second-biggest city is a relaxed and graceful place with plenty to attract the casual visitor. This is due in part to two destructive cyclones that ripped the foreshore apart in 1997 and 1998, prompting a A$29-million restoration along The Strand. The resultant 2.2-km (1½-mile) stretch of white sand, swaying palms, water parks, play areas and casual restaurants redefined Townsville as a tropical resort city of considerable appeal. Townsville's residents congregate here to sunbake, barbecue, browse and bird-watch.

Flinders Street, the main thoroughfare, has notable late 19th-century architecture, including many of the city's 58 National Trust-listed buildings. At its northern end the **Museum of Tropical Queensland** (daily 9.30am–5pm; tel: 07-4726 0600; www.mtq.qld.gov.au; entrance fee), its atrium dominated by a huge cross-section of an 18th-century naval frigate, provides a good child-friendly introduction to the history, peoples and geology of the area.

Next door, **Reef HQ** (daily 9.30am–5pm; tel: 07-4750 0800; www.reefhq.com.au; entrance fee) has a huge coral-reef aquarium as its centrepiece.

Overlooking everything is the craggy Castle Hill. In a typical display of civic pride, an early resident deduced that if Castle Hill were just a few metres higher, it could officially be called a mountain. He began carting soil up the hill and dumping it on top. The town never got its mountain, but the project was in itself a kind of monument to obscure endeavour everywhere. Climb, or more likely drive, to the top for a different perspective of the city and look out to sea where **Magnetic Island** can be seen anchored offshore.

It's only a 20-minute ferry ride from Townsville but Magnetic Island feels worlds away. Hire a Mini Moke and hop from one bay to another, follow one of the many trails into the forest, maybe stumble over an old wartime lookout post. There are plenty of places to stay at all budgets.

Townsville's relatively green hinterland strip is bordered by rocky mountain ranges that eventually give way to the inland savannah. About 10 km (6 miles) north of Ingham, as you reach the top of a steep hill, you are suddenly treated to one of the most breathtaking sights of the whole coastal trip. Be ready to stop and admire the view of **Hinchinbrook Island** across the narrow mangrove-lined channel. *(see page 260).*

Gorges and beaches

From Cardwell northwards the highway sticks pretty close to the coast, offering plenty of diversions to peaceful little spots for picnics, fishing and water sports. A trip up **Tully Gorge**

Map on page 226

Paragliding at sunset on Magnetic Island.

BELOW:
Alma Bay on Magnetic Island.

Gold Towns

Head west from Townsville to gold country and the vistas along the Flinders Highway rapidly turn from lush green to the parched semi-arid savannah of Australian myth. **Charters Towers**, 135 km (84 miles) inland, owes its heyday to an Aboriginal boy who found gold in 1872, while on an expedition with prospector Hugh Mossman. A tiny town boomed. Of the splendid architecture that resulted, the restored Stock Exchange in the historic Royal Arcade is one of the city's 19th-century highlights. Gold is still produced locally, with companies reworking old sites. One is in **Ravenswood**, 38 km (24 miles) south of the Flinders Highway, where among deserted shacks and derelict equipment two ancient pubs still function and there's a small museum.

The Esplanade at Cairns.

BELOW: Kuranda scenic railway.

(with a pause to wonder at the Big Gumboot in Tully itself) offers dramatic scenery and the opportunity to take in some whitewater rafting.

Mission Beach ⓱, an 18-km (11-mile) detour off the highway, is a relaxed, low-rise destination. The beach is perfect, the restaurants are good and there's always the option of a quick trip across to Dunk Island if you crave a spell on a westward facing strand for a change.

This is the beginning of the area devastated by Cyclone Larry in March 2006 but the brunt of the damage was inflicted on **Innisfail**, 49 km (30 miles) to the north. Even before that, locals' claims that this would be the next happening place in the region aroused some scepticism, but it's a nice enough town and its art deco architecture and Chinese temple are worth a look.

Gateway to paradise

And so on to **Cairns** ⓲, pulsating visitor centre of tropical north Queensland. Until the 1980s, this was a sleepy provincial backwater wallowing in a swamp. Not terribly much had changed since it was founded just over a century before, on some not very picturesque mangrove flats, to service the gold and tin fields further inland. Then the tourism boom hit. There's still a core of old-style tropical charm in the languid pubs and distinctively Queensland-style porches, but today Cairns, with a population of 124,000, has a modern international airport, bustling shopping malls, and a vast variety of restaurants. Almost any sporting activity – diving trips to the Reef, bungy jumping, whitewater rafting, tandem parachuting, hiking the Atherton Tableland – can be arranged from its hotels and travel agencies.

The focus of Cairns remains the **Esplanade**, a great place for people-watching. The waterfront is lined by high-rise hotels and backpacker accommodation, and there's always an array of picnicking locals beneath the Moreton Bay figs and palms. Its centrepiece is a huge landscaped swimming lagoon, classic red and yellow-garbed lifeguards in attendance, its lawns carpeted with minimally clad sunbathers, and with a full-time picnic atmosphere.

A seven-day leisure retail shopping centre, the Pier Marketplace is still struggling to impose itself, but weekend markets, and a marina for the region's marlin fishing fleet and pleasure boats give verve to the waterfront.

The **Cairns Historical Museum** (corner Lake and Shields streets; Mon–Sat 10am–4pm; tel: 07-4051 5582; www.cairnsmuseum.org.au; entrance fee) has exhibits on the more rough-and-ready past of the area, while the elegant **Regional Art Gallery** (corner Abbot and Shields streets; Mon–Sat 10am–5pm, Sun 1–5pm; tel: 07-4046 4800; www.cairnsregionalgallery.com.au; entrance fee) has local artists' work on display as well as visiting exhibitions.

But the real attractions of Cairns lie beyond the town limits; either out to sea for the **Great Barrier Reef** (see page 256) or inland where the lush, cool plateau of the **Atherton Tableland** deserves extensive exploration. Like the rest of the region, it was opened up by prospectors in the 1870s. It is now a major dairy farm area, with a range of B&Bs and farm-stay accommodation with faintly chi-chi names (see panel on next page).

However, for many tourists there is only time for a day-trip package. This means taking the pleasant 64-km (44-mile) return trip from Cairns to the village of **Kuranda**; one way by train, with vintage coaches climbing tortuously through spectacular scenery, tunnels and past impressive waterfalls; the other half of the journey by Skyrail, a cable car that almost brushes the rainforest tree tops. In consequence Kuranda is one big shopping opportunity with a craft market (Wed–Fri and Sun), galleries, didgeridoo outlets and a host of restaurants and cafés. Beyond that, the station is charming and there's a butterfly sanctuary and two aviaries.

The far north

North of Cairns, the Cook Highway runs through one of the most classically gorgeous parts of Australia. Strings of uncrowded, palm-fringed beaches (including those of the beachside suburbs of Trinity, Kewarra and exclusive Palm Cove) look as Hawaii must have done before developers arrived. Having said that, developers are moving in en masse and for Palm Cove in particular it's worth checking in advance on the likely impact that the latest building works may have on your holiday haven.

The Great Barrier Reef comes within 15 km (9 miles) of the shoreline, and from various ports diving boats head out to the sand cays and coral reefs. One of the most popular starting points lies some 80 km (50 miles) north of Cairns. **Port Douglas** , like most of the coastal settlements, was founded after a gold rush in the 1870s, when the Gugu-Yalangi Aborigines were forced from their land. For a time it was more important than Cairns, but it died when the gold ran out. For the next century, Port Douglas boasted little more than two pubs and a pie shop. Today, the pubs and pie shop are still there, but they've been joined by glitzy new resorts like the Sheraton Mirage, which continues to attract

Map on page 226

TIP

Drop in at the century-old Cairns Yacht Club to meet barnacled locals while washing down prawns with beer. Hemmed in on all sides by high-rises, the club has been assured that its two-storey weatherboard headquarters will remain unmolested by developers – for now. Its veranda is a fine place to sip a beer.

BELOW: the upmarket Sheraton Mirage Resort in Port Douglas.

TIP

Heading north from Port Douglas, you pass cane farms and exotic fruit plantations to Miallo, famous as the place where actress Diane Cilento established her 500-seat Karnak Playhouse (tel: 07-4098 8111; www.karnakplayhouse .com.au) with her late husband, the playwright Anthony Shaffer. It's worth a look just for the setting.

RIGHT: Daintree River cruise boats.

world leaders and household names from the entertainment industry. There are some fine restaurants and chic boutiques on Macrossan Street, even nightly cane-toad races in one of the bars, but the palm-fringed village atmosphere that could still be enjoyed in the 1990s has long gone.

However, Four Mile Beach is among the region's most beautiful, while every morning dozens of boats head out from the marina for day trips on the Reef. Just offshore are the immensely popular Low Isles, and a string of excellent snorkelling spots is only an hour away *(see page 261)*. Passages are available on everything from tiny yachts catering for only a dozen passengers right up to the massive Quicksilver catamarans that can shuttle hundreds of people at a time.

Rainforest

Returning to the highway, just north of the Port Douglas turn-off is Mossman and the road to **Mossman Gorge**. A 3-km (2-mile) walking circuit runs past mountain streams and lush, dripping foliage. Slightly further north, past rich

sugar-cane country, the village of **Daintree** is the starting point for river trips. Just after dawn, the bird life is extraordinary (parrots, ospreys, great white herons). Later in the day, you'll see saltwater crocodiles lounging in prehistoric bliss.

Cross the Daintree River by ferry (6am–midnight) and drive for 36 km (23 miles) to **Cape Tribulation** ⑳. It's an incongruous name for one of Australia's most serene corners, but then Captain Cook was in a poor mood after his ship, the *Endeavour*, ran onto a reef in 1770. "This was where our troubles began," he noted in his log, and his subsequent naming of Mount Misery, Cape Sorrow and the like indicate a man who hadn't perked up.

Troubles returned in the early 1980s, when the Queensland government decided to push a road through the rainforest to improve access for tourists and remote Aboriginal communities. Hundreds of "greenies" descended on "Cape Trib" to throw themselves in front of the bulldozers. Ironically, this focused so much attention on the area that Cape Trib became

The Atherton Tableland

The hill country inland from Cairns offers respite from the tropical heat of the coast and with its sprinkling of attractive townships, inviting lakes, picturesque waterfalls and towering forests, it is deserving of proper investigation over a few days. With its elevatiion and associated rainfall, this fertile plateau at the northern end of the Great Dividing Range is prime dairy country. In the early days of settlement great areas of forest were cleared of valuable timber, leaving today's rolling pastureland.

It was the Chinese, originally drawn by tin and gold mining in the region, who led the way in agriculture and evidence of their presence is manifest in **Atherton**, the main town in the area. The 1903 Hou Wang Temple (Herberton Road; daily 10am–4pm; www.houwang .org.au) was the focal point of Chinatown.

Yungaburra, a few kilometres to the east, is dotted with heritage buildings and has a famed 500-year-old curtain fig tree, as well as a good spot to see platypus – by the bridge. **Malanda** is worth a look and **Millaa Millaa** is a pretty place to join a "waterfalls circuit" taking in four examples, with Millaa Millaa Falls perhaps the highlight.

Millstream Falls are the widest in the country and can be found outside **Ravenshoe** if you're not detained by the town's stream train.

a household name in Australia, and is now firmly on the tourist map. The road was eventually completed, but meanwhile the outcry prompted a United Nations World Heritage listing for the Daintree area, which is now part of a national park.

Today, the isolated, otherworldly atmosphere of Cape Trib appears to have barely changed. There is a scattered community with a few grocery stores and, except for a couple of hours in the middle of the day, when tour buses arrive from Cairns, there are usually few people on the beaches. Meanwhile, nestled in rainforest-covered hills are a cluster of new high-quality "eco-lodges". Although far fewer people come here than go to Port Douglas, there are coral reefs close to the shore, a very unusual phenomenon.

The contentious coastal road to Cooktown is now a reality – although barely. You need a four-wheel-drive vehicle to bounce through tunnels of virgin forest, plough across shallow rivers and up 45-degree inclines. Although you glimpse the sea rarely, the views and sense of isolation are worth it. The road is open all year with extreme caution – but watch the tide at Bloomfield River unless you'd like to contribute to the crocodiles' diet. Otherwise, in a conventional vehicle, you can make the journey from Cairns on the inland Cape York Development Road, which was only fully sealed in 2006. Call in at the Lion's Den pub, just off the highway at Helenvale – it's one of the oldest in north Queensland, with the original wooden bar, piano and a vast array of pickled snakes.

Cooktown

At the end of the line is **Cooktown ㉑**, a place that has always had a Wild West reputation as an isolated tropical refuge which you could escape to when nowhere else would have you. It is located on the mangrove estuary where Captain Cook spent seven weeks repairing the *Endeavour*. The local Gugu-Yalangi people were friendly, and it was the most significant contact between Aborigines and Europeans to that date, allowing Sir Joseph Banks to make more detailed studies of local wildlife than he had

Map on page 226

Cooktown marks Captain Cook's enforced stay with a statue and a festival in June re-enacting his arrival in 1770.

BELOW: one of a clutch of old hotels in Cooktown.

The World's Oldest Rainforest

The rainforest stretching from Cairns through to Mossman, Cape Tribulation and Cooktown is at least 100 million years old (compared with the Amazon's paltry 10 million) and a vital component in Queensland's tourist industry.

All the earth's rainforests are thought to have begun around present-day Melbourne some 120 million years ago, when Australia was a part of the great continent of Gondwanaland. When Oceania broke away, 50 million years ago, the drier land began to replace tropical conditions. The rainforests that once covered Australia retreated to less than 1 percent of the continent; logging since European settlement has reduced that by more than half

North Queensland's rainforest – now protected as part of the Wet Tropics World Heritage area and a patchwork of national parks – has the highest diversity of local endemic species in the world. Fully one-fifth of Australia's bird species, a quarter of its reptiles, a third of its marsupials, a third of its frogs and two-fifths of its plants are here in a tiny fraction of the Australian landmass.

Conservationists waged battles with the timber industry and the Queensland government throughout the 1980s. Ultimately, the "greenies" triumphed over the bulldozers and today most North Queenslanders accept the importance of the wet zones. With its capacity to attract visitors, it doesn't do the local economy any harm either.

As for the seething tangle of vines and ferns itself, it has always deployed a wide array of defences against intruders. First off, there's the taipan snake, whose bite is 300 times more toxic than a cobra's. Some other native snakes are nearly as dangerous. However, deaths by snakebite are rarer than deaths by lightning strike.

The local (non-venomous) python is hardly worth a mention, although the largest recorded scrub python, found in the Tully area, measured 8.5 metres (28 ft) long. The saltwater crocodiles that lurk in the remoter rivers here only grow up to about 6 metres (20 ft) – but that's still enough to grab the unwary by the legs and spoil their day with the "death-roll" they use to disable and eventually kill their victims.

If you see a tree goanna – a giant speckled lizard with enormous claws – don't startle it: it may confuse you with a tree, climb up your leg and disembowel you. Why it would attack a tree in the first place isn't entirely clear. A kick from a frightened cassowary – a 2-metre (6-ft) high flightless bird with a bony crown – can tear open your ribcage so, if you meet one in the bush, give it plenty of room.

The barking or bird-eating spider, with a leg-span up to 15 cm (6 inches), may be found in areas bordering on rainforest and can deal you a nasty bite.

Dangerous plants

Even some plants are armed and dangerous. The heart-shaped leaves of the Gympie vine, for example, injects silica spines into any skin unlucky enough to brush it. It's "like a blow-torch being applied to your flesh," apparently

Now while this gives infinite material for the droll musings of Bill Bryson, the chances of actually encountering any of these horrors is minimal. The whole point of declaring a World Heritage Area is conservation so access for visitors is tightly controlled and any sightseeing is likely to be from well-defined paths or boardwalks, where the route is marked by interpretive boards. The tramp of tourists will have frightened off wildlife long ago.

You can take it a step further by visiting the **Daintree Discovery Centre** where the whole rainforest experience is packed into a fenced compound and enjoyed from either the raised boardwalk on the forest floor or an ariel walkway. ❑

LEFT: following a rainforest trail.

been allowed at Botany Bay. (Banks was introduced to a creature they called the kangaru, although it was actually a wallaby.)

When an Irish prospector struck gold at Palmer River in 1873, Cooktown became one of Australia's busiest ports, with 94 pubs (many little more than shacks) and 35,000 miners working on the claims. There's a mural in the Middle Pub depicting those days when miners blew thousands of pounds' worth of gold dust in a single night, chased women such as the legendary Palmer Kate, passed out on drugged whisky and then woke up penniless in the swamps.

Cooktown still thrives on the memories, and it has maintained a languid charm. Poking between palm trees on the wide main street are many late 19th-century buildings, including the three surviving watering holes (to avoid confusion, known as the Top, Middle and Bottom pubs).

The **James Cook Historical Museum** (corner of Helen and Furneaux streets; daily 9.30am–4pm; tel: 07-4069 5386; entrance fee) is one of the best in Australia and is located in the former convent of St. Mary; exhibits include the original anchor of the *Endeavour*, retrieved from the Reef. The Cooktown cemetery, just north of town, is full of its own stories of the old pioneers.

The last frontier

Beyond Cooktown sprawls the **Cape York Peninsula**, a popular destination for four-wheel-drive expeditions in the dry season. The red-dust road runs from one lonely bush pub to the next, past anthills, forests full of screaming cockatoos and vast sandstone bluffs rich in Aboriginal rock art. It can take several days to get to Australia's northernmost point, the tip of Cape York, and experience of serious off-roading is essential. Even then, it's best to go in convoy with at least one other vehicle.

The tiny township of **Laura** ㉒ at the southern tip of the Lakefield National Park (an expanse of marshland, lagoons, mangrove swamps and rainforest that is rich in flora and fauna) is one of the last accessible spots without a four-wheel-drive vehicel as long as you stay outside the park. It's worth the trip to see some fabulous Aboriginal rock art. Split Rock can be explored on your own and other sites can be enjoyed in the company of Aboriginal guides booked through the Quinkan Regional Cultural Centre (tel: 07-4060 3457).

Heading north, the journey passes the bauxite-mining town of **Weipa** and the Jardine River Crossing (which has a ferry). At the end of the line, at the Torres Strait, there are campgrounds, and 6 km (4 miles) to the northeast, at Punsand Bay, is the closest population to the continent's northernmost tip.

Boats run from Red Island Point (Bamaga) to Thursday Island, administrative centre of the Torres Strait Islands, many of which were named by Captain Bligh when he passed through on an open longboat after the *Bounty* mutiny. From June to September, the ferry also operates from Punsand Bay.

Map on page 226

TIP

Lizard Island, 27 km (19 miles) off the coast and about 100 km (60 miles) north of Cooktown, is a dry, rocky, mountainous island with superb beaches for swimming and pristine reef which makes for great snorkelling and diving. Charter flights operate from Cairns and Cooktown.

BELOW: a guide explains Aboriginal rock art at Laura.

Traditional Torres Strait Island dances are performed by pupils from the Thursday Island High School during festivals and for special events.

Thursday Island **㉓** (pop. 3,500) was once one of the world's great pearling stations. Although there are no tourist traps nor beaches of note, "T.I." is a pleasant enough place to lay up after the rigours of the road. Its cosmopolitan mix of inhabitants are a carefree and friendly crowd who like to party. There are four old pubs, the more modern Jardine Motel, and a Japanese cemetery from pearling days.

A special way to take a close look at the far north Queensland coastline and the Torres Straits, is a five-day return voyage from Cairns on the MV *Trinity Bay*, a working cargo ship supplying the remote Cape York communities all the way up to Thursday Island. It's air conditioned and comfortable, and dress and conversation are informal. (Tel: 7 4035 1234; www.seaswift.com.au)

The Queensland Outback

Most of Queensland's key tourist destinations and by far the majority of the population are to be found on the coast, and yet much that is most fascinating about the place is to be found inland. It's impossible to get a real handle on the state until you've headed off into the Outback. There are countless ways to do it, but with the idea of describing a circuit (which hardly anyone would actually do unless they had considerable time) let's look at a journey moving inland from Cairns. This is the starting point of the Savannah Way, which eventually winds up in Broome in northern Western Australia. The land is vast and there may be hundreds of kilometres between destinations so keep a keen eye on the fuel gauge.

Chillagoe **㉔**, 215 km (134 miles) west of Cairns, is not actually on the Savannah Way but worth a visit. It's a town built on mining with plenty of detritus from the industry to provide character. Limestone bluffs around the town add drama to the harsh terrain, while underground spectacular caves in the **Chillagoe-Mungana National Park** can be explored on your own or with guided tours.

More subterranean wonders are to be found at the **Undara Lava Tubes** **㉕** a few kilometres south of the Savannah Way, one of the best examples of lava-tube formation anywhere on the planet. These are created when lava follows the line of river beds, the lava surface cools but the molten material within flows out, leaving a tube behind. Some of the tubes are 15–20 metres (50–65 ft) in diameter. Full resort accommodation is offered in beautifully restored vintage rail carriages relocated there for the purpose. It's also a Savannah Guide Station.

The Savannah Way continues on through **Georgetown** where there are a few significant buildings and the **Terrestrial Centre** in Low Street (Apr–Sept daily 9am–5pm, Oct–Mar Mon–Fri 8.30am–4.30pm; tel: 07-4062 1485; entrance fee) which highlights the importance of minerals to the area. It's another 148 km (92 miles) to **Croydon** **㉖**, a friendly township with a well-preserved timber pub and an interesting historic precinct. From here there's an old railway service, the

Gulflander, which runs through to **Normanton**, just a short distance from the **Gulf of Carpentaria**.

Towards the border with the Northern Territory, where the terrain is becoming drier and less hospitable, **Lawn Hill Gorge** ㉗ provides a green oasis and stakes a claim to be one of the most spectacularly beautiful locations in the state. Not many get out this far but, for those who do, there are kayaks to paddle down between sheer red sandstone cliffs, and easy hikes through the surrounding Boodjamulla National Park. A half-hour drive away is the World Heritage-listed Riversleigh Fossils site.

It's mines, all mines

Track south down dirt roads to **Mount Isa** ㉘ and discover the full significance of the finds at the **Riversleigh Fossil Display & Interpretive Centre** attached to the Outback at Isa complex (tel: 07-1300 659 660; www.outbackatisa .com.au; entrance fee). Mount Isa is a mining city truly in the middle of nowhere. A rich lode of lead, silver, copper and zinc was discovered here in 1923, and a tiny tent settlement rapidly developed into Australia's largest company town, dominated by the looming presence of the mine and its tailings. Surface tours are available or you can take a two-hour underground tour of the ersatz Hard Times Mine, through the Outback at Isa operation.

The municipal boundaries of "The Isa" extend for 41,000 sq. km (15,830 sq. miles) – an area the size of Switzerland. Away from the mines, people relax at the artificial Lake Moondarra or socialise in any of the numerous licensed clubs, which welcome visitors. In August, Mount Isa hosts a three-day rodeo, the largest and richest in Australia.

The School of Distance Education (formerly the School of the Air), first established in Cloncurry, now operates from here, providing children on remote properties with direct radio and internet contact with a teacher. Its premises adjoin the Kalkadoon High School on Abel Smith Parade and can be toured (Abel Smith Parade; tours Mon–Fri 9am and 10am in term time; tel: 07-4744 9100; entrance fee).

Map on page 226

TIP

For a scenic overview of Mount Isa, head for the **City Lookout** (a short drive off Hilary Street), preferably at dusk when the mine lights up. You can see the whole city sprawled out across a flat valley, backed by low hills, and all dominated by the mine.

BELOW: bareback riding in the Mount Isa rodeo.

The Flying Doctor Service was started in Cloncurry in 1928 by the Revd John Flynn to provide "a mantle of safety" over the Outback. Its first plane was supplied by the Queensland and Northern Territory Aerial Service (QANTAS).

BELOW: the Ernest Henry Mine.

Cloncurry ㉙ is also a mining town but in this case the main employer, the vast open-cut **Ernest Henry Mine**, is a bus ride away from the centre. Conducted tours are comprehensive and informative (tel: 07-4742 1361; entrance fee). Among the attractions in town, John Flynn Place (corner Daintree and King streets; Mon–Fri 8.30am–4.30pm all year, Sat–Sun 9am–3pm May–Sept; tel: 07-4742 4125; entrance fee) contains a museum devoted to the Royal Flying Doctor Service and its founder.

Waltzing in Winton

The Matilda Highway heads south-east through **McKinlay**, home of the pub used in the *Crocodile Dundee* films and now rechristened the Walkabout Creek Hotel.

Some 241 km (150 miles) further on sits **Winton ㉚**, a town full of character and home to the Waltzing Matilda Centre (50 Elderslie Street; daily 8.30am–5pm; tel: 07-4657 1466; www.matildacentre.com.au; entrance fee), which celebrates the song, its composer "Banjo" Paterson and all aspects

of Outback life. This is also dinosaur country *(see panel below)*.

From Winton the Matilda Highway continues to **Longreach ㉛** where two major attractions await. A local manufacturer helped develop the **Australian Stockman's Hall of Fame** (Landsborough Highway; daily 9am–5pm; tel: 07-4658 2166; www.outbackheritage.com .au; entrance fee) as a fascinating tribute to the cattle drovers, shearers, jackaroos and entrepreneurs who opened up Australia to European settlement. It's an interesting building too.

Longreach was also where Qantas set up its first operational base in 1922, and its original hangar, with the old sign still on it, has become part of the multimillion-dollar **Qantas Founders' Outback Museum** (Landsborough Highway; daily 9am–5pm; tel: 07-4658 3737; www.qfom.com.au; entrance fee), which displays a retired Qantas Boeing 747 jumbo jet (still in flying condition), replicas of its early fleet of biplanes, and a comprehensive record of the national airline's growth.

Barcaldine ㉜ to the east is notable for a collection of fabulous vintage

Dinosaur District

Detour south from Winton to **Lark Quarry Dinosaur Trackways** (tours at 10am, noon, 2pm; tel: 07-4657 1812; www.dinosaurtrackways.com.au; entrance fee), where petrified footprints denote a dinosaur encounter millions of years ago.

The theme is maintained in two towns to the north: **Richmond** has Kronosaurus Korner (91–93 Goldring Street; daily 8.30am–4.45pm; tel: 07-4741 3429; www.kronosauruskorner.com.au; entrance fee), a marine fossil museum, and **Hughenden** features the Flinders Discovery Centre (37 Gray Street; daily 9am–5pm; tel: 07-4741 1021; entrance fee), with a replica of a dinosaur skeleton found locally. A concrete dinosaur in the middle of town presses the point home. Nearby is the majestic **Porcupine Gorge** with its 120-metre (400-ft) high walls.

hotels and pubs, and as home to the **Workers' Heritage Centre** (Ash Street; Mon–Sat 9am–5pm, Sun 10am–5pm; tel: 07-4651 2422; www.australianworkersheritagecentre.com.au; entrance fee), where a varied collection of heritage structures houses displays commemorating the role played by workers in the social and political development of Australia.

The Matilda Highway continues south all the way to **Charleville** ㉝. The usual assortment of historic buildings are worth a look but the points of difference are the **Cosmos Centre** (Qantas Drive; Apr–Oct daily 10am–6pm, Nov–Mar 10am–5pm; tel: 07-4654 7771; www.cosmoscentre.com; entrance fee), an observatory and museum which makes the most of clear night skies to host astral viewing sessions; and the **Steiger Gun**, a bizarre device designed in 1902 to fire hot air into the sky in order to create rain.

Miles ahead

Heading east now through **Roma** and then **Miles** ㉞, with its charming **Historical Village** (Murilla Street; daily 8am–5pm; tel: 07-4627 1492; entrance fee), would eventually lead back to the east coast. But that would be to ignore two of Queensland's iconic sites. **The Dig Tree**, right on the border with South Australia, is the location of the famous base camp of the Burke and Wills expedition where the two explorers just missed a rendezvous with the men who could have rescued them from starvation, exhaustion and death *(see page 215)*.

Finally, there is **Birdsville** ㉟. This isolated far western settlement only has a population of 100, but each September that grows by five or six thousand for the Birdsville Races, when about 300 light aircraft cram the airport, with their pilots and passengers camped under the wings. The 1884 Birdsville Hotel is one of Australia's legendary watering holes. West of here are only the sand dunes of the Simpson Desert, an endless wasteland reaching towards Alice Springs. A huge sandhill called **Big Red**, 36 km (22 miles) to the west, marks the beginning of the famous Birdsville Track and is a popular spot for sunset parties. ❑

Café proprietor in Wyandra, 100 km (60 miles) south of Charleville.

BELOW:
the Australian Stockman's Hall of Fame.

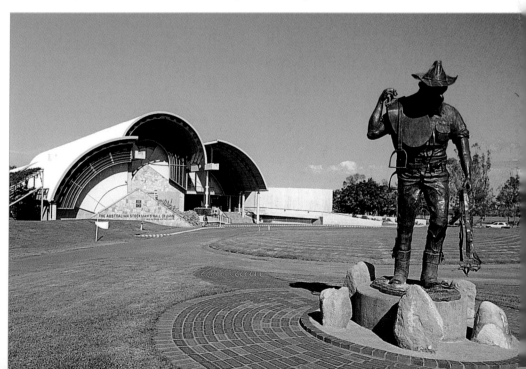

Map on page 226

RESTAURANTS & BARS

Restaurants

Brisbane

E'cco
100 Boundary Sreet (corner Adelaide Street East)
Tel: 07-3831 8344
www.eccobistro.com
Open: L Tues–Fri, D Tues–Sat. $$$$
One of Brisbane's most-awarded bistros. Philip Johnson stresses simplicity. Essentially, his food relies on fresh ingredients and unfussy preparation.

The Green Papaya
898 Stanley Street,
East Brisbane
Tel: 07-3217 3599
www.greenpapaya.com.au
Open: L Fri, D Tues–Sat. $$
Chef Lien Yeomans offers classic and contemporary Vietnamese cuisine. BYO.

Michael's Riverside Restaurant
123 Eagle Street, Riverside Centre. Tel: 07-3832 5522
Open: L Sun–Fri, D daily. $$$
Beautifully positioned, overlooking two reaches of the Brisbane River, Michael's offers impeccable food and flawless service. The menu has a lingering resonance of old-style fine dining.

Gold Coast

Absynthe
Q1 complex, 9 Hamilton Avenue, Surfers Paradise
Tel: 07-5504 6466
www.absynthe.com.au
Open: L Mon–Fri, D Mon–Sat. $$$$
Celebrated French chef Meyjitte Boughenout lends a dash of Gallic élan to the 80-storey Q1 building. He is famous for juxtaposing the most unlikely of flavours to create taste sensations that are as beguiling as they are unexpected. His Golden Egg, for example, combines an egg mousse bisque with soya jelly and edible gold leaf.

The Broadbeach Tavern
Old Burleigh Road, corner of Charles Avenue, Broadbeach
Tel: 07-5538 4111
www.broadbeachtavern.com.au
Open: L & D Mon–Sat. $
Good food from an extensive and surprisingly inexpensive menu. However, most people come here for the live entertainment, on seven nights a week.

Ristorante Fellini
Marina Mirage, Seaworld Drive, Main Beach
Tel: 07-5531 0300
Open: L & D daily. $$
Brothers Carlo and Tony Percuoco dish up superb Italian cuisine within their elegant, award-winning restaurant.

Noosa

Berardo's On The Beach
On the beach, Noosa
Tel: 07-5448 0888
www.berardos.com.au
Open: L & D daily. $$
A delightful location for acclaimed chef Bruno Loubet's version of Noosa cuisine. The menu offers such delights as sugar-cured salmon with creamed lime mayonnaise.

Bundaberg

Rendezvous Restaurant
220 Bourbong Street
Tel: 07-4153 1747
Open: D Mon–Sat. $$
Well-regarded and long-established restaurant serving modern Australian food.

Spinnaker Bar and Bistro
1a Quay Street
Tel: 07-4152 8033
Open: L Tues–Fri, D Tues–Sat. $$
A Bundaberg institution and arguably the smartest restaurant in town. Emphasis is on seafood dishes such as Moreton Bay bugs with lemon risotto.

Rockhampton

The Allenstown Hotel
8 Upper Dawson Road,
Tel: 07-4922 1853
Open: L & D daily. $$
Sophisticated dishes such as double-roasted duck and spiced pork belly with blue swimmer-crab salad. Pub food in the bars.

Mackay

Church on Palmer Street
15a Palmer Street,
North Mackay
Tel: 07-4944 1477
Open: D Mon–Sat. $$
Stylish restaurant specialising in steak and seafood. Modern Australian dishes with a French influence.

Latitude 21
Clarion Hotel, Mackay Marina
Tel: 07-4955 9400
Open: L & D daily. $$

LEFT: chefs at work in Brisbane.

Intelligent blending of Asian, African and European food served alfresco. Views over the marina.

Townsville

C Bar Café
Gregory Street Headland, The Strand
Tel: 07-4724 0333
Open: L & D daily. **$$**
Attractively situated on an artificial headland, right on the beachfront, offering open-air dining with great sea views. Café menu by day, and more up-market dining by night.

Bistro One
30–34 Palmer Street
Tel: 07-4771 6333
Open: B, L & D daily. **$$**
Chic modern local fare with a Mediterranean influence.

Cairns

The Red Ochre Grill
43 Shields Street
Tel: 07-4051 0100
www.redochregrill.com.au
Open: L Mon–Fri, D daily. **$$$**
Renowned for innovative handling of bush tucker and native species. Consider smoked wild spice-crusted kangaroo, crocodile wonton and emu paté.

Palm Cove

Sebel Reef House Restaurant
99 Williams Esplanade
Tel: 07-4055 3633
www.reefhouse.com.au
Open: L & D daily. **$$$**
Renowned chef Philip Mitchell's fare exhibits deceptive simplicity. By day, he offers mezze plates; by night, complex cosmopolitan feasts.

Port Douglas

Flames of the Forest
Bus picks up diners from 6pm.
Tel: 07-4098 2755
www.flamesoftheforest.com.au
Open: D Thur–Sat. **$$$**
Dine in the rainforest and listen to Aboriginal stories. Guests are picked up from town and transported to the Mowbray Valley where flames light a path to a clearing and candles flicker beside a stream. More candles illuminate tables, immaculately set. It's Lord of the Rings meets Alice in Wonderland – a magical experience.

Nautilus Restaurant
17 Murphy Street
Tel: 07-4099 5330
www.nautilus-restaurant.com.au
Open: D daily. **$$$**
Everybody in Port Douglas goes to the Nautilus at least once. All the celebs have been – along with thousands of others who soak up the tropical ambience while troughing.

Bars

Brisbane

Cru Wine Bar
22 James Street, Fortitude Valley
Tel: 07-3252 2400
www.crubar.com
Open: L & D daily. **$$**
Part bottle shop, part bar and part café, Cru serves great wine and tapas through most of the day.

Gold Coast

Charlie's 24-Hour Café, Restaurant & Bar,
Cavill Avenue,

Surfers Paradise
Tel: 07-5538 5285
www.charlies24hours.com.au
Open: 24 hours a day. **$**
Everyone ends up here, it's said, while in Surfers Paradise. Well-located and affordable, Charlie's hasn't closed its doors since 1976.

Cairns

Beethoven Café
105 Grafton Street
Tel: 07-4051 0292
Open: L Mon–Fri. **$**
Bread of all descriptions with interesting fillings and, the clincher, spectacularly good cakes.

Croydon

Club Hotel
Corner Sircon and Brown streets
Tel: 07-4745 6184.
Open: D daily. **$**
Standard Outback pub menu is enriched by won-

deful old wooden building and friendly locals.

Mount Isa

Keen's Bar and Grill
Mount Isa Irish Club,
1 Nineteenth Avenue
Tel: 07-4743 2577
Open: B, L & D daily. **$$**
Mount Isa is flush with social and working social clubs (visitors welcome). The Irish is one of the biggest. Keen's offers an all-day breakfast in the coffee shop and a lunch buffet in the Members' Bar.

RIGHT: quenching a Queensland thirst.

RAINFOREST

Tropical or temperate, rainforest is one of Queensland's defining characteristics, as well as a key tourist attraction

High rainfall – at least 2 metres (6½ ft) – is a prerequisite for rainforest, and then it's generally a matter of latitude and proximity to the ocean which defines it as tropical or temperate. Queensland is big enough to have both.

Rainforests are nature *in extremis*. Two-thirds of all the earth's plant and animal species can be found within them, and in north Queensland the highest diversity of local endemic species in the world is present. It is the last bastion for some of them, while others are still being discovered, particularly in the upper regions under the canopy, an area only recently appreciated for the richness of its various flora and fauna.

It is estimated that the tropical rainforest stretching from just north of Cairns to Cape Tribulation and on to Cooktown is in the region of 110 million years old, and constitutes the last remnant of the forest that used to cover all of Australia and, before that, Gondwanaland. Now protected as an element of the Wet Tropics World Heritage Area, it is a key attraction for monied tourists, and so the economic rationale that has seen the destruction of forests elsewhere in Australia and round the world would probably now protect it, irrespective of the heritage listing.

ABOVE: Queensland's rainforests are home to several species of tree frog, from the nursery frog at only 2.5cm (1 inch) in length to the giant tree frog, which can reach up to 140cm (5½ inches).

BELOW: one of the best places to spot the elusive platypus is in the rivers and streams of the Atherton Tableland where the climate is temperate. They are nocturnal animals but are often active in early morning and at dusk. Try looking beside the bridge in Yungaburra.

ABOVE: the flightless cassowary can still be found in small pockets of dense rainforest; if you do happen to spot one, give it a very wide berth, as they are known to lash out with their sharp claws.

LEFT: the frill-necked lizard may be seen in trees and sometimes on the ground and searching for food: insects, termites and centipedes. The ruff usually lies flat against its neck and shoulders and only fans out when the lizard is frightened (and its jaws will be agape for extra effect). Despite this show of bravado, the frill-necked lizard is not a poisonous or dangerous creature, and is most likely to run away when confronted, first on four legs, and then on two as it gathers speed, earning it the nickname "bicycle lizard".

THE DAINTREE

Some of the most easily accessible rainforest, and therefore most visited, is in the Daintree National Park. There's a well-worn route from Cairns or Port Douglas up to Cape Tribulation, and every tour bus or expedition will stop at least once for a walk in the woods. In several places there are short boardwalk circuits from handy parking spots, and the way is marked by a series of interpretive boards. This makes it easy for the visitor to explore and also helps in managing the forest by keeping tourists away from more pristine areas.

The complete packaged rainforest experience can be enjoyed at the Daintree Discovery Centre, a short distance north of the Daintree ferry. Boardwalks wend along the forest floor, and a steel walkway through the canopy allows an entirely different perspective on life as the birds see it. Audio guides are available and there are more of the ubiquitous interpretive boards. The cassowaries here seem used to visitors.

LEFT: brolgas (Grus rubicundus), a type of crane, can be found in most of northern and eastern Australia, especially where there is marshland or shallow water, which they favour as a nesting site. They are best known for their elegant and elaborate dance, which involves leaping, shaking, strutting and loud calling.

RIGHT: tropical rainforest tends to have so much rain that bushfires rarely affect it. However, in more temperate areas woodland can be susceptible, particularly in the dry season, and restrictions are introduced on campfires, barbecues and the use of some machinery in times of high to extreme fire danger.

RIGHT: smaller types of marsupial, such as this pademelon, spend their time scurrying around the forest floor, mostly at night. Being the smallest in the kangaroo family, they tend to be susceptible to introduced predators such as cats and foxes, and prefer to graze close to thick forest or undergrowth into which they can flee if necessary. Their numbers have also been reduced by rabbits, as well as by wallabies and kangaroos, which sometimes compete for the same grazing areas.

THE GREAT BARRIER REEF AND THE ISLANDS

The Reef is not only Queensland's major tourist attraction, it is one of the natural wonders of the world. It is the largest coral reef on earth, one of the most accessible and happens to have a selection of stunning islands close by

BELOW:
a fringing reef,
Lady Elliot Island.

The world's largest coral reef in fact consists of over 2,500 separate, inter-connected reefs stretching over 2,300 km (1,430 miles) from just above the tip of the Cape York Peninsula in the north to just north of Bundaberg in the south.

In the nomination that saw the Reef given a World Heritage listing, one of the supporting arguments was that "Biologically the Great Barrier Reef supports the most diverse ecosystem known to man. Its enormous diversity is thought to reflect the maturity of an ecosystem which has evolved over millions of years..."

At the heart of that ecosystem is the polyp, a tiny animal consisting of little more than a mouth and surrounding tentacles to feed it – plus a limestone carapace into which it withdraws during the day. It is the skeletal remains of these that form the basis of the reef. Individual polyps are linked by body tissue, thereby sharing the colony's food, but the main nutrient for a photosynthetic coral's food is algae cells within its tissue called zooxanthellae, which convert the sun's energy into nutrients.

Major threat

Over millions of years this has created what is effectively the largest living entity in the world. This structure is fragile, however, and it only takes small environmental changes to disrupt a delicate balance that has pertained for millennia. Coral bleaching is the major threat. If the water temperature rises by just a degree or two over a sustained period, the corals expel their zooxanthellae, lose their capacity for photosynthesis and become colourless. The process is not irreversible but if the water does not cool within a month or so the coral will die.

Severe damage was caused by extended hot spells in 1997–8 and again in 2002, and most marine scientists believe that global warming not only exists but had a direct bearing on these incidents. The Australian Gov-

Map on page 258

ernment has said it is committed to reducing annual greenhouse gas emissions, although it has not signed up to the Kyoto Protocol.

There are other dangers too. Human traffic can cause significant damage to coral, whether through chains and anchors from boats, or by snorkellers and divers who may brush against polyps and kill or damage them. The Reef is also under pressure from the effects of poor water quality, which is often caused by soil and fertiliser runoff from the shore, not helped by the wash from periodic cyclones.

The Great Barrier Reef Marine Park was established in the 1970s to help protect this magnificent resource and the Great Barrier Reef Marine Park Authority monitors the effects of tourism, fishing and research.

The islands

While only a few are literally coral islands, the 20 or so resort islands inside the Great Barrier Reef Marine Park offer many attractions. Lodging varies from five-star resorts to backpacker hostels and campgrounds.

Some islands are dry, barren and windy; others are lush and covered with rainforest.

The South

Lady Elliot Island ❶ A quiet and beautiful 42-hectare (103-acre) coral cay at the bottom of the Reef, with bungalow accommodation and some permanent tents. It is 80 km (50 miles) from Bundaberg and reached by air. Its coral setting ensures easy access to good diving and snorkelling.

Lady Musgrave Island ❷ A tiny uninhabited cay available only for day trippers or campers (with a National Parks permit). Access is by boat from Bundaberg. It offers diving and snorkelling within a brilliant blue lagoon.

Heron Island ❸ Only 1 km (⅔ mile) long, this is the Reef's most famous coral cay and, according to aficionados, number one for diving (along with Lizard at the northern fringe of the Reef). The Reef is certainly at its most accessible: where the beach ends, the coral begins, with its abundant marine life. There is easy access from Gladstone by plane or by fast catamaran but visitors

Not all of the Reef's islands are made of coral. In fact, nearly all of the popular resort islands are continental in nature – the tips of offshore mountain ranges. The true coral cays of the real Reef are more numerous but tend to be smaller and more fragile.

BELOW:
Heron Island.

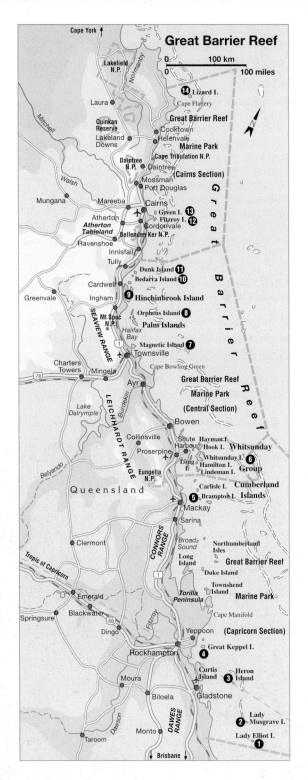

Great Barrier Reef

0 — 100 km
0 — 100 miles

Cape York

Lakefield N.P.
Normanby
Laura
Quinkan Reserve
Lakeland Downs
Mungana
Walsh
Mitchell
Mareeba
Atherton
Atherton Tableland
Ravenshoe
Innisfail
Tully
Cardwell
Ingham
Greenvale
SEAVIEW RANGE
Mt Spec N.P.
Halifax Bay
Charters Towers
Mingela
Ayr
Lake Dalrymple
Belyando
Clermont
Tropic of Capricorn
Emerald
Blackwater
Springsure
Dingo
Moura
Biloela
Taroom
Monto

14 Lizard I.
Cape Flattery
Great Barrier Reef
Cooktown
Helenvale
Marine Park
Cape Tribulation N.P.
Daintree N.P.
Daintree
(Cairns Section)
Mossman
Port Douglas
Cairns
13 Green I.
12 Fitzroy I.
Gordonvale
Bellenden Ker N.P.
11 Dunk Island
10 Bedarra Island
9 Hinchinbrook Island
8 Orpheus Island
Palm Islands
7 Magnetic Island
Townsville
Cape Bowling Green
Great Barrier Reef
Marine Park
(Central Section)
Bowen
Collinsville
Shute Harbour
Hayman I.
Hook I.
Whitsunday
Proserpine
Whitsunday I.
6 Hamilton I.
Long I.
Lindeman I.
Group
Eungella N.P.
Carlisle I.
Cumberland
5 Brampton I.
Islands
Mackay
Sarina
Broad Sound
Northumberland Isles
Long Island
Great Barrier Reef
Duke Island
Townshend Island
Marine Park
Torilla Peninsula
Cape Manifold
Yeppoon
(Capricorn Section)
4 Great Keppel I.
Rockhampton
Curtis Island
3 Heron Island
Gladstone
2 Lady Musgrave I.
1 Lady Elliot I.

Queensland
LEICHHARDT RANGE
CONNORS RANGE
DAWES RANGE
Fitzroy
Dawson
Burdekin
Great Barrier Reef

↑ Cape York
↓ Brisbane

must stay at the Heron Island Resort. **Great Keppel Island 4** The resort used to sell itself on the slogan "Get wrecked on Great Keppel", but it was re-branded with a "family" image and these days anyone can enjoy it. There are excellent white sandy beaches, long hiking trails, views of the mainland, and plenty of social activities. Great Keppel is not directly on the Reef (although there is coral in most of the bays), so short cruises run out for divers. Access is by air from Rockhampton or by sea from Rosslyn Bay. **Brampton Island 5** A mountainous island 32 km (20 miles) from Mackay, Brampton has one resort set in a tropical garden. Sailing, water sports, good beaches and rainforest walks are the attractions. Access is from Mackay and Shute Harbour but not for day-trippers.

The Whitsundays 6

Lindeman Island At the southern end of the archipelago, Lindeman's resort is Australia's first Club Med, and beyond the buildings it has retained the beauty of its natural setting. There is tennis, swimming and fishing, and 20

km (12 miles) of bushwalking trails through 500 hectares (1,230 acres) of national park. Access is from Mackay, Hamilton Island and Proserpine.

Long Island Three very different resorts co-exist, and it is only a short boat trip from Shute Harbour. Club Crocodile is for all ages, and particularly popular with the young. Peppers Palm Bay is ideal for a back-to-nature holiday with lovely beaches, clear water and coral, and solitude. The self-catering Whitsunday Wilderness Lodge provides camping cabins.

Hamilton Island The largest, most aggressively marketed Whitsunday resort has a high-rise hotel, a floating marina, an airstrip with direct flights to major cities and a full sports complex. With a pseudo-South Seas main street once described as "Daiquiri Disneyland", Hamilton Island is not the place for a quiet island sojourn.

Whitsunday Island The largest of the group, covering 109 sq. km (42 sq. miles), Whitsunday has no resort, but the fabulous Whitehaven Beach – a great option for campers (with permits).

South Molle Island A self-contained resort on a large, hilly island. It is popular with families, and diving, swimming, sailing, golf, fishing and shopping are all offered. Travel is from Shute Harbour or Hamilton Island.

Daydream Island A popular family resort with all the necessities for a good time at a reasonable all-inclusive tariff. Great beaches and a wide range of activities including memorable crazy golf, and all just 15 minutes from Shute Harbour or Hamilton Island.

Hook Island The second-largest island in the Whitsundays provides budget camping and cabins as well as services for visiting yachts. There is an excellent underwater observatory here and Aboriginal cave painting at Nara Inlet.

Hayman Island An exclusive five-star resort set in a coral-trimmed lagoon, close to the outer Reef and a favourite with honeymooners. Fine beaches and fishing are complemented by resort facilities, on which no expense has been spared. It goes without saying that dining on Hayman is gourmet and silver service. Access is from Hamilton Island, Proserpine, Shute Harbour and Townsville. No riff-raff.

Map on opposite page

Electric buggies are the popular way for tourists to get around Hamilton Island.

LEFT: a key venue for Hamilton Island's thriving wedding industry. **BELOW:** diving and snorkelling are the islands' principal business.

Map on page 258

Kayaks for hire on the islands.

The Centre to the North

Magnetic Island ❼ A large (5,000-hectare/12,400-acre) island and a national park, this pleasant, populated (2,300) haven is almost an outer suburb of mainland Townsville. A wide range of accommodation and facilities for day-trippers. Plenty of walks in the rainforest, or up to the 500-metre (1,640-ft) Mount Cook. Horseshoe Bay has a koala and wildlife park. Bikes, scooters and Mini Mokes can be rented.

Orpheus Island ❽ In the Palm group northeast of Townsville and very close to the outer Reef. An exclusive resort hidden among the trees has good accommodation and entertainment. Seaplane access from Townsville.

Hinchinbrook Island ❾ Accessible from Cardwell by boat, the jagged peaks, golden beaches and luxuriant rainforests of Hinchinbrook National Park can be fully explored by experienced hikers, and at least sampled by the less adventurous. There's one small resort, otherwise it's camping. The island's signature east coast trail has limits on walker numbers so bookings

need to be made months ahead. **Bedarra Island ❿** A small fragment of the Family Islands, with an exclusive resort set in rich rainforest. For a fabulous fee, guests stay in bungalows that make them feel as if they are alone on the island. Pure white beaches and tranquil coves. Go via Dunk Island.

Dunk Island ⓫ Where the recluse E.J. Banfield lived for 26 years at the turn of the 20th century, writing his *Confessions of a Beachcomber*. A rainforested national park with a large resort nestled in one corner and a camping ground alongside it. Access is from Townsville, Cairns and Mission Beach.

Fitzroy Island ⓬ Totally surrounded by coral reef, a great place for diving and fishing. There is a budget resort. Access is from Cairns.

Green Island ⓭ A tiny coral cay just off Cairns with a good underwater observatory. Mostly for day-trippers.

Lizard Island ⓮ The most northerly island and home, in season, to the marlin boats. Lizard allows access directly from the beach to the Reef and has stunning diving. Fly from Cairns. ❏

RESTAURANTS & BARS

Restaurants

Hamilton Island

The Beach House
Hamilton Island Resort
Tel: 07-4946 9999
Open: L & D daily. $$$
www.hamiltonisland.com.au
Everything from wood-fired pizza to fine dining in an atmosphere of laid-back luxury

Mariners Seafood Restaurant
Marina Village
Tel: 07-4946 8628
Open: D Mon–Sat. $$$
The Coral Reef Platter is the ultimate choice at this haven for seafood lovers. Harbour views.

Daydream Island

Mermaids Restaurant
Daydream Island Resort
Tel: 07-4948 8488
Open: L daily. $
Offers café-style fare such as "tropical" open grilled sandwiches and salt and pepper calamari.

Dunk Island

Beachcomber
Dunk Island Resort
Tel: 07-4068 8199
www.dunk-island.com
Open: B & D daily. $$$
The island's main resort restaurant, specialising in tropical cuisine and buffets.

Magnetic Island

Barefoot Art Food Wine
5 Pacific Drive, Horseshoe Bay
Tel: 07-4758 1170
Open: L & D Thur–Mon. $$
There's a bit of everything here. The wine list has more than 100 entries, and the food is Mod Oz with Asian touches.

Geckos
Maggie's Beach House, Pacific Drive, Horseshoe Bay
Tel: 07-4778 5144
Open: L & D daily. $
Café and bar with a beach location ideally placed for admiring spectacular sunsets. It is geared towards budget travellers.

Green Island

Emerald Restaurant
Green Island Resort
Tel: 07-4031 3300
Open: L & D daily. $$$
This restaurant leaves no stone unturned in its effort to present fabulously luxurious cuisine. The service is flawless, the setting superb.

PRICE CATEGORIES

Prices are for a three-course meal per person with house wine:
$ = A$60 and under
$$ = A$60–A$100
$$$ = A$100 and over

Visiting the Reef

The easiest way to visit the Reef is not to stay on an offshore island but to take a day trip from **Cairns** or **Port Douglas**. Every morning dozens of fully equipped diveboats and catamarans head out from the two centres to various pre-selected sites. You can also take Reef trips from **Cape Tribulation**. Trips from some of the island resorts or coastal towns further south, such as Townsville, tend to be less commercialised and sophisticated and, indeed, less frenetic.

About an hour later, wherever you leave from, you'll be moored by the coral. Because the water is so shallow, snorkelling is perfectly satisfactory for seeing the marine life (in fact, many people prefer it to scuba diving; even so, most boats offer tanks for experienced divers and "resort dives" for people who have never dived before). Above the waves, the turquoise void might be broken only by a sand cay crowded with sea birds, but as soon as you poke your mask underwater, the world erupts. It's almost sensory overload: there are vast forests of staghorn coral, whose tips glow purple like electric Christmas-tree lights; brilliant blue clumps of mushroom coral; layers of pink plate coral; bulbous green brain coral.

Tropical fish with exotic names slip about as if showing off their fluorescent patterns: painted flute-mouth, long-finned batfish, crimson squirrelfish, hump-headed Maori wrasse, cornflower sgt-major.

A venomous killer

Thrown into the mix are scarlet starfish and black sea cucumbers (phallic objects that you could pick up and squeeze, squirting water out of their ends). You definitely don't pick up the sleek conus textile shells – they shoot darts into anything that touches them, each with enough venom to kill 300 people. There are 21 darts in each shell and so, as one captain notes, "if they don't get you the first time, they'll get another try".

Almost all Reef trips follow a similar format. There's a morning dive or snorkel, followed by a buffet lunch; then, assuming you haven't eaten too much or had too much free beer, an afternoon dive. There should be a marine biologist on board to explain the Reef's ecology. Before you book, ask how many passengers the boat takes: they vary from several hundred on the Quicksilver fleet of catamarans to fewer than a dozen on smaller craft.

RIGHT: life on the largest coral reef on earth.

Regardless of your reason for visiting the Great Barrier Reef, weather will play an important part in your enjoyment of its scenic attractions. From late April through to October it's at its best, the clear skies and moderate breezes offering perfect conditions for coral viewing, diving, swimming, fishing and sunning. In November the first signs of the approaching "Wet" appear: variable winds, increasing cloud and showers. By January it rains at least once most days. And when the winds are up and the waters are stirred, visibility in and under the water diminishes. Furthermore, in rough seas excursion boats have fewer places to anchor and may be restricted to areas which have been over-visited and where, consequently, the coral has been damaged. Pick your time carefully.

In general, the further out the boat heads, the more pristine the diving (the Low Isles, for example, near Port Douglas, have suffered). But don't be conned by hype about the "Outer Reef"; as the edge of the continental shelf it may be the "real" Reef, but it looks exactly the same as other parts. Even in the winter months, the water here is never cold, but it is worth paying a couple of dollars extra to hire a wet suit anyway; most people find it hard not to go on snorkelling for hours in this extraordinary environment.

For an entirely different perspective, try sightseeing from a seaplane, light plane or helicopter.❏

THE WORLD'S LARGEST LIVING THING

The Great Barrier Reef is top of the list on many tourists' itineraries, but its fragility means it's important to follow the park's guidelines

The Great Barrier Reef may be the largest mass of living organisms on earth, but it is also extremely fragile. Rising sea temperatures have added to the already considerable risk posed by tourism, pollution and natural enemies like the crown-of-thorns starfish, and protecting the reef has become more important than ever. The reef's astonishingly complex and diverse ecosystem will disappear forever if precautions aren't taken now.

The appeal of the Great Barrier Reef to visitors is undeniable and tourism is big business, but should you decide to visit the park there are a number of things you can do to limit your environmental impact. Scuba diving is one of the main tourist draws to the reef but it can take an average of 25 years for the coral to recover from accidental knocks and scrapes from inexperienced divers. The main way to avoid causing damage to the reef is to take scuba lessons before you go and then to make sure you choose a recognised dive operator to take you to the site. Smaller groups of divers are also preferable as they are less likely to cause disturbance to the coral and its inhabitants.

If you plan on fishing make sure you use the Marine Park Authority's zoning maps, which will let you know of any restrictions in the area, and return any unwanted or undersized fish to the water as quickly as possible. Use official campsites and take all litter, including fishing lines, away with you.

BELOW: The shovel-nosed lobster (also called the slipper lobster) is one of the thousands of species of crustacea that inhabit the Reef. It uses its "shovel" to plough up the sea-bed in search of food.

ABOVE: Not all corals use the sun's rays to provide their food. Some, such as this tubastrea, or sun coral, live in the shade in strong currents, and feed by filtering food from the water.

BELOW: For a moray eel, a coral cave is a convenient hiding place from which to ambush prey. The moray grows to 2 metres (6½ ft) in length and is a ferocious predator, with excellent camouflage, sharp teeth and a savage bite. The moray prays on fish, molluscs and crustaceans, but also sometimes on other moray eels.

THE REEF'S GREATEST ENEMY?

For years, the most famous threat to the Reef was thought to be the crown-of-thorns starfish (above), an ugly creature that clamps on to coral and effectively spits its stomach out. Its digestive juices dissolve the polyps and leave great expanses of coral bleached and dead. The crown-of-thorns is poisonous to other fish and almost indestructible: it can regenerate to full size from a single leg and a small piece of intestine. Altogether, it's an unpleasant creature but at least it was once relatively rare. With only a few around, it was easy to ignore its depradations on the reef. But in the early 1960s the pattern changed. Instead of a few crown-of-thorns starfish, suddenly there were millions. Green Island was the first to see the plague, in 1962. From there it spread southwards, reaching the reefs around Bowen by 1988. Surveys between 1985 and 1988 established that about 31 percent of the reefs examined had been affected. Even after millions of dollars' worth of research, no one knows what caused the proliferation of the starfish. Furthermore, no economic way to get rid of the pest has presented itself.

Recently, however, marine biologists have decided to let the crown-of-thorns run its destructive course. The latest wisdom posits that it isn't a genuine threat at all but a natural, if poorly understood, part of the reef's life-cycle.

ABOVE: The Cod Hole is a spot on the outer reef 40 minutes by boat from Lizard Island. A popular scuba-diving spot, it is noted for its concentration of very large fish, such as this giant potato cod, which probably weighs 60 kg (130 lb).

RIGHT: There are some 300 species of stony (hard) coral, of which Acropora or staghorn corals are the most common. They appear in many forms and many colours, including the beautiful lilac version here. They are particularly susceptible to bleaching.

RIGHT: The clown fish has a symbiotic relationship with the sea anemone. The anemone is an animal, closely related to coral, consisting of one large polyp. Anemones live attached to rocks in shallow waters and small ones feed on particles and plankton that drift by. Although the anemone has stinging tentacles, the clown fish is immune to their charge and uses them to hide from predators. In return, it scares off the butterfly fish, which would otherwise eat the anemone. Any damage to the reef therefore has an impact not only on the anemones, but also on the clown fish.

LEFT: The sea fan belongs to a group known as gorgonians (other members include sea whips and sea feathers). They all have a flexible spine of horn-like material, with the polyps living on the outside. The sea fan feeds on plankton. The intricate colony that makes up a sea fan can grow to 3 metres (10 ft) in diameter and can be very brightly coloured. Unlike other oganisms on the reef, sea fans do not attach themselves to rocks or coral but to sand or mud on the ocean floor.

NORTHERN TERRITORY

Fewer than one in 100 Australians live in the vast Northern Territory, an untamed region with a climate, a landscape and a history all its own

The Northern Territory, or just "NT", is Australia in epic mode. Things here are larger than life – the sky, the distances, people's dreams and visions, the earth itself. An area of 1.35 million sq. km (521,240 sq. miles) – more than double the size of France, yet inhabited by just 203,000 people – provides plenty of room to move.

The locals are a breed apart: tough, laconic, beholden to no one. Like the inhabitants of any inhospitable environment, they possess friendliness by the bucketful, a truly egalitarian spirit, and a wicked sense of humour.

Many urban Australians visiting NT's Outback feel as though they have entered foreign land. They find a kind of detachment, a floating feeling of insubstantiality inspired by the uncomfortable knowledge that nothing human beings do here can ever touch the soul or the brute power of this ancient, beaten-down land.

Long distances

Despite its size, Northern Territory fits neatly into a travel itinerary. There is the Red Centre – Alice Springs and the stunning hinterland in the Territory's south; various points along "The Track" (the Stuart Highway) heading north; and the "Top End", Darwin, Kakadu and surroundings.

The distance between points of interest can be intimidating – roughly 1,600 km (1,000 miles) from Alice to Darwin – but only by driving through

NT do you get a true sense of its grand and ancient terrain.

Apart from the Top End, which is swamped by a tropical monsoon each February–March, most of the Territory is an arid zone. Rainfall is minimal, averaging about 250 mm (9.8 inches) a year. But, when rain does come, it comes Outback-style: no half measures.

The Red Centre

Australia's Red Centre is the heart of the country in more ways than one. For many visitors, Australia is primarily a

Map on page 268

PRECEDING PAGES:
Ayers Rock (Uluru).
LEFT: hiking in Standley Chasm.
BELOW: camping out.

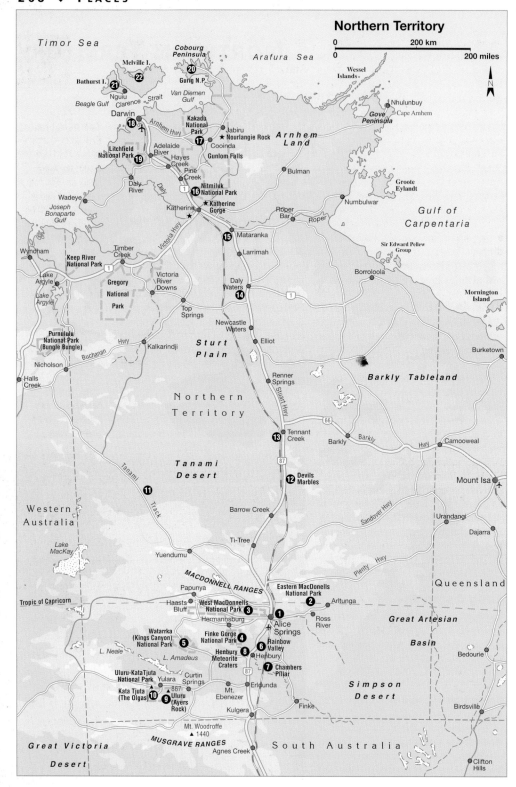

Northern Territory

0 — 200 km
0 — 200 miles

N

Timor Sea

Arafura Sea

Cobourg Peninsula

Melville I.

20 Gurig N.P.

Wessel Islands

Bathurst I.

21 Nguiu

22

Van Diemen Gulf

Nhulunbuy

Cape Arnhem

Beagle Gulf

Clarence Strait

Darwin

18

Kakadu National Park

Jabiru

★ Nourlangie Rock

Gove Peninsula

Arnhem Land

Arnhem Hwy

17

Cooinda

Gunlom Falls

Bulman

Groote Eylandt

Adelaide River

Litchfield National Park

19

Hayes Creek

Pine Creek

16 Nitmiluk National Park

Numbulwar

Gulf of Carpentaria

Daly River

Daly

Katherine

★ Katherine Gorge

Roper Bar

Roper

Sir Edward Pellew Group

Wadeye

Joseph Bonaparte Gulf

15 Mataranka

Larrimah

Wyndham

Timber Creek

Keep River National Park

Victoria Hwy

Daly Waters

14

Borroloola

Mornington Island

Lake Argyle

Lake Argyle

Gregory National Park

Victoria River Downs

Top Springs

Newcastle Waters

Elliot

Sturt Plain

Barkly Tableland

Burketown

Purnululu National Park (Bungle Bungle)

Hwy

Kalkarindji

Buchanan

Renner Springs

Stuart Hwy

Nicholson

Northern Territory

Halls Creek

Tanami Track

Tanami Desert

13 Tennant Creek

66

Barkly

Barkly Hwy

Camooweal

Mount Isa

87

12 Devils Marbles

Lake MacKay

Western Australia

11

Barrow Creek

Urandangi

Dajarra

Ti-Tree

Sandover Hwy

Yuendumu

MACDONNELL RANGES

Queensland

Tropic of Capricorn

Papunya

Haasts Bluff

West MacDonnells National Park

3

Eastern MacDonells National Park

2

Arltunga

Plenty Hwy

Great Artesian

Hermannsburg

1 Alice Springs

Ross River

Basin

Watarrka (Kings Canyon) National Park

5

Finke Gorge National Park

4

Rainbow Valley

6

Bedourie

L. Neale

L. Amadeus

8 Henbury Meteorite Craters

Henbury

7 Chambers Pillar

Simpson Desert

Uluru-KataTjuta National Park

Yulara

Curtin Springs

Erldunda

Kata Tjuta (The Olgas)

10

867

9 Uluru (Ayers Rock)

Mt. Ebenezer

Finke

Birdsville

Kulgera

Great Victoria

Mt. Woodroffe ▲ 1440

MUSGRAVE RANGES

South Australia

Clifton Hills

Desert

Agnes Creek

nature trip, and it is here in central Australia that the continent's greatest natural feature stands – **Uluru**, or **Ayers Rock**. But just as two-thirds of The Rock's awesome mass lies hidden beneath the ground, so Uluru and the other main tourist sights represent the mere tip of the great inselberg that is the Outback.

Incidentally, "Red Centre" isn't just a cute name. The sand and rock around here is red because of iron oxides found in the sandstone. The skins of the "white" inhabitants are more often a ruddy red. The sun is red when it drops, and red scars mark the flow of mineral-rich, ultra-healthy water. Even some of the kangaroos are red.

Alice Springs

Alice Springs ❶ – or "The Alice" – is the natural base for exploring the Red Centre. It is a grid-pattern, sun-scorched town of squat, mostly modern buildings, which crouches in one of many gaps (or Outback oases) in the rugged **MacDonnell Ranges**. These hills – which turn an intense blue at sunset, as if lit internally – act like a wagon train, a protective ring that might just keep the expanse of the Outback at bay.

Alice has enjoyed a tourist boom, based on Uluru and Aboriginal art and culture. Its present population of 27,500, one-tenth of which is Aboriginal, represents the greatest demographic concentration for 1,500 km (900 miles) in any direction.

By no means a picture-postcard town, Alice none the less has strange powers of attraction: visitors find themselves drawn again and again to this incongruous outpost, and many who come here for short-term work wake up 10 years later and wonder what happened. It's not always easy to meet someone who was actually born in Alice.

White settlement began here in 1871 in the form of a repeater station on the Overland Telegraph Line, constructed beside the permanent freshwater springs. Lying 4 km (2½ miles) north of the present township, the **Telegraph Station** (tours daily from 8am) and **Springs** form a popular tourist site. Then, as now, water dictated all human movement and settlement, and the line, running from Adelaide through Alice and up to Darwin, followed virtually the same route as the track does now. The line linked the cities of Australia's south and southeast with the rest of the world, as it continued from Darwin through Indonesia to Singapore, Burma, British India and across Asia and Europe to colonial headquarters in London. Keeping the line open was a full-time job, and it is still possible to see some of the original telegraph posts, now disused, rising from the hard earth.

Alice developed slowly; in 1925, it had just 200 residents. Four years later, the coming of "The Ghan" – which at that time ran from Adelaide via Oodnadatta to Alice and is named after Afghan camel drivers who pioneered transport in these parts – saw things pick up, but the trip was fraught with hazards. In the mistaken

Map on opposite page

Alice Springs gained fame through Neville Shute's 1950 novel A Town Like Alice, *filmed in 1956 with Peter Finch and in 1981 as a TV series with Bryan Brown. Its title echoes the longings of an Aussie prisoner of war in Malaya in World War II. Shute (1899–1960), a prolific London-born novelist, emigrated to Australia after the war.*

BELOW: the old telegraph station at Alice Springs.

The Royal Flying Doctor service operates more than 50 aircraft and has around 500 full-time staff. It can make over 160 landings and deal with more than 600 patients each day, nearly 100 of whom will need an aerial evacuation.

BELOW:
a ranger points out swallow nests at Alice Springs.

belief that the Outback never flooded, the track was routed across low-lying terrain; consequently, the train was often stranded in nowheresville, with additional supplies having to be parachuted in to the hapless passengers. A new, flood-proof route was completed in 1980, and the Ghan remains one of Australia's great rail journeys. In February 2004 Alice Springs ceased to be the end of the line, when the Alice–Darwin 1,420-km (880-mile) extension was completed. The event fulfilled a century-old promise of a key economic and tourism link.

The Flying Doctor

In Alice, spend your first sunset on **Anzac Hill** to get the lie of the land. One of the town's most popular attractions is the **Royal Flying Doctor Service Visitors' Centre** (tours Mon–Sat 9am–4pm, Sun 1–4pm, free). The service, established in 1928 by the Rev. John Flynn – who now graces the $20 bill – provides essential medical treatment to many isolated communities and cattle stations the

length and breadth of the Outback. Flynn's grave is 7 km (4 miles) west of Alice on Larapinta Drive – he is pinned down in perpetuity by one of the Devil's Marbles, poor chap.

Another popular spot is the **Alice Springs School of the Air** on Head Street, which services the educational needs of far-flung children. The school, unique in the world, conducts primary-level classes via radio, and the most notable of its 26 bases across the Outback is in Alice, covering an area of 1.3 million sq. km (500,000 sq. miles). It is the world's biggest classroom, and visitors can listen to lessons being taught there.

The **Alice Springs Desert Park**, situated just outside Alice at the base of the MacDonnell Ranges, is a must-see primer for anyone about to explore the desert. Its 35 hectares (86 acres) contain 320 arid-zone plant species and more than 400 desert-dwelling animals. The birds of prey nature theatre, where wild birds interact with park rangers in an astonishing way, is unforgettable.

The **Alice Springs Cultural Precinct**

Map on page 268

(10am–5pm; entrance fee) on Larapinta Drive contains the Strehlow Research Centre, the Namatjira Gallery, the Museum of Central Australia, the Memorial Cemetery, the Central Australian Aviation Museum and the Araluen Centre, with four galleries.

The **Strehlow Research Centre** chronicles the life and work of Ted Strehlow, who was born at Hermannsburg, the Lutheran mission established in 1877. He became a patrol officer and researcher among the Arrernte people, winning their trust, and artefacts from his comprehensively documented collection that are not culturally sensitive are on display at the centre.

For non-aviators, the **Aviation Museum** is uninspiring; the cemetery is more interesting because the famous Aboriginal landscape painter, Albert Namatjira, and the legendary gold seeker Harold Lasseter (whose lives form a pretty comprehensive recent history of the region) are buried there, as are a number of Afghans, in a separate section at the back, facing Mecca.

If you find yourself in Alice in September, don't miss the **Henley-on-Todd Regatta**. This grandly named event is a boat race unlike any other. The "boats" are bottomless wraparounds, and teams of about eight runners inside each one race along the dry bed of the Todd River. Much merriment is had by all, and it is the one time in the year that the white population takes over the bed of the Todd, usually inhabited by groups of Aborigines camping under the gums.

Around Alice

Alice's immediate surroundings offer numerous attractions. To the east, in the **Eastern MacDonnell Ranges** ❷, **Emily Gap**, **Jesse Gap**, **Trephina Gorge**, **N'dhala Gorge** and the old gold town of **Arltunga** are interesting excursions.

Stretching west from Alice is the **West MacDonnell National Park** ❸, incorporating many of the gaps in the ranges. These include **Simpson's Gap**, accessible via an excellent cycle path from Alice; **Standley Chasm**, whose steep walls become alive with colour

The Todd River was named after Charles Todd, the postmaster-general of South Australia, who began the telegraph line from Adelaide to Darwin in 1870. The springs discovered in the dry river bed were named after his wife, Alice Todd.

LEFT: "The Ghan", taking 48 hours from Adelaide to Darwin.
BELOW: the Henley-on-Todd Regatta.

an hour either side of midday; **Serpentine Gorge**; the **Ochre Pits**, used by Aborigines for centuries; **Ormiston Gorge and Pound**, with some fine walking trails; **Glen Helen Gorge**, with a comfortable lodge nearby; and **Redbank Gorge**. A 223-km (138-mile) walking track, the **Larapinta Trail**, constructed by local prisoners, connects many of the attractions of the MacDonnells. Guided treks along the whole track can be arranged in Alice.

To the south is **Finke Gorge National Park ❹**, featuring the picturesque Palm Valley, with its distinctive red cabbage palms, and the Finke River, whose watercourse is one of the oldest in the world at 350 million years in some areas. This park is accessed via Hermannsburg, by four-wheel-drive only.

Due west of here is one of Central Australia's star attractions – spectacular **Kings Canyon** and **Watarrka National Park ❺**. The 350 million-year-old canyon shelters a permanent rockpool, aptly named the Garden of Eden and visited during the magnificent four-hour **Canyon Rim Walk**. The nearby Kings Canyon Resort

BELOW:
Finke Gorge
National Park.

offers a range of accommodation. There is also accommodation 36 km (22 miles) from the Canyon Rim Walk at Kings Creek station, which offers basic cabins and a camping ground.

The new **Mereenie Loop Road** is a dirt road that connects Watarrka National Park with Namatjira Drive and attractions like Glen Helen Gorge. The track skirts the desert's eastern edge and should not be tackled by a conventional vehicle without local advice. Beware of crossing camels.

Rainbow Valley

South of Alice lies **Pine Gap**, off-limits to visitors but notable as the largest US communications and surveillance base in the Asia-Pacific region. Most of the 400-odd Americans employed here live in Alice; they hold weekend barbecues and baseball games in town parks, and blend with the local community.

The Aboriginal rock carvings at **Ewaninga**, of undetermined age, remain cryptic and alluring. Kaleidoscopic **Rainbow Valley ❻** is a stunning rock formation (with primitive camping conditions), as is **Chambers Pillar ❼**, a solitary upstanding red ochre outcrop inscribed with the names and dates of early explorers, who used it as a convenient landmark.

The **Henbury Meteorite Craters ❽**, just off the highway, consist of 12 indentations, about 5,000 years old, the biggest of which (180 metres/590 ft wide by 15 metres/49 ft deep) was caused by four meteors, each the size of a 200-litre (44-gallon) drum. The craters have become occasional pools, sprouting plants and attracting a variety of animal life.

En route to Uluru is **Curtin Springs**, a sprawling cattle station established in 1930 to breed horses for the British Indian Army. The road-side pub may look like a showroom for weird and wonderful tourist paraphernalia, but it's a hotbed of controversy. For years local Aborigines were writing themselves off on the highways after drinking here,

and an Aboriginal women's group has persuaded government to restrict the drinking of blacks – a rare case of positive reverse discrimination.

Dominating the horizon is **Mount Conner**, a table-top monolith that many people initially mistake for Uluru. Conner, at 700 million years old, is 150 million years older than Uluru and Kata Tjuta and just 4 metres (13 ft) lower than Uluru. The only ways to visit Mount Conner are by helicopter or with Discovery Ecotours, both based in Yulara.

Uluru

From here, the road leads to Australia's great Outback icon, **Uluru ❾** (**Ayers Rock**; entrance fee for a three-day pass), whose surrounding Uluru-Kata Tjuta National Park was World Heritage-listed for its natural significance in 1987, and for its cultural significance in 1994. It was first sighted by a European in 1872 when explorer Ernest Giles noted a prominent hill in the distance. The following year, William Gosse discovered that the "hill" was in fact "one immense rock rising abruptly from the plain". After climbing it barefoot and soaking up its mystical aura, he enthused: "This rock appears more wonderful every time I look at it." The observation remains true.

Uluru means "meeting place", and many Aboriginal Dreaming tracks or "songlines" intersect here. Spirituality is often grounded in common sense and Uluru, with its permanent waterhole, abundant animal life, shelter and firewood, has been saving lives for millennia. The rock is sacred to the local Anangu people, who resumed ownership of the lands inside the national park in 1985, in a historic "hand-back" ceremony. The Anangu have a controlling interest on the park's board of management; the chairperson is Anangu, and the meetings are bilingual (Pitjantjatjara and English). No park policy or development occurs without consultation. The Anangu receive over $2 million in revenue under the terms of the hand-back, but there is a caveat: tourists are allowed to climb over the rock on a defined path, although their sacred places are still out of bounds.

Map on page 268

Uluru is the world's largest monolith. It stands 348 metres (1,142 ft) tall and its circumference at the base is almost 9 km (5½ miles).

BELOW: the red sand around Uluru.

Titjikala

Cultural awareness is the new trend, with many tourists wanting to experience life in remote Aboriginal communities. This is not always possible with the permit system for travel into the communities (now under federal review) but one community making a determined effort to forge close links with its visitors is **Titjikala**, 120 km (75 miles) south of Alice Springs. Gunya-Titjikala arranges for visitors to stay at a tented camp site, joining Aboriginal families for witchetty grub hunts, picnics to scenic spots and kangaroo cooking in open pits.

The women will take you out into the bush for the witchetty grubs, digging around the roots of acacia trees with a crowbar to prise them from their burrows inside the roots. They will then quickly cook them in the ashes of a fire, and it is up to you to decide what they taste like. It's men's business to cook the kangaroo, burying the singed carcass upside down in a pit fire. The meat may be tasty but it comes out very rare.

Such activities provide an insight into Aboriginal life, with the activities run by the community itself – but it doesn't come cheap. An overnight stay in comfortable tent accommodation will cost $1,300 per person. Promotional material suggests this is a luxury resort, but don't expect satin sheets and turned-down beds. It's comfortable enough if you're prepared to accept a certain rough and ready ambience. For bookings call 02-8347 1159 or see www.gunya.com.au.

The Yulara Resort has seven different tiers of accommodation, ranging from a camping ground to a luxury resort. Its water supply is drawn from underground rivers.

BELOW:
a low-maintenance
form of transport.

Climbing Uluru is a major attraction for many visitors, but is considered by resident park rangers and rescue teams to be a dangerous activity. More than a dozen climbers have been killed, and every few days someone has to be rescued. The Anangu would prefer that no-one climbed, but at the same time they respect tourists' urge to do so. In one local language, the word for the ubiquitous tiny black ant is *minga* – it is also the word for tourist. This cutting-edge ecotourism is about as happy as this sort of cross-cultural marriage of convenience gets.

Recognising that the climb cannot be closed until more alternative activities are in place, the board of management opened a cultural centre in 1995 to mark the 10th anniversary of handback. An alternative to climbing is the 9.4-km (5.8-mile) "base walk" around the rock, which is well marked. A self-guiding brochure is available from the cultural centre and numerous interpretive signs are displayed.

While more walks in the rock's vicinity are scheduled, **Kata Tjuta ❿** or **The Olgas** has a number of excellent trails, including the three-hour **Valley of the Winds** circuit. No climbing of Kata Tjuta (which means "many heads", referring to the 36 domes) is permitted and, just in case you get the urge to take home any souvenir rocks or sand, bear in mind that it is disrespectful to Aboriginal sentiments and that park authorities receive, on average, two letters a week from visitors returning rocks they had taken, claiming that their luck has been bad ever since their stay in Uluru.

The 380,000-odd annual visitors to the national park are serviced by the award-winning **Yulara Resort**, which has been given a major refurbishment. There is a wide range of tours and activities available, and the sight of a sunset traffic jam has to be seen to be believed. Uluru, like the entire Red Centre, will humble you with its scale and overwhelm you with its beauty.

The first attempt at luxury tented accommodation on the edge of the Uluru-Kata Tjuta National Park burnt down when an official bush burn got out of control. **Longitude 131** is now back in business, with 15 air-conditioned tents *(see page 359)*.

Up the track

Anyone seeking the old-style Outback experience of endless long, hot, dirt roads may like to leave the highway 21 km (13 miles) north of Alice Springs and head northwest along the **Tanami Track ⓫** to rejoin "civilisation" 1,050 km (660 miles) away at Halls Creek in the Kimberley. But, for most tastes, the 1,500-km (930-mile) route along a good paved road to Darwin will suffice.

Heading north from Alice, one passes through the tiny community of **Barrow Creek**, before reaching the **Devil's Marbles Conservation Reserve ⓬** (403 km/250 miles from Alice), a series of granite boulders that litter either side of the highway for several kilometres. Some of the larger ones stand precariously balanced on tiny bases. It's thought they were once part of one solid block, broken and gradually rounded by wind and water erosion. The local Aboriginal people believe them to be the eggs of the rainbow serpent.

Tennant Creek

Tennant Creek ⓭ (504 km/313 miles from Alice) is a gold town, although only one major mine is still in production. Gold was discovered in 1932 but the rush was short-lived and it seemed destined to become a ghost town, until the discovery of copper in the 1950s brought new prosperity. The town is 12 km (7 miles) from the creek; the story goes that a cart carrying timber to build the first pub for the miners became bogged here. It was too much trouble to continue, so the hotel was erected on the spot. With a tree-lined double highway and a population of over 3,500, the town bears few signs of such a haphazard beginning.

To explore the remote **Barkly Tableland**, take the Barkly Highway east for 185 km (115 miles), then turn north onto the Tablelands Highway and towards the remote township of **Borroloola** (pop. 600), just inland from the Gulf of Carpentaria and famous for its barramundi fishing. Like any journey that involves driving into the true Outback, this route requires ample preparation, including fuel, emergency rations and water. The last leg to Borroloola is on the Carpentaria Highway, an excellent sealed road.

North of Tennant Creek, the tiny township of **Renner Springs** marks a geographical and climactic end to the long, dry journey through the Red Centre: this is the southern extremity of the monsoon-affected plains of the "Top End". But the changes are slow and subtle. Termite mounds are fascinating features of this scrubby country. They are usually about 3 metres (11 ft) high and point north–south, a position that allows termites the maximum benefit of both heat and shade. This orientation inevitably led to them being called "magnetic anthills", and at first glance it does look as if they are built on compass bearings.

At **Elliott**, golfers can enjoy the far-out experience of playing nine holes on a desert course with well-kept greens.

Newcastle Waters is an historic stock-route junction town established

Map on page 268

TIP

Visitors to Tennant Creek can tour the underground gold mine at Battery Hill Mining Centre, about 1.5 km east of the town centre. There's an enormous ore crusher plus two museum buildings. Tel: 08-8962 3388. www.tennantcreek tourism.com.au

BELOW: Nobles Nob gold mine, Tennant Creek.

as a telegraph station. In 1872 at **Frew's Ironside Ponds**, some 50 km (31 miles) north of Newcastle Waters, the respective ends of the telegraph wire were joined to establish the overland communication link.

The **Daly Waters Pub** is worth a pause for a drink and rest. Built in the 1930s as a staging post for Qantas crew and passengers on multi-hop international flights, it is full of related memorabilia. **Mataranka** ⓳ is a small town that was really put on the map only when an earlier rail track from Darwin was laid in 1928. Before that, it was part of the huge Elsey farming property (in 1916 Mataranka Station was established as an experimental sheep run, a project doomed to failure in this classic cattle country). Today, the surprise attraction is the **Mataranka Homestead Tourist Resort**, a 4-hectare (10-acre) section of tropical forest, including palms and paperbark trees adjoining the **Elsey National Park**. The nearby sparkling **Mataranka Thermal Pool**, with a water temperature of 34°C (93°F), is a real oasis amid the north's arid surrounds. Also adjacent to the tourist park

Jeannie Gunn, the author of the 1908 Outback novel We of the Never Never, *was the wife of the manager of Elsey Station, and the first white woman to set foot in this area. The saying goes that those who live in the region can "never never" leave.*

BELOW:
cooling off at Edith Falls, Nitmiluk National Park.

is a replica of the Elsey Station homestead, made for the 1981 film *We of the Never Never*.

Katherine, 103 km (63 miles) to the north, is the Top End's second most important town after Darwin. It has a population of 10,500 and a well-developed infrastructure of shops, camping grounds, hotels and motels. Since colonial days, Katherine has been an important telegraph station and cattle centre.

Katherine Gorge

To the east of the township, **Katherine Gorge** is one of the best-known features of the Territory. It's a massive stretch of sandstone cliffs rising to more than 100 metres (330 ft) above the Katherine River, with 13 main canyons. The gorge is best explored by water. Tour boats operate mostly on the lower two canyons, but the more inquisitive traveller can explore the other 11 gorges upstream – by either hiring a canoe or swimming – for a total of 12 km (7 miles) before the river widens out again. (The small crocodiles looking on are freshwater and don't attack humans, although they can be unnerving.) In recent years "saltie" crocs have been found; this has led to a ban on swimming.

The gorge system is part of the 1,800-sq. km (695-sq. miles) **Nitmiluk National Park** ⓰ that deserves at least a couple of days. There are also several walking trails in the park that follow the top of the escarpment, looking down into the gorge. Katherine is also home to a Savannah Guide Station. These eco-accredited specialist guides focus on heritage, culture, and the preservation of the natural environment.

From Katherine the Victoria Highway strikes west towards the Kimberley region of Western Australia. Just before the WA border, there is a turn-off to **Keep River National Park**. Like the better-known formations across the border in the Purnululu National Park, Keep River features a

series of fascinating banded sandstone towers that shelter a wide range of vegetation and animal life.

The richness of Kakadu

One of the brightest jewels in the whole array of Australian wilderness lies to the north of Katherine, at **Kakadu National Park** ⑰. The park's prime accommodation and commercial centre is Jabiru, 250 km (155 miles) southeast of Darwin. The richness of Kakadu defies description. Here, where the Arnhem Land escarpment meets the coastal floodplains, scenic splendour, ancient Aboriginal culture and paintings and an incredible array of flora and fauna come together in a brilliant, coherent whole.

The statistics of Kakadu – which is now on the World Heritage list – give some indication of what this area has to offer. The park covers 19,804 sq. km (7,200 sq. miles), with further extension likely. It is home to a quarter of all Australian freshwater fish, over 1,000 plant species, 300 types of birds, 75 species of reptiles, many mammals and innumerable insects. Its world-

famous galleries of Aboriginal art – particularly at Nourlangie and Ubirr rocks – give a significant insight into early man more than 20,000 years ago. In Kakadu the oldest evidence for the technology of edge-ground stone axes has been found.

Coming into Kakadu from the south, via the road from **Pine Creek**, one should detour into **Gunlom**, with its magical combination of waterfall and plunge pool. This oasis featured in the 1986 movie *Crocodile Dundee* and is even more beautiful than its celluloid image.

Most visitors approach Kakadu along the sealed **Arnhem Highway** from Darwin. This road terminates at **Jabiru**, a service town for the Ranger Uranium Mine; the mine operates in an enclave surrounded by the national park and near to **Arnhem Land**, a great expanse of Aboriginal land that is closed to tourists. The juxtaposition of national park and uranium mine has provided ongoing controversy in Australian politics for years.

A good introduction to Kakadu is a boat tour on **Yellow Water**, at Cooinda,

Map on page 268

It is possible that the earliest paintings at Ubirr Rock are up to 23,000 years old – which would make them the oldest art works known anywhere on earth.

BELOW: Kakadu National Park.

which offers the finest natural wildlife viewing anywhere in Australia. You are likely to see saltwater crocodiles, Jabiru storks, brolga cranes and a host of water birds, resident and migratory – but only during the dry season (May–Sept). During The Wet, when water is plentiful, the animals disperse across the region, and successful viewing is more haphazard.

Other easily accessible sights within the park are the paintings of **Ubirr Rock** and the towering faces of **Nourlangie Rock**. The splendid **Bowali Visitor Centre** has a permanent display setting out the features of the park. The **Marrawuddi Gallery** features displays of Aboriginal art, books and gifts.

To see what makes Kakadu special, however, head out to one or more of the water holes nestled at the base of the escarpment.

The most popular conjunction of swimming hole and waterfall is **Jim Jim Falls**. The deep, cool pool and the nearby sandy beach are remarkably attractive and have the distinct benefit of being easy to visit, at least

The majestic landscape of Kakadu National Park.

BELOW: rock paintings at Mount Borradail, Kakadu National Park.

when the access road is open (June–Nov). Effort is well rewarded for those who decide to walk into nearby **Twin Falls**, where the two strands of water drop right onto the end of a palm-shaded beach. However, don't swim there because large and possibly hungry crocodiles have been known to move in. Both Jim Jim and Twin Falls turn into seething maelstroms during wet-season flooding, at which time they are inaccessible to anyone without a helicopter. In the dry season, they are tranquil places of exquisite beauty, but you will need a four-wheel drive vehicle.

The Adelaide River

On the Arnhem Highway to Darwin you cross the **Adelaide River**, and at that point you'll find the *Adelaide River Queen* (tel: 08-8988 8144). which can take you on a short (90-minute) river cruise to see the "jumping crocodiles", which leap almost clear of the water when offered a slice of steak, just as they do when catching birds and bats in mid-air. There are more croc cruises situated just down the river.

Darwin

Darwin , capital of the Northern Territory, is a city with two histories: pre-Tracy and post-Tracy. It was founded in 1869, after more than four decades of failed settlements in the north – abandoned one after another because of malaria outbreaks, cyclones, Aboriginal attacks and supply failure due to the sheer distance from the other white settlements. Named after the naturalist Charles Darwin, one of whose shipmates on the *Beagle* discovered the bay in 1839, it drifted on in a tropical stupor for decades, punctuated only by the discovery of gold at Pine Creek in 1870, a minor "revolution" in 1919. Some 243 people were killed and another 300 injured in the first savage surprise Japanese bombing attack in February 1942, and Darwin suffered repeated raids over the following 18 months.

Asian influences

Today's Darwin has a pace that might – almost – be described as brisk, at least by Northern Territory standards. Once the neurotic front line of white Australia, the city's populace now reflects its proximity to Asia: the mix of some 50 cultures including Aborigines, Vietnamese, Filipinos, Malays, New Guineans, Pacific Islanders, Japanese and Indonesians – and Greeks and white Australians – provides a strong cosmopolitan flavour. That mix might have become more predominantly Asian had the Japanese advance in World War II not been stalled at New Guinea. When the Japanese bombed Darwin's port, there was mass panic, desertions, the evacuation of the civilian population, and the looting of homes by some of the army marshals who remained. The desperate dash for safety in the south became known derisively as the "Adelaide River Stakes".

Discoveries of oil and gas in the Timor Sea have led to an influx of mining engineers, refinery workers and skilled tradesmen, feeding an economic boom. In turn, this has led to a housing boom, with apartment blocks proliferating and real estate prices rocketing. Many locals have cashed in on the housing boom, while doomsayers predict that the levels of economic

Map on page 268

TIPS

● As an alternative to walking, explore Darwin on the Tour Tub, an open-topped minibus that allows you to get on and off anywhere on its circular route.

● It can often be unbearably hot in the middle of the day. If exploring the city on foot, take your tour in the early morning or late afternoon.

BELOW: Kitty O'Shea's Bar in Darwin.

Cyclone Tracy

In four furious hours on Christmas Eve 1974, Cyclone Tracy swept in from the north and flattened the city. With gusts up to 280 km (175 miles) an hour, the hurricane destroyed more than 5,000 homes – 80 percent of the city. The dead and missing totalled 66 in one of the most dramatic natural disasters in Australian history. With massive government funding, the city was rebuilt in the knowledge that the character and ambience of the old Darwin had been blown away forever.

Most of the old-style Darwin was levelled, to be replaced by a modern, more commercialised city. But of the over 30,000 residents evacuated in the nation's fastest-ever mass population shift, the majority returned. Today the city has 102,000 inhabitants.

and housing activity are not sustainable in the long term, and that the downturn will surely come. Meanwhile, the defence forces give another boost to the economy, with army, navy and airforce personnel spending at least two years in Darwin as part of their service.

Everywhere there is a spirit of optimism, although population mobility remains an important factor. Many people leave the Territory on retirement to head south where health and aged care facilities are better.

The focal point of the city's defence was the **Old Navy Headquarters** . This simple stone building, dating from 1884, was a police station and courthouse. It and other historical buildings such as **Fannie Bay Gaol** (1883) and **Brown's Mart** (built in 1885, and the oldest in the city centre) contrast with Darwin's new cyclone-proof architecture, represented by the city's high-rise hotels, **Sky City Casino** and **Parliament House**.

Despite the changes, it is Darwin's natural charm and the relaxed "Top End" lifestyle that give the new city its appeal. The town is flanked by great expanses of golden sandy beaches and in the dry season – April to October – the vision of sand, clear blue skies and tropical flora makes Darwin immensely attractive.

For six months of the year **Darwin Harbour** ❸ becomes the playground of the area's boating populace. Many people swim here, even though huge saltwater crocodiles are regularly pulled from the water. It may be more relaxing to swim at nearby **Mindil Beach** or **Vestey's** (named after the cattle company that once employed most Darwinians). Mindil Beach is the scene of a popular sunset market every Thursday evening (Apr–Oct 5–10pm). The Asian food stalls are marvellous.

Other markets are in **Parap** on Saturday morning (8am– 2pm) and in **Rapid Creek** on Sunday (8am–1pm).

Fannie Bay

When the tides are right in early August at **Fannie Bay**, about 4 km (2½ miles) from the city centre, Darwin conducts its famous **Beer Can Regatta**. Thousands of beer cans are used to build a fleet of wildly imaginative,

Darwin's weekly Mindil Beach Market.

BELOW: Darwin's Parliament House.

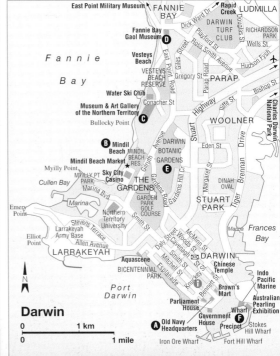

semi-seaworthy craft. The whole city turns out to watch them race or wallow in the bay. This event is in keeping with Darwin's reputation as the world's beer-drinking capital.

Thanks to post-Tracy funding, in 1981 the ambitious **Museum and Art Gallery of the Northern Territory** ⓒ (Mon–Fri 9am–5pm; Sat, Sun 10am–5pm; free) was opened. Its five galleries include one of the world's best collections of Aboriginal art and cultural artefacts, and archaeological finds from the Pacific region. Don't miss the fine collection of Aboriginal contemporary art, the Tiwi Pukumani burial poles and "Sweetheart", a stuffed saltwater crocodile 5 metres (17 ft) long.

The **Fannie Bay Gaol Museum** ⓓ (daily 10am–4.30pm; free) displays old cells and gallows from the prison's grim past.

Darwin's tropical nature makes a visit to the 34-hectare (84-acre) **Botanical Gardens** ⓔ worthwhile, and fish-feeding at the **Aquascene** in Doctor's Gully Road, near the corner of Daly Street and the Esplanade, is lots of fun, especially with children. Fish can be hand-fed at

high tide every day, at times advertised in the local paper.

Finally, the **Wharf Precinct** ⓕ has undergone a major renovation: on any balmy afternoon, head out to the end of the pier, where dozens of restaurants have set up outdoor tables. It's the perfect place to drink in the tropical air, or drop a line to catch a passing Spanish mackerel. By 2010 the waterfront will have expanded to include a convention centre, high-rise apartments, offices and retail outlets and a wave pool for surfers. The total cost of the project will be $1 billion.

Exploring the Top End

About 60 km (40 miles) south of Darwin on the Cox Peninsula Road, the **Territory Wildlife Park** provides a potted display of the Top End's varied bird, marine, and bush wildlife, and an aquarium representing an entire Top End river system, viewed from a shuttle train that potters around the 400-hectare (988-acre) property.

A two-hour drive to the southwest of Darwin is **Litchfield National Park** ⑲, 153 sq. km (59 sq. miles) of sandstone

Map on page 268

Taking a spin through the Top End's mangroves.

BELOW: termitarium at Litchfield National Park.

Map on page 268

TIP

However tempting the sea might seem, it is unwise to swim off the coast of NT between October and May. Box jellyfish, whose sting can be fatal, are usually present in great numbers. Always observe the warning signs.

BELOW:
a Tiwi guide demonstrates how to hold a possum.

plateau with pockets of rainforest. It is one of the best areas in the Top End for bushwalking, but is even more popular for its waterfalls and clear pools, which provide excellent swimming.

Darwin is the ideal base for exploring the remote, mangrove-filled north. Easily reached by light plane is the **Cobourg Peninsula ⑳**. Because it is on Aboriginal land, permission is required before visiting, but that will be arranged by the tour operators. Cobourg was the site of one of the earliest attempts to establish a British base in northern Australia. Through a series of misadventures and bungles, Port Essington failed, but the bay in which it was built is a place of extravagant beauty in one of the most remote corners of the continent. **Seven Spirit Bay** here is perhaps the most out-of-the-way five-star resort in the world.

The Tiwi Islands

Splaying out to the north of Darwin like a giant ink blot, the two Tiwi Aboriginal islands, **Bathurst ㉑** and **Melville ㉒**, are among Australia's most isolated outposts. Although the

mainland is only 80 km (50 miles) away, dugout canoes rarely survived the journey, so the Tiwi culture and language developed separately from that of other Aboriginal groups. Early Dutch explorers met with hostility, and when the British set up an outpost on Melville in 1824 it lasted less than five years, owing to Tiwi sieges and tropical disease. As a result, the Tiwis largely escaped the scorched-earth period of Australia's colonisation.

Control of their own affairs was returned to the Tiwis in the 1970s; most crucially, since they have never been moved, their land rights have never been disputed. This confident sense of possession may be why they are so outgoing; despite their once-fearsome reputation, they now bill their lands as the "Friendly Islands".

Visiting them requires a permit, organised by the Tiwi-owned tour company *(see box below)*. It's worth the journey: this remote coastline alternates between croc-infested mangrove swamps and blinding white beaches where you can walk for miles without seeing another person. ❑

Visiting the Tiwi Islands

The best time to visit is in late March or early April, during the Aussie Rules Tiwi Islands Football League Grand Final. On the same Sunday there is also the Tiwi Islands Annual Art Sale, where local jewellery, paintings, carvings, ceramics, weavings and fabrics are sold.

Visitors can only go on an organised tour by boat or plane. The catamaran *Arafura Pearl* takes day-trippers to Nguiu on Bathurst Island for a visit to the art centre during the dry season. A charter plane allows visits to the three art centres on Bathurst and Melville Island ($500 for a day trip). Call **Tiwi Art Network** on 08-8941 3593; or visit www.tiwiart.com.

Two-night plane charter visits to the islands are also available from **Aussie Adventure Tours** (tel: 08-8923 6523; www.aussieadventure.com.au). The visits involve camping accommodation.

RESTAURANTS & BARS

Restaurants

Darwin

Char Restaurant
Admiralty House,
70 The Esplanade
Tel: 08-8981 4544
www.charrestaurant.com.au
Open: L Mon–Fri,
D Mon–Sat. **$$$**
Char's reputation rests
on their high-quality
steaks. Located in the
former navy HQ, this is
alfresco dining among
magnificent fig trees
and frangipani. Superb
inner-city location.

Magic Wok
22 West Lane Arcade
Tel: 08-8981 3332
Open: L Mon–Fri,
D Mon–Sat. **$**
Set-price menu cooked
up in "turbo-wok" as you
watch. You choose and
load your plate from an
extensive menu. This is
an eclectic Chinese
meal using a mix of
Asian and Aussie ingre-
dients; return for second
or third helpings and
Bring your appetite.

Vietnam Saigon Star
60 Smith Street
Tel: 08-89811420
Open: L, Mon–Fri, D daily. **$**
Best Vietnamese nosh
in the Territory; and
cheap for such good-
quality dishes. BYO and
licensed.

Pee Wee's at the Point
Alec Fong Lim Drive,
East Point Reserve
Tel: 08-8981 6868
www.peewees.com.au
Open: D daily. **$$$**
Alfresco dining on the
shores of Fannie Bay.
Darwin's most up-
market restaurant with
prices and exotic menu
to match. The place for
that special occasion.
Essential to book.

Hanuman
93 Mitchell Street
Tel: 08-8941 3500
www.hanuman.com.au
Open: L Mon–Fri, D daily. **$$$**
Highly spiced, superbly
presented Indian and
Thai dishes renowned
for consistent quality.
It's the restaurant locals
take their visitors to
show off Darwin's culi-
nary delights. Excellent,
if pricy, wine list and
imaginative menu with
classy ambience.

Wisdom Bar and Café
48 Mitchell Street
Tel: 08-8941 4866
Open: B, L & D daily. **$**
Bright, breezy eatery in
former dental surgery
(hence the name) on the
main tourist strip. Offers
more than 50 beers
from around the world,
and if you drink them all
(not necessarily on the
same day) your name
goes up on the Wall of
Wisdom. The place to
drop in for a snack and
a catch-up with friends.

Victoria Hotel
27 Smith Street Mall
Tel: 08-8981 4011
Open: L & D daily. **$**
The oldest pub in town
(built 1890). The Vic's
historic sandstone walls
have survived several
cyclones, its latest
reincarnation being a
backpacker's watering
hole. The Vic is a lively
entertainment centre
year-round with music,
pub nosh and fun and
games nightly during the
dry season. It even has
a mini-museum in the
beer cellar.

Shenannigans
69 Mitchell Street
Tel: 08-8981 2100
Open: L & D daily. **$**
www.shenannigans.com.au
Another old-style, ram-
bling pub with a crowded
beer menu and fair-
quality food in cheerful
outdoor setting. The
kind of middle-ranking
pub that fills rapidly on
Friday nights; music and
dancing on Friday and
Saturday. Always busy.

Top End Hotel
Corner Mitchell and Daly
streets
Tel: 08-8981 6511
Open: L & D daily. **$**
Once an institution in
Darwin for its heavy rock
ambience, the old pub
has been knocked down
to make way for apart-
ments, leaving two
extensive bars on two
levels. One of the bars
is a TAB and sports out-
let. Overall the theme is
sporty, with the food an
adjunct to drinking.

Ducks Nuts Bar and Grill
76 Mitchell Street
Tel: 08-8942 2122
www.ducksnuts.com.au
Open: L & D daily. **$$**
Trendy eatery with good
coffee, a vodka bar and
occasional live music.
The sort of place to
unwind after a hard day
on the tourist trail.
Meals are good value,
with plentiful servings.

Buzz Café
Cullen Bay
Tel: 08-8941 1141
Open: L & D daily. **$$**
Located over the water
at the beautiful and
trendy Cullen Bay
marina, Buzz is one of
the most popular eater-
ies along a boardwalk of
fine restaurants. Worth
a visit just to hang over
the marina's splendid
turquoise waters.

Alice Springs

Hanuman Restaurant
Crowne Plaza Hotel, 82 Barrett
Drive
Tel: 08-8953 7188
Open: L, D Mon–Fri, D from
6pm Sat–Sun. **$$$**
Run by the owner of
Hanuman's in Darwin,
the Alice restaurant
maintains the same
quality of Thai and
Indian food. A fine dining
experience in a desert
setting.

PRICE CATEGORIES

Three-course dinner with a
half-bottle of house wine:
$ = under A$50
$$ = A$50–A$75
$$$ = over A$75
B = breakfast, L = lunch,
D = dinner, BYO = bring your
own alcohol

WESTERN AUSTRALIA

Two thirds of the population of "WA" live in its attractive capital, Perth. The vast emptiness beyond includes barren desert, lush forests, rugged canyons and far-flung gold-mining towns

Western Australia is, quite simply, enormous. Covering more than 2½ million sq. km (960,000 sq. miles), it is much larger than Alaska and Texas combined. In fact, if "WA" was a separate country, it would be the ninth largest in the world – and the emptiest. India is about the same size, with a population of 700 million, whereas the whole vast, dry expanse of Western Australia is inhabited by just 2 million people, three-quarters of whom live in Perth.

Being so far from the main Australian population centres on the east coast, WA conveys a feeling of utter isolation. **Perth** is the world's remotest state capital city, closer to Bali than it is to Sydney. Most of the state is parched and barren, but the north is lushly tropical and the southwest temperate. In springtime, between September and November, many visitors travel from the eastern states just to see the profusion of wildflowers that turn the south into a riot of colour. WA's vastness, small population and rugged scenery give this state a strong sense of being a new frontier, an impression heightened when only a few hours' drive from Perth takes you into pure Outback scenery.

When planning a trip in WA, it's a good idea to keep an eye on the map scale and distances. It's all too easy to outline a weekend tour through an apparently tiny proportion of the state – only to add up the distances and find this would mean driving some 1,600 km (1,000 miles). If you are based in Perth, with limited time to spare, consider joining an organised excursion. Several Perth tour operators run day, overnight and longer tours to WA's scenic highlights, such as Margaret River, Albany, Kalbarri National Park and the Pinnacles.

The first arrivals

Western Australia was the arrival point for the first Australians. It is thought that, more than 50,000 years ago, the forebears of today's Australian Abo-

Map on page 292

PRECEDING PAGES: flags fly over the central business district.
LEFT: a replica of the 1606 *Dyfken*.
BELOW: street performer outside London Court.

Statue of James Stirling, the colony's first governor, outside the Town Hall.

rigines sailed across on bamboo rafts from what is now Indonesia, arriving in waves over many centuries. From the northwest, they gradually spread to occupy the whole continent.

The first recorded European view of the west Australian coast occurred in 1616, when Dirk Hartog, a Dutch captain, sailed to what is now Dirk Hartog Island near Carnarvon. The first English explorer known to have visited Australia was William Dampier, who was on the *Cygnet* in 1688 when it was repaired at what is now Cygnet Bay in the Kimberley. He was unimpressed with what he saw, finding the land useless and the Aborigines the "miserablest people in the world".

In 1827, amid fears that the French might seize the vast coastline, Captain James Stirling was despatched from Sydney to find a potential site for a western settlement. In 1829 the first colonists arrived to set up shop on a site he had spotted 16 km (10 miles) upstream on the Swan River. Surrounded by black swans, a village of some 300 residents was founded and named Perth.

Inducing other colonists to head

west was no easy matter. An acute labour shortage led to convicts being imported in 1850, much to the disgust of many founding fathers. By 1858, the population of Perth was still barely 3,000; far fewer white settlers ventured into the hinterland.

But gold changed all that. When news of the great finds of the 1890s at fields at Kalgoorlie to the east reached the outside world, Perth became the leaping-off point for one of the last great gold rushes. Still, many parts of the northeast were among the last to be settled in Australia, when some of the world's largest cattle stations were opened in the Kimberley. Throughout the 20th century, the discovery of mineral deposits throughout the state provided the main basis of its wealth – from uranium to gas and oil on the northwest shelf.

Perth

As in the gold-rush days, almost all visits to the wild west still start in **Perth ❶**, whose population now stands at 1.47 million. Set on the west coast, a high-tech counterweight to the older, heavily populated eastern cities,

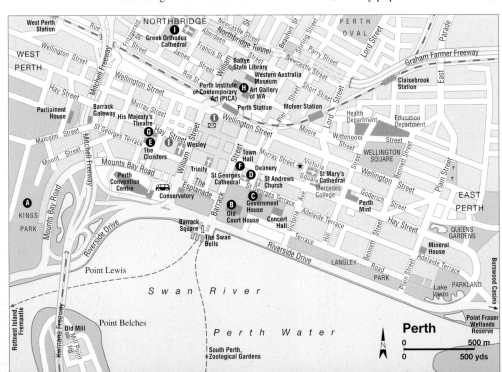

the place has become a symbol of Australian confidence – many would say over-confidence.

Perth still lives in the shadow of the roaring 1980s, when it was the base of a posse of high-profile multimillionaires, exemplified by Alan Bond, who worked so closely with the Labor politicians of the time that the state was referred to as "WA Inc". But the powerful alliance collapsed in the wake of the 1987 Wall Street crash, when one tycoon after another was implicated in corrupt dealings, charged and jailed. Today, Perth is a much-chastened city, but it remains well worth the long flight from the east.

The city takes full advantage of its setting on the serpentine Swan River. The dominant view is over **Perth Water** where the **Swan River** widens into a broad bay about 1 km (⅔ mile) across. A little further downstream, fringing the river mouth, is a string of surfing beaches. On the edge of the business district, set high on an escarpment, is **Kings Park Ⓐ**, a 400-hectare (988-acre) reserve of botanical gardens and bushland offering panoramic views over the

city and the river. Dominating the jetty on Riverside Drive are the sail-shaped copper wings of the tower containing the **Swan Bells** (daily from 10am, closing times vary seasonally; to ascend the tower; entrance fee), a gift from the church of St Martin-in-the-Fields, Trafalgar Square, London, to mark Australia's bicentenary in 1988.

Successive mining booms since the 1970s have led large multinational and West Australia-based companies to build high-rise office blocks in Perth. Their presence has dramatically changed the city skyline, causing older residents to complain that the city has lost its intimate country-town feel. But the odd architectural gem can still be found. Tucked into the back of **Stirling Gardens** is **Old Court House Ⓑ** (1837), Perth's first brick building, which has a modest facade of Doric columns. On the whole, however, buildings pre-dating the state's 1890s gold rush are rare. **Government House Ⓒ** (also in Stirling Gardens) stands as a true reflection of the beginning of the state. Constructed in the 1860s by convict labour, it placed a regal stamp of

Map on opposite page

TIP

City-centre buses are free. The free service applies to all regular buses while they're in the central zone, as well as CATS (Central Area Transit), distinctive buses – red, blue or yellow, depending on the route – linking main tourist sights and running from early morning until early evening.

BELOW:
a view of Perth business district.

The Caller, *a*
sculpture by Gerhard
Marks outside the
Art Gallery of
Western Australia.

BELOW:
the Town Hall.

authority on the new settlement. Some say the emerging Australian "larrikin" characteristic shows through in the upstairs windows, which are in the shape of a broad arrow – the motif on the uniforms of the convict builders.

Other early buildings include the **Deanery Ⓓ**, on the corner of Pier Street, opposite Stirling Gardens, built by paroled convicts in 1859, and the Elizabethan-style **Cloisters** building **Ⓔ**, at the western end of St George's Terrace, established in 1858 as the first public school for boys. The old **Town Hall Ⓕ** (Hay Street Mall) was the last building in Perth to be built by convict labour (commenced in 1867). It has been the site of various entertainments as well as formal civic ceremonies and political meetings. It was a rallying-point for conscription in both World Wars.

The city architecture of the 1890s gold rush includes **His Majesty's Theatre Ⓖ** ("The Maj") at the west end of Hay Street. To discover more about the gold rush and its pivotal role in the city's development, visit the 1899 **Perth Mint** (eastern end of Hay Street, Mon–Fri 9am–5pm, Sat–Sun 9am–

1pm; guided tour every 30 minutes; entrance fee), among the world's oldest operating mints. Try picking up a block of gold worth A$250,000, minting your own medallion, or watch gold being smelted.

Two sections of town with contrasting histories are **London Court** and **East Murray Street Precinct**. London Court dates back to 1937, a monument to mock-Tudor kitsch whose curiosities include a clock tower at each end: one a replica of London's Big Ben, the other of the Gros Horloge in Rouen, France. East Murray Street, by contrast, is the genuine colonial item. It appears on the original town plans of 1838 and now stands lined by early 20th-century buildings and old public offices.

On the northern side of the railway station, across the lovely **Horseshoe Bridge**, lies the **Perth Cultural Centre Ⓗ**, comprising the **Art Gallery of Western Australia** (daily 10am–5pm; www.artgallery.wa.gov.au; free entrance and guided tours) and the Western Australian Museum. The art gallery displays more than 1,000 works of art, including one of the continent's best collections of Aboriginal art. One painting that is almost always included in a guided tour is *The Foundation of Perth* by George Pitt, depicting the wife of an early dignitary ceremoniously felling a tree to mark the city's founding. A copy of this painting was given to every WA school to mark the state's centenary celebrations in 1929.

The **Western Australian Museum** (daily 9.30am–5pm; www.museum.wa.gov.au; free) traces the history of the state from the formation of the Australian continent 120 million years ago to the present day. Don't miss the fascinating natural history section or the illuminating Katta Dijinoong Gallery devoted to Aboriginal history and culture.

In the museum's beautifully preserved **Old Gaol** (1856), life in the early days of the colony has been recreated in a collection of period interiors,

including a 1917 pharmacy and an original court room. There is also a good little courtyard café here.

Just along from the Art Gallery of WA, and also forming part of the cultural centre, is the **Perth Institute of Contemporary Art** (www.pica.org.au; gallery Fri 11am–9pm; Tues, Thurs, Sun 11am–6pm; free), which offers a lively programme of exhibitions, installations and events, as well as a great café-bar.

The cultural centre stands on the doorstep of **Northbridge ❶**, where Perth's ethnic diversity is displayed on a plate, as it were. You can walk past tanks of live mud crabs and crayfish, smell the sharp tang of lemongrass, chew on chickens' feet or dim sum at eight in the morning, sip cappuccino in the Italian cafés or have a beer on the balcony of a pub, watching all the action on the streets below. Northbridge also has nightclubs and discos as lively as any in Sydney.

Another fruitful neighbourhood for restaurants and bars is **Subiaco**, a fashionable suburb on the western side of town (direct access on the Perth–Fremantle railway). Come here for brunch on Friday or Saturday and visit its funky weekend markets (**Station Street** and **Pavilion**), perhaps after a walk in nearby Kings Park.

Perth's seaside

Fremantle ❷, just 19 km (12 miles) from Perth's city centre but deemed a city in its own right, was brushed up for the America's Cup race in 1987 and has since become one of Western Australia's most popular attractions. Unlike glittering Perth, the old port's colonial charms remain intact, including the **Round House** (which actually has 12 sides), WA's oldest public building (1830) and its first jail, built where Captain Fremantle landed to claim Western Australia for the Crown.

If you arrive by ferry you will disembark at Victoria Quay, at the far end of which you will notice the sail-like roof of the excellent **Maritime Museum** (daily 9.30am–5pm; www.mm.wa.gov.au; entrance fee) exploring all aspects of Fremantle's seafaring heritage from whaling and pearling to its role in World War II and as the place of disembarkation for thousands of post-

Maps:
City 288
Area 292

TIP

Fremantle is a 30-minute train ride from Perth railway station, and Transperth buses to Fremantle leave from St George's Terrace. But try to arrive by boat along the Swan if you can. The ferry from Barrack Street Jetty takes about an hour.

LEFT: leafy, laid-back Northbridge.
BELOW: the Round House.

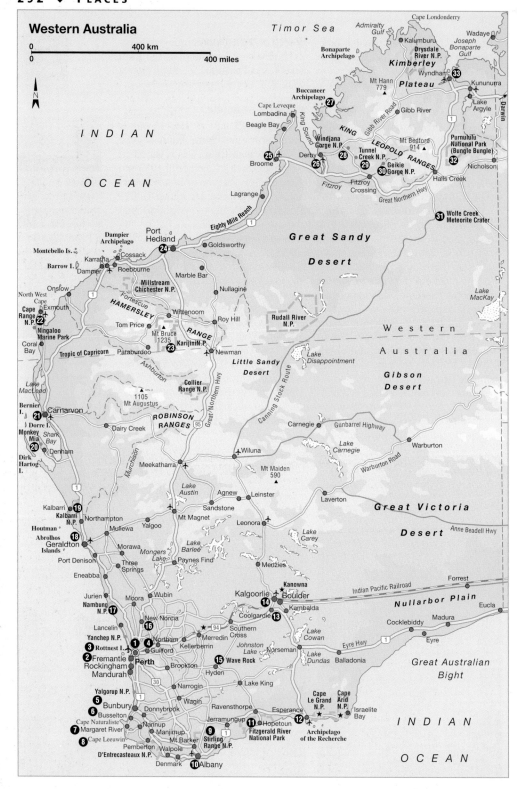

Western Australia

0 _____ 400 km
0 _____ 400 miles

INDIAN OCEAN

Timor Sea

Cape Londonderry

Admiralty Gulf

Kalumburu

Wadaye

Joseph Bonaparte Gulf

Bonaparte Archipelago

Drysdale River N.P.

Kimberley

Wyndham

33

Kununurra

Mt Hann 779

Plateau

Darwin

Buccaneer Archipelago

27

Gibb River Road

Gibb River

Lake Argyle

Cape Leveque

Lombadina

KING

Mt Bedford 914

Purnululu National Park (Bungle Bungle)

32

Beagle Bay

Windjana Gorge N.P.

LEOPOLD

Nicholson

Derby

28

Tunnel Creek N.P.

25

26

29

Geikie Gorge N.P.

RANGES

Halls Creek

Broome

30

Fitzroy Crossing

Fitzroy

Great Northern Hwy

Lagrange

31

Wolfe Creek Meteorite Crater

Eighty Mile Reach

Great Sandy

Port Hedland

24

Goldsworthy

Desert

Dampier Archipelago

Cossack

Montebello Is.

Karratha

Roebourne

Marble Bar

Lake MacKay

Barrow I.

Dampier

Nullagine

Onslow

Millstream Chichester N.P.

North West Cape

HAMERSLEY

Wittenoom

Western

Cape Range N.P.

22

Exmouth

Fortescue

Roy Hill

Tom Price

RANGE

Ningaloo Marine Park

Rudall River N.P.

Australia

Coral Bay

Mt Bruce 1235

Karijini N.P.

23

Tropic of Capricorn

Paraburdoo

Newman

Lake MacLeod

Little Sandy Desert

Lake Disappointment

Gibson Desert

Ashburton

Collier Range N.P.

Bernier I.

21

Carnarvon

1105 Mt Augustus

ROBINSON RANGES

Carnegie

Gunbarrel Highway

Dorre I.

Dairy Creek

Canning Stock Route

Warburton

Monkey Mia

20

Shark Bay

Denham

Murchison

Meekatharra

Lake Carnegie

Warburton Road

Dirk Hartog I.

Wiluna

Mt Maiden 590

Lake Austin

Agnew

Leinster

Great Victoria

Kalbarri

19

Kalbarri N.P.

Northampton

Mullewa

Yalgoo

Sandstone

Laverton

Desert

Anne Beadell Hwy

Houtman Abrolhos Islands

18

Geraldton

Mt Magnet

Leonora

Morawa

Lake Barlee

Port Denison

Lake Carey

Three Springs

Mongers Lake

Paynes Find

Menzies

Eneabba

Forrest

Jurien

Moora

Wubin

Kalgoorlie

Kanowna

Indian Pacific Railroad

Nullarbor Plain

Nambung N.P.

17

Boulder

Eucla

Lancelin

16

New Norcia

Coolgardie

14

Kambalda

Cocklebiddy

Madura

Yanchep N.P.

Southern Cross

Merredin

13

Lake Cowan

Eyre

3

Rottnest I.

Northam

Kellerberrin

Johnston Lake

Eyre Hwy

1

4

Guilford

Norseman

Balladonia

2

Fremantle

Perth

Brookton

15

Wave Rock

Lake Dundas

Great Australian Bight

Rockingham

Mandurah

Hyden

Lake King

Yalgorup N.P.

5

Narrogin

6

Bunbury

Wagin

Ravensthorpe

Cape Le Grand N.P.

Cape Arid N.P.

INDIAN OCEAN

Busselton

Donnybrook

Jerramungup

11

Hopetoun

12

Israelite Bay

Cape Naturaliste

Nannup

7

Margaret River

Manjimup

9

Stirling Range N.P.

Fitzgerald River National Park

Esperance

Archipelago of the Recherche

8

Cape Leeuwin

Pemberton

Mt Barker

D'Entrecasteaux N.P.

Walpole

Denmark

10

Albany

Southern Cross

war immigrants. The **Shipwreck Galleries** (same hours as the Maritime Museum, but free) on Cliff Street, is devoted to marine archaeology. It has relics from some of the many ships wrecked off WA's coast over the centuries, including original timber (partially reconstructed) and treasures from the Dutch ship *Batavia (see page 301).*

Fremantle Prison (daily 10am– 5pm; entrance fee), a maximum security prison until 1991, offers a variety of tours including a "torchlight tour". Ghost sightings are not guaranteed but the tours incude the gallows yard and hellish cell blocks built by convict labour in 1855.

One of the chief pleasures of Fremantle is to wander at random, soaking up the laid-back atmosphere and admiring the frilly ironwork of the gold-rush architecture. It has no shortage of restaurants and coffee shops (explore South Terrace, aka Cappuccino Strip), and plenty of interesting shops. On Fridays and weekends dip into the the splendidly restored **Fremantle Markets** (corner of South Terrace and Henderson Street) for interesting crafts and souvenirs.

Perth's beaches

From Fremantle a string of soft sandy beaches stretches all the way to Hillary's Boat Harbour, 50 km (30 miles) north. Development, though continuous, is almost without exception low-rise and low-key, set well back from the shore. Each of the beaches has its fans. For surfing, head for **Scarborough** or **Trigg**; for a lively apres-beach scene, choose **Cottesloe**, where the Indiana Tea Rooms *(see page 310)* offer good food, cocktails and fabulous sunset views.

For family-friendly attractions head for **Hillary's Boat Harbour**, where AQWA (Aquarium of Western Australia; daily 10am–5pm; www.aqwa.com.au; entrance fee) recreates WA's five coastal environments. The highlight here is the walk-through aquarium, representing the "shipwreck coast", where sharks, loggerhead turtles, and stingrays glide smoothly overhead within inches of the upturned faces watching them. Other highlights include a touch pool, saltwater crocodiles of the far north coast and tropical fish of the coral coast.

Map on page 292

Leighton and Port Beaches are best for windsurfing.

BELOW: the huge sun-dial at Cottesloe beach.

Margaret River's Voyager Estate combines fine wines and 18th-century architecture inspired by Cape Town.

RIGHT:
the boardwalk of the Western Cape, Rottnest Island.

Rottnest Island

Hillary's Boat Harbour is, along with Barrack Street Jetty in Perth and Fremantle, one of the springboards for **Rottnest Island ❸**, an idyllic getaway just 19 km (13 miles) offshore. First settled as a natural prison for West Australian Aborigines, "Rotto", as it is known locally, is now a favourite holiday spot for Perth families. Because private motor vehicles aren't allowed on the island, visitors tend to wobble along on bicycles, re-discovering long-lost skills. Cycles can be brought on the ferry or rented in situ.

Visitors can spend their time boating, golfing, playing tennis or just lazing on a quiet beach. In summer, divers come here to explore the world's southernmost coral reef. The island's pub, the Quokka Arms, originally served as the official residence of the Australian state governor; it now has live music on summer evenings. Facilities are fairly basic. Accommodation is limited to the Quokka Arms and Rottnest Lodge, and at peak times is allocated by public ballot, as demand is so high. If you want to stay overnight or longer, book well in advance.

The Swan Valley

If you have limited time during your stay in Perth, and can manage only one out-of-towner, it is worth venturing into the **Swan Valley**. A major wine-producing area, it offers vineyard tours and elegant towns such as **Guildford ❹**, one of the earliest settlements in Western Australia, and only 30 minutes by train or road from the CBD. To follow the Swan Valley food and wine trail, a 32-km (20-mile) loop linking some of the best vineyards and micro-breweries, as well as the Margaret River Chocolate Company, leave the town via the West Swan Road and return by the Great Northern Highway. Also along the route is **Caversham Wildlife Park**, the best place in the region for kangaroo-spotting for visitors too short of time to "go bush". Caversham forms part of Whiteman Park (www.whitemanpark.com.au), packed with family attractions, including an excellent **Motor Museum** (daily 10am–4pm; entrance fee).

Getting to Rottnest Island

Rottnest's proximity to the mainland makes it an easy day trip by ferry from Perth. Boat Torque Cruises (tel: 08-9430 5844; www.boattorque.com.au) operates from Northport and the C Shed at Fremantle, and Barrack Street, Perth. Hillary's Fast Ferries (tel: 08-9246 1039; www.hillarysfastferries.com.au) run from Hillary's Boat Harbour, while Oceanic Cruises (tel: 08-9325 1181; www.oceancruises.com.au) set out from the B Shed at Fremantle, and Barrack Street Jetty, Perth. It takes approximately 25 minutes to get to the island from Fremantle, around 45 minutes from Hillary's and 90 minutes from Perth. The cost of the ferry crossing includes the entrance fee to the island. The ferry crossing to Rottnest can get choppy. If you're prone to seasickness, or have children with you, take tablets beforehand.

The beauty of the island is perhaps best appreciated from the air, so you may want to consider taking the Rottnest Air Taxi (tel: 08-9292 5027; www.rottnest.de) instead of the ferry. You will also get there alot quicker – taxis spend just 12 minutes in the air. Flights leave from Jandakot Airport in Perth for Rottnest Aerodrome at times arranged to suit you (cost is approximately AU$80 return per person, based on three people sharing a four-seater aircraft).

The Southwest of WA

Head south of Perth for the region's top wineries and dense karri and jarray forests.

Immediately south of Fremantle the landscape is fairly industrial apart from **Rockingham** (47 km/30 miles south of Perth), a springboard for Penguin Island, named for its colony of 1,100 penguins, and **Mandurah** (74 km/40 miles from Perth), a fast-growing but nonetheless delightful town on the Peel Estuary. In high season the towns and camp sites around Mandurah are busy with holiday-makers, but for the rest of the year they can be enjoyed in relative peace.

Further down the coast (140 km/75 miles from Perth) is the dairy town of **Harvey**, dating back to 1890. The nearby **Yalgorup National Park** can be reached by the old coast road. It is a sanctuary for water birds and wildlife, though it is its colony of living, rock-like creatures known as thrombolites, the earliest known life on earth and very rare, that makes it special. The only access point is via the coast road, 25 km (15 miles) south of Mandurah, indicated by a large brown sign for the Lake Clifton platform, an observation walkway built across the shallows containing the thrombolites.

The city of **Bunbury** ❺ (180 km/ 110 miles south of Perth) is a busy port that owes its existence to Lt Henry St Pierre Bunbury, who travelled overland to the coast from Pinjarra in 1836. At **Koombana Beach**, just north of town, visitors can feed a community of bottlenose dolphins that visit the beach daily at the Dolphin Discovery Centre (daily 9am–3pm in winter, 8am–4pm in winter; entrance fee).

Forests and vineyards

It was logging of the nearby forests that brought prosperity to the region; jarrah and blackbutt hardwoods abound in the area, and can be seen in much of the early architecture. Bunbury sits at the northern end of **Geographe Bay**, a large sheltered waterway that has **Cape Naturaliste** as its northern spur. From

here a cape-to-cape hiking trail leads south to Cape Leeuwin, 135 km (84 miles) away.

On the southern coast of the bay, the resort town of **Busselton** ❻ has a fine setting on the Vasse River. Its 2-km (1¼-mile) jetty, the longest in the southern hemisphere, has an interpretive centre and a multimillion dollar underwater observatory (daily Dec–Apr 8am–5pm, May–Sept 10am–4pm, Oct–Nov 9am–5pm; entrance fee) that takes visitors 8 metres (26 ft) below sea level for amazing views of fish and coral.

Margaret River ❼, 280 km (173 miles) from Perth, is internationally famous for estate-grown and bottled wines. Names like Leeuwin, Xanadu, Moss Wood, Devil's Lair and dozens more rival the world's best. This is crafted wine and a far cry from the mass-production of Australia's eastern states. Margaret River's success sparked a Western Australian wine revolution that has encouraged quality production from Swan Valley down to the Great Southern region. Surfing the big waves, visiting spectacular caves such as **Mammoth**, **Lake** and **Jewel**,

Map on page 292

A wedgetail eagle at the Eagle Heritage Raptor centre, Margaret River.

BELOW:
friendly face at the Dolphin Discovery Centre, Bunbury.

Drive carefully at dusk and at night, when wildlife is most active. If a kangaroo jumps in front of your car, don't swerve. Most fatal road accidents involving wildlife occur when drivers swerve, hit loose gravel on the side of the road and lose control.

BELOW:
the Valley of the Giants Treetop Walk, Walpole.

and browsing in arts and crafts shops are alternatives to wine (and beer) sampling.

Cape Leeuwin ❽ marks the south-west extremity of Australia and the junction of the Indian and Southern oceans. This point is written into the marine lore of many navies and marked the start of Matthew Flinders' odyssey when he set out to circumnavigate and chart the Australian coastline in 1790.

Inland lies **Pemberton**, surrounded by three national parks – a region of giant karri and jarrah trees. Some of the trees are over 50 metres (160 ft) tall – the world's tallest hardwoods. The adventurous can climb the **Gloucester Tree** to the fire tower, 60 metres (190 ft) above the ground.

Travelling east along the coast road towards Denmark and Albany, stop at **Walpole** to view the ancient Tingle Forest from the Treetop Walk (daily 9am–4.15pm and 8am–5.15pm; wheelchair access; entrance fee), a lofty ramp looping over the Valley of the Giants. Further east is the **Stirling Range National Park ❾**, its conical hills and jagged peaks rising to 1,000 metres (3,300 ft), presenting challenging

walks. A seasonal centre for wildflowers, including native orchids, it receives Western Australia's only snowfalls.

To the south, **Albany ❿** is where white settlement was first established in the western half of Australia. On Christmas Day 1826, Major Lockyer arrived from Sydney in the brig *Amity*, attracted by the splendid expanses of **King George Sound**, an enclosed waterway twice as large as Sydney Harbour. Today tourists flock here from July to November to spot whales – an ironic attraction for a town that till 1978 was the last operating whaling station in the southern hemisphere. A museum, **Whaleworld** (daily 9am–5pm, until 6pm in Jan; guided tours at 10am and 4pm; entrance fee) tells the story.

Albany is also one of Australia's most picturesque towns, with a wonderful bay-side location and well-preserved 19th-century streetscapes. At nearby **Strawberry Hill** stands the state's oldest house, built in 1836 for the first government resident, Sir Richard Spencer. There is plenty of exploring to be done here. The **post office** with its shingled tower, is the oldest in Western Australia,

and the **Church of St John the Evangelist**, built in 1848, is the earliest house of worship in the state. Overlooking King George Sound is a memorial to the **Australian Light Horse** who served in Egypt and Gallipoli in World War I. It was moved here from Port Said, Egypt after the 1956 Suez War. Nearby Mount Adelaide, a military history precinct, looks down on the waters where the ANZAC Dardanelles invasion fleet assembled in 1914.

Perhaps the most spectacular park in the region is **Fitzgerald River National Park ⑪**, 185 km (115 miles) northeast of Albany. It includes an impressive stretch of coastal landscape and also contains a group of mountains known as the **Barren Range**, with dramatic views of the Southern Ocean.

The easternmost town of **Esperance ⑫** is 750 km (465 miles) from Perth. Local attractions include the salt-rich **Pink Lake** and the grave of Tommy Windich, an Aboriginal guide who accompanied explorer John Forrest on his two overland treks to Adelaide in 1870 and 1874.

Cape Le Grand and **Cape Arid** national parks offer superb beaches, an abundance of bird life and some terrific camp sites. Offshore lies a maze of beautiful islands called the **Recherche Archipelago**. On the road from Albany to the capes, opportunities for camping, fishing and surfing presents themselves at almost every turn.

The East

Around 200 km (125 miles) north of Esperance is the crossroads town of **Norseman**, from where the Eyre Highway heads east across the vast Nullarbor Plain to eastern Australia, crossing the border into South Australia after 725 km (450 miles). Alternatively, the route north heads to Kalgoorlie and the goldfields.

The goldfields

The birthplace of the West Australian goldfields was **Coolgardie ⑬**, 190 km (118 miles) north of Norseman. In Sep-

tember 1892 it was the site of Australia's richest strike at that time – producing 85 kg (200 lb) of gold in a single month. By 1900, it was a town of 15,000 people with a score of hotels, half a dozen banks, three breweries, two stock exchanges and seven newspapers. By 1905, however, the lode was running out. Today Coolgardie is an attractive, historic township with elegant buildings.

Kalgoorlie ⑭, 40 km (25 miles) away, started off as Coolgardie's twin city, but it has survived as a thriving mining town of 29,000, the hub of a region of boom and bust. When an Irishman, Paddy Hannan, discovered gold here in 1893, it was soon realised that the wealth of the Kalgoorlie find far exceeded anything else ever found in Australia. Kalgoorlie's "Golden Mile" became the richest piece of real estate in the world.

However, water hereabouts was in short supply, so the celebrated engineer C.Y. O'Connor built a pipeline from Mundaring Weir near Perth, more than 500 km (300 miles) away. Today, the area continues to yield 241 million grams (850,000 ounces) of gold a year.

Map on page 292

Emus are a fairly common sight in the roadside bush.

BELOW: the Super Pit at Kalgoorlie.

TIP

The best time to view Wave Rock is Aug–Dec when wildflowers are in bloom. Other interesting rock formations in the immediate area are Hippo's Yawn, a 20-minute walk away, and the Humps and the Breakers. For details on how to get to these rocks, check with the tourist office at the Wave Rock Wild Flower Shop and Visitor Centre (tel: 08-9880 5182).

BELOW:
Wave Rock.

Kalgoorlie's architecture retains much of its early charm, with the **Palace Hotel** being a fabulous example of Edwardian excess. The business district of Kalgoorlie is a leafy refuge from the moonscape of the mines; the continuing trade in beer, prostitution and minerals still reflects much of the town's earlier freebooting ways. For miners who gamble on the earth's riches every day, other less "legitimate" forms of gambling thrive – especially "two-up", a uniquely Australian game based on the toss of two pennies. When the Burswood Casino was about to open in Perth, the manager visited Kalgoorlie to see how Australia's most famous two-up school operated.

The main reason for visiting Kalgoorlie is to see the **Super Pit**, a working goldmine of awe-inspiring proportions. It runs tours on the third Sunday of every month, departing from the Super Pit shop in Kalgoorlie. Those whose visit does not coincide with the guided tours should head for the Super Pit lookout (daily 7am–9pm; free), just off the Goldfields Highway. It is best to come at night when the pit is lit up by high voltage-lights.

Many towns haven't fared as well as Kalgoorlie. Ghost towns such as **Gwalia** and **Kanowna** dot the area, while many outposts have seen their populations dwindle so much that they, too, will soon be deserted. In many of these centres stand the imposing relics of Australia's Wild West era.

Wave Rock

The most famous inland attraction of the southwest is **Wave Rock** , approximately 350 km (250 miles) from Perth. This natural feature appears on almost every tourist brochure of Western Australia. The rock, a few kilometres east of **Hyden**, is at once exciting and disappointing to visit. From below, this 15-metre (50-ft) high lip of solid granite looks set to curl over and crush bystanders. But, taking a wider perspective, one sees that the wave is just one wall of a huge granite dome, underscoured by erosion; and a walk along the top rather shatters the illusion.

While you are in the area of Wave

Rock, you may like to take time to visit other interesting rock formations in the immediate area. **Hippo's Yawn** is a 20-minute walk away, and the **Humps** and the **Breakers** are also nearby. For details on how to get to these rocks pop into the tourist office at the Wave Rock Wild Flower Shop and Visitor Centre (tel: 08-9880 5182).

Due west of the goldfields, farmers harvest the state's other golden bounty: wheat. **Merredin** is a busy town at the heart of one of the world's great grain belts. It was founded in 1891 around a water hole on the way to the goldfields, and has since become a research centre for improving the wheat yield of the area. Merredin's annual agricultural show is one of the most prestigious in the state. The town's tree-lined main street is best in November when the jacarandas bloom.

Situated on the Avon River, **Northam** is the central hub of the western wheat fields, and also the scene of a hell-for-leather river race each August, when hundreds of canoeists and power-boaters dash madly downstream in the Avon River Descent.

It wasn't until Robert Dale led an expedition over the Darling Range and into this 150-km (90-mile) stretch of fertile valley that the early settlers could be certain that the west held land capable of sustaining livestock and crops. The valley's towns were settled soon after Perth. For an insight into the pioneering history, **York**, with its extravagantly designed town hall, **Toodyay** and **Mahogany Creek** are well worth exploring.

North of Perth

The Perth to Darwin route is Australia's longest capital-to-capital haul, and its most desolate. At 4,027 km (2,502 miles), it is even longer than the Melbourne to Darwin trek.

A major attraction of taking the Great Northern Highway inland route rather than the coastal Brand Highway is **New Norcia** ⑯, 130 km (80 miles) from Perth. The settlement was established by Benedictine monks in 1846 as an Aboriginal mission. The monastery is still operating, although many of the town's more impressive buildings are closed to the public. However, the

Map on page 292

Traffic is scarce in rural areas. However, you are bound to encounter the massive "road trains" which can be several trailers long.

BELOW:
New Norcia's St Gertrude's College, adorned with art deco frescoes.

TIP

To discover more
about Western
Australia's history and
heritage, visit the
**Greenough Historical
Hamlet** (9am–5pm,
museum 10am–4pm;
fee includes a guided
tour) on Brand High-
way, a 20-minute drive
south of Geraldton. Its
collection of 19th-
century colonial
buildings, restored by
the National Trust,
include a church and
a schoolhouse.

BELOW:
the Pinnacles.

Spanish architectural influence is interesting and the museum and art gallery
(Aug–Oct 9.30am–5pm, Nov–July
10am–4.30pm; entrance fee) provide
fascinating insights into pioneer life.
Guided tours of the settlement are available, or visitors can take a self-guided
2-km (1½ mile) walk linking the major
sites, including the Abbey Church, decorated with locally inspired sgraffito
and an image of Our Lady of Good
Counsel, said to have been held up to
repel a bushfire in 1847. Be sure to
come away with some of the delectable
treats such as New Norcia nut cake and
Dom Salvado Pan Chocolatti, produced
by the monastery's bakery.

Heading up the coastal Brand Highway, the tiny town of **Gingin** – 82 km
(51 miles) north of Perth – is a good
first stop. There are excellent fishing
grounds off the coast, 48 km (30 miles)
to the west: estuaries such as the
mouth of the Moore River at **Guilderton** are ideal for casting a line. Just to
the south of Guilderton is the **Yanchep
National Park** (vehicle entrance fee),
offering wetlands, woodlands, bushwalks, caves and an Aboriginal her-

itage trail. **Sun City**, one of WA's
newer golf courses, is nearby.

Further north along the coast road is
Lancelin, 127 km (79 miles) north of
Perth, protected by two large rock
islands and surrounded by towering
sand dunes. Gutsy winds off the Indi-
dan Ocean make it ideal for windsurfing and surfing. It attracts top
international surfers, but also caters to
novices keen to learn.

The Pinnacles

The only way of proceeding north of
Lancelin is to follow the Brand Highway. Though considered the "coastal
route", it is quite a distance inland,
and you must turn off it in order to
see the ocean.

Nambung National Park ⑰, 29 km
(18 miles) south of the coastal town of
Cervantes and 245 km (153 miles) from
Perth, shouldn't be missed. The **Pinnacles Desert** within the park (*see below*)
is a bizarre sight: a world of limestone
spires – varying from the size of a truck
to smaller than a finger – all rising from
smooth sand dunes. When Dutch
explorers first saw the Pinnacles from

The Pinnacles

Most organised tours north of Perth
include a stop at the Pinnacles in
Nambung National Park. These strange
limestone formations known as the
Pinnacles were shaped around 30,000
years ago by winter rain leaching in to
the sand dunes and turning the lower
levels of the lime-rich sand into a soft
limestone. Plants then grew upon the
surface of the dunes, accelerating the
leaching process and causing a hard
cap to form around the roots of the
plants. Wind erosion eventually removed
the surrounding sand, leaving the
hard rock exposed and moulding it into
weird and wonderful shapes. The
process continues to this day:
submerged sections of the Pinnacles
are thought to be as deep as the
exposed sections are high.

their vessels, they thought they had found the ruins of a long-deserted city. In fact, they are entirely natural. A circular track leads around the spires (vehicle entrance fee).

A short distance up the coast is **Jurien**, a lobster-fishing centre set on the shores of an attractive sheltered bay, framed by spectacular sand dunes. **Port Denison** (now referred to as Dongara-Denison), 170 km (105 miles) further up the coast, has Australia's biggest rock lobster grounds; over 400 fishing boats work the area.

Maritime Geraldton

From the Pinnacles, continue north along Brand Highway towards Geraldton. About 25 km (13 miles) south of the city, look out for **Greenough Historical Hamlet** (daily 9am–5pm; entrance fee including a guided tour), a collection of 19th-century colonial buildings, restored by the National Trust, that presents a vivid picture of life for the early settlers.

Geraldton ⓲, 425 km (265 miles) north of Perth, supports a population of about 20,000 and is the administrative centre for West Australia's mid-coast region. It has a near-perfect climate, superb fishing conditions and fine sandy beaches that stretch north and south of Champion Bay. This stretch of coast saw many shipwrecks when early Dutch mariners heading for the East Indies were swept too far south.

The **Abrolhos Islands**, 64 km (40 miles) offshore, have claimed many ships over the years, including the Dutch East Indiaman *Batavia*, which ran aground in 1629. Survivors waited behind while the captain and a few crew headed off for Java in an open boat. While the survivors were awaiting rescue, a mutiny broke out, driving loyal crewmen to a separate island. When the captain finally returned from his epic journey, many of the mutineers were hanged; two others were cast ashore to fend for themselves.

The Abrolhos sit on one of the finest reefs on the west coast, and divers can visit various wrecks. Many relics rescued from the deep are on view in the **Western Australian Museum** (daily 10am–4pm; entrance by donation) in Geraldton and at Fremantle's Ship-

Map on page 292

Map on page 292

TIP

Skywest flies to Geraldton daily, departing from Perth domestic terminal. In Geraldton, hire a car from Avis, Budget or Hertz, which all have offices at the airport, and self-drive to Greenough and surrounding areas.

BELOW: Geraldton.

*The **Kalbarri Wild Flower Centre** (Ajana Road, Jul–Nov daily 9am–5pm, the: 08-9937 1229) provides a nature trail or a guided walk through Kalbarri's Native Botanic Garden.*

BELOW: wildlife spotting cruises leave from Monkey Mia.

wreck Gallery where the hull of the *Batavia* is on display.

For panoramic views of the area surrounding Geraldton, head for **Waverley Heights**. **Ellendale Bluffs** are notable for their sheer cliffs, at the base of which is a permanent waterhole. Locals will advise you to visit **Chapman Valley**, at its most spectacular in spring (Sept–Nov) when the wildflowers are in bloom.

A century ago, **Northampton**, 48 km (30 miles) north of Geraldton, was an important rural outpost. Recently it has been spruced up by residents to create an unusually pretty Outback town. Buildings such as **Chiverton House Museum** (Fri–Mon 10am –noon and 2–4pm; free) were built by convict labour; the cemetery in the grounds of Gwalia Church records the passing of the convicts and free settlers who first came to the area.

About 20 km (12 miles) away is **Horrock Beach**, with fine sand expanses and bays. When there is water in it, don't be surprised to see **Lake Hutt**, near Port Gregory, turn pink in the midday sun – a bizarre phenomenon caused by light refraction and naturally occurring beta carotene in the water.

Kalbarri National Park

Comprising 186,000 hectares (460,000 acres), **Kalbarri National Park** ⓳ (tel: 08-9937 1140) features a combination of stunning river gorges and towering sea cliffs. The park is set around the lower reaches of the Murchison River, which weaves its way to the Indian Ocean past the multi-hued sandstone formations of Red Bluff.

South of Carnarvon is the great system of peninsulas and inlets of **Hamelin Pool** and **Denham Sound**. These two huge expanses of water are protected in the northeast by **Dirk Hartog Island**. A pewter plate, nailed in 1616 to a post on Cape Inscription by the Dutch explorer Hartog, marked the first known landing of Europeans on Australia's west coast. A replica of this plate is in the **Shark Bay Shire Office** (the original is in Amsterdam).

Dolphins at Monkey Mia

Despite its name, **Shark Bay** is one place where every visitor ventures into

Exploring Kalbarri

To get the most out of Kalbarri National Park and the multitude of adventure activities on offer, especially when time is limited, you may want to sign up with a specialist tour operator.
● **Kalbarri Safari Tours**, tel: 08-9937 1011.
● **Kalbarri Boat Hire**. For a canoe safari, tel: 08-9937 1245.
● **Kalbarri Abseil**, tel: 08-9937 1618.
● **Kalbarri Sand-Boarding**, tel: 1800 886 141.

For deep-sea fishing or whale-watching tours, contact **Kalbarri Explorer Ocean Charters**, tel: 08-9937 2027, or **Kalbarri Reefwalker Tours** Coastal Cruises, tel: 08-9937 1356.

Kalbarri Aquarium (daily 10am– 4pm, tel: 08-9937 2027) provides a good overview of the local marine life,

the water. That's because this is the site of **Monkey Mia** ⑳, perhaps one of Australia's most delightful tourist attractions. In the small bay near Denham township, wild dolphins come to shore to be fed and mingle with visitors. This came about when local fishermen started tossing fish scraps overboard to following dolphins – by 1964, they were coming in to be hand-fed. This unique interaction between humans and dolphins is still very delicate, so follow the rangers' instructions.

Monkey Mia is only the best-known corner of Shark Bay, which was declared a World Heritage area in 1991. Covering 2.3 million hectares (5.7 million acres), it comprises a series of cliff-lined peninsulas and islands with some 145 species of plants (28 endemic to the region, having developed in isolation). The extraordinary salinity of the southern parts of Shark Bay have allowed the growth of stromatolites at Hamelin Pool – giant masses of algae that are considered the oldest form of life on earth (they probably first formed 3 billion years ago). Somewhat more exciting to observe are

the many dugongs, humpback whales and green and loggerhead turtles that roam the splendid arc-shaped bays.

On Shark Bay's slender land prongs, scientists are reintroducing furry marsupials with quaint names like burrowing bettongs and western barred bandicoots. These native species, almost eaten to extinction by introduced foxes and cats, now live behind predator-proof fences.

The tropical north

Carnarvon ㉑ is 1,000 km (600 miles) north of Perth on the beautiful **Gascoyne River**. Sitting just below the Tropic of Capricorn, Carnarvon has warm winters and tropical summers that encourage vibrant tropical wildlife, yield a huge banana crop and boatloads of succulent prawns. The town was established in 1883, though Dutch explorer Willem de Vlamingh first landed nearby in 1697. Game fishermen relish the area, and picturesque **Pelican Point** is good for swimming. **Miaboolya Beach** is worth a look, as is the **Bibbawarra artesian bore**, where water surface temperatures are 70°C (158°F).

Map on page 292

A pair of pelicans at Monkey Mia.

BELOW: Kalbarri National Park.

Further north, a spectacular coastline unfolds, with blowholes, sheltered beaches and wild seascapes. The landlocked **Lake MacLeod**, is famous for salt production. Inland, southwest of **Exmouth** is the **Cape Range National Park ㉒**, based along a rugged, dry limestone ridge. Boat trips through Yardie Creek Gorge are good, with predictable sightings of rock wallabies.

Offshore, **Ningaloo Reef** in its protected marine park stretches 260 km (160 miles) from Amherst Point around North West Cape into the Exmouth Gulf. Western Australia's largest coral reef, with 250 species of coral and more than 500 fish types, Ningaloo is an unspoilt delight for divers. Coral outcrops can be reached just 20 metres (65 ft) from the beach, though they extend 7 km (12 miles) into the ocean. Dolphins, dugongs, manta rays, giant cod and sharks abound. Whale sharks visit the reef from March to June.

Coral Bay, 1,132 km (703 miles) from Perth, is renowned for fishing and diving. Snorkelling tours go out from here or Exmouth.

The Pilbara

To the east of Exmouth lies the region called **The Pilbara**, focal point of the state's mineral wealth and one of the world's richest series of holes in the ground. Here, iron ore is king, and company towns seem to appear overnight amid the spinifex. Ore mined at such places as Tom Price and Mount Newman is freighted by rail systems to the coastline, where it is shipped off for national or overseas processing.

The northwest was first explored by the English pirate and explorer William Dampier in 1688 and 1699, so names based on *Buccaneer*, *Cygnet* and *Roebuck* (his vessels) litter the coast. The **Dampier Archipelago** includes **Barrow Island**, the centre for the North West Shelf oil and gas fields. Far from being an environmentally threatened area, it is classified as a wildlife sanctuary and has some unusual animal, bird and plant life.

Roebourne is the oldest town in the northwest, but in recent years its importance has waned because of the clout of the newly established mining towns. The ghost town of **Cossack** is a reminder of the one-time might of the local pearling industry (before it moved north to Broome and beyond), while a jaunt up the **Fortescue River** reveals the lush area around the Millstream, a bountiful supply of fresh water for many Pilbara towns. The **Millstream-Chichester National Park** is a fine outing for naturalists or hikers.

The magnificent **Karijini National Park ㉓** (previously Hamersley Range National Park), with spectacular gorges and bluffs, can be reached from **Tom Price**. Karijini's visitor centre (daily, times vary seasonally; tel: 08-9189 8121) is worth a look. Designed to withstand bushfires, the centre is shaped like a goanna (an animal sacred to the local Banyjima Aboriginal people) and contains information on the natural and cultural history of the area. Karratha, 40 km (25 miles) from the port of Dampier, has been developed as the work base for the mighty Hamersley Iron concern.

For an indication of just how much ore might be coming out of the ground, take a look at the loading facilities at **Port Hedland** ㉔. This seaside town, which copes with more tonnage than any other port in Australia, is almost exclusively geared to handle the iron ore from the huge open-cut and strip mining centres of The Pilbara. Port Hedland is built on an island linked to the mainland by three long causeways. Visitors can view the loading from the wharves where some of the world's largest ore carriers dock. The Port Hedland visitor centre offers daily tours of the BHP-Billiton Nelson Point and Port Authority workings and half-day tours of Dampier Salt and BHP's Boodarie Iron.

Port Hedland has no shortage of drawbacks. Its tropical setting makes it prone to cyclones; its seas are considered unsafe for swimming, thanks to sharks and stonefish; and its industrial and mineral landscape might not be to everyone's liking. But the local fishing is excellent, there are nearby Aboriginal carvings, bird life is abundant, and you can cool off in the town swimming pool or at Pretty Pool inlet.

To sample a real Western Australian Outback town, detour 193 km (120 miles) southeast to **Marble Bar**. With a population of less than 400, it owes its existence to the discovery of gold in 1891 and 1931. The disused **Comet Gold Mine**, 10 km (6 miles) south of town, has a museum and visitor centre.

Pearling centre

Coming from the south, along the vast monotony of the road between Port Hedland and Broome, the highway describes a gentle arc along a stretch of coastline known aptly as the **Eighty Mile Reach**.

During the 1920s, **Broome** ㉕ was the capital of the world pearling industry, with more than 300 luggers (pearling vessels) competing for finds off the northwest coast of Australia. For the mostly Japanese divers, the real wealth lay in the mother-of-pearl shell, which was used in jewellery and for buttons; a pearl was an unexpected bonus. But it was a dangerous job, as the Japanese Cemetery testifies. Broome went into the doldrums when plastic buttons flooded the market after

Map on page 292

The outback town of Marble Bar is renowned as the hottest place in Australia. Daytime temperatures can regularly soar past 38°C (100°F), even in winter. In Dec–Jan, temperatures higher than 45°C (113°F) are common.

BELOW:
Karijini
National Park.

*A Broome pearl
in an elegant
Spanish pendant.*

BELOW:
Manning Gorge
in the Kimberley.

World War II. The recent development of cultured pearls has revitalised the industry (although the harvesting now occurs in remote aquatic farms) and several Broome jewellery shops, including one owned by the dominant pearling operator, Paspaley Pearls, sell fine pearls in a variety of settings. A stroll through the timber dwellings of Chinatown, with its multilingual street signs, provides an insight into what the town was like in the pearling days.

With a large Asian population, Broome has retained enough character to be one of Australia's most fascinating communities. Aboriginal culture thrives here, with an Aboriginal radio and TV station (Goolari, known as "GTV"), which broadcasts partly in local dialect. The town comes alive each August when fishermen, farmers, miners, drovers and tourists swell the population tenfold for the Shinju Matsuri – Festival of the Pearl.

Residents will point out such exotic attractions as the "Golden Staircase to the Moon", an optical illusion created when moonlight reflects on the ocean bed at low-water spring tides. At **Gant-heaume Point**, when the tide is low, giant dinosaur tracks considered to be 130 million years old can be viewed.

The 22-km (14-mile) **Cable Beach** was named after the underwater communication link between Broome and Java (and on to London) was established in the 19th century. Today it is the core of Broome's tourist industry, with an up-market resort and crocodile farm complementing the glorious ocean beach. A ride on a camel train along the beach at sunset is a great experience.

Outback of the Outback

For Australians, the **Kimberley** region is the final frontier. About half the size of Texas but with only 26,000 inhabitants, encompassing ½ million-hectare (1.2 million-acre) cattle ranches and enormous Aboriginal tribal lands, it was first explored in the 1890s but has opened to travellers only over the past 20 years. The landscapes here are awe-inspiring, even by Antipodean standards. The blood-red desert is sliced by lush, forest-filled gorges, where freshwater crocodiles and stingrays swim;

the coastline is torn by tropical fjords with tidal waterfalls that flow horizontally. Everything is on a gargantuan scale: vast meteor craters, petrified coral reefs and desert rivers that swell from 100 metres (330 ft) wide in the dry season to 13 km (8 miles) wide in the wet.

Generations of isolation have left the Kimberley region the most Aboriginal part of Australia, with some immense tracts of tribal land. Remote communities have their own language, newspapers and radio stations; Aboriginal guides work at the national parks and conduct tours of ancient cave paintings; and it has one of Australia's few Aboriginal-owned resorts (at Cape Leveque).

This independence was hard-won. White ranchers arrived here in the 1890s after the world's longest – and most gruelling – cattle drive across central Australia. Soon the Kimberley was the scene of a little-known Aboriginal uprising and of several massacres of indigenous peoples by settlers. Aboriginal bushrangers roamed the Kimberley, easily evading mounted police posses in the rugged terrain. Newspaper readers in faraway Sydney were both thrilled and horrified by their exploits.

Derby ㉖, 216 km (134 miles) along the highway northeast from Broome, is the administrative centre for the huge cattle-producing region of West Kimberley. Unlike bustling Broome, with a population of 10,000, Derby is a sleepy town where little seems to have changed over the decades. From here, sightseeing is mostly by light plane: taking a flight from Derby over **King Sound** and the **Buccaneer Archipelago** ㉗ beyond will unfold one of the world's most spectacularly beautiful coastlines, a maze of islands, red cliffs and white beaches – uninhabited except for the mining communities of **Cockatoo Island** and **Koolan Islands**. Cruise vessels also operate along the coast.

From Derby, you can either follow the main all-weather **Great Northern Highway** or turn off onto the "Beef Road", the **Gibb River Road**, which cuts through the heart of the Kimberley. Seven km (4¼ miles) outside Derby is a huge boab tree that is reputed to have been used as an overnight prison when transporting prisoners in colonial

Map on page 292

TIP

The only sensible time to visit the Kimberley, whose landscapes are hallucinatory even by Antipodean standards, is Apr–Sept. At other times it is unbearably hot and humid, with a good chance of being isolated by flash floods.

BELOW: a camel train on Cable Beach, near Broome.

times. The boab (a close relation of the southern African baobab tree, is often known as the "bottle tree" and can have a circumference greater than its height – the girth frequently exceeds 10 metres (33 ft).

Windjana Gorge National Park ㉘ (tel: 08-9191 1426), 145 km (90 miles) to the east, is worth a visit for its eerie Wandjina figures in Aboriginal rock paintings, and its huge flocks of spooky, screeching white cockatoos. **Tunnel Creek National Park** ㉙, 35 km (22 miles) further on, allows you to walk through an underground stream course populated by bats. Only recently has this part of the Kimberley become accessible to people other than the toughest pioneers, cattlemen or prospectors. The roads are constantly being improved as the area opens up to tourism.

East of Derby, on the Fitzroy River near the township of Fitzroy Crossing, is **Geikie Gorge** ㉚, 14 km (9 miles) long, with limestone cliffs up to 30 metres (100 ft) high. This is one of the most spectacular gorges in the northwest and a pleasant camping spot.

Western Australia has 10,000 species of wild flowers, 6,000 of them native to the state. Make sure you travel in spring if you want to see the state in all its floral glory (see pages 312–3).

BELOW: cruising Geikie Gorge.

Interesting tours conducted by Aboriginal rangers can be taken along the river, where fresh water crocodiles sunbake at the water's edge; down below, you can see sawfish and stingrays that have adapted to life in freshwater. On the eastern side lies **Fossil Downs**, a huge private cattle station (over 405,000 hectares/1 million acres), founded in 1886. It is the only Kimberley cattle station still owned by descendants of the original pioneers, the MacDonalds.

Regional centre

The Great Northern Highway cuts along the southern perimeter of the Kimberley before entering the new township of **Halls Creek** which, with its comfortable hotels and air-conditioned supermarkets, serves as a base for the regional pastoral industry. At "Old Halls Creek", remnants of the 1884 gold rush can be seen. The rush made a few prospectors rich, but the harsh environment and shortage of water ruined a good many more.

South of Halls Creek, 130 km (80 miles) away, is the meteorite crater at

Wolfe Creek ③, the second largest in the world – although it really comes into visual perspective only from the air.

The turn-off 110 km (68 miles) north of Halls Creek leads to a 4WD track to one of the most astonishing natural features in the world: the **Bungle Bungle Range**. The "Bungles" cover some 640 sq. km (247 sq. miles) of the Ord River Valley with a labyrinth of orange and black (caused by the black lichen and orange silica) horizontally tiger-striped, domed mountains. Within the canyons and gorges of the **Purnululu National Park** ② are palm-filled grottoes, enormous caves and white-sand beaches. It's a wonderland with variations that no human mind could have envisaged. The rough track from the highway deters many, so a thriving industry has arisen in **Kununurra** to fly tourists over (and, more recently, into) the Bungle Bungles.

A true gem of the Kimberley lies to the north of Purnululu: **Argyle Diamond Mine** is the world's largest, extracting some 1,000 kg (6.5 tonnes) of diamonds each year. The Argyle Diamond Pipe was discovered in 1979 and remains the only source of deep-pink diamonds. Air tours to the mine are available from Kununurra.

Wyndham ③ is the most northerly port in Western Australia, a small scattered community that has changed little since the days of the gold rush. You can see large crocodiles lying on the mudflats below the Wyndham wharf. Cattle that miss their footing when being loaded onto ships provide an occasional meal.

The Ord River was dammed in 1971 to harness the monsoon runoff for irrigation; in recent years, this has opened up the East Kimberley to the cultivation of tropical crops. To the south, Lake Argyle in the **Carr Boyd Range** is the main reservoir (boat tours are conducted around it). The damming of the Ord River would have submerged **Argyle Downs Homestead**, home of one of the northwest's great pioneering families, the Duracks, so it was moved to a new location to escape the rising waters. It is now a museum about life for the early settlers of the Kimberley.   ❑

Map on page 292

The Kimberley is such an isolated region that the extraordinary "Bungles" were unknown to all but a few locals until 1983, when a photographer came upon them by chance.

BELOW: the Bungle Bungles.

RESTAURANTS & BARS

Perth

Fraser's Restaurant
Fraser Ave.
Tel: 08-9481 7100
www.frasersrestaurant
.com.au
Open: B, L & D daily. $$$
Top-quality local produce is used abundantly, from roast kangaroo loin with potato and celeriac crumble, beetroot and caramelised onion, to chargrilled WA rock lobster with spicy tomato sauce. The restaurant is situated in Kings Park.

Matilda Bay Restaurant
3 Hackett Drive, Crawley.
Tel: 08-9423 5000.
www.matbay.com.au
Open: B Sun, L & D daily. $$$
Situated on the banks of the Swan at Matilda Bay, this restaurant is popular for its beautiful views. The menu has rotisserie items, fresh crayfish, plus favourites such as chargrilled sirloin and rack of lamb.

C Restaurant Lounge
St Martin's Tower, level 33/
44 St George's Terrace.
Tel: 08-9220 8333.
www.crestaurant.com.au
Open: L & D, everyday except Sat, D only. Open until late every night. $$$$
Located on the 33rd storey of one of the city's office buildings, this revolving restaurant offers superb views. The modern-Australian food is also excellent.

Jackson's
483 Beaufort Street, Highgate.
Tel: 08-9328 1177.
www.jacksonsrestaurant.
com.au
Open: D Mon–Sat. $$$$
One of Perth's top places to dine. Expect interesting combinations, such as apple risotto with grilled chorizo and scallops.

Lamont's
11 Brown Street.
Tel: 08-9202 1566.
www.lamonts.com.au
Open: B Sat and Sun, L Tues–Sun, D Wed–Sat. $$$$
Kate Lamont is one of Perth's best-loved foodies, and her riverside East Perth property has become a local institution. Showcases the best in local produce.

Indiana Tea House
99 Marine Parade, Cottesloe.
Tel: 08-9385 5005.
www.indiana.com.au
Open: L & D daily. $$$
This majestic building sits perched above the sands at Cottesloe Beach. The style is colonial, but the food ranges from pasta to sushi. Get an oceanside table and watch the sunset.

The Southwest

Albany Area

Maleeya's Thai Café
1376 Porongurup Road, Porongurup.
Tel: 08-9853 1123.
Open: L & D Fri–Sun. $$–$$$
One of the best dining options in the southwest. The food is fresh and fantastic. Many of the organic vegetables and herbs are grown in the gardens. Booking essential.

Bunbury

Vat 2
2 Jetty Road, Bunbury.
Tel: 08-9791 8833.
www.vat2.com.au
Open: B, L & D daily.$$$
Located near the water in the Marlston Hill development, Vat 2 caters for those looking for a light snack (chicken salad with prosciutto, for example) or a more substantial meal (grilled meats and pastas).

Bunker Bay

Other Side of the Moon
Bunker Bay Road,
Tel: 08-9756 9100.
Open: B, L & D daily. $$$$
Located in the up-market Bunker Bay resort, with views over olive trees and the pool to the ocean. The food is Modern Australian and uses the best and freshest local produce, such as Pemberton marron and lamb. The desserts are divine.

Busselton and Vasse

Bay Organics
63 Duchess Sreet, Busselton.
Tel: 08-9751 1315.
Open: B & L Mon–Sat. $
Bay Organics is a little cottage-like café selling delicious healthy food. The lentil burger is outstanding, as are the salads. The owners grow all the vegetables and herbs organically, and there is also a small organic grocery store inside. Worth a visit even if you're not particularly in to healthy food.

The Goose
Geographe Bay Rd, Busselton.
Tel: 08-9754 7700.

LEFT: lunch at Matilda Bay Restaurant, Crawley.

www.thegoose.com.au
Open: B, L & D daily. $$$
Overlooking the ocean, right next to the Busselton Jetty, The Goose is a light and airy restaurant serving quality food. The modern menu changes regularly. Sample dishes include *nasi goreng* and seared tuna steaks. Gorgeous views whatever the weather.

Margaret River Region

Cape Lavender
Lot 4 Carter Road, Metricup.
Tel: 08-9755 7552.
www.capelavender.com.au
Open: L daily. $$$
Cape Lavender has won several Gold Plate awards for its food. The menu includes items such as individual tarts filled with spinach, roast pumpkin, capsicum and feta topped with a rocket and olive salad, as well as more substantial meals. The farm also grows lavender, which is made into a variety of products, including lavender scones and lavender sparkling wine.

Lamont's
Gunyulgup Valley Drive, Yallingup.
Tel: 08-9755 2434.
www.lamonts.com.au
Open: B & L daily, D Sat. $$$$
The elegant food is matched by the wonderful setting – perched over a lake in the middle of the bush. The menu includes sugar-cured Margaret River venison, black pepper shortbread and tapenade, and Pemberton marron, roasted

baby potatoes, green veg, lime and chive *beurre blanc*.

Wino's
85 Bussell Highway, Margaret River. Tel: 08-9758 7155.
Open: L Sat, Sun, D daily. $$$
Located in the heart of Margaret River, this is a chilled restaurant serving excellent food. The dark wood floors and the extensive tapas menu are European in character. There is an extensive wine selection, as you would expect.

Vasse Felix
Corner Caves and Harman's South roads, Yallingup.
Tel: 08-9755 5425.
www.vassefelix.com.au
Open: L daily. $$$
Vasse Felix is a top winery, and this is a top restaurant serving high-quality modern Australian food. The timber and stone building is a great place to sit and relax while you look out over the vineyards.

Walpole & Nornalup

Nornalup Teahouse Restaurant
South Coast Highway, Nornalup.
Tel: 08-9840 1422.
www.nornalupteahouse.com.au
Open: B, L & D Wed–Mon. $$$
This beautifully converted cottage has an idyllic setting. The food is also excellent. Call ahead because the opening times change from time to time, and booking on popular nights is recommended. A hidden treasure.

East

Kalgoorlie

Saltimbocca
90 Egan Sreet, Kalgoorlie.
Tel: 08-9022 8028.
Open: L Wed–Fri, D Mon–Sat. $$$
The house speciality here is the veal saltimbocca, in a creamy prosciutto, sage and white wine sauce. Known for its homemade pastas.

York

The Ragged Robin
27 South Street, York.
Tel: 08-9641 1266.
www.raggedrobin.com.au
Open: L Sun, D Thur–Sat. $$$
A relaxed and intimate fine dining experience in a heritage-listed building. A typical dish is seared scallops on braised pork belly with pineapple and cauliflower purée.

North

Geraldton

Skeeta's Restaurant and Café
101 Foreshore Drive.
Tel: 08-9964 1619.
Open: B, L & D daily. $$$
Specialises in seafood, but they cater for non-fish eaters covered, too, with pasta, steak and chicken dishes. The whiting fillets served with crispy gourmet potatoes and salad are a favourite, as is the seafood platter for two.

Kalbarri

Echo Beach
Porter Street, Kalbarri.
Tel: 08-9937 1033.

Open: B, L & D daily. $
The food and ambience are great, whether you want a simple coffee for a morning wake-up or a proper meal. The interior is fresh and modern.

Black Rock Café
80 Grey Street.
Tel: 08-9937 1062.
www.blackrockcafe.com.au
Open: B & L Tues–Sun, D Tues–Sat. $$$
Interesting food ranging from strawberry pancakes at breakfast to surf-and-turf dinners, potato rosti and salad. The view of the Murchison River as it meets the Indian Ocean is spectacular.

The Grass Tree Café and Restaurant
94–96 Grey Street.
Tel: 08-9937 2288.
Open: B, L & D Thur–Tues. $$$$–$$$$
With its sweeping ocean views, the Grass Tree brings a touch of sophistication to this relaxed town. The food is part Asian and part European; the signature dish is shelled crayfish in creamy whisky sauce.

THE BUSH BLOOMS ETERNAL

In spring, the bush is ablaze with wildflowers, from bold and brilliant banksias to delicate ice daisies

Western Australia is known for its beautiful wildflowers and people travel from all around the country – and the world – to view the impressive display. The flowering is most spectacular during spring (August through to November), though at almost any time of the year you will find some flowers brightening the olive- and sage-greens of the bush. Banksias, for example, often bloom in autumn or winter. It might seem strange that such a dry landscape should produce so many wildflowers and there are various reasons for their success. For millions of years western Australia has avoided the sort of landmass upheaval that have caused species in other parts of the continent to die out. The flowers have also benefitted from the lack of shade-casting trees and instead have enjoyed the protection of smaller, less engulfing, plants and shrubs.

The state has some 10,000 species of wildflowers, 6,000 native to the state, and journeys in spring will be rewarded by stunning roadside displays. But some areas are particularly well-endowed: Kalbarri National Park, the karri forests around Pemberton, and the Stirling Ranges north of Albany. The southwest is known for its delicate flowers such as orchid, kangaroo paw and mountain bell. It also has one of the world's highest distributions of different flower varieties.

Closer to Perth, John Forrest National Park is another rich area, or you could simply visit Kings Park Botanic Garden, especially during its Wild Flower Festival in September. We recommend you pack a picnic and a camera and take your time enjoying the rich palette of the blooms. The Western Australian Visitor Centre in Perth has maps to ensure you make the most of the wildflower season.

ABOVE: a typical roadside display near Kalbarri in spring. If you have a special interest in wildflowers it is worth taking an escorted wildflower tour, an option offered by most of the day-tour operators in Perth.

ABOVE: Albany bottlebrush. Bottlebrush is more commonly associated with the eastern states (it was one of the plants the naturalist Joseph Banks collected on Cook's voyage of 1770), but you will also find it in WA, especially in damp habitats.

BELOW: in spring, daisies of many types and colours carpet forest clearings, heathlands and fields.

GRASS TREES

Even if you are not in Western Australia during the wildflower season, the bush is a fascinating landscape with a rich biodiversity that is at last being championed by conservationists after well over a century of indiscriminate land clearance for agriculture.

Among the many types of eucalyptus (gum trees), paper bark, banksias, etc, the tree that perhaps stands out above all others is the grass tree *(Xanthorrhoea)*, with their distinctive fire-blackened trunk surmounted by a mop of spiky grass and spear-like flower shaft.

Grass trees are very slow-growing (about 1 metre/3 ft every 100 years) but can live for hundreds of years, and their ability to survive in tough conditions has made them a symbol of the Australian Outback. Like many other bush plants, they have evolved to withstand bushfires, and germination is actually assisted by fire. The distinctive flower shaft will often shoot up in the year following a bushfire, providing valuable food to wildlife in an otherwise charred, barren landscape. In contrast to the slow-growing trunk, the flowering stalk grows rapidly after germination, at a rate of 2–3 cm (1 inch) a day.

The trees are known as balga (black boys) to the Aborigines, who traditionally used a waterproof resin produced from the base of the plant to make glue. The shafts could also be used as spear heads, and the dried flower shafts could be rubbed together to create fire. The tender shoots could be eaten, and the nectar from the flowers of the plant was used to make a sweet drink. In their turn, the settlers had various uses for the resin, for furniture polish among other things. Today they are prized by horticulturalists – plants saved from the developers' bulldozers can, with great skill and care, be transplanted and coaxed into life.

RIGHT: succulents, such as these in a forest near Karridale, also flourish, especially in the south. Succulents are plants that survive in hot, arid areas. Their characteristic fleshy leaves, stems and roots store water and their compact shape reduces dehydration. The best-known type of succulent is the cactus, but there are many other forms.

BELOW: there are 12 species of the delightfully named kangaroo paw (the flower resembles a paw tipped with small white claws). The distinctive red and green kangaroo paw *(Anigozanthos manglesii)* is Western Australia's floral emblem. Kangaroo paw grows easily in native soils and is a common feature in Western Australian gardens.

LEFT: Banksias have large cone-shaped flowers comprising hundreds of tiny individual flowers. The temperate southwest corner of WA supports some 60 different species, many of which flower in winter. Banksias are named after Joseph Banks, Captain Cook's botanist, and were celebrated in the *Snugglepot and Cuddlepie* book and bush baby drawings of the children's author and illustrator May Gibbs (1877–1969).

TASMANIA

Australia's smallest and remotest state is also the most temperate. It has no arid Outback but there's an abundance of cool forests, rugged mountains, highland lakes, lush pasture and fruitful orchards

"How beautiful is the whole region, for form, and grouping, and opulence, and freshness of foliage, and variety of color, and grace and shapeliness of the hills, the capes, the promontories; and then, the splendor of the sunlight, the dim rich distances, the charm of the water-glimpses!" Such was the view of inveterate traveller Mark Twain, commenting on his voyage to Tasmania in the 1890s.

However, he then went on to point out the irony behind this observation: "And it was in this paradise that the yellow-liveried convicts were landed, and the Corps-bandits quartered, and the wanton slaughter of the kangaroo-chasing black innocents consummated on that autumn day in May, in the brutish old time. It was all out of keeping with the place, a sort of bringing of heaven and hell together."

This is the paradox of Tasmania, nowhere more so than at the Port Arthur Penal Settlement, the most popular of the state's myriad tourist attractions. It sits in a jaw-droppingly gorgeous setting: an amphitheatre of rolling green meadow leading down to the tranquil blue waters of Mason Cove, dotted with picturesque sandstone ruins glowing golden yellow in the watery sunlight. Even without the sun, there is something magisterial and uplifting about the setting. Yet this must be reconciled with its original role as a setting for a prison regime, which was considered by many to be the harshest in the British Empire.

Van Diemen's Land

That was in the days when the island was Van Diemen's Land (after being so named by Abel Tasman in 1642) and when British colonists were establishing their second toehold on the Australian continent. It was a struggle to tame the inhospitable land and establish viable agriculture. Today there are still vast stretches of Tasmania which are only accessible by tough walking tracks. Even in populated regions, there is a sense of space. It's to be expected in an island the size of Ire-

Map on page 322

PRECEDING PAGES: hiking across the southwestern wilderness.
LEFT: the bridge at Richmond.
BELOW: the blowhole at Bicheno.

Salamanca Market.

BELOW: Hobart is beautifully situated between mountain and water.

land but with an eighth of the latter's 4 million people.

So Twain's first observations still apply today. Tasmania's appeal resides in the range and beauty of its landscapes and natural features, from the lakes and mountains of the central highlands, culminating in the iconic Cradle Mountain, to the deserted beaches of the east coast where the aquamarine of the seas is offset by the vibrant orange lichen on the rocks that run down to it.

And if this isn't enough, try the islands in the Bass Strait where, such is the sparseness of the population, every motorist acknowledges every other.

Few venture to such far-flung outposts on their first visit though. There are no international flights to Tasmania and just the odd cruise ship so most visitors come via the mainland, either on the *Spirit of Tasmania* ferries from Melbourne to Devonport or by air into Hobart or Launceston.

Hobart

If you follow Twain's lead and make **Hobart ❶** the first port of call, you'll find a small distinguished city nestling between the waters of the Derwent and the brooding bulk of Mount Wellington. These features have prevented the urban sprawl that affects the mainland cities, while a spell in the economic doldrums in the 1960s and 1970s meant that much of the old colonial architecture was spared from development. Today, here and across the state, there are numerous well-preserved Georgian and Victorian buildings to give character and a nod back to old England.

Hobart's waterfront is a magnet. There are the classic views across to Mount Wellington and plenty of remnants of the thriving 19th-century port. At **Victoria Dock ❹**, the beautifully restored IXL **Jam Factory** is on the site of the first wharf and now contains the remarkable, award-winning **Henry Jones Art Hotel**, and the University of Tasmania's **Centre for the Arts**.

Visit both, then wander across to the adjoining **Constitution Dock**. Consider fish and chips from one of the floating stalls, then head to **Salamanca Place ❸**. This is the site of a pulsating Saturday morning market, but even without that, the old stone warehouses

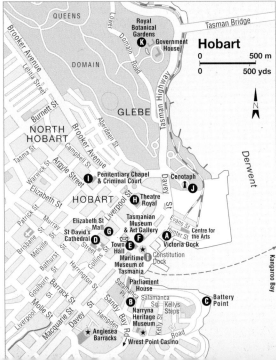

are atmospheric and appealing. They house a lively arts centre as well as the usual selection of galleries, bars and cafés. Behind them is the pedestrianised **Salamanca Square**, a modern development that successfully latches on to the original buildings.

East along Salamanca Place turn up Kelly's Steps to the eyrie of **Battery Point Ⓒ**, where a pristine collection of the city's earliest dwellings is to be found. At its centre is Arthur's Circus, doing a fine impression of a village green, while Hampden Road's range of eateries includes the peerless **Jackman & McRoss** bakery/café. The **Narryna Folk Museum** (Tues–Fri 10.30am–5pm, Sat–Sun 2–5pm; tel: 03-6234 2791; entrance fee) preserves a merchant's house in Victorian splendour.

Westwards along Salamanca Place brings you to the administrative centre of the state. The discreet sandstone-clad modernism of the **Supreme Court** on the left is balanced by the more conventional Victorian bulk of **Parliament House** on the right (tours when houses not sitting; Mon–Fri 2–5pm; tel: 03-6233 2200; www.parliament.tas.gov.au; free).

Macquarie Street

A block further back, Macquarie Street has **St David's Cathedral ⒟** – the Georgian-style seat of the local Anglican bishop; the **Treasury Building** facing onto the formal gardens of Franklin Square; the **General Post Office**, built with the grandeur that characterises these buildings; the **Town Hall ⒠**; the art deco sleekness of the **Mercury Newspaper Building**; and the **Tasmanian Museum and Art Gallery ⒡** (daily 10am–5pm; tel: 03-6211 4177; www.tmag.tas.gov.au; free).

The museum is a repository for colonial and contemporary art, local fauna, a collection of Chinese antiquities, and material illustrating early polar exploration. The **Maritime Museum of Tasmania** (daily 9am–5pm; tel: 03-6234 1427; www.maritimetas.com.au; entrance fee) is small but worthwhile.

Another block back from the water, the main downtown shopping area centres on **Elizabeth Street Mall ⒢**.

North, beyond the mass of the Royal Hobart Hospital, the old **Theatre Royal ⒣** on Campbell Street is well worth a visit. It's plush auditorium can usually

The Maritime Museum of Tasmania.

BELOW: Sir John Franklin's statue in Franklin Square.

Maps:
Area 322
City 318

be inspected if you employ a touch of charm at the box office, and it is well worth a look to appreciate the set-builder's art. The auditorium was completely rebuilt in 1984 after a fire.

A few blocks up Campbell Street the **Penitentiary Chapel and Criminal Courts** ❶ (tours daily 10am, 11.30am, 1pm, 2.30pm; ghost tour 8pm; tel: 03-6231 0911; entrance fee) are all that remain of the original vast Hobart Gaol. Splendid tours are run by knowledgeable National Trust volunteers.

The Queens Domain

If you head north-east and can manage to cross some busy highways, **Queens Domain** has, since the early days, been a place of recreation, remembrance and, for the occupant of Government House, residence. The **Cenotaph** ❿ is flanked by a couple of interesting modern glass and stone pyramids that incorporate audio tributes to those lost in combat. The **Royal Botanical Gardens** ⓚ were established in 1828 and still appear to be faithful to the early vision of the founders by collecting every conceivable variety of flora.

North Hobart has a plethora of cosmopolitan bars, restaurants and entertainment venues. Further north still, **Runnymede** in New Town is an early 1830s homestead maintained by the National Trust (61 Bay Road, New Town; daily Aug–June 10am–4.30pm; tel: 03-6278 1269; entrance fee) and worth a stop on the way to the **Moorilla Estate**. This winery not only claims one of Tasmania's leading restaurants but also houses a purpose-built **Museum of Antiquities** gathered from around the globe (Main Road, Berriedale; daily 9am–4pm; tel: 03-6277 9900; www.moorilla.com.au; free).

Kids can go wild in the suburb of Claremont, either at the eccentric **Alpenrail Swiss Model Village and Railway** (82 Abbotsfield Rd, West Claremont; daily 9.30am–4.30pm; tel: 03-6249 3748; entrance fee), or on a tour of the **Cadbury Chocolate Factory** (Mon–Fri 8am–2.30 pm, half-hourly; bookings essential; tel: 03-1800 627 367; entrance fee). In the latter, mildly disturbed chocoholic guides obsess about the product, pausing only to hand out samples.

An African figure made from beads at the Museum of Antiquities, part of Moorilla Estate Winery.

BELOW: old and new structures at the Cenotaph. **RIGHT:** a performance of *Louisa's Walk* at the Female Factory.

West of the city centre, Mount Wellington provides superb views of the city, and make sure that you visit the **Cascade Brewery** (Cascade Road, South Hobart; daily, times vary; bookings essential; tel: 03-6224 1117; entrance fee). Relish the picturesque setting, the 90-minute tour, and the opportunity to drink your way through the sampling room. The brewery is also the starting point for *Louisa's Walk*, a promenade through the **Female Factory** in which professional actors enact a gripping chapter in history (Mon–Fri 9am–4.30pm, until 4pm Jan–Apr; tel: 03-6223 1559; entrance fee). You can visit the site on your own too.

On the other side of the Derwent, the suburb of **Bellerive** fans out from **Kangaroo Bluff Battery**, an emplacement designed to guard the city from attack. The **Tasmanian Cricket Museum** (Tues–Thur, 10am–3pm, Fri 10am–noon match days 1–3pm; tel: 03-6211 4206) is located at **Bellerive Oval**, where state and international cricket is played in a village-green atmosphere.

Leaving Hobart via the **Tasman Bridge** is the first step towards the Tasman Peninsula, where so much colonial history was forged.

Richmond

The direct route goes across Sorell Causeway, but that would be to neglect the wonderful colonial township of **Richmond ❷**. It sits in the Coal River Valley, its convict-built stone bridge offset by the English village-style church on the hill beyond. This is the kind of setting that led Mark Twain to observe that "wherever the exiled Englishman can find in his new home resemblances to his old one, he is touched to the marrow of his being; the love that is in his heart inspires his imagination, and these allied forces transfigure those resemblances into authentic duplicates of the revered originals." Most of the town was built between 1824 and 1840, and it is the consistency in style that gives Richmond its charm. There's the obligatory gaol for this staging post on the Hobart to Port Arthur road, as well as a couple of churches. More recent attractions include a maze and the **Old Hobart Town Model Village** (21 Bridge Street; daily 9am–5pm;

Maps:
City 318
Area 322

TIP

A joint venture between various agencies has seen the publication of a free booklet, *Great Short Walks*, which outlines 60 treks in some of the most beautiful areas in the state. There are information boards at the start of each route co-ordinated with the design of the booklet.

BELOW: combining cricket and sunbathing.

tel: 03-6260 2502; entrance fee).

Pass through Sorell and pause, if you must, at the Colonial and Convict Collection (self-proclaimed as junk) at **Copping** before continuing to **Eaglehawk Neck**. This isthmus to the Tasman Peninsula is where the infamous "Dog Line" was set. A team of ferocious fidos was chained to a row of posts so that no convict could cross without coming into range of at least one of them. See the fearsome statue.

There are gentler attractions nearby. The **Tesselated Pavement** suggests that nature has tiled the shoreline, while across the isthmus the **Tasman Arch** and **Devil's Kitchen** are popular stops on the bus tours to Port Arthur.

The **Tasmanian Devil Park** (daily 9am–6pm; book for Devils in the Dark by 5pm; tel: 03-6250 3230; www .tasmaniandevilpark.com; entrance fee) at Taranna has a recommended night tour, although you may already be committed to a ghost tour at the **Port Arthur Penal Settlement ❸** (daily 8.30am–dusk; tel: 03-1800 659 101; www.port arthur.org.au; entrance fee). *See page 324.*

Don't miss the **Coal Mines Historic Site**. Convicts provided the labour and the ruins reveal grim evidence of their travails (daily 24 hours; free).

The East Coast

The Tasman Highway runs up the east coast, arriving first at the sleepy resort of **Orford**. Continue to Louisville Point where ferries depart for **Maria Island ❹** (9.30am, 1.30pm, 3.15pm; tel: 03-6234 2999). Originally a penal settlement, it is now a national park and a haven for wildlife and walkers. No traffic is permitted unless you take a bicycle and the only accommodation is in unpowered bunkhouses in the settlement at **Darlington**. There are many natural wonders – **Fossil Cliffs** and the **Painted Cliffs** amongst them.

Up the coast the old **Spiky Bridge**, and pristine **Spiky Beach** are untrumpeted gems.

Swansea is a low-key resort with lovely views across Great Oyster Bay to the pink granite peaks of the **Hazards** on the Freycinet Peninsula, another of Tasmania's big tickets.

It's quite a long drive to get there, but the rewards are worth it. First stop is

Fishermen can often be seen unloading their catches at harbours all along the east coast.

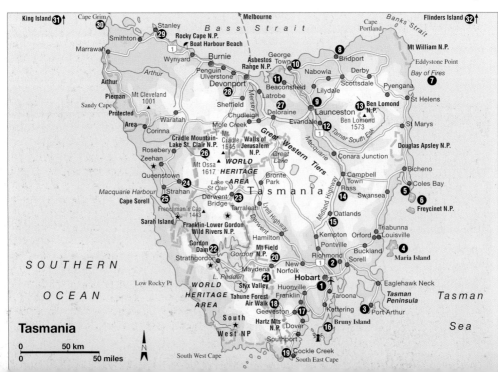

Coles Bay ❺, the service and accommodation centre that happens to have some rather fabulous beaches. However, the main attraction is **Freycinet National Park** ❻ (daily 9am–4.30pm; tel: 03-6256 7000; www.parks.tas.gov.au) and its headline act, **Wineglass Bay** (*see panel below*).

Bicheno, to the north, is a family resort with a pretty fishing boat shelter, the Gulch, and a big blowhole (*picture on page 317*). The **Douglas-Apsley National Park** has a natural water hole and is a popular picnic spot.

The north-east

After a handful of other beach resorts you wind round into **St Helens** on sheltered George's Bay. With a population around the 2,000 mark, it is the largest town on the east coast. It's a nice enough place, but better to follow the road out to **Binalong Bay** at the southern end of one of the world's great coastal stretches, the **Bay of Fires** ❼.

It consists of 30 km (19 miles) of some of the finest beach in the world and much of it is inaccessible by road. There are four-day guided walks which

include a couple of nights at a stunning modern lodge, but otherwise you have to fend for yourself. Northern access is via the **Mount William National Park**, where the lighthouse at **Eddystone Point** marks the top of the bay.

The road inland from St Helens climbs steeply into tin country. A turn off to **Pyengana** reveals cheese factory, the **Pub in the Paddock** where Priscilla the beer-drinking pig dwells, and the less-contrived appeal of **St Columba's Falls**. Further inland, **Derby** has its **Tin Mine Centre** (daily 9.30am–4.30pm; tel: 03-6354 2262; entrance fee) to provide a glimpse back to the days when the area's prosperity lay beneath the ground.

Scottsdale is notable for the architecturally adventurous **Forest EcoCentre** (daily 9am–5pm, 9am–3pm winter; tel: 03-6352 6458; free), where Forestry Tasmania uses the exhibition space to promote sustainable forestry. The road north runs to **Bridport** ❽ with its mix of holiday shacks and a tired resort playing host to fans of fishing and beaches. The acclaimed new **Barnbougle Dunes Golf Links** is a short distance out of town and is bring-

Map on page 322

George's Bay has plenty of variety on offer for anglers. Estuary and bay fishing offers bream, salmon, flathead and trevally; deep-sea fishing adds trevalla, gemfish, blue grenadier and others; offshore reef options include stripey trumpeter, cod, perch and squid.

LEFT:
Wineglass Bay.

Freycinet National Park

There are few places in the world where the elements of landscape combine so winningly as at Freycinet. The mix of mountains, forest, beaches and achingly blue sea, not to mention the abundant wildlife, is hard to match and impossible to beat. Best just to surrender to it and allow as much time as possible to take it all in. And the best way to see it is to get out there and walk.

The most popular trek is the fairly stiff climb up to the saddle between two of the Hazards: Mount Amos and Mount Mayson. This houses the **Wineglass Bay** lookout. Even for regulars, the view down can take you aback; there's the faultless symmetry of the curve that gives the bay its name and, if you're lucky and the sun's out, the searing azure of the sea. For the first-time visitor, it is just breathtaking. It is not unusual to find groups of people settled on the benches or clumped on nearby rocks, gazing down in silence, lost in contemplation. Or getting their breath back. Some turn back now, while others scramble down to the beach, perhaps as part of a longer hike which could take in **Mount Graham** or **Mount Freycinet**, or to return via **Hazards Beach**. There are several shorter walks too, at **Cape Tourville**, **Sleepy Bay** or **Little Gravelly Beach**, for instance. Pick up a map at the visitor centre just inside the park.

The Gulag Peninsula

Port Arthur was designed from scratch to be the ultimate prison. Establishments in Hobart, Sarah Island and Maria Island pre-date it but all had their problems. The new place had to be secure and remote enough to make escape difficult, if not impossible, but it was also to employ the "enlightened" punishment regime favoured at the time.

In this setting, 110 km (68 miles) from Hobart, remoteness was not a problem, nor was security; even if convicts did escape, the dogs at Eaglehawk Neck were there to stop them. Letting it be believed that sharks patrolled the sea didn't exactly encourage a swim to freedom either.

So, with a population of prisoners, soldiers and settlers miles from anywhere, this was not just a prison but a penal settlement – and a settlement on an industrial scale. These convicts weren't basket-weaving but shipbuilding and timber felling; they were grappling with agriculture and animal husbandry. A thriving village grew up around the prison, with farms, shops and Australia's first railway system (pulled by convicts instead of mules). To a large extent the population needed to be self-sufficient and for this to happen there had to be strong organisation and a firm grasp of logistics.

As tourists flood in today, it could be argued that little has changed. Visitors have to be "managed" through the site, but it's all done with subtlety and style. On buying your ticket you are allocated a time for a boat cruise and another for the guided tour, ensuring that the constant flow of visitors is fed through as comfortably as possible. The quieter times are first thing in the morning before the bus tours arrive from Hobart, and mid-afternoon onwards when most of them have departed.

You are also given a playing card to use in the "Lottery of Life" exhibition that leads out to the main site. Each card corresponds to an inmate whose history you follow through the display. You may have been transported for stealing bread but worked your way through the system to win the prized ticket of leave. Or you may be a recidivist who meets a sticky end.

After this and the guided tour you can start exploring. The best-known building in Port Arthur is the long, squat sandstone **Penitentiary**, a former flour mill converted in 1848 into a 136-cell prison for the worst offenders, although they were allowed out during the day to work. Two bushfires in the late 1890s gutted this and other edifices.

Take a stroll up the path to the left to the **Commandant's House**, with an extraordinary view over the bay and the site. It was one of the few wooden houses to survive the flames.

The path away from the bay runs past the eerie ruined hospital to the **Separate Prison** – built in the 1850s on a radical concept of punishment being developed in Britain. Instead of physical pain, prisoners were subjected to total sensory deprivation: kept in tiny cells for 23 hours a day, they were not allowed to talk nor interact with others. Not surprisingly, the treatment led to more derangement than rehabilitation; indeed Port Arthur was used as a mental asylum in later years.

Harbour cruises run out around the **Isle of the Dead** and **Point Puer Boys' Prison**, and twice a day you can land on the former, which became the cemetery for the prison colony. A lone convict lived on the island to dig the graves.

On the way back to the visitor centre, the shell of the Broad Arrow Café is part of a **Memorial Garden** to the victims of a gunman who massacred 35 people in and around the site in April 1996. Visitors should not broach the subject with staff.❏

LEFT: many of the buildings were destroyed by bush-fires which ravaged Port Arthur in 1897.

ing in a new breed of pleasure seekers.

Purple people head to **Bridestowe Estate Lavender Farm** (daily; Nov–Apr 9am–5pm; May, Sept–Oct 10am–4pm; June–Aug by appointment; tel: 03-6352 8182; free except Dec–Jan), a blanket of colour in December and January just before the crop is harvested. **Lilydale**, on the road winding down towards Launceston, has an attractive main street notable for historic **Bardenhagen's General Store**, and the imaginative paint jobs that have been applied to the town's power poles.

Launceston

Tasmania's second city has undergone a revival in recent years due, to some extent, to the advent of cheaper air fares from the mainland and also to some shrewd investments in tourist infrastructure. Of particular note has been the development of the old railway workshops at Inveresk, especially the new site operated by the **Queen Victoria Museum and Art Gallery** (daily 10am–5pm; tel: 03-6323 3777; www.qvmag.tas.gov.au; free). This impressive complex combines art galleries

with museum space marking the industrial history of the area. The Blacksmith Shop, complete with deafening "soundscape", gives an impression of the labours of the past.

Launceston 9 has more than its share of distinguished Victorian architecture on its undulating streets and much pleasure comes from simply walking around the city centre. Indeed, Cameron Street, with its redbrick terraces replete with filigree ironwork, must be one of the best-preserved streets of the era in Australia. It leads off **Civic Square**, which gathers up the grandiose **Town Hall**, the **Library** and the simple **Macquarie House**, a stone warehouse from 1830.

The main shopping area radiates out from **Brisbane Street Mall** and includes graceful **Quadrant Mall** and hapless modern construct, **Yorktown Square**. The **Old Umbrella Shop** (Mon–Fri 9am–5pm, Sat 9am–noon; free) in George Street has remained unchanged for the best part of a century and is now run by the National Trust.

To the east of the centre **City Park** is laid out Victorian style with original

Map on page 322

Artist at work in the Blacksmith Shop of the Queen Victoria Museum and Art Gallery.

BELOW: Cameron Street, a typically well-preserved area of Launceston.

Cataract Gorge.

BELOW: vintage motorcycles at the National Automobile Museum of Tasmania.

fountains, rotundas and a conservatory. A monkey enclosure contains macaques that have been exciting local children for years. Other highlights around the city include the original **Queen Victoria Museum** (daily 10am–5pm; tel: 03-6323 3777; www.qvmag.tas.gov.au; free), the **Design Centre of Tasmania** (daily 9.30am–5.30pm; tel: 03-6331 5506; www.twdc.org.au; entrance fee), the **National Automobile Museum of Tasmania** (Sept–May 9am–5pm, June–Aug 10am–4pm; tel: 03-6334 8888; entrance fee) and **Boag's Brewery** (Mon–Fri 8.45am–4.30pm; tours Mon–Fri 9am; tel: 03-6332 6300; www.boags.com.au; free), where enthusiasts can take a tour and, well, drink beer.

The riverfront has enjoyed a revival with **Seaport**'s hotel, restaurants and bars making the most of the setting, and a boardwalk eastwards runs past **Ritchies Mill**, home to **Stillwater**, one of several outstanding city eateries.

Few cities have such a remarkable phenomenon as **Cataract Gorge** within walking distance of the centre. The gorge has paths along its steep walls – the southern one tough, the northern one easy. If walking is out then pleasure boats sail part of the way up the South Esk River. Walkers can go all the way to the **Cliff Grounds** area where the gorge opens out into a basin, with gardens and a rotunda on one side, and grassy banks and an open-air swimming pool on the other. A chairlift and suspension bridge link the two sides.

The Tamar Valley

Launceston's playground lies to the north in the **Tamar Valley**, an area best known for its vineyards. Although there is an officially sanctioned **Tamar Valley Wine Route**, with special signage (blue grapes on yellow), just as much fun can be had by following your nose.

Make a stop in **George Town ⑩**, where the first settlers on the Tamar pitched up. The **Watch House Museum** (Macquarie Street; Sept–May Mon–Fri 10am–4pm, Sat–Sun noon–2pm; June–Aug Mon–Fri 10am–3pm, Sat–Sun noon–2pm; donation) tells the story, and **The Grove** (25 Cimitiere Street; Sun–Fri 10.30am–4pm; tel: 03-6382 1336; entrance fee) provides insight into prosperous colonial life.

Low Head at the mouth of the Tamar has the atmospheric **Pilot Station** where whitewashed houses, some for rent, are dotted around a green. There's a **Maritime Museum** (daily 9am–5pm or "late"; tel: 03-6382 1143; www.lhhp .com.au; entrance fee) and the chance to watch a pilot boat at work guiding vessels up the tricky river.

Batman Bridge is the only fixed crossing above Launceston. Turn right for **Beaconsfield** ⓫, a town which gained global notoriety when two miners were trapped in its gold mine in 2006. The impressive **Grubb Shaft Museum** (daily; Oct–Apr 9.30am–4.30pm, May–Sept 10am–4pm; tel: 03-6383 1473; entrance fee) is housed in old mine buildings.

Beauty Point's attractions are on its wharf. **Seahorse World** (daily 9.30am–4pm; tours every half hour; tel: 03-6383 4111; www.seahorseworld.com.au; entrance fee) has seahorses, funnily enough, you can guess the main attraction at the neighbouring **Platypus House** (daily 9.30am–3.30pm; tel: 03-6383 4884; www .platypushouse.com.au; entrance fee).

Detours from the road back to Launceston may include **Grindelwald**, a resort hotel for those yearning for a faux Swiss village, and **Tamar Island**, just north of the city, a wetlands reserve with an easily accessible boardwalk.

The Midland Highway

The Midland Highway runs down to Hobart and takes in some of the best of the colonial villages. **Longford** has numerous listed buildings, especially along Wellington Street, and **Brown's Big Store** has grand Victorian style. Close by are two country estates, both open to the public. **Woolmers Estate** has an exuberant mansion and extensive grounds containing a coach house, stables, cottages, and a working woolshed. Also at Woolmers is the **National Rose Garden** which will eventually feature over 500 varieties (daily 10am–4.30pm; regular guided tours of the house; www.woolmers.com.au; tel: 03-6391 2230;

entrance fee). **Brickendon Estate**'s **Historic Farming Village** has great character (Tues–Sun 9.30am–5pm; tel: 03-6391 1383; www.brickendon.com.au; entrance fee).

Evandale ⓬, to the east of the highway, makes much of hosting the National Penny Farthing Championships each February, but there are numerous other pretexts for a visit: the two churches to St Andrew – one Anglican, the other, a more extravagant Uniting Church; the interior to **Brown's Village Store**; and the **Clarendon Arms**.

For a break from historic villages, follow the steep, winding C401 from Evandale up towards **Ben Lomond National Park** ⓭. Once you've negotiated the tortuous Jacob's Ladder, you arrive at the **Alpine Village**. In winter this is one of two snowfields in the state (the other is at Mount Field) and during the rest of the year there are some lovely alpine walks.

Return to the Midland Highway for **Campbell Town**'s **Heritage Highway Museum** (Mon–Fri 10am–3pm; tel: 03-6381 1353; free). Elsewhere

Map on page 322

A miner's cottage at the Grubb Shaft Museum in Beaconsfield.

BELOW: a home maid – time has stood still at the Grove in George Town.

TIP

Day entry to national parks in Tasmania costs A$20 per vehicle and can be purchased upon arrival with cash to be left in envelopes provided. For multiple visits a two-month pass costs A$50 but it can only be bought from staffed national park offices or visitor centres, as well as some state visitor information centres, so plan ahead.

BELOW:
the bridge at Ross.

the theme is bricks. Millions of them in the convict-built **Red Bridge**, and a few thousand set into the pavements on both sides of the highway as part of a project which will eventually see one brick for each of the 68,000 people who were transported to Van Diemen's land.

Ross ⓮ is arguably the most unspoiled of all the historic towns. **Church Street** is unsurpassed in its Georgian structures and includes **Ross Village Bakery** from where, sticky cake in hand, you can relax. Continue down to the stone **bridge** and follow the path behind the Uniting Church to the remains of the **Female Factory**.

Ross benefits from being bypassed by the highway, as does **Oatlands** ⓯. It has dozens of old sandstone buildings and the towering **Callington Mill** (daily 9am–4pm; free), but, lacking the shady elms that contribute so winningly to Ross's ambience, it attracts fewer visitors. Make the most of this and follow the town's walking trail in peace.

Kempton is the last town worth perusing, and then it's a straight run into Hobart, unless the Romanesque church of St Mark in **Pontville** detains you.

The Huon Valley

South from Hobart, the **Huon Valley** is an area that people don't necessarily see on their first visit to the island, but its gentle pleasures reward those who make the effort. For long draped with the orchards that gave the "Apple Isle" its name, the area is as likely to reveal vineyards or berries in its rolling meadows these days. In fact its providores and gourmet restaurants have made it something of a foodie's haunt.

Sticking to the coast road, check out the **Shot Tower** (daily 9am–6pm; tel: 03-6227 8885; entrance fee) at **Taroona**, perhaps the exhibition in the foyer of the **Australian Antarctic Division HQ** (Mon–Fri 9am–5pm; tel: 03-6232 3516; free) outside Kingston, and the novel snorkel trail at **Tinderbox**, where you swim out and read a series of information boards on plates on the seabed.

Kettering has a sparkling cove but most people are there for the ferry to **Bruny Island** ⓰. It could be viewed

Truganini

Truganini was born around 1812 on Bruny Island. Her mother was killed by whalers, her two sisters abducted and sold into slavery, and her fiancée killed as he tried to save her from her sisters' fate. In 1830 she was one of a group of the "last" Aboriginals shipped to Wybalenna on Flinders Island under the so-called protection of George Augustus Robertson. In 1856, the few who had survived were relocated to the mainland. Truganini, the last of this group, died in Hobart in 1876. She was buried at the Female Factory but exhumed two years later and her remains put on display in a Hobart museum. It wasn't until 1976 that she was finally cremated and her ashes scattered in the sea off Bruny Island. It is not all verifiable but carries great symbolic weight in the lore of Aboriginal oppression.

as two islands joined by a narrow isthmus ("The Neck") and locals refer to North Bruny and South Bruny. Either way, it's a lengthy 63 km (39 miles) from top to bottom. **Adventure Bay** on the more rugged South Bruny is the main holiday centre, if you can call it that. Most activity involves walking or fishing, and maybe visiting **Cape Bruny Lighthouse** or **Fluted Cape**. A boat excursion stars seals, dolphins and any other aquatic life that turns up.

The Neck has a penguin viewing point and, at a lookout reached by a steep flight of steps, a memorial to Truganini, supposedly the last pure-bred Tasmanian Aboriginal *(see page 328)*.

On the mainland, make your way to **Huonville**, the area's commercial centre, where visitor interest focuses on the river. There are easy walks or rigorous tests of your capacity to withstand intense G-forces on the **Huon Jet** boat.

Continuing south, **Franklin** is but a street along the river bank. However, the **Wooden Boat Centre** (daily 9.30am–5pm; tel: 03-6266 3586;

entrance fee) is an interesting stop. For a small fee, you can follow the progress of students on an 18-month boatbuilding course. At the end of their studies they will have combined to build a complete vessel.

Into the woods

Geeveston ⓱ is a timber town. The clues are easy to spot: the two huge trunks either side of the road as you drive in, the life-size carved wooden figures placed along the streets, and the **Forest and Heritage Centre** that doubles as the visitor centre in the middle of town. Geeveston is on the edge of a huge area of managed forest, and beyond that there's only the uninhabited wilderness of **Southwest National Park**, a World Heritage Area.

The spectacular **Tahune Forest Air Walk** ⓲ (daily 9am–5pm, later in summer peak time; tel: 03-6297 0068; charge), a 28-km (17-mile) drive west, is a 600-metre (1,970-ft) steel walkway high in the canopy, which gives a new perspective on life in the forest. Part of it is cantilevered out over the banks of the Huon River. Quieter, and

Map on page 322

A carved statue in Geeveston, where the principal industry is timber.

BELOW: the beach on the Neck has protected areas for penguins and mutton birds.

just as alluring, is the **Hartz Mountains National Park**, where trails take a few minutes or several hours.

Pass through somnolent **Dover** and then turn inland to the **Hastings Caves and Thermal Springs** (daily Jan–Feb 9am–6pm; Mar–Apr & Sep–Dec 9am–5pm; May–Aug 10am–4pm; tel: 03-6298 3209; entrance fee). Bask in one and enjoy a guided tour of the other.

A dirt road leads to **Cockle Creek** **❶**, the most southerly point you can drive to in Australia. Consecutive settlements failed at whaling, logging and mining. Now it just attracts tourists. Walkers can take on the multi-day **South Coast Track**. Many just walk the two hours each way to **South Cape Bay** and back. And everyone else does the stroll to a bronze whale by the bay.

Wilderness

Visitors can penetrate furthest into the World Heritage Area along the Gordon River Road to Strathgordon.

Follow the course of the Derwent north from Hobart and dawdle for a while in **New Norfolk**, a town with a lumpen paper mill but also scenic stretches of hop gardens and their associated oast houses. The **Oast House** (daily 9am–6pm; tel: 03-6261 1322; entrance fee) in Tynwald Park has a museum devoted to the industry. Elsewhere there are a pair of sturdy old inns and, in **St Matthew's**, traces of the oldest church in the state, buried beneath all the subsequent renovations.

It's just a few kilometres to the blissful tranquillity of the **Salmon Ponds Heritage Hatchery and Garden** (daily 9am–5pm; tel: 03-6261 5663; entrance fee). Its history as a breeding ground of early introduced species is interesting, but the main pleasure is in just strolling in the glorious gardens.

Not far along the Gordon River Road **Mount Field National Park** **❷** can get busy with day-trippers from Hobart so be prepared to share the boardwalks to the most accessible sights including **Russell Falls** and, above it, **Horseshoe Falls**. The **Tall Trees** trail provides a first taste of the giants of the forest, and another hour's walk brings **Lady Barron Falls** into range. Go deeper into the park for alpine uplands and the snow fields.

Junee Cave, in Maydena, is the entrance to an extensive karst system. Then just beyond the village, after a bridge, take a track on the right which winds round to the **Styx Valley** **❷**. At **Big Tree Reserve**, there's a boardwalk loop taking in some of the highest trees in the country, all *Eucalyptus regnans* or swamp gum. There have been long battles by conservationists to save these and others like them from the loggers; the evidence is in scrawled rebuttals to the "propaganda" on the information boards erected by Forestry Tasmania.

Enjoy the long drive through wild mountain scenery to **Strathgordon**, where there's a lodge and restaurant with views across **Lake Pedder**. Drive the final few kilometres for the engineering marvel of the **Gordon Dam** **❷** in all its grey concrete glory.

Playground in Mount Field National Park.

BELOW: the Tahune Forest Airwalk.

The Lyell Highway

As the Lyell Highway from New Norfolk climbs up to the Central Plateau, look for hydroelectric activity, with power stations and old workers' camps at **Tarraleah** and **Bronte Park**. Fishing fans should turn right down the Marlborough Highway for **Great Lake**. It has amazing trout and a remarkable collection of shack communities. Otherwise continue to **Derwent Bridge ㉓**.

This is where hikers finish the Overland Track at the visitor centre at the end of **Lake St Clair**. Casual visitors can embark on shorter walks, take a cruise up the lake, or combine the two by chugging to the far end and walking back. A more recent local attraction is **The Wall**, a long-term project by sculptor Greg Duncan to carve a 100-metre (328-ft) long relief depicting the life and history of the Central Highlands (daily Sept–Apr 9am–5pm; May–Aug 9am–4pm; tel: 03-6289 1134; entrance fee).

The drive continues past access points to the **Franklin River** for kayakers and whitewater rafters, until the landscape changes from lush green hills to bleak brown and grey. Gold, and then copper, was discovered here in the late 1800s. Trees were lopped to fuel the smelters, and sulphurous outpourings put paid to any remaining vegetation. The land is now entirely denuded. It's bleak but also strangely compelling.

In the midst of all this sits **Queenstown ㉔**, a rough-and-ready mining town, which now receives a daily influx of tourists who arrive on the steam-drawn (at least for the last few kilometres) **West Coast Wilderness Railway** from Strahan on the west coast. They may take in the old-fashioned **Galley Museum** (1 Driffield Street; tel: 03-6471 1483; Oct–Mar Mon–Fri 9.30am–6pm, Sat–Sun 12.30–6pm; Apr–Sept 10am–5pm, Sat–Sun 1–5pm; entrance fee), the **Miners Siding** public sculpture or maybe just have a drink in the historic **Empire Hotel**.

Macquarie Harbour

Strahan ㉕ (pronounced *strawn*) began life as a timber town, thrived on the copper that passed through and always

Map on page 322

The Miners Siding, *a sculpture in Queenstown.*

BELOW: the road spirals down from the mountains into Queenstown.

Cradle Mountain Lodge offers luxury accommodation on the edge of the National Park.

BELOW: Strahan harbour with one of the Gordon River excursion boats.

supported a small fishing fleet. Now, however, it's driven by tourism. And this is down to its position on **Macquarie Harbour**

It's almost obligatory for visitors to take a cruise (World Heritage Cruises daily 9am; tel: 03-6471 7174; or Gordon River Cruises, daily 8.30am; tel: 03-1800 628 288), which includes a swing through **Hell's Gates** at the mouth of the harbour, a look at a fish farm and then a tramp around the ruins on **Sarah Island**.

Probably the toughest penal establishment in the colony, Sarah Island was for the worst recidivists. From 1822 they were put to work fashioning ships from the local Huon pine and had to suffer appalling living conditions for the 11 years the establishment existed before all convicts were transferred to Port Arthur.

The cruise continues on to the **Gordon River** and a stop for a walk through the rainforest. Back at Strahan look into the visitor centre where, in a small theatre, the play *The Ship That Never Was* tells a story of Sarah Island (daily 5.30pm, plus Dec–Jan 8.30pm;

tel: 03-6471 7622; entrance fee).

The road north from Strahan passes the extensive **Henty Dunes**, which stretch for miles behind Ocean Beach, and then turns inland to more mining towns. **Zeehan** is the most significant, having boomed in the 1900s on the back of silver. In those days the magnificent **Gaiety Theatre**, currently under restoration, could fill its 1,000 seats nightly with the biggest names of the era. The stimulating **West Coast Pioneers' Museum** (Main Street; tel: 03-6471 6225; daily 9am–5pm; entrance fee) has extensive displays on mining, minerals and local history.

Cradle Mountain

Continue through Rosebery and Tullah before making for Cradle Valley. The first sighting of **Cradle Mountain ㉖** looming up across Dove Lake must rate alongside the first view of the Opera House in Sydney in the chart of magical travel moments; you've got a pretty good idea what it should look like but are still blown away by the real thing. Drink it in, then it's a matter of picking your walk. Most choose the **Dove Lake** circuit, which takes up to two hours, but there are plenty of other options, all outlined on the maps available at the visitor centre.

Hardy hikers will tackle the 80-km (50-mile) **Overland Track** (*see panel*).

If the weather closes in – and it often does – look around "Waldheim", the lodge occupied by Gustav Weindorfer, who first campaigned to get the area designated a national park.

Continuing eastwards along the edge of the Great Western Tiers, there is hiking to be done in the vehicle-free **Walls of Jerusalem National Park**, but it is not to be undertaken lightly.

Detour north for **Sheffield**, which has put itself on the tourist map by commissioning murals to cover every available wall; and maybe have a look at the wilfully eccentric **Tazmazia** and the associated **Village of Lower**

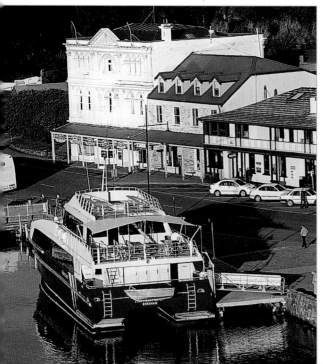

Crackpot (500 Staverton Road; daily 10am–5pm; tel: 03-6491 1934; www .tasmazia.com.au; entrance fee), with its comical model houses.

Mole Creek Karst National Park is abundant with caves. Tours go into Marakoopa Cave (tel: 03-6363 5182; daily 10am–4pm; call for tour times; entrance fee), which contains glow worms, underground rivers and the superb Great Cathedral; and the smaller King Solomon's Cave (tel: 03-6363 5182; daily 10.30am–4pm; call for tour times; entrance fee).

Chudleigh has an acclaimed honey farm and then you're in to Deloraine ㉗. It's a pretty town on the banks of the Meander River and a rewarding way of exploring it is to follow the trail of sculptures that winds along the main street and down by the river banks.

The north

The Bass Highway snakes its way north, but detour to Latrobe for its Victorian high street, and the Australian Axeman's Hall of Fame (daily 9am– 5pm, closed Tues May–Aug; tel: 03-6426 2099;

entrance fee), where proprietor and legend, David Foster, may be on hand to explain wood-chopping.

Devonport ㉘ is the home port for the *Spirit of Tasmania* ferries that traverse the Bass Strait. The centre need not detain you but there is a good Maritime Museum (Tues–Sun 10am– 4.30pm summer, 10am–4pm winter; tel: 03-6424 7100; entrance fee) near the foreshore, and on Mersey Bluff, the Tiagarra Aboriginal Culture Centre and Museum (daily 9am–4.30pm; tel: 03-6424 8250; entrance fee). Besides historical artefacts, Tiagarra has a collection of 10,000-year-old rock art.

The Bass Highway continues along the north coast to Ulverstone, a comfortable family destination with nice parks, and a smattering of Victoriana. In Penguin, you can pose by a giant concrete penguin above the beach and the penguin-shaped litter bins along the streets.

Industry hits you with a thud at Burnie, where a massive paper mill (tours available) and the state's biggest container port dominate. The Pioneer Village Museum (Mon–Fri 9am–5pm,

Penguin's penguin.

BELOW: most walkers spend five nights on the Overland Track.

The Overland Track

Australia's most renowned walk, the Overland Track usually entails six days of hard walking and five nights camping out or staying in the regularly spaced huts. It's not easy but the rewards more than justify it as you traverse buttongrass moorlands, myrtle and sassafras forests, glittering tarns and broken, snowcapped peaks. You're alone out there and need to carry all your supplies and equipment with you. Okay, not quite alone. The walk has become so popular that in the high season (1 Nov–30 Apr) there is now a A$100 fee, a limit of 60 hikers per day and everyone must start at the Cradle Valley end and finish at Cynthia Bay at Lake St Clair. Bookings on www.parks.tas.gov.au; tel: 03-6233 6047; or Cradle Mountain-Lake St Clair National Park visitor centres.

Map on page 322

Cape Wickham lighthouse on King Island.

BELOW:
Patriarch Inlet,
Flinders Island.

Sat–Sun 1.30–4.30pm; tel: 03-6430 5746; entrance fee), with its reconstituted 1900 street scene, is impressive, as are some of the works in the **Burnie Regional Art Gallery** (Mon–Fri 10am–4.30pm, Sat–Sun 1.30–4.30pm; tel: 03-6430 5875; free). And a short ride inland to **Fern Glade** provides a good chance of spotting platypus in the wild.

Wynyard has discreet appeal and **Table Cape** demands a visit in spring when the tulip farm is in full flower, but the lighthouse and the views from it are worth a look at any time.

Possibly the finest bay is at **Boat Harbour Beach**, but plans are afoot for a new resort hotel so get in now (unless you're waiting for the hotel, obviously).

Visitor favourite **Stanley** ㉙ is dominated by The Nut, a huge plug of volcanic rock at the end of a spit. You can walk or take the chairlift to the top if you don't mind the wind. Down below, Alexander Terrace has well-kempt cottages, one of which was the original home of Joe Lyons, the first Tasmanian prime minister.

The Van Diemen's Land Company (VDL) was crucial to Stanley. The old company store can be found near the wharf, while the clifftop situated **Highfield** (Sept–May daily 10am–4pm, Jun–Aug, call; tel: 03-6458 1100; entrance fee) was company HQ.

An incarnation of VDL still manages the **Woolnorth** estate that covers the state's north-western tip. The only way to visit is on a tour (daily if enough interest; tel: 03-0417 390 241; charge) taking in a wind farm placed to take full advantage of the Roaring Forties, and dramatic **Cape Grim** ㉚.

The Bass Strait Islands

King Island ㉛ is best known for cheese from **King Island Dairy**; there's a shop to visit but no tours, so try **Currie**, the main town (if a handful of streets warrants the term), with its quaint harbour where giant crabs and crayfish are landed. There's a small museum, too, just below the lighthouse (Lighthouse Street; tel: 03-6462 1698; daily 2–4pm; entrance fee).

Ships have often come to grief here but **Cape Wickham Lighthouse**, on the northern tip, has played its part in keeping the numbers down, although it came too late for many. At **Yellow Rock Beach**, wreckage from a paddle steamer can still be seen in the surf.

In the south there's the intriguing **Calcified Forest**, while the **Kelp Industries** centre explains why tons of the stuff is hanging out to dry.

King Island is relatively flat and windswept, whereas **Flinders Island** ㉜, in the north-east, has some serious hills, culminating in **Mount Strzelecki**. The southern corner also has the immaculate sands of **Trousers Point** and **Fotheringate Beach**. The main town is **Whitemark**, but the important **Furneaux Museum** (daily 1–5pm summer, Sat–Sun 1–5pm winter; tel: 03-6359 2010 to confirm opening; entrance fee) is up at **Emita**. Many of the exhibits stem from the time of the forced exile of Tasmania's Aboriginal population in 1838, and the chapel at nearby **Wybalenna** is on the site of their settlement. ❑

RESTAURANTS & BARS

Restaurants

Hobart

Amulet
333 Elizabeth Street, North Hobart
Tel: 03-6234 8113
Open: L & D daily. **$$**
www.northhobart.com/amulet
Considering the quality of the produce and the complexity of some of the dishes, Amulet is one of the most reasonably priced eateries in town and with a good wine list too.

Gondwana
22 Francis St, Battery Point
Tel: 03-6224 9900
Open: L Tues–Fri, D Mon–Sat. **$$$**
www.restaurantgondwana.com
The building might be old but the dining concept is modern. Local produce is thoughtfully and sometimes inventively teamed with complex sides.

Republic Bar and Café
299 Elizabeth Street, North Hobart
Tel: 03-6234 6954
Open: L & D daily. **$**
www.republicbar.com
Music, poetry, politics and beer are the priorities and they do an excellent steak marinated in Jack Daniels.

The Source
Moorilla Estate, 655 Main Road, Berriedale
Tel: 03-6277 9900
www.moorilla.com.au
Open: L daily, D Wed–Sat. **$$**
This relatively new first-floor winery dining room is one of Hobart's most spectacular. Chef Justin North is a strong supporter of local producers.

St Helens

Captain's Catch
The Wharf
Tel: 03-6376 1170
Open: L daily. **$**
Possibly the best fish and chips in Tasmania. It is a big call for a boat moored in the St Helens Harbour, but ask the locals.

Launceston

Mud Bar and Restaurant
28 Seaport Boulevard
Tel: 03-6334 5066
Open L & D daily. **$$**
www.mudbar.com.au
One of the most satisfying dining experiences in town, everyone loves Mud's delicious Italian-inspired dishes. Add knowledgeable service, a relaxed mood, and a waterside location.

Stillwater River Café
Ritchies Mill, Paterson Street
Tel: 03-6331 4153
Open: L daily, D Mon–Sat. **$$$**
www.stillwater.net.au
The largely Asian-inspired dishes are beautifully balanced and always exciting – highly recommended for food lovers. The degustation menu, matched with wine choices, is a great way to immerse yourself in it.

Huon Valley

Peppermint Bay
3435 Channel Highway, Wood-bridge. Tel: 03-6267 4088
www.peppermintbay.com.au
Open: L daily, D Sat. **$$$**
One of Australia's best regional restaurants, Peppermint Bay also has one of the most beautiful aspects. Chef Steve Cumper has cultivated an impressive array of local suppliers, and creates distinctive, seasonal dishes.

Latrobe

Glo Glo's
78 Gilbert Street, Latrobe
Tel: 03-6426 2120
Open: D Mon–Sat. **$$**
www.gloglos.com.au
Superb food, excellent service and a great wine list make this one of the best restaurants in the region.

Stanley

The Shingle Inn
25 Church Street
Tel: 03-6458 2083
Open: D daily. **$**
A charming dining room with a menu that includes cooked-to-order pies, Thai and Indian curries, a steak sandwich, braised lamb shanks, along with spag bol. The place is not easily categorised.

PRICE CATEGORIES

Prices for a three-course dinner with a half-bottle of house wine:
$ = under A$50
$$ = A$50–A$80
$$$ = A$80–A$120
$$$$ = over A$120
L = lunch, D = dinner, BYO = bring your own alcohol

RIGHT: a not-so-light snack.

FREYCINET

Wineglass Bay is the headline attraction in Freycinet National Park, but there is plenty more to see and keen walkers could easily spend a few days here

Without overstating it, the Freycinet Peninsula must be one of the most beautiful places in the world. The combination of mountains, forest, beaches and blisteringly blue sea, not to mention the abundant wildlife, is hard to match and impossible to beat. Best just to surrender to it and allow as much time as possible to take it all in. Pitch a tent just back from the beach and get close to nature (but not too close; secure food from inquisitive wallabies and wombats who can sniff a bonanza every time they hear a tent peg being hammered in). Alternatively, follow the path to luxury and book into the Freycinet Lodge, inside the park boundary, for a couple of nights of hedonism. Settle on the balcony of your cabin and watch the scurrying animals in the undergrowth below.

In summer there is good swimming to be had, while fishermen are spoilt for choice. Above all, though, this is a place for walking. The Wineglass Bay Track is a must, whether it's just a climb up to the saddle for the view, or perhaps as part of a longer trek which could take in Mount Graham or Mount Freycinet. People with mobility problems or young children can still take on the shorter walks, some with views of Wineglass Bay. Another option is to join one of the boat trips around the peninsula which embark from Coles Bay.

ABOVE: they're cute and friendly but visitors are warned not to feed the wallabies in Freycinet because some processed foods can cause a fatal bony growth called lumpy jaw.

BELOW: the bright orange deposits on boulders along the shoreline in Freycinet and all along the east coast are in fact a type of rock lichen. They are a complex mixture of fungi and algae which extract nutrients from the rocks they're attached to.

ABOVE RIGHT: the waters around the Freycinet peninsula are rich in marine life so fishing is popular among visitors. However, it tends to be the professionals who procure giant crabs like this.

LEFT: the Cape Tourville walk, which affords partial views of Wineglass Bay, is an easy 20-minute stroll around the lighthouse. The walk is accessible to wheelchair users. While you walk, keep your eyes and ears open for any unusual birds. Freycinet's visitors include yellow-tailed black cockatoos (you'll probably be able to hear them before you see them), and the rare white-bellied sea eagle.

VISITOR FACILITIES

The visitor centre is just a few hundred metres inside the park on the right-hand side. This is where park permits can be purchased and maps and guides picked up. Even those who have already paid their park fees should find a stop rewarding as there are displays about many aspects of the park's history and geology, as well as useful pointers towards the weather and the state of the various walks.

One of the walks starts immediately behind the visitor centre. The Great Oyster Bay walk is a 5-minute amble down to Richardson's Beach where the cormorants play, and the Hazards loom above.

The Centre is also the place to register for the camp sites, which need to be booked in advance at all times. Indeed some, such as those at Honeymoon Bay (open only at Easter and in the summer) are so popular that a ballot system is used to allocate spaces. There are powered sites for caravans and RVs, and unpowered for tents. Electric barbecue facilities are provided at various points as all campfires are banned, although portable fuel stoves are allowed.

RIGHT: Sleepy Bay is one of many blissful spots in the park and can be accessed just five minutes from the car park. The way down to the beach is a bit of a scramble but more than worth the effort. At times the bay is anything but sleepy and the sea can be rather choppy.

ABOVE: nothing beats that first view of Wineglass Bay which, for most people, comes as a generous reward for the steep climb up to the saddle between Mount Amos and Mount Mason.

RIGHT: it can take a good 15 to 20 minutes to walk to the end of the beach at Wineglass Bay, and then the choice must be made whether to return via the saddle or take the longer, less steep route via Hazards Beach.

LEFT: a ranger from the Parks and Wildlife Service promotes the campaign to keep foxes out of Tasmania and increase awareness of the devastating consequences for indigenous animal and bird life if this predator were to gain a toehold in the state. Several species, already wiped out on the Australian mainland would be endangered, including quolls and bandicoots.

INSIGHT GUIDES

TRAVEL TIPS

AUSTRALIA

TRAVEL TIPS

T RANSPORT

GETTING THERE
AND GETTING AROUND

GETTING THERE

By Air

Almost all foreign visitors travel to Australia by air. Brisbane, Cairns, Melbourne and Sydney are the major international tourism gateways, with daily flights arriving from Asia, Europe and North America. Less frequent flights also arrive directly in Adelaide, Darwin, Cairns, Perth and Hobart. More than 35 international airlines currently fly to and from Australia (see Major Airlines list).

Getting to Australia can be expensive. Fares vary widely, so it is important to seek advice from a knowledgeable travel agent before buying a ticket. A departure tax of A$38 is included in the cost of your international ticket, so it no longer has to be paid at the airport when you leave.

Note that domestic flights are available to international travellers at lower fares than to Australian residents.

There may be price advantages in pre-booking your domestic travel along with your flight to Australia; however, since the launch of budget carriers Virgin Blue and Jetstar (see Domestic Flights), competition has lowered domestic fares considerably. The early birds often secure the best deals. Special pre-booked packages tend to incorporate inexpensive hotel and car rental rates.

Qantas usually offers good deals to Australia (it also operates Qantas Vacations). Tickets can be booked by calling 800-348 8145 (in the US), 800-348 8137 (in Canada), or 020-8222 9199 (in the UK).

Major Airlines Flying to Australia

Air Canada
Tel: 1300-655 767
www.aircanada.com

Air France
Tel: 1300-390 190
www.airfrance.com

Air New Zealand
Tel: 132-476
www.airnewzealand.com

British Airways
Tel: 1300-767 177
www.britishairways.com

Cathay Pacific Airways
Tel: 131-747
www.cathaypacific.com

Emirates Airlines
tel: 1300-303 777
www.emirates.com

Gulf Air
Tel: 1300-366 337
www.gulfairco.com

Japan Airlines (JAL)
Sydney based:
tel: 02-9272 1111
www.jal.co.jp.en

Malaysia Airlines
Tel: 132-627
www.malaysiaairlines.com

Qantas
Tel: 131-313
www.qantas.com.au

Singapore Airlines
Tel: 131-011
www.singaporeair.com

South African Airways
Sydney based:
tel: 1300-435 972
www.flysaa.com

Thai Airways International
Tel: 1300-651 960
www.thaiair.com

United Airlines
Tel: 131-777
www.united.com

Virgin Atlantic
Tel: 1300-727340
www.virgin-atlantic.com

GETTING AROUND

Domestic Flights

Australia's national domestic airline is Qantas. Its main competitor, Ansett Australia, unexpectedly folded in September 2001, but competition was restored on most routes by fast-growing **Virgin Blue** (tel: 136-789, www.virginblue.com.au), and Qantas launched its own budget domestic airline, **Jetstar** (tel: 131-538, www.jetstar.com). Each of these airlines operates regular scheduled flights between all capital cities and regional centres throughout Australia. Both Jetstar and Pacific Blue (a subsidiary of Virgin Blue) operate from Australian cities to a number of Asian and Pacific destinations. **Qantas** (tel: 131-313, www.qantas.com.au) also operates regular scheduled flights between all capital cities and regional centres throughout Australia.

Although many domestic flights are often fully booked, cheaper standby and advance-purchase seats are available on most routes, and

Flying Times

Sydney–Melbourne, 1 hr
Sydney–Perth, 4 hrs 50 mins
Melbourne–Adelaide,
1 hr 20 mins
Melbourne–Canberra, 1 hr
Brisbane–Sydney, 1 hr 25 mins
Brisbane–Melbourne,
2 hrs 20 mins
Adelaide–Alice Springs, 2 hrs
Perth–Adelaide, 3 hrs
Canberra–Sydney, 50 mins

you can save around 20 percent off the regular economy fare.

Within Australia, discounts of up to 50 percent off the full fare are available when purchasing return economy fares in advance. You must book and pay for your ticket at least 10–14 days before departure and you cannot alter your booking within those times. Other, smaller, discounts apply if you are prepared to fly at off-peak times or book via the internet.

Excursion fares, discounts and packages are available from time to time. Some of the best deals include both air travel and accommodation outside the main holiday seasons – check with airlines for special offers.

There are also regular price wars between airlines, which can result in some great deals. Check out the advertisements in the newspapers.

Each state is serviced by a number of regional airlines such as QantasLink and Rex, providing access to more remote destinations.

From the Airport

Sydney

Situated approximately 8 km (5 miles) from the Central Business District (CBD), Sydney Airport is best reached by car, taxi or train. Just 10 minutes to the domestic terminals and 12 minutes to the international, trains run from Central Station up to eight times an hour on weekdays, and four times an hour on weekends. The only bus to the airport from the city is the No. 400, which runs from Bondi Junction and takes 40 minutes. For exact times and information visit www.airportlink.com.au, or tel: 131 500.

BELOW: A Queensland taxi cab waits for a fare.

Canberra

Canberra airport is 7 km (4 miles) from the city centre. An Airliner Shuttle bus charges A\$7 each way; other bus companies run regular services into town too. The taxi fare is about A\$20.

Melbourne

Melbourne's airport is 22 km (14 miles) from the city centre. A taxi costs about A\$36–50; for about half that price, the Skybus departs every half hour.

Adelaide

The dual international/domestic airport, 8 km (5 miles) from the city centre, has a Skylink shuttle bus, which runs about every 30 minutes, stopping at major hotels (tel: 08-8413 6197; www.skylinkadelaide.com). Adelaide Metro runs buses through the city to the airport seven days a week from 4.50am to midnight. A taxi into the city centre costs about A\$20.

Brisbane

The domestic and international airport terminals lie 16 km (10 miles) from the city centre. At any time when flights are arriving or departing, a combination of bus and fast rail transport options provides easy connections between Brisbane Airport, Brisbane city and the Gold Coast. The hub is the city coach/rail terminus, and the "Trans-info" service (tel: 131-230), or the information desks at the airport will help you identify the easiest and most convenient way to get from A to B.

Darwin

Darwin airport is 12 km (7½ miles) from the CBD, and a taxi costs around \$30. For the 15-km (9-mile)

Bargains by Bus

If you plan extensive bus travel in Australia, several discount plans offer unlimited travel within various time frames. There are also set-duration and set-distance fares.

journey to Alice Springs, the fare is around \$25–30. Both cities are serviced by cheap airport shuttles.

Perth

Taxis from the domestic and international airports to Perth city cost around A\$26 and A\$32 respectively and to Fremantle A\$44. One shuttle bus meets all flights and runs to accommodation in the city, while another travels between Fremantle and the airport (pick-ups must be pre-arranged by phone, preferably the day before). For the Perth shuttle, tel: 08-9277 7958. One-way trips are \$15 for adults from the international terminal and \$12 from the domestic terminals. Bookings for the Fremantle service are on tel: 08-9335 1614.

Hobart

The Airporter Bus meets all flights into Hobart International Airport and drops off at hotels in the city centre and inner suburbs. Charges are A\$11 for adults one way or A\$19 return; children and concessions A\$5. A taxi to the city centre will cost about A\$30.

By Bus

Long-Distance Buses

Lively competition between the major bus companies means many bargains are available when travelling by bus in Australia. The biggest company, with the most services, is **Greyhound Australia** (tel: 131 499; www.greyhound.com.au).

The standard of buses is high, with most having reclining seats, seats for the disabled, videos, washrooms and air conditioning. Smoking is prohibited on all buses. Bus terminals are well equipped with toilets, showers and shops and are generally very clean. However, you should be aware that distances are enormous in Australia, so think twice before hopping onto the Brisbane–Cairns leg because it takes more than 24 hours.

Greyhound has various money-saving passes including ones that are based on kilometres travelled.

There are many other bus companies in Australia, offering a variety of transport/hotel packages departing regularly from capital cities. Prices are per day inclusive of bus travel, accommodation and various day tours or driver "feature commentary". Some of the more adventurous routes are taken by deluxe four-wheel drive vehicles, incorporating camping and are accompanied by a cook.

City Buses and Trams

Sydney Sydney has an extensive bus service with main terminuses at Circular Quay, Wynyard and Central Station. For all route information visit the Transport Infoline website: http://131500.com.au or tel: 131 500. At Circular Quay there is an information kiosk at the centre of the row of bus stops, on the opposite side of the street (Alfred St) from the ferry wharfs.

The easy-to-spot, red **Sydney Explorer** bus leaves every 18 minutes daily from Circular Quay and runs a continuous loop around 26 of the city's main tourist sites with running commentary. You can hop off as many times as you like or stay on for the full 100-minute journey.

The blue **Bondi Explorer** bus takes in 19 spots around the eastern suburbs. Departing from Circular Quay daily, this hop-on hop-off service covers a 30-km (19-mile) route right up to Watsons Bay.

Canberra In Canberra, ACTION bus services are adequate and modern, but you need to study a map and timetable together. It is possible to purchase daily and off-peak daily bus passes that allow unlimited rides on the buses. A red double-decker bus offers a 24-hour pass and you can get on and off as often as you like. Tel: 131 710; www.action.act.gov.au.

Melbourne Called Metlink or the Met, Melbourne's public transport system is one of Australia's best. Trams form the basis of the system. There are over 750 trams venturing as far as 20 km (12 miles) out of the city. Buses are the secondary form of public transport, often taking over when trams are out of service. Trains connect an underground city loop to the outer suburbs.

A good idea is to visit the Met Shop. Located at Melbourne Town Hall on the corner of Swanston and Little Collins streets in the city, it has

Melbourne Transport

For telephone information on all public transport in Melbourne call the **Met Public Transport Information Centre**, tel: 131 638; open 6am–10pm daily or visit www.metlinkmelbourne.com.au.

Sydney Transport and Passes

The State Transit Authority operates the buses in Sydney, and **CityRail** the trains. Ferries are run by **Sydney Ferries**. For information on buses, trains and ferries from 6am–10pm daily, tel: 131 500. Or check www.131500.com.au, www.cityrail.info, www.sydneyferries.info, or www.sydneybuses.info. The front of the White Pages phone book also has information on Sydney's transport.

The **Sydney Pass** is an all-inclusive sightseeing ticket that

gives you unlimited travel on all ferries, buses and trains for 3, 5 or 7 days. Including harbour cruises, Explorer buses and return transfers on Airport Link trains, the pass also offers discounts on some major attractions. For more information visit www.sydneypass.info. Travel passes offer cheaper weekly rates and a **Travel 10** ticket gives a discount for 10 trips. Buy these passes from locations and stores displaying the transport symbol.

a useful "Discover Melbourne" kit and provides all the information you could ever need. There is a wide choice of tickets that enable travel over various periods of time and throughout the various zones of the city (zone 1 is big enough to cover most visitors' purposes). There are daily and weekly options, and tickets for use on both trams and buses. A brochure from the Met Shop outlines the options and advises which are the best tickets for your plans.

Adelaide A free **Bee Line bus** follows the city shopping circuit from Victoria Square to the railway station along King William Street; it runs at 7.40am, 7.50am and 8am then every 5 minutes until 6pm daily except Friday when it continues every 10 minutes to 9.20pm. There are fewer buses on weekends so check timetables. The **City Loop** is another free bus; running every 15 minutes, it does a wider circuit of the city stopping at or near most main sights. Detailed maps are available from Tourism South Australia, tel: 1300 655 276; www.adelaide.southaustralia.com.

All information regarding the Adelaide transport system is available from the Office of Public Transport's InfoCentre on the corner of King William and Currie streets, tel: 08-8210 1000 or 1800-182 160; www.adelaidemetro.com.au.

Brisbane For information on city buses in Brisbane, go to the underground bus station beneath the Myer Centre in the Queen Street Mall, open weekdays 8.30am–5pm. Apart from the regular city buses, there are **Cityxpress** buses, which connect certain suburbs to the city, and **Rockets**, which are peak-hour commuter services. Fares are based on a zone system and there are a number of special deals such as day or weekly passes.

Darwin and Alice Springs Both Darwin and Alice Springs have town bus services that connect accommodation precincts with the

CBD. **Darwinbus** (tel: 08-8924 7666) has tourcards that allow unlimited travel for one or seven days. **ASBUS** buses leave the interchange on Railway Terrace in Alice Springs, near the Coles supermarket. Comfortable, frequent and fast buses connect the three central attractions – Darwin, Alice Springs and Ayers Rock.

Greyhound Australia (tel: 131 499; www.greyhound.com.au) runs daily services between Alice Springs and Yulara (Ayers Rock). It is 460 km/ 286 miles each way.

Perth Perth has five bus routes aboard the Central Area Transit (CAT), four train lines including one to Fremantle, and ferries cross some sections of the Swan River. The "Perth Tram" (actually a bus) operates a circuit of tourist attractions. Regular bus services have fares based on a zone system, with discount passes. For maps and on-the-spot information about all forms of public transport, a Transperth office is in the Plaza Arcade (off the Hay Street Mall), tel: 136 213; www.transperth.wa.gov.au.

High-speed ferries travel from Perth, Fremantle and Hillarys to Rottnest Island.

Tasmania Metro Tasmania runs an extensive network of bus services in Hobart and they are an easy way to reach sights that are more than a casual stroll from the town centre such as Hobart's beaches, the Taroona Shot Tower, the Cadbury Factory and Cascade Brewery. Buses run Mon–Thur 6.30am to 10.30pm and until midnight on Friday and Saturday. There is a limited service on Sunday and holidays.

By Train

A wide network of modern railways operates from coast to coast. The principal lines follow the east and south coasts, linking the cities of Cairns, Brisbane, Sydney, Melbourne, Adelaide and Alice Springs. The most comprehensive service is operated by **Countrylink**: reservations are required; tel: 132 232 (Australia-wide); www.countrylink.info.

The line between Sydney and Perth via Adelaide is the famous **Indian–Pacific** run (linking the Indian Ocean to the Pacific Ocean). On its 4,352-km (2,700-mile) journey, taking 65 hours (three nights), the train crosses the treeless Nullarbor Plain, with the longest stretch of straight track in the world. Comforts include an observation lounge and bar. If money is no object you can travel in the historic Prince of Wales carriage, complete with wood panelling and cathedral glass doors.

Other popular scenic rail journeys run by Great Southern Railway (tel: 132 147 or 08-8213 4592; www.trainways.com.au) include the **Overland**, an overnight journey between Melbourne and Adelaide, and the **Ghan**, which runs from Adelaide to Darwin. The recently extended Ghan runs straight through the middle of the country, from Adelaide in South Australia through Alice Springs and on to Darwin. The two-night, 3,000-km (1,864-mile) trip can be broken in Katherine for short sightseeing tours by boat or helicopter, and Alice Springs for longer stopovers.

For travel in Western Australia it is possible to take a bus or train to the southern and southwest regions in the area bounded by Kalbarri, Meekathara, Kalgoorlie, Esperance, Albany and Augusta. For more details contact **Transwa**, tel: 08-9326 2600 or 1300-662 205, or visit www.transwa.wa.gov.au.

Tickets

The classes available are first, holiday and economy. First-class

passengers have sleeping berths with showers in their cabin, a first-class restaurant and lounge. Other classes get aeroplane-style reclining seats and a buffet car.

An **Ausrail Flexipass** entitles international visitors to unlimited travel on **Countrylink**, **Queensland Rail** and **Great Southern Railway** services. It is valid for 15 or 22 days of travel within a six-month period.

The **Countrylink Backpacker Rail Pass** is only available to foreign passport holders and is valid for 14 days to six months of unlimited economy-class travel, plus some metropolitan train travel.

City Trains

Sydney The city's growing traffic issues means that trains are the most time-efficient way to navigate Sydney. With a fairly frequent service most of Sydney's main areas are covered, including the central "City Circle" stations – Central, Town Hall, Wynyard, Circular Quay, St James and Museum. Most do not run between midnight and 4.30am, when a **Nightrider** bus service takes over.

The **Airlink** trains run about every 10 minutes between the city and the domestic and international terminals and the journey to Sydney's Central Station takes about 15 minutes.

Sydney's **monorail** glides from Central Station to the inner-west suburb of Lilyfield. Stops include Paddy's Markets, Star City Casino and the Sydney Fish Markets at Pyrmont.

The electric **Citytrain** services are very efficient. They all pass through the city stations of Roma Street, Central and Brunswick on their way out to the suburbs. The Public Transport Information Centre is

Brisbane Ferries

Brisbane ferries provide pleasant river crossings to Kangaroo Point, South Bank Parklands and along the river to other locations.

They depart from Eagle Street Pier and Edward Street on the corner of the Botanic Gardens. They are fast, efficient, inexpensive – and under-appreciated by Brisbane folk.

located in Central Station. There are tickets that enable unlimited travel in one day.

Canberra There are no train services in Canberra.

Melbourne The city has an extensive train service, with all lines radiating from the central Flinders Street Station to the outer suburbs. The Met Shop (Melbourne Town Hall, cnr Swanston and Little Collins streets; tel: 131 638) provides timetables and maps and sells tickets (also valid on city buses and trams). Apart from the underground city loop, stations are above ground. Train services on most lines depart every 15 or 20 minutes on weekdays, every 20 minutes on Saturdays, and about 30 minutes on Sundays.

Adelaide Train services are limited and are mostly used by locals to get out to far-flung suburbs. Generally speaking, you will need to rely on other forms of transport in Adelaide. One exception is the tram route linking Victoria Square in the city to the popular beach-side suburb of Glenelg, which tends to get quite busy in the summer months.

Brisbane The electric **Citytrain** services are very efficient. They all pass through the city stations of Roma Street, Central and Brunswick on their way out to the suburbs. The Public Transport Information Centre is located in Central Station. There are tickets that enable unlimited travel in one day.

Darwin There are no city trains serving Darwin.

Perth Wellington Street is Perth's central station, with an underground terminal planned for the nearby Mandurah line. **Transperth** trains run south through Perth to Fremantle; north to Joondalup; and by mid-2007, will go down the coast to Mandurah.

Hobart Regular passenger rail services ceased in Tasmania in the 1980s, but there are a few tourist/heritage railways operating in the state. Visit www.puretasmania.con.au and www.donriverrailway.au for more information.

Sydney Ferries and Cruises

Weather permitting, which it usually is, ferries are by far the most picturesque way of travelling around Sydney. Departing from the wharfs at Circular Quay, all tickets and timetables can be found at the Sydney ferries office.

The trip to Manly is the longest ferry run, covering 11 km (7 miles) in 30 minutes. The alternative **Jetcat** service offers the same trip in half the time for slightly more money. There are currently temporary timetables in place for both services while the east side of Manly Wharf is redeveloped. Visit www.sydneyferries.info for exact times.

Ferries are a great way of getting

to Taronga Zoo, Kirribilli and Watsons Bay, not to mention a good opportunity to see the harbour, bridge and Opera House from all angles.

The **Rivercat**, a high speed catamaran, cruises all the way up the Parramatta River.

Harbour cruises are a great way to relax while seeing Sydney off dry land. Daily cruises start at 10.30am and depart from Wharf Four. With comfy seating and unlimited tea and biscuits, these STA cruises are less expensive than private options and the commentary provides an interesting addition to the scenic backdrop.

By Sea

After arriving in Australia, a number of the international cruise lines continue around the coastline at a leisurely pace, stopping at Sydney, Brisbane and Cairns on the east coast, Melbourne, Hobart and Adelaide on the south coast, and at Fremantle in the west.

Day trips and cruises operate between mainland towns and the islands on the Great Barrier Reef. Six-day cruises run from Cairns to Cape York. The coral-fringed Whitsunday Islands are one of the best cruising and yachting locations in Australia (rent yachts from operators at Airlie Beach →the motto is, if you can drive a car, you can sail a yacht). River cruises and houseboat rentals are available on major rivers such as the Hawkesbury north of Sydney, along the River Murray, or the Myall Lakes on the NSW north coast, and the Murray River on the Victoria/NSW border.

The only regular maritime services are the passenger and car ferries called *Spirit of Tasmania I* and *II*, operating between Melbourne and Devonport.The trip from Victoria can be rough and takes about 11 hours. Tel: 1800-634 906 (in Australia) or see www.spiritoftasmania.com.au.

Taxis

Sydney All taxis are metered, so do not ride unless the meter is on. There is an initial A$2.90 hiring charge (called "flag fall"), then A$1.68 per kilometre thereafter. Between 10pm and 6am, this rate increases by 20 percent. A phone booking costs A$1.50 extra. There may be additional charges for road, bridge, ferry, tunnel and airport tolls. For information on taxis in NSW see the Taxi Council of NSW website, www.nswtaxi.org.au.

Premier Cabs: 131-017
Taxis Combined: 133-300
Legion Cabs: 131-451
RSL Cabs: 02-9581 1111
Silver Service: 133-100

In addition, there are companies that operate water taxis on the harbour. These are quite expensive – the price depends on the distance and time of day.

Water Taxis Combined: 02-9555 8888
Yellow Water Taxis: 02-9299-0199
Melbourne Melbourne's transport system tends to curl up and go to sleep around midnight, after which taxis are the only form of transport available. **Melbourne City Taxis**, tel: 03-9335 3536; **Silver Top Taxis**, tel: 131 008.
Canberra If you're waiting at a Canberra cab rank with no cabs in sight call **Canberra Taxis** on tel: 132-227 and they'll send one along. All cabs are metered, with flag fall costing A$3.20, and a charge of A$1.56 per km after that. Between 9pm and 6am, the rate goes up to A$1.80 per km. For more information, visit www.cancabs.com.au
Adelaide There are a number of taxi services available. **Adelaide Independent Taxi Service**, tel: 132 211; **Suburban Taxi**, tel: 131 008; **Yellow Cabs**, tel: 132 227.
Brisbane The city's officially recognised sevices are **Yellow Cabs** (tel: 131 924) and **Black and White Cabs** (tel: 131 008). Both charge a booking fee of A$1, with flag fall fixed at A$2.50 on weekdays 7am–7pm, after which it is A$1.38 per km. After-hours flag fall is A$3.70.
Darwin Darwin has three major taxi companies: **Darwin Radio Taxi**, tel: 131 008, **Arafura Shuttle**, tel: 08-8981 3300 and **Yellow Cab**, tel: 131 924.
Perth Hail taxis on the street, find them at a rank, or phone **Black and White** on 08-9333 3333 or **Swan** on 13 13 30, for up to four passengers. Black and White also have maxicabs (up to 10 passengers) and a service for the disabled (tel: 136 294 for these). Rates are reasonable: a small flag fall charge followed by a rate per kilometre.
Hobart Taxis can be hired in the street if their "vacant" sign is lit. All cabs use meters and tipping is not necessary. **Tasmanian Cabs**, tel: 131 008, will connect you to cab companies in most of the major towns in Tasmania, including **City Cabs** in Hobart.

Motorcycles and Bicycles

Both are available for hire throughout Australia. Thoughtfully designed systems of bicycle paths provide good views or access to tourist sites – a pleasant, healthy and environmentally friendly alternative to the city bus tour.
Sydney Bonza Bike Tours (www.bonzabiketours.com) offers 2–5-hour tours of the city from A$50, as well as bike hire. A range of mountain, hybrid and children's bikes, including

dragsters, choppers and tandems, are for hire in **Sydney Olympic Park** (www.sydneyolympicpark.com.au). *Cycling Around Sydney* by Bruce Ashley is a useful guide available at **Bicycle NSW**'s offices at Level 5, 822 George St (tel: 02-9218 5400), or from book and bike shops.
Canberra Cycling is perhaps the most pleasant choice for sightseeing in Canberra, as the terrain is flat and bike paths are extensive. Bicycles can be hired by the hour, by the day, or by the week. If you intend hiring a bike make sure to get a copy of the *Canberra Cycleways* map from the tourist office or bookshops.
Melbourne Melbourne is fairly flat, which affords the cyclist a number of good long tracks. Bike paths lie along the Yarra River, the Maribyrnong and the Merri Creek. For general cycling information, contact **Bicycle Victoria** at Level 10, 446 Collins Street, tel: 03-8636 8888; www.bv.com.au.
Adelaide Running alongside the Torrens River in Adelaide is the 35-km (22-mile) long Linear Park Bike and Walking Track, one of the best in Australia. You can hire bikes from **Linear Park Bike Hire**, tel: 04-0059 6065. You can also get free use of a bike for two hours within the city limits under a scheme run by **Bicycle SA** and **Adelaide City Council** called the City Bike Scheme. Once the two hours are up, an hourly rate applies. For more information see the Adelaide City Council website (www.adelaidecitycouncil.com) or contact the Cycling Information Centre at 46 Hurtle Square (tel: 08-8232 2644). Bikes can also be picked up from **Cannon Street Backpackers** on Franklin Street, opposite the central bus station.
Brisbane Brisbane City Council has built more than 500 km (310 miles) of cycleways across the city. The riverside Bicentennial Bikeway, a flat path that follows the river from the CBD along Coronation Drive to Toowong, is one of the most pleasant. Maps of popular cycleways can be found on the council's website www.brisbane.qld.gov.au.
Darwin You can hire motorcycles along Mitchell Street. Try **Darwin Scooter Hire**, corner Peel and

Mitchell streets. 50cc scooters are very popular for running out to the beaches around Darwin. Bicycles can be hired from some of the backpacker hotels, and some five-star hotels offer their guests cycle hire. There are plenty of cycle tracks; especially the one to East Point around Fannie Bay.

Perth Cycle paths have been developed all around Perth, alongside the freeway and coast, into the hills and cross-country. The **Perth Bicycle Network** (www.dpi.wa.gov.au/cycling) is a useful source of information. Maps are available from bike shops, or the **Bicycle Transportation Alliance** (2 Delhi Street, West Perth, tel: 08-9420 7210). **All About Bikes** on the corner of Riverside Drive and Plain Street, tel: 08-9221 2665, rents bikes, double bikes and quadcycles, as well as in-line skates.

Hobart Tasmania's longest dedictaed cycleway is the 15-km (9-mile) Intercity Cycleway in Hobart. The bike club **Bicycle Tasmania** (www.biketas.org.au) has all the information you'll need.

By Car

Car Hire

By international standards, renting a car in Australia is expensive. The big three rental companies are **Avis**, **Hertz** and **Budget**, whose rates are just about identical. **Thrifty** and **Europcar** are also big players in the market. The small outfits are usually much cheaper and offer special deals (such as weekend and standby rates), but they may not offer all the services and extras of the major companies – which can be extremely useful. These include substantial discounts for pre-booking overseas, and the ability to return the car to another city at no extra charge. Also be aware that many rental cars have manual, rather than automatic, gears (the latter are pricier).

The big three have offices in almost every town, as well as at airports and rail terminals. They offer unlimited kilometre rates in the city but when travelling in the Outback, rates are usually per kilometre. Compulsory third-party insurance is included in car rentals but collision damage waiver is an add-on. More comprehensive insurance plans are available for an additional fee, or your travel insurance may cover them. Most companies have 25 as their minimum driver age, or will charge a premium for drivers aged between 21 and 25.

Since driving a conventional

vehicle off sealed roads may invalidate your insurance, four-wheel drive (4WD) cars are expensive but worth considering for safe Outback touring. Camper vans are popular, especially in Tasmania; they aren't cheap, however, and it might work out more economical to rent a regular car and stay at budget hotels.

If you're getting around the Outback independently, you must constantly remind yourself that you're in seriously frontier country. Do plenty of research and planning before you head off.

Carrying adequate water, notifying people of your intentions, using reliable vehicles and protecting yourself from sunburn should be high on your list. Picking up hitchhikers is, in general, a bad idea.

Independent travellers should be aware that significant tracts of the Outback are designated as Aboriginal land, and a permit may be required to enter them.

Motoring Advice

If you do opt to explore Australia by car, keep in mind that distances are often huge and towns may be few and far between. Many visitors on short-term trips opt to fly between major cities and rent cars for shorter excursions.

The major highways linking capital cities are all sealed and of a good standard, but you don't have to go far to find yourself on dirt roads. If you're heading into the Outback, great care should be taken. Make sure you have spare tyres, enough fuel and water, and that somebody knows where you're going. In remote areas such as Cape York and the Kimberley, most 4WDs travel in pairs or teams, to assist one another when bogged.

The speed limit in a built-up area is 60 kmph (37 mph) and sometimes 50 kmph (31 mph) or 40 kmph (25 mph) in suburban residential areas; in the country it is usually 100 kmph (62 mph), unless otherwise signposted. Darwin has the most open roads in the country. Beyond city limits there is a maximum speed limit of 130 kmph (81 mph).

Drink driving is a major problem. There is random breath testing for alcohol in most states. If you exceed .05 percent blood-alcohol level (ie, more than three drinks), a hefty fine and loss of licence are automatic.

Fuel comes in super, unleaded, super-unleaded, LPG (gas) and diesel. becoming more expensive in remote country areas.

For extended touring, visitors

sometimes buy a new or used car and sell it at the end of their journey. Each state has an Automobile Association which will supply you with excellent maps and literature. For a small membership fee, they also provide a free, highly recommended, nationwide emergency breakdown service. Motoring organisations in your own country may have reciprocal arrangements with Australian ones so do check before you leave home.

Automobile Associations

Sydney: National Roads and Motorists' Association (NRMA), 74–6 King Street, tel: 131 111; www.nrma.com.au
Melbourne: Royal Automobile Club of Victoria (RACV), corner Little Collins Street and New Chancery Lane; tel: 131 111; www.racv.com.au
Canberra: National Roads and Motorists Association (NRMA), Canberra Centre Shop CG5/6 Canberra Centre, City Walk, Civic, ACT 2600, tel: 131 111; www.nrma.com.au
Perth: Royal Automobile Club of Western Australia Inc. (RAC WA), 832 Wellington Street, West Perth, WA 6839, tel: 131 111; www.rac.com.au
Brisbane: Royal Automobile Club of Queensland (RACQ), GPO Building, 261 Queen Street, Brisbane 4000; tel: 131 111; www.racq.com.au
Adelaide: Royal Automobile Association of South Australia (RAA), 55 Hindmarsh Square, Adelaide, SA 5000, tel: 131 111; www.raa.net
Darwin: Automobile Association of the Northern Territory (AANT), 79–81 Smith Street, Darwin, NT 0800, tel: 131 111; www.aant.com.au

BELOW: Left or right?

ACCOMMODATION

HOTELS, YOUTH HOSTELS, BED & BREAKFAST

Accommodation

Generally speaking, the standard of accommodation in Australia is high. In the capital cities and tourist areas you will find all the international hotel chains such as Hyatt and Sheraton as well as privately managed properties.

While some destinations cater more to well-heeled international visitors (such as Port Douglas, QLD), other regions have recognised the income generated by the young backpacker market and can provide an excellent choice of budget accommodation (for example, Darwin, NT). Log onto www.tntmagazine.com.au for information on Australia's youth hostels.

Sydney's hotels are significantly more expensive than anywhere else in Australia. Seasonal fluctuations in price often apply in heavily touristy areas. One way to reduce the cost is to book accommodation online through one of the last-minute websites such as www.wotif.com or www.lastminute.com.au. Hotels from five-star down to three-star, self-contained cottages and bed and breakfasts throughout Australia use these websites to fill empty rooms, often at a significantly reduced rate, and it is now possible to book accommodation through these sites up to 28 days in advance.

Also check the hotel's own website for last-minute packages and special deals. Some hotel chains guarantee that the rate they offer on their website will be lower than could be found on any other booking website.

Farms and Homes

For a holiday with a difference, you can stay as a paying guest with Australian families in a private home or on a working farm.

B&Bs come and go, so the best source of current information is the **Bed and Breakfast and Farmstay Australia** (BBFA); visit www.australianbedandbreakfast.com.au

The BBFA is comprised of the state and territory B&B and Farmstay associations, with overall responsibility for more than 1,000 B&Bs and Farmstays, and its excellent website details them state by state. The Farmstays include everything from small dairy farms in the hills to vast grain farming and sheep- and cattle-grazing properties.

ACCOMMODATION LISTINGS

NEW SOUTH WALES

Sydney

Sydney has an almost overwhelming choice of hotels. The best method for making a decision, after budgetary considerations, is where in Sydney you would like to be. Most of the de-luxe hotels are located in the historic Rocks and city area. This has the major advantage of being right on Sydney Harbour, but there are other inner-city suburbs with harbour views. Potts Point, for example, has a wealth of accommodation, much of it moderately priced; it provides quick access to the city and has many fine restaurants and cafés.

Budget accommodation is mainly found in Kings Cross, the central business district, Bondi or Manly. Victoria Street in Kings Cross has a score of privately run hostels for backpackers; it's also the place to network with other travellers in arranging lifts, buying cheap flights, or buying a car for that extended road odyssey around Oz. A short trip from the city, through the eastern suburbs, will take you to beautiful Bondi Beach. Glebe is also an attractive student neighbourhood with inexpensive options. Manly is a beach suburb with more of a family feel, with ferry transport to and from the city.

For details of the huge range of B&Bs on offer in Sydney, log onto www.australian bedandbreakfast.com.au

CBD - *Central Business District*

Hilton Sydney
488 George Street
Tel: 02-9265 6045
After a A$200-million makeover, Hilton Sydney reopened it's doors in July 2005, and is now one of the most coveted hotels in the city. Central and super chic, it boasts the city's largest health centre, top-class restaurants and bars and stunning harbour views from the Executive Lounge.
$$$$

Hotel Inter-Continental
Corner of Bridge and Phillip streets
Tel: 02-9253 9000
www.sydney.intercontinental.com
Grand historic Treasury building provides the introduction to a spectacular central skylit courtyard, with accommodation rising above. Many rooms with classic harbour views. Located in the Circular Quay area, within minutes of the Opera House and harbour. **$$$$**

The Observatory Hotel
89–113 Kent Street
Tel: 02-9256 2222
www.observatoryhotel.com.au
Discreet and elegant alternative to large hotels, tucked away behind Observatory Hill in The Rocks. Sydney's most sumptuous suites with antique-style furnishings, deep baths and excellent service. Facilities include a stunning star-ceilinged indoor pool and health spa, as well as an excellent restaurant. Popular with small groups of well-heeled business folk and romantic Sydneysiders. **$$$$**

Park Hyatt Sydney
7 Hickson Road, The Rocks
Tel: 02-9241 1234
www.sydney.park.hyatt.com
Rated as the most luxurious hotel in Sydney, where every attention is paid to personal service. Spacious, supremely comfortable rooms have privileged water-level views of the harbour and Opera House. Ideal location in The Rocks area. **$$$$**

Quay West Sydney
98 Gloucester Street, The Rocks
Tel: 02-9240 6000
or 1800-805 031
www.mirvachotels.com.au
Another of the modern towers that front Sydney Harbour, but this one has self-contained luxury apartments, as well as executive penthouses. There's also a Roman bath-style swimming pool. For a different view – looking back towards the Harbour Bridge from near the Opera House – Mirvac also owns a similar luxury apartment development called Quay

Grand. $$$$
Shangri-La Grand Hotel
176 Cumberland Street, The Rocks
Tel: 02-9250 6000
or 1800-222 448
Fax: 02-9250 6250
www.shangri-la.com
Quintessential harbour views can be had from every room of this award-winning, 573-room modern tower hotel, one of several in The Rocks/Circular Quay area. **$$$$**

Sheraton on the Park
161 Elizabeth Street
Tel: 02-9286 6000
www.sheraton.com/sydney
Huge rooms with dramatic city and Hyde Park park views. **$$$$**

Sir Stamford at Circular Quay
93 Macquarie Street
Tel: 02-9252 4600
or 1300-301 391
www.stamford.com.au
Classical French furnishings and beautiful paintings create a distinguished atmosphere. Located in the business district, this is a "clubby" place, popular with business people. The excellent restaurant is *the* place to close a deal. **$$$$**

The Waldorf Apartment Hotel
57 Liverpool Street
Tel: 02-9261 5355
www.warldorf.com.au
Glitzy tower containing one- and two-bedroom apartments with good views over the city centre and Darling Harbour. At the high end of this price range. **$$$**

YWCA (Hyde Park)
5–11 Wentworth Avenue
Tel: 1800-994 994
Tel: (overseas): +61 2-9264 2451
Fax: +61 2-9285 6288
Email:enquiry@yhotel.com.au
www.yhotel.com.au
Great inner-city location, with over 100 beds. Safe, clean and good facilities. Close to Oxford Street, over the road from Hyde Park. **$**

Inner Eastern Suburbs

Blue Sydney, A Taj Hotel
6 Cowper Wharf Road
Tel: 02-9331 9000
On the buzzing Wharf at Woolloomooloo, this boutique hotel has a choice of views from its

many rooms, including the de-luxe Ultra Loft. Blue's high standard of service and eclectic mix of heritage timber and modern minimalist interior will suit the younger, monied traveller who wants top-class restaurants and uber-trendy bars on site. **$$$$**

Sir Stamford Double Bay
22 Knox Street, Double Bay
Tel: 02-9362 4455
www.stamford.com.au
Fastidious interior decoration, with valuable original artworks. Each room has a carefully designed theme – there's even a Manhattan loft-style room. Double Bay is a wealthy suburb close to the city, known primarily for its fashionable shopping. **$$$$**

Kirketon Boutique Hotel
229 Darlinghurst Road
Darlinghurst 2010
Tel: 02-9332 2011
or 1800-332 920
www.kirketon.com.au
In the epicentre of hip Darlinghurst, ultra-modern, minimalist-style accommodation with restaurants and bars. **$$$**

Medina on Crown Executive
359 Crown Street,
Surry Hills
Tel: 02-8302 1000
or 1300-633 462
www.medinaapartments.com.au
Surry Hills is an attractive and peaceful terrace-house suburb not far from the city centre, with a concentration of galleries, antiques shops and restaurants. These are serviced apartments. **$$$**

Oaks Hyde Park Plaza
38 College Street, Sydney
Tel: 02-9331 6933
or 1800 222 442
www.theoaksgroup.com.au
Overlooking Hyde Park in the centre of the business district, large apartment-style rooms including full kitchen facilities. Functional design. **$$$**

Simpsons of Potts Point
8 Challis Avenue, Potts Point
Tel: 02-9356 2199
www.simpsonspottspoint.com.au
Beautifully restored historic house with authentic period decoration throughout.

ABOVE: Lord Howe Island.

Potts Point is known for fashionable restaurants and cafés; easy access to the city by bus or train. **$$$**

The Grantham
1 Grantham Street, Potts Point
Tel: 02-9357 2377
or 1800 249 706
www.thegrantham.com.au
Many of these apartments have great views across the city skyline to the Botanic Gardens and Sydney Harbour. Functionally designed rooms with all the facilities you need. Good value for money. **$$**

Morgan's of Sydney
304 Victoria Street, Darlinghurst
Tel: 02-9360 7955
www.morganshotel.com.au
Fashionably located boutique hotel aimed at successful young business people, Morgan's is stylish and comfortable; the downstairs bar is the scene for "beautiful" people. Paid parking only. **$$**

Regents Court
18 Springfield Avenue, Potts Point
Tel: 02-9358 1533
www.regentscourt.com.au
The friendly management set up this designer hotel for a clientele of arts-orientated professionals. Nestled in a peaceful backstreet of otherwise seedy Kings Cross, these huge sparse rooms of ultra-modern design lack views, but guests meet for drinks on the rooftop garden. **$$**

PRICE CATEGORIES

Price categories are for a double room without breakfast:
$ = under A$80
$$ = A$80–130
$$$ = A$130–200
$$$$ = over A$200

TRANSPORT · **ACCOMMODATION** · **ACTIVITIES** · **A – Z** · **LANGUAGE**

Sydney Marriott
36 College Street
Tel: 02-9361 8400
www.marriott.com
Facing Hyde Park, this
241-room hotel enjoys a
fine reputation for the
quality of its service.
Amenities include rooftop
pool and spa, and modern
Australian cuisine in the
Windows on the Park
restaurant. **$$$**

Victoria Court Hotel
122 Victoria Street, Potts Point
Tel: 02-9357 3200
or 1800-630505
www.victoriacourt.com.au
Historic boutique hotel and
B&B in elegant Victorian
terraced house. Central,
quiet location in the heart
of Sydney's gastronomic
precinct. **$$**

For backpackers, there is
the **Jolly Swagman** hostel in
Kings Cross, tel: 02-9358 6400;
www.jollyswagman.com.au **$** and
the **Sydney Central
Backpackers** in the same
street, tel: 02-9358 6600;
www.sydneybackpackers.com.au **$**

Inner Western Suburbs

Australian Sunrise Lodge
485 King Street, Newtown
Tel: 02-9550 4999
www.australiansunriselodge.com
Newtown is a fairly
bohemian student suburb,
about 10 minutes' drive
from the city, with great-
value ethnic restaurants,
pubs with live bands, and
an interesting vibe. A
modern hotel with sunny
double, triple and family
rooms. **$$**

**Broadway University
Motor Inn**
25 Arundel Street, Glebe.
Tel: 02-9660 5777
www.goldenchain.com.au
Located just opposite the
University of Sydney, an
area well known for its
alternative lifestyle and a
wide range of cafés. **$$**

Cremorne Point Manor
6 Cremorne Road,
Cremorne Point
Tel: 02-9953 7899
www.cremornepointmanor.com.au
A ferry ride across the
harbour connects the
charming suburb of
Cremorne Point to the city.
This is a restored

Federation mansion with
excellent harbour views. **$$**

Eastern Suburbs

**Coogee Bay Boutique
Hotel**
9 Vicar Street, Coogee
Tel: 02-9315 6055
www.coogeebayhotel.com.au
Heritage-style seaside pub,
nicely renovated. Located
opposite picturesque
Coogee Beach with ocean
views from the front
rooms. Bus to city takes
about 40 mins, taxi 15
mins. **$$**

The Hotel Bondi
178 Campbell Parade, Bondi Beach
Tel: 02-9130 3271
www.hotelbondi.com.au
Bondi's landmark historic
pub, right on the main
street, has undergone a
series of renovations and
can now offer a moderate
standard of accommo-
dation, with five bars, café
and entertainment. The
pub is a bit raucous, so
it is worth staying here
only if you get a front
room with ocean view; for
these, you need to book
well in advance. **$$**

Sinclairs of Bondi
11 Bennett Street, Bondi
Mobile: 0414-342 010
www.sinclairsbondi.com.au
500 metres/yards east
of Bondi Junction. Cooking
facilities. Also at Surry
Hills. **$**

North Sydney

Harbourside Apartments
2A Henry Lawson Avenue,
McMahons Point
Tel: 02-9963 4300
www.harboursideapartments.com.au
Terrific harbour views of the
Opera House underneath
the Sydney Harbour Bridge.
Compact but comfortable –
and the city ferry is right on
the doorstep. **$$$**

Blue Mountains

Less than two hours' drive
from Sydney, the Blue
Mountains are a popular
getaway destination with a
choice of accommodation
in the main towns.

**Blueberry Lodge and The
Loft**
Waterfall Road, Mount Wilson
Tel/fax: 02-4756 2022

www.bluemts.com.au/blueberry
Chalet in historic Blue
Mountains village. **$$$$**

Echoes Boutique Hotel
3 Lilianfels Avenue, Katoomba
Tel: 02-4782 1966;
www.echoeshotel.com.au
Modern luxury and old-
fashioned atmosphere in
this immaculately
renovated boutique hotel
with tremendous views.
$$$$

Lilianfels Blue Mountains
Lilianfels Avenue, Katoomba
Tel: 02-4780 1200;
www.lilianfels.com.au
Well-managed, tranquil
resort located near most
Blue Mountains attractions.
Popular indoor pool/health
club. Wonderful restaurant
in early 20th-century guest
house makes for a special
evening. **$$$$**

Rural NSW

Milton Park
Horderns Road, Bowral
Tel: 02-4861 1522
www.milton-park.com.au
One and a half hours'
drive from Sydney, in the
Southern Highlands,
Milton Park is an elegant
estate, offering horse
riding, golf, tennis, bush
walking and peaceful
solitude. Fine cuisine
using fresh seasonal
produce. **$$$$**

North of Sydney

Casuarina Country Inn
Hermitage Road, Pokolbin,
Hunter Valley
Tel: 02-4998 7888
Striking garden and
vineyard views are provided
from nine fantasy-themed
suites. **$$$$**

Hunter Valley Gardens
Broke Road, Pokolbin
Tel: 02-4998 4000
www.hvg.com.au
A kind of garden theme
park over 300 hectares
(740 acres). There are
three different places to
stay ranging from three- to
four-star. **$$$**

Kim's Beach Hideaway
Charlton Avenue, on the beach,
Toowoon Bay
Tel: 02-4332 1566
www.kims.com.au
Ninety minutes north of
Sydney, Kim's has been a

much-loved resort for
generations. Now more
luxurious than ever, it offers
private beach houses, many
facing directly onto the bay.
And Kim's tradition of fresh
hearty seafood dishes
prevails. **$$$$**

Pips Beach Houses
14 Childe Street, Byron Bay
Tel/fax: 02-6685 5400
For romantic beach-front
privacy, these are cabins
hidden in the bush on the
dunes of Belongil Beach.
$$$$

Rae's on Watego's
8 Marine Parade,
Watego's Beach, Byron Bay
Tel: 02-6685 5366
Near the Queensland
border and designed after a
1920s Mediterranean villa
with Indonesian-inspired
interiors. Guests enjoy five-
star cuisine in a terraced
restaurant overlooking the
beach. No children under
13. **$$$$**

Byron Bay Beach Resort
Beside The Beach
Bayshore Drive
Byron Bay
Tel: 02-6685 8000
or 1800-028 927
www.byronbaybeachresort.com.au
This resort offers 78 self-
contained cabins set
among native gardens of
large beach-front property.
$$$

Peppers Convent
Halls Road, Pokolbin, Hunter Valley
Tel: 02-4998 7764
www.peppers.com.au
Early 20th-century Roman
Catholic convent with
guest rooms and
restaurant. **$$$**

Peppers Guest House
Ekerts Road, Pokolbin,
Hunter Valley
Tel: 02-4993 8999
www.peppers.com.au
The extensive gardens are
ablaze in spring and autumn,
but Peppers is perhaps most
famous for its restaurant –
Chez Pok. **$$$**

PRICE CATEGORIES

Price categories are for a
double room without
breakfast:
$ = under A$80
$$ = A$80–130
$$$ = A$130–200
$$$$ = over A$200

AUSTRALIAN CAPITAL TERRITORY

Canberra

Because Canberra is so spread out, location is important. While some hotels are close to the shopping and business district, others are within walking distance of the National Gallery and Parliament House. Each outer suburb has its own shopping complex and restaurants.

Hyatt Hotel Canberra
Commonwealth Avenue
Yarralumla
Tel: 02-6270 1234
www.hyatt.com
This is the place to stay in Canberra if your budget allows it, and well worth a visit if it doesn't. A part of the city's history, the Hotel Canberra is an elegant example of Australian Art Deco. Custom-designed 1920s carpets, period-outfitted staff and interior balconies. Set on extensive landscaped gardens and located within the Parliamentary Triangle. **$$$$**

Canberra Rex Hotel
150 Northbourne Avenue
Braddon
Tel: 02-6248 5311
www.canberrarexhotel.com.au
Reliable four-star hotel, popular with business

people. An easy walk from the central business district, with an indoor pool, sauna and gymnasium. **$$$**

The Crowne Plaza Hotel Canberra
1 Binara Street, City
Tel: 02-6247 8999
www.crowneplaza.com.au
Centrally located next to Canberra Casino and Convention Centre, close to shopping, theatres, cinemas and restaurants, the Crowne Plaza has 24-hour room service, a health club and undercover parking. **$$$**

Olims Canberra Hotel
Corner of Limestone and Ainslie avenues, Braddon
Tel: 02-6243 0000;
Freecall: 1800-475337
www.olimshotel.com
Only about 1 km (⅔ mile) from the city centre and very close to the war memorial, this Heritage-listed property has split-level apartments designed around a central courtyard. **$$$**

Rydges Lakeside Canberra
London Circuit
Canberra City
Tel: 1800-857922
www.rydges.com
Closer to the commercial centre of the city, rooms provide great views of the lake and surrounding mountains. There are several pleasant bars in which to unwind. **$$$**

Diplomat Boutique Hotel
Corner of Canberra Avenue and Hely Street, Griffith
Tel: 02-6295 2277;
Freecall: 1800-026367
www.diplomathotel.com.au
Canberra's boutique hotel offers honeymoon packages in a spa suite. Large rooms, extensive facilities, 3 km (2 miles) from city centre. **$$$**

Forrest Inn and Apartments
30 National Circuit, Forrest
Tel: 02-6295 3433;
Freecall: 1800-676372
www.forrestinn.com.au
Close to Parliament House and the National Gallery; in leafy surrounds. Some rooms have park views. **$$$**

Oxley Court Serviced Apartments
Oxley and Dawes streets
Kingston
Tel: 02-6295 6216;
Freecall: 1800-623960
www.oxleycourt.com.au
A good choice for families and small groups. Spacious fully self-contained apartments a short drive from the city centre. **$$$**

Hotel Heritage
203 Goyder Street, Narrabundah
Tel: 02-6295 2944;
Freecall: 1800-026346
www.domahotelscanberra.com.au
Hotel rooms and family apartments 12 minutes from the city centre and

close to many tourist attractions. **$$**

Canberra City yha Hostel
7 Akuna Street, Canberra City
Tel: 02-6248 9155
www.yha.com.au
One of the best YHA hostels in Australia. Within walking distance of shops, restaurants, nightclubs and the Jolimont Centre. Facilities include a rooftop barbecue area, an indoor pool, spa and sauna. Some double/twin and family rooms. **$**

Victor Lodge
29 Dawes Street, Kingston
Tel: 02-6295 7777
www.victorlodge.com.au
Friendly place, close to the railway station, 5 minutes drive from Parliament House. Offers twins or bunk rooms with shared bathrooms. Breakfast included, and bicycles available to rent. **$**

Outside Canberra

Brindabella Station
Brindabella Valley Station
Brindabella
Tel: 02-6236 2121
www.brindabellastation.com.au
Historic homestead set in classic Australian bush, between two national parks. A superior country retreat, with five comfortable rooms. **$$$**

VICTORIA

Melbourne

Melbourne has a wide range of accommodation dispersed throughout the city. There are a number of designer or boutique hotels with fashion-conscious interiors, as well as a range of apartment-style accommodation, which often provide more space and facilities for the same price as a hotel. The seaside suburb of St Kilda offers moderate accommodation. The classified columns of *The Age* newspaper on Wednesdays and Saturdays are also a good guide to

new and off-beat places.
Budget-priced hotels lie mainly at the Spencer Street end of the city, around the bus and train terminal and the new blocks rising around the Docklands development are increasing apartment availability in that area.

Adelphi
187 Flinders Lane
Tel: 03-9650 7555
www.adelphi.com.au
An ultra-modern hotel in the heart of the city. Fabulous room-service choices. Spectacular views from the rooftop bar and the pool, which is cantilevered over

the street and has sauna and steam rooms alongside. **$$$**

Albert Heights Serviced Apartments
83 Albert Street
East Melbourne
Tel: 03-9419 0955
Freecall: 1800-800117
www.albertheights.com.au
Modern apartment units, all facing a central garden courtyard and spa pool. Functional but tasteful, the units include all expected facilities. **$$**

Batmans Hill Hotel
623 Collins Street
Tel: 03-9614 6344;
www.batmanshill.com.au

Old-fashioned and friendly style under an elegant, historic exterior. **$$**

Carlton Clocktower Quest Inn
255 Drummond Street, Carlton
Tel: 03-9349 9700;
Freecall: 1800-062966
www.clocktower.com.au
Stylish apartments in the bustling Lygon Street area. **$$**

Crown Promenade Hotel
Southbank
Tel: 03-9292 6688;
Freecall: 1800-776612
www.crownpromenadehotel.com.au
This 39-floor hotel towers above the Yarra River and a vast casino and

entertainment complex that includes cinemas, restaurants and live entertainment. **$$$$**

Downtowner on Lygon
66 Lygon Street, Carlton
Tel: 03-9663 5555
Freecall: 1800-800130
www.downtowner.com.au
Carlton is the cosmopolitan location of this hotel near the university. Stylishly decorated rooms. Guests receive gold membership to the Melbourne City Baths. **$$**

The Explorers Inn
16 Spencer Street
Tel: 03-9621 3333
Freecall: 1800-81616
www.explorershotel.com.au
A modern hotel with simple but good rooms. **$**

Georgian Court
21–5 George Street
East Melbourne
Tel: 03-9419 6353
www.georgiancourt.com.au
Comfortable Bed & Breakfast situated on a tree-lined street, across from beautiful Fitzroy Gardens and just a short walk to the city centre. Thirty-one rooms; dinner available most nights. **$**

Hotel Grand Chancellor
131 Lonsdale Street
Tel: 03-9656 4000
Freecall: 1800-753379
www.ghihotels.com
Comfortable rooms, close to Melbourne Cricket Ground and shopping district. **$$**

Grand Hyatt Melbourne
123 Collins Street
Tel: 03-9657 1234/131234
www.melbourne.grand.hyatt.com
Ostentatious display of brass and marble right down to the huge black-marble bathrooms. Popular for business conventions. The hotel is currently undergoing major renovatios but remains open. Visit the website for details. **$$$$**

Hotel Como
630 Chapel Street,
South Yarra
Tel: 03-9825 2222;
Freecall: 1800-033400
www.mirvachotels.com.au
The Como wins awards year after year for its attention to comfort and uniquely designed suites.

In the fashionable South Yarra district, famous for its fine restaurants and boutiques. **$$$$**

Jasper Hotel
489 Elizabeth Street
Tel: 03-8327 2777
Freecall: 1800-468359
www.ywca.net
Old but comfortable, secure and well-maintained downtown complex. All rooms have showers and toilets. **$**

The Langham
Southgate Avenue,
Southbank
Tel: 03-8696 8888
www.langhamhotelmelbourne.com.au
Central to the Southgate Development, this highrise promotes an aura of untramelled luxury with the bonus of exceptional city views. Private promenade to the shopping district. **$$$$**

Manor House Apartments
36 Darling Street,
South Yarra
Tel: 03-9867 1266
www.manorhouse.com
Well-furnished apartments in the exclusive restaurant and shopping district of South Yarra. **$$$**

Melbourne Metro YHA
78 Howard Street, North Melbourne
Tel: 03-9329 8599
www.yha.com.au
Huge property with fine facilities. Breakfast and dinner service. **$**

The Nunnery
116 Nicholson Street, Fitzroy
Tel: 03-9419 8637
Freecall: 1800-032 635
www.babs.com.au/nunnery
Converted Victorian building close to the city, with comfortable heated rooms, good facilities and a friendly atmosphere. Some dormitory-style accommodation for under A$30. **$**

Olembia Guest House
96 Barkly Street, St Kilda
Tel: 03-9537 1412
www.olembia.com.au
Cosy and friendly guesthouse with dorm rooms, singles and doubles. Very good facilities, heating, parking and a pleasant guest lounge. **$**

Rialto Hotel on Collins
495 Collins Street

Tel: 03-9620 9111;
Freecall: 1800-331 330
European-style hotel in historic building, within walking distance of the casino, World Congress Centre and business district. **$$$**

The Sofitel
25 Collins Street
Tel: 03-9653 0000
www.sofitelmelbourne.com.au
Guest rooms start on the 36th floor and offer sweeping views across Melbourne and Port Phillip Bay. The fancy restaurant may have gone, but the bar and café at the top still welcome visitors who want the view without the room. **$$$$**

Vibe Savoy
630 Little Collins Street
Tel: 03-9622 8888
www.vibehotels.com.au
This intimate 1920s hotel promotes an elegant, club-like atmosphere. **$$$**

The Victoria Hotel
215 Little Collins Street
Tel: 03-9669 0000;
Freecall: 1800-331147
www.victoriahotel.com.au
Budget, standard and superior rooms offered in this good standard hotel. Within walking distance of the CBD. **$$**

The Westin
205 Collins Street
Tel: 03-9635 2222
www.westin.com.au
Facing City Square in Swanston Street, it's hard to get more central than this. Combine that with sleek interiors and fine service. **$$$$**

The Windsor
103 Spring Street
Tel: 03-9653 6000
www.thewindsor.com.au
For the old wealth of Melbourne, there is no question about the Windsor's supremacy. This majestic National Trust building in the centre of Melbourne is one of the few in Australia originally built as a hotel. Intended in 1883 to provide the most luxurious accommodation in Melbourne, the Windsor in many respects still holds that title. Excellent service, combined with old-world

interiors and a famous high tea at 3pm. **$$$$**

Outside Melbourne

Amaroo Caravan Park and YHA Hostel
Corner of Church and Osborne streets, Cowes
Tel: 03-5952 2548
In the main town of Phillip Island, this is the best budget accommodation by far. Friendly hostel and caravan park with evening meals, bicycles for hire and organised tours to the Penguin Parade and Wilsons Prom. **$**

Comfort Inn Shamrock
Corner of Pall Mall and Williamson streets, Bendigo
Tel: 03-5443 0333
www.shamrockbendigo.com.au
Grandiose country hotel from the gold-mining period. Ornate roof structure and surrounding balconies. Rooms range from inexpensive traditional rooms to de-luxe suites. **$$$**

Cumberland Lorne
150 Mountjoy Parade,
Lorne
Tel: 03-5289 2400
Freecall: 1800-037 010
www.cumberland.com.au
A memorable scenic drive down the Great Ocean Road, and you're in one of Victoria's favourite seaside playgrounds. The hotel offers a variety of suites with wonderful views and complimentary recreational activities, right in the heart of the friendly town. **$$$**

Hotel Pension Grimus
224 Breathtaker Road,
Mount Buller
Tel: 03-5777 6396
www.pensiongrimus.com.au
A great hotel in Victoria's premier ski-resort area. Legendary skiier hosts Hans and Lotte Grimus (Hans has a ski named after him) run a friendly, great-value lodge. All rooms

PRICE CATEGORIES

Price categories are for a double room without breakfast:
$ = under A$80
$$ = A$80–130
$$$ = A$130–200
$$$$ = over A$200

have double spa baths. Families welcome; babysitting available. **$$$**
Lake House
King Street, Daylesford
Tel: 03-5348 3329
www.lakehouse.com.au
Located in "Spa Country", this is a luxurious retreat on the shore of Lake Daylesford with one of Victoria's finest restaurants. Everything from the pastries to the

preserves are made on the premises. You can visit local wineries, a sheep station and Hanging Rock (scene of the picnic in Peter Weir's classic film). **$$$$**
Mount Buffalo Chalet
Mount Buffalo
Tel: 03-5755 1500
Freecall: 1800-037038
www.mtbuffalochalet.com.au
Spectacularly situated atop an escarpment in Victoria's high country, the chalet

offers a range of activities. Sweeping views of the Great Dividing Range and the green valleys below. **$$$$**
Mt Ophir Estate
Stillards Lane
Rutherglen
Tel: 02-6032 8920
www.mount-ophir.com
Historic winery buildings, plus two homesteads with four bedrooms in each. There is an emu and elk farm, vineyards and

forests, as well as an organic cropping farm. **$$**
Southern Grampians Cottages
33–5 Victoria Valley Road
Dunkeld
Tel: 03-5577 2457
www.grampianscottages.com.au
Attractive log-style cabins, self-contained with wood fires, spas and kitchens, in a bushland setting. Located next to a national park full of wildlife and nature walks. **$$**

SOUTH AUSTRALIA

Adelaide

Adelaide has been spaciously planned, so if you need to be within walking distance of the Festival Centre, South Australian Art Gallery, and lively East End neighbourhood, make sure to stay in the Central Business District. However, North Adelaide is just a short distance across the Torrens River and has a wealth of historic B&Bs with views of the Adelaide Hills. The suburb of Glenelg is an attractive beach-front community with many Mediterranean-style houses and restful ocean views. Budget accommodation in central Adelaide is limited, with hostels clustered around the Central Bus Station on Franklin Street – a wider selection can be found in the attractive beachside suburb of Glenelg.

Central Adelaide (CBD)
Hyatt Regency Adelaide
North Terrace
Adelaide
Tel: 08-8231 1234
www.adelaide.regency.hyatt.com
Luxurious tower accommodation and a casino housed in an historic railway station downstairs. Best location in the centre of town, right beside the Adelaide Festival Centre. Rooms provide excellent views of the city. **$$$$**
Stamford Plaza Adelaide
150 North Terrace
Adelaide

Tel: 08-8461 1111
www.stamford.com.au
Adelaide's original five-star hotel has been refurbished and includes a delightful terrace garden for breakfasts and buffets. In the centre of town with city views. **$$$$**
Hilton Adelaide
233 Victoria Square
Tel: 08-8217 2000
www.adelaide.hilton.com
Located adjacent to the Central Markets as well as Gouger Street restaurants with views over Victoria Square. The Grange restaurant located downstairs is highly acclaimed and has won numerous industry awards. **$$$$**
Medina Grand Adelaide Treasury
2 Flinders Street
Tel: 08-8112 0000
Serviced one- and two-bedroom apartments and studios in the centre of town on Victoria Square. Located in the grand Heritage-listed treasury building. **$$$**
Hotel 208
208 South Terrace
Tel: 08-8223 2800 or 1300-797208
www.hotel208.com
With views of the attractive South Parklands directly opposite, this four-star property is 15 minutes' walk to the city and close to the business centres of Parkside, Unley and Wayville. **$$**
Mercure Grosvenor Hotel
125 North Terrace
Tel: 08-8407 8888
www.mercure.com.au

Opposite the Skycity Adelaide, the casino in the centre of town, this makes an ideal base for walking to all major attractions. **$$$**
Adelaide Backpackers Inn
112 Carrington Street
Tel: 08-8223 6635
Freecall: 1800-247 725
www.adelaidebackpackersinn.net.au
Dormitories and annexe with singles and twins. Free hot apple pie and ice cream every night. **$**
Adelaide Youth Hostel
135 Waymouth Street
Adelaide
Tel: 08-8414 3010
www.yha.com.au
A modern YHA hostel with good facilities; movies every night. Family rooms and doubles/twins with private bathrooms available. **$**

North Adelaide
All Seasons Adelaide Meridien
21–37 Melbourne Street
North Adelaide
Tel: 08-8267 3033
Freecall: 1800-888 228
www.adelaidemeridien.com.au
Fashionable street in North Adelaide known for its cafés, boutiques and parklands. Modern terraced structure comprises standard and executive suites. **$$$**
North Adelaide Heritage Apartments & Cottages
Various locations in North Adelaide
Tel/fax: 08-8272 1355
www.adelaideheritage.com
Manages many B&Bs in Heritage-listed properties – including manor houses, a fire station and iron-lace

villas – in the historic boulevards of North Adelaide. **$$$**
Princes Lodge
73 Lefevre Terrace
North Adelaide
Tel: 08-8267 5566
www.princeslodge.com.au
Friendly management and good location in North Adelaide, within walking distance of the city. Light breakfast is served. **$$**

Glenelg (beach)
Stamford Grand
Moseley Square
Glenelg
Tel: 08-8376 1222
www.stamford.com.au
Beautiful views of the ocean or the Adelaide Hills from this grand highrise resort in seaside Glenelg. Award-winning hotel provides extra-large rooms and touches of the Victorian era. **$$$$**
Glenelg Beach Hostel
1–7 Moseley Street
Glenelg
Tel: 08-8376 0007
www.glenelgbeachhostel.com.au
Everything from seven-bed dorms to family rooms – and no bunk beds. **$**.

Outside Adelaide
Adelaide Hills
Thorngrove Country Manor
2 Glenside Lane
Stirling
Tel: 08-8339 6748
www.slh.com
About 20 minutes by car from Adelaide, this is a Gothic fantasy complete with turrets and gables.

Although it sounds tacky, the Manor offers five-star luxury with large private suites furnished with valuable antiques, and a fine restaurant. $$$$

Mt Lofty House
74 Mt Lofty Summit Road,
Crafers,
Adelaide Hills
Tel: 08-8339 6777
www.mtloftyhouse.com.au
Historic country estate that is now a boutique hotel. Located in the Adelaide Hills with views of the Piccadilly Valley and only a 20-minute drive from the city. $$$

Barossa Valley

Collingrove Homestead
Eden Valley Road
Angaston
Tel: 08-8564 2061
www.collingrovehomestead.com.au
National Trust-listed homestead in the Barossa Ranges with

extensive English-style gardens and antiques; ideal for a peaceful escape. $

Langmeil Cottages
89 Langmeil Road
Tanunda
Tel/fax: 08-8563 2987
www.langmeilcottages.com
Beautiful views from self-contained units, with the use of bicycles, barbecue and swimming pool. $

Kangaroo Island

Lighthouse Keeper's Cottage
Cape Borda,
Kangaroo Island
Tel: 08-8559 7235
www.parks.sa.gov.au/flinderschase
Stay in one of the unique heritage cottages in Kangaroo Island's wilderness. Bookings handled by National Parks & Wildlife, South Australia, Flinders Chase National Park, Kangaroo Island. $

*Coonawarra
(wine region)*

Padthaway Estate Homestead
Riddoch Highway
Padthaway
Tel: 08-8765 5555
www.padthawayestate.com
Magnificent 19th-century mansion amid the Padthaway Estate vineyards, home of fine Australian champagne-style wines. Six rooms, cosy lounges with fireplaces and a relaxed friendly service. $

Outback

Arkaroola Tourist Resort & Wildlife Sanctuary
Arkaroola, northern Flinders Ranges via Port Augusta
Tel: 08-8648 4848;
Freecall: 1800-676 042 (reservations)
www.arkaroola.com.au
A rugged Outback landscape 600 km (373 miles) north of Adelaide, rich in native flora and

fauna. Winner of SA Tourism Awards. $$

Desert Cave Hotel
Hutchison Street
Coober Pedy
Tel: 08-8672 5688
www.desertcave.com.au
De-luxe underground hotel in Australia's most famous opal-mining Outback community 850 km (528 miles) north of Adelaide. Most residents live below ground as an escape from the desert sun. Choose underground suites with their naked rock walls and impressive skylit foyer. $$$

The Underground Motel
Catacomb Road
Coober Pedy
Tel: 08-8672 5324;
Freecall: 1800-622 979
www.theundergroundmotel.com.au
A more economical choice in (or under) Coober Pedy, also with natural rock walls; friendly comfortable place with a guest kitchen for self-catered breakfasts. $$

QUEENSLAND

Queensland's coastline is a near-continuous strip of excellent beaches, with hundreds of holiday resorts. While Brisbane itself has no beaches, it is an excellent base or jumping-off point for exploring the south of Queensland. Cairns in the far north is the direct arrival point for visitors to the Great Barrier Reef and Cape York. An hour further north, the village of Port Douglas is smaller, more charming and more convenient (it also has the Four Mile Beach, while Cairns faces mudflats).

Camping

For an excellent guide to Queensland camping grounds, contact:
The Environmental Protection Agency, PO Box 155, Brisbane Albert Street, Queensland 4002.
Tel: 07-3227 8197
Fax: 07-3227 8749
Or vist them at www.epa.qld.gov.au. They publish a Queensland

National Parks and Wildlife Service booklet entitled *Camping in Queensland*, detailing over 280 places to camp in national parks, state forests and water reserves. Bookings are recommended to avoid disappointment.

Brisbane

Acacia Inner City Inn
413 Upper Edward Street
Tel: 07-3832 1663
Friendly inner-city facility with a range of accommodation choices, and a sociable environment. Continental breakfast inclusive. $$

Brisbane City YHA Hostel
392 Upper Roma Street
Brisbane
Tel: 07-3236 4999
www.yha.com.au
Excellent facilities in this backpacker-orientated youth hostel. Located in trendy Paddington, close to the city, the hostel has an inexpensive restaurant for breakfast and dinner. $

Brisbane Palace Backpackers
308 Edward Street
Tel: 07-3211 2433
Freecall: 1800-676 340 (reservations only)
www.palacebackpackers.com.au
Smack opposite Central Station and with everything you need, including the famous Down Under Bar. $

Carlton Crest Hotel
King George Square, corner of Ann and Roma streets
Tel: 07-3229 9111
Freecall: 1900-777 123 (reservations only)
www.carltonhotels.com.au
City-centre location with a choice of four-star Crest Tower, or five-star Carlton Tower accommodation. $$$$

Conrad Treasury
William and George streets
Tel: 07-3306 8888
Freecall: 1800-506 889 (reservations only)
www.conradtreasury.com.au
The Treasury building – which houses Brisbane's casino – is one of the finest 19th-century structures in the city. Accommodation is

in individually decorated suites, featuring many of the original furnishings. $$$$

Dockside Central Apartment Hotel
44 Ferry Street
Kangaroo Point
Tel: 07-3981 6644
www.centralgroup.com.au
Spacious self-contained apartments, each with a sweeping view from a private balcony. Across the river from the city but there's a ferry at the bottom of the garden. $$$

Explorers Inn
63 Turbot Street
Tel: 07-3211 3488
Freecall: 1800-623 288
www.explorers.com.au
Budget-style accommodation in the Brisbane CBD, 150 metres/yards from the Queen Street Mall and a range of bars and restaurants. $$$

The Marque Hotel Brisbane
103 George Street
Tel: 07-3221 6044
www.chifleyhotels.com
Refurbished 99-room hotel

with a distinctive casual elegance. A 5-minute walk to the Southbank Parkland across the river. **$$$**

Mercure Hotel Brisbane
85–7 North Quay
Tel: 07-3237 2300
www.mercurebrisbane.com.au
Great location on the Brisbane River overlooking the Cultural Centre, Southbank Parkland, and more. Comfortable accommodation just a few minutes' walk from the Central Business District and casino. **$$$$**

Il Mondo Boutique Hotel
25-35 Rotherham Street
Kangaroo Point
Tel: 07-3392 0111
A boutique hotel where every room is individually decorated. Close to Kangaroo Point. **$$$**

Quay West Suites Brisbane
132 Alice Street
Tel: 07-3853 6000
Freecall: 1800-672 726
(reservations only)
www.mirvachotels.com.au
One- and two-bedroom apartment accommodation in the city centre, overlooking the Botanic Gardens. All suites have balconies. **$$$$**

Ryan's on the River
269 Main Street
Kangaroo Point
Tel: 07-3391 1011
www.ryans.com.au
Attractive property in a great location in Kangaroo Point on the walking and cycle pathway. Close to the CBD but a world away. **$$**

Spring Hill Terraces
260 Water Street
Spring Hill
Tel: 07-3854 1048
www.springhillterraces.com
Modern and comfortable self-contained apartments and budget rooms in a good location, about 5 minutes' drive from the city centre. **$$**

Stamford Plaza Hotel
By the Botanic Gardens (corner of Margaret and Edward streets)
Tel: 07-3221 1999
Freecall: 1800-301391
(reservations only)
www.stamford.com.au
Brisbane's finest luxury hotel, located in the city centre beside the historic

Botanic Gardens. Impressive oil paintings of early Queensland grace the lobby, which extends alongside a serene central courtyard, providing a haven from the inner city. Elegant rooms of generous country-style proportions overlook the winding Brisbane River. Try the excellent Siggi's at the Port Office restaurant for special occasions. **$$$$**

Hotel Watermark Brisbane
551 Wickham Terrace
Tel: 07-3831 3111
Freecall: 1800-777 702
(reservations only)
www.albertparkhotel.com.au
Up-market hotel with European-style decor, located near Roma Street Parkland and Transit Centre. **$$$$**

Southern Queensland Outback

Talgai Homestead
Allora–Ellinthorp Road, Allora, Southern Darling Downs
Tel: 07-4666 3444
A small, friendly hotel with country-style cooking in a National Trust-listed homestead furnished with antiques. Total relaxation guaranteed. **$$$$**

Central Queensland Outback

Albert Park Motor Inn
Matilda Highway
Longreach
Tel: 07-4658 2411
Very comfortable with modern facilities, within walking distance of the Stockman's Hall of Fame and the Qantas Founders' Outback Museum. **$$**

Carnarvon Gorge Wilderness Lodge
Carnarvon Gorge, via Rolleston, Queensland
Tel: 07-4984 4503
Freecall: 1800-644 150
(reservations only)
www.carnarvon-gorge.com
Unique timber and canvas safari cabins have their own Outback charm, and make a good base for exploring the gorge with its ancient plant life and fossilised Aboriginal rock art. **$$$$**

Gold Coast

There are dozens of generic highrises along this 35-km (20-mile) stretch of sand, which includes Surfer's Paradise, but most people who come here have their hotel already organised through package tours. There are also many small motels for the independent traveller.

Broadwater Keys Quest Inn
125 Frank Street
Labrador
Tel: 07-5531 0839
www.broadwaterkeys.com.au
About 100 metres/yards from the Broadwater, self-contained units available on daily and weekly rates. **$$**
Motels such as **Sunset Court** in Surfers Paradise (tel: 07-5539 0266), are typical of the cheap Aussie vacation hangouts here – functional, often with a kitchen, and not far from the beach. **$$**

Palazzo Versace
94 Sea World Drive
Main Beach
Tel: 07-5509 8000
Freecall: 1800-098000
www.palazzoversace.com
The world's first hotel designed by Versace is predictably over the top. **$$$$**

Sheraton Mirage Resort and Spa
Sea World Drive
Main Beach
Tel: 07-5591 1488
Freecall: 1800-073 535
(reservations only)
www.sheraton.com
Low-rise luxury resort with comprehensive health club facilities. Restaurants highly rated. **$$$$**

Sunshine Coast

Hyatt Regency Coolum Golf Resort & Spa
1 Warran Road
Coolum
Tel: 07-5446 1234
www.coolum.hyatt.com
About 90 minutes' drive north of Brisbane, a championship golf-course resort set in natural bushland with ocean

beachfront, and its own lifeguard on duty. **$$$$**

Noosa Blue Resort
16 Noosa Drive
Noosa
Tel: 07-5447 5699
Freecall: 1800-463854
www.noosablue.com.au
A stylish boutique resort perched high on Noosa Hill, with sweeping views of Noosa's coastline and hinterland, and only 450 metres/yards from its Hastings Street social and shopping centre. Luxury self-contained suites with spas and fine attention to detail. **$$$$**

Fraser Island

Kingfisher Bay Resort and Village
North White Cliff, Fraser Island
Tel: 07-4120 3333;
Freecall: 1800-072555
www.kingfisherbay.com
The only de-luxe property on this stunningly beautiful World Heritage-listed island. (Arrive by car ferry or catamaran from Urangan, approx 3½ hours' drive north of Brisbane.) For a fee the resort provides tours to scenic sites, or you can rent a four-wheel drive. **$$$$**

Lamington National Park

Binna Burra Mountain Lodge
Beechmont
Tel: 07-5533 3622
www.binnaburralodge.com.au
Award-winning eco-accredited lodge in world-heritage area with over 160 km (100 miles) of hiking tracks. Packages include rustic cabin accommodation, all country-style meals, abseiling, and flying fox, rainforest and bird-spotting walks. Camping sites and

PRICE CATEGORIES

Price categories are for a double room without breakfast:
$ = under A$80
$$ = A$80–130
$$$ = A$130–200
$$$$ = over A$200

permanent safari tents also available. **$$$**
O'Reilly's Rainforest Guest House
Lamington National Park Road
Via Canungra
Tel: 07-5502 4911
Freecall: 1800-688 722
(reservations only)
www.oreillys.com.au
Friendly family-run guesthouse which has been providing accommodation, naturalist guide services, touring and special events in this beautiful world-heritage region for over 80 years. About 2 hours' drive southwest from Brisbane. **$$$**

Far North Queensland

Archipelago Studio Apartments
72 Macrossan Street
Port Douglas
Tel: 07-4099 5387
www.archipelago.com.au
Self-contained apartments right on Macrossan Street and only 50 metres/yards from Four Mile Beach. Proprietors Christel and Wolfgang are a goldmine of local knowledge. **$$$**
Gilligan's Backpackers Hotel & Resort
57–89 Grafton Street
Cairns
Tel: 07-4041 6566
www.gilligansbackpackers.com.au

Only a couple of years old this luxury backpackers offers rooms with air conditioning, en-suites and balconies. **$$**
The Lakes Cairns Resort & Spa
2 Greenslopes Street
Cairns
Tel: 07-4053 9411
(reservations) or 07-4053 9401 (reception)
www.thelakescairns.com.au
Adjoining the Botanical Gardens and close to the city action without complete immersion, a thoughtfully designed resort in natural surroundings. **$$$**
Port O'Call Lodge
Corner of Port Street and
Craven Close
Port Douglas
Tel: 07-4099 5422
www.portocall.com.au
YHA associate. The best option for budget accommodation, about 1 km (⅔ mile) from the town. Four-share and private rooms, cooking facilities, bar and bistro, a pool and courtesy bus to and from Cairns (Mon–Sat, conditions apply). **$**
The Reef Retreat
10–14 Harpa Street
Palm Cove
Tel: 07-4059 1744
www.reefretreat.com.au
Good-value resort accommodation in Palm Cove, 20 minutes' north of

Cairns. Natural tropical setting, idyllic beach, bars and al-fresco dining. **$$**
Sebel Reef House & Spa
99 Williams Esplanade
Palm Cove
Tel: 07-4055 3633
www.reefhouse.com.au
Elegant tropical resort only 25 minutes north of Cairns on Palm Cove's golden beach. The design is refreshingly light and spacious. **$$$$**
Sheraton Mirage Port Douglas
Davidson Street
Port Douglas
Tel: 07-4099 5888
Freecall: 1800-818 831
(reservations only)
www.sheraton-mirage.com.au
The glitziest resort in the fast-developing town of Port Douglas. All the man-made five-star luxury you can imagine, including 2 hectares (5 acres) of swimmable blue lagoons and an 18-hole international-standard golf course. **$$$$**
Sofitel Reef Hotel Casino
35–41 Wharf Street
Cairns
Tel: 07-4030 8888
Freecall: 1800-808 883
www.reefcasino.com.au
This luxury development in Cairns includes a nightclub, rainforest conservatory, five restaurants and a casino. All suites have balconies and modern woodgrain furnishings in a vaguely tropical Queensland fashion. **$$$$**
Sovereign Resort Hotel
128 Charlotte Street
Cooktown
Tel: 07-4069 5400
www.sovereign-resort.com.au
A relaxed "plantation-style" resort hotel in the heart of Cooktown. Excellent balcony restaurant, and the air conditioning is welcome at the end of a warm day. Airport courtesy pick-up by arrangement. **$$$$**
Yungaburra Pub
6-8 Kehoe Place
Yungaburra
Tel: 07-4095 3515
www.yungaburrapub.com.au
A fine example of Federation-style architecture in the quiet village of Yungaburra and a comfortable base for

exploring the rolling hills of the Atherton Tablelands. The rooms are simple but pleasantly decorated, there's good pub food and staff are friendly. **$$**

Far North Eco Resorts

For a more natural and unspoilt environment, the following resorts provide a glimpse of real North Queensland.
Cape Trib Beach House
Cape Tribulation Road
(38 km/24 miles from the ferry)
Tel: 07-4098 0030
www.capetribbeach.com.au
Dormitory and family cabins as close to the beach as the National Parks Authority will allow. Kitchen/laundry facilities, swimming pool and bistro/bar. **$$**
Cape Tribulation Exotic Fruit Farm B&B
Lot 5 Nicole Drive, Cape Tribulation
Tel: 07-4098 0057
www.capetrib.com.au
A fruit-tasting and farm tour in a permaculture orchard; will add another dimension to your rainforest experience. **$$$$**
Daintree Eco Lodge & Spa
20 Daintree Road, Daintree
Tel: 07-4098 6100;
Freecall: 1800-808010
www.daintree-ecolodge.com.au
Comfortable lodges set in the rainforest opposite the tropical Daintree River. Only 90 minutes' north of Cairns on a sealed road – no ferry crossing. Multi award winner for its spa and eco-tourism incorporating indigenous culture. **$$$$**
The Horizon at Mission Beach
PO Box 150, Mission Beach
Tel: 07-4068 8154
www.thehorizon.com.au
South of Cairns and high above historical Tam O'Shanter Point, surrounded by rainforest, with command-ing views of Dunk and Bedarra islands. Spacious verandas look out to sea and a short stroll leads to a private beach. **$$$$**
Kewarra Beach Resort
Kewarra Beach
Tel: 07-4057 6666
www.kewarra.com
Private de-luxe bungalows

BELOW: luxury living at the Sheraton Mirage Port Douglas.

hidden in tropical beach-front property 20 minutes from Cairns. Quiet relaxation after busy North Queensland day trips. Fine collection of Aboriginal and Torres Strait art and historical artefacts. **$$$$**

Peppers Bloomfield Lodge
PO Box 966, Cairns
Tel: 07-4035 9166
www.bloomfieldlodge.com
Remote and beautiful location abutting Cape Tribulation National Park. Private cabins hidden in the rainforest, overlooking the Coral Sea. Possible to continue by four-wheel drive to historic Cooktown and surrounds. Minimum four-night packages include all meals, flight transfers from Cairns and a guided rain-forest walk and river cruise. **$$$$**

Red Mill House
11 Stewart Street, Daintree Village
Tel/fax: 07-4098 6233
www.redmillhouse.com.au
Excellent B&B in an old Queenslander house set in spacious gardens near the Daintree River. Caters espe-cially to keen bird watchers and nature lovers. **$$**

Silky Oaks Lodge and Healing Waters Spa
Finlayvale Road
Mossman River Gorge
Tel: 07-4098 1666
Freecall: 1800-134044
www.silkyoakslodge.com.au
Some 27 km (17 miles) from Port Douglas, this rainforest hideaway lies on the edge of Mossman Gorge, which adjoins Daintree National Park. The treehouses and river houses have all the creature comforts you need, plus a spa, restaurant, and rainforest excursions and canoe trips on the Mossman River. **$$$$**

Undara Lava Lodge
Mount Surprise
Tel: 07-4097 1900
www.undara.com.au
Accommodation is in quaint refurbished railway carriages on the edge of the Undara Volcanic National Park. Qualified savannah guides conduct interpretive tours through ancient caverns. Also has a camping area. **$$**

Voyages Coconut Beach Rainforest Lodge
Cape Tribulation Road
Cape Tribulation
Tel: 07-4098 0033
Freecall: 1300-134044
(reservations only)
www.voyages.com.au
Hideaway accommodation nestled in the rainforest, and only minutes to the beach from its Cape Restaurant. A "canopy crane" is an innovative way to view the rainforest treetops from above, and the resort has its own boat for reef trips. **$$$$**

Cape York

Punsand Bay Camping Resort
Via Bamaga, Cape York
Tel: 07-4069 1722
This resort, which offers camping facilities and air-conditioned cabins for Cape York's annual influx of four-wheel drive adventurers as well as air travellers (via Bamaga or Horn Island), provides access to some of the remotest, most historic and beautiful sites on the Cape York Peninsula – virgin rainforest, clear, fast-flowing streams, and endless unpopulated beaches. **$$**

Great Barrier Reef & Whitsunday Islands

A number of the more up-market island resorts – Lizard, Bedarra, Dunk, Silky Oaks, Heron and Brampton – are owned by Voyages and accessed by road, by sea, or (more commonly) by air. The freecall number in Australia for Voyages is 1300-134 044; fax: 02-9299 2103. Their website is www.voyages.com.au

Bedarra Island Resort
Bedarra Island, via Mission Beach
Freecall 1800-134044
www.bedarraisland.com
Bedarra Island Resort has created a mystique surrounding its rich and famous guests. Privacy is the draw, since only 15 individual luxury villas are nestled in the beachfront foliage. Guests (no under-16s) are free to explore the

island by motor dinghy and find their private beach to settle down on with their champagne-filled picnic hampers. **$$$$**

Brampton Island
Via Mackay
Tel: 07-4951 4499
Tel: 1300-134044 (reservations)
www.brampton-island.com
Intimate resort on an island which is almost entirely on national parkland, and where you can take the mini-train to the daily fish feeding. Located 32 km (20 miles) northeast of Mackay (a 20-minute flight or 50-minute launch trip). Activities include golf, catamaran sailing and plenty of other sports. Reef trips and seaplane flights additional. **$$$**

Daydream Island Resort and Spa
Whitsunday Islands
Mackay
Tel: 07-4948 8488
Freecall: 1800-075040
(reservations only)
www.daydream.net.au
Family-style resort on a smallish, pretty tropical island with a wide range of free activities including outdoor cinema. Day trips to Outer Reef and Whitehaven Beach. **$$$**

Dunk Island
Via Townsville
Tel: 07-4068 8199
Tel: 1300-134044
(reservations)
www.dunk-island.com
Almost completely rainforested, Dunk is home to richly diverse native flora and fauna. It has walking trails, an Australian farm and game fishing, and is 45 minutes by ferry from Mission Beach. Good for families with a full range of activities, four levels of accommodation and child-minding facility. **$$$**

Fitzroy Island Resort
Fitzroy Island
PO Box 2120, Cairns
Tel: 07-4051 9588
www.fitzroyisland.com.au
A continental or "high" island reached by catamaran from Cairns, Fitzroy features beach cabins with private facilities and beach bunkhouses with communal facilities. **$$$**

Great Keppel Island Resort
Via Rockhampton
Tel: 07-4939 5044
www.greatkeppelresort.com.au
Catering to couples and families, the resort is 25 km (15 miles) of white sandy beach and provides land- and water-based activities, ranging from water-skiing and sailing to tandem skydiving. **$$$**

Great Keppel Island Holiday Village
Great Keppel Island
Tel: 07-4939 8655
Freecall: 1800-180 235
This Youth Hostel Association site offers camping, safari tents and on-site cabins. Book well ahead for this popular location. Snorkel gear for rent, bushwalks and other activities. Facilities include café and shop. **$$$**

Green Island Resort
PO Box 898, Cairns
Tel: 07-4031 3300
Freecall: 1800-673 366
www.greenislandresort.com.au
Forty-five minutes by fast catamaran from Cairns, Green Island Resort is a luxury eco-tourist develop-ment built on a coral cay. Also popular with large numbers of day visitors. **$$$$**

Hayman Island Resort
Great Barrier Reef
North Queensland
Tel: 07-4940 1234
www.hayman.com.au
One of the Whitsunday Islands, located between the coast and the Great Barrier Reef, Hayman Island is another "total luxury" resort. A modern, three-level complex overlooks a vast pool and the sea. Unlike some luxury resorts, young children are welcome and a crèche and baby-sitting are available.

PRICE CATEGORIES

Price categories are for a double room without breakfast:
$ = under A$80
$$ = A$80–130
$$$ = A$130–200
$$$$ = over A$200

Even so, it's a popular honeymoon venue. **$$$$**

Heron Island Resort
Via Gladstone
Tel: 07-4972 9055
Tel: 1300-134044
(reservations only)
www.heronisland.com
A coral cay located right on the Great Barrier Reef and one of the world's top dive sites, the island is a pristine national park, bird sanctuary and turtle rookery. Turtles come in summer to lay their eggs, and tiny hatchlings emerge from December to April. Whales arrive in August and September. During the mating season hundreds of indigenous birds are joined by migrating species to nest and rear their young in the lush forest of pisonia trees. No televisions in the rooms. High standard of tropical cuisine; fishing trips; guided walks; sunset wine and cheese cruises; overnight camping trips to uninhabited Wilson Island.

Hinchinbrook Island Wilderness Lodge and Resort
Tel: 07-4066 8270
www.hinchinbrookresort.com.au
Accommodation is in architect-designed tree houses linked by an aerial boardwalk. If you're scared of heights, take a beach cabin instead. **$$$$**

Island Leisure Resort
4 Kelly Street, Nelly Bay
Magnetic Island
Tel: 07-4778 5000
www.islandleisure.com.au
A short ferry ride from Townsville, a family-style resort comprising 17 self-contained units in a tropical village garden setting only 50 metres/yards from the beach. **$$$**

Lizard Island
Via Cairns
Tel: 07-4060 3999
Freecall: 1800-737768
www.lizardisland.com.au
Thoroughly exclusive atmosphere on the most de-luxe resort island of the Barrier Reef. The

northernmost Reef island, Lizard's natural beauty includes excellent dive sites and idyllic calm waters with a colony of giant clams. Sophisticated cuisine and world-class game fishing. No facilities for children under six. **$$$$**

Long Island Resort
Tel: 07-4946 9400
www.clubcroc.com.au
Relaxed resort on its own bay with the emphasis on water sports and fun, but quiet woodland walks if you want to get away from it all. **$$$$**

Orpheus Island Resort
Private Mail Bag 15
Townsville Mail Centre
Tel: 07-4777 7377
www.orpheus.com.au
Designed as an intimate, secluded resort, with only 21 beach-front rooms available. Emphasis on couples and romantic picnics. Surrounded by national park on an island 11 km (7 miles) long and 1.5 km (1 mile) wide. **$$$$**

Pumpkin Island
South of North Keppel Island
PO Box 1151,
Kenmore,
Qld 4069
Tel: 07-4939 4413
www.pumpkinisland.com.au
Five large cabins are available; each accommodates five or six people and has solar power and gas appliances. You'll need to bring food and linen. Transport to the island is by charter boat arranged when you book. **$$$**

Reef View Hotel
Hamilton Island
Tel: 07-4946 9999
www.hamiltonisland.com.au
There are a range of room types on this self-contained island, all of which are expensive. Choose from the Beach Club, Reef View Hotel, Whitsunday Apartments and the Palm Bungalows and Terrace. Palm Terrace is the cheapest while the exclusive Beach Club is at the other end of the spectrum. **$$$$**

NORTHERN TERRITORY

Darwin

Darwin is spread over a large area and although many hotels can be found in the city centre, a number of pleasant options are located a short drive away. Keep in mind that the rates are often significantly higher during the dry season of May–October.

Since Darwin is the starting point for so many adventure travel options, a good selection of accommodation for backpackers and the budget-conscious is on offer, much of it conveniently near the Transit Centre.

Crowne Plaza Darwin
32 Mitchell Street
Darwin
Tel: 08-8982 0000
Tel: 1300-363 300 (reservations)
www.crowneplaza.com.au
Centrally located highrise, views of the harbour and city. Spa and health club. **$$$$**

Skycity Darwin
Gilruth Avenue
Darwin
Tel: 08-8943 8888
Freecall: 1800-891118
www.skycitydarwin.com.au
A beach-side casino hotel on 7 hectares (18 acres) adjoining a golf course and the Botanic Gardens. **$$$$**

Marrakai Luxury All Suites
93 Smith Street
Darwin
Tel: 08-8982 3711
www.marrakai.com.au
Located in the city area, this is a highrise of balcony apartments close to the mall. Barbecue area. Ideal for families or groups. Secure underground car park. **$$$$**

Novotel Atrium Darwin
100 The Esplanade
Darwin
Tel: 08-8941 0755
www.noveldarwin.com.au
On the Esplanade in downtown Darwin, just a short walk from the city

centre, with its own indoor tropical rainforest. Spacious hotel rooms and two-bedroom suites. **$$$$**

Parap Village Apartments
39–45 Parap Road
Parap
Tel: 08-8943 0500
Freecall: 1800-620913
Five minutes' drive from the city centre and 10 from the airport, standard or de-luxe large apartments overlooking two swimming pools. **$$$**

Saville Park Suites
88 The Esplanade
Darwin
Tel: 08-8943 4333
www.savillesuites.com.au
On the Esplanade overlooking Darwin Harbour, foreshores, tropical parklands and the city skyline. Apartment style or traditional hotel services. **$$$$**

Botanic Gardens Apartments
17 Geranium Street
The Gardens, Darwin

Tel: 08-8946 0300
www.botanicgardensapts.com.au
High on a hill overlooking the Botanic Gardens and the Arafura Sea. **$$$$**

Mirambeena Resort Darwin
64 Cavenagh Street
Darwin
Tel: 08-8946 0111
www.mirambeena.com.au
In the heart of the city, with lush tropical pool area. Treetops restaurant, poolside bar and café, mini-golf and gym. **$$**

Palms City Resort
64 The Esplanade
Darwin
Tel: 08-8982 9200
Freecall: 1800-829 211
www.palmscityresort.com
Modern motel rooms or tropical-style villas with balcony barbecues. **$$$**

Steeles at Larrakeyah
4 Zealandia Crescent
Darwin
Tel: 08-8941 3636
Mobile: 0411-442373
www.steeles-at-larrakeyah.com.au

Price categories are for a double room without breakfast:
$ = under A$60
$$ = A$60–130
$$$ = A$130–160
$$$$ = over A$160

Private, quiet B&B close to shops, tourist facilities, Mindil Beach markets and Botanic Gardens. Hosts Janette and Roger are knowledgeable long-term Territorians. **$**

**Frogs Hollow
Backpackers Lodge**
27 Lindsay Street
Darwin
Tel: 08-8981 4145
Freecall: 1800-068686
www.frogs-hollow.com.au
Popular spacious hostel in city, 10-minute walk to Transit Centre. Spas, travel info. Clean and friendly; off-season rates. **$**

Kakadu

**Gagudju Crocodile
Holiday Inn**
1 Flinders Street
Jabiru (Kakadu)
Tel: 08-8979 9000
www.gagudju-crocodile.holidayinn.com
Shaped like a giant crocodile, with the swimming pool as its stomach, this is the only deluxe hotel in the Kakadu National Park. **$$$$**

**Seven Spirit Bay
Wilderness Lodge**
Garig Gunak Barlu National Park
Arnhem Land
Tel: 08-8979 0281
www.sevenspiritbay.com
A 45-minute scenic flight from Darwin transports you to the sea breezes, sights, sounds and natural harmony of the tropics – day and night. Guests stay in free-standing, airy, hexagonal "habitats", each with an open-air bathroom, set in a tropical garden. Located in Garig Gunak Barlu National Park in Aboriginal Arnhem Land, where entry is by permit only and extremely limited. Two-night packages start at A$1,300 for twin rooms. **$$$$**

Katherine

All Seasons Katherine
Cypress Street (off Stuart Highway)
Katherine
Tel: 08-8972 1744
www.accorhotels.com.au
A 3-hour drive from Darwin brings you to this historic town and tours of the stunning Katherine Gorge. Two levels of accommodation. **$$**

Gagudju Lodge
Cooinda
Tel: 08-8979 0145
Freecall: 1800-500401
www.gagudjulodgecooinda.com.au
Situated on the Yellow Water Billabong, 1 km (½ mile) from the Warraadjan Cultural Centre. Provides both comfortable units and budget rooms. **$$**

Alice Springs

Alice Springs is the service town for the whole Central Australian desert area, although many striking attractions within a short driving distance make it worth considering as part of your itinerary. Uluru (Ayers Rock) is about six hours' scenic desert drive away; and the small village of Yulara caters for its visitors.

**Crowne Plaza Alice
Springs**
82 Barrett Drive
Alice Springs
Tel: 08-8950 8000
www.ichotelsgroup.com
Low-rise luxury resort with spectacular views of the MacDonnell ranges. **$$$$**

Lasseters Hotel Casino
93 Barrett Drive, Alice Springs
Tel: 08-8950 7777
www.lassetershotelcasino.com.au
Comfortable rooms in radiating wings to three-storeys high. Casino facilities and the glitz of gambling does not impinge on those who prefer to wander the spacious gounds with its large swimming pool. **$$$$**

Alice Springs Resort
34 Strott Terrace
Alice Springs
Tel: 08-8951 4545 or
1300-134 044 (reservations)
www.alicespringsresort.com.au
Five minutes' walk to town, quality rooms, oasis-style pool area and à la carte restaurant. **$$$**

Desert Palms Resort
74 Barrett Drive
Alice Springs
Tel: 08-8952 5977
Freecall: 1800-678037
www.desertpalms.com.au
One kilometre (⅔ mile) from town, great-value air-conditioned villas with private verandas and lush tropical pool area. **$$**

Todd Tavern
1 Todd Mall
Alice Springs
Tel: 08-8952 1255
www.toddtavern.com.au
The only traditional pub left in Alice. Meals are served noon–9pm. **$**

Pioneer Youth Hostel
Corner of Parsons Street and Leichhardt Terrace
Alice Springs
Tel: 08-8952 8855
www.yha.com.au
Built within the walls of a Heritage-classed outdoor movie theatre; close to shops, cafés and pubs. **$**

Uluru (Ayers Rock)

Longitude 131
Yulara
Tel: 1300-134 044 (reservations)
www.longitude131.com.au
A line of individual tents make up the accommodation of this five-star eco-resort just 9 km (5 miles) from Uluru. Guest numbers are restricted to 30 at a time. **$$$$**

**Sails in the Desert Hotel
(part of the Ayers Rock
Resort)**
Yulara Drive
Yulara
Tel: 1300-134044 (reservations)
www.voyages.com.au
The premier hotel at Yulara, famous for its soaring white "sails" which shelter outdoor areas from the intense desert sun. **$$$**

**Outback Pioneer Hotel
and Lodge**
Yulara Drive
Yulara
Tel: 08-8957 7888 or
1300-134044 (reservations)
www.voyages.com.au
Ayers Rock location with both comfortable private rooms and dormitory-style accommodation. **$$**

Kings Canyon

Kings Canyon Resort
Luritja Road
Watarrka National Park
Tel: 08-8956 7442 or
1300-134 044 (reservations)
www.kingscanyonresort.com.au
Six kilometres (4 miles) from the spectacular canyon, providing all levels of accommodation. **$$$**

Kings Creek Station
via Lasseter Highway or Mereenie Loop Road from Alice Springs
Tel: 08-8956 7474
www.kingscreekstation.com.au
Basic cabins under canvas and camping ground on working farm wth camels. **$**

BELOW: roomy Palm Bungalow, Hamilton Island, Queensland.

WESTERN AUSTRALIA

Perth

Aarons Hotel
70 Pier Street, 6000
Tel: 08-9325 2133
Toll free: 1800-998133
Fax: 08-9221 2936
www.aaronsperth.com.au
Centrally placed, on free CAT bus route around Perth. Modern and comfortable rooms, and a bright bar and grill; good, friendly service. **$$**

Bailey's Parkside Hotel-Motel
150 Bennet Street, 6004
Tel: 08-9220 9555
Toll free: 1800-199477
www.baileysmotel.com.au
Homely hotel opposite park within walking distance of the centre or 5 minutes on free city buses. Comfortable units with air conditioning, swimming pool and barbecue. The restaurant serves home-style cooking, and the room tariff includes continental breakfast. **$**

Bel Eyre Motel
285 Great Eastern Highway
Belmont
Tel: 08-9277 2733
www.beleyremotel.com.au
Convenient location, courtesy airport transfers and swimming pool. **$$**

Broadwater Resort Apartments
137 Melville Parade,
Como 6152
Tel: 08-9474 4216
Toll free: 1800-644414
www.broadwaters.com.au
South of the river, minutes away from shopping, Perth Zoo and restaurants. Heated swimming pool, spa and tennis court, and Australian cuisine restaurant with al-fresco courtyard. Apartments have full kitchen. **$$$**

Criterion Hotel Perth
560 Hay Street, 6000
Tel: 08-9325 5155
Toll free: 1800-245155
Fax: 08-9325 4176
www.criterion-hotel-perth.com.au
Central, beautifully restored Art Deco building in main shopping area, with "British" pub in basement. **$$**

Durham Lodge
165 Shepperton Road,
Victoria Park 6100
Tel: 08-9361 8000
Fax: 08-9361 8101
www.durhamlodge.com
South of the river, a short drive/bus to the centre and southern attractions: the zoo and Burswood. Elegant old home with baby grand piano and comfortable furnishings. Private guest wing; spa bath or showers, air conditioning, TV, DVD, phone, bar and fridge. **$$**

Duxton
1 St George's Terrace, 6000
Tel: 08-9261 8000
Toll free: 1800-681118
www.duxton.com
Beautifully renovated hotel in a heritage building, formerly Perth's old tax office. Close to the Concert Hall, State Governor's Residence, Swan River and shops. **$$$$**

Hotel Ibis Perth
334 Murray Street
Tel: 08-9322 2844
www.ibishotels.com.au
In the centre of Perth, with popular restaurants and bars. **$$**

Kings Perth Hotel
517 Hay Street
Tel: 08-9325 6555
www.kingshotel.com.au
Central location near the Mall and Swan River; good value. **$$**

Seasons of Perth
37 Pier Street
Tel: 08-9325 7655
Freecall: 1800-999004
(reservations)
www.seasonsofperth.com.au
Boutique hotel featuring a large swimming pool in a spectacular courtyard. Ideally located close to the best shopping and the Swan River. **$$**

Sheraton Perth
207 Adelaide Terrace
Tel: 08-9224 7777
www.sheraton.com/perth
De-luxe and centrally located; all rooms have breathtaking views of the Swan River or the city skyline. **$$$$**

The Witch's Hat
148 Palmerston Street
Tel: 08-9228 4228
Freecall: 1800-818358
www.witchshat.com
Near the bus terminal and

Perth railway station. A Victorian residence with al-fresco dining and internet café. **$**

YMCA Jewell House
180 Goderich Street
Tel: 08-9325 8488
www.ymcajewellhouse.com
Large, with clean, comfortable rooms. A 15-minute walk to the city, or catch the free Transperth Red CAT bus, which passes outside. **$**

Freemantle and Perth Environs

The Loose Box
6825 Great Eastern Highway
Mundaring
Tel: 08-9295 1787
www.loosebox.com
Located in the ranges 35 km (20 miles) east of Perth, six private cottages are available to guests of the restaurant, acknowledged as one of the finest in Australia. **$$$$**

Rendezvous Observation City Hotel
The Esplanade, Scarborough Beach
Tel: 08-9245 1000
www.rendezvoushotels.com
Luxury hotel on the beach, a rare example of a highrise building on the coast. Wide-ranging facilities include several restaurants and bars, nightclub, pool, spa, tennis courts and gym. **$$$**

Esplanade Hotel – Fremantle
Corner of Marine Terrace and Essex Street, Fremantle
Tel: 08-9432 4000
www.esplanadehotelfremantle.com.au
Elegant gold rush-era building with atrium, two pools, three spas, fitness centre, bar and two restaurants. Most rooms have private balconies with views overlooking popular parklands, tropical gardens and pools. Across Marine Terrace lawns is Fishing Boat Harbour, with restaurants and entertainment. **$$$$**

Pier 21 Apartment Hotel
7–9 John Street, North Fremantle
Tel: 08-9336 2555
www.pier21.com.au
On the banks of the Swan,

with river views, fully serviced one- and two-bed air-conditioned apartments with kitchen, TV, VCR and DVD. Indoor and outdoor pools overlooking the river marina, two spas, tennis and squash courts. Barbecue area. **$$**

Ocean Beach Hotel
Corner of Eric Street and Marine Parade, Cottesloe Beach
Tel: 08-9384 2555
www.obh.com.au
Overlooking the Indian Ocean, refurbished, modern and lively location with seafront restaurant, café, pizza-bar and two bars heavily used by younger clientele. **$$**

Flag Motor Lodge
129 Great Eastern Highway
Rivervale
Tel: 08-9277 2766
Freecall: 1800-998044
www.flagmotorlodge.com.au
Inexpensive units, some with cooking facilities. Restaurant and room service; swimming pool, bus to city. **$–$$**

Kilkelly's B&B
82 Marine Terrace,
Freemantle, 6160
Tel: 08-9336 1744
Fax: 08-9336 1571
www.wt.com.au/~kilkelly
Renovated 1883 mariner's cottage opposite Fishing Boat Harbour. Stroll to restaurants, markets and shops. **$$**

Around Perth

Atrium Hotel
65 Ormsby Terrace,
Mandurah, 6210
Tel: 08-9535 6633
Fax: 08-9581 4151
www.the-atrium.com.au
Within walking distance of the beach, this hotel is centred on an impressive atrium with a palm-fringed, heated indoor pool and spa, cocktail bar and restaurant (7am until late). One-, two- and three-bed apartments with full cooking facilities. There's another pool outdoors, plus sauna, tennis, and game room. **$$**

Hansons
60 Forest Road,
Swan Valley, Henley Brook 6055
Tel: 08-9296 3366

Fax: 08-9296 3332
www.hansons.com.au
This is a cool and elegant hotel with a fine restaurant featuring local ingredients prepared in style. Close to the vineyards and microbreweries of the Swan Valley, and with lovely views over the surrounding countryside. With a swimming pool and access to the river. Six spa rooms and four en-suite rooms leading to either a balcony or courtyard. The tariff includes breakfast. **$$**

Margaret River/ Southwest

Cape Lodge
Caves Road
Yallingup
Tel: 08-9755 6311
www.capelodge.com.au
Stunningly beautiful and tranquil country retreat between Yallingup and the

Margaret River. This mansion within a plantation and gardens overlooks a private lake and features de-luxe suites and rooms, both in the homestead and in the new A$3-million development. **$$$$**
Chandlers Smiths Beach Villas
Smiths Beach Road, Yallingup 6282
Tel/fax: 08-9755 2062
www.chandlerssmithsbeach.com.au
On a hill side surrounded by national park, 15 comfortable villas, all with beach and ocean views. The villas are 4 km (2½ miles) south of Yallingup and 5 minutes from Smiths Beach for swimming and surfing; two-bed villas have full kitchen facilities, TV and VCR. Laundry and barbecue on site. **$$**
The Grange on Farrelly
18 Farrelly Street, 6285
Tel: 08-9757 3177
Toll free: 1800-650100
Fax: 08-9757 3076
www.grangeonfarrelly.com.au
Small, stylish motel set in gardens; short stroll to the main street, restaurants and shops. Some rooms have spas, some four-poster beds; all have en-suite, air conditioning, TV and tea/coffee facilities. The restaurant is in a

historic building serving good Asian-influenced food. **$$**
Margaret River Holiday Cottages
Lot 2, Boodjioup Road
Margaret River
Tel/fax: 08-9757 2185
Home-style two-bedroom cottages in a tranquil park setting; fully equipped and ideal for families. There are bushland walks to see kangaroos and flora. **$$$**
Merribrook
Armstrong Rd
off Cowaramup Bay Road
Cowarumup
Tel: 08-9755 5599
www.merribrook.com.au
Small and relaxing luxury resort comprising nine private chalets. Treatments such as aromatherapy massage and reflexology are complemented by superb food. Prides itself on providing an hospitable and eco-friendly experience. **$$$**
Wellington House B&B
Station Road, Walpole 6398
Tel: 08-9840 1103
www.wellingtonhouse.com.au
Set in 14 hectares (35 acres) of natural forest near the Valley of the Giants and Tree Top Walk. Has three large, well-furnished, en-suite rooms, and another with a separate bathroom.

There is a communal lounge with log fire, TV and VCR, and a sun deck with great views to the forest. **$$**

Broome/Kimberley

Cable Beach Club Resort
Cable Beach Road
Broome
Tel/fax: 08-9192 0400
www.cablebeachclub.com
Located on beautiful Cable Beach. De-luxe bungalows in the style of pearling-masters' houses reflect Broome's Asian heritage, with wide verandas and lattice screens. There are lush tropical gardens, waterfalls and swimming pools. **$$$$**
El Questro
Gibb River Road
Kununurra
Tel: 08-9169 1777
www.elquestro.com.au
A vast cattle station in the Kimberley, on the edge of the Chamberlain Gorge, El Questro offers many classic Outback activities like barramundi fishing, night crocodile spotting and mustering by helicopter. Choice of stays, from inexpensive campsites to luxurious suites and gourmet cuisine at the homestead. **$–$$$$**

TASMANIA

Hobart

Adelphi Court YHA
17 Stoke Street
Newtown
Tel: 03-6228 4829
www.yha.com.au
Hostel as well as guesthouse accommodation within easy range of the restaurant and entertainment strip of North Hobart. **$**
Central City Backpackers
138 Collins Street
Tel: 03-6224 2404
www.centralbackpackers.com.au
Massive building, with a maze of rooms, sparse but clean. Dormitories and private rooms. **$**

Graham Court Apartments
15 Pirie Street, New Town
Tel: 03-6278 1333
www.grahamcourt.com.au
Helpful and friendly management make this a favourite for families or groups happy to be north of the CBD. **$$**
Hotel Grand Chancellor
1 Davey Street
Hobart
Tel: 03-6235 4535;
Freecall: 1800-625138
This de-luxe hotel is situated in the historic Docks area, within walking distance of popular restaurants. Panoramic river views. **$$$**
The Henry Jones Art Hotel
25 Hunter Street
Tel: 03-6210 7700

www.thehenryjones.com
Stunning conversion of the old jam factory on the waterfront. The art hotel concept is to have paintings by contemporary artists hung throughout the building, all for sale. Everything a top hotel should be. **$$$$**
Hobart Tower Motel
300 Park Street
Newtown
Tel: 03-6228 0166
www.hobarttower.com.au
One of the best-value options in Hobart. The rooms are spacious and provide a high standard of comfort and facilities. Family units available. **$$**
Lenna of Hobart
20 Runnymede Street
Battery Point

Tel: 03-6232 3900;
Freecall: 1800-030633
www.lenna.com.au
Award-winning colonial hotel ideally located in Battery Point, the historic headland above Salamanca Place which is the home of Hobart's trendy restaurants and cafés. **$$$**
Quest Waterfront Serviced Apartments
3 Brooke Street
Tel: 03-6224 8630
www.questwaterfront.com.au
Spacious, immaculately finished apartments, in the heart of the waterfront action. **$$$**
Rydges Hobart
Corner of Argyle and Lewis streets, North Hobart
Tel: 03-6231 1588;

Freecall: 1800-801 703
www.rydges.com
Grand historic hotel in leafy
North Hobart, minutes from
the city centre, offering
luxury antique suites or
contemporary decor. **$$$**
Theatre Royal Hotel
31 Campbell Street
Tel: 03-6234 6925
Idiosyncratic management
style can test guests'
initiative but good rooms in
great location offer very
good value. **$$**

Battery Point
There are many small,
historic B&Bs in the Battery
Point area. Although quite a
few have succumbed to Ye
Olde Twee and are decked
out with throw-pillows and
beaming hosts, the location
is excellent.
Crelin Lodge
1 Crelin Street
Battery Point
Tel: 03-6223 1777
Fully self-contained one-
and two-bedroom holiday
apartments. **$$$**

Outside Hobart

Wherever you go in
Tasmania, you're never far
away from quality historic
accommodation. In popular
destinations, such as
Launceston, Strahan,
Stanley and the Tasman
Peninsula, there are a

number of beautiful
cottages and a spattering
of luxury lets in larger
homes.

Tasman Peninsula
Stewart Bay Lodge
Arthur Highway
Port Arthur
Tel: 03-6250 2888
www.stewartsbaylodge.com
Award-winning natural-
design log cabins all with
log fires, overlooking
Stewarts Bay; a short walk
from the Port Arthur
Historic Site. **$$$**

Strahan
Franklin Manor
The Esplanade, Strahan
Tel: 03-6471 7311
www.franklinmanor.com.au
Situated at the edge of
Macquarie Harbour with a
range of accommodation,
including rooms within the
historic mansion and in the
old stables, within a short
walk of Strahan harbour.
$$$$
Piners Loft
The Esplanade, Strahan
Tel: 03-6471 7036
www.pinersloft.com.au
Amazing pole-house
construction overlooking
Macquarie Harbour.
Features innovative design
in timber using recycled
huon pine, celery-top pine
and other prized local
timbers. This is a place

where travelling groups of
two to six people can
experience luxury at a
reasonable cost. **$$$**

East Coast
**Bicheno Backpackers
Hostel**
11 Morrison Street, Bicheno
Tel: 03-6375 1651
Recommended as the
budget option. **$**
Bicheno Gaol Cottages
81 Burgess Street, Bicheno
Tel: 03-375 1430
Stay in the old prison and
be within walking distance
of all the town's
attractions. **$$$**
Edge of the Bay Resort
2308 main Road,
Coles Bay
Tel: 03-6257 0102
www.edgeofthebay.com.au
Right above the beach
there is a mixture of sleek
modern one-bedroom units
with floor-to-ceiling views of
the Hazards, or slightly
older two-bedroom cabins
where the design hasn't
been honed quite so well.
$$$$
Freycinet Lodge
Freycinet National Park
via Coles Bay
Tel: 03-6257 0101
www.freycinetlodge.com.au
Environmentally sensitive
resort development in
unspoilt coastal setting.
Comfortable private bush
cabins lead down to tiny

beach areas. Restaurant
and bar overlook Great
Oyster Bay. Seasonal whale
watching, diving with seals,
hiking and special tour
programmes available.
$$$$
Piermont Retreat
Tasman Highway, Swansea
Tel: 03-6257 8131
www.piermont.com.au
Magnificent stone-built
cottages overlooking their
own beach. This is the
place to recharge the
batteries between trips to
the pool and the tennis
court. **$$$$**

The Midlands
**Brickendon Historic
and Farm Cottages**
Woolmers Lane, near Longford
Tel: 03-6391 1251
www.brickendon.com.au
Have the old farm to
yourself after the visitors
have left and enjoy these
superb wooden cottages.
$$$
Colonial Cottages of Ross
12 Church Street, Ross
Tel: 03-6381 5354
www.rossaccommodation.com.au
A choice of four
immaculately restored
cottages sleeping between
two and six. **$$$**
Millhouse on the Bridge
2 Wellington Street, Richmond
Tel: 03-6260 2428
About as sumptuous a
bed and breakfast as you
could ask for, the clincher
is its position right next
to Richmond Bridge with
gardens running down to
the river. **$$$**
**Oatlands Lodge Colonial
Accommodation**
92 High Street, Oatlands
Tel: 03-6254 1444
The most effusive welcome
in the state at this well-run
cosy B&B. **$$$**
Ross Bakery Inn
Church Street, Ross
Tel: 03-6381 5246
Plenty of treats from the
bakery if you choose this
historic B&B. **$$$**
Woolmers Estate
Woolmers Lane
near Longford
Tel: 03-6391 2230
www.woolmers.com.au
Live it up on the estate in
these settlers' cottages.
$$$

BELOW: Edge of the Bay Resort in Coles Bay.

Derwent Valley

Lake Pedder Chalet
Gordon River Road, Strathgordon
Tel: 03-6280 1166
Originally the camp for workers on the dam project, it still accommodates some of them but offers clean, serviceable rooms to tourists. Substantial meals available at the restaurant. **$$**

Old Colony Inn
21 Montagu Street, New Norfolk
Tel: 03-6261 2731
Attractive old pub now given over to bed and breakfast. The mock-tudor half timbering extends inside. **$$**

Woodbridge on the Derwent
6 Bridge Street, New Norfolk
Tel: 03-6261 5566
Sheer luxury in this strikingly renovated place just by the bridge. **$$$$**

The North

Abbey's Cottages
1 Marshall Street, Stanley
Tel: 1800 222 397
A collection of cottages close to the centre of Stanley, all full of character and original features and offering very good value for money. **$$$**

Boat Harbour Beach House
12 Moore Street, Boat Harbour Beach
Tel: 03-6445 0913
A house with everything you could possibly need, including a huge deck with views out to sea. Another house on the beach is rented out by the owners. **$$$**

Calstock
Lake Highway, Deloraine
Tel: 03-6362 2642
A Georgian mansion set in extensive gardens, Calstock offers elegant rooms, exquisite French cuisine and no reason to leave. **$$$**

Devonport Historic Cottages
66 Wenvoe Street, Devonport
Tel: 03-6424 1560
Three refurbished two-bedroom cottages on offer. **$$$**

Furners Hotel
42 Reiby Street, Ulverstone
Tel: 03-6425 1488
Gloriously ornate exterior isn't quite matched by the rooms but still a sound choice. **$$**

Mersey Bluff Caravan Park
Devonport
Tel: 03-64248655
Plenty of space for camping near the sea and some cabins available too. **$**

Silver Ridge Retreat
46 Rysavy Road, Mount Roland, via Sheffield
Tel: 03-6491 1727
www.silverridgeretreat.com.au
Idyllic rural getaway featuring self-contained accommodation located right at the foot of breathtaking Mount Roland. There are great walks, especially to Roland summit. It is also only a 40-minute drive to Cradle Mountain. **$$$**

Tall Timbers Hotel Motel
3–15 Scotchtown Road, Smithton
Tel: 03-6452 2755
www.talltimbershotel.com.au
A symphony to timber indeed, this woody establishment has rooms in a range of styles and prices as well as a pool, bistro and bar. **$$**

Waterfront Wynyard Motor Inn
1 Goldie Street, Wynyard
Tel: 03-6442 2351
A steady if unremarkable motel to be chosen for its location. **$$**

Central Highlands

Bronte Park Highland Village
Bronte Park, 6 km (4 miles) north of the Lyell Highway (Lake Country)
Tel: 03-6289 1126
A half hour's drive from Lake St Clair, this utterly peaceful holiday village features converted hydro-electric workers' huts, now a favourite with fishermen. Well-designed private cottages and an inexpensive restaurant serving simple but excellent fish dinners. Access by Tasmanian Wilderness Transport from Launceston or Devonport. **$$**

Central Highlands Lodge
Haddens Bay, Miena
Tel: 03-6259 8179
Pleasant motel units behind the lodge. In the lodge there's an enticing bar and dining room where fishermen can eat their catch and enthral slow-footed tourists with tales of how they caught it. **$$$**

Cradle Mountain

Cradle Mountain Lodge
Cradle Mountain
Tel: 03-6492 1303;
Freecall: 1800-737 678
www.cradlemountainlodge.com.au
Wilderness retreat with secluded cabins and alpine spa at the entrance to the Cradle Mountain–Lake St Clair National Park. There are over 20 walking tracks and the chance to breathe what the Australian scientists claim is some of the purest air in the world. **$$$**

Bass Strait Islands

Furneaux Tavern
11 Franklin Parade, Lady Barron, Flinders Island
Tel: 03-6359 3521
Excellent cabins up the hill behind this welcoming modern pub. **$$**

Healing Dreams Retreat
855 trousers Point Road, Flinders Island
Tel: 1800-994477
Beautifully put together modern house operating as an up-market B&B, with the option of bringing a chef in in the evenings. Its Californian owner originally kept the place meat and alcohol free but Flinders wasn't ready for that. Now, if she were to tackle that name. **$$$$**

King Island Holiday Village
Grassy, King Island
Tel: 03-6461 1177
Fly from Wynyard or Melbourne; hire cars are available. This clean, green Bass Strait island is well worth holidaying in. It produces Australia's finest beef and cheese and is the shipwreck capital of the Southern Hemisphere, with more than 60 wrecks in the past 200 years. An ex-mining town, Grassy has a population of around 50. Look out over gorgeous empty beaches and experience three coasts within an hour's drive. **$$**

Launceston

Penny Royal Motel & Apartments
147 Paterson Street, Launceston
Tel: 03-6331 6699
www.pennyroyalworld.com.au
Historic watermill-turned-hotel with rooms or self-contained apartments, restaurant and tavern. Five minutes' to Cataract Gorge. **$$$**

Peppers Seaport Hotel
28 Seaport Boulevard, Launceston
Tel: 03-6345 3333
Chic modern development with a range of trendy bars and restaurants on the boardwalk below. **$$$$**

The Sebel
St John Street, Launceston
Tel: 03-6333 7555
www.cornwallhotel.com.au
It's got a lot of rooms for a boutique hotel but they are all executed with such taste and intelligence that you can almost justify paying the prices being asked. **$$$$**

Tamar Valley

Pilot Station
399 Low Head Road
Tel: 03-6382 1143
Simple cottages but a terrific atmospheric place to stay within the museum precinct. **$$**

Pier Hotel Motel
5 Elizabeth Street, George Town
Tel: 03-6382 1300
www.pierhotel.com.au
Pleasant rooms and apartments overlooking the river and well-served by the pub's accomplished bistro. **$$$**

Tamar Valley Resort Grindelwald
7 Waldhorn Drive, Grindelwald
Tel: 03-6330 0400
High-class accommodation in nutty Swiss-themed resort. **$$$**

PRICE CATEGORIES

Price categories are for a double room without breakfast:
$ = under A$80
$$ = A$80–130
$$$ = A$130–200
$$$$ = over A$200

A CTIVITIES

The Arts, Nightlife, Sports, Shopping and Festivals

The Arts

Theatre

Sydney

The **Sydney Opera House** is a focal point of fine performances, including concerts, opera, ballet, theatre and films, but it isn't the only venue. Among the larger performance venues are the Capitol Theatre, the State Theatre and the Theatre Royal.

The Sydney Theatre Company has a harbourside home in the Wharf Theatre – a renovated old wharf in the Rocks – and presents an extensive schedule of productions. The Sydney Dance Company occasionally performs here and at the newer Sydney Theatre across the road. The **Seymour Centre** stages a variety of unusual shows and the **Belvoir Street Theatre** has a history of experimentation. Smaller venues include the **Darlinghurst Theatre** and **Griffin Theatre** in Kings Cross, the **New Theatre** in Newtown, the **Footbridge Theatre** at Sydney University and the stunning **Ensemble Theatre** at Milsons Point.

The best guide to entertainment in Sydney is in the *Sydney Morning Herald's* Metro section every Friday.

Canberra

The **Canberra Theatre Centre** on Civic Square (tel: 02-6243 5711; www.canberratheatre.org.au) contains a theatre, playhouse and gallery, and presents everything from Shakespeare to rock music. **Tilley's Devine Café Gallery**, corner of Brigalow and Wattle streets, Lyneham (tel: 02-6247 7753; www.tilleys.com.au), is one of

Canberra's more bohemian venues, featuring national and local musicians, storytellers, poetry readings and art exhibitions. It was originally set up as a centre for women only, but the outcry forced Canberra to change its sex-discrimination laws and it is now open to all.

Consult the *Fly* section in the Thursday edition of the *Canberra Times* for what's on. Also the free monthly magazine *BMA* lists bands and other events.

Melbourne

Melbourne is noted for its high-quality live performances of comedy, theatre and music. There are always theatre productions at the city's major arts venue, the **Arts Centre**, which has three theatres. Other major commercial theatres include the grand **Princess Theatre**, 163 Spring Street; **Her Majestys**, 219 Exhibition Street; the **Comedy Theatre**, 240 Exhibition Street and the spectacularly refurbished 2,000-seat **Regent Theatre**, 191 Collins Street. The Melbourne Theatre Company is the major theatrical company, performing at the Arts Centre. More adventurous work can be found at the **Malthouse**, 113 Sturt Street, Southbank; **Red Stitch**, 2 Chapel Street, St Kilda; and **La Mama**, 205 Faraday Street, Carlton.

The best listings for Melbourne's lively arts scene can be found in the Entertainment Guide in every Friday issue of *The Age* newspaper or the free weekly street press: *Inpress* and *Beat*.

Adelaide

The home of performing arts is the **Adelaide Festival Centre**

(www.adelaidefestivalcentre.com.au). The centre has regular performances of theatre, dance and concerts and is the main venue for the Adelaide International Festival of Arts (www.adelaidefestival.com.au). The State Theatre Company of South Australia appears regularly at the Festival Centre. **The Bakehouse Theatre** on Angas Street is a more intimate venue where smaller theatre troupes perform. While they regularly tour the country and overseas, Australian Dance Theatre is based in Adelaide and can be seen at the Adelaide Festival Centre or **Her Majesty's Theatre** on Grote Street. The free magazine *Adelaide Review* lists theatres and galleries.

Brisbane

Brisbane's main theatre company is the Queensland Theatre Company, based at the **Performing Arts Complex**. The Brisbane **Powerhouse** also offers regular performances and exhibitions, and downtown you'll find a plethora of new acts playing in pubs, clubs and restaurants.

Darwin

Darwin's multicultural arts festival runs for three weeks in August. The focus is on indigenous artists with dance, music and an open-air festival club each night. Local plays are performed at **Brown's Mart**, a historic sandstone building on Smith Street opposite the Supreme Court. Folk music can be heard on weekends at **Happy Yess (ok) Club** on Bennett Street in the city.

Perth

Perth has a vibrant cultural life and is the proud home of Australia's longest-running arts event, the Perth

International Arts Festival, which takes place in February and March (www.perthfestival.com.au).

Outstanding drama is regularly presented by the **Black Swan Theatre Company**, **Perth Theatre Company** and **Deckchair Theatre**.

Children's events, such as international arts festival, the Awesome Festival in November–December, include contributions by **Barking Gecko Theatre** and **Spare Parts Puppet Theatre**. Given Perth's Mediterranean climate, outdoor concerts and performances are popular in the summer months.

Perth's multitude of theatres and concert venues offer year-round entertainment. The **Perth Concert Hall** is the performance home for the West Australian Symphony Orchestra; **His Majesty's Theatre** houses the West Australian Ballet and Opera companies, and the **Playhouse** is the base for the Perth Theatre Company and the Black Swan Theatre Company. Other city-based venues offering plays, musicals and cabarets are the **Burswood Casino's Theatre**, the art deco-style **Regal Theatre** and the **Subiaco Theatre Centre**. Bookings and enquiries on Perth's two booking services: BOCS Ticketing, tel: 08-9484 1133, freecall: 1800-193 300, www.bocsticketing.com.au; and Ticketmaster7, tel: 136 100, www.ticketmaster7.com.au.

Hobart

The **Playhouse Theatre** (tel: 03-6234 1536) presents a mix of Shakespeare, old favourites and more modern performances. The **Theatre Royal** (tel: 03-6233 2299) is Australia's oldest working theatre with walls of convict-carved stone.

Comedy

Sydney

Tuesday is popular comedy night in Sydney, and the **Sydney Comedy Store** at the Entertainment Quarter hosts some of the world's top comics every week. Many other local bars also have popular comedy nights, including **The East Village**, **Palmer Street** and **Fringe Bar** on Oxford Street.

Canberra

Canberra Irish Club holds a comedy competition called Green Faces (www.irishclub.com.au). **The Canberra Theatre Centre**, **Street Theatre** and **Royal Theatre Canberra** host touring comedians and travelling comedy roadshows. Check out the entertainment section of www.outincanberra.com.au

ABOVE: His Majesty's Theatre on Hay Street, Perth.

Melbourne

The Last Laugh was the birthplace of Melbourne's reputation as comedy capital and it is still going strong. It is situated in the **Athaenum Theatre** at 188 Collins Street. The **Melbourne International Comedy Festival** offers three weeks of the best comedy in Australia *(see Events, page 372)*. The festival website, www.comedyfestival.com.au, is also a good source of information on comedy happenings year-round.

Adelaide

March is the best time for comedy when venues all over the city burst with shows by comics who flock from around the world to perform in the **Adelaide Fringe** festival.

The **Rhino Room** on Frome Street hosts home-grown and international comics each Wednesday night. The Adelaide casino **Sky City** has also started to host comedy nights on Thursdays, while **PJ O'Briens** on East Terrace has a regular comedy night on Tuesdays.

Brisbane

The **Dockside Comedy Bar** (www.docksidecomedybar.com.au), by the river, at the bottom of the Dockside Hotel building on Ferry Street, hosts some of the best of Australia's comics Wed–Sat nights. The **Sit Down Comedy Club**, at 186 Given Terrace in the Paddington area, is an established comedy venue; details of events can be found on www.standup.com.au.

Darwin

There are no comedy clubs in Darwin but the **Darwin Entertainment Centre** and **Brown's Mart** occasionally put on comedy events.

Perth

Perth's comedy scene centres around the **Comedy Lounge**, Thursday nights at the Hyde Park Hotel (corner Bulwer and Fitzgerald streets, North Perth; tel: 08-9328 6166; www.comedylounge.com.au).

Hobart

Comedy is just beginning to establish a toehold in Hobart with three venues hosting events, if somewhat sporadically. And they don't go overboard on promotion either; the "Big Laughs in the Little Pub" on the last Wednesday of the month in the **New Sydney Hotel** invites customers to "come along and support local comedy and be pleasantly surprised". That'll get 'em.

The focal point is the **Hobart Comedy Festival**, which runs over a couple of weeks each January. It claims to be "the world's smallest cultural event".

Cinema

Sydney

For foreign films, art films and generally good films, go to the **Verona** or **Academy** in Paddington and the **Dendy** at Opera Quays or Newtown. The more commercial films are shown at multi-cinema complexes on George Street in the city and Bondi Junction. The majestic old **State Theatre** in the city is the site of the annual Sydney Film Festival.

Every June, art cinemas in Sydney showcase the best new films selected from recent film festivals around the world.

Canberra

There are cinema complexes around the Civic Square area. The eight-screen **Dendy Electric Shadows** (tel: 02-6247 5060; www.electricshadows.com.au) complex in the new Canberra Centre on Bunda Street shows art-house and foreign-language films. The **National Film and Sound Archives** opened a state-of-the-art 25-seat cinema in early 2007, screening a broad variety of films (www.nfsa.afc.gov.au).

Melbourne

Quality art and independent films are shown at the fabulous original art deco **Astor Cinema** in St Kilda and the **Kino** in Collins Street, **Cinema Nova** in Carlton and the **Australian Centre for the Moving Image (ACMI)** in Federation Square.In the summer there are outdoor screenings in the **Royal Botanic Gardens** and there's even a roof-top cinema on one of the office blocks in the CBD.

Adelaide

Art films are shown at the **Nova** and the **Palace**, both in Rundle Street; also at the **Trak** in Toorak Gardens, the **Picadilly** in North Adelaide and at the art deco cinema in Goodwood, **Capri**.

Brisbane

Greater Union Hoyts Regent Cinema at 167 Queen Street has a sweeping marble staircase and high, ornately decorated ceilings. Brisbane has a good range of summer outdoor cinemas, including the **Sunset Cinema** at the City Botanic Gardens and the **Moonlight Cinema** (www.moonlight.com.au) at Brisbane Powerhouse in New Farm Park. Check www.ourbrisbane.com for comprehensive film listings.

Darwin

Outdoor cinema is popular in the dry season at the **Deckchair Cinema** (that's what you sit in), Jervois Road off Kitchener Drive near the Wharf Precinct; mainly art-house films rotated through a weekly programme. Tel: 08-8981 0700. Multiplexes showing first-release mainstream films are located in **Mitchell Street** in Darwin city and at **Casuarina Square** shopping centre complex 8 km (5 miles) from the city (bus route 4).

Perth

Two major chains, **Greater Union and Hoyts**, carry big-distribution films, but Perth is full of small, independent cinemas. Buy the *West Australian* newspaper for programme details. The **Astor** on 659 Beaufort Street, Mount Lawley is an art deco building showing modern and classic films. The **Somerville Auditorium** at the University of WA, Nedlands is the main venue for Perth Festival Films, which takes place in February.

Hobart

The independent **State Cinema** (tel: 03-6234 6318) is well known and well loved for its eclectic programming – it screens anything from surf films to world cinema and the latest Australian releases. Other venues include **Eastlands Village Cinemas** (tel: 03-6245 1033) and **Hobart Village Cinemas** (tel: 03-6234 7288).

Music

Sydney

Whatever your taste in music may be, it can be satisfied in Sydney. The Sydney Symphony Orchestra is an international-class orchestra; it appears regularly with leading Australian and international conductors at the **Opera House**.

To listen to jazz, try the **Basement** (29 Reiby Place), **Soup Plus** (1 Margaret Street in the city) or **Vanguard** at 42 King Street in Newtown.

The band scene is nearly always in pubs, which are scattered throughout the city and suburbs; almost every little place will have live music on Friday and Saturday nights. In general, the best rock pubs are in Surry Hills, Newtown and Annandale: try the **Hopetoun** in Surry Hills and the **Annandale Hotel** in the inner-west. Other good bets are the **Metro Theatre** in the city centre and **The Gaelic Club** in Surry Hills. Better-known and international rock acts tend to play the **Enmore**.

Canberra

Canberra's only professional music group, the Canberra Symphony Orchestra, performs half a dozen times a year. Most of the concerts take place at **Llewellyn Hall**, but the popular Proms concert, held every February, takes place in the grounds of the governor-general's residence, **Government House**.

Popular jazz nights are held at the **Hippo Bar** at Garema Place on Wednesday nights, and the last Sunday of every month at the **Kamberra Wine Company Cellar Door** in Lyneham.

The student community of the ANU (Australian National University) has live bands perform at the **ANU Union Bar** during term; big-name touring bands and DJs play at the **Refectory**.

Melbourne

The Melbourne Symphony Orchestra performs at a variety of locations from March to October.

Much of Melbourne's rock and jazz scene is found in its thriving pub venues. Listen to the gig guide on the FM stations 3RRR, 3MMM and 3PBS. The **Esplanade Hotel** (Espy) and the **Prince of Wales Bandroom**, both in St Kilda, have been a good rock bet for years, as have the **Corner Hotel** in Richmond, the **Hi-Fi Bar** in the city and the **Evelyn Hotel** in Brunswick Street. Relative newcomer, the **Northcote Social Club** has proved its credentials very quickly. A popular jazz venue is **Bennetts Lane** in the city. Cover charges vary widely depending on what night of the week and what band is playing. Shows are free on

BELOW: most Aussie nightlife revolves around the pub.

some nights, but generally cost from around A$10.

The best listings for Melbourne's lively music scene can be found in the Entertainment Guide (EG) in every Friday issue of The Age newspaper, or the free weekly street press: Inpress and Beat.

Adelaide

Check the Gig Guide in Thursday's edition of the Advertiser newspaper, or the free publication Rip It Up, for what's on in Adelaide. The free magazine Adelaide Review also lists musical events.

The Adelaide Symphony Orchestra regularly performs at the **Grainger Studio**, a refurbished art deco building in the heart of Adelaide's West End. There are also regular gigs and concerts at the **Festival Centre** including the popular Adelaide Cabaret Festival each June. There is a healthy live pub scene in Adelaide and some notable venues include the **Grace Emily** on Waymouth Street for local bands and **The Royal Oak** in North Adelaide for jazz. There are also a number of pubs on and around the east end of Rundle Street that regularly host live music.

Brisbane

Brisbane has a lively pop and rock scene; **The Zoo**, **The Troubadour** and **The Rev**, all in Fortitude Valley, are the most popular venues.
For classical music, the home of the prestigious Queensland Orchestra is the 1800-seat QPAC **Concert Hall**, one of Australia's most spectacular concert venues, situated on the corner of Grey and Melbourne streets. For jazz, the **Brisbane Jazz Club**, on the river at 1 Annie Street, Kangaroo Point, is ever-popular.

Darwin

Darwin Symphony Orchestra gives concerts at the **Darwin Entertainment Centre** on a regular basis. Visiting artists perform at the **Botanical Gardens** in the dry season, and in the grounds of the Skycity casino near Mindil Beach. There are free concerts on the **Esplanade** during the Festival of Darwin.

Perth

Perth Concert Hall at 5 St George's Terrace (tel: 08-9231 9900), home to the Western Australia Symphony Orchestra, is the hub of the city's classical music scene. The prestigious Conservatorium at WAAPA (**West Australian Academy of Performing Arts**) attracts a wealth of jazz musicians. JAZZWA (www.jazzwa.com) has a complete rundown of current events.

Perth hosts live rock and pop concerts almost every night; check listings on www.wagigguide.com

Hobart

The responsibility for providing Tasmania with its classics falls to the Tasmanian Symphony Orchestra. The TSO, established in 1948, performs most of its concerts at **Federation Concert Hall** (tel: 1800 001 190) in Hobart or, when in Launceston, at the **Princess Theatre**.

Big names in pop, rock and comedy tend to play at the **Derwent Entertainment Centre** in Hobart's northern suburbs. Elsewhere there are numerous pubs with live music; the **Republic Bar and Café** in north Hobart probably has the best range of local and visiting artists. Other pubs with good live music are **Knopwood's Retreat**, **Irish Murphy's** and **Bar Celona**, all in Salamanca Place. Check the local press for details.

NIGHTLIFE

Sydney

In some of the Sydney clubs and rock pubs you will be uncomfortable if you are over 30; in others if you are under 30. Dress codes vary, from up-to-the-minute designer fashion only to "neat casual". Sloppy or dirty clothing will often keep you out on the street. If you are one of those who look eternally young, you must have ID to prove that you're over 18 (the minimum legal drinking age). For up-to-date listings, consult the weekly Drum Media, Friday's Sydney Morning Herald Metro entertainment supplement, or check out www.sydney.citysearch.com.au.

Canberra

Because of Canberra's liberal licensing laws, quite a few bars are open 24 hours a day. The **Canberra Casino** at Glebe Park (21 Binara Street) is open from noon to 6am daily.

Melbourne

Melbourne offers a huge choice of nightclubs and wine bars offering cheap gigs. Just stroll along Brunswick Street, Fitzroy and take your pick. St Kilda still buzzes as it has for years, while newer hubs for an action-packed night out include Sydney Road, Brunswick, and High

Street, Northcote – both to the north of the city centre.

Laneways in the CBD provide a mixed bag of bars, clubs and live music venues. Many of these places are to be found behind anonymous doorways and attract punters through a mixture of word of mouth and discreet advertising. Most of the nightclubs in the "West End" King Street strip now exist as table-dancing and men's clubs.

Check out The Age for listings of gay and lesbian venues.

Adelaide

The grand old railway station on North Terrace now houses a **casino**, for those inclined. The "sin centre" of Adelaide is Hindley Street, although few will be shocked by it. Interspersed with excellent restaurants you'll find strip clubs, bars, porno bookstores and the usual persons of the night. The west end of Hindley Street, between Morphett Street and West Terrace, has a cleaner vibe and some good bars, pubs and nightclubs.

Brisbane

The busy late-night spots in Brisbane are the Riverside Centre, Elizabeth Street, Petrie Terrace and Fortitude Valley. New eating places are constantly cropping up in New Farm.

Pick up a copy of the two free entertainment guides – Time Off and Rave – from any café, as well as the Thursday edition of Brisbane's daily newspaper, The Courier Mail, for an up-to-the-minute guide to what's on.

A useful website containing lots of information on events, accommodation and attractions is www.ourbrisbane.com.

Darwin

Darwin pubs are popular meeting places for the locals, with a varied nightlife ranging from rowdy live-band performances to the relative sophistication of imported casino entertainers. Although the city's hard-drinking, macho/sexist culture is on the wane, pubs are still the centre of social life. A good start is the **Tourist & Entertainment Precinct**, running the length of Mitchell Street.

Perth

A variety of publications including Scoop and Perth's Cultural Guide are available from hotels and the Western Australian Visitor Centre. Daily updates are available in the entertainment segment of the West

Australian newspaper and every Thursday in *X-Press*, a free magazine with details of bands, exhibitions and clubs. Online Citysearch (www.citysearch.com.au) is a fast way to find out what is happening in Perth.

Hobart

Hobart nightlife is fairly quiet. Most of the action is in the Docks area and Salamanca Market.

The other area where there is a cluster of restaurants, bars and venues, as well as a vibe that suggests there might be life after 10pm, is the Elizabeth Street strip in North Hobart.

Wrest Point Hotel Casino was Australia's first casino – it also houses a restaurant, accommodation and a nightclub. The casino opens at 1pm and operates Sun–Thur until 3am, Friday and Saturday until 4am.

For other entertainment – cinemas, pub bands and the burgeoning club scene – check the *Mercury* newspaper for a guide to what's on.

SPORT

Participant

Sydney

Yachting In Sydney, the yachting season runs September–March. Races and regattas are held nearly every weekend between the 18-footers. A spectator ferry leaves Circular Quay at 1.30pm every Saturday and occasionally on other days. Spectators also turn out in full

BELOW: spoilt for choice

force each year for the Sydney-to-Hobart Yacht Race, on 26 December.

Surfing Surfing carnivals are held at one of Sydney's ocean beaches on most Saturdays between October and March. These consist of swimming races, surf-boat races and board-paddling events. There are also professional and amateur surfboard-riding competitions in the summer and autumn months, but the location is often not selected till the day of the contest to take advantage of the best surf.

Golf and Tennis There are more than 80 golf courses within Sydney, nearly all of them open to the public. And for the tennis player, Sydney has public courts and private tennis clubs.

Canberra

Water Sports Lake Burley Griffin is the scene of the action during the summer months, with rowing, sailing, and kayaking all popular. Swimmers can do laps at one of the city's aquatic centres, or cool off in one of the natural swimming holes, such as Pine Island, Point Hutt Crossing and Kambah Pool.

Horse riding and Golf Canberra has 22 km (13 miles) of equestrian trail winding through the surrounding bushland. It also has a number of quality golf courses including the Federal Gold Club at Red Hill and Yowani Golf Club at Lyneham.

Melbourne

Water Sports Port Phillip offers excellent sailing conditions, and yacht clubs are plentiful; the Melbourne Sailing School (www.melbsailing.com.au) offers a range of courses. Swimmers should head to the Melbourne Sports and Aquatic Centre (MSAC), the largest integrated sports complex of its type in Australia, on the edge of Albert Park Lake on Aughtie Drive. Melbourne's Yarra River is great for canoeing and kayaking.

Tennis Melbourne Park, home of the Australian Open, has four indoor courts and 22 outdoor courts available for public hire seven days a week, except in January.

Golf Melbourne harbours some of Australia's top courses in the famed "sandbelt" region in the south-eastern suburbs. All "sandbelt" clubs are private, though golf tour operators such as Gimme Golf (www.gimmegolf.com.au) can organise access to exclusive courses, provided players meet clubs' strict requirements. Failing that, Melbourne has some of the nation's best public links.

Adelaide

Cycling An excellent cycling and walking trail called Linear Park follows the length of the River Torrens, which runs through the centre of the city. Adelaide is also very flat so cycling is an easy way to get around. Thousands of spectators line the streets each January for the Tour Downunder that features some of the world's best cyclists.

Golf There are plenty of golf courses in Adelaide and most are open to the public. The Royal Adelaide Golf Club in Seaton is South Australia's oldest and among the best in Australia (bookings essential). Closer to the city centre, the City of Adelaide Golf Links caters for all levels. The course winds its way through North Adelaide and offers great city views.

Water-skiing The River Murray is an easy day trip from Adelaide and its glassy waters in the mornings and evenings make it excellent for water-skiing and other water sports.

Brisbane

Running and Jogging Brisbane's river banks offer many kilometres of flat running tracks, and the bay provides plenty of opportunities both to the north and south of the city.

Golf and Tennis Brisbane has several lovely courses including the Brookwater Golf Club, the North Lakes Resort Golf Club and the Royal Queensland. For tennis, head to the University of Queensland's Tennis Centre at Blair Drive, St Lucia, which has 21 floodlit courts and equipment for hire, and is open to all.

Water Sports Just outside Brisbane, the Moreton Bay Islands (www.moretonbayislands.com.au) are the place for surfing and kiteboarding. Bribie Island's Woorim Beach is a popular spot for swimmers and board riders, with its own surf school. Jetskiing, waterskiing, and para-sailing are also possible here.

Darwin

Cycling Darwin City Council have produced a map, titled *Making Tracks*, which shows cycle paths in and around the city.

Golf There are numerous golf courses in the Northern Territory but most public courses are located outside Darwin.

Tennis Public tennis courts are located in Ross Smith Avenue, Aralia Street in Nightcliff and Chrisp Street in Rapid Creek.

Perth

Surfing Reliable conditions mean you can catch a wave year-round in

Perth; check in first with the experts at Surfing WA (tel: 08-9448 0004; www.surfingaustralia.com). Courses are held at Trigg Beach, which with Scarborough has Perth's best surf.

Kayaking Wildlife sea kayaking among seals, sea lions and penguins around Seal Island just south of Perth is a one-day excursion offered by Rivergods Paddle Adventures (tel: 08-9259 0749; www.rivergods.com.au). No experience is necessary on this supervised trip, including transport, lunch, equipment, etc.

Running and Jogging Running is popular in Perth, and the 10-km (6-mile) circuit around the bridges is well used. WA Masters Athletics Club (tel: 08-9330 3803; www.mastersathleticswa.org) welcomes visitors of all ages and abilities to events on Sunday mornings at locations around the city.

Hobart

Golf and Tennis The Tasmania Golf Council (tel: 03-6244 3600) is a good starting point for golfers from abroad looking to play a round. The local club in Hobart is the Royal Hobart Golf Club, tel: 03-6248 6161. A good stop for tennis information is Tennis Tasmania (tel: 03-6334 4237; www.tennistasmania.com.au). The Domain Tennis Centre in Hobart (tel: 03-6234 4805) has courts for hire.

Water Sports There are several scuba-diving operators based in Hobart. To make contact with a local diver, try the Tasmanian Scuba Diving Club (tel: 0418 138 293). Sea kayaking options range from day paddles in sheltered waters to

exposed crossings to the offshore islands. Try Blackaby's Sea Kayaks, tel: 0418 124 072. Based in Hobart, Rafting Tasmania (tel: 03-6239 1080) offers half-day, full-day or extended tours of the Derwent, Huon, Picton, North Esk and Franklin rivers.

Sailing Getting out on the water is an integral part of Tasmanian culture. To find out about the Tasmanian yachting scene have a look at the Tasmanian Yachting Association website (www.tas.yacting.org.au).

Fishing Tasmania offers the ultimate in fishing, in idyllic surroundings. For more information see www.fishonline.tas.gov.au. Hobart-based Fish Wild Tasmania (tel: 0418 348 223) offers one- to five-days tours, principally in trout waters.

Spectator

Sydney

Football Four types of football are played in Sydney, the most popular being rugby league. Games are played in winter months at the Sydney Football Stadium at Moore Park and at other ovals in Sydney.

Cricket One of Sydney's main summer sports is cricket. The season runs October–March with international and interstate matches. You can watch cricket at the Sydney Cricket Ground at Moore Park.

Canberra

Rugby Canberra's local rugby league teams are still young, but they have a loyal following. The Canberra Raiders, launched in the 1980s, quickly became one of the strongest teams in the national league, but have fared

less well in recent years. The Brumbies, the city's Rugby Union team, is even younger – its current incarnation was launched a decade ago – but have also put in a strong showing.

Women's Basketball Catch a Canberra Capitals game, and you may get to see a genuine champion in action. Local girl Lauren Jackson, one of the top players in the WNBA in the United States, plays for her hometown team during the WNBA off-season, lending her star power to an already strong team. However, injury has recently forced her to take some time off.

Motor Sports Forget the roar of the crowd – it's the roar of the rally cars that really penetrates, as they race through the forests around Canberra every March during the Rally of Canberra.

Horse Racing A more genteel atmosphere is found at Canberra's Thoroughbred Park, where race meets are held throughout the year.

Melbourne

To see the locals cast away their Victorian reserve, any major sporting event will do – but football and horse racing are the surest bets. **Australian Rules Football** – a mixture of rugby, soccer and Gaelic football – is at its best in Melbourne. Matches are held every Saturday, some Friday nights and Sundays during the April–September season. The finals pit the two top teams at the Melbourne Cricket Ground before more than 100,000 fanatical supporters.

Horse Racing The city has six tracks. Randwick is the closest and principal track, but races are held

BELOW: another glorious day at the cricket at Bellerive Oval, Hobart.

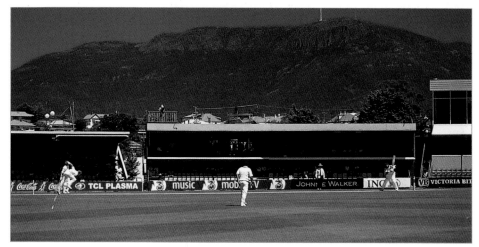

throughout the year at Canterbury, Rosehill and Warwick Farm. Trotting (harness) races are held Friday nights at Harold Park Paceway, and greyhound races on Monday and Saturday nights at Wentworth Park.

Horse racing is held year-round on the metropolitan courses at Flemington, Caulfield, Moonee Valley and Sandown. Flemington is the home of the **Melbourne Cup**, an internationally famous racing event held on the first Tuesday in November. On this day, the entire nation stops to follow the race on radio or television. Meanwhile, all Melbourne is at the track where huge amounts of champagne and betting money flow. It's also the fashion event of the season.

Cricket December to February is the season for international Test cricket matches played at the Melbourne Cricket Ground, where the Boxing Day Test forms the year's highlight.

Tennis In January the Australian Open grand-slam tournament is held on the banks of the Yarra.

Motor Racing Early March is the time for the Melbourne Formula 1 Grand Prix in Albert Park and in October, bikers flock to Phillip Island for the Moto G.

Soccer has blossomed since a national league was set up in 2005 and, following the natonal team's success at the 2006 World Cup, crowds have been reaching record proportions. Melbourne Victory had its first 50,000+ attendance in 2006.

Adelaide

Football During winter, AFL is the sport of choice for most locals. Adelaide is home to two AFL teams who you can see play during the winter months at the AAMI Stadium in West Lakes. The locals love their teams and the matches are usually a colourful affair.

Cricket In the summer months locals flock to the historic Adelaide Oval to watch Australia clash with international teams in Test matches and the faster-paced one-day internationals.

Cycling The Tour Downunder is a cycling event held each January. It attracts competitors from around the world as well as thousands of roadside spectators.

Motor Racing The city's streets play host to the Clipsal 500 each March, one of Australia's leading motorsport events featuring V8 cars. In November the Classic Adelaide Rally winds its way through 34 stages that take drivers through the Adelaide Hills and nearby wine regions.

Brisbane

Rugby Rugby League is the most popular spectator sport in Brisbane. There are two state teams, the North Queensland Cowboys, based in Townsville, and the Brisbane Broncos. Home games are played at Suncorp Stadium.

Cricket The Queensland Bulls are the state's top cricket team. Their home ground is the infamous Gabba at Woolloongabba.

Football AFL (Australian Football League) is hugely popular in Brisbane, thanks to the Brisbane Lions who have taken home a string of national titles in recent years. Home games are played at the Gabba.

Darwin

Football Australian Rules Football is played in the wet season (incredibly sweaty conditions for the players) Most major sporting events are conducted at the Marrara sports complex, Abala Road, Marrara (near the airport), where each major sport has its own dedicated ground. Soccer, rugby, cricket and hockey are all popular.

Horse Racing Popular all year round at the Darwin Turf Club at Fannie Bay. The locals celebrate the running of the Darwin Cup on the first Monday in August with a public holiday.

Motor Racing Held at the Hidden Valley raceway off Tiger Brennan Drive.

Perth

Cricket The WACA ground (Western Australian Cricket Association; Nelson Crescent, East Perth; tel: 08-9265 7222) is HQ of state cricket and venue for all important matches.

Horse Racing Perth has two racetracks, each a short ride from the centre. Ascot (tel: 08-9277 0777) is used for summer meetings, while Belmont Park (tel: 08-9470 8222), on the river with enclosed facilities, is popular in the winter months. Entry is generally free mid-week, unless there is a special meeting, and cheap (around A$10) at weekends.

Hobart

The main action in Tasmania occurs on water; otherwise the only option for watching sports in Hobart are international and national **cricket** matches. Bellerive Oval (tel: 03-6211 4000) hosts all the major cricket tournaments.

Sydney to Hobart and Melbourne to Hobart Yacht Races These famous races finish at Constitution Dock.

Launceston hosts a handful of **Aussie Rules (AFL)** games each season – technically home matches for Melbourne side, Hawthorn – and draws large crowds to the Aurora Stadium.

Its other crowd-pleaser is **motor racing**, with a round of the V8 Supercars championship held at the Symmons Plains circuit, just south of the city, each November.

BELOW: the Edwardian-style Brisbane Arcade at Queen Street Mall, Brisbane.

SHOPPING

Sydney

Sydney's main shopping district is bounded by Martin Place, George, Park and Elizabeth streets. Here you'll find large department stores like **David Jones** and **Myer**, the elegantly restored **Queen Victoria Building (QVB)** on George Street, the **Royal**, **Strand** and **Imperial** arcades, and the four-level **Centrepoint** shopping arcade that runs between Pitt and Castlereagh streets. Bargains include opals and sheepskin products.

Sydney's busiest area is around **Martin Place** and **Pitt Street Mall**. These pedestrian plazas provide seating for weary shoppers and at lunch time on weekdays, office workers and shoppers gather to hear free entertainment.

A visit to **Paddington Markets** is a Saturday afternoon ritual: they're at the corner of Oxford Street and Newcombe. **The Rocks** markets operate all weekend.

The **Westfield** shopping centre at Bondi Junction offers you all your shopping needs under one roof. With 453 stores, it also offers a state-of-the-art gym, restaurants and an 11-screen cinema.

Canberra

London Circuit is the business and civic heart of Canberra. A series of shopping complexes lie close to **Civic Square**, with department stores, boutiques, cafés and gift shops.

Each suburb has its own comprehensive shopping complex. South of the lake, **Manuka Shopping Centre** is an up-market location, including a cinema centre, several bars and stylish eateries. Canberra's city shops are open Mon–Thurs 9am–5.30pm, Friday 9am–9pm, Saturday 9am–5.30pm and Sunday 10am–4pm.

The **Old Bus Depot Markets** (tel: 02-6292 8391; www.obdm.com.au) in Kingston are the place to find everything from handcrafted jewellery to fresh produce, Sundays 10am–4pm. One Saturday a month it is home to a Regional Farmers Market.

Melbourne

Melbourne sees itself as Australia's major fashion centre. In fact, "shopping tours" have become one of the city's biggest tourist draw cards:

Sydney Tower

For the best bird's-eye view of Sydney (and even the Blue Mountains), take a trip up Sydney Tower on top of the Centrepoint complex. Located on Market Street between Pitt and Castlereagh, the tower is 305 metres (1,000 ft) high and comprises a viewing gallery, sky- lounge café and revolving restaurant. Open 11.30am–10.30pm daily; until 10.30pm on Saturdays.

they include lunch and take in Melbourne's famous factory outlets and seconds shops. Try Shopping Spree Tours, tel: 03-9596 6600.

In the city centre the major department stores are **Myer** and **David Jones**. Shopping centres include the **Melbourne Central** complex, with its multi-level glass atrium, the **QV Centre** in a whole block in Swanston Street, and the refurbished post office, **GPO** on the corner of Bourke and Elizabeth streets. **Collins Place** offers over 40 stores and hosts an "Australian-Made Art & Craft Market" every Sunday. The **Sportsgirl Centre** is a well-designed modern complex, and **Australia on Collins** features over 60 stores, many with imported fashions. Suburban shopping complexes are also huge. **Chadstone** is the largest in Australia and still growing. In South Yarra and Toorak, **Chapel Street** and **Toorak Road** are for the well-heeled only. Younger, cooler designers tend to congregate along **Brunswick Street**, Fitzroy. Richmond has a popular strip of factory outlets and bargain clothing shops where you can also buy clothes by young designers.

Melbourne has several famous shopping arcades. The oldest, the **Royal Arcade**, dates from 1870 and, along with the intimate **Block Arcade**, is one of Melbourne's landmarks. Street markets are also very popular here: there's the lively **Queen Victoria Market**, while the comprehensive **Prahran Market** attracts the Melbourne gourmands.

Adelaide

Adelaide's main shopping area is **Rundle Mall**. Adelaide's Central Market between Gorger and Grote streets offers a wide array of gourmet goodies and fresh produce. Wines can be bought from the cellar doors of many wineries in the Barossa Valley, Clare Valley, McLaren Vale, Adelaide Hills and the

Coonawarra. The Retail Art and Craft shop at the **Tandanya National Aboriginal Cultural Institute** sells a wide range of quality indigenous art, craft, books, music and clothing, as well as the essential didgeridoos and boomerangs (tel: 08-8224 3200; www.tandanya.com.au). At the **JamFactory** on Morphett Street you can tour craft and design studios and buy locally made contemporary ceramics, glass and jewellery.

Brisbane

Every Sunday, 8am–4pm, the vast **Riverside (Eagle Street) Market** is held at the Riverside Centre in Brisbane, with 150 craft stalls and many cafés. The **South Bank Markets** also offer craft and clothing on Friday evenings and weekends. The **Brisbane Powerhouse** in New Farm is the scene for a rapidly growing farmers' market on the second and fourth Saturdays of the month.

The main shopping centres in Brisbane are located around the Queen Street Mall, with the **Myer Centre** being the most comprehensive. Large arcades include **Wintergarden on the Mall**, **T&G**, **Rowes** and **Post Office Square**.

Darwin and Alice Springs

Darwin and Alice Springs are two of the best places to buy Aboriginal arts and crafts. Darwin is known for art from Arnhem Land and the Tiwi Islands, while Alice offers some of the best desert art (traditional dot painting style). In Darwin, try the up-market **Karen Brown Gallery** near Parliament House, **Mason's** at 21 Cavenagh Street, **Maningrida Arts and Culture**, 32 Mitchell Street or **Framed**, 55 Stuart Highway, north of the city centre.

In Alice, head for the **Todd Street Mall** for a plethora of desert art galleries, such as Papunya Tula and Gondwana. Nearby is the marvellous, comprehensive **Mbantua Gallery** at Lot 71 in Gregory Street with its diversity of styles and reasonable prices.

Perth

Out-of-town shopping centres have multiplied around Perth. **Centro Galleria** (Old Collier Road, Morley; tel: 08-9375 3228) in the city's north and **Westfield Carousel** (1382 Albany Highway, Cannington; tel: 08-9458 6344) to the south stand out as typical, American-style mega-centres. Still large, but compact and more "select" locations like **Karrinyup** (Karrinyup Road; tel: 08-9446 8454) also include food and furnishing outlets but major in clothes, shoes and more luxurious consumables.

The new suburban malls are booming, but none matches Perth city centre for its huge range – both "regular" shops and the many specialising in good-value, genuine Australian produce. Central Perth also benefits from extra trading on Friday nights and Sundays *(for retail hours, see page 377)*.

Other areas have their own specialities – **Fremantle** for arts and crafts, **Subiaco** and **Claremont** for style and fashion, **Guildford** for antiques.

Hobart

Elizabeth Street Mall and the adjoining **Cat and Fiddle Arcade** and **Centrepoint Hobart Shopping Centre** form the retail hub of Hobart, with all the major department stores and retail chains.

Go to **Salamanca Place** for arts and crafts, especially on a Saturday when the market is held.

If you are in search of antiques, **Bathurst Street** and **Battery Point** are good places to look.

FESTIVALS

The peak months for the arts in general are March, during the **Adelaide Fringe Festival**, and October for the **Melbourne International Festival of the Arts**, the **Fringe Festival** and the **Writers Festival**.

A list of some of the annual events held in Australia follows. Dates may vary, so refer to the Australian Tourist Commission's very comprehensive calendar booklet of current dates.

January
Australia-wide
Australia Day (26 Jan). There are parades, concerts and fireworks around the country, including concerts at Sydney's Darling Harbour and fireworks at Melbourne's Federation Square.
Hobart
Hobart Summer Festival (early Jan)
Melbourne
The *Australian Open* is a world-class Grand Slam partner to the French Open, the US Open and Wimbledon.
Tamworth (NSW)
Country Music Festival.
Sydney, Melbourne, Gold Coast, Adelaide and Perth
Big Day Out (late Jan–early Feb). One-day outdoor rock music festival.

February
Canberra
Royal Canberra Show. Typical agricultural show: animals, crafts, wood chopping, fireworks, etc.
Hobart
Australian Wooden Boat Festival. One of the world's leading maritime festivals. Held biennially (2007, 2009) *Hobart Cup Carnival.* Tasmania's premier horse racing event. *Royal Hobart Regatta.*
Launceston
Festivale Music. Arts, food and wine festival held over a weekend.
Melbourne
Heineken Classic. Golfing title. *Melbourne Fashion Festival.* Designers and retailers in a stylish array of parades and special events.
Perth
Perth International Arts Festival. Three weeks of arts and multicultural activities.
Rottnest Channel Swim. Swimmers attempt the 20 km (12 miles) between Cottesloe Beach and Rottnest Island.
Sydney
Sydney Gay and Lesbian Mardi Gras (throughout Feb). The parade on the last Saturday evening is the world's biggest gay and lesbian mardi gras.

February/March
Adelaide (SA)
The city comes alive during the Adelaide Festival, held every two years (2006, 2008, etc.) in February and March. Street theatre is everywhere, spontaneous and usually very funny, with non-stop partying. The festival includes a mainstream schedule of international performances in the Festival Centre, plus the ever-popular Fringe Festival which is now a yearly event – three weeks of stand-up comedy, alternative theatre and visual arts. Similar in concept and quality to the Edinburgh Fringe Festival, the Adelaide Fringe draws comedians and other acts from around the English-speaking world and it is well worth making a trip to Adelaide to experience its variety and fun.

At the same time, Writer's Week brings important scribblers from around the world and a huge audience of adoring listeners to hear them read and discuss their work. There is also a Visual Arts Festival, a showcase of cutting-edge artworks, which can take place in any form – even in the homes of artists. During the festival, there are extra information booths in Rundle Mall and a number of free publications which give listings and information about the daily events.
Adelaide Fringe (held annually). New

theatre, comedy, visual arts and music. The cutting-edge counterpart to the *Adelaide Festival of Arts (see The Arts, page 364).*

March
Adelaide (SA)
Adelaide Cup. South Australia's premier horse racing event.
Womadelaide. World and roots music festival held annually.
Clipsall 500. Motor-sports festival.
Ballarat (Vic)
The Ballarat Begonia Festival. World-famous begonia display and ten days of festival activities.
Brisbane (Qld)
Ideas Festival. Four days of focus on ideas, innovation and invention.
Canberra (ACT)
Celebrate Canberra. A 10-day celebration of the nation's capital with fireworks and hot-air ballooning.
Rally of Canberra. Biggest car rally event on the eastern coast.
Gold Coast (Qld)
Australian Surf Lifesaving Championships.
Margaret River (WA)
Salomon Masters. Annual allcomers surfing event.
Melbourne (Vic)
March is usually the best time of year in Melbourne, packed with events taking a punt on the good weather.
Moomba, one of Australia's largest outdoor festivals, is held in the first two weeks of March. Moomba is an Aboriginal word meaning "let's get together and have fun".

Over 200 activities include the world's best water-skiers on the Yarra, the bizarre birdman contest for amateur aviators, and games, music and rides in the Alexandra Gardens.

Also look out for the *Melbourne Food and Wine Festival* and the start of the *Melbourne International Comedy Festival.*
Fosters Australian Grand Prix. Four-day opening round of the FIA Formula 1 World Championship.
Australian International Airshow. Australia's biggest aviation and areospace event, held biennially (2007, 2009).

March/April
Bendigo (Vic)
Awakening of the Dragon Festival (date is variable). The world's longest imperial dragon parades through the streets every Easter Monday.
Broome (WA)
Broome Arts and Music Festival. The remote pearling community comes alive with Aboriginal art shows, artists' markets and more.
Margaret River (WA)
Margaret River Pro. Draws top

surfers from around the world.
Newcastle (NSW)
Surfest. An annual surfing event with surf film competition included.
Port Fairy (Vic)
Folk Festival (Labour Day weekend).

April
Australia-wide
Anzac Day (April 25). Australia's day to commemorate all who fought in wars. Marked by parades by former soldiers and dawn ceremonies.
Byron Bay (NSW)
East Coast International Blues and Roots Festival.
Canberra (ACT)
Celebrate Canb Balloon Fiesta. See dozens of hot-air balloons take to the skies from the forecourt of Old Parliament House.
National Folk Festivals (Easter weekend). Gathers fiddlers and folk musicians from all over Australia.
Fremantle (WA)
Fremantle Street Arts Festival. Celebrating the art of busking.
Melbourne (Vic)
Melbourne International Comedy Festival. One of the world's best.
Melbourne International Flower and Garden Show. Australia's premier horticultural show.
Sydney (NSW)
Royal Easter Show. Agricultural show and amusement park extravaganza.
Tasmania (Tas)
Targa Tasmania. Major car-racing event covering Tasmania's scenic coastline and mountain passes.
10 days on the Island (held every second odd year). Event celebrating island identity.

May
Alice Springs (NT)
Bangtail Muster. A day of Outback fun including a parade in honour of all cattlemen from Central Australia.
V8 Supercar Championships.
Barossa Valley (SA)
Riverland Balloon Regatta. Beautiful visions of dawn and late-afternoon skies dotted with colourful balloons.
Paniyiri. Australia's largest Greek festival.
Clare Valley (SA)
Clare Gourmet Weekend. Wineries join with prominent restaurants for the complete gourmet experience.
Sydney (NSW)
Sydney Writers Festival. Australian and international authors convene.

June
Alice Springs (NT)
Beanie Festival. Quirky event with special classes to make "beanies" (close-fitting woollen caps).
Finke Desert 200 km Race. Cars, bikes and buggies race along the dry river bed from Alice to Finke, stop overnight and race back. Spectators camp along the river bank.
Alpine resorts
Opening weekend. The Queen's birthday weekend is the signal for the opening of the ski season – snow or no snow!
Barmera (SA)
Riverland Country Music Festival. Country music of all varieties in over 20 venues.
Barunga (NT)
Barunga Festival. Aboriginal people gather for four days of dancing, athletics, arts and crafts. Advisable to bring a tent.

Geelong (Vic)
National Celtic Folk Festival. Celebration of Scottish, Welsh, Irish and Cornish heritage with theatre, music, crafts, sports and food.
Laura (Qld)
Dance and Cultural Festival. Biennial Aboriginal event at a dedicated site 15 km (9 miles) from Laura.
McLaren Vale (SA)
McLaren Vale Sea and Vines Festival. The McLaren Vale wineries present food and wine to visitors.
Mildura (Vic)
Mildura International Balloon Fiesta. Incorporating the Ballooning World Cup and National Championships.
Sydney
Sydney International Film Festival. A month-long festival.

July
Australia-wide
NAIDOC Week. Celebrates the history, culture and achievements of Aboriginal and Torres Strait Islander people.
Alice Springs (NT)
Lions Camel Cup. Camels are brought from all over Australia to compete. A day of fun, with fireworks.
Brisbane (Qld)
Brisbane Festival. The arts shindig held every two years (even numbers).
Darwin (NT)
Darwin Cup Festival. Cup Day is accompanied by loads of live music.
Beer Can Regatta (date is variable). Traditional Darwin water race, where competing vessels must be constructed entirely of beer cans.
Melbourne (VA)
Melbourne International Film Festival.
Stroud (NSW)
Stroud International Brick and Rolling Pin Throwing Contest. Four towns called Stroud (also in England, Canada and the USA) simultaneously hold this bizarre contest.

August
Adelaide River (NT)
Adelaide River Show Rodeo, Campdraft and Gymkhana. Activities range from a bush dance to a country music talent quest. Big money prizes.
Alice Springs (NT)
Alice Springs Rodeo. Bareback bull riding, steer wrestling and calf roping from the Northern Territory's best.
Henley on Todd Regatta. Waterless regatta held on the dry bed of the Todd River. The "Sea Battle" is fought with flour bombs and water canons between four-wheel drive "boats".
Barossa Valley (SA)
Barossa Classic Gourmet Weekend (August). Wineries combine with restaurants to provide samples of gourmet fare.

BELOW: rumba at the Fremantle Festival in Western Australia.

Brisbane (Qld)
Ekka. City-meets-country show.
Darwin (NT)
The*Darwin Festival* celebrates the
end of the tropical dry season with
entertainment, arts and cultural
events in parks and venues around
Darwin. The festival strongly
reflects the Asian-Pacific and
Aboriginal communities of Darwin.
It overlaps with the *Darwin Fringe
Festival*, which showcases local
visual and performing arts.
Darwin Festival. Eighteen days of
dance, cabaret, outdoor concerts,
film, visual arts and comedy.
Geraldton (WA)
Sunshine Surfmaster. Big prizes.
Hervey Bay (Qld)
Hervey Bay Whale Festival. Marks the
opening of the whale season.
Melbourne (Vic)
Melbourne Writers Festival. Australian
and foreign writers discuss their works,
tel: 03-9645 9244.
Mount Buller (Vic)
World Aerials. The international aerial
ski championships.
Mount Isa (Qld)
Mount Isa Rotary Rodeo. Australia's
biggest rodeo, held since 1959.
Noosa (Qld)
Noosa Jazz Fest. Live jazz including
the famous "Woods" Picnic Concert.
Gove Peninsula (Arnhem Land; NT)
Garma Festival is a celebration of
the Yolngu culture of East Arnhem
Land, with a different theme each
year. It is part-conference, part-
festival, part-education seminar.
Delegates live in a tent city for up
to five days. A unique experience
on a coastal scarp 30 km (18
miles) from the mining town of
Nhulunbuy.
Toowoomba (Qld)
Australian Heritage Festival.
Jondaryan Woolshed hosts a week of
historic rural Australian activities
featuring bullock teams, steam
engines and hand shearing.

September
Adelaide (SA)
Royal Adelaide Show. Adelaide's
major agricultural show.
Bathurst (NSW)
*Bathurst 1000 Touring Car Motor
Race*. Popular Mount Panorama
event.
Birdsville (Qld)
Birdsville Races. Horse races in aid
of the Royal Flying Doctor Service.
Brisbane (Qld)
River Festival. A ten-day event
celebrating Brisbane's waterways.
Brisbane Writers Festival.
Broome (WA)
Shinju Matsuri Festival of the Pearl.
A ten-day festival honouring

Broome's Asian heritage. Pearl
jewellery, Chinese feasts and more.
Canberra (ACT)
Floriade. Australia's largest spring
floral festival.
Perth (WA)
Perth Royal Show. Perth's major
agricultural event.
Western Australia Wildflower Festival.
Huge range of unique Australian wild-
flowers at their best at Kings Park.
Sydney (NSW)
Festival of the Winds. The sky above
Bondi Beach is filled with kites.
Sydney Marathon.

October
Alice Springs (NT)
Masters Games. Veteran athletes
compete in many sports.
Gold Coast (Qld)
Indy 300. Four days of car racing.
Melbourne (Vic)
Antipodes Festival. Australia's
largest ethnic celebration and
reputedly the biggest Greek
festival in the world.
*Melbourne International Festival of
the Arts* & *Melbourne Fringe Festival*.
Noosa (Qld)
Noosa Triathlon Multi-sport Festival.
See them run, swim, cycle and play
golf and volleyball.
Phillip Island (Vic)
The Australian Motorcycle Grand Prix.
Wynyard (Tas)
Tulip Festival.

November
Australia-wide
Melbourne Cup Day. Australia's
premier horse-racing event is
celebrated throughout the country.
On the first Tuesday in November
the whole of Australia stops for the
running of this famous race at the
Flemington Racecourse. It's
accompanied by a huge carnival in
Melbourne where the locals don their
finest and most outrageous hats to
attend.
Fremantle (WA)
Festival of Fremantle. Exhibitions,
concerts, and a huge street carnival.
Perth (WA)
Awesome Festival. Entertainment
and workshops for the under-25s.
Wangaratta (Vic)
Festival of Jazz.

December
Eltham (Vic)
*Montsalvat National Poets, Spoken
Word and Vision Festival*. Poetry
performed in beautiful grounds.
Hobart (Tas)
*Summer Festival, including Taste of
Tasmania festival (late Dec–early
Jan)*. Food and entertainment add up
to a non-stop party on the docks.

Sydney–Hobart
Sydney to Hobart Yacht Race.
Famous blue-water yacht race has its
dramatic Boxing Day start in Sydney
Harbour.

CHILDREN'S ACTIVITIES

There are many ways to keep even
the most demanding children happy
while holidaying in Australia.
Below are some highlights from
each major city guaranteed to
keep kids amused (at least
momentarily). Alternatively,
Australia's beaches and national
parks provide a stunningly diverse
playground.

Sydney

Conveniently, two of Sydney's leading
attractions are located in Darling
Harbour: the **Monorail** (kids love it) and
Tumbalong Park, with a free playground and a stage for free concerts.
The "Search and Discover"
section on the second floor of the
Australian Museum lets children
get their hands on all sorts of
exciting exhibits that most
museums would keep out of
bounds. **The Powerhouse Museum**
has stimulating Kids Interactive
Discovery Spaces (KIDS), designed
to involve younger children in
hands-on activities related to the
themes in the museum's
exhibitions. They explore subjects
such as music, machines, life in the
home, film and television.
The **Opera House** runs children's
events such as the Babies Proms,
which allows toddlers to get close to
the musical instruments (tel: 02-9250
7111). **The Art Gallery of New South
Wales** holds special family events on
Sundays, such as renditions of
Aboriginal Dreamtime stories
(tel: 02-9225 1700).

Canberra

Two major attractions with appeal to
kids are the **National Zoo and
Aquarium** (tel: 02-6287 8400) and
the **National Museum of Australia**
(tel: 02-6208 5000), with its KSpace
FutureWorld gallery. Kids also love
the **Questacon** (**National Science
and Technology Centre**; daily
9am–5pm; tel: 02-6270 2800;
www.questacon.edu.au). This distinctive
drum-shaped structure on the lake
shore specialises in hands-on
science and technology exhibitions.
Allow at least three hours for a
fascinating visit.

Melbourne

The **Royal Melbourne Zoo** is a famously well-designed zoo, and one of the oldest in the world. Royal Melbourne Zoo lies just north of the city centre in Parkville and provides creative walk-through environments, a butterfly enclosure, an excellent gorilla forest and a revamped elephant section. During January/ February the zoo is open until 9.30pm for Zoo Twilights concerts. Open Mon–Fri 9am–4.30pm, Sat and Sun until 5pm; tel: 03-928 9300; www.zoo.org.au.

The **Melbourne Museum** has an excellent children's section and the complex now also features an Imax cinema.

Alternatively, the **Scienceworks Museum** (see page 175) has tactile displays that aim to make science and technology fun, and includes a Planetarium and Pumping Station.

Adelaide

Adelaide Zoo (see page 205) located next to the Botanic Gardens, Adelaide Zoo is noted for its Australian birds, including pelicans, penguins, lorikeets, and blue and gold macaws. There are also sea lions, big cats and a reptile house.

For high-octane fun, head to **The Beachouse** in Glenelg. This new entertainment complex has waterslides, dodgems, mini golf, a bouncy castle and ferris wheel. For more information tel: 08-8295 1511; www.thebeachouse.com.au

Brisbane

There are plenty of exciting attractions aimed at children in Queensland. Theme parks on the Gold Coast have everything from water slides at **Wet'n' Wild Water World** to movie sets at **Warner Brothers Movie World**. Dolphins and polar bears can keep smaller kids amused at **Sea World**, while the rides at **Dreamworld** cater to older children.

Australia Zoo on the Sunshine Coast was set up by the late Steve Irwin, otherwise known as the Crocodile Hunter. There are 14 shows daily, and, although crocodiles may be the main attraction, the zoo allows visitors to feed the Asian elephants and cuddle koalas. Cuddly koalas can also be found at the **Lone Pine Sanctuary** (tel: 07-3378 1366) near Brisbane, the first and largest koala sanctuary in the world.

The **Queensland Museum** on Brisbane's South Bank is full of inspiring interactive exhibitions for kids. They can learn how to measure an earthquake, play a thongophone and piece together a human jigsaw. At the **Cobb & Co. Museum** at Toowoomba are examples of transport from the horse-drawn era. The excitement of huge cattle sales can be seen on Wednesdays at **Dalrymple Sales Yards** (tel: 07-4761 5300) on the Flinders Highway at Charters Towers. At **Tjapukai Aboriginal Cultural Park** in Cairns (tel: 07-4042 9999) the daily shows include an evening of corroboree around a fire.

Darwin

Kids will enjoy exploring the Northern Territory's diverse wildlife at the **Territory Wildlife Park**, which has a walk-through aquarium, as well as kangaroos and wallabies roaming free.

A much needed rest can be had while the children splash around at the **Howard Springs Nature Park**, which has a children's pool fed by freshwater springs (just outside Darwin; tel: 08-8983 1001).

Perth

Extra events and projects are put on at venues during school holidays: details from the Perth Visitor Centre, tel: 08-9483 1133.

Some of best activities to keep kids occupied in Perth include The **Perth Zoo** (20 Labouchere Road, South Perth; tel: 08-9474 0444), which has great collections of native and exotic animals in natural enclosures; children's activities include an overnight stay in the summer months. Open 9am–5pm daily.

Apart from being a genuinely interesting visit any time of the year, the **Western Australian Museum** (Perth Cultural Centre, James Street, tel: 08-99212 3700) organises special children's activities during school holidays.

At **Adventure World** (179 Progress Drive, Bibra Lake; tel: 08-9417 9666; Oct–Apr 10am–5pm, daily during school holidays, closed Tues and Wed out of holiday times) there's unlimited use of all the rides and attractions once you have paid the rather steep entry fee to enter. "The Rampage" is the scariest ride of all, not for the faint-hearted.

Hobart

The Discovery Space at the **Tasmanian Museum and Art Gallery** (40 Macquarie Street; tel: 03-6211 4177) has hands-on action and its summer holiday programmes can include anything from a sneak preview of the taxidermist's latest work to putting butterflies under the microscope.

The **Terrapin Puppet Theatre** (77 Salamanca Place; tel: 03-6223 6834) introduces under-12s to the magic of performance via Hans Christian Andersen stories with an Aussie twist and other contemporary tales.

The **Imaginarium Science Centre** (Wenvoe Street, Devonport; tel: 03-6423 1466) has interactive exhibits that are changed every school term.

BELOW: admiring a wombat at Lone Pine Sanctuary in Queensland.

A HANDY SUMMARY OF PRACTICAL INFORMATION, ARRANGED ALPHABETICALLY

A dmission Charges

Compared with the UK and USA, admission charges to sight s and attractions are fairly low, and often free for museums, though you may find that they charge for entry to temporary exhibitions. The "worlds" – including Dreamworld and Sea World in Queensland for example – have some of the highest admission charges, but usually offer discounted family tickets, which can help keep a lid on costs if travelling with children. Concession prices are often available on production of a student or senior card.

For more information contact the relevant tourist office (tourist offices are listed on page 382, while contact information for Australia's National Parks and National Trust offices are listed under Useful Addresses on page 383).

B udgeting for Your Trip

The cost of living in Australia is generally lower than Europe and the USA (although manufactured goods tend to be more expensive

in Australia). The one exception to the general rule in Australia is Sydney where property prices are up there with cities like London and New York and day-to-day expenses such as public transport and dining out tend to be noticeably higher as well. As you move away from the east coast, where most of Australia's population lives, to cities like Adelaide, Hobart, Darwin and Perth, the cost of living is lower again. However, there is an exception once more which is the isolated towns and settlements of the Outback where the cost of transporting supplies long distances drives petrol and food prices upwards.

In general accommodation can cost as little as A$40–60 for a double room in a country pub, A$100 for self-contained cabin-style accommodation in the country, A$120 for a basic hotel room and A$200 upwards per night for five-star hotels. Mid-week rates tend to be cheaper than weekends.

The variety of climates means Australia grows lots of fresh produce that is of a high quality

although the standard in super-markets is much lower than what you will find in markets and fruiterers. A takeaway or dine-in café meal costs anywhere from A$5–15, a main in a restaurant ranges from $15–30 and a main in a fine dining restaurant ranges from A$25–40. In major cities, some of the most affordable and best quality food can be found in and around Chinatown.

Travel tends to be expensive because of the distances involved and high fuel prices. Car hire can start from around A$60 per day including insurance although significant discounted rates apply for longer rental periods. Budget airlines Virgin Blue and Jetstar continue to have price wars and you can pick up flights from Sydney to Cairns, some 2,500 km (1,550 miles), for A$149 one way. An airfare between Sydney and Melbourne can cost as little as A$75 last-minute or around A$110 if you book a few weeks ahead. The train between Sydney and Melbourne can cost around A$100 but when you take into account the 12 hours travel time versus only 1½ hours on a plane, its easy to see why most people prefer to fly.

Business Hours

General retail trading hours for stores are Mon–Sat 9am–5pm. Most shops open 10am–4pm on Sunday too. Late-night shopping (until 9pm) takes place at least one night a week in the capital cities – usually a Thursday or Friday.

Restaurants and snack bars, bookshops and local corner stores are open until later in the evening; at times all weekend. Australians still enjoy the tradition of the weekend holiday and most offices are closed on Saturday and Sunday.

Banks open Mon–Thur 9.30am–4pm and until 5pm on Friday. Some selected branches are open on Saturday morning as well. All banks, post offices, government and private offices, and most shops close on public holidays (see Public Holidays, page 381).

C limate

The seasons in Australia are the reverse of the northern hemisphere's. September to November is spring, December to February summer, March to May autumn, and June to August winter. Since fine, mild weather occurs during all seasons, any time can be recommended for a visit to Australia – although some months are warmer and drier than others.

About 40 percent of the country lies in the tropical zone north of the Tropic of Capricorn. In the Top End around Darwin (the monsoon belt) and near Cairns, there are only two seasons: the dry (April–November) and the wet (December–March). In the dry, there are warm days, clear blue skies and cool nights. The wet, however, is usually characterised by heavy rain alternating with sunny hot weather. On the Great Barrier Reef most rain falls in January and February.

In the southern temperate zone seasons are more distinct. Winter's days in Sydney are usually sunny with a maximum of 15°C (60°F) – chilly enough to require an overcoat – while humid summer temperatures can regularly hit 30°C (90°F) and higher. Snow falls on the southern mountain ranges, but not in the cities (except Hobart). Melbourne is pleasant in spring, summer and autumn, but winter can be grey and miserable, especially in July and August. Tasmania, the island state off the southern tip of the continent, is the coolest: summers are by far the best time to visit here, as winters can be damp and depressing.

South Australia has a Mediterranean climate: summers are hot and dry with temperatures regularly above 30°C (85°F), and highs of 40°C (105°F) and above are not uncommon.

Western Australia also has a Mediterranean climate. There are four distinctive seasons and moderate temperatures in its southern parts, while the north is in the tropical zone, so Top End conditions prevail.

In central Australia, summer temperatures are generally too high for comfort. In winter, the nights may be cool, with clear warm days.

Visitors should also bear in mind the various Australian school holidays; Christmas coincides with the long summer school break, which lasts throughout January. Easter is another big break. If you are travelling during these seasons, book well in advance.

Crime and Safety

When it comes to crime, Australia is a relatively safe country. That being said, you should use the same common sense and precautions as you would elsewhere regarding your possessions and personal security. Issues surrounding prostitution, drugs and drunken behaviour occur in all cities. However, these are unlikely to affect travellers. If an incident occurs, report it to the police or, for urgent attention, call the emergency services by dialling **000**.

When it comes to safety, non-human elements can pose more of a risk in Australia. Bushfires occur regularly each year and it is important to be aware of fire bans or restrictions. If you are out in the bush and notice smoke it is important to take it seriously and head for the nearest open space.

It is also important you thoroughly prepare if you are bushwalking or exploring the Outback. Take plenty of water and supplies, a good map and let a friend or the local ranger know of your plans in case you get stranded. Daily temperatures can reach the extremes with searing heat during the day and freezing nights.

In northern Australia saltwater crocodiles are a real danger and have been known to take humans. They can be found in rivers, creeks, waterholes and around the coast. In popular tourist areas, croc-inhabited waterholes are regularly signposted. However, if you are unsure whether a place is croc-free, it is best not to risk swimming at all.

Box jellyfish are another danger in the far north during the wet season (November to May). Their venomous sting is extremely painful and can be fatal. During these months make sure you only swim in the special "stinger" enclosures.

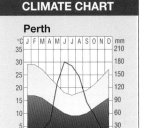

CLIMATE CHART
Perth

☐ Maximum temperature
■ Minimum temperature
— Rainfall

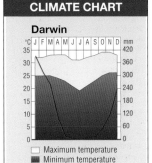

CLIMATE CHART
Darwin

☐ Maximum temperature
■ Minimum temperature
— Rainfall

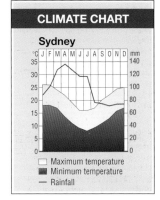

CLIMATE CHART
Sydney

☐ Maximum temperature
■ Minimum temperature
— Rainfall

TRANSPORT

ACCOMMODATION

ACTIVITIES

A – Z

LANGUAGE

Unsuspecting tourists can easily find themselves in trouble when swimming at Australian surf beaches. Lifesavers patrol popular beaches and put up red and yellow flags that swimmers should stick between. If an undertow or "rip" drags you out, raise an arm if you need help and a surf lifesaver will come to your aid.

Customs

Customs

There are no customs charges on personal belongings intended for use during your stay. Non-dutiable allowances are 250 grams (8oz) of tobacco goods and 2.25 litres (2.4 quarts) of alcohol. You may also import dutiable goods to the value of A$900 in personal baggage. Visit www.customs.gov.au.

Australian produce is of a very high standard because it is free from many insect pests and diseases common to other countries. This is due in part to the strict control on the importation of insects, animal and plant products, fruit, vegetables and seeds.

Laws strictly prohibit the export of protected Australian wildlife and products made from the skins, feathers, bones, shells, corals, or any part of protected species.

Quarantine

Australia is free of rabies, anthrax and foot-and-mouth disease, so all incoming animals are placed in quarantine. Cats and dogs (including guide dogs) are quarantined for up to 6 months, depending on the animal's country of origin – from the UK the period is 30 days. See www.affa.gov.au.

D isabled Travellers

Most new buildings, public transport and tourist attractions have wheelchair access and other facilities for the disabled. The major rental car companies have a small number of cars with hand controls (reserve at least seven days in advance). Advance notice with relevant details of your disability will facilitate the best possible assistance from airlines, hotels or railway offices. Taxi fleets in state capitals all have cars that can carry wheelchairs. Tourism Australia has further information on its website (www.australia.com). Also, the National Information Communications Network (NICAN) provides a directory of accessible accommodation, recreation and other facilities. Contact NICAN at: Unit 5,

48 Brookes Street, Mitchell, ACT 1220, tel: 02-6241 1220; freecall: 1800-806 769; www.nican.com.au.

The state automobile associations publish accommodation directories which include information on disabled access.

E lectricity

The power supply is 220–240 volts AC. Sockets are three-pin flat plugs. You may be able to find adaptors in hardware stores or at some hotels.

Embassies and Consulates

If you need help with matters such as legal advice or a stolen passport while in Australia, most countries have diplomatic representations, with embassies in major cities.

Melbourne

Canada
Level 50, 101 Collins Street, tel: 03-9653 9674.
Japan
Level 45, Melbourne Central Tower, 360 Elizabeth Street, tel: 03-9639 3244.
UK
17th Floor, 90 Collins Street, tel: 03-9652 1600.
USA
553 St Kilda Road, Melbourne, tel: 03-9526 5900.

Sydney

A comprehensive list of every country represented in Australia is available on the Australia Department of Foreign Affairs and Trade website www.info.dfat.gov.au. A small selection of the consulates in Sydney follows:
Canada
Consulate-General of Canada Level 5, Quay West, 111 Harrington Sreet, tel: 02-9364 3050;

Canberra Embassies

Over 60 countries have diplomatic representation in Canberra, and their buildings form a tourist attraction in their own right. The embassies are mostly south and west of Capital Hill, scattered through the suburbs of Red Hill, Forrest and Yarralumla. Many of the buildings have been designed in the architectural style of the country the mission represents, such as the US Embassy in a red-brick Williamsburg Mission style and the Thai Embassy with its upswept roof corners and gold-coloured roof tiles.

http://geo.international.gc.ca/asia/australia/
China/Hong Kong
Consulate General of the P.R of China/Hong Kong, 39 Dunblane St, St Camperdown Pvt Boxes, NSW 4450
Surry Hills, tel: 02-8595 8002 (9am–12.30pm)
www.australia.org.hk
France
Consulate-General of France, Level 26, 31 Market Street, St Martin's Tower, tel: 02-9261 5238;
www.consulfrance-sydney.org
Japan
Consulate-General of Japan, Level 34, 52 Martin Place, Colonial Centre, tel: 02-9231 3455;
www.japan.org.au
USA
Consulate-General of the United States of America, Level 5, 19–29 Martin Place, MLC Centre, tel: 02-9373 9200; http://usembassy-australia.state.gov/sydney/

Brisbane

China
Level 9, 79 Adelaide Street, tel: 07-3210 6509-206.
Italy
Level 14 AMP Place, 10 Eagle Street, tel: 07-3229 8944.
UK
Level 26, Waterfront Place, 1 Eagle Street, tel: 07-3236 2575.

Perth

Canada
Third Floor, 267 St George's Terrace, tel: 08-9322 7930
UK
Level 26, Allendale Square, 77 St George's Terrace, tel: 08-9224 4700.
USA
13th Floor, 16 St George's Terrace, tel: 08-9231 9400.

Adelaide

Germany
23 Peel Street, tel: 08-8231 6320.
Italy
398 Payneham Road, Glynde, tel: 08-8337 0777.
UK
Level 22, 25 Grenfell Street, tel: 08-8212 7280.

Darwin

British Consulate (emergencies only) 02 44 22 22 80.

Canberra

Canada
Commonwealth Avenue, Yarralumla, tel: 02-364 3050.
Ireland
20 Arkana Street, Yarralumla, tel: 02-6273 3022.

Japan
112–114 Empire Circuit, Yarralumla, tel: 02-6273 3244.
Malaysia
7 Perth Avenue, Yarralumla, tel: 02-6273 1543.
New Zealand
Commonwealth Avenue, Yarralumla, tel: 02-6270 4211.
Singapore
17 Forster Cresent, Yarralumla, tel: 02-6273 3944
UK
Commonwealth Avenue, Yarralumla, tel: 02-6270 6666; www.uk.emb.gov.au/.
USA
21 Moonah Place, Yarralumla, tel: 02-6214 5600.

Overseas Missions
Canada – Ottawa
Australian High Commission, Suite 710, 50 O'Conner Street, Ottawa, Ontario, K1P 6L2, tel: 1 613-236 0841.
Toronto
Australian Consulate-General, Suite 1100 South Tower, 175 Bloor Street East, Toronto, Ontario, M4W 3R8, tel: 1 416-323 1155.
Vancouver
Australian Consulate, Suite 1225, 888 Dunsmuir Street, Vancouver, BC V6C 3K4, tel: 1 604-684 1177.
China (Hong Kong)
Australian Consulate-General, 23/F Harbour Centre, 25 Harbour Road, Wan Chai, tel: 852 2827 8881.
Ireland
Australian Embassy, 7th floor, Fitzwilton House, Wilton Terrace, Dublin 2, tel: 353 1-664 5300.
Japan
Australian Embassy, 2-1-14 Mita, Minato-Ku, Tokyo 108-8361, tel: 81 35232 4111.
New Zealand – Wellington
Australian High Commission, 72–76 Hobson Street, Thorndon, Wellington, tel: 64 4473 6411.
Auckland
Australian Consulate-General, Level 7 PricewaterhouseCoopers Tower, 186–194 Quay Street, Auckland, tel: 64 9921 8800.
Singapore
Australian High Commission, 25 Napier Road, Singapore 258507, tel: 65 6836 4100.
UK
Australian High Commission, Australia House, The Strand, London WC2B 4LA, tel: 44 20-7379 4334.
USA – Washington DC
Australian Embassy, 1601 Massachusetts Avenue, Washington DC NW 20036-2273, tel: 1 202-797 3000.

New York
Australian Mission to the UN, 150 East 42nd Street, 33rd floor, New York, NY 10017-5612, tel: 1 212-351 6600.
San Francisco
Australian Consulate-General, 575 Market Street, Suite 1800, San Francisco CA 94105-2185, tel: 1 415-5361970.
Atlanta
Australian Consulate-General, Atlanta Financial Center, 3353 Peachtree Road, NE, Suite 1140, Atlanta GA 30326, tel: 1 404-7603408.

Emergencies

Call **000** for police, fire and ambulance. This number is toll-free from any phone in Australia and can be made from public phones without a phonecard or coins. **112** is the international standard emergency number that can be dialled from mobile phones.

Entry Requirements

Visitors to Australia must have a passport valid for the entire period of their stay. All non-Australian citizens also require a visa – except for New Zealand citizens, who are issued with a visa on arrival in Australia.
ETA visas The Electronic Transfer Authority (ETA) enables visitors to obtain a visa on the spot from their travel agent or airline office. The system is in place in over 30 countries, including the US and the UK. ETA visas are generally valid over a 12-month period; single stays must not exceed three months, but return visits within the 12-month period are allowed. ETA visas are issued free, or

Toll-free Phone Calls

Toll-free or freecall numbers are common in Australian business. Numbers beginning with 13 (ie. Qantas domestic 131 313) can be called from any phone in Australia at local-call rates; numbers starting with 800, 1300 or 1800 are freecall numbers (toll-free) when dialled from within Australia.

you can purchase one online for A$20 from www.eta.immi.gov.au.
Tourist visas These are available for continuous stays longer than three months, but must be obtained from an Australian visa office, such as an Embassy or Consulate. A A$20 fee applies. Those travelling on tourist and ETA visas are not permitted to work while in Australia. Travellers are asked on their applications to prove they have an adequate source of funding while in Australia (around A$1,000 a month).
Temporary residence Those seeking temporary residence must apply to an Australian visa office, and in many cases must be sponsored by an appropriate organisation or employer. Study visas are available for people who want to undertake registered courses on a full-time basis.
Working holiday visas Under a reciprocal arrangement, visitors from a list of 19 countries including the UK, Canada and Japan, who are between the ages of 18 and 30, are eligible for a Working Holiday visa. This entitles them to a stay of up to 12 months and some casual employment during that time. Such visas can only be applied for in the traveller's country of origin.

BELOW: Australia's distinctive coat of arms.

Entry requirements for Australia are continually updated. Information and applications for visas should be made to the nearest Australian Government representative in your home country well before travelling (see Overseas Missions, page 379), or visit www.immi.gov.au, which gives information on all the different types of visas, and allows online applications.

G ay and Lesbian Travellers

Australia is popular with gay and lesbian travellers, although homophobic attitudes do exist, mostly in areas away from inner cities and popular tourist spots. One of the main attractions is Sydney's annual gay and lesbian **Mardi Gras** each March, one of the greatest celebrations of its kind in the world. Sydney's Oxford Street is where all the action takes place and outside of Mardi Gras it remains a popular gay and lesbian hub, along with Newtown. **Midsumma** (www.midsumma.org.au), held each January/February, is the major gay and lesbian festival in Melbourne.

Major cities have gay and lesbian newspapers and magazines, available from many inner-city cafés, bars and pubs. Gay and Lesbian Tourism Australia (GALTA) is a network of gay-friendly tourism operators (www.galta.com.au).

H ealth and Medical Care

Australian doctors, dentists and hospitals all have modern equipment, high-level training and extensive facilities. They are also expensive.

BELOW: pain killers Aussie-style.

New Zealand, Finland, Italy, Malta, the Netherlands, Norway, Sweden, the UK and Ireland have reciprocal health-care agreements with Australia, so visitors are entitled to free hospital treatment and Medicare (the Australian national health plan) benefits for GP treatment. Taking out a travel insurance policy that covers your health, before travelling to Australia, is recommended however.

Vaccinations are not required if you are flying directly to Australia and have not passed through an epidemic zone or a yellow fever, cholera or typhoid-infected area in the 6 days prior to your arrival.

The sun in Australia has extremely strong ultraviolet rays, so extended exposure is not recommended, especially when the sun is at its fiercest between 11am and 4pm. A wide-brimmed hat and adequate-strength sunscreen are essential.

M aps

Tourist information centres usually have free, quality local maps that also include useful tourism information. If you are travelling by car most car-hire companies supply road atlases. You can also pick up Australian road atlases from any good bookshop. Australia is a vast country and it is easy to get lost once you head to the Outback so it is recommended you purchase maps that detail geography as well as road and track types for Outback travel and long-distance bushwalking.

The Tourism Australia website (www.australia.com) has a wide range of state, city and localised maps which can be useful for planning your itinerary.

Media

Each major city has one daily newspaper and in some cases two. The *Sydney Morning Herald* (www.smh.com.au) and the *Melbourne Age* (www.theage.com.au) are the two most important capital-city dailies, and can usually be found around Australia. The only national daily newspapers are *The Australian* and *The Financial Review*. Numerous weekly magazines are sold alongside local editions of international publications, such as *Newsweek* (included in *The Bulletin*) and *Time*. The largest-selling papers are the tabloids in Sydney (the *Daily Telegraph*) and Melbourne (the *Herald-Sun*, online at www.heraldsun. com). There are about 120 newspapers catering to Australia's ethnic minorities, which are

published in either English or one of 40 languages.

Australia has a high readership of magazines: in addition to 1,200 magazine titles, airmail copies of overseas newspapers and journals are readily available at specialist newsagents and numerous bookstores in major cities.

The number of free-to-air television stations varies around the country. In some remote areas, the ABC (Australian Broadcasting Corporation) may be the only station. This is the national, advertisment-free, television and radio network – the equivalent of Britain's BBC. The capital cities also offer three commercial stations and the excellent SBS (Special Broadcasting Service) multicultural station, with shows in many languages with subtitles.

On radio, there is always ABC (FM and AM), plus a full spectrum of commercial and public broadcast stations, offering everything from rock to classical music.

Money

Australia's currency is in dollars and cents. The coins come in 5-, 10-, 20- and 50-cent silver pieces and 1- and 2-dollar gold coins. Notes are A$5, 10, 20, 50 and 100. Amounts of over A$10,000 must be declared on entering and leaving Australia.

The larger hotels will usually exchange cash and well-known traveller's cheques. Nearly all places accept major credit cards such as American Express, Visa, Diners Club and MasterCard.

Banks The four big banks in Australia are the National, the Commonwealth, Westpac and ANZ. Trading hours are generally Mon–Thur 9.30am–4pm, until 5pm on Friday. A few of the smaller banks and credit unions open on Saturday mornings.

Traveller's cheques in any currency can be readily cashed at international airports and banks. Bureaux de change offices are open seven days a week and are located throughout major cities – but usually charge a significant fee, so try to change money at banks when you can, despite limited opening hours.

Credit/Debit Cards and ATMS Carrying a recognised credit or debit card such as Visa, MasterCard, American Express or Diners Club is always a good idea when travelling. A credit card should provide access to EFTPOS (electronic funds transfer at point of sale), which is the easiest and often the cheapest way to exchange money – amounts are automatically debited from the selected account. Many Australian businesses are connected to EFTPOS.

Australian currency cash withdrawals can be made from automatic banking machines (ATMs) that are linked to overseas banks. Since credit card companies generally start charging interest on cash withdrawals immediately, and charge a fee on top, it is usually cheaper to withdraw cash using a debit card rather than a credit card. Some UK banks charge a fee for using debit cards overseas, so check this out before travelling to avoid any nasty surprises on your bank statement when you return home.

Some of the islands and the Outback towns have limited banking facilities, so make sure you have plenty of cash before heading into these less populated areas.

ABOVE: regional publications for sale at New Norcia, Western Australia.

P ostal Services

Post offices open Mon–Fri 9am–5pm. The service is reasonably efficient but not cheap.

Post offices provide fax services at urgent or ordinary rates, the cost depending on the rate selected and the destination.

The front pages of the telephone directory give further information on all postal services, including telephone interpreter service, community service and recorded information service.

Post Restante: post offices will receive and hold mail for visitors. American Express offices will also hold mail for members.

Public Holidays

Public and school holidays affect availability of transport and hotel reservations, which often results in higher prices. The public holidays observed Australia-wide are as follows:

1 January	**New Year's Day**
26 January	**Australia Day**
late March/	**Good Friday,**
early April	**Easter Saturday and Monday**
25 April	**Anzac Day**
2nd Monday in June	**Queen's Birthday**
Early October	**Labour Day**
25 December	**Christmas Day**
26 December	**Boxing Day**

In addition, the states have their own public holidays, such as Victoria's Melbourne Cup Day (first Tuesday in November).

R eligion

Australia is a multicultural society and numerous religions are practised. The major cities are where you will find all types of places of worship. Christianity has the most adherents and you won't be hard pushed to find church services for major denominations in cities and towns. The major cities have some magnificent cathedrals that are worth attending.

Buddhism, Islam, Judaism and Hinduism also have large followings in Australia. Muslim communities can be found in the western suburbs of Sydney, concentrating around Lakemba, and the northern suburbs of Melbourne around Broadmeadows. A strong Jewish community exists in Melbourne around St Kilda East.

S tudent Travellers

Australia is popular with international students and backpackers so there is an abundance of budget tourism operators and accommodation providers. STA Travel has offices in every state and offers a range of products and services aimed at students. Look out for free copies of TNT Magazine for budget travel tips and information (www.tntmagazine.com. au). Universities also offer a range of services and local advice for international students, including affordable accommodation on campus.

T elecommunications

Emergency numbers: **police, ambulance, fire, tel: 000, or 112 from mobile telephones.**

Australia has several telecommunication operators including Telstra, Optus and AAPT. Rates vary between companies for long distance, but local calls on all networks are untimed.

Internet Cafés

Internet cafés are easily found all over Australia, particularly in the larger towns and cities – anybody from a concierge to a cop will happily point you in the right direction. We have not included any listings, as they change so frequently.

Making Calls

Public telephones are located throughout cities and towns. Most public telephones take phonecards, which can be bought at newsagents and stores in various denominations. Dialling from hotel rooms is much more expensive than from a public or private phone.

Subscriber Trunk Dialling (STD) for calling long distance is available on all private and most public telephones. Dial the regional code (say 02 for NSW, 03 for Victoria, etc) followed by the local number. STD calls are cheapest after 7pm and before 8am.

International Calls

Direct-dialled international calls may be made from any ISD-connected private or public phone. International public phones are located at city GPOs, rail termini and airports. There are off-peak rates to most countries which generally apply all day Saturday and 11pm–6am Sunday to Friday. Dial 0011 followed by the relevant country code.

Time Zones

Australia has three time zones: Eastern Standard Time for the east coast states (Tasmania, Victoria, New South Wales, Queensland), 10 hours ahead of GMT; Central Standard Time (covering Northern

Territory and South Australia) 30 minutes behind the east coast, 9½ hours ahead of GMT; and Western Standard Time (Western Australia), 2 hours behind the east coast, 8 hours ahead of GMT.

During the summer most states introduce Daylight Saving Time, moving the clock forward by 1 hour. New South Wales and Australian Capital Territory run daylight saving November–February; South Australia and Victoria November–March; and Tasmania October–March. Neither Queensland nor Western Australia uses Daylight Saving Time

Tipping

Tipping is not the general custom in Australia – waiters are given a decent hourly wage. Most Australians round up the amount in restaurants, or leave the change. In the more formal places, it is becoming customary to give a little more than that – about 10 percent of the total.

Porters at luxury hotels once never received tips, but since many overseas visitors give them a dollar or two, there is an increasing look of expectancy. Porters at air-ports and taxi drivers do not expect to be tipped, but will hardly throw the money back if you do. "It's up to you" has become the common advice from Australians. In other words: nobody really expects a tip, but it's always appreciated.

Toilets

In their typical no-nonsense fashion, Australians manage without euphemisms for "toilet". "Dunny" or "thunder box" is the Outback slang, but "washroom", "restroom", "Ladies" and "Gents" are all understood. Public toilets are often locked after certain hours, but you can generally use the facilities in any pub or cinema without making a purchase. Toilets are generally clean, even in the Outback.

For those who like to plan their rest stops, the government has produced the Toilet Map, available at www.toiletmap.gov.au, with details of the various public toilets in each of Australia's states.

Tourist Offices in Australia

Tourist information within Australia is handled principally by state tourist offices. These offices are generally open seven days a week, and will provide brochures, maps, price lists and other information. They can often book accommodation, tours and transport on your behalf. Most towns also have a local tourist information office.

ACT – Australian Capital Territory
Canberra and Region Visitors Centre, 330 Northbourne Avenue, Dickson, ACT 2602
Tel: 1300-554 114 or 02-6205 0044

Fax: 02-6205 0776
www.visitcanberra.com.au
New South Wales
Sydney Visitor Centre, George Street, The Rocks, Sydney NSW 2000
Tel: 132-077 or 02-9240 8788
Also at 33 Wheat Road, Darling Harbour.
Tel: 1800-067 676 or 02-9240 8788
Fax: 02-9252 8738
www.sydneyvisitorcentre.com
www.visitnsw.com.au
Northern Territory
Tourism NT, 43 Mitchell Street, Darwin, NT 0800
Tel: 08-8999 3900
Fax: 08-8999 3888
www.travelnt.com
Queensland
Queensland Travel Centre, 30 Makerston Street, Brisbane 4000
Tel: 1300-872 835
Fax: 07-3535 4044
www.tq.com.au
South Australia
South Australian Visitor and Travel Centre, 18 King William Street, Adelaide SA 5000
Tel: 1300 655 276 or 08-8303 2220
www.southaustralia.com
Tasmania
Tasmanian Travel and Information Centre, 22 Davey Street Hobart, Tas 7000
Tel: 1300-655 145 or 03-6230 8233 (for international enquiries)
www.discovertasmania.com.au
www.tastravel.com.au
Victoria
Melbourne Visitors Centre, Federation Square (corner of

BELOW: the tourist information centre at the Outback town of Cunnamulla, Queensland.

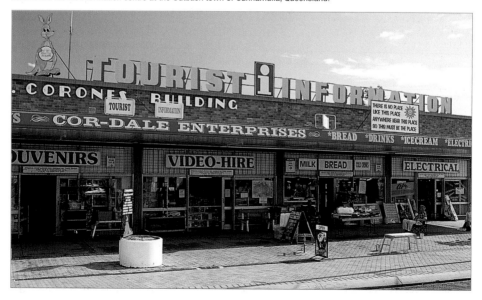

Flinders/Swanson streets), Melbourne
Tel: 03-9658 9658
www.visitvictoria.com

Western Australia
Western Australian Visitor Centre, Albert Facey House, Forrest Place (corner of Wellington Street), Perth
Tel: 1300-361 351 or 08-9483 1111
Fax: 08-9481 0190
www.westernaustralia.net

Useful Addresses

Tourist Information Abroad

Tourism Australia supplies excellent information for travellers wishing to plan their trip:

London:
Australia Centre, Australia House, 6th Floor, The Strand, London, WC2B 4LG
Tel: 020-7438 4601
Fax: 020-7240 6690

Los Angeles:
6100 Center Drive, Suite 1150, Los Angeles, CA 90045
Tel: 310-695 3200
Fax: 310-695 3201

Hong Kong:
Suite 6706, Central Plaza, 18 Harbour Road, Wanchai
Tel: 852-2802 7700
Fax: 852-2802 8211

Singapore:
101 Thompson Road, United Square 08-03, Singapore 307591
Tel: 65-6255 4555
Fax: 65-6253 8431

Local Office of Tourism Australia:
Tel: 1300-361 650 or 02-9360 1111
Fax: 612-9361 1388

National Trust Offices

The National Trust in Australia owns and preserves more than 180 historic properties. All of them are open to the public and Trust members are entitled to free entry. If you intend to visit a number of Australia's historic buildings it may be worth joining. Annual membership costs A$89 for an individual, A$113 for families. Non-members can pay to see particular properties. To join call toll-free in Australia 1800-246 766 or contact one of the state offices. A reciprocal arrangement exists with similar organisations in other countries, so bring their cards with you to Australia.

National
The Australian Council of National Trusts, 14/71 Constitution Avenue, Campbell, ACT, 2612. Tel: 02-6247 6766; www.nationaltrust.org.au

Australian Capital Territory
1st Floor, North Building, Civic Offices, Civic Square, Canberra, ACT

2608. Tel: 02-6230 0533; www.nationaltrust.org.au

New South Wales
Observatory Hill, The Rocks, Sydney, NSW 2001. Tel: 02-9258 0123; www.nsw.nationaltrust.org.au

Queensland
Ground Floor, 91–95 William Street, Brisbane Qld 4001. Tel: 07-3229 1788; www.nationaltrustqld.org

South Australia
Level 2, 27 Leigh Street, Adelaide 5000. Tel: 08-8212 1133; www.nationaltrustsa.org.au

Tasmania
Franklin House, 413 Hobart Road, Launceston, Tas 7250. Tel: 03-6344 6233. www.nationaltrusttas.org.au

Victoria
4 Parliament Place, East Melbourne, Vic 3002. Tel: 03-9656 9800; www.nattrust.com.au

Western Australia
The Old Observatory, 4 Havelock Street, West Perth, WA 6005. Tel: 08-9321 6088; www.ntwa.com.au

National Parks

Some national parks require you to purchase permits before entry. Visitor centres and regional offices where you can obtain information and permits are located throughout Australia and are often in or close to popular parks. National parks information can also be obtained from these regional offices:

ACT: National Parks and Wildlife Service
Tel: 02-6229 3201
www.npaact.gov.au

NSW: National Parks and Wildlife Service
Level 14, 59 Goulburn Street, The Rocks, Sydney, NSW 2000. Tel: 1300-361 967 or 02-9995 5000
www.nationalparks.nsw.gov.au

NT: Parks & Wildlife, Northern Territory
Goyder Centre, 25 Chung Wah Terrace, Palmerston, NT 0830. Tel: 08-8999 5511
www.nt.gov.au/nreta/parks

Qld: Parks & Wildlife Service
160 Ann Street, Brisbane, Qld 4000. Tel: 07-3227 8185
www.epa.qld.gov.au

SA: Environment & Heritage
Tel: 08-8204 1910 (info line)
www.parks.sa.gov.au

Tas: Parks and Wildlife Service
134 Macquarie Street, Hobart 7000. Tel: 1300-135 513
www.parks.tas.gov.au

Vic: Parks Victoria
Level 10/535 Bourke Street
Melbourne Victoria 3000.
Tel: 03-8627 4699; or 131963

(within Australia) for information centre and 24-hour emergency hotline
www.parkweb.vic.gov.au

Weights and Measures

Australia uses the metric system of weights and measures. Despite the change from the imperial to the metric system in the 1970s, a 183-cm person is still frequently referred to as being "6 feet tall" and many people still give their weight in stones (14 lb to the stone).

The main conversions are as follows:

1 metre	3.28 feet
1 kilometre	0.62 mile
1 kilogramme	2.2 pounds
1 litre	2.1 pints (US)
1 litre	1.8 pints (UK)
0°C	32°F
(Centigrade)	(Fahrenheit)

What to Bring

Clothing

Generally, Australians are informal dressers, especially when the weather is warm: comfort comes before tradition. However, for special occasions or dining in fine restaurants, formal attire or neat casual dress is required. While a jacket and tie are rarely required for men, the more elegant establishments would not welcome gym shoes or shorts. In other words, dress more or less as you would in other cosmopolitan cities.

If you visit Australia during summer, include at least one warm garment for the occasional cold snap. If travelling to the southeastern states during winter, include warm clothing, a raincoat and an umbrella – temperatures in Melbourne can reach freezing at night. The weather in northern Queensland and the Top End of the Northern Territory is rarely chilly, even in August.

At any time of the year, waterproof, solid walking shoes are essential if you intend to go bushwalking. If exploring the Great Barrier Reef, bring along an old pair of trainers for reef walks. And always pack a hat.

Women Travellers

Women are generally safe in Australia, though the same degree of caution should be used as you would use elsewhere. Some backpacker hostels such as Base Backpackers (www.basebackpackers.com) offer women-only dorms and floors designed for use by female travellers only.

L ANGUAGE

UNDERSTANDING THE LANGUAGE

Aussie Slanguage

Despite the stereotype, Australians don't actually wander around yacking at each other like cockney parodies. However, there are some definite peculiarities in the vernacular, often called "Strine". The term derives from saying the word "Australian" through both closed teeth and the nose – a local accent that some scholars claim arose out of a need to keep the trap (mouth) shut against blowies (blow flies).

The lingo has a laconic, poetic originality ("he was flash as a rat with a gold tooth…") and can be colourfully coarse ("…and as thin as a streak of pelican shit").

Following are a few oddities and words that are used in Australia and are worth knowing:

A

ABC Australian Broadcasting Corporation
ACT Australian Capital Territory (Canberra)
ACTU Australian Council of Trade Unions
ALP Australian Labor Party
ASIO Australian Security Intelligence Organisation
Across the ditch Across the Tasman Sea: i.e. New Zealand
Alf Stupid Australian
Alice, The Alice Springs
Amber fluid Beer
Ankle-biter Young child
ANZAC Australian & New Zealand Army Corps (World War I)
Arvo Afternoon
Avago Have a go (popular at sporting events: as in "avagoyamug!" if you think the sportsperson could try harder)
Avo Avocado

B

BHP Broken Hill Proprietary, a mining corporation
B&S Bachelors' and Spinsters' Ball (usually held in the country)
Back of Bourke Far Outback
Back of beyond Further Outback
Bag of Fruit Suit
Bail up To rob, hold up
Banana bender Queenslander
Barbie Barbecue
Barrack To cheer for, encourage
Bastard Term of endearment (when it's not a term of dislike)
Bathers Swimming costume (men and women)
Battler One who struggles for a living
Beaut Short for "beautiful" (very good, great, fantastic, as in "you beaut!")
Bible basher Religious preacher
Biker Non-gang motorbike rider
Bikey Biker gang member
Billabong Waterhole in semi-dry river. Features in many Outback songs and stories
Billy Tin container used for boiling water to make tea
Bitser Mongrel dog ("bits a this and bits a that")
Black Stump, The Where the back of Bourke begins (as in the phrase "beyond the black stump")
Blind Freddie could have seen it Something obvious
Bloody Universal expletive, as in "shootin' kanga-bloody-roos"; also "very"
Bloody Oath! True
Blowie Blowfly
Blow in Stranger
Bludger Slacker
Blue A fight
Bluey A redhead
Bogan Unsophisticated and uncultured

Bogin Start eating
Bomb A bad car
Bonzer Terrific
Boomer Huge kangaroo
Boomerang Aboriginal hunting instrument and now found in tourist shops as a souvenir
Booze bus Police breathalizer
Boozer Pub
Bottler Terrific (esp Beauty Bottler!)
Bottle-o Liquor Shop
Brissie Brisbane
Bris Vegas Brisbane
Buckley's Chance One chance in a million
Bug Small edible crustacean, as in Balmain Bug/Moreton Bay Bug
Bullamakanka Mythical, far distant place
Bull Dust Bullshit
Bunyip Australia's Yeti, Big Foot or Loch Ness monster. Lives in a billabong
Burl A try (give it a burl)
Bush The countryside
Bushie Person who lives in the Bush
Bushranger Highwayman, outlaw
Bushweek Traditionally a period of licence when rural folk hit the towns. Now used when you think someone is putting something over on you (in the expression, "What do you think this is…bushweek?")
BYO Bring Your Own (liquor to a restaurant)

C

Cadbury A cheap drunk (as in "a glass and a half")
Cark it Die
Cask Boxed bag of cheap wine
Chips Crisps (unless hot and fried)
Chockers Full
Chook Chicken
Chuck a U-ey Do a U-turn
Chunder Vomit. (Other quaint expressions include – chuck, pave-

ment pizza, kerbside quiche, techni-colour yawn)

Cobber Antique version of "mate"
Cockie Farmer or a cockatoo
Coldie A beer
Come a gutser Make a bad mistake
Compo Workers' Compensation
Coolabah Box eucalyptus tree
Cop it sweet To take the blame or the loss agreeably
Corroboree Aboriginal ceremonial gathering
Cossie Swimming costume
Cow Cockie Cattle grazier
Counter Lunch A pub lunch
Crikey! An exclamation
Crissie Christmas
Crook Broken, sick or no good
Cut lunch A lunch mainly consisting of sandwiches

D

Dag Mild term for fool or unfashionable person; the popular adjective is daggy
Daks Trousers
Damper Unrisen bread, usually cooked in a campfire (a staple of bush tucker)
Dero Derelict person
Didgeridoo Aboriginal droning instrument
Digger Australian soldier, or any old male character
Dill Idiot
Dingo Australian native dog
Dinkie die The truth
Dinkum Genuine or honest
Do yer block Lose your temper
Dob To report on someone. ("To dob in")
Don't come the raw prawn Don't try and fool me

BELOW: subtle Aussie humour.

Doona Quilted eiderdown (duvet)
Drongo Idiot
Dumper A roundly crashing wave, unsuitable for bodysurfing
Dunny Toilet ("Useless as a glass door on a dunny")
Dunny budgie Blowfly
Dynamo A cheaper drunk than a "cadbury"

E–F

Ear-bashing Nagging
Esky Portable cooler for drinks, food
Fair dinkum Same as "Dinkie die" and "dinkum," above
Fair go A chance
Figjam F★★★ I'm good, just ask me (used derogatively as in "He's figjam")
Flake Shark meat
Flat out Busy/fast
Flash as a rat with a gold tooth Showing off
Flog Sell
Footpath Pavement or sidewalk
Footy Aussie Rules football
Fossicking To search for gold in abandoned works, rummage

G–H

G'day Good day/hello
Galah Fool or idiot (after the parrot of same name)
Garbo Garbageman
Give it the flick Get rid of it
Gong, The Wollongong
Good on ya Well done
Greenie A conservationist
Grog Alcoholic drink
Grundies Underwear
Gurgler, down the Down the toilet, wasted
Heaps A lot
Heart starter First drink of the day
Hoon Loudmouth young motorised hooligan
Hotel Some hotels are pubs, some hotels are hotels, some are both (simple eh?)
Humpy Aboriginal shack

I–J

Icey-pole ice lolly
Jackaroo Male managment trainee on an Outback station
Jillaroo Female same
Job To punch
Jocks Men's underpants
Joe Blake Snake
Joey Baby kangaroo
Journo Journalist
Jumbuck Lamb/sheep

K

Kangaroos loose in the top paddock Intellectually inadequate
Karked it Died
Kelpie Australian sheep dog
Kip To sleep. Also an instrument

used to toss pennies in the gambling game "two-up"
Knuckle To punch

L

Lair A show-off
Lamington Aussie dessert: cubes of sponge cake, covered in chocolate and desiccated coconut
Larrikin Previously a street hoodlum. Now a cheeky or mischievous youth
Loaf To do nothing ("just loafing about"). Also means a head ("use yer loaf")
Lob Arrive ("To lob in")
Lolly Candy or sweet
Lurk A racket, a "dodge" or illegal scheme

M

Mad as a cut snake Particularly crazy
Mate's rate A cheap deal
Mick A Roman Catholic
Middy 285 ml/10oz glass of beer (in NSW)
Mob A group of persons or things (not necessarily unruly)
Mozzie Mosquito
Mug A gullible fool

N

Neck oil Beer
Nervy A nervous attack (To "chuck a nervy")
Never-never Far off in the Outback, middle of nowhere
Nick Steal
Nipper Young surf lifesaver
Nit Fool, idiot
No-hoper Same as above, but worse
Nong Fool
Nuddy, in the Nude

O

O.S. Overseas
Ocker Quintessential Aussie bumpkin-loudmouth, a favourite target of comedians
Outback The bush; uncivilised, uninhabited country
Oz Australia

P

Panic merchant Chronic anxiety case
Pashing Kissing
Perve To ogle at an attractive person
Pie Floater A meat pie in a bowl of pea soup
Piece of piss Easy
Pie-eyed Drunk
Pinch Arrest, or steal
Pissed Off Angry
Plonk Cheap wine
Poker machine Slot machine (a.k.a. "pokie")
Pom English person
Postie Mail person

Prezzy Present
Private school For fee-paying pupils
Public school State school

Q–R

Quarts Pints, but only in Queensland
RSL Returned Servicemen's League, known for their entertainment clubs
Rack off Get lost/go away
Ratbag Trouble-maker (also a friendly term of abuse)
Rat shit Lousy, ruined. Abbreviation "RS" also used
Rego Registration (car)
Rid Insect repellent
Ridgi-didge Genuine, true
Ringer Stockman or woman on an Outback station
Ripper Good
Road train Outback truck with up to three trailers
Roo Kangaroo
Roof rabbits Possums or rats in the attic
Root Sexual intercourse
Rooted Exhausted
Ropable Very angry
Running round like a chook with its head cut off useless, frenetic activity

S

Saltie Salt-water crocodile
Salvo Member of the Salvation Army
Sanger Sandwich
Scab Technically a strike-breaker; often used to describe someone who's cheap and/or underhand; can also be used to mean borrow ("Can I scab a dollar off you?")

Schooner Large beer glass (particular to NSW)
Scrub Bushland
Scunge A dirty, untidy person
Semi-trailer Articulated truck
Servo Petrol/gas station
She'll be apples It'll be right
She's sweet Everything is all right
Sheila Female (derogatory)
Shoot through Leave unexpectedly, escape
Shonky Unreliable
Slats Ribs
Smoke-o Work break (archaic)
Snags Sausages
Speedos Nylon swimming trunks
Spit the dummy Get upset
Sprog Baby
Spunk Good-looking person
Squatter Large landholder in early colonial times
Station Large farm or ranch
Stickybeak Busybody
Stinger Box jellyfish
Stirrer Trouble maker
Stockman Cowboy, station hand
Stonkered Exhausted
Strain the potatoes (or spuds) Urinate
Strewth! An exclamation
Strides Trousers
Strine Vernacular Australian
Stubby Small bottle of beer, kept cold in a "stubby holder"
Stuffed Tired
Stunned Mullet Someone who looks shocked
Sunbake Suntan/bathe
Swag Canvas bed for camping
Swagman Vagabond, rural tramp
Sydney or the Bush All or nothing

T

TAB Totalisator Agency Board, legal offtrack betting shop
Tall poppies High achievers (as in the expression "tall poppy syndrome", to describe Australians' habit of attacking anyone who has achieved something)
Tassie Tasmania
Taswegian resident of Tasmania
Telly Television, also the *Sydney Telegraph Mirror*
Thongs Flip-flop sandals and, increasingly, string undergarments
Tinnie Can of beer, also a small aluminium boat
Togs Swimsuit (sometimes called "bathers", or "cossie")
Top End Northern Territory/far north Australia
Too Right! Absolutely!
Troppo Unhinged by tropical weather
True blue Patriotic
Tube Can of beer or innermost section of breaking surf wave
Tucker Food
Turps Any form of alcohol ("On the turps" – to be drinking)
Two-pot screamer Person unable to hold their drink
Two up Popular gambling game involving two pennies thrown in the air

U

Uni University
Unit Apartment, flat
Urchin Baby or small child
Useless as tits on a bull Incompetent
Ute "Utility" truck – a pickup truck

V–W

Vegemite Brown yeast sandwich spread which Australians grow up on but is regarded by most foreigners as semi-toxic (the British equivalent is Marmite)
Walkabout Travelling on foot for long distances – an Aboriginal tradition – usually involves disappearing entirely for long periods at a time
Wheeties Weetabix or most other breakfast cereals
Whinge Complain (often used in relation to "whingeing Poms")
Wharfie Dockworker
Wog Minor disease or flu
Wowser Killjoy, prude

X–Y

XXXX Beer
Yabber Chatter
Yabbie Small freshwater crayfish
Yack To talk
Yahoo An unruly type
Yakka Work
Yobbo Hoon, loudmouth – Pacific redneck
Your blood's good enough to bottle I like you

The Unofficial National Anthem – *Waltzing Matilda*

Once a jolly swagman camped by a
  billabong
Under the shade of a coolibah tree
And he sang as he watched and
  waited 'til his billy boiled
You'll come a-waltzing matilda
  with me

Waltzing matilda, waltzing matilda
You'll come a waltzing matilda
  with me
And he sang as he watched and
  waited 'til his billy boiled
You'll come a-waltzing matilda
  with me

Down came a jumbuck to drink at
  that billabong
Up jumped the swagman and
  grabbed him with glee
And he sang as he stuffed that
  jumbuck in his tucker-bag
You'll come a-waltzing matilda
  with me

(repeat chorus)
Up rode the squatter, mounted on
  his thoroughbred
Up rode the troopers, one, two,
  three
"Where's that jolly jumbuck you've
  got in your tucker-bag?"
You'll come a-waltzing matilda
  with me
(repeat chorus)

Up jumped the swagman and
  sprang into that billabong
"You'll never take me alive!",
  said he
And his ghost may be heard as you
  pass by that billabong
You'll come a-waltzing matilda
  with me
(repeat chorus)

[words attributed to "Banjo"
  Patterson, c.1890]

FURTHER READING

TRANSPORT

General

Australian Geographic Book of the Kimberley by David McGonigal.
Australia. The Greatest Island by Robert Raymond.
The Heritage of Australia: The Illustrated Register of the National Estate.
The Penguin Good Australian Wine Guide by H Hooke and R Kyte-Powell.
Tucker Track – A curious history of food in Australia by Warren Fahey.
Unreliable Memoirs by Clive James.
Wine Western Australia by Mike Zekulich.

History

The Commonwealth of Thieves: The Story of the Founding of Australia by Thomas Keneally.
Crackpots, Ratbags and Rebels by Robert Holden.
The Explorers edited by Tim Flannery.
The Fatal Shore by Robert Hughes.
The Floating Brothel by Sian Rees.
Gallipoli by Les Carlyon.
Leviathan: the Unauthorised Biography by John Birmingham.
Manning Clark's History of Australia by Manning Clark.
A New History of Australia by F.R. Crowley.
Patriots: Defending Australia's Natural Heritage 1946–2004 by William J. Lines.
A Secret Country by John Pilger.
A Shorter History of Australia by Geoffrey Blainey.
The Spirit of Kokoda by Patrick Lindsay.
Terra Australis introduced by Tim Flannery.
Turning Points in the Making of Australia by Michael Page.

Social History

Claiming a Continent: A New History of Australia by David Day.
The Fatal Shore by Robert Hughes.
Great Southern Land, a New History of Australia by Frank Welsh.
At Home in Australia by Peter Conrad.
A Traveller's History of Australia by John H. Chambers.

Natural History

Australia, the Wild Continent by Michael Morcombe.
Australian Wildlife: Best-known Birds, Mammals Reader's Digest.
Country by Tim Flannery.
Australia's Natural Wonders by Michael Richardson.
Green Guide: Mammals of Australia by T Lindsey.
Green Guide: Snakes and Other Reptiles of Australia by G Swan.
Wild Australia Reader's Digest.
Wilderness Australia by David McGonigal.

Travel

Digger by Max Anderson.

Down Under by Bill Bryson.
Drive by Cathy Savage and others.
Explore Australia by Four-Wheel Drive by Peter and Kim Wherrett.
Into the Blue: Boldly Going Where Captain Cook Has Gone Before by Tony Horwitz.
One for the Road by Tony Horwitz.
The Songlines by Bruce Chatwin.
Tracks by Robyn Davidson: Pan Macmillan.

Aboriginal Australia

Aboriginal Australians by Richard Broome.
Aboriginal Myths, Legends and Fables by A.W. Reed.
Archaeology of the Dreamtime by Josephine Flood.
The Artist is a Thief by Stephen Gray.
Australian Dreaming: 40,000 Years of Aboriginal History. Compiled and edited by Jennifer Isaacs.
Australia's Living Heritage: Arts of the Dreaming by Jennifer Isaacs.
Balanda: My Year in Arnhem Land by Mary Ellen Jordan.
Central Queensland by W.E. Roth.
A Change of Ownership by Mildred Kirk.
Dreamings: The Art of Aboriginal Australia edited by Peter Sutton.
My Place by Sally Morgan.
Prehistory of Australia; John Mulvaney and John Kamminga.
Songman by Allan Baillie.
Triumph of the Nomads by Geoffrey Blainey.
Why Warriors Lie Down and Die by Richard Trudgen.
Why Weren't We Told? by Henry Reynolds.
Wings of the Kite-Hawk: A journey into the heart of Australia by Nicholas Rothwell.

Australian Language

Dictionary of Australian Colloquialisms by G.A. Wilkes.
The Dinkum Dictionary by Susan Butler.
G'Day! Teach Yourself Australian by Angus and Robertson.
John Blackman's Australian Slang Dictionary by John Blackman.

ACCOMMODATION

ACTIVITIES

A – Z

LANGUAGE

Let's Talk Strine by Afferbeck Lauder.

The Macquarie Dictionary Macquarie University.

New South Wales Aboriginal Place Names by F.D. McCarthy.

Fiction/Poetry

There are many excellent choices from Australia's recognised writers. Here is a selection of some of best titles:

The Bodysurfers by Robert Drewe.
Capricornia by Xavier Herbert.
Cloudstreet by Tim Winton.
Collected Poems by Judith Wright.
Collected Poems by Les Murray.
   Death of a River Guide by Richard Flanagan.
Dirt Music by Tim Winton.
Eucalyptus by Murray Bail.
Fly Away Peter by David Malouf.
For the Term of His Natural Life by Marcus Clarke.
A Fortunate Life by Albert Facey.
Gould's Book of Fish by Richard Flanagan.
The Idea of Perfection by Kate Grenville.
Illywhacker by Peter Carey
Last Drinks by Andrew McGahan.
The Man from Snowy River by Banjo Paterson.
Matthew Flinder's Cat by Bryce Courtenay.
Morgan's Run by Colleen McCullough.
My Brilliant Career by Miles Franklin.
The Office of Innocence by Thomas Keneally.
Oscar and Lucinda by Peter Carey.
Over the Top with Jim by Hugh Lunn.
Remembering Babylon by David Malouf.
The Secret River by Kate Grenville.
Short Stories by Henry Lawson.
The Sound of One Hand Clapping by Richard Flanagan.
Territory by Judy Nunn.
Theft by Peter Carey.
The Thorn Birds by Colleen McCullough.
Tree of Man by Patrick White.
The True History of the Kelly Gang by Peter Carey.
The Vivisector by Patrick White.

Other Australian authors worth checking out include: Helen Garner, Germaine Greer, Beverley Farmer, Elizabeth Jolley, Thea Astley, Alex Miller, Janet Turner Hospital and Kaz Cooke.

Works by Christina Stead, Patrick White, Ruth Park, Kylie Tennant, Eleanor Dark and D'Arcy Niland may be easier to come by in second-hand book shops.

Children's Books

Blinky Bill by Dorothy Wall.
The Magic Pudding by Norman Lindsay.
Possum Magic by Julie Vivas & Mem Fox.
Snugglepot & Cuddlepie by May Gibbs.
Wombat Divine by Mem Fox and Kerry Argent.
The Australian Government website has a page on children's authors with links to other sites:
www.cultureandrecreation.gov.au/articles/childrensbooks

Other Insight Guides

Insight Guides

Like this guide, Insight Guides are known for their superb photography and in-depth background reading. Other titles in the Insight Guide range that highlight destinations in this region include **Insight Guides** to **Australia & New Zealand's Best Hotels & Resorts**, **Bali**, **Indonesia, Japan** and **Southeast Asia**.

In addition there are three Australian titles in Insight's regional series: **Insight Guide: Queensland**, **Insight Guide: New South Wales** and **Insight Guide: Tasmania**. The regional series comes with a free touring map.

Insight City Guides

The Insight City Guides are written by locally-based writers, who show you how to make the most of your destination city. Includes detailed listings and a free restaurant guide map to locate the city's best restaurants. Australian titles in this series include **Insight City Guide: Perth & Surroundings** and **Insight City Guide: Sydney**.

Insight Pocket Guides

Insight Pocket Guides to **Perth**, and **Brisbane and the Gold Coast**, are available. These books provide a series of timed itineraries for short-stay visitors and come with a pull-out map.

We also recommend **Berlitz Pocket Guide: Australia** and **Berlitz Pocket Guide: Sydney**.

ART & PHOTO CREDITS

PICTURE SPREADS

Cartographic Editor: Zoë Goodwin
Map Production: Polyglott Kartographie,
Berndtson and Berndtson Publications,
Elsner & Schichor
© 2007 Apa Publications GmbH & Co.
Verlag KG (Singapore branch)

INDEX

Numbers in italics refer to photographs, in bold refer to major entries.